READERS, TEACHERS, LEARNERS

Expanding Literacy Across the Content Areas

READERS, TEACHERS, LEARNERS
Expanding Literacy Across the Content Areas

Third Edition

William G. Brozo
Texas A & M University—Corpus Christi

Michele L. Simpson
University of Georgia

Merrill, an imprint of Prentice Hall
Upper Saddle River, New Jersey *Columbus, Ohio*

Library of Congress Cataloging-in-Publication Data

Brozo, William G.

Readers, teachers, learners : expanding literacy across the content areas / by William G. Brozo, Michele L. Simpson.—3rd ed.

p. cm.

Includes bibliographical references and index.

ISBN 0-13-647272-9

1. Reading (Secondary)—United States. 2. Language arts (Secondary)—United States. I. Simpson, Michele L. II. Title.

LB1632.B7 1999

428.4'071'273—dc21 97-50270

CIP

Editor: Bradley J. Potthoff
Production Editor: Mary M. Irvin
Design Coordinator: Karrie M. Converse
Text Designer: Linda M. Robertson
Cover Designer: Tom Mack
Production Manager: Pamela D. Bennett
Director of Marketing: Kevin Flanagan
Advertising/Marketing Coordinator: Krista Groshong
Marketing Manager: Suzanne Stanton

This book was set in Garamond by Carlisle Communications, Inc., and was printed and bound by R. R. Donnelley & Sons Company. The cover was printed by Phoenix Color Corp.

Photo credits: Scott Cunningham/Merrill, 5, 51, 361, 393; Anne Vega/Merrill, 29, 145, 181, 271; Anthony Magnacca/Merrill, 97, 317, 437; KS Studios/Merrill, 227.

Printed in the United States of America

10 9 8 7 6 5 4 3 2 1

ISBN: 0-13-647272-9

Prentice-Hall International (UK) Limited, *London*
Prentice-Hall of Australia Pty. Limited, *Sydney*
Prentice-Hall of Canada, Inc., *Toronto*
Prentice-Hall Hispanoamericana, S. A., *Mexico*
Prentice-Hall of India Private Limited, *New Delhi*
Prentice-Hall of Japan, Inc., *Tokyo*
Simon & Schuster Asia Pte. Ltd., *Singapore*
Editora Prentice-Hall do Brasil, Ltda., *Rio de Janeiro*

For Carol, Hannah, and Genevieve

—William G. Brozo

For Tom

—Michele L. Simpson

PREFACE

In every case, it is the reader who reads the sense; it is the reader who grants or recognizes in an object, place or event a certain possible readability; it is the reader who must attribute meaning to a system of signs, and then decipher it. We all read ourselves and the world around us in order to glimpse what and where we are. We read to understand, or to begin to understand. We cannot do but read. Reading, almost as much as breathing, is our essential function.

—*Alberto Manguel (1996)**

Those of us who "cannot do but read" are part of a culture of letters that can be traced from the first Sumerian tablets of the fifth millennium, B.C., to Greek scrolls; from the codices of St. Augustine to CD-ROMs. Every word read is part of a history of language and sense filled with tales of anarchy, censorship, triumph, and passion. To read and write, then, is to become part of that history.

As habitually and naturally as we, the authors, pick up a book for the exhilaration of residing in the world between its covers, we know all too well that countless American adults and young adults habitually avoid reading. Gustave Flaubert said, "Read in order to live," but too many among us are choosing to live without reading; to squander our privilege of literacy. To be a nonreader, however, is not without its consequences. Beyond the more esoteric benefits of literacy, nonreaders lose reading skills, are less capable of understanding complex text, may be less likely to find well-paying jobs, and may fail to impart positive values of literacy to their children. Being an active reader, on the other hand, can expand life and career options and enlarge one's sense of self.

This book is about widening life and career options for students in the middle and upper grades through literacy. We make one overarching assertion in this book: that teachers of all subjects can create engaging learning environments where readers and learners use literacy for personal pleasure and as a tool for mind expansion. To demonstrate the viability of this assertion we continue in this third edition to communicate to teachers through teachers. With fresh and exciting reading, writing, and literacy research as a backdrop, we have tried in a collaborative spirit to empower teachers with the confidence to make their own best decisions about the learning that goes on in

---

*Manguel, A. (1996). *A history of reading.* New York: Viking.

their classrooms. As in our previous two attempts, we have made a serious effort to avoid prescribing, offering "canned" answers, or demanding certain behaviors from teachers—answers or behaviors that ignore the realities of the everyday world of middle and secondary schools, where the major goal is to teach content-area material.

We hope another clear message of the book is that teachers inform us as much as we inform them. In a very real sense, the growth and improvement of students' language processes in middle and secondary schools will depend on the strength of the transaction between teachers in higher education and teachers in public schools.

In this edition we present even more actual teaching scenarios than in the first and second editions, including additional examples from content areas such as math, science, art, music, and kinesiology. In each of the scenarios we demonstrate the valuable lessons to be learned from content-area teachers struggling and triumphing as they implement stimulating reading, writing, and learning strategies. Theory and research frame these vignettes and examples, which provide glimpses of teachers making literacy and content acquisition work.

IMPORTANT NEW FEATURES OF THIS THIRD EDITION

Anyone familiar with our previous editions will immediately notice some major new additions to this book in both format and content.

Format

- **Marginal Gloss**—As an aid to comprehension and study, we have included throughout the book summary statements and paraphrases in the margins of each page that signal important content and ideas.
- **Anticipation Guides**—At the beginning of each chapter, the reader is asked to fill in an anticipation guide made up of thought-provoking statements related to the chapter. In the book, we advocate the use of anticipation guides for content-area teachers and have found such guides highly useful for helping adult readers develop meaningful purposes for reading and an appropriate mindset for the content. We encourage readers to return to the guide after reading and studying the chapter to reconsider their original assumptions and hunches.
- **Framework of Instruction for Content-Area Literacy**—At the beginning of chapters 1 through 11 is a graphic organizer of the broad topics in this book, entitled "Framework of Instruction for Content-Area Learning." The organizer is an attempt to depict the relationships among the major chapter topics. The particular topic of each chapter is highlighted on the organizer at the beginning of that chapter to remind readers of the connection between topics and how they can support greater content learning. The organizer is explained in Chapter 1.

- **Chapter Photographs**—To help make this edition more visually appealing we have included photographs near the beginning of each chapter. These pictures help create a more tangible image of the teaching and learning dynamics we advocate and demonstrate throughout the book.

Content

- **Middle School and Secondary School Emphasis**—A major addition to this new edition is the inclusion of many more examples of content-area teaching and learning for students in the middle grades. The strategies, ideas, and teaching scenarios in this book now range from sixth through twelfth grades. In this way we demonstrate a wider range of application for the content-area literacy strategies we describe.
- **Book Title Change**—As a result of the growing emphasis in this book on content area literacy for a wider grade and age range, we decided to rename the third edition to reflect this change. The new title is: *Readers, Teachers, Learners: Expanding Literacy Across the Content Areas.* We believe that the new title more accurately describes the intent of the book—to provide sound literacy and learning strategies for students not only in the upper grades of secondary school but also for middle and junior high school students.
- **New Chapter on Technology**—The topic of technology and its role in promoting content-area literacy and learning has evolved from a few paragraphs in our first edition, to a small section in the second edition, to a complete chapter in this edition. The mounting advances in classroom applications of computer technology warrant a much fuller description of this electronic learning tool. Chapter 10, Expanding Literacy and Content Learning Through Computer Technology, provides a conceptual and research framework for the use of computers in the middle and upper grades, as well as many detailed examples of subject-area teachers using this technology to expand students' learning.

ASSUMPTIONS UNDERLYING THE READING AND WRITING STRATEGIES IN THIS THIRD EDITION

A major theme of this book is that teachers who employ language-based strategies are more likely to build active learners and expand literacy for students in the middle and upper grades. Throughout the book we describe strategies that exploit students' beliefs and backgrounds and provide students with new, imaginative experiences that will help them find reasons to learn. The strategies we discuss demonstrate how teachers can move students to become active learners by building independence. Above all, the strategies in this book strive to make learning fun and accessible for all.

We believe that students develop misconceptions about literacy and learning as a result of their experiences in school. The strategies and ideas in this third edition stem from the belief that students can become interested and enthusiastic users of literacy to expand their sense of reality and their sense of themselves. One of the dominant themes in literacy research today is student motivation, and much of the work on motivation for literacy by prominent scholars and educators is included in this book. This work has shown us that students are touched and moved by learning when teachers bring together teaching and learning experiences in positive and authentic ways, when learning is meaning centered, when teachers and students work together to shape the learning environment, and when students are given real-world reasons to learn.

Several assumptions, therefore, underpin the strategies in this book. These assumptions form the theoretical foundations on which our ideas for teaching and learning rest.

1. **Teaching is more than dispensing information, because learning is more than receiving and remembering information.** Learning is the construction of meaning, an active process on the part of the learner. Teaching is creating classroom contexts that support the acquisition of new knowledge through literacy.
2. **A major goal of education should be the development of critical thinkers and active, independent learners.** Students should be provided opportunities to play active roles in the meaning-making process. Students should be engaged in learning experiences that help them critically evaluate their worlds and participate in active problem solving or real-world concerns.
3. **To be literate is to use literacy as a tool for learning.** In supportive learning environments, students can learn to use literacy as vehicles for meaningful and functional learning.
4. **Content and process should be taught simultaneously.** Students should be led to see that *what* is learned is inextricably tied to *how* one learns.
5. **Content area teachers need to develop students' will to learn.** Literacy and learning skills are of little help if students are unmotivated to learn. Motivation results when teachers create interesting learning environments and help students develop their own personally relevant reasons for learning.

ORGANIZATION OF THE BOOK

This text is designed to help you teach your content more effectively and to develop independent learners who can think about your content in creative and critical ways. This text is also designed to help you envision the possibilities for exciting teaching and learning in your classroom. To this end, we have filled the book with actual, practical examples, teaching scenarios, and classroom dialogues. Using an informal tone, we share our own teaching experiences as well as those of many middle and secondary school classroom teachers. We provide many alternatives, not with the intent that you should adopt every one, but with the expectation that you will select the strategies that best suit your subject area, your students, and your teaching style.

As in previous editions, Chapter 1 provides a thorough description of major trends in literacy, themes in this new edition, and principles of language-based teaching and learning, as well as an updated explanation of the benefits of cooperative learning. A new principle of language-based teaching has been added that reflects our growing concern that teachers of all subjects account for student motivation. Chapters 2 and 3 are critical in that they explain the processes involved in developing active learners. We recommend that you read these first three chapters before reading the others, because the remaining chapters build on the foundations we establish in Chapters 1, 2, and 3.

Regardless of the content that you teach or plan to teach, each chapter can provide you with insights into effective classroom interactions and practical examples of teaching strategies. Even when these examples of strategies and classroom applications do not come from your particular subject area, they can be invaluable as guides for helping you modify instructional practices within your own classroom context. Therefore, we recommend that you read each one and, as you do, rather than implementing the strategies exactly as explained and presented here, consider how the strategies can be adapted to your content, student, classroom, and teaching style.

Woven throughout the 12 chapters of this new edition are many common threads. For instance, although we devote an entire chapter to writing in the content areas (Chapter 7), writing strategies—in combination with other literacy processes as vehicles for learning in a variety of classroom settings—are offered in nearly every chapter. The same holds true for using young adult literature and trade books to engender interest and spice up content learning (Chapter 8).

Chapters 2 through 12 include case studies. The case study format asks you to consider a particular problem or issue from an actual teaching scenario related to the content of the chapter. At the conclusion of the chapter, the case study is revisited, and you are invited to offer teaching or problem-solving suggestions. This process makes your reading and study more interactive and it is hoped that the text will become more useful to you. We urge you to take full advantage of the case studies as you process chapter information, ideas, and strategies.

Finally, readers of this third edition will be especially pleased with all of the updated references to professional literature. Although this book is clearly a practical teaching reference, we want all of our readers to be mindful of the importance of scholarship in supporting the strategies and methods we describe.

FINAL THOUGHTS ON OUR THIRD EDITION

It is with great confidence that we stand behind the methods and strategies discussed within this book. In fact, many of the teaching scenarios and examples come from our own teaching and research experiences with middle school, junior high, and high school teachers and students. Other examples come from past students who have told us about or invited us to view their successful creation of literacy innovations or application of strategies in the content areas.

We have taken great pains not to write another instructional recipe book that lists activities without connections to actual classroom environments, without a grounding in theory and research, without a focus on process. Dorothy Watson suggests that "instructional cookbooks carry teachers from one activity to the next, but do not empower them with knowledge that leads to flexibility in future decision making" (in Gilles, et.al., 1988). Instead, we have tried to provide the encouragement, strategies, and examples needed to help you transform your classroom world into a learning place where you and your students' mutual desire to learn will constantly be nurtured.

ACKNOWLEDGMENTS

These opening remarks would be incomplete without a very special thanks to Brad Potthoff, our editor at Merrill. Without his guidance and perception, as well as his faith in the power of our message about content-area literacy, this third edition would never have become a reality. Thanks as well go out to our production editor, Mary Irvin, and to our copy editor, Helen Greenberg. We are, of course, indebted to our diligent reviewers—Gerald J. Calais, McNeese State University; Cindy Gillespie, Bowling Green State University; Betty McEady, California State University-Monterey Bay; and Robert J. Rickelman, University of North Carolina-Charlotte—whose helpful insights made this third edition a better text. We thank all the students and teachers whose experiences inspired us and continue to influence our work. We are especially grateful for the wisdom and generosity of our mentors: for Bill, Dr. Paul Berg and Dr. Ronald Schmelzer, and for Michele, Dr. Keith Thomas and Dr. Ned Ratekin.

In physics they call it the "butterfly effect"—small influences creating dramatic effects—derived from the idea that the mere flap of an insect's wing in your backyard can cause a hurricane on the other side of the globe. This book is dedicated to small influences that bring about big changes in the way students and teachers in middle and secondary schools interact and the quality of student learning.

Contents

READERS, TEACHERS, LEARNERS

Expanding Literacy Across the Content Areas

CHAPTER 1

Readers, Teachers, Learners: An Introduction

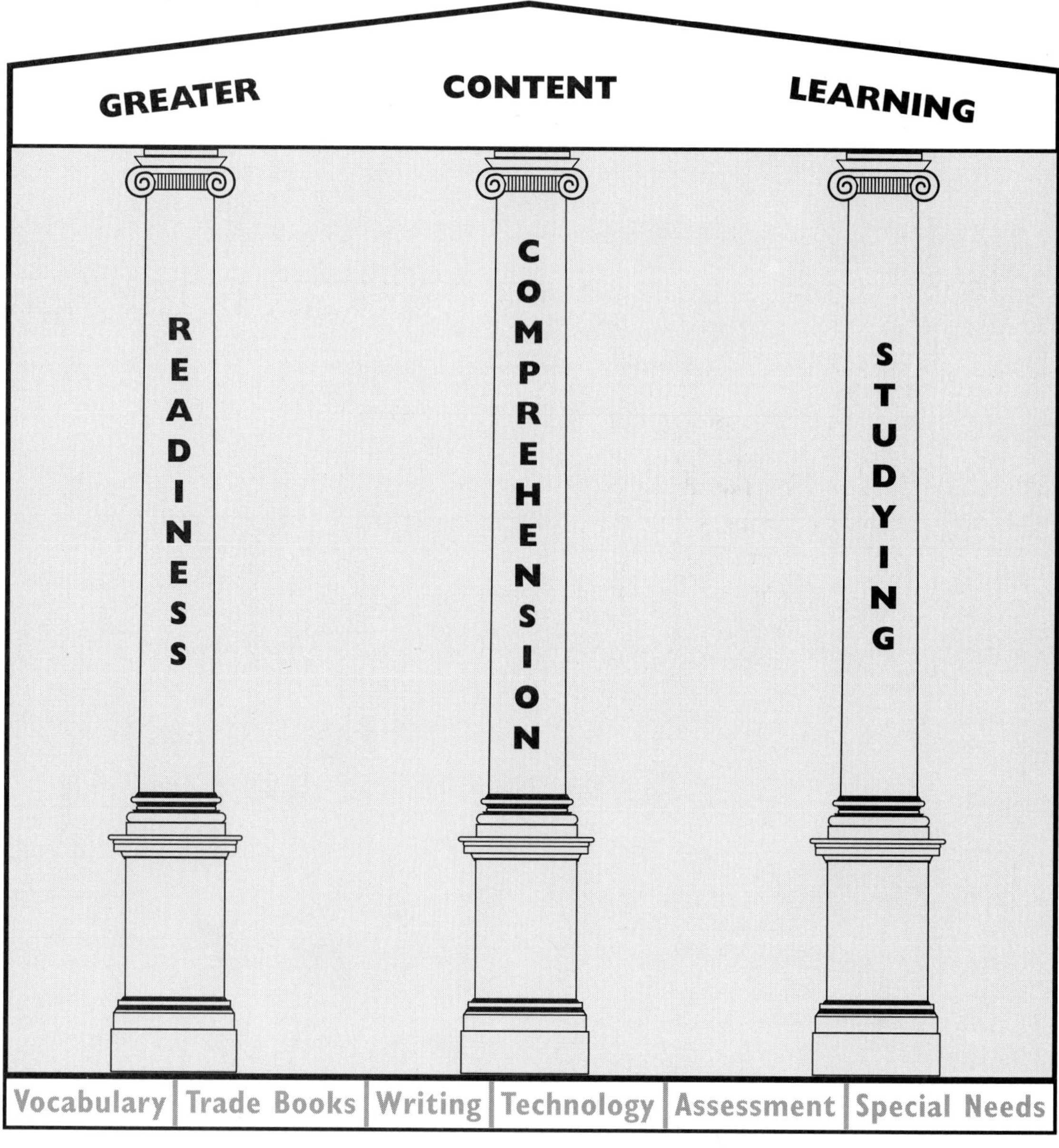

ANTICIPATION GUIDE

Directions: Read each statement carefully and decide whether you agree or disagree with it, placing a check mark in the appropriate *Before Reading* column. When finished reading and studying the chapter, return to the guide and decide whether your anticipations need to be changed by placing a check mark in the appropriate *After Reading* column.

	BEFORE READING		**AFTER READING**	
	Agree	*Disagree*	*Agree*	*Disagree*
1. Students are better able to read at higher levels than in the past.	______	______	______	______
2. Literacy means being able to read words correctly.	______	______	______	______
3. All teachers should reinforce literacy skills for students.	______	______	______	______
4. *Aliteracy* means being unable to read.	______	______	______	______
5. Literacy can be used to achieve social and economic improvement.	______	______	______	______
6. Learning is most effective when students learn on their own.	______	______	______	______

. . . [P]lausible argument, substantiated over three hundred years of insight and research, is that knowing is an activity, not a condition or state, that knowledge implies the making of connections, not an inert body of information, that both teachers and students are learners, that discourse manifests and realizes the power to learn, and that teaching entails creating incentives and contexts for learning, not a reporting of data. Specifically, learning is the process of an individual's mind making meaning from the material of its experience.

—Knoblach and Brannon (1983)

This book is about readers, teachers, and learners in middle and secondary school; it is about contexts for learning; and it is about how students can be supported in their use of language processes for learning course content and expanding their sense of self.

Purpose of Chapter 1

Our purpose in this chapter is fivefold: (1) to share our philosophy of literacy; (2) to build a case for why literacy processes should be integral to middle and secondary-content classroom instruction; (3) to describe what we believe to be important principles of language-based teaching; (4) to lay down the assumptions about literacy and learning underpinning the strategies and ideas contained in this text; and (5) to present a framework of instruction showing the interrelatedness of the important topics and themes of this book.

WHAT IS LITERACY AND ITS ROLE IN MIDDLE AND SECONDARY SCHOOL?

To be literate in middle and secondary school means many things. It means using literacy to bring pleasure and expand one's sense of self. It means using literacy to become a more fully realized and participatory citizen in a democratic society such as ours. And it means being able to use reading, writing, speaking, and listening to acquire and apply knowledge in content-area classrooms.

With regard to using literacy for pleasure and personal growth, it seems to us that middle and secondary school teachers must take as much care in reaching adolescents as they do in teaching them the curriculum. As if to confirm a long-held supposition about the relationship between reading widely for pleasure and reading achievement, recent national reading test results clearly demonstrate that middle- and upper-grade students who read for pleasure achieved higher scores on the test (Campbell, Donahue, Reese, & Phillips, 1996). A big part of reaching students is to trust the voices of our students, to be learners ourselves, and to take risks. Glasgow (1996) and others (Hill & Van Horn, 1995) have found that one of the best ways to reach young adults at all ability levels is through books. Sharing books that help students work through a personal or interpersonal crisis, that excite their imaginations, or that support their "need to know" communicates the clear message that the teacher cares about students

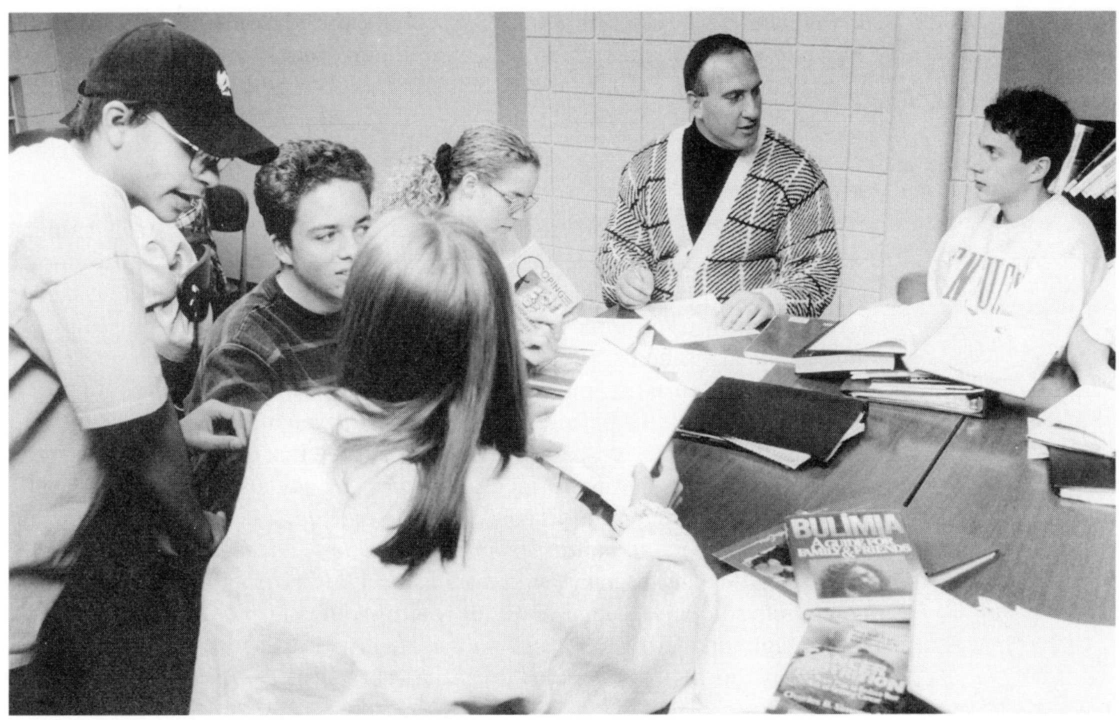

Students Will Improve Their Reading and Learning When They Find Them Enjoyable

and values reading and learning outside the traditional boundaries of the school or class curriculum. To be a companion in literacy, however, requires that we ourselves read and know books. Linda Rief, a junior high school teacher, talks about how she rediscovered reading in a summer course and how she was shocked into awareness of her own reading habits:

> She asked each of us to bring five favorite books we were currently reading, or had recently read, to the first class. I couldn't find five recently read books. I realized I wasn't reading. I thought I didn't have time. That scared me. Reading was part of my curriculum. How could I have neglected it so badly? (1992, p. 3)

Becoming knowledgeable about books, and regularly reading and writing ourselves, puts us in the perfect position to introduce young adults to the pleasures and functional uses of literacy.

Literacy as a Tool for Change

Helping students become critical, participatory citizens may be one of the most important yet most neglected aspects of literacy teaching and learning in middle and secondary schools (Goodman, 1992; Willinsky, 1990). This may be due to the way schools are structured. Gregory and Smith (1987) sum up the plight of American schools:

> In our view the typical American . . . school is much more effective as an instrument for controlling and confining . . . than as a means for

> teaching. . . . Very little of the . . . school experience is congruent with the findings of learning research or of common sense. Rather, it is about the fragmentation of knowledge, the emphasis on coverage at the expense of establishment of personal meaning, the tyranny of a time schedule that precludes lengthy discourse or introspection, and a concept of mass education that emasculates attempts to individualize learning. (p. 5)

The harshness of these criticisms makes us uncomfortable; yet, many students and parents appear to agree with them (Bintz, 1993). This book is an attempt to counter the diatribes of biased researchers as well as a critical public by presenting numerous examples of effective teaching and useful learning in middle and secondary schools. We believe our prescient forebears, such as Thomas Jefferson and Benjamin Franklin, foresaw the critical role schools could play in preparing students to be intelligent, functioning members in the democratic process. In fact, over 200 years ago, they suggested that the biggest threat to national security was an uninformed populace. Literacy teaching and learning in junior and senior high schools could provide the necessary experiences for adolescents to take on the political, social, and economic challenges in the near and long term. Making literacy and learning meaningful on a sociopolitical level could help students look more critically at their own lives, as well as the lives of their neighbors and society, and imbue them with the courage to become involved in the improvement of our political, social, and economic condition (King & Brozo, 1992).

With regard to learning content material, unfortunately, students are rarely taught reading, writing, and reasoning processes that enable them to use these literacy skills as tools for learning in their daily schoolwork (Bintz, 1993). A traditional perspective of reading development assumes that students become fluent readers by third or fourth grade, just at about the time they begin encountering textbooks in science, social studies, health, and so on. But the processing demands of simple stories, which comprise nearly all of the material for reading instruction in the early grades, contrast sharply with the processing demands of expository texts from which middle and secondary students are expected to read and learn. Consequently, when students experience difficulty with expository reading in their content classes, it is often assumed that they have not learned to read properly, and they may be recycled through a program of basic reading skills. This practice leaves little hope of ever developing interested or sophisticated readers. When we consider the complexity of textbook reading, even greater time should be devoted to providing instruction in processing expository text at the middle and secondary levels than is provided for story reading at the elementary level.

Thus, reading is meaningful for older students when they can apply literacy processes for pleasure and personal growth, to better understand and influence their world, and to expand understanding of content textbooks and other school-related reading materials. The development of these critical reading, writing, and reasoning skills cannot be left to reading teachers or English teachers alone. Teachers in all academic areas should be responsible for reinforcing literacy skills as they apply to the understanding of their particular content, as well as helping adolescents appreciate the personal pleasures of literacy. While we are certainly not the first to make these admonitions, the idea that all teachers should assume responsibility for supporting students' various needs to be literate is difficult for some to grasp. We ask you to accept the following premise as critical for content-area literacy and learning: None of us—teachers and students alike—at any point in time have "arrived" as readers, writers, and thinkers. Instead, our literacy skills are in a continual process of growth and refinement.

All Teachers Should Help Students Develop Literacy Skills

DEFINITION OF LITERACY: A MODEST PROPOSAL

Given the multifarious nature of literacy, perhaps it is futile to attempt to include all of its dimensions in a single terse definition. We believe, therefore, that it is more helpful to define literacy by sharing scenes and instances of literacy teaching and learning. In other words, we try in this book to make the concept concrete by demonstrating how teachers and students in middle and secondary schools continually stretch the boundaries of literacy possibilities. As you might infer, we believe there is no single best static definition of literacy. Nonetheless, we outline in general terms the variables inherent in literacy acts in schools. Following is our modest definition of literacy, which will form the basis for all of the discussion and methods in this book. This definition combines current theory and research with our own and others' teaching experiences.

Definition of Literacy

> *Literacy* (including reading, writing, speaking, and listening) is a meaning-making and meaning-using process. Meaning is constructed through the interaction between the learner (in all of his or her complexity), the text (in all of its complexity), and instructional variables within the context of the learning situation. *Meaning* is used in direct relation to the level of interest in the learner and the level of functionality of the learning. The degree of interaction and use varies as a function of factors such as the learner's culture, prior knowledge, skills and strategies, motivation and interests, the type of text, the classroom environment, the instructional strategies, the meaningfulness of learning activities, and a host of other contextual factors.

Notice in this definition that our overall goal as learners is to make sense of our world through the use of literacy. Like all good thinkers, your ability to make meaningful interpretations of this book and use what you learn from it is directly related to (1) how much you already know about the topic of literacy (prior knowledge); (2) your experience with printed language (prior knowledge about the organization and structure of texts); (3) your interest in and motivation for reading this text; (4) your strategies for studying and retaining the ideas and information; (5) your purpose for reading it in the first place; (6) if you are reading it for a college course, how the instructor uses the book and the kinds of classroom experiences you are provided for learning the concepts and strategies in the book; and (7) how well we as authors have communicated to you as the reader. As classroom teachers, the more instruction we provide that braids literacy processes with the curriculum, that is connected to the interests and experiences of the learner, that allows for the exploration and generation of engaging texts, and that makes learning meaningful and functional, the more we improve how students make and use meaning (Calkins & Harwayne, 1991; Guthrie et al., 1996; Many, Fyfe, Lewis, & Mitchell, 1996).

The remainder of this chapter is devoted, first, to describing some growing concerns about literacy trends and habits of American youth and adults to clarify why literacy in middle and secondary school is so important. Next, we describe important principles of language-based teaching that underpin the scenes and strategies used in this text. We conclude with a description of the organizing instructional framework for the topics and strategies in this book.

THE LITERACY LANDSCAPE

Three growing trends in the American literacy landscape deserve our serious consideration. First, national assessment data on reading and writing continue to point to the fact that many middle and secondary school students cannot read or write beyond basic levels. A second and insidious trend is that greater and greater numbers of able readers are choosing not to read. Finally, ample evidence supports the contention that students' levels of critical literacy are falling. Taken together, these trends pose many awesome challenges for middle and secondary school educators concerned about the literacy growth of their students. Each is developed in more detail in the following discussion.

Low Levels of Literacy

The National Assessment of Educational Process (NAEP), a congressionally mandated project, has been conducting national surveys of the reading competency of 4th, 8th, and 12th graders since 1969 and of writing competence in the same grades since 1984. In its most recent reading assessment in 1994 (Campbell, Donahue, Reese, & Phillip, 1996), the following major results were observed:

- The average reading proficiency for 4th-grade students declined slightly since the 1992 assessment, remained unchanged for 8th-grade students, and declined significantly for 12th-grade students.
- For Hispanic students in Grade 4, as well as for white, black, and Hispanic students in Grade 12, there was a nationwide decline in reading proficiency from 1992 to 1994.
- Virtually all students displayed rudimentary reading skills and strategies characterized by the ability to perform relatively uncomplicated, discrete reading tasks successfully. However, very few students in any assessment

reached the highest levels of reading proficiency, reflecting their difficulty in comprehending passages that are more lengthy and complex or that deal with specialized subject matter.

- In the most recent report on writing proficiency (Applebee, Langer, Mullis, Latham, & Gentile, 1994), the NAEP authors make the following assertion about writing progress: "Whatever successes schools may claim in writing instruction, many students at each grade level continue to have serious difficulty in producing effective informative, persuasive, or narrative writing" (p. 3).

Together these findings make it clear that middle and secondary students are not making the kinds of reading gains all of us would like to see. Also, the few changes in writing proficiency that have occurred since 1984 suggest that not enough attention to writing as a regular and important form of communicating and meaning making is being given in junior and senior high schools. Attention to fostering higher levels of literacy and problem-solving abilities among young adults seems imperative because our world is becoming increasingly complex and increasingly challenges the intellectual and creative energies of all our citizens.

Students Need Training in Higher-Level Reading and Writing Skills

There is some good news on this front, however. American students in the fourth and ninth grades compare quite favorably to students in other countries in reading achievement. The International Association for the Evaluation of Educational Achievement (IEA), in their International Reading Literacy Study (Binkley & Williams, 1997), found that American fourth graders ranked among those of the top three countries, behind Finland and Sweden, outperforming those of such industrialized nations as Germany and France. American ninth graders fared less well but were among the top 10 countries in the study. Results such as these from international studies of reading achievement among elementary and secondary school children help erode the myth that students in the United States are inferior to those from other countries. A word of caution should be added to this discussion, however. IEA emphasizes that the tests used to measure reading comprehension focused almost exclusively on lower levels of thinking. In other words, to demonstrate success on the IEA test, students had to answer "questions directly related to the passage" (p. 14). On the other hand, successful performance on NAEP's tests of reading required students to interpret and examine passage meaning, summarize, develop their own ideas about text information, and evaluate limitations of documents. In some ways, therefore, the IEA study corroborates the NAEP results. In both cases, students performed fairly well on measures of reading comprehension requiring lower levels of thinking; yet, advanced literacy skills were found wanting on the NAEP test, though they were not measured on the IEA test.

We believe advanced literacy skills will develop when teachers place a special emphasis on helping students make thoughtful, critical elaborations of ideas and understandings that come from the materials they read and from their prior knowledge and experiences. To accomplish this, classroom teachers must shift away from learning that requires only simple memorization and superficial reading (Campbell et al., 1996). Nearly every year, the national science and math teachers' associations call for a move away from teaching science and math as a collection of minute facts and details, which students tend to memorize for quizzes and tests and then forget, toward improving the way students think and reason about science and math and making these subjects more functional and meaningful. We strongly endorse this recommendation because, like these educators, we believe that as students' thinking abilities improve, their interest in and motivation to learn science will increase and their ability to learn and retain important science and math facts will improve. Science and math educators are not alone in their desire to transform science and math learning from a rote exercise to a functional, problem-solving process; similar curricular recommendations have been made by national social studies organizations under the rubric of "globalism," whereby students are led to see how broad social, political, and economic issues relate to their everyday experiences.

In all the subjects students study, countless opportunities exist for developing higher-level literacy skills. Experiences that allow them to tap their own prior knowledge, to connect their experiences with the topic, to develop their own interpretations of what they read, to question, rethink, self-assess, and elaborate on text information and ideas, are what literacy instruction in the content area classroom should be about (Campbell et al., 1996).

The NAEP results also make clear the need to support students in their literacy efforts at home. Students at all three grade levels demonstrated higher reading proficiency if they (1) had a wider array of literacy materials in their homes, (2) read for fun on their own time, (3) had more frequent home discussions about their studies, (4) watched less television, and (5) read five or more pages each day of homework (Campbell et al., 1996).

Aliteracy

Barbara Hoover (1989), a syndicated columnist, tells a seriocomic story of falling in love with an attractive, enjoyable, and affectionate man. Not long into the relationship, however, she discovered that he owned just four books—a couple of business manuals, a dictionary, and a success guide. Her better judgment clouded temporarily by the newness of the romance, she minimized this observation and started bringing her own books to read during idle moments in their time together. After a couple of difficult years, they finally broke up. It was then, she says, that she realized an important truth: "There are two kinds of people: those who read and those who don't. And sometimes they run out of things to say to each other" (p. 3B).

Aliteracy Defined

While more and more money is spent on remedial reading and learning disabilities programs in public schools and on adult functional literacy programs, a growing number of people, like Hoover's ex-boyfriend, are in fact reading less and, in some cases, choosing not to read at all. This decision of literate individuals not to use their literacy has come to be known as *aliteracy.* Evidence for this growing phenomenon abounds.

U.S. presidents Ronald Reagan and George Bush might be characterized as aliterates. Of course, they knew how to read; they simply chose not to. When interviewed at the end of his administration, Reagan was hard pressed to remember the last time he'd read a book, let alone what the title was. And Bush boasted that he read fishing magazines (even as his wife, Barbara, headed a national drive for literacy). We are not trying to single out these two presidents for criticism but rather to draw attention to how pervasive aliteracy has become in our country.

Statistics from the American Enterprise Institute (AEI), a Washington, D.C.,-based organization involved in increasing public familiarity with contemporary issues, reports that by age 15, the average American child has spent more time in front of a television set than in the classroom or in doing homework (Thimmesch, 1985). Our current generation of youngsters also spends many additional hours playing video games in arcades or at home. Not only are children watching more and more TV, so are adults. Interior decorators and home builders in wealthy suburbs report that large homes are being built and remodeled without libraries, studies, or bookshelves. The owners simply aren't reading. Instead, these homes are being furnished with lavish entertainment centers (Hoover, 1989).

Television news programs claim as many viewers as this nation's approximately 1,700 newspapers have readers. Yet, while television news is expanding, newspaper circulation is steadily declining. From 1970 to the present, the daily circulation of newspapers has dropped by nearly 1 million. Studies have shown heavy TV viewers to be more suspicious of people than those described as avid readers. People who rely exclusively on television to size up political candidates make far more subjective judgments than people who rely largely on written accounts about those candidates and the issues (Thimmesch, 1985).

This increasing proclivity toward evaluating candidates based on their television presence has far-reaching implications. For instance, we're coming to discover that, more often than not, political candidates who outspend their opponents in campaigns win elections. The great bulk of campaign spending, especially at the state and national levels, is for television advertising. So, while our more cynical instincts tell us that this may have always been the case, increased television viewing may actually be playing into the hands of politicians with the deepest campaign chests. All of us would agree that a democracy is on a less than firm foundation if its citizenry elects not the representatives who have the best ideas, but those who have the most money. Politicians appear to be well aware of these contemporary truisms of campaign financing, as evidenced by the alarming number of scandals related to their obsession with raising money.

Studies have found that the average college student had not read a book in 4 years after graduating. Another study found that less than a majority of Americans read books regularly, with less than 25% characterized as moderate to heavy readers (defined as reading 10 to 30 books or more per year) (Campbell, 1985).

Even College Graduates Are Reading Less

Finally, Robert Duffey (as reported by Campbell, 1985) conducted a study indicating that, for the most part, teachers do not read. It is difficult for adults, whether parents, teachers, successful businesspeople, or politicians, to impart the love of reading or even a positive attitude toward reading to American youth unless they themselves value literacy enough to make it an integral part of their lives.

We argue, therefore, that teachers are foot soldiers in the fight against aliteracy. Those of us who work directly with middle- and upper-grade students are in the best position to foster positive perceptions and attitudes toward literacy while giving students regular and frequent opportunities to practice and grow as literate learners.

No Place for Critical Literacy

Lankshear (1993) talks about the need to infuse school curricula with a critical literacy perspective whereby reading and writing become processes for educating students to be critical participatory citizens. In his view, as well as those of Goodman (1992) and others (Giroux, 1987; King & Brozo, 1992), school learning should provide the context for students to become critical and self-determined thinkers. Unfortunately, as increasing economic and political pressures dictate the teaching and learning possibilities for teachers and students, the curriculum in many middle and secondary schools has been reduced to a warehouse of knowledge to be passed on to waiting customers. Teachers often find themselves in the role of information disseminator, forced to find ever more efficient means to "cover the material."

Symptomatic of a curriculum that has become devoid of a critical component is the preoccupation among adolescents with getting a job or doing better than Japan. This single-minded thinking about the purpose of schooling reflects the prevailing condition of much of our content-area curriculum. Middle and secondary schools that make it a priority to educate students to make choices and think critically can help students develop the confidence and conviction that they can make a difference in the world. This sense of power can result from instruction concerned with making connections between and among teachers and students, within and among classrooms, and inside and outside of schools. Critical literacy fosters an understanding of the ways we are all interconnected and interdependent, and teaches that in caring for others we are in fact caring for ourselves (Goodman, 1992).

Critical Literacy Can Be Used to Solve Real-World Problems

When conceptualizing a curriculum of critical literacy that attends to the real-world needs, concerns, and aspirations of youth, we can't help but think of the monumental problems facing us as a nation that beg for creative and humane solutions. Those same problems could be the focus of our curriculum in middle and secondary schools: for example, conditions of urban and rural poverty, overpopulation and world hunger, environmental degradation, unresponsive government, and the energy crisis. We believe that schools can become sites for entertaining, working toward, and remedying the social, political, economic, and environmental ills of our communities, nation, and world.

In the concluding section of this chapter, we outline essential principles of language-based teaching. Based on our experience as teachers and our knowledge of the research and applied literature in literacy, we believe that these principles hold the most promise for meeting the challenges posed by aliteracy, falling levels of literacy, and lack of critical literacy.

PRINCIPLES OF LANGUAGE-BASED TEACHING

Language-based teaching involves much more than the narrow notion of reading and writing techniques. It is a philosophy of teaching that sees the teacher's role as one of agitator, creator of conceptual conflicts, challenger of conventional wisdom, and, above all, facilitator of students' own knowledge construction and use. Within language-based learning environments, students should be allowed to grow into critically thinking members of society, while teachers engage in the processes of reflecting, researching, and learning in order to become more effective teachers.

Following are the principles we consider essential for effective language-based teaching:

1. Language-based teachers understand that learning is a social process.
2. Language-based teachers know that the best learning occurs when it is whole, functional, and meaningful.
3. Language-based teachers know that students improve their reading and writing when given abundant opportunities to use reading and writing as vehicles for learning.
4. Language-based teachers understand the importance motivation plays in learning.
5. Language-based teachers are continually moving toward better literacy and content teaching.

Principle 1: Language-Based Teachers Understand That Learning Is a Social Process

It has long been recognized that we know what we know only when we reflect our knowledge in others (Blumer, 1969). Harste (1988) offers these insights into the significance of the social nature of learning:

> I am convinced that we know nothing by ourselves. It is only in juxtaposition with others that we know, and know what we know differs from others' knowledge. (p. 13)

Literacy is a social process (Green, 1990; Myers, 1992; Turner, 1995). Even when you curl up with a book in the "private" act of reading, you are not alone—you are interacting with an author who holds other ideas, points of view, styles of expression. A useful construct here is **intertextuality,** or ways in which an individual's construction of meaning depends on other meanings (Hartman, 1995). Bloome and Egan-Robertson (1993) have demonstrated that when teachers provide for intertextual tying between and among students in the social world of the classroom, greater language learning takes place. In their research, students made obvious connections between their written texts and those of classmates because they were provided opportunities to observe another author at work and to talk with that author in order to develop and expand on their own ideas. Similar discoveries of the power of cooperative meaning making have been made by Unrau and Ruddell (1995).

Social Learning Promotes Intertextual Tying

The instructional implications of the social nature of learning are many and varied. On a general level, students can build shared meanings of literacy, language, and concepts when they are encouraged to make use of demonstrations provided by their peers and teachers and are given opportunities to interact informally with other authors and learners in the classroom community. On a practical level, the classroom itself should be arranged to encourage social interaction among student meaning makers. Instead of arranging desks in rows, forcing students to talk to the back of others' heads and making easy eye contact only with the teacher, we recommend a more flexible seating arrangement that encourages student-student dialoguing and problem solving. One such approach that has been found to improve not only the academic achievement of students but also their level of interpersonal attraction (Jules, 1990) is cooperative learning.

Cooperative Learning

Johnson and Johnson (1989) describe three basic learning experiences that students are likely to have in schools: individualistic, competitive, and cooperative. Of the three, cooperative learning better facilitates a teacher's constructive use of student interaction and gives rise to an "increase in the pro-social orientation among students" (Kagan, 1990, p. 9).

Cooperative Learning Defined

Cooperative learning groups consist generally of three or more students grouped heterogeneously and linked by a common goal. The emphasis in the groups is on the completion of an academic assignment, as well as the promotion of social skills. Cooperative learning has become immensely popular since the early 1980s because of its positive effect on achievement, self-esteem, interpersonal dynamics, and motivation. Figure 1.1 presents the essential elements for successful cooperative learning.

The use of cooperative groups as a dynamic method for teaching content-area comprehension and learning has been consistently supported by a history of voluminous research (Abrami & Chambers, 1996; Slavin, 1996). Cooperative learning enables students to assume responsibility for their learning and to develop confidence in their ability to learn. In heterogeneous classroom situations, where social interaction plays an important role in the facilitation of learning (Jordan & LeMatais, 1997), cooperative learning provides students who view themselves as unsuccessful learners, when grouped with others of low ability

1. *Positive interdependence:* "We sink or swim together!"
   Methods to promote this attitude include
   - Mutual goal
   - Group accountability
   - Shared/limited materials
   - Group rewards
   - Complementary and interconnected roles
   - Division of labor
2. *Individual accountability:* "No hitchhiking!"
   Methods to promote this attitude include
   - Individual tests
   - Random selection of a group member
   - Random selection of one paper
3. Face-to-face interaction
   - Eye to eye, knee to knee
   - Oral exchange
   - Conducive physical arrangement
4. Appropriate use of collaborative skills
   - Skills should be taught
   - Skills should be practiced
   - Students should be motivated to use skills
   - Skills should be assessed by teacher or group members

FIGURE 1.1 Essential Elements of Cooperative Learning

(Ediger, 1995), the opportunity to make significant contributions to group decisions. Further, cooperative learning gives students the opportunity to share what they have learned, to listen to the ideas and opinions of fellow students, to be taught by their peers, and to assume the role of teacher (Johnson & Johnson, 1996; Jules, 1990; Kagan, 1990; Sapon-Shevin & Schniedewind, 1990). As a result of cooperative learning, greater literacy and content learning have been observed in a variety of classroom contexts (Gillies & Ashman, 1997; Jacobson, 1990; Nelson, 1996; Sullivan, 1996; Thistlewaite, 1990). Cooperative learning has also been shown to promote active comprehension and to develop the language abilities in the content areas (Noll, 1994; Wood, 1991). When teachers use cooperative learning, they communicate to students that their input is valued and that their contributions broaden the understanding of the topic for the community of learners in the classroom. We demonstrate applications of this powerful teaching and learning strategy throughout this book.

Cooperative Learning Helps Students Become Responsible for Learning

Principle 2: Language-Based Teachers Know That the Best Learning Occurs When It Is Whole, Functional, and Meaningful

The term *whole* in this principle has many different aspects. In one sense, it refers to complete and genuine text sources that students read and write.

Commercially prepared learning materials, such as textbooks, are bound by countless restrictions that result inevitably in "pointlessly arid prose" (Tyson-Bernstein, 1988). Genuine text, on the other hand, is created by authors who simply have an urge to communicate their perspectives and information on a topic. Consider, for instance, the difference between the treatment of the Vietnam War in a 10th-grade history textbook compared with Elizabeth Becker's (1992) *America's Vietnam War: A Narrative History.* The textbook, because of space limitations, offers only a few pages on the topic. The textbook publisher makes sure that issues about the war that might be considered too controversial are not included; concerns about readability force the authors of the textbook to exclude certain imaginative terms and phrases. By comparison, Becker's book provides an in-depth, critical view of the issues surrounding the Vietnam War, from the history of American involvement to the fall of Saigon. Unbounded by the publisher restrictions, such as those placed on textbook authors, Becker presents the topic in a lively and engaging way that is sure to draw adolescent readers into a more thoughtful study of Vietnam. So although textbooks often form the core of learning in most secondary classrooms, we suggest that textbooks alone aren't enough because they fail the test of wholeness.

Students Learn More from Authentic Texts

With respect to writing, we advocate that teachers allow students to compose complete texts through the writing process (discussed in detail in Chapter 7). Instead of being confined to certain topics and forms of writing, as often as possible students should be free to select the discourse mode best suited to their needs of expression. For example, in writing about the Vietnam War, students required to write a two-page report on the battle of Dien Bien Phu or the Gulf of Tonkin incident would likely be less engaged in and enthusiastic about learning than if they were asked to put themselves in the place of a participant or a victim of the war (e.g., a Viet Cong villager, a witness to the My Lai massacre, an American living in Canada to avoid the draft, a parent of a soldier who is missing in action) and write, for instance, a letter, diary entry, or story. Better yet, students could be asked to respond in writing, using a variety of discourse options that help them rework the content. When given options, students may choose to write poetry, song lyrics, or dialogue for a drama to be enacted impromptu by a small group. In this way, students become much more invested in the learning process as they develop a sense of ownership of their ideas and their learning.

Students Need to Write Genuine Communications

Another aspect of whole learning is the notion of *integrated learning.* Students should be involved in activities and projects that require integrating reading, writing, speaking, and listening. Writers workshops (see Chapter 7), for example, can be used to bring all the language systems to bear on learning content material. Integration also refers to tying together learning from many areas of the secondary school curriculum. This aspect of holistic teaching can be the most challenging for secondary teachers, largely because of the highly departmentalized nature of most junior and senior high schools. Consider this example of integration: Students learning about the Vietnam War could be learning about the U.S. government's evolving foreign policy as it relates to Southeast Asia in one classroom, the culture and customs of Southeast Asia in another, and

Linking Curriculum Leads to Greater Learning

the economic ramifications of the war in another. Students meanwhile could read works of fiction by Southeast Asian authors or about this region and its people. Making the curriculum whole allows students to see the interconnectedness of content in order to develop a broader understanding of topics. We present strategies for teachers working together to bring cohesion to the curriculum in Chapter 12.

Webster's Dictionary defines *functional* as "connected with." We like this definition because it implies that when teachers make learning functional, students connect with it; they find linkages between classroom content, on the one hand, and needs and purposes in their personal lives, on the other. We agree with Edelsky, Altwerger, and Flores (1991), who argue that "learners' purposes and intentions are what drives learning" (p. 25). If the sole purpose of learning is external to the learner (e.g., pleasing the teacher, getting a good grade), then it doesn't really matter what is learned. In content-area classrooms where the purposes of learning are always and unilaterally determined by the teacher, we have seen a condition of "learned helplessness" (Diener & Dweck, 1978) set in. Students can become so conditioned to respond only to teachers' directives that they rarely if ever initiate learning, attack problems independently, or seek out information on their own. By contrast, students in classrooms that support their own explorations of functional learning are engaged, enthusiastic, and independent.

An excellent example of functional learning comes from a senior high school French class where the teacher provided the necessary support for students to explore their career options in a French language profession or aspects of French culture about which students desired more information. One student, Deanna, interviewed translators from international businesses (e.g., Michelin) and gained insights into the educational and experimental prerequisites for such a career. Terrell read about and spoke directly to French poets and writers whose topics dealt with race relations in France. Kimme's interest in becoming a buyer for a major department store led her to study the French fashion world. And Charles looked into French wines and cuisine with the intent of using this knowledge to conduct eating tours in France. These students kept a log of their information-gathering process, including following leads, phone conversations, and written correspondence, as well as personal reflections on their research. They also shared their findings with the class. Their demonstrations clearly reflected the power of making learning functional.

Functional Learning Is Tied to Students' Lives

Meaningfulness refers to ways of making learning personally meaningful for the learner. If we assume that the only way to make students learn is to force them to learn, then we may be left with no choice but to use force every time we try to teach. Think about an alternative self-fulfilling prophecy. What if we demonstrated trust in students' own natural curiosity, their own need to know more, their ability to make meaning? Imagine the transformation that might take place in classrooms where students are supported in their efforts to find meaningful connections to their own lives and their realities outside school with topics and content being considered in school! In working with Chicago youth, we discovered that students who were considered problems became engaged in learning when they were supported in their efforts to bring their real-world issues and concerns into the classroom. Using a reader-response writing strategy (described in detail in Chapter 7), students in an eighth-grade social studies class read magazine and newspaper articles about problems common to most inner-city communities and then wrote responses connecting their own experiences with those in the readings. Raymond, a former "graffiti artist," responded to an article in the *Chicago Tribune* about gangs and graffiti by relating it to his experiences. Raymond claimed that while most graffiti artists were not gang members, the mayor was linking all of them to gangs to mobilize more resources to eradicate graffiti. The teacher of this class found that by supporting her students' efforts to bring their lives into the content of their writing, students like Raymond became more engaged learners and more animated participants in class discussion.

Principle 3: Language-Based Teachers Know That Students Improve Their Reading and Writing When Given Abundant Opportunities to Use Reading and Writing as Vehicles for Learning

Earlier, we described the result of aliteracy: Children and youth adopt the attitude that using literacy is not critical to functioning in the adult world. As one avoids literacy experiences more and more, one's reading, writing, and critical thinking skills wither. Frank Smith's (1985) pithy axiom that "We learn to read by reading" (p. 88) captures the essence of this principle. All of us must take responsibility for expanding literacy for our students. This is not the purview of any single teacher or of parents alone. And to do so, we must all be prepared to involve students in literacy experiences that contribute to their language development and their ability to think more expansively about themselves and their worlds.

Characteristics of Language-Based Classrooms

Middle and secondary school learning environments that embody this principle of language-based teaching possess characteristics of immersion, demonstration, interaction, and transaction. **Immersion** refers to involving students in environments that are language-rich, filled with real-world artifacts of the adult literate community and opportunities for critical analysis of school, text, and personal truths. **Demonstration** reminds us that teachers should know the literacy processes from the inside out to credibly model teaching as learning and teaching as inquiry. **Interaction** refers to giving students opportunities to learn from one another, value one another, and critique one another's truths. The teacher's truths should be subject to the same level of scrutiny as anyone else's. **Transaction** suggests that for students to learn principles of cooperation, participation, and critical citizenship, they should be directly involved in shaping the curriculum so that it is more closely aligned with their personal and career needs and goals.

In content-area classrooms, this principle means that teachers create supportive learning environments for students to use the language processes of reading, writing, speaking, and listening to better understand the curriculum. Such an environment would likely include process writing (see Chapter 7) wherein students work together to write drafts, receive feedback, and rewrite until their work is ready to be graded and/or published. A content-area teacher who encourages students' literacy growth while expanding their knowledge of content also makes available to students and makes integral to the curriculum a variety of resources, such as trade and reference books and, as mentioned, a variety of literacy material from the adult world, in addition to the textbook. Not only can these alternative reading materials generate more enthusiasm for reading and learning, they are also excellent resources for broadening students' understanding of topics as they read and consider the topics from various perspectives.

In middle and secondary classrooms where this principle is practiced, teachers in all content areas provide sustained, uninterrupted periods for students and themselves to read and write. In this way, a literate culture is developed wherein teachers model healthy, adaptive literacy behavior while nurturing the literacy habits of their students.

Virtually every chapter of this book offers ideas and strategies for getting students more actively and frequently involved in using the language systems as vehicles for learning and for personal growth and pleasure.

Principle 4: Language-Based Teachers Understand the Importance Motivation Plays in Learning

Motivation is a topic researchers of learning can never ignore. Behaviorists may try to argue that children can be taught to learn school-based information and content much the same way they can be taught to dribble a basketball or swim the breast stroke—that is, by breaking learning down into minute parts and steps, working discretely with each one until all have been mastered before putting the parts together into a meaningful whole. Missing, of course, in the behavioral approach to instruction, is whether or not the learner has the **will** to master discrete parts of learning. Without a student's acquiescence, all of our attempts at drill and practice of small, fragmented parts of learning will meet with disappointment. A principal offered these enlightened words to us recently on this topic: "We can force students to attend school, but we can't force them to learn."

Not surprisingly, motivation has reemerged as one of the most popular areas of interest to researchers and practitioners in literacy and content learning (Guthrie & Wigfield, 1997). Over the past decade, research has offered us many important new insights into how to motivate students to read by using interesting books (Allington, 1991; Elley, 1992; Gambrell, 1996) and how this motivation can translate into significant improvement in reading achievement (Taylor, Frye, & Maruyama, 1990).

Turner (1995) has provided extensive research-based descriptions of school contexts that are motivating for students. These motivating contexts consist of the "six C's" (Turner & Paris, 1995):

Choice. When students can choose the tasks and texts they are interested in, they spend more energy trying to learn and understand the material.

Challenge. Moderately challenging tasks, as opposed to simple, feel-good tasks, are often the most engaging and cognitively useful to students.

Control. Students need to have some control of their learning in order to develop independence and versatility as learners.

Collaboration. Social interaction and cooperation are fundamental to motivation because they increase effort and persistence.

Characteristics of Motivating Learning Environments

Constructing meaning. Active meaning construction promotes motivation by placing responsibility on students to make sense of their learning. When students are denied this responsibility, they often become passive and nonparticipatory.

Consequences. Students should be helped to see the connection between effort and outcome. When tasks are controllable, students are more likely to take responsibility for them and more willing to learn from mistakes.

As you proceed through this book, pay attention to how the teachers in the many scenarios we describe incorporate the six C's into their instructional approach.

Principle 5: Language-Based Teachers Are Continually Moving Toward Better Literacy and Content Teaching

A theme running throughout this book is that language-based teaching is a process. This book is meant to encourage and support content-area teachers as they move from teaching practices that focus exclusively on content to those that develop and apply students' language processes and, in this way, help students come to value literacy as an integral part of their lives. Advocates of a content/process model of middle and secondary school teaching for improving students' ability to learn content material, as well as for expanding students' sense of themselves as learners and as critical, independent decision makers, have been around for some time (see Herber, 1978). Nonetheless, changes in the ways teachers teach junior and senior high students have been slow and painstaking. Administrators, professors, "experts," teachers, and students all share some of the responsibility for this uneven progress. O'Brien, Stewart, and Moje (1995) and others (Moje, Brozo, & Haas, 1994) explain how the realities of middle and secondary school teaching, including curricular demands and institutional and peer pressures, can seem to leave teachers little choice but to employ efficient but unengaging and unauthentic instructional methods (e.g., lecturing, objective testing). We understand the realities of change and, therefore, emphasize the value of making transitions.

After working with a junior high school teacher, Robin, for a year as she implemented cooperative learning for the first time after 12 years of teaching, we found that two overarching generalizations hold true with regard to making transitions in teaching: Transitions take time, and they involve helping students make transitions.

Transitions Take Time

Robin wanted to change but found that when her students didn't respond in ways she had expected, she became filled with self-doubt and wondered about returning to an information-dissemination model of teaching. It was only after 3 or 4 months of the school year, as her students began to take on their cooperative roles with enthusiasm and independence, that she saw the tangible benefits of this new approach to teaching and learning. Robin realized that through exploration, experimentation, and reflection she eventually appreciated the powerful transformation taking place in her classroom. So, as Robin allowed time for change, students began to change; these positive changes in the students then made it easier for Robin to accept and support further transitions to more language-based, cooperative teaching.

Good Teachers Are in a Constant State of Transition

Transitions Involve Helping Students Make Transitions as Well

We often forget, in our enthusiastic support of teacher change, that as challenging as it may be for teachers themselves to make the transition to new models of teaching, it may be even more challenging for students in a changing classroom environment. In Robin's classroom, we discovered that students were not prepared initially for the demands of cooperative learning and, therefore, could not make an abrupt transition from their role as receivers of information to active participants in shared learning. As discussed, the interrelationship between the students' reluctance to change and Robin's perseverance to work through change was critical. What helped was Robin's willingness to provide more modeling, more opportunities for students to take risks and experiment with their new roles. Perhaps most critical, however, was the self-assessment that was built into the process of cooperative learning. Through this process, students were able to take a new look at themselves as learners and turn to Robin for support. In this process, too, Robin watched herself change from "purveyor of truth" to someone who created the process and environment that allowed students to see each other as learning resources.

LITERACY AND CONTENT LEARNING: A FRAMEWORK FOR INSTRUCTION

This book is filled with hundreds of ideas and strategies for teaching. While these ideas and strategies are presented in various chapters, we do not want them to be viewed in isolation. Instead, we want you to see how many different strategies can work together to form a complete set of teaching and learning experiences for you and your students.

To assist you in your exploration and study of the ideas and strategies in this book, study the graphic of an instructional framework at the opening of this chapter. This graphic appears at the beginning of Chapters 2 through 11

The Strategies in This Book Are Linked

to remind you of how the ideas and strategies in a particular chapter should be linked to an overall lesson structure. All content-area lessons in middle and secondary schools should comprise three primary elements, represented by the pillars in the graphic. First, students should be introduced to new learning by engaging them in interesting purpose-setting readiness activities. Second, comprehension strategies should be taught and used in the process of exploring texts related to the topic. Third, students should be given study strategies for retaining and demonstrating their new understandings. Supporting these three pillars of instruction are several additional aspects of teaching and learning that should be included to create an effective content-area lesson (represented at the base of the graphic): vocabulary, trade books, writing, technology, assessment, and special needs. Strategies based on these topics can be integrated into any phase of the lesson.

SUMMARY

This opening chapter has set the stage for the ideas, examples, and strategies presented in this book. We have discussed the challenges all of us must face in attempting to encourage middle and secondary students to become active, full participants in the learning process. Findings from national reports on literacy skills and on the habits of adolescents and adults paint a rather disturbing picture. Low levels of literacy are apparently becoming acceptable in our schools, and an attitude of indifference toward reading appears to be growing among adults; meanwhile, our youth are becoming increasingly passive learners. At the same time, the potential power of literacy as a tool for promoting social, political, and economic transformation is largely ignored in middle and secondary schools. To reverse these trends, we suggest that teachers, with the help of their students, create learning environments in content classrooms that are language based, where students use literacy to acquire new knowledge, to grow personally, to find pleasure, and to transform themselves and their world. Finally, as illustrated in the graphic at the chapter opener, we discuss a framework of instruction to help organize the ideas and strategies contained in this book and urge teachers to frame their content-area lessons within this structure to increase the likelihood of greater content learning.

REFERENCES

Abrami, P., & Chambers, B. (1996). Research on cooperative learning and achievement: Comments on Slavin. *Contemporary Educational Psychology, 21,* 70–73.

Allington, R. L. (1991). The legacy of *slow it down and make it more concrete.* In J. Zutell & S. McCormick (Eds.), *Learner factors/teacher factors: Issues in literacy research and instruction.* Chicago: National Reading Conference.

Applebee, A., Langer, J., Mullis, I., Latham, A., & Gentile, C. (1994). *NAEP 1992 writing report card.* Washington, DC: Educational Testing Service.

Becker, E. (1992). *America's Vietnam war: A narrative history.* New York: Clarion Books.

Binkley, M., & Williams, T. (1997). *Reading literacy in the United States.* Washington, DC: U.S. Department of Education.

Bintz, W. (1993). Resistant readers in secondary education: Some insights and implications. *Journal of Reading, 36,* 604-615.

Bloome, D., & Egan-Robertson, A. (1993). The social construction of intertextuality in classroom reading and writing lessons. *Reading Research Quarterly, 28,* 304-333.

Blumer, H. (1969). *Symbolic interactionism: Perspectives and method.* Englewood Cliffs, NJ: Prentice-Hall.

Calkins, L., & Harwayne, S. (1991). *Living between the lines.* Portsmouth, NH: Heinemann.

Campbell, J. (1985). The "reading to learn" approach. In N. Thimmesch (Ed.), *Aliteracy.* Washington, DC: American Enterprise Institute.

Campbell, J., Donahue, P., Reese, C., & Phillips, G. (1996). *NAEP 1994 reading report card for the nation and states.* Washington, DC: Educational Testing Service.

Diener, C., & Dweck, C. (1978). An analysis of learned helplessness: Continuous changes in performance, strategy, and achievement cognitions following failure. *Journal of Personality and Social Psychology, 34,* 451-462.

Edelsky, C., Altwerger, B., & Flores, B. (1991). *Whole language: What's the difference?* Portsmouth, NH: Heinemann.

Ediger, M. (1995). Cooperative learning and heterogeneous grouping. *Reading Improvement, 32,* 135-143.

Elley, W. (1992). *How in the world do students read?* Hamburg, Germany: International Association for the Evaluation of Educational Achievement.

Gambrell, L. (1996). Creating classroom cultures that foster reading motivation. *The Reading Teacher, 50,* 14-25.

Gillies, R., & Ashman, A. (1997). The effects of training in cooperative learning on differential student behavior and achievement. *The Journal of Classroom Interaction, 32,* 1-10.

Giroux, H. (1987). Critical literacy and student experience: Donald Graves' approach to literacy. *Language Arts, 64,* 175-181.

Glasgow, J. N. (1996). Motivating the tech prep reader through learning styles and adolescent literature. *Journal of Adolescent and Adult Literacy, 39,* 358-367.

Goodman, J. (1992). Towards a discourse of imagery: Critical curriculum theorizing. *The Educational Forum, 56,* 269-289.

Green, J. (1990). Reading as a social process. In J. Howell, A. McNamara, & M. Clough (Eds.), *Social context of literacy.* Canberra, Australia: ACT Department of Education, Canberra.

Gregory, T., & Smith, G. (1987). *High schools as communities: The small school reconsidered.* Bloomington, IN: Phi Delta Kappa.

Guthrie, J., Van Meter, P., McCann, A., Wigfield, A., Bennett, L., Poundstone, C., Rice, M., Faibisch, F., Hunt, B., & Mitchell, A. (1996). Growth of literacy engagement: Changes in motivations and strategies during concept-oriented reading instruction. *Reading Research Quarterly, 31,* 306-333.

Guthrie, J., & Wigfield, A. (1997). *Reading engagement: Motivating readers through integrated instruction.* Newark, DE: International Reading Association.

Harste, J. (1988). Tomorrow's readers today: Becoming a profession of collaborative learners. In J. Readence & R. S. Baldwin (Eds.), *Dialogues in literacy research.* Chicago: National Reading Conference.

Hartman, D. (1995). Eight readers reading: The intertextual links of proficient readers reading multiple passages. *Reading Research Quarterly, 30,* 520-561.

Herber, H. (1978). *Teaching reading in the content areas.* Englewood Cliffs, NJ: Prentice-Hall.

Hill, M., & Van Horn, L. (1995). Book club goes to jail: Can book clubs replace gangs? *Journal of Adolescent and Adult Literacy, 39,* 180–189.

Hoover, B. (1989, April 16). Is anybody reading? *The Detroit News,* Section E, p. 1.

Jacobson, J. (1990). Group vs. individual completion of a cloze passage. *Journal of Reading, 33,* 244–251.

Johnson, D., & Johnson, R. (1989). *Cooperation and competition: Theory and research.* Edina, MN: Interaction Book Company.

Johnson, D., & Johnson, R. (1996). Cooperative learning and traditional American values: An appreciation. *NASSP Bulletin, 80,* 63–66.

Jordan, D., & LeMatais, J. (1997). Social skilling through cooperative learning. *Educational Researcher, 39,* 3–12.

Jules, V. (1990). Cooperative learning and work-mate preferences in classrooms in secondary schools. *Contemporary Education, 61,* 65–70.

Kagan, S. (1990). On cooperative learning: A conversation with Spencer Kagan. *Educational Leadership, 47,* 8–10.

King, J., & Brozo, W. G. (1992). Critical literacy and the pedagogies of empowerment. In A. Frager & J. Miller (Eds.), *Using inquiry in reading education.* Oxford, OH: College Reading Association.

Knoblach, C. H., & Brannon, L. (1983). Writing as learning through the curriculum. *College English, 45,* 465–474.

Lankshear, C. (1993). Curriculum as literacy: Reading and writing in *New Times.* In B. Green (Ed.), *The insistence of the letter: Literacy studies and curriculum theorizing.* Pittsburgh: University of Pittsburgh.

Manning, M. L., & Lucking, R. (May/June 1991). The what, why, and how of cooperative learning. *The Social Studies, 17,* 120–124.

Many, J., Fyfe, R., Lewis, G., & Mitchell, E. (1996). Traversing the topical landscape: Exploring students' self-directed reading-writing-research processes. *Reading Research Quarterly, 31,* 12–35.

Moje, E., Brozo, W. G., & Haas, J. (1994). Portfolios in high school classrooms: Challenges to change. *Reading Research and Instruction, 33,* 275–292.

Myers, J. (1992). The social contexts of school and personal literacy. *Reading Research Quarterly, 27,* 297–333.

Nelson, B. (1996). Cooperative learning. *The Science Teacher, 63,* 22–28.

Noll, E. (1994). Social issues and literature circles with adolescents. *Journal of Reading, 38,* 88–93.

O'Brien, D., Stewart, R., & Moje, E. (1995). Why content literacy is difficult to infuse into the secondary school: Complexities of curriculum, pedagogy, and school culture. *Reading Research Quarterly, 30,* 442–463.

Rief, L. (1992). *Seeking diversity: Language arts with adolescents.* Portsmouth, NH: Heinemann.

Sapon-Shevin, M., & Schniedewind, M. (1990). Selling cooperation without selling it short. *Educational Leadership, 47,* 63–65.

Slavin, R. (1996). Research on cooperative learning and achievement: What we know, what we need to know. *Contemporary Educational Psychology, 21,* 43–69

Smith, F. (1985). *Reading without nonsense.* New York: Teachers College Press.

Sullivan, J. (1996). Implementing a cooperative learning research model: How it applies to a social studies unit. *The Social Studies, 87,* 210–217.

Taylor, B., Frye, B., & Maruyama, G. (1990). Time spent reading and reading growth. *American Educational Research Journal, 27,* 351-362.

Thimmesch, N. (1985). *Aliteracy.* Washington, DC: National Enterprise Institute.

Thistlewaite, L. (1990). Critical reading for at-risk students. *Journal of Reading, 33,* 586-593.

Turner, J. (1995). The influence of classroom contexts on young children's motivation for literacy. *Reading Research Quarterly, 30,* 410-441.

Turner, J., & Paris, S. (1995). How literacy tasks influence children's motivation for literacy. *The Reading Teacher, 48,* 662-673.

Tyson-Bernstein, H. (1988). *A conspiracy of good intentions.* Washington, DC: Council for Basic Education.

Unrau, N., & Ruddell, R. (1995). Interpreting texts in classroom contexts. *Journal of Adolescent and Adult Literacy, 39,* 16-27.

Willinsky, J. (1990). *The new literacy.* New York: Routledge.

Wood, K. (1991). Meeting the social needs of adolescents through collaborative learning experiences. In J. Irvin (Ed.), *Transforming middle level education.* New York: Allyn & Bacon.

CHAPTER 2

Active Learning in Language-Based Classrooms

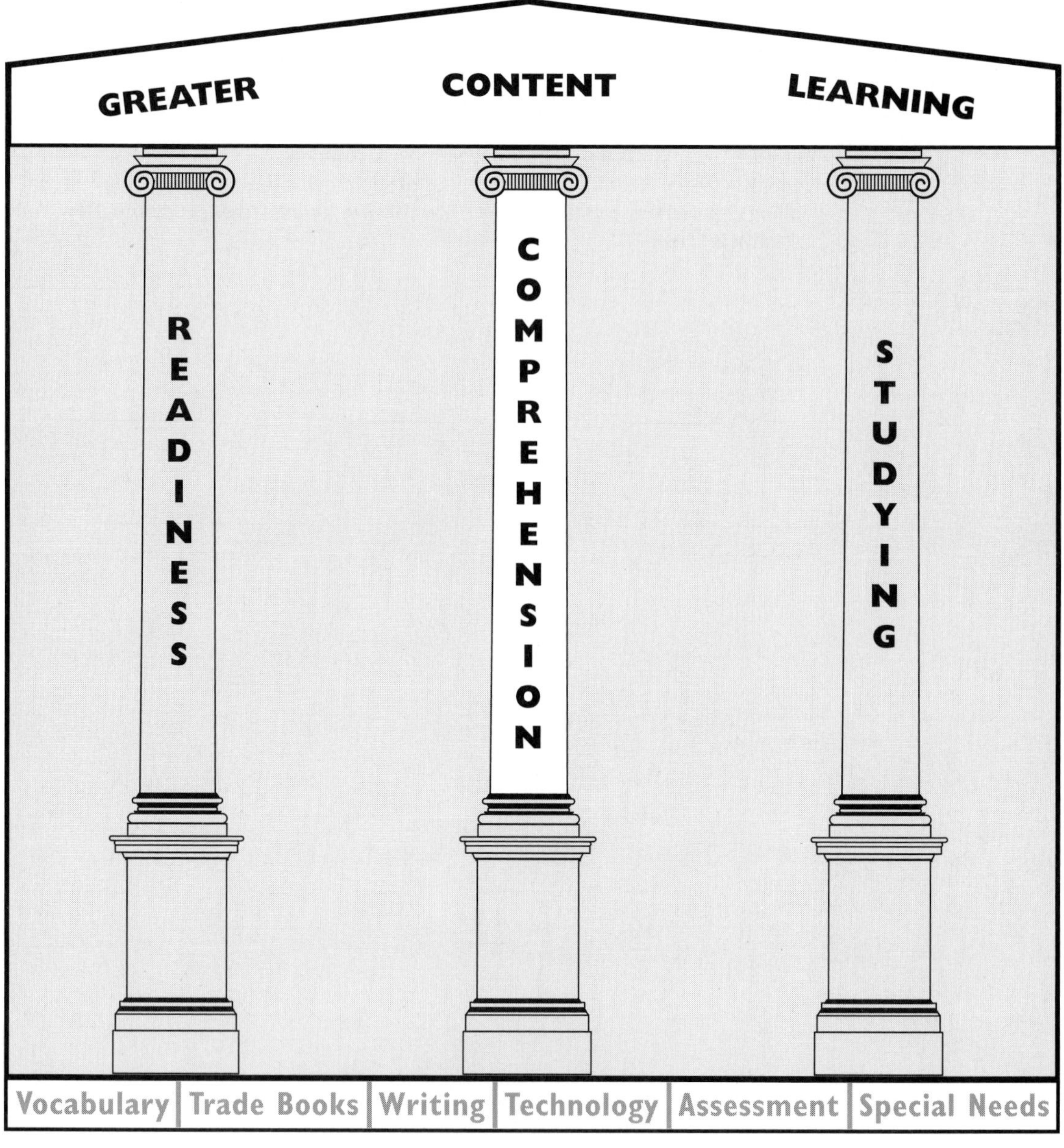

ANTICIPATION GUIDE

Directions: Read each statement carefully and decide whether you agree or disagree with it, placing a check mark in the appropriate *Before Reading* column. When finished reading and studying the chapter, return to the guide and decide whether your anticipations need to be changed by placing a check mark in the appropriate *After Reading* column.

	BEFORE READING		**AFTER READING**	
	Agree	*Disagree*	*Agree*	*Disagree*
1. Our students' ability to read and think critically has improved significantly.	_____	_____	_____	_____
2. What you know about a topic has little influence on how much you will remember once you begin reading.	_____	_____	_____	_____
3. Narrative and expository writing place equal demands on readers.	_____	_____	_____	_____
4. Most middle school and secondary school textbooks have been written so that they are very easy to understand.	_____	_____	_____	_____
5. As students grow older, they are better able to identify concepts they do not understand.	_____	_____	_____	_____
6. If students learned one or two strategies, they would be prepared for any task in any class.	_____	_____	_____	_____
7. Active learning is an inherited trait that cannot be coached or taught.	_____	_____	_____	_____

Active learning works not only because it helps motivation and feedback but also because active learners are more likely to be attentive and to be thinking about the topic, relating new knowledge to previous learning, and elaborating the implications of what they have learned.

—McKeachie (1994)

Local school boards, administrators, teachers, and parents have long been concerned about the results of national studies indicating that schools need to do more to improve students' higher-level reading and critical thinking skills. For example, the 1994 NAEP found a statistically significant decline of 4 percentage points between 1992 and 1994 in the proportion of 12th graders who could read at the "proficient level" (Campbell, Donahue, Reese, & Phillips, 1996). Students at this level can draw inferences and conclusions, make connections between what they have read and their personal experiences, and analyze literary devices. Although this statistic appears somewhat pessimistic, we believe that all students can improve their higher-level comprehension and critical thinking skills. This chapter describes a model of active learning that can apply to all content-area classrooms where readers and teachers focus on understanding, critical thinking, and learning. Because we know that many middle school and high school teachers use discussions, demonstrations, projects, and activities to help them teach their course objectives and may never use the traditional textbook, we wish to stress the universality of this model of active learning. Rather than focusing on just higher-level comprehension or critical thinking strategies oriented only to textbooks, we propose a model that will assist students in their meaning-making processes for any content-area class and any text, written or oral. Hence, when we discuss texts in this chapter and the other chapters, we refer to all the written and oral texts from which students must learn. The five theoretical principles that guide students' active learning from these texts are as follows:

Principle 1: Active learners use their prior knowledge in the meaning-making process.

Principle 2: Active learners understand and use text structure to organize their meaning making.

Principle 3: Active learners think critically about text and create their own elaborations.

Principle 4: Active learners are metacognitively aware.

Principle 5: Active learners possess and employ a wide range of reading and learning strategies.

In Chapter 3 we demonstrate how middle school and secondary school teachers can use this model and these five principles to help their students become active learners. We would be remiss if we did not also point out that almost

every chapter in this textbook presents practical ideas and teacher-directed strategies for promoting active learning across the content areas.

FIVE PRINCIPLES THAT PROMOTE ACTIVE LEARNING

Principle 1: Active Learners Use Their Prior Knowledge in the Meaning-Making Process

Active learners know that what they take from a text depends on how much they bring to it. In other words, what learners already know, their prior knowledge, and what they want to know will affect the ease or difficulty of their meaning making or understanding and their subsequent learning. This premise is consistent with a **schema-theoretic** perspective of comprehension (McNamara, Miller, & Bransford, 1991). **Schemata** (plural of *schema*) are abstract frameworks that organize knowledge in memory by putting information into the correct "slot," each slot containing related parts (Wilson & Anderson, 1986). For instance, your schema for going to an airport probably includes taxis, ticket counters, crowds, the smell of jet fuel, claiming baggage, and so on. These clusters of related knowledge in memory—of experience, ideas, and feelings—guide our interpretations, inferences, expectations, and attention as passages are comprehended. It is theorized that learners comprehend a text when they bring to mind a schema that gives a good account of the objects and events described in the message. Schemata guide comprehension; without them, we could make little sense of a text. Without some unifying idea to help tie together the information, without connections to our own prior knowledge and experience, without a foundational understanding of the concept, we might as well be looking at words in a foreign language.

To demonstrate the important role schemata play in students' comprehension and meaning making, read the following passage and see if you can activate an appropriate schema to help you understand it.

> The southpaw touched the rubber, kicked, and dealed. The big number 38 sent one up the chute. Smith raced from the hot corner and camped under it. He tripped, however, on the artificial turf, and it fell behind him and just in front of Murphy from left—38 had a two-bagger on a Texas leaguer. Cries of "kill the bum" echoed throughout the place as number 16 strode up. He was a sub for the dh and stood in, brandishing a 40-ounce stick menacingly. He crushed one through the hole at short. Perez stabbed at it, but it rolled all the way to the warning track. 38 touched home, and it was over.

Did you understand this passage? What does it mean if you can't understand it? Chances are that you had no difficulty with saying the words, so much of the difficulty you may have had making sense of this short passage can be attributed to an underdeveloped schema: a lack of prior knowledge about baseball, especially baseball terminology.

Prior Knowledge Influences Your Students' Comprehension of What They Read

Prior knowledge may be one of the most potent variables in the overall process of understanding (McKeown, Beck, Sinatra, & Loxterman, 1992). Active learners consciously or unconsciously use their schema or prior knowledge in many ways. For example, a student with diabetes who has been assigned to read a chapter on the endocrine system probably already possesses a partially developed schema for this content. This schema helps the student assimilate new information into what she already knows about the pancreas and the hormone it secretes, insulin. She would cautiously approach the topic as one in which she has some related information but needs a great deal more. Perhaps the student might even take the time to preview (see Chapter 9) the chapter to determine what glands and hormones in the endocrine system the author deemed important and compare that information to what she already knows.

Active Learners Realize that Textbooks are Never Explicit

Active learners also use their schema to make inferences or to fill in gaps in their comprehension (Pressley, Johnson, Symons, McGoldrick, & Kurita, 1989). They know that textbooks, lectures, discussions, or demonstrations are never completely explicit, and they often have to think between the lines and piece ideas together to construct a full interpretation. For example, if a video shown in a government class refers briefly to the confidence levels of polls, such as the Gallup, but does not fully define confidence levels, active learners would use their prior knowledge to construct a definition. Active learners who had never heard of a confidence level in polling would also seek alternative information sources such as the dictionary, an index, or a teacher to fill this gap in understanding.

Middle school and high school students often experience difficulty comprehending technical concepts because of their limited prior knowledge.

Conversely, students with extensive prior knowledge of a given topic will likely understand and learn more, whether that information comes from a textbook or a class discussion. Of course, prior knowledge occurs in degrees and is not necessarily an all-or-none condition. In a fascinating study of prior knowledge, Bransford and Johnson (1972) presented the following statement to students from differing sociocultural backgrounds:

> Jane decided not to wear her matching silver necklace, earrings, and belt because she was going to the airport. (p. 719)

Students from backgrounds that had provided them with many direct and related prior experiences with airports and airplane travel had no problems explaining Jane's reasoning: The heavy jewelry could trigger the metal detector; therefore, she left it at home. Students from backgrounds that precluded opportunities for visiting airports and flying, however, came up with explanations such as "She was afraid of getting ripped off." The point of this research, as well as of other related studies, is that the amount of information students possess on any topic may vary widely, leading to alternative interpretations.

Students Do Not Automatically Use Their Prior Knowledge

What is more, many students do not automatically draw on their prior experiences when learning in school settings (Pressley et al., 1990). For many students, learning is a compartmentalized procedure in which the different subjects they study and their own background knowledge may never interact or come together. For example, what students have learned in a seventh-grade physical education class about the role of adrenalin in a competitive event may never be used when they study human glands in a science class. Hence, teachers must cue and encourage students to use their prior knowledge from one setting in another.

Misconceptions Affect Students' Understanding of What They Read or Listen To

Although most researchers agree that prior knowledge facilitates comprehension, some have shown that students may possess "incorrect" prior knowledge or "naive" conceptions (Alvermann & Hynd, 1989) that can interfere with learning important information (Guzzetti, Snyder, Glass, & Gamas, 1993). For example, many of us have entrenched beliefs about the laws of motion that are not scientifically defensible. Researchers have also found that many students are likely to hold on to their misconceptions (Hynd & Guzzetti, 1993). These findings reinforce the critical importance of exploring students' prior knowledge for and conceptions of topics before they read a text or listen to a lecture. In this way, you can discover any misconceptions and create instructional conditions that enable students to reject their existing misconceptions (Hynd & Guzzetti, 1993).

To summarize, active learners use their schema or prior knowledge flexibly to construct meaningful interpretations of texts. The instructional implication of the importance of prior knowledge for middle school and secondary school teachers can be simply stated: To maximize learning, teachers need to assist students in developing relevant background knowledge and in relating their own experiences to what they learn (Alexander & Kulikowich, 1991; Pritchard, 1990). In the next chapter and in Chapter 5, we examine some teaching strategies for helping students activate and use a relevant prior knowledge.

Principle 2: Active Learners Understand and Use Text Structure to Organize Their Meaning Making

Are you surprised that the reading materials first-grade children are introduced to are stories? Can you imagine passing out science books and welcoming children to their first readers? We begin teaching children to read with stories because they are already familiar with the structure of stories. **Narrative,** according to Sawyer (1987), is a fundamental mode of meaning making through language.

Stories, whether oral or written, are based on the narrative structure. Because most of us prefer the narrative structure, interest in stories rarely wanes throughout our lives. However, most textbooks and classroom presentations do not typically use a narrative structure. Rather, most learning situations in school are organized around an **expository** or explanatory structure that is more formal and demanding than our oral language. Try to recall the last time you relished the opportunity to crack open one of your textbooks before going to bed. Most of us rarely do, and the same is true of students. We have observed students plow through their assigned government and science reading, anxious to finish so that they can put the book down. Students in middle and secondary school must learn to deal with the formal expository styles of writing and speaking if they are to be successful readers and learners.

Expository Text Is More Demanding Than Narrative Text

Text structure refers to the discernible organizational patterns of narrative and expository texts. Researchers have been identifying the general structures of text and demonstrating the importance of using knowledge of these structures for effective comprehension (Armbruster, Anderson, & Ostertag, 1989; Graesser, Golding, & Long, 1991; Roller, 1990).

Stories or narrative text have predictable structures or patterns, called *story grammars* (Mandler, 1987). For instance, stories have settings; they have characters; the main character is usually en route to a goal; to reach his or her goal, the main character must confront obstacles (essentially conflict); and conflict is resolved in some way. Apparently, as readers or listeners receive constant exposure to well-structured stories, they internalize these grammars in the form of a story schema, which assists them in understanding and writing stories. Theoretical and instructional aspects of story schemata are presented in Chapter 9.

Texts Have Predictable Structures or Organization

Although several organizational structures exist for expository text, Meyer's (1979) system, which examines five groups of logical relationships, is representative:

- *Antecedence/consequence or covariance showing a causal relationship between ideas.* For example, a paragraph taken from a biology textbook explaining the direct and indirect cell damage caused by radiation would be organized using the antecedent/consequent pattern.
- *Response relationships, including problem-solution, question-answer, and remark-reply.* For example, in an ecology textbook, one chapter is devoted to the problems caused by water and air pollution, and the next chapter focuses on possible solutions to the problems caused by the pollution.

- *Comparison relationships dealing with likenesses and differences between ideas.* For example, in a chapter about igneous rocks, students learn how intrusive and extrusive rocks are similar in some ways but different in others.
- *Collection relationships showing that ideas are related to each other by a common factor or factors.* In a geometry class it is important for students to understand that triangles, quadrilaterals, pentagons, hexagons, octagons, and decagons are all examples of polygons and, hence, have the same common features. Such reasoning is an example of the collection relationship or pattern of thinking.
- *Description relationships presenting attributes or explanations of a topic.* This type of relationship exists in all content areas. For example, when a physical education teacher explains a sport such as tennis to her students, she probably not only presents the goals and rules of the game but also describes the characteristics of an expert tennis player. She provides descriptions and attributions because she knows they will help her students understand the nuances of tennis.

Knowledge of Text Structure Can Improve Students' Comprehension

When researchers have trained students to identify and use these text organizational relationships, their comprehension has improved (Richgels, McGee, Lomax, & Sheard, 1987; Slater, Graves, & Piche, 1985). However, the videos teachers show in class, the presentations they make during labs, or the chapters they assign rarely conform to one organizational structure. Even so, when teachers provide direct instruction on how to use text structure as an organizing device for meaning making, students will benefit (Garner & Gillingham, 1987).

In addition to text structure, another useful way to characterize a written or oral text is to describe its degree of **considerateness.** According to Anderson and Armbruster (1986), a considerate text is coherent, a characteristic they claim plays a prominent role in students' comprehension and learning. To be coherent, a text must cohere both globally and locally. When texts are **globally coherent,** the ideas are arranged logically in an easily identifiable organization or structure. Research indicates that well-organized text is better understood and more easily recalled than poorly organized text (Sinatra, 1991). When the organization of a text is implicit or less obvious, the text is more difficult to understand (Horowitz & Samuels, 1987).

Active learners are sensitive to a text's global structure through the use of signaling devices (Kintsch & Yarbrough, 1982; Meyer, 1979). Signals tell students something about a text's organization or emphasize certain ideas in the content. Types of signals include the following:

There Are Many Types of Clues or Signals That Students Should Use When They Read

- Summary statements
- Previews or introductory statements
- Typographic clues such as underlining, italics, and boldface print or headings (see Chapter 9)
- Pointer words and phrases, such as "the most important reason why"

The other factor in making a text considerate is **local coherence,** the linguistic mortar that connects ideas together in a text (Tierney & Mosenthal, 1982). A text is locally coherent if the pronoun referents, substitutions, connectives, and conjunctions are explicitly stated and clear to the reader. When textbook authors or speakers fail to be locally cohesive, their texts are less structured, the ideas are not woven together, and there is no flow of meaning from one idea to the next. This kind of text places a particularly heavy burden on students because it forces them to bridge many ideas inferentially that could have been tied together explicitly by the author. The point here is that the more inferences the learner has to make, the greater the chance for the author's message to be misconstrued (Pearson & Camperell, 1985).

Fortunately, active learners can identify text structure in spite of its disconnectedness (Brozo, 1986; Brozo & Curtis, 1987). The two paragraphs that follow provide an example of a disconnected text and show how active learners normally impose their own structure on the text to understand it.

Disconnected Text

In the evening, the light fades. Photosynthesis slows down. The amount of carbon dioxide in the air space builds up again. This buildup of carbon dioxide makes the guard cells relax. The openings are closed.

How the Good Reader Makes Connections

The fading light of evening causes photosynthesis to slow down. A plant's ability to "breathe," *however* [italics added here and following], does not depend on light and thus continues to produce *carbon dioxide*. The *carbon dioxide* in the air spaces builds up again, which makes the *guard cells relax*. The *relaxing of the guard cells* closes the *leaf openings*. *Consequently*, the *leaf openings* close in the evenings as photosynthesis slows down (Anderson & Armbruster, 1984, p. 206).

In the first example, the author's use of short, simple sentences often obscures the relationships among the ideas in the text. In the second example, the reader echoed words that ended the previous sentence by placing them at or near the beginning of the following sentence and inserted, inferentially, words that tied together the text and made the relationships more obvious (see the italicized words).

Many Textbooks Are Not Considerate

When a text has global and local coherence, it becomes considerate and, thus, makes understanding and learning more possible for students. Unfortunately, many middle school and secondary school textbooks have a high degree of inconsiderateness: They contain misleading titles and subtitles, lack explicit main ideas, omit crucial information, contain contradictory information, and are ambiguous (Pressley, Yokoi, van Meter, Van Etten, & Freebern, 1997). Many textbook writers, editors, and publishers have attempted to deal with these inconsiderate and difficult texts by altering the surface-level features of sentences and word length, two indices typically used in readability formulas.

Readability formulas such as Fry's (1968) use these easily quantifiable indices to yield either a grade level or a score on a scale roughly correlated with a grade level. Often textbooks are purposely rewritten or written with short, simple sentences and few multisyllable words to superficially simplify their level so that a match can be made between students' supposed reading level and a text's estimated readability. The rewritten text, while judged to be easier by a readability formula, often becomes more ambiguous and difficult for students (Davidson & Green, 1988). The first paragraph in the preceding example about photosynthesis vividly illustrates this phenomenon. This paragraph has only 5 sentences, 35 words, and 52 syllables, yet it remains inconsiderate and difficult for students to understand.

Thus, when selecting a textbook, teachers should focus on whether it is considerate rather than on superficial features that may give the impression of considerateness but actually make the text less readable. Although no textbook is perfect, some are more considerate and have better learnability characteristics than others. Sometime in your teaching career, you probably will be asked to join a committee to select the "perfect" new textbook for your students. Do you know what to look for beyond content that would promote learnability? Theresa, an eighth-grade health education teacher, was given the checklist in Figure 2.1 by her district-level curriculum coordinator. She found it extremely helpful in reviewing the many textbooks the publishers had sent her. With the checklist, she had specific characteristics to evaluate that exceeded content and concepts in the field of health. You may wish to use this checklist to analyze the textbooks you are using, to review possible new adoptions, or even to critique this book.

There Are Some Features That You Should Consider When Selecting a Textbook

In Chapter 3 we discuss some specific teaching strategies that can help your students overcome comprehension barriers of inconsiderate text by becoming more actively involved in the meaning-making process.

Principle 3: Active Learners Think Critically About Text and Create Their Own Elaborations

Mr. Kuzak, a ninth-grade science teacher, told his students to write a summary of a section in their textbook that discussed water and land pollution. He likes to give this assignment early in the year to determine which of his students have difficulty in thinking about scientific concepts. Susan's and Derrick's summaries in Figure 2.2 typify what Mr. Kuzak receives from his freshmen. Which student is the active learner? What did that student do to make his or her summary better?

As you probably determined, Susan's summary is more effective than Derrick's for several reasons. What reasons did you list? If you listed any of the following, you identified some of Susan's thinking processes.

- Susan focused on the overall structure of the section—the four types of pollution and the solutions to water pollution. Derrick focused on details and facts, with no sense of organization.

Directions: Check the column that best describes the textbook's use of these characteristics that promote active and successful learning.

	Excellent	**Good**	**Poor**
1. Difficult new vocabulary words are highlighted, italicized, underlined, or defined in the margins.	______	______	______
2. Concepts are presented clearly in relatively direct and understandable sentences.	______	______	______
3. The chapter's main idea(s) or purposes for reading are explicitly stated at the beginning.	______	______	______
4. The authors present a list of objectives, questions, or organizational structure to guide the students while reading/studying.	______	______	______
5. The authors use explicit and appropriate words to signal the text's structure and organization (e.g., *on the other hand*).	______	______	______
6. The authors use practical real-life situations, examples, or analogies that students can relate to and have an interest in.	______	______	______
7. The authors use boldface headings and subheadings that are logical to the concepts being discussed and useful to students with little or no prior knowledge.	______	______	______
8. The authors internally summarize key concepts and present useful summaries at the end of the chapter.	______	______	______
9. The authors help students use appropriate prior knowledge by reviewing or reminding readers of previously learned concepts (e.g., *in the last chapter we discussed . . .*).	______	______	______
10. The text includes quotations from primary sources and authorities to support and add interest.	______	______	______
11. When there are questions at the end of the chapter, different kinds (e.g., true–false) of questions are supplied that require higher levels of thinking (e.g., on my own) and responses using students' own words.	______	______	______
12. The table of contents shows a logical development of the subject matter.	______	______	______
13. Captions under graphs, tables, diagrams, and pictures are clearly written.	______	______	______
14. Math and science problem examples match the concepts and steps previously discussed.	______	______	______
15. The authors inform the students when information contained in graphs, tables, or diagrams is not also contained in the text.	______	______	______
16. When the text refers to a graph or table, that aid is on the same page as the textual reference.	______	______	______
17. The authors suggest other resources and activities for students motivated to explore the area or for students who have difficulties with specific objectives or specific tasks.	______	______	______

FIGURE 2.1 Criteria for Measuring a Textbook's Learnability

Susan's Summary

According to this section of our textbook, there are four sources of water pollution: agriculture, industry, domestic, and other sources such as oil spills. Perhaps the most dangerous source of pollution comes from industry, though oil spills, such as the one in Alaska, have certainly had a large impact on our wildlife and on our economy. Pesticides, fertilizers, and animal waste, the three types of agricultural pollution, are usually not direct but indirect. A notorious example of a pesticide is DDT. There are three kinds of industrial pollution: chemical, thermal, and radiation. The problems associated with radiation seem to be the most severe in that skin cancer and leukemia are possible results of exposure. Organic waste and detergent builders are the main sources of domestic pollution. Both seem to have an adverse effect on our lakes and rivers so that the balance of nature is upset. This section of the chapter ended by discussing some solutions to the problem of water pollution—all of which are costly but very important.

Derrick's Summary

This section of the chapter discussed different kinds of water pollution. Pesticides such as DDT are dangerous to use because they are not biodegradable. Some nitrates are toxic to animals and humans. Nitrates can be reduced to nitrites, which interfere with the transport of oxygen by hemoglobin in the blood. Mercury vapor is highly toxic and can be absorbed through the lungs. There are two types of radiation cell damage, direct and indirect. Detergents and organic wastes can also harm our water sources. Oil spills hurt our aquatic life.

FIGURE 2.2 Susan's and Derrick's Summaries on Water Pollution

- Susan used personal examples (e.g., the Alaskan oil spill) that were not included in the text. Derrick's summary used only textbook information, even though water pollution is a highly controversial and often debated topic in the news today.
- Susan formed some conclusions and drew some inferences from the text. For instance, she inferred that radiation is the most dangerous form of water pollution.

In sum, Susan's summary provided more evidence of critical thinking and elaborations than did Derrick's summary. When students think critically about what they read or hear, they identify the basic elements of thought such as purpose, assumption, interpretation, concepts, implications, and point of view. Then they assess those elements using universal intellectual criteria and standards such as clarity, accuracy, precision, relevance, depth, and logic (Ennis, 1996). When students think elaboratively about text, they add information that is not explicitly stated (Wittrock, 1990).

There are various ways in which students can think elaboratively about the texts they read or listen to in class. Wittrock (1990) has listed several learner-created elaborations that include many of Susan's processes and many others that Susan did not use. The following is a modification of Wittrock's ideas:

There Are Many Ways Students Can Elaborate Upon Texts

Compose titles, headings, and subheadings when they are missing.

Underline, circle, or *check* words and sentences that are important or troublesome.

Develop questions.

Paraphrase key ideas in your own words.

Relate text to personal experiences.

Seek interrelationships among ideas and across text.

Sense the overall structure of the text.

Create examples, analogies, or metaphors.

Make predictions, inferences, or conclusions.

Draw pictures, tables, or graphs for difficult operations.

Solve problems or create new problems.

Apply principles to new situations.

Students who think critically about text and create their own elaborations will increase their understanding, as well as their interest and enjoyment in their reading (Garner, Alexander, Gillingham, Kulikowich, & Brown, 1991; Pintrich & Garcia, 1994; Wittrock, 1991). Just asking students to think of examples of concepts they have studied can significantly increase their remembering and understanding on both multiple-choice and essay test formats (Simpson, Olejnik, Tam, & Supattathum, 1994). We know, however, that more middle school and secondary students are like Derrick than like Susan. That is, most students do not know how to think about text in elaborative ways because the ability to elaborate does not develop naturally (Pressley, Woloshyn, Lysynchuk, Martin, Wood, & Willoughby, 1990). When the Derricks in most classrooms read an assignment or listen to a class discussion, they choose to rely on lower-level thinking, such as memorizing and rereading, to remember and understand key ideas (Pressley, 1995; Simpson & Nist, 1997). Fortunately, teachers can use a variety of strategies to help students move toward a more sophisticated level of thinking in order to become active learners. Most of these teacher-directed strategies begin by providing students with examples, demonstrations, and activities that require them to go beyond memorization. Then, gradually, students are challenged to accept responsibility and ownership in initiating their own critical and elaborative thinking. In Chapter 3 we discuss how classroom teachers can teach students to think critically and elaboratively about concepts and ideas.

Principle 4: Active Learners Are Metacognitively Aware

Thus far, we have discussed three characteristics of active learners. Briefly, the active learner is one who understands the interactive nature of the reading process, the unique characteristics of texts, and elaborative strategies for maximizing understanding and critical thinking. The fourth principle describes active learners as those who are metacognitively aware.

Think about a typical reading experience: You're moving through a passage on automatic pilot, absorbing information and ideas, seemingly without effort. Suddenly, your eyes fix on the word *propinquity*. Within a mere 2 or 3 seconds, you realize you don't know what the word means, quickly reread the sentence in which it was found, and decide that, at least for the time being, its definition is not critical to your present level of comprehension. Back on automatic pilot, you realize after two more paragraphs that the meaning of *propinquity* has become more significant. You return to the word, frame its meaning in context, guess, and finally consult a dictionary.

This scenario essentially describes the process of **monitoring,** one aspect of metacognition. According to Baker and Brown (1984), **metacognition** is the "knowledge and control we have over thinking and learning activities" (p. 2). Students who can self-monitor their reading or listening can detect errors or contradictions in a text, identify topics or ideas they do not understand, and use a variety of task-appropriate reading and learning strategies to "fix up" or alleviate their difficulties in understanding. Active learners use a variety of self-monitoring strategies such as self-questioning, paraphrasing, comparing key ideas, and using their prior knowledge.

Many Students Do Not Monitor Their Understanding

Self-monitoring plays a vital role in determining whether or not students have successful reading experiences. In fact, research indicates major differences between the metacognitive abilities of novice and expert readers and between successful and less successful students (Garner & Alexander, 1989; Simpson & Nist, 1997). There also appear to be developmental differences in students' ability to self-monitor. Researchers have found that older students seem better able to regulate and control their understanding processes than younger students (Brown, Armbruster, & Baker, 1986; Pressley, Goodchild, Fleet, Zajchowski, & Evans, 1989).

Students Can Be Trained to Monitor

These findings do not mean, however, that you can expect your students to be able to monitor their reading, listening, and understanding. On the contrary, research studies with entering college freshmen have found them to be very passive learners who do not monitor and evaluate their understanding (Pintrich & Garcia, 1994; Simpson & Nist, 1997). Fortunately, high school and middle school students can profit greatly from some form of self-monitoring training (Garner, 1990). When Haller, Child, and Walberg (1988) analyzed the effects of metacognitive instruction on reading comprehension in 20 different research studies, they found that it was effective at all grade levels, but particularly for seventh- and eighth-grade students.

In addition to self-monitoring, metacognition involves **task knowledge** and **self-knowledge.** *Task knowledge* can be classified according to the products that teachers require of students and the thinking processes involved in completing the products (Doyle, 1983). Typical products include tests, papers, classroom discussions, projects, experiments, and demonstrations. Each product requires certain types of thinking processes, making some products more challenging than others. For example, some multiple-choice tests require students to memorize certain facts and details. The following question illustrates a factual test question in a science course:

Task Knowledge Involves Students in Understanding Products and Thinking Processes

> What are the two basic types of igneous rocks?
>
> a. clastic sedimentary and breccia
>
> b. intrusive and extrusive
>
> c. metamorphic and organic
>
> d. foliated and nonfoliated

Other tasks require higher levels of thinking because they involve drawing conclusions, taking a stand on an issue, or applying a concept to a new situation. The following question, taken from a 10th-grade psychology course, illustrates an application-level question concerning Freud's concept of a defense mechanism:

> Theo has a girl friend whom he accuses of being unfaithful. Interestingly, Theo is the one who has been unfaithful because he has been seeing three other girls. Which defense mechanism is Theo using when he accuses his girl friend of being unfaithful?
>
> a. rationalization
>
> b. denial
>
> c. projection
>
> d. repression

The correct answer to the question, (c), required students to understand the concept of defense mechanism, the various kinds of defense mechanisms, and examples of each. Questions such as these require students to think and elaborate on what they read in their texts or hear in class discussions so that they can identify new situations or examples of concepts.

Thus, task knowledge involves an understanding of the product to be created and the thinking processes involved in creating it. When active learners possess task knowledge, they realize that understanding directions to a physics laboratory experiment, for example, requires a different kind of reading and thinking than does understanding a poem, such as "Richard Cory," so that they can write a paper for their English teacher. Students who understand the academic tasks specified by their teachers and select the appropriate strategies and approaches to accomplish those tasks are generally the ones who are academically successful (Pressley, 1995; Simpson, Hynd, Nist, & Burrell, 1997).

Students with *self-knowledge* understand themselves as readers and learners. Specifically, they are aware of their motivations, beliefs, and strengths as they read, listen, and think about ideas. When active learners are aware of themselves in relation to the texts they are reading and the tasks they are assigned, they are in a better position to use strategies and approaches effectively

(Pintrich & Garcia, 1994). Motivation is perhaps the most important aspect of self-knowledge because it contributes to students' positive views of themselves as individuals who control what and how much they learn. Bandura (1986) has described this motivational view as **self-efficacy** and has found that students with a high sense of self-efficacy tend to exert greater effort to meet their academic challenges. Moreover, students who perceive themselves as having control over their learning are more likely to choose learning strategies and approaches that require them to use deep thinking processes or elaborative approaches (Pintrich & Garcia, 1994). In contrast, students with low self-efficacy are those who tend to give up quickly, doubt their ability when they confront a difficult or novel situation, and resort to memorization even when it is not appropriate.

Students Who Believe They Can Learn and Control Their Learning Will Be More Successful

Another aspect of self-knowledge consists of the beliefs that students have about what constitutes knowledge and learning. According to Schommer (1993), who has conducted extensive research with secondary school students, these beliefs, or personal **epistemologies,** include several knowledge dimensions. For example, some students may perceive knowledge to be absolute, something handed down by authority that can be acquired quickly, with little effort. In contrast, other students view knowledge acquisition as a tentative, gradual process derived from reason and thought after considerable effort. How students define learning is also very revealing. According to Gibbs (1990), students can view learning as an increase in knowledge, as memorizing, as acquiring facts or procedures that they will use, or as something that demands their attempt to abstract meaning and make sense of a phenomenon. These conceptions seem to exist on a continuum from surface to deep approaches to learning. In general, students who use deeper approaches to learning that encourage them to elaborate are the ones who learn more and do better in their courses (Pintrich & Garcia, 1994).

Students' Beliefs About Learning Influence What They Do in Class

Metacognition is probably the mindset that makes learning possible. Students who are metacognitively aware are the ones who understand all the nuances of academic tasks, who can monitor their learning in order to identify when they do not understand, and who can identify strategies to help them learn more effectively. Most important, students who are metacognitively aware are the ones who see themselves as individuals who control what and how much they learn. In Chapter 3 and elsewhere in this textbook, we discuss strategies that content-area teachers use to encourage their students to become more metacognitively aware.

Principle 5: Active Learners Possess and Employ a Wide Range of Reading and Learning Strategies

Strategies are the behaviors or actions that students use during learning to influence their understanding, thinking, and retrieval of new information or concepts (Weinstein & Mayer, 1986). To be effective, students need strategies to make sense out of their texts, monitor their understanding, and clarify what they do not understand. In addition, to cope with the difficult tasks that demand higher levels of thinking, middle school and secondary school students need strategies to help them elaborate, organize, and synthesize information from multiple sources and evaluate. Such a list of requirements implies that there is no one technique or strategy that will work for students in all situations (Simpson, Hynd, Nist, & Burrell, 1997). Rather than a generic approach, active learners have a repertoire of strategies and know when to select the most appropriate one(s) for the subject area and for the task described by the teacher.

To select the most appropriate strategy, active learners must have three different kinds of strategic knowledge (Paris, Wasik, & Turner, 1991). The first is **declarative** knowledge. For example, a student with declarative knowledge of previewing knows that previewing is done before reading and that it involves such steps as reading the introduction and summary. The second kind of strategic knowledge is **procedural.** Active learners with declarative and procedural knowledge of the preview strategy can preview and describe the procedures for previewing in detail. In addition to these two types of strategic knowledge, active learners possess **conditional** knowledge, perhaps the most critical form of strategic knowledge (Pressley, 1995). When active learners have conditional knowledge, they know when and why to use various strategies. Thus, with the previewing strategy, they know that it may be appropriate to preview only certain texts. Active learners know that the time involved in previewing a chapter before they read is time well spent because it allows them to check the author's organization, establish what they may already know about the topic, set purposes for reading, and divide the reading into meaningful chunks. Students must develop all three kinds of strategic knowledge if they are to control and transfer the strategies we teach in the classroom to their own reading and learning tasks outside the classroom (Pressley, 1995).

There Is No One Best Strategy

In sum, students must have a wide repertoire of strategies to match the different types of academic tasks they will encounter across the content areas. In addition, students must know where, how, and why they should use these strategies. Throughout this textbook, we discuss a variety of strategies and explain ways in which they can be taught.

Strategy Transfer Requires the Three Types of Strategic Knowledge

THE INFLUENCE OF THE CLASSROOM CONTEXT ON ACTIVE LEARNING

In Chapter 1 we gave considerable attention to the idea that learning does not take place in a vacuum; rather, students become active learners within supportive learning environments that teachers create. It is important to keep in mind, therefore, that students will not develop all the characteristics of active learners described previously unless teachers actively promote independent learning within a classroom context that is inviting, engaging, and nurturing of students' risk taking.

You can create an environment that fosters active learning in a variety of ways. Most important, you need to model or demonstrate the strategic behavior you want your students to emulate. For example, if there is a specific strategy you want them to use in solving math story problems, you must demonstrate and explain that process so that it becomes external and accessible. The mental steps you intuitively employ must be made explicit to your students; otherwise, the chances of their understanding and applying the strategy to their own story problems will be greatly reduced (Dole et al., 1991; Vygotsky, 1978).

You can also encourage active learning by providing students with challenging and diverse tasks that require them to think critically and elaboratively. Students will not try out new strategies if they believe their usual routines will work. Their resistance to change makes sense if you think about it. Would you change your tennis serve if you were constantly winning all your matches? Moreover, you should stress that learning is often hard, even for the most capable learners. If students view learning as difficult but not impossible, they will be more likely to use active learning strategies (Pressley, 1995). Of course, the key to these two instructional principles is finding the balance between assigning your students impossible tasks and inviting them to engage in challenging tasks that they can accomplish with your support. Throughout this textbook, you will read about teachers who have found that delicate balance necessary for encouraging their students to become active learners.

There Are Many Ways to Challenge Our Students to Become Active Learners

SUMMARY

In this chapter we have proposed a holistic perspective of active learning. We have suggested that active learners are strategically involved in the reading process. More specifically, we outlined five important principles that characterize active learners. These five principles are not discrete and mutually exclusive, as in the skills model of reading comprehension, but rather are interactive and interdependent. The first principle concerns learners' use of prior knowledge to interact with text. The second principle focuses on active learners' use of structure to guide their meaning construction. The third principle explains how active learners think critically about text and create their own elaborations in order to enhance their understanding and recall. The fourth principle explains how active learners who are metacognitively aware monitor their understanding, understand their academic tasks, and view themselves as learners who have control of what and how much they learn. The fifth principle states that active learners possess and use a wide variety of strategies that encourage them to make sense of what they read, monitor their understanding, and clarify what they do not understand.

In Chapter 3 we address these five principles within a methodological framework. We explain and demonstrate how you can use and devise specific strategies for your classroom. Some of these strategies will be teacher directed and some will be student initiated. As you read the remaining chapters of this book, you will be frequently reminded of how a particular strategy is intended to force students out of familiar passive roles and impel them to become active participants in the learning process.

REFERENCES

Alexander, P., & Kulikowich, J. (1991). Domain knowledge and analogic reasoning ability as predictors of expository text comprehension. *Journal of Reading Behavior, 23,* 165–190.

Alvermann, D., & Hynd, C. (1989). Study strategies for correcting misconceptions in physics: An intervention. In S. McCormick & J. Zutell (Eds.), *Cognitive and social perspectives for literacy research and instruction.* Chicago: National Reading Conference.

Alvermann, D., & Swafford, J. (1989). Do content area strategies have a research base? *Journal of Reading, 32,* 388–395.

Anderson, T. H., & Armbruster, B. B. (1984). Content area textbooks. In R. Anderson, J. Osborn, & R. Tierney (Eds.), *Learning to read in American schools: Basal readers and content texts.* Hillsdale, NJ: Erlbaum.

Anderson, T. H., & Armbruster, B. B. (1986). Readable textbooks, or, selecting a textbook is not like buying a pair of shoes. In J. Orasanu (Ed.), *Reading comprehension: From research to practice.* Hillsdale, NJ: Erlbaum.

Armbruster, B., Anderson, T., & Meyer, J. (1991). Improving content-area reading using instructional graphics. *Reading Research Quarterly, 26,* 393–416.

Armbruster, B., Anderson, T., & Ostertag, J. (1987). Does text structure/summarization instruction facilitate learning from expository text? *Reading Research Quarterly, 22,* 331–346.

Armbruster, B., Anderson, T., & Ostertag, J. (1989). Teaching text structure to improve reading and writing. *The Reading Teacher, 43,* 130–137.

Baker, L., & Brown, A. (1984). Metacognitive skills and reading. In P. D. Pearson (Ed.), *Handbook of reading research.* New York: Longman.

Bandura, A. (1986). *Social foundations of thought and action: A social cognitive theory.* Upper Saddle River, NJ: Prentice Hall.

Bransford, J., & Johnson, M. (1972). Contextual prerequisites for understanding: Some interesting investigations of comprehension and recall. *Journal of Verbal Learning and Verbal Behavior, 11,* 717–726.

Brown, A., Armbruster, B., & Baker, L. (1986). The role of metacognition in reading and studying. In J. Orasanu (Ed.), *Reading comprehension: From research to practice.* Hillsdale, NJ: Erlbaum.

Brown, A., & Day, J. (1983). Macrorules for summarizing text: The development of expertise. *Journal of Verbal Learning and Verbal Behavior, 22,* 1–14.

Brozo, W. G. (1986). Recognizing and manipulating connectives: A reading/writing strategy for secondary students. *Reading Improvement, 23,* 7–11.

Brozo, W. G., & Curtis, C. L. (1987). College readers' comprehension of connected and disconnected text. *Research and Teaching in Developmental Education, 3,* 21–26.

Campbell, J. R., Donahue, P. L., Reese, C. M., & Phillips, G. W. (1996). *NAEP 1994 reading report card for the nation and the states: Findings from the National*

Assessment of Educational Progress and Trial State Assessment (Report No. NCES-95-045). Washington, DC: U.S. Department of Education. (ERIC Document Reproduction Service No. ED 388 962).

Davidson, A., & Green, G. (1988). *Linguistic complexity and text comprehension: Readability issues reconsidered.* Hillsdale, NJ: Erlbaum.

Dole, J., Duffy, G., Roehler, L., & Pearson, P. D. (1991). Moving from the old to the new: Research on reading comprehension instruction. *Review of Educational Research, 61,* 239–264.

Doyle, W. (1983). Academic work. *Review of Educational Research, 53,* 159–199.

Ennis, R. (1996). *Critical thinking.* Upper Saddle River, NJ: Prentice Hall.

Fry, E. B. (1968). A readability formula that saves time. *Journal of Reading, 11,* 513–516, 575–578.

Garner, R. (1990). When children and adults do not use learning strategies: Toward a theory of settings. *Review of Educational Research, 60,* 517–529.

Garner, R., & Alexander, P. (1989). Metacognition: Answered and unanswered questions. *Educational Psychologist, 24,* 143–158.

Garner, R., Alexander, P., Gillingham, M., Kulikowich, J., & Brown, R. (1991). Interest and learning from text. *American Educational Research Journal, 28,* 643–659.

Garner, R., & Gillingham, M. (1987). Students' knowledge about text structure. *Journal of Reading Behavior, 29,* 247–259.

Gibbs, G. (1990). *Improving student learning project briefing paper.* Oxford: Oxford Centre for Staff Development, Oxford Polytechnic.

Graesser, A., Golding, J., & Long, D. (1991). Narrative representation and comprehension. In R. Barr, M. Kamil, P. Mosenthal, & P. D. Pearson (Eds.), *Handbook of reading research* (Vol. 2). New York: Longman.

Guzzetti, B. J., Snyder, T. E., Glass, G. V., & Gamas, W. S. (1993). Meta-analysis of instructional interventions from reading education and science education to promote conceptual change. *Reading Research Quarterly, 28,* 116–161.

Haller, E. P., Child, D. A., & Walberg, H. J. (1988). Can comprehension be taught?: A quantitative synthesis of "metacognitive studies." *Educational Researcher, 17,* 5–9.

Horowitz, R., & Samuels, S. J. (1987). *Comprehending oral and written language.* San Diego, CA: Academic Press.

Hynd, C., & Alvermann, D. (1986). The role of refutation text in overcoming difficulty with science concepts. *Journal of Reading, 29,* 440–446.

Hynd, C., & Alvermann, D. (1989). Overcoming misconceptions in science: An on-line study of prior knowledge activation. *Reading Research and Instruction, 28,* 12–26.

Hynd, C., & Guzzetti, B. J. (1993). Exploring issues in conceptual change. In D. J. Lew & C. K. Finzer (Eds.), *Examining central issues in literacy research, theory, and practice.* Chicago: National Reading Conference.

Irwin, J., & Baker, I. (1989). *Promoting active reading comprehension strategies.* Upper Saddle River, NJ: Prentice Hall.

Kintsch, E. (1990). Macroprocesses and microprocesses in the development of summarization skill. *Cognition and Instruction, 7,* 161–195.

Kintsch, W., & Yarbrough, C. (1982). Role of rhetorical structure in text comprehension. *Journal of Educational Psychology, 74,* 828–834.

Mandel, H., Stein, N., & Trabasso, T. (1984). *Learning and comprehension of text.* Hillsdale, NJ: Erlbaum.

Mandler, J. (1987). On the psychological reality of story structure,. *Discourse Processes, 10,* 1–29.

McKeachie, W. J. (1994). *Teaching tips* (9th ed.). Lexington, MA: D. C. Heath.

McKeown, M., Beck, I., Sinatra, G., & Loxterman, J. (1992). The contribution of prior knowledge and coherent text to comprehension. *Reading Research Quarterly, 27,* 79–93.

McNamara, T., Miller, D., & Bransford, J. (1991). Mental models and reading comprehension. In R. Barr, M. Kamil, P. Mosenthal, & P. D. Pearson (Eds.), *Handbook of Reading Research* (Vol. 2). New York: Longman.

Meyer, B. J. (1979). Organizational patterns in prose and their use in reading. In M. L. Kamil & A. J. Moe (Eds.), *Reading research: Studies and applications.* 28th Yearbook of the National Reading Conference. Rochester, NY: National Reading Conference.

Meyer, B. J. (1985). Prose analysis: Purposes, procedures and problems. In B. K. Britton & J. B. Black (Eds.), *Understanding expository text: A theoretical and practical handbook for analyzing explanatory text.* Hillsdale, NJ: Erlbaum.

Nist, S. L., & Simpson, M. L. (1988). The effectiveness and efficiency of training college students to annotate and underline text. In J. Readence & R. S. Baldwin (Eds.), *Dialogues in literacy research.* Chicago: National Reading Conference.

Paris, S. (1987, December). *Does metacognition inhibit or facilitate reading comprehension?* Paper presented at the annual meeting of the National Reading Conference, St. Petersburg, FL.

Paris, S., Wasik, B., & Turner, J. (1991). The development of strategic readers. In R. Barr, M. Kamil, P. Mosenthal, & P. D. Pearson (Eds.), *Handbook of reading research* (Vol. 2). New York: Longman.

Pearson, P. D., & Camperell, K. B. (1985). Comprehension of text structures. In H. Singer & R. Ruddell (Eds.), *Theoretical models and processes of reading* (3rd ed.). Newark, DE: International Reading Association.

Perkins, D., & Salomon, G. (1989). Are cognitive skills context-bound? *Educational Researcher, 18,* 16–25.

Pintrich, P. R., & Garcia, A. (1994). Self-regulated learning in college students: Knowledge, strategies, and motivation. In P. R. Pintrich, D. R. Brown, & C. E. Weinstein (Eds.), *Student motivation, cognition, and learning.* Hillsdale, NJ: Erlbaum.

Pressley, M. (1995). More about the development of self-regulation: Complex, long-term, and thoroughly social. *Educational Psychologist, 30,* 207–212.

Pressley, M., Goodchild, F., Fleet, J., Zajchowski, R., & Evans, E. (1989). The challenges of classroom strategy instruction. *Elementary School Journal, 89,* 301–342.

Pressley, M., Johnson, C., Symons, S., McGoldrick, J., & Kurita, J. (1989). Strategies that improve children's memory and comprehension of text. *The Elementary School Journal, 90,* 3–32.

Pressley, M., Woloshyn, V., Lysynchuk, L., Martin, V., Wood, E., & Willoughby, T. (1990). A primer of research on cognitive strategy instruction: The important issues and how to address them. *Educational Psychology Review, 2,* 1–58.

Pressley, M., Yokoi, L., van Meter, P., Van Etten, S., & Freebern, G. (1997). Some of the reasons why preparing for exams is so hard: What can be done to make it easier? *Educational Psychology Review, 9,* 1–38.

Pritchard, R. (1990). The effects of cultural schemata on reading processing strategies. *Reading Research Quarterly, 25,* 273–295.

Richgels, D., McGee, L., Lomax, R., & Sheard, C. (1987). Awareness of four text structures: Effects on recall of expository text. *Reading Research Quarterly, 22,* 177–196.

Roller, K. (1990). The interaction of knowledge and structure variables in the processing of expository prose. *Reading Research Quarterly, 25,* 79-89.

Sawyer, W. (1987). Literature and literacy: A review of research. *Language Arts, 64,* 33-39.

Schommer, M. (1993). Epistemological development and academic performance among secondary students. *Journal of Educational Psychology, 85,* 406-411.

Schommer, M., & Surber, J. R. (1986). Comprehension-monitoring failures in skilled adult readers. *Journal of Educational Psychology, 78,* 353-357.

Simpson, M. L., Hynd, C. R., Nist, S. L., & Burrell, K. I. (1997). College academic assistance programs and practices. *Educational Psychology Review, 9,* 39-87.

Simpson, M. L., & Nist, S. L. (1997). Perspectives on learning history: A case study. *Journal of Literacy Research, 29,* 363-395.

Simpson, M. L., Olejnik, S., Tam, A., & Supattathum, S. (1994). Elaborative verbal rehearsals and college students' cognitive performance. *Journal of Educational Psychology, 86,* 267-278.

Sinatra, R. (1991). Integrating whole language with the learning of text structure. *Journal of Reading, 34,* 424-433.

Slater, W. H., Graves, M. F., & Piche, G. L. (1985). Effects of structural organizers on ninth graders' comprehension and recall of four patterns of expository text. *Reading Research Quarterly, 20,* 189-202.

Tierney, R. J., & Mosenthal, P. J. (1982). Discourse comprehension and production: Analyzing text structure and cohesion. In J. H. Langer & M. T. Smith-Burke (Eds.), *Reader meets author/bridging the gap: A psycholinguistic and sociolinguistic perspective.* Newark, DE: International Reading Association.

Trends in academic progress (1991). Princeton, NJ: Educational Testing Service.

Vygotsky, L. S. (1978). *Mind in society: The development of higher psychological processes.* Cambridge, MA: Harvard University Press.

Weaver, C., & Kintsch, W. (1991). Expository text. In R. Barr, M. Kamil, P. Mosenthal, & P. D. Pearson (Eds.), *Handbook of reading research* (Vol. 2). New York: Longman.

Weinstein, C. E., & Mayer, R. E. (1986). The teaching of learning strategies. In M. C. Wittrock (Ed.), *Handbook of research on teaching.* New York: Macmillan.

Wilson, P. T., & Anderson, R. C. (1986). What they don't know will hurt them: The role of prior knowledge in comprehension. In J. Orasanu (Ed.), *Reading comprehension: From research to practice.* Hillsdale, NJ: Erlbaum.

Wittrock, M. C. (1990). Generative processes of comprehension. *Educational Psychologist, 24,* 345-376.

Wittrock, M. C. (1991). Contemporary methodological issues and future directions in research on the teaching of English. In J. Flood, J. Jensen, D. Lapp, & J. Squire (Eds.), *Handbook of research on teaching the English language arts.* New York: Macmillan.

CHAPTER 3

Comprehension Strategies: The Tools of Literacy

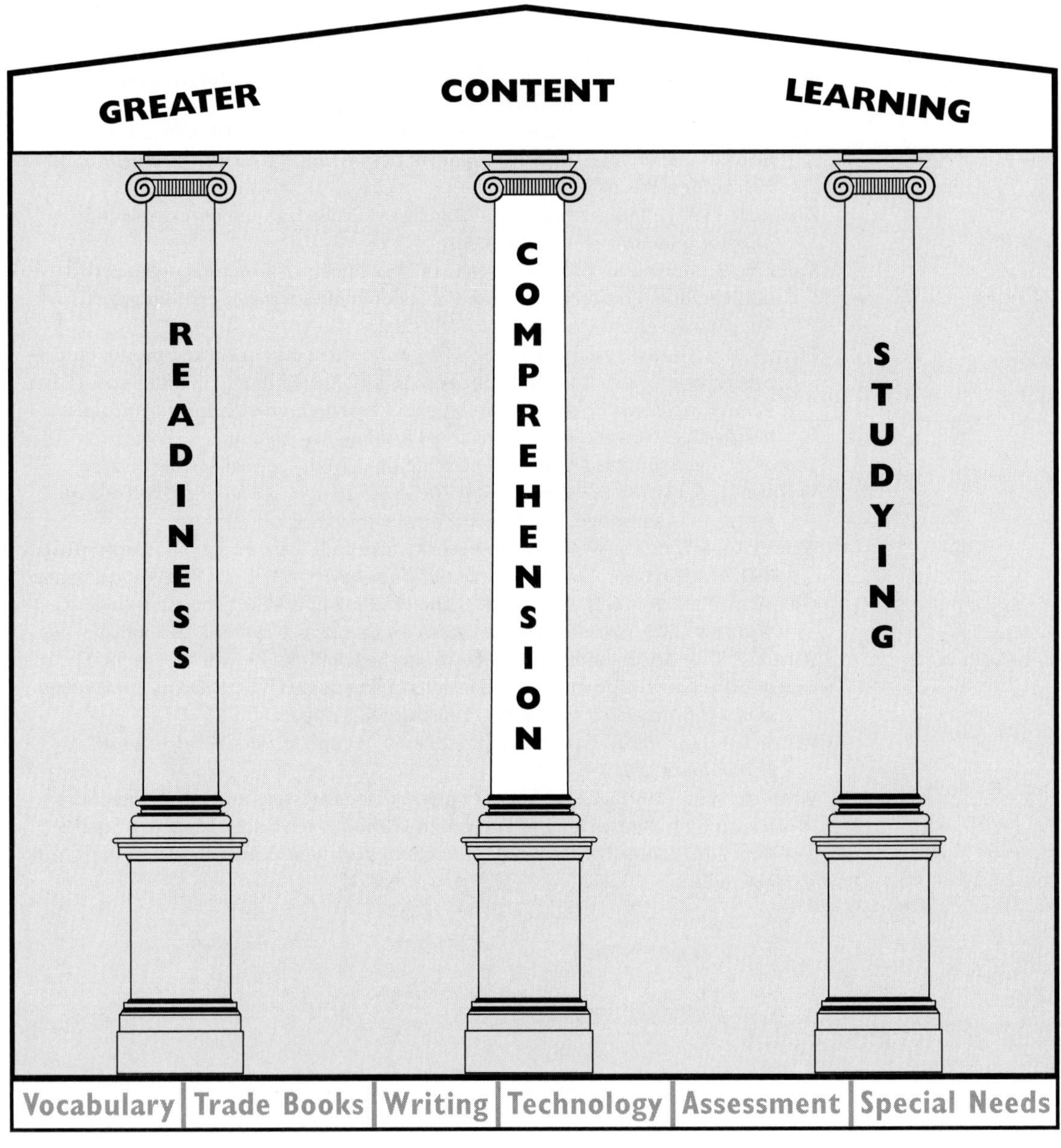

ANTICIPATION GUIDE

Directions: Read each statement carefully and decide whether you agree or disagree with it, placing a check mark in the appropriate *Before Reading* column. When you have finished reading and studying the chapter, return to the guide and decide whether your anticipations need to be changed by placing a check mark in the appropriate *After Reading* column.

	BEFORE READING		**AFTER READING**	
	Agree	*Disagree*	*Agree*	*Disagree*
1. Testing is the most efficient way to discover your students' lack of knowledge about a concept.	_____	_____	_____	_____
2. Students should learn how to identify writing patterns.	_____	_____	_____	_____
3. The best way to teach students how to monitor their learning is by having them answer questions at the end of a chapter.	_____	_____	_____	_____
4. Most students believe that answers to questions will be found in the text.	_____	_____	_____	_____
5. The brighter students are the ones who profit most from instruction on how to think critically.	_____	_____	_____	_____

To fail to teach students strategies they do not use and from which they could benefit is to fail the students, to neglect to show them ways of reaching reading and studying in optimal ways. To teach crops and arithmetic facts and science principles and battles without teaching students how they can learn more about any of this or about other content is to risk that children will not become effective independent learners.

—Garner (1988)

As discussed in Chapter 1, we believe that the major goal of education should be the development of critical thinkers and independent learners who can use the literacy processes to pursue knowledge and solve problems. To become independent learners, students need strategies that actively involve them in the process of constructing meaning in reading and writing and using new understandings in a functional way. In this chapter we present teacher-directed comprehension strategies for facilitating the growth of independent learners. The first four principles outlined in Chapter 2 provide the organizing framework for our discussion; the fifth principle will be discussed in detail in Chapter 9. These principles, however, are not mutually exclusive. That is, a strategy discussed under the first principle—helping students use prior knowledge and schemata in the meaning-making process—could easily help your students with the second, third, fourth, or fifth principles describing active learning. In fact, each chapter in this book will in some way present another approach to helping your students become active readers and writers and, thus, effective independent learners.

CASE STUDY

Charles teaches 10th-grade general biology in a large consolidated high school in the Midwest. After 3 years of teaching, he has noticed that many of his students (1) generally have a difficult time understanding the textbook, (2) do not complete homework reading assignments, and (3) seem to be trying to memorize information while failing to learn to observe and think about scientific phenomena. Charles is highly interested in discovering ways to help his students become more enthusiastic about science learning and better able to deal with and benefit from textbook reading.

Midway through the first semester of the new school year, Charles has begun a 2-week unit on genetics. Within the unit he wants to emphasize students' understanding of genetic engineering and the implications of this technology for their personal lives. In the preceding 2 months, his students studied the scientific method, the cell, and classification of living things, including the life cycle and basic requirements of life.

To the Reader:

As you read and work through this chapter on comprehension strategies, think about and be prepared to generate some strategies that could help Charles accomplish his goals. Consider how the strategies described in this chapter and those generated from your own experience and imagination could be adapted to the teaching and learning of science material.

■ ■ ■

ACTIVE LEARNERS USE THEIR PRIOR KNOWLEDGE IN THE MEANING-MAKING PROCESS

The principle that active learners use prior knowledge in the meaning-making process (as discussed in Chapter 2) is concerned with the extent to which readers *apply* appropriate schemata in meaning making. You can use many strategies to help students engage and use relevant prior knowledge as they read. In this section, we discuss three very effective ways of helping students access and use their relevant prior knowledge to comprehend and make meaning of the texts they read: the PReP procedure, learning logs, and the Content Area DR-TA. We explain how middle school and high school teachers implement these strategies in their classrooms to meet their students' needs. Teaching considerations related to prior knowledge are taken up in other chapters in this book as well (e.g., Chapter 5).

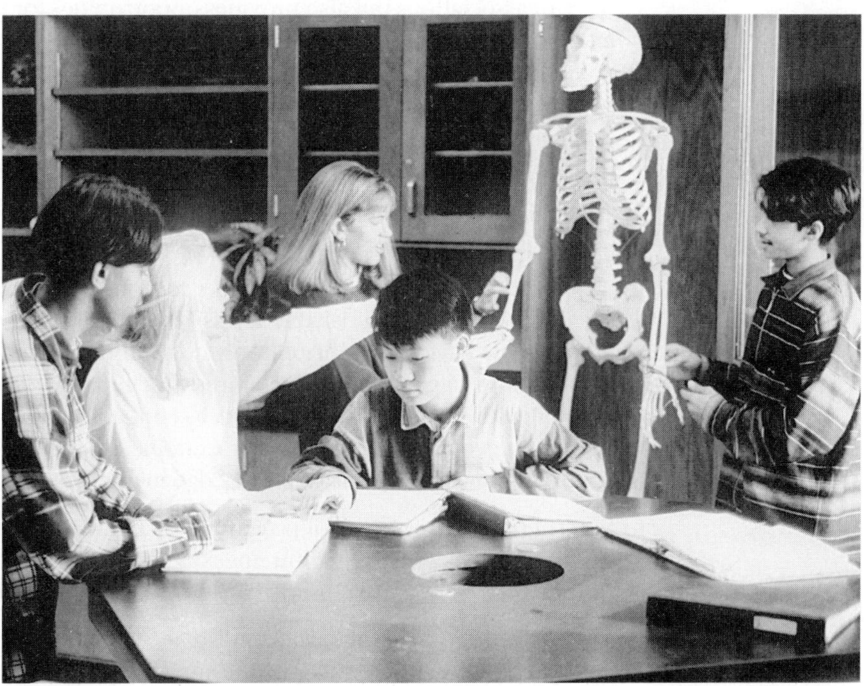

The PReP Procedure

The PReP Procedure Has Many Classroom Uses, Especially When Used with Follow-Up Writing Activities

PReP, the Prereading Plan (Langer, 1981), is an instructional procedure that can activate your students' prior knowledge about a particular topic and provide you with information about the adequacy of that knowledge. By analyzing your students' responses during the discussion phases of PReP, you can determine how their prior knowledge is organized, assess the quality and quantity of their oral language, and identify any potential misconceptions that may interfere with their learning.

According to Langer, when teachers use the PReP procedure, they guide students through three phases of discussion: the initial association with the concept, reflections on the initial associations, and the reformulation of knowledge.

1. **Initial association with the concept.** During this phase of discussion, ask students for their **initial associations with a concept** or topic by saying, "Tell me anything that comes to mind when. . . ." For example, you might ask students to say anything that comes to their minds when they hear the words "stock market." As students respond, you or another student record these comments on the board. During this phase, students have an opportunity to find associations between the topic about to be studied and their own prior knowledge about that topic, as well as the benefit of hearing their classmates' associations.

2. **Reflections on initial associations.** Ask students for their reflections on those initial associations with a question such as "What made you think of . . . ?" This phase not only helps students develop an awareness of their network of associations but also provides opportunities for them to hear their classmates' explanations.

3. **Reformulation of knowledge.** In this third phase, you might ask, "Based on our discussion and before we read the text, have you any new ideas about . . . ?" This question gives students the opportunity to verbalize associations that have been elaborated or changed through the discussion. By the close of this phase, students are usually making more refined statements about the concept to be studied.

Langer (1981) claims that students' responses to these questions can be classified into three distinguishable levels. The first level of response indicates that the students have "much prior knowledge" about the concept being discussed. Students with a great deal of prior knowledge will respond in the three phases of PReP with superordinate (main idea) concepts, definitions, analogies, or linkages of one concept to another. For example, on the concept of pollution, a student with considerable prior knowledge might respond as follows:

> There are three kinds of pollution—air, water, and land. All three deal with the process of harming our environment by making it unclean. Land and water pollution are closely related through the hydrologic cycle.

The second level of response, "some prior knowledge," indicates that students can discuss the concept in terms of examples, attributes, or characteristics. A student with some prior knowledge might state that pollution is bad because it ruins our air, land, and water with impurities. Students at both this level and the first level should be able to comprehend the assigned text with some guidance by the teacher.

Students responding at the third level, "little prior knowledge," have underdeveloped schemata for the topic to be studied. Their responses focus on low-level associations such as other words that sound like the targeted word or unrelated firsthand experience. For example, a student operating at this level might say this about pollution:

> Pollution—yes, I have seen pollution at my grandmother's lake in southern Georgia. I used to fish there during the summer.

Students responding in this manner will likely need additional information to fill in gaps in their prior knowledge to ensure adequate understanding of the assigned text. Although the PReP procedure is useful for the activation and discussion of students' prior knowledge about a particular topic, it does not provide additional support or strategies to guide students in their meaning making. Hence, it is important to combine PReP with other strategies to help students interact actively with assigned material. For example, the PReP procedure, or a modification of it, can be used in conjunction with learning logs. In the next section we will examine how a math teacher and a science teacher use this combination with their students.

Learning Logs

Learning Logs Can Be Used by Math Teachers as Well as Other Content Area Teachers

Learning logs involve students in keeping a notebook where they can record ideas, questions, and reactions to what they have read, observed, or listened to in class. Learning logs can also be used to help students prepare for learning by thinking about new knowledge in terms of their preexisting knowledge (Santa & Havens, 1991). Clarese, an eighth-grade mathematics instructor, asks her students to write a learning log entry for each unit of study. Her students respond to a variety of open-ended questions similar to those contained in PReP. For a unit on the real-number system, she asks her students to respond to the following questions:

> What do you think of when I say *whole numbers, rational numbers,* and *irrational numbers?*
>
> If you wrote anything in answer to my first question, what or who made you think of that response?

Clarese believes that writing activities such as these help her plan her lessons because she learns so much about her students' prior knowledge or lack of knowledge.

Toni, a 10th-grade biology teacher, also likes to have her students write in their learning logs before she begins a new unit of study. Sometimes she initiates her students' thinking and writing by asking them to preview the next assigned chapter. When students preview chapters in their biology textbook, they examine the title, headings, subheadings, charts, pictures, and questions. Based on this preview, the students then write in their learning logs what they already know or think they know about the topic. After reading the text chapter or a section of it, students write another entry focusing on what they learned and noting any misconceptions in their original log entries (Santa & Havens, 1991).

The following example shows one student's entries before and after reading a chapter on the human brain.

Learning Log Entry Written Before Reading

In this chapter I'm going to learn about the human brain. I know the brain is split into a right and left half. I think the halves control different things, but I'm not sure what. I also know that when someone has a stroke, blood vessels break in the brain.

Learning Log Entry Written After Reading

I learned that the two halves of the brain are called the right and left cerebral hemispheres. But, really, there are four main parts of the brain: the medulla oblongata, which controls involuntary movements like breathing, the pons, which controls auditory and muscular coordination, the cerebellum, which controls fine motor movements, and the cerebrum, which is the largest part, made up of two hemispheres, and controls speech, intelligence, and emotions. I also learned that a stroke is caused by a blockage in the arteries in the brain. This keeps the brain from getting enough oxygen, and it becomes damaged.

As these entries demonstrate, the student was able to use writing as an aid in the process of meaning making. The first entry served as a reflection of prior knowledge, whereas the second entry allowed the student to reconsider his initial understandings (e.g., about the nature of strokes) and derive new understandings based on text reading. Toni reinforces this reader–text interaction and metacognitive processing by asking students to include in their logs process comments that answer the broad question "How did writing about your ideas before and after reading affect your ability to learn the content?" Here is what the same student wrote in response:

Process Comments

I felt more interested in reading about the brain because I thought more about it before I read the chapter. I was surprised I knew even the little bit I did know about the brain before reading. Writing helped me think about what I already knew. It also made me more curious about what I was going to read because I wanted to find out if I was right. Knowing that I was going to have to write after reading made me read more carefully than I usually read stuff for school. I got more out of it. I wasn't real happy about doing it at first, but I think it helps.

Toni invites students to share their process comments with the whole class, which often sparks lively discussion about strategies for learning. Toni tries to focus class discussion on how writing helps connect prior knowledge to the ideas and information in the text, promotes active reading, and can lead to self-monitoring of learning.

Content Area Directed Reading-Thinking Activity (DR-TA)

The **Content Area DR-TA** (Haggard, 1985) was developed to activate students' prior knowledge about a topic and to involve them actively in what they are learning. Although the steps or procedures of the DR-TA are flexible and can be modified for almost any situation or content area, students are usually involved in (1) activating their prior knowledge, (2) predicting what will be discussed in the text, (3) reading, and (4) confirming and revising their predictions with the information they learned from the text.

Phil, a sixth-grade science teacher, uses a modification of the DR-TA with his students because he believes that it arouses their curiosity and motivates them to read more intently. When he taught a unit on humans and the environment, he started by asking his students to meet with their study partner in order to brainstorm and list all the information they predicted would be covered in the unit. After a few minutes of brainstorming, Phil led a large group discussion in which the study partners shared their lists as he wrote them on the chalkboard. As you can see in Figure 3.1, their ideas were very concrete, focusing on personal experiences. Chanda and her study partner listed ideas that pertained to littering because their youth group had just finished a project in which they volunteered to remove litter from the county road near their church.

The Content Area DR-TA Involves Students in Predicting, Brainstorming, Discussing, and Writing

Phil followed up the prediction step of DR-TA by suggesting that the students organize these predictions around possible problems that we have with our environment and possible solutions to these problems. He asked them to reread the list and identify the problems first. As the students volunteered their responses, he made another list on the board under the heading "Problems." When he asked the students to identify possible solutions, several of them pointed out that their predictions did not include any solutions except for the one about Chanda's church group. "Can you think of any solutions to our environmental problems besides picking up trash?" Phil asked. The students then volunteered the idea of recycling, and Phil added that to the "Solutions" list.

At this point, Phil told the students to read the first five pages of the chapter, which focused on the use and misuse of natural resources and the consequences of pollution. He directed them to "read carefully in order to determine the accuracy of our predictions and to identify information that we can add to our problems and solutions lists." Because Phil likes to have his students start their assignments during class, he gave them the last 10 minutes to begin their reading.

The next day, Phil asked the students to copy the list of predictions on the board. He then asked them to identify situations in which the predictions matched the information in the text that they had been assigned to read. As the

FIGURE 3.1 Students' Brainstorming as a Part of a Content Area DR-TA Lesson

Ideas Brainstormed

smelly garbage
litter
rats in garbage cans
garbage pits
a trip to a landfill
a dirty lake by my grandmother
unclean air in Chicago—my sister lives there
clay soil in Georgia
farmers using irrigation to grow cotton
the high cost of food
tainted food, like hamburgers and apples
not enough rain
oil on the beach in Brunswick
dead whales
people dying from bad food or water
newspapers, cartons, cigarettes on roadsides
picking up trash on Saturday morning

students eagerly volunteered, he placed a check mark by the relevant information on the master list. Then Phil told them to meet with their study partner to identify the problems or solutions discussed in the text but not included in their original predictions. After allowing 5 minutes for the partners to work, Phil led a large group discussion of the problems related to pollution and the environment. Figure 3.2 illustrates the information the students added to the master list.

Phil uses the Content Area DR-TA because he likes the fact that his students are engaged in brainstorming, discussing, writing, and reading to verify their predictions. In addition, he believes that the steps involved in DR-TA help his students become more aware of the active role they must assume when reading content area material.

The PReP procedure, learning logs, and the DR-TA are strategies that not only provide considerable diagnostic information about students and their prior knowledge but also, because they are excellent stimuli for student discussion and writing, promote more critical reading and thinking. In the next section, we discuss strategies that help students use text organization and structure to improve their understanding and learning.

ACTIVE LEARNERS UNDERSTAND AND USE TEXT STRUCTURE TO ORGANIZE THEIR MEANING MAKING

Teachers who want their students to be more sensitive to the structure and characteristics of text have a wide range of strategies available. In this section, we first discuss two methods of teaching students how to capitalize on the local co-

Problems in Our Environment

Before We Read

dead whales
people dying from bad food or water
newspaper, cartons, cigarettes on roadsides
oil on beaches
dirty water in lakes and oceans
unclean air
smelly garbage

After We Read

mercury from industrial waste
acid mine waste
pesticides with DDT
detergents with phosphates
fertilizers with phosphates
animal wastes
thermal pollution
radiation

Solutions to the Problems

Before We Read

picking up trash

After We Read

landfills with liners
outlawing chemicals
sewage treatment
contour farming
reclamation projects
public awareness

FIGURE 3.2 Students' Ideas Before and After Reading Organized into a Problem–Solution Format

herence of text: the use of connectives and the interlocking exercise. Then we explain three methods for teaching students about global coherence: charting, expository passage organizers, and text organization visualization. These strategies, as well as the related strategies of previewing and mapping (see Chapter 9), are intended to help students use a text's structure and organization to locate key ideas, understand relationships in the text, and store information in their long-term memory for future recall.

Creating Local Coherence with Connectives

Rita teaches 9th- and 10th-grade history in a large suburban high school, where she has developed a method for helping her students use connectives in comprehending their history textbook. **Connectives** are the signal words or phrases used to join ideas in our written and oral text, such as *because* or *on the other hand.* The following example describes her work in teaching connectives to students at the beginning of a unit on the American Civil War.

In groups of three or four, students were asked to generate a couple of statements about the Civil War that reflect what they already know about the topic.

Afterward, the groups read their statements to the whole class. Rita copied the statements on the board. She studied the list for a moment and then placed stars next to six of the sentences:

The Civil War was fought for many reasons.
The major reason the Civil War was fought was to free slaves.
The Civil War was not fought with a foreign country.
American fought American in the Civil War.
Abraham Lincoln was president during the Civil War.
Many soldiers from both sides died in the Civil War.

Besides laying the foundation for manipulating connectives, Rita provided students with a stimulus for prior knowledge activation with this activity. Plenty of interesting discussion ensued as groups of students offered their statements. For instance, when the statement "The major reason the Civil War was fought was to free slaves" was read, another student quickly commented that she didn't think that was quite true, and a small debate commenced over that issue. The students finally agreed that the slave issue was one of the significant reasons for the war. During this period, Rita did not direct the discussion but facilitated it by prodding and asking open-ended questions.

Teachers Can Model the Importance and Use of Connectives

Rita then passed out a list of connecting words (see Figure 3.3), provided information about the significance of the words, and modeled how she would use them in her speaking and writing. Then she wrote these two sentences on the board:

The wine glass broke.

Mary grabbed the broom.

Rita described how important it is to understand how sentences relate to each other, and she mentioned that the ability to connect sentences with a word that accurately reflects the relationship between sentences is part of what good readers do. She asked for some possibilities from the students' list of connectives that would join the sentences. Some students said "so" and "therefore," which created one meaning, while others offered "as" and "when," which created another meaning. Rita capitalized on these responses by pointing out how important it is to have a connective joining these sentences to match the author's intended meaning more closely.

Next, Rita asked her students to open their history textbooks to the Civil War chapter and identify any connectives they found on the first couple of pages. As connecting words were found, Rita and her students discussed the role each played in context by considering the meaning of adjoining ideas and their relationship as signaled by the connective.

At this point, Rita asked her students to work in small groups and write a paragraph using connecting words to join together the statements the class generated about the Civil War. The groups then read their paragraphs aloud. After each reading, Rita asked for reactions, especially comments about whether the

then	in spite of	notwithstanding
moreover	by this time	in comparison
also	another	instead
likewise	in addition	finally
for this reason	as well as	next
because	in order to	furthermore
hence	so that	since
accordingly	thus	therefore
soon	as a result	consequently
at that time	at last	until
while	subsequently	but
in the meantime	meanwhile	otherwise
however	even though	nevertheless
although	yet	rather
on the other hand	on the contrary	even so

FIGURE 3.3 Connectives Used to Join Ideas

connectives signaled the correct relationships among the sentences. Here is the way one group connected the statements:

> *Although* the Civil War was fought for many reasons, the major reason the Civil War was fought was to free slaves. The Civil War was not fought with a foreign country; *rather,* American fought American, *and* many soldiers from both sides died. *At that time,* Abraham Lincoln was president.

After reminding the students to keep a watchful eye out for structures provided by the author that help explain how ideas are related and stating that they would be working with connectives throughout the year, Rita proceeded with the unit. With only about 10 minutes left in the period, she began to read aloud from a book containing letters written by and to soldiers and officers during the Civil War. Not wishing to waste an opportunity to reinforce her recent instruction, she paused after reading a connective or some other structure of cohesion and, thinking aloud, modeled why she thought the author chose that structure.

Rita also takes some time within every unit to reinforce students' knowledge of how connectives operate in text. She gives students passages from their textbooks with the connectives removed. Students are expected to supply these missing links. Rita has found that when students are sensitized to the role of connectives in text, they not only improve their comprehension by becoming better able to compensate for disconnected text, but they also compose more cohesive themes, essays, and stories.

Creating Local Coherence with the Interlocking Exercise

Interlocking Exercises Can Also Help Students Use and Interpret Connectives

Another way to teach students to become more sensitive to connectives is through the use of an interlocking exercise (Thomas, 1979). Thomas developed the **interlocking exercise** to help students become more aware of the role of connectives in signaling a text's structure and organization. Calvin, a seventh-grade teacher of career education, uses the interlocking exercise with his students because it improves their text comprehension. The following example is an exercise he developed to help his students become aware of the use of the connectives signaling advantages and disadvantages and ideas in a list. The key connectives that Calvin wanted his students to notice are printed in italics in the example but would be omitted from the students' guide.

> Every household has at one time or another received some type of advertising message sent directly to the home, such as a catalog, a circular, a letter, or a free sample. Direct-mail advertising is *advantageous* if an advertiser desires to get a wide coverage for products. The circulars announcing a grocer's specials for the week, the catalog announcing a summer or spring sale of merchandise, or a letter offering a special purchase are *examples* of direct-mail advertising. There are *two* major *advantages* of direct-mail advertising. *First,* the message can be directed to specific customers and thus it is selective; *second,* it can be spread over a wide territory. Both large national companies and small, local retailers effectively use direct-mail advertising (Pickle & Abrahamson, 1980, p. 71).

As you can see from the example, the selections used for the interlocking exercise are brief and require students to replace the omitted word. The selections can be taken from textbooks, newspaper or magazine articles, or content from a demonstration, video, or class discussion.

The following steps Calvin used in constructing this exercise can be followed in developing your own interlocking exercise:

1. He located a passage that represented an obvious organizational structure and contained several connectives that cued the organization.
2. He typed the passage on a separate sheet of paper, placing a blank of uniform size in place of the connectives. He then made handouts and a transparency for overhead projection.
3. Before students were assigned to read the chapter, he introduced the concept of connectives, similar to the way Rita did with her 9th and 10th graders. Then he asked his students to read the passage and alerted them to the fact that some of the words were purposely left out.
4. After the students read the excerpt, he asked them to reread and fill in the blanks with the appropriate words. He emphasized that the excerpt must make sense with the inserted connectives.
5. He read the excerpt aloud, pausing at each blank, and asked students to insert their connective and provide a rationale.

6. He summarized the strategy and experience by reminding them of the usefulness of connectives—information can be recalled more easily when a structure is imposed on a text.

Calvin provided an excellent follow-up to this exercise by asking students short-answer questions about the excerpt that required them to integrate text structure knowledge with textual information. For example, one of the questions he asked was "What is one advantage and one disadvantage of direct-mail advertising?"

Creating Global Coherence with Charting

Charting Can Help Students See the Big Picture

A critical aspect of instruction designed to promote active learning is for teachers to phase out of their instructional role and for students to phase in and take on more responsibility for their own learning. One method that supports this transfer is charting, a strategy that eventually can be used by students once teachers have provided sufficient examples and guided practice.

Charting helps students summarize key ideas and visually sense the interrelationships between these ideas. The chart in Figure 3.4 is one that Tad, a biology teacher, used to help his sophomores understand a film they had watched about recent research and experiments involving the pituitary gland. Tad first distributed the partially completed chart and described how the act of creating a chart can help improve understanding and recall. He then told his students to complete the chart after viewing the film. The next day in class, he asked his students to work in small groups to check and discuss the information in their charts. After allowing students to work in small groups, he brought the class together for a discussion of the function and location of the pituitary gland. During the rest of the unit entitled "Hormones, Nerves, and Muscles," he created a variety of charting formats so that his students could see their versatility. Tad's long-term plan was to require his students to work in pairs to create their own charts for the next unit of study.

Tad relied on the structure of his supplementary materials and the textbook to organize the charts for his units of study. Although this organizational structure suited his instructional objectives and his students, you may have to make some adjustments, depending on the extent to which the information in your units of study is explicitly organized. Charting then becomes one way of imposing order on information that may not be organized in a suitable way for your students.

Clarese, the math instructor referred to earlier, uses charting to improve her students' skills in solving word problems. The following motion problem is typical:

> The speed of a stream is 4 miles per hour. A boat travels 6 miles per hour upstream in the same time it takes to travel 12 miles downstream. What is the speed of the boat in still water?

To help her students achieve the reading precision necessary for motion problems, Ann asks them to organize the data in a chart with the headings *t, r,* and *d,* representing time, rate, and distance. She explains her lesson this way:

The Pituitary Gland				
Hormone	Function	Location	Scientific Name	Chemical Composition
TSH	influences the thyroid by negative feedback	anterior lobe; 1 of 4 tropic hormones	thyroid-stimulating hormone	glycoprotein
FSH	stimulates ovarian follicle	anterior lobe; 1 of 4 tropic hormones	follicle-stimulating hormone	glycoprotein
ACTH				
LH				
Growth				

FIGURE 3.4 Sample Chart for Biology Chapter

My students already know that $R \times T = D$. I also have them represent rate downstream as $b + c$, where b is the rate of the boat, c is the rate of the current or stream, and $b - c$ is the rate upstream. I point out how the boat and current work together downstream, hence $b + c$, and against each other upstream, hence $b - c$. Therefore, before looking at the specifics of the problems, the student can make a chart as follows:

	t	r	d
upstream		$b - c$	
downstream		$b + c$	

My students then can read further and fill in the appropriate information, so the chart looks like this:

	t	r	d
upstream	$\frac{6}{b - c}$, or $\frac{6}{b - 4}$	$b - c$, or $b - 4$	6
downstream	$\frac{12}{b + c}$, or $\frac{12}{b + 4}$	$b + c$, or $b + 4$	12

Here is the process they follow. Four is substituted for the stream speed. Six and 12 are substituted for distance up- and downstream, and the time is represented as distance divided by rate. To set up an equation, students must look for a relationship, and hopefully they read "same time," so they set the representations for time equal to each other. In other words, the equation is:

$$\frac{6}{b-4} = \frac{12}{b+4}$$

My students seem to catch on to these motion problems much quicker with the charting idea.

Clarese knows that she needs to maximize the interactions between her students and their math textbook by employing a variety of strategies. While some would suggest that good textbooks should take care of that interaction, we know that textbooks do not teach—teachers do.

Creating Global Coherence with Expository Passage Organizers

EPOs Improve Students' Comprehension and Recall of Expository Text

Another useful way to help students become more aware and take advantage of a text's global coherence is with **expository passage organizers (EPOs).** EPOs were designed to help students see the structure of expository text and how the organization of ideas in text can affect comprehension (Miller & George, 1992). The proponents of EPOs have documented their utility for (1) focusing attention on critical components of expository text structure and (2) providing students models for organizing their ideas for writing exposition. Providing organizers for reading and writing of expository text has been shown to improve students' comprehension and recall (Mayer, 1996), as well as their writing and their attitude toward writing (Miller, 1988).

Teachers in a variety of content areas can design EPOs that match their particular texts or lessons. For example, in the EPO in Figure 3.5, a seventh-grade health teacher provided his students with an EPO for a problem–solution text on AIDS. Here is how the EPO was generated and how the teacher used it with his students:

First, he identified the various structural elements of the text—in this case, a chapter from a book entitled *AIDS: How It Works in the Body* (Greenberg, 1992), by (1) listing the overall passage pattern (problem–solution); (2) labeling the critical components of the text structure (e.g., introduction, problem, body); and (3) providing the partially completed main idea and detail statements within each of the critical components. As students work through the chapter, they fill in the remaining information on the EPO, such as additional details and/or main idea statements.

The teacher uses EPOs such as the one on AIDS not only to promote students' understanding and recall of text material but also to further develop their expository writing skills. The organization of the EPO helps students conceptualize the overall structure of the author's ideas about AIDS from the specification of the problems to a discussion of particular solutions. The teacher extends the utility of EPOs

AIDS: How a Virus Becomes an Epidemic

Directions: Complete the following EPO by looking back at the passage.
Passage Pattern: Problem–Solution

Introduction—Problem—Paragraph 1

Detail: HIV can be passed to another person during sexual intercourse if body fluids are exchanged.
Detail: Blood-to-blood contact ____________________
Detail: Mothers with AIDS ____________________
Main Idea: HIV enters the body in only three ways.

Body—Solution—Paragraph 2

Main Idea: ____________________
Detail: AZT has been shown to interfere with the production of HIV.
Detail: Natural immune substances ____________________

Body—Solution—Paragraph 3

Main Idea: Scientists continue to search for better ways to treat the infections that attack people with AIDS.
Detail: Chemotherapy, radiation ____________________
Detail: Antibiotics ____________________
Detail: Early detection of HIV can improve the chances of successful treatment.

Conclusion—Result—Paragraph 4

Main Idea: With no scientific cure in sight, changing behavior in the face of this growing danger may be the best preventive act.
Detail: ____________________

FIGURE 3.5 EPO for a Problem–Solution Text

by writing an essay himself using an expository text pattern consistent with the cause–effect patterns in the text and then fashioning an EPO for it. Both the essay and the EPO are shared with students and critiqued. Using EPOs to interact with text on a global structural level helps students recognize that their expository writing should have an overall organizational pattern as well. In recognizing how authors produce well-written exposition, students learn to model their compositions on these excellent examples. For instance, in the problem–solution essay on AIDs, students see how the author's citing of the problem is a main idea and her elaborations on the problem are supporting details. They notice how the author uses examples to support points and become better at providing appropriate supporting examples when composing their own expository texts (Miller & George, 1992).

Creating Global Coherence by Visualizing Text Organization

Another method for helping students better understand the organization of expository text is a holistic strategy that helps them visualize the abstract structures of exposition (McNeil, 1987; Sinatra, 1991).

Text Structure
Cause and effect
Enumeration
Description
Problem–solution
Comparison–contrast

Visual Display
Suggest, using pictures of slides, that an event took place as a result of a prior event. For example, a cause-and-effect relationship can be portrayed by showing melting snow and heavy rain and then the resulting damage from river flooding.

Arrange a display that shows a picture representing a group or class surrounded by a variety of pictures that exemplify that class. For example, a picture of a weasel could be surrounded by other animals in the weasel family.

Pictures should be organized so that each adds a bit more detail to the overall display. For example, in a horizontal plane, pictures showing the process of recycling aluminum or paper could be arranged.

Pictures of a problem situation or event should be followed by pictures showing how the problem was solved. For example, photos depicting the size and complexity of early computers followed by photos of today's personal computers would demonstrate how computers have been made more accessible and "friendly" by their reduced size.

Pictures should be displayed that show likenesses and differences among events, people, and places. For example, British soldiers in battle formation and dress could be accompanied by the battle tactics and dress of the colonial army during the American Revolution.

FIGURE 3.6 A Guide to Visual Displays for Expository Text Structure

Visual Text Organization Displays Can Improve Students' Reading and Writing

One of the best ways of assisting students in **visualizing text organization** is with pictures. You can use visuals to promote the learning of text organization in two ways. First, students can make their own visual essays with photographs, slides, or magazine or newspaper pictures and arrange them to form visual compositions. A visual display that is shared with the whole class can serve as a powerful organizer for students' oral presentations and written compositions. Second, you can help students prepare their visual essays and teach them to use frames and storyboards in representing text organization. The process of selecting pictures and arranging visuals that tell or imply how an expository text is organized reinforces for students a sense of global coherence, that is, of text structure (Sinatra, 1986).

We recommend you give students a guide to structuring visual compositions for text organization such as the one in Figure 3.6. With this guide, students could be asked to work in small groups to prepare visual essays. On large charts, they can arrange and attach their pictures while planning their verbal accounts to accompany the visuals. Students can be shown how to draw lines to connect pictures and show relationships; in this way, they create a visual schema for a particular organizational structure. Before writing compositions that mirror the text structure inherent in the visual essay, students should be given opportunities to share their displays with the class. During the "talk-through" period, they can refine their thinking as a result of questions and feedback from their peers.

Assisting students in becoming more sensitive to the structure of text or imposing structure on a text that lacks considerateness (see Chapter 2) can lead them to active and meaningful learning.

ACTIVE LEARNERS THINK CRITICALLY ABOUT TEXT AND CREATE THEIR OWN ELABORATIONS

Many teachers will tell you that the students who frustrate them the most are those passive students who rarely do the reading or assignments but listen well enough in class to "just get by." For these passive nonparticipants, learning is memorization of facts, and teachers are the dispensers of information. Teachers are always searching for solutions to problems associated with passive learners. Although there is no panacea for passivity, the four strategies included in this next section invite students to participate actively in their own learning. We discuss teacher modeling, question–answer relations used in cooperative learning situations, study guides, and discussion webs.

Demonstrating Active Reading Processes

Because we know that active learners think about and focus on key ideas when they read or listen, researchers have been investigating how readers construct main ideas for paragraphs and passages (Afflerbach, 1990; Hare, Rabinowitz, & Schieble, 1989). This interest in main idea comprehension is not surprising when we consider the following: (1) national reports on literacy habits conclude that students in the middle and upper grades cannot think inferentially about text (*Trends in Academic Progress,* 1991); (2) direct teaching of comprehension skills rarely takes place in reading and content classrooms (Dole, Duffy, Roehler, & Pearson, 1991); and (3) analyses of textbooks that students must read show that only a minority contain topic sentences or explicit main idea statements (Pressley, Yokoi, van Meter, Van Ellen, & Freeburn, 1997).

To find out how active learners construct main ideas, researchers are investigating how a reader thinks while reading. Pressley and Afflerbach (1995) and others (e.g., Brown & Day, 1983) asked for a sample of mature, expert readers to describe their thought processes while they read. This technique, known as *verbal reporting* or *think alouds,* afforded the researchers the opportunity to eavesdrop on how good readers make sense of text. They discovered that good readers use certain rules in constructing main ideas for paragraphs and passages, including:

- Deleting irrelevant or unimportant information
- Generalizing categories for lists of items or actions
- Selecting a main idea statement when the author provides one
- Constructing a main idea statement if none is provided

Even At-Risk Students Can Be Taught to Think About Main Ideas in a Content Area

These research findings have profound instructional implications. For instance, Brown and Day (1983) found that when less able readers were trained to use the same procedures used by experts, their ability to summarize and comprehend expository text improved significantly. Furthermore, these rules of main idea construction can be modeled by the teacher. Thus, thinking out loud becomes a means of reading comprehension instruction.

Sandy's seventh-grade social studies class was confronted by the following passage about the Bay of Pigs invasion in their textbooks. Sandy's interaction with her class exemplifies the power and effectiveness of modeling and demonstrating comprehension processes for teaching students to focus on key ideas in text.

> In 1959 a revolution, led by Fidel Castro, had taken place in Cuba. At first, the United States supported the revolution. But when Fidel Castro was shown to be a communist, the United States withdrew its support for him and started planning ways to overthrow him.
>
> Under President Eisenhower, plans were made to overthrow Castro by starting another revolution in Cuba. The U.S. gave arms, money, and training to a number of Cubans who had left their country and had come to the U.S. during the revolution because of their dislike for Castro and communism. After Eisenhower, John Kennedy was elected President. He continued to support the Cubans in the U.S. who were planning to overthrow Castro.
>
> In April 1961, the Cubans with U.S. assistance landed at the Bay of Pigs in eastern Cuba. But because they were not well prepared, they were quickly defeated by Castro's soldiers. Shortly afterward, Kennedy went on television to accept the blame for the defeat of the Cubans at the Bay of Pigs. (Graff, 1980, p. 676–677)

Sandy: Okay, let's see if we can make sense out of this passage. First of all, let's talk about some of the words in here and some of the words referred to.

Student 1: I know what a "revolution" is. It's when the people of a country go against their president.

Sandy: Great, so how does that fit with the first sentence?

Student 1: Well, there was a revolution in Cuba.

Sandy: Okay, who is Fidel Castro?

Student 1: He must be from Cuba if he led the revolution.

Sandy: Did Castro revolt by himself? No, of course he didn't. Other Cubans helped him. How do we know this?

Student 2: He "led" people.

Sandy: Right. Does anyone know anything else about Castro?

Student 3: Isn't he still the president of Cuba?

Sandy: Yes he is, and he's considered a communist. Do you remember reading about communism a few weeks ago? What did you learn?

Student 3: The Russians were communist.

Student 4: It's when everyone works for the government.

Sandy: Okay, I've heard two things about communism. How does communism compare with how we live in the United States?

Student 4: People work for themselves here. They can keep their own money.

Student 5: In some communist countries there's no religion. Nobody believes in God.

Sandy: Okay, so that's another difference when compared with our system. We have freedom of religion. Now, what do you think the topic of this passage is?

Student 3: The Bay of Pigs.

Sandy: Can anyone be more specific?

Student 4: What happened before and after the Bay of Pigs?

Sandy: Excellent, so the first paragraph is talking about what happened before. Can someone give me the main idea for the first paragraph?

Student 6: The United States supported Castro until they found out he was a communist. Then they stopped.

Sandy: How many agree with Todd's main idea? Excellent, Todd. Do you now see why we would reject Castro? What does the passage say that supports this main idea?

Student 6: It says we didn't support him anymore when we found out he was a communist.

Sandy: Great. Now, what can you tell me about Presidents Eisenhower and Kennedy?

Student 2: I know, Kennedy was shot by Oswald.

Student 5: Eisenhower was some kind of general or something before he was president.

Sandy: Okay, who can tell me what's going on in the next paragraph?

Student 5: Well, it sounds like some Cubans who had left Castro didn't like him and wanted to go back to Cuba.

Sandy: Right. Why do you think these Cubans who had left Cuba didn't like Castro?

Student 5: Because they liked our government?

Sandy: Very good answer. So what can we say is the main idea for this paragraph?

Student 7: Eisenhower helped Cubans overthrow Castro.

Sandy: Okay, does anyone disagree with this?

Student 6: And Kennedy helped too.

Sandy: So give me a complete main idea.

Student 6: Eisenhower and Kennedy helped Cubans overthrow Castro.

Sandy: The overthrow didn't actually happen, did it?

Student 3: No.

Sandy: So what if we say that Eisenhower and Kennedy helped Cubans who were living in the United States plan the overthrow of Castro?

Class: That's good.

Sandy: What support do we have for this main idea?

Student 1: It says the United States gave arms and training.

Sandy: It sure does. Excellent work, group!

It is important to notice that Sandy does not tell students the key ideas, nor does she simply hand out chapter questions. Instead, she teaches students how to develop key idea statements. Notice, too, how Sandy's interaction with her students stimulated their prior knowledge of the topic, regulated their attention to the important points and supporting information in the text, provided a model of her own thinking about main ideas, and reinforced students' main idea thinking. Sandy spends a few minutes during nearly every class discussion in a similar way, collaborating with students in the process of generating key ideas while assisting them in the overall task of making sense of the entire text. She solidifies the importance of reading for key ideas with homework, papers, and tests that require students to demonstrate elaborate levels of comprehension.

We have seen that modeling and demonstrating comprehension processes are very effective strategies for Sandy. Her students are aware that she is their partner in constructing meaningful interpretations of their class texts. These teaching strategies, however, have broad applications for helping improve students' thinking and learning. As you will see, examples of teacher modeling and demonstrating appear in nearly every chapter of this book with a wide variety of content and in a number of classroom settings.

Identifying Sources of Information in Answering Questions

Another way you can encourage elaborative and critical thinking about content area concepts is through a questioning strategy that sensitizes students to the interaction of the text with their prior knowledge during question answering. Using a questioning framework known as **question–answer relations (QAR)** (Raphael & Pearson, 1985), students can learn how to locate and use many **sources of information** when answering comprehension questions along the continuum of text processing:

- *Right There:* The answer can be found in the text. The question cues the reader by echoing words from the text. The information source is mostly text based.
- *Think and Search:* The answer is not directly stated but requires the reader to combine ideas in the text with prior knowledge to form inferences.
- *On My Own:* The source of information for answering this type of question is the reader's prior knowledge. Processing is almost entirely reader based.

The QAR Framework Encourages Students to Go Beyond the Text and Think Critically about Content Area Concepts

QAR refutes the common misconception held by students that the text tells all. Reliance on the text as the sole source of information limits students' interactions with text and consequently their depth of understanding. A study with college remedial readers (Brozo, Stahl, & Gordon, 1985) found that before training in QAR, most students believed that the answers to all reading comprehension test questions were stated directly in the text. Their comprehension scores reflected this faulty line of reasoning—all had failed a state-mandated reading test for matriculation into college. However, after 4 weeks of developing their question-answering abilities based on QAR, significantly more of these students passed the reading test compared with a control group. In a study by Wixson (1983), fifth-graders were conditioned to answer questions about an informational passage on either the reader-based end of the continuum or the text-based end. Then, after a week, the students were asked to recall the passage. Recalls were provided at a level of understanding consistent with the level of questions students had been trained to answer. In other words, students who had answered text-based questions gave superficial, detail-level recalls, while elaborate and meaningful recalls were provided by students who had answered questions that required more reader-based processing. This finding demonstrates the powerful learning potential of questioning. If students are asked questions at the think-and-search and on-my-own levels of processing, they will remember textual information and ideas at those levels; if they are asked questions at the right-there level, they will likely remember only information at the verbatim-recall level.

To provide you with firsthand experience with identifying sources of information for questions, following is a QAR activity for you to complete. The experience will give you a much better grasp of the processing requirements placed on students in a typical QAR exercise. Read the following passage; then group the questions and answers according to the source of information for answering them (right there, think and search, on my own).

The Story of Buck Billings

"Buck" Billings left Teddy's Rough Riders the very day peace was signed with the Spanish. There were wild stories about gold in the Klondike, and he couldn't wait to claim his stake. In the port of Havana he planned to pick up a boat to Tampa, then head north by train. After 3 days' trek through mosquito-infested swamps, he found that all the boats were packed with soldiers and civilians leaving for the States. He hopped aboard a ship bound for Venezuela. From there he found passage on a banana boat heading for South Carolina. The boat was turned back by a hurricane and forced to dock in Santiago Harbor. On a small sailing vessel he was finally able to reach the southern coast of Florida. He walked for 2 days to a train depot. After several weeks, he made it through the southern plains and eventually arrived in Denver, the town of his birth. Since it was already November, he moved back into his Aunt Dolly's boarding house, where he planned to stay for the next 4 months. During that winter, however, his yellow fever returned, and he succumbed to it on the first day of the new year.

1. Why was the boat forced to turn back? (Because of a hurricane.)
2. Where is Aunt Dolly's boarding house? (Denver.)
3. Where is the Klondike? (In Alaska.)
4. Where was Buck's ship forced to dock after the hurricane? (In Santiago Harbor.)
5. If Buck intended to head back to the States, why did he take a boat to Venezuela? (Because all the boats heading for the States were packed, and he thought he could get back to the States from Venezuela.)
6. Where did Buck get yellow fever? (Cuba.)
7. What was the boat carrying that was heading for South Carolina? (Bananas.)
8. Did Buck make it to the coast of South Carolina? (No, the boat was forced back by a storm.)
9. Where was Buck the day peace was signed with the Spanish? (Cuba.)
10. Who is Teddy? (Teddy Roosevelt.)

Think about how you categorized these questions and answers as you read our categorization and rationales. We placed questions 1 and 4 in the right-there category because these questions cue the reader to the answers with words taken directly from the relevant sentence in the text.

Questions 2, 5, 7, and 8 we identified as think-and-search questions. Question 2 requires the reader to combine ideas from two sentences—the one stating that Buck arrived in Denver and the next one stating that Buck moved back with his aunt. The inference is that Buck is from Denver and has lived with his aunt before. To answer question 5 also requires some inferential reasoning.

Buck was unable to go directly north to the States because all the ships were filled. By heading south first, he hoped to get there from Venezuela by avoiding Cuba altogether. Unfortunately, he found himself back in Cuba anyway. Question 7 asks the reader to make a low-level inference that connects the words in the question "What was the boat carrying?" to the sentence in the text that refers to the boat heading for South Carolina as a "banana boat." To answer question 8, the reader must combine information from two sentences—one stating that Buck was on a boat bound for South Carolina and the next one stating that the boat was forced to dock in Santiago Harbor. To answer "no" to this question requires more inferencing than may initially meet the eye. Notice that the reader must realize that Santiago Harbor is not in South Carolina, and because no other mention of South Carolina is made in the passage, it can be assumed that Buck never arrived there.

We grouped questions 3, 6, 9, and 10 in the on-my-own category. Certainly, to answer question 3, the reader must already know the geographical location of the Klondike. The text provides no clue. If the reader also realizes that peace with the Spanish over Cuba was signed at around the turn of the century, this knowledge could reinforce the time frame for the Alaskan gold rush. To know that Buck probably contracted yellow fever in Cuba (question 6) means that the reader has prior knowledge that yellow fever is a tropical disease and that many soldiers suffered and died from it as a result of their experiences in the war with Spain over Cuba. To answer question 9, the reader must integrate several bits of textual information with a great deal of prior knowledge. The reader must possess knowledge about the Rough Riders and Teddy Roosevelt and know that they fought the Spanish in Cuba. Question 10 requires prior knowledge related to question 9; certainly, the reader must know that it was Teddy Roosevelt who commanded the Rough Riders.

Teaching Question–Answer Relations Using Cooperative Learning

The ultimate goal of QAR is not simply to train students to identify information sources for answering questions. Instead, QAR training should be seen as a method of sensitizing students to the idea that there are various ways of thinking about a text. Through QAR they can use their existing knowledge to interact more elaboratively and meaningfully with the texts they read.

Following is a description of an actual eighth-grade science classroom in which students were involved in **cooperative learning** experiences for reinforcing their understanding of QAR. Beth, the teacher, exploits the powerful learning potential of cooperative groups throughout the school year with nearly every topic she and her students explore. Students in this class develop a deeper understanding of science content through interactions with their peers by speaking, listening, reading, and writing. All students are provided greater opportunities to articulate and reinterpret text concepts and vocabulary, raise questions, discuss answers, and become more active class members.

The topic the class was considering was "What Makes Ice Ages?" Beth first asked students to form into their **study reading groups,** three to a group. Her students were used to many different grouping arrangements that allow them to move in and out of groups, interacting with different students, depending on the purpose of the group. For instance, two other common grouping patterns in Beth's classroom were **interest groups** and **research groups.** Beth briefly rehearsed the "Rules for Group Membership," which students had in their notes and which were also written in bold letters on the side wall bulletin board.

There Are Many Different Ways to Group Students

- Each member must be strongly committed to doing the work and carrying out his or her specific role within the group.
- Each member should understand and follow the directions for completing assigned work.
- Each member should respect other members' input.
- A member who disagrees with another member should defend his or her own point of view, giving specific reasons based on the text or on personal experience.
- No member should dominate or withdraw; every member should add something to the discussion.
- Each member should be positive and encourage other members.

Beth then introduced the idea of QAR using an overhead transparency to focus the discussion. She discussed with the students how becoming more sensitive to the sources of information for answering questions can improve their ability to get more out of their textbook reading. She explained each of the levels of QAR and provided a handout with the labels and explanations. Beth asked students to open their science textbooks to the beginning of the section on ice ages. Using an overhead transparency, she presented a series of questions accompanied by answers covering the first page of this section. In their groups, students discussed among themselves why a question belonged in a particular category. Afterward, students shared their responses and rationales with the whole class. Beth allowed students to debate their answers, providing support, feedback, and demonstrations of her own thinking in identifying information sources for the questions.

The next phase of QAR instruction involves assigning responsibilities to each of the three group members. Beth asked each student in the groups to generate questions with answers for one of the three levels of QAR. The questions were written on the next page of the text. The groups then went over their questions, helping each other focus on the appropriate question for the assigned level. Beth then asked groups to exchange questions, emphasizing that the questions not be labeled. The groups worked with their new questions, determining sources of information and rationales. During this time, Beth sat in on each group's discussion, answering questions, providing necessary input, and reinforcing group efforts. Questions were then given back to their owners with comments. Students then reworked their questions based on input from the other groups.

To get a better idea of the kinds of group discussions students had as they worked cooperatively on identifying QARs, refer to the following excerpt. This discussion took place between three students trying to determine whether a question required think-and-search or on-my-own processing.

Student 1: The question is, "If the greenhouse effect is true, what kind of climate will Chicago have in 50 years?"

Student 2: What's the answer?

Student 1: It says "6 to 12 degrees warmer. Like Florida."

Student 3: How are we supposed to know that?

Student 1: We can figure it out. We have to look in the book first to make sure it doesn't tell us about Chicago.

Student 3: I don't remember anything about Chicago.

Student 2: It doesn't, I'm looking right now. I can't find anything about it.

Student 1: It does say that if carbon dioxide keeps getting worse, the world temperature is going to go up. You see where I am, on page 128.

Student 3: It's for sure not a right-there or in-the-book question.

Student 1: Does it say by how many degrees? I'm looking down here. Yeah, here it is. It says that "if carbon dioxide levels continue to increase at the present rate, in 40 to 50 years the greenhouse effect will cause temperatures worldwide to increase by about 6 to 12 degrees centigrade."

Student 2: So, big deal, that doesn't sound like very much. How could that make us as warm as Florida?

(Students attend to the text.)

Student 3: Look, I found this part up here that says that a 100 million years ago the earth was a lot warmer even at the poles. So maybe if the poles were warm, we would be really warm too. What do you think?

Student 1: I like it. This is a hard one.

Student 2: So we're saying it's what, an on-my-own type or a think-and-search?

(They ponder.)

Student 3: I think it's sorta like both. You can find some of the information in the book, but you have to figure it out by yourself when it comes to the part about Chicago.

Student 1: Don't we have to say one or the other?

Student 3: I don't think so. She said they could be one or the other or anywhere in between.

(Student 1, designated as the recorder, writes down the group's rationale. They move on to the next question.)

Students Must Eventually Learn How to Create Their Own Questions

QAR training promotes sensitivity to various information sources for answering comprehension questions; thus, students learn to process text in a more elaborative fashion. To move toward greater independence in reading comprehension, students should be generating their own questions that reflect the important information and ideas in the text. In Chapter 9, self-questioning is discussed as a strategy for improving students' understanding and metacognitive awareness.

Using Study Guides

To facilitate students' elaborative processing and to promote more critical thinking, teachers can provide students with **study guides** (Herber, 1978). Study guides are designed to stimulate students' thinking during or after their reading, listening, or involvement in any content area instruction. Guides also help students focus on important information and ideas, making their reading or listening more efficient (Herber & Nelson-Herber, 1993).

Study Guides Can Be Used for Almost Any Reading, Listening, or Viewing Experience in a Content Area Classroom

If you are not familiar with study guides, we invite you to complete the sample in Figure 3.7. First, look at the guide and directions. Then read the passage that accompanies it. After reading, complete the guide.

Now that you have finished the guide, a few comments are in order. Did you notice that, like QAR questions, the statements seemed to require a greater degree of mental activity as you moved from level I to level III? The reason is that the statements were written to tap various levels of comprehension. We think about a text as existing on a sliding scale or continuum. On one end of the continuum is the kind of text processing that requires recall of directly stated material. We might call this **text-based processing** or *memory-level comprehension* because the information is based almost entirely on the text. To respond to level I of the study guide, you employed mostly text-based processing because the answers were basically right there. As we move along the continuum, processing becomes less and less text based and increasingly reader based. By **reader based,** we mean that comprehension requires readers to connect their prior knowledge about a topic with the information in text. Level II of the guide required you to combine your prior knowledge with textual information to form inferences. At level III, comprehension of these statements that seem to go far beyond the directly stated information in the text required you to rely heavily on prior knowledge and to process text in an elaborative fashion by applying and predicting. Thus, the goals of a study guide are to help learners assimilate information into their existing schemata and to think critically about ideas.

Something else you may have noticed about your study guide experience is that the statements in the guide form an excellent basis for class discussion. In fact, we urge you to take advantage of the discussion-generation potential of study guides; otherwise, students might eventually come to view them as just more busy work. The important advantage of study guides for teachers is that students must read the assigned textbook and think about the assignment rather than skim or scan the pages for answers to text-based questions. In short,

Directions: Read the following passage; then read the statements about it. In the space to the left of each statement, put an *A* if you agree with the statement and a *D* if you disagree. Base your decisions on the information and ideas in the passage, as well as on what you already know about the topic.

Jesse Jackson's Broadening Political Base

In 1984, during his first presidential campaign, Jesse Jackson identified a constituency of the American public he believed had been, up to that time, underrepresented. Minorities of all colors and ethnic backgrounds, as well as women, the poor, and other groups, rallied around Jackson and were to become his *rainbow coalition.* Jackson claimed that politicians had forgotten about these groups of Americans. He charged that many were victims of poverty, homelessness, joblessness, poor working conditions, low salaries, sexual harassment, and subtle and overt racism. Many had chosen not to vote out of hopelessness. They looked at the slate of presidential candidates, claimed Jackson, and despaired, realizing that none had their concerns at heart.

In spite of grass-roots support and impassioned oratory, Jackson lost his bid for the presidency in 1984. Many said the country was not ready for a black president. However, political analysts speculated that Jackson's lack of success was attributable more to his narrow appeal than to his color. Indeed, in the 1988 presidential election, Jackson broadened his political base of support and mounted a far more serious challenge for the Democratic Party nomination. While holding on to the rainbow coalition, he reached out to farmers, factory workers, and the Democratic mainstream. He brought many delegates to the Democratic National Convention in Atlanta, where he brokered his political power and exerted leverage on Michael Dukakis to help shape the Democratic planks and platform.

Level I

______ Jackson broadened his political base of support in 1984.
______ Jackson first ran for president in 1984.
______ The Democratic National Convention was held in Atlanta in 1982.
______ The rainbow coalition was made up of the white middle class.

Level II

______ Jackson might have been more successful in 1984, but the country was not ready for a black president.
______ Jackson charged that the presidential candidates engaged in racism.
______ Jackson supported equal pay for women.
______ Affordable housing would not have been on Jackson's platform in 1984.

Level III

______ Presidential candidates who appeal to farmers and factory workers are likely to be fairly successful.
______ Jackson should continue to broaden his political base of support if he expects to be successful in 1996.
______ Americans will not vote for a black president in the foreseeable future.
______ Jackson lost his bid for the presidency in 1988.

FIGURE 3.7 Sample Study Guide Activity

students who are required to complete study guides cannot come to class unprepared; the guides force them to become active learners.

A few other important features of study guides are especially pertinent. To make guides more motivating and attractive to students and, consequently, to increase the likelihood that they will complete them and use them, the response formats should require students to do very little writing other than make a simple mark or check or write a few words. The idea is that guides should not resemble the typical discussion questions students are used to seeing and are forced to respond to with extensive written answers. The extent of the response on the guides should not, however, be construed as indicating the extent of thinking demanded of students. A colleague puts it well, describing study guides as "short on responding but long on thinking." As you undoubtedly noticed when working through the level III statements in Figure 3.7, your single-letter responses were made after considerable mental activity. In the directions to the guide, you are asked to base your responses on evidence from the text and your prior knowledge. Emphasis on this point will discourage students from responding arbitrarily, especially when they will be held accountable for their work in small-group or whole-class discussions.

The Response Format Is Very Important to a Study Guide

Finally, like most strategies, study guides can become drudgery if misused or overused. Use discretion in employing them. Not every text lesson or topic will demand or lend itself to guides. A science teacher's point about study guides is instructive: "I use them with topics that typically give my students the most difficulty. They agree that it helps them organize the information and ideas and prepares them for my tests. But I don't use them all the time because other approaches work well too." Study guides are only one way to promote elaborate text processing.

As With All Strategies, It Is Important Not to Overuse Study Guides

Designing and Teaching with Guides

There are no set procedures for creating study guides. The types of guides are as varied as the teachers who construct them. In this section, we present various examples of teacher-constructed study guides from many different content areas. However, although guides can take a number of different forms, you must make some important and necessary decisions before designing them:

1. Read the text material thoroughly and decide what information and concepts need to be emphasized. You will be reminded of this step at several points throughout this book because it is the same process you should go through when, for instance, deciding key vocabulary to teach, appropriate readiness activities, and relevant trade books to accompany the text.
2. Determine how much assistance your students will need to process the information at an elaborative and meaningful level. If students already possess a basic understanding of the content, your guides can focus exclusively on higher levels of critical thinking. If, on the other hand, your students lack a basic understanding of the content, then guides should focus more on key ideas.
3. Ask yourself, "What format will stimulate my students to think about the content in an elaborative fashion, as well as motivate and appeal to them?" In our experience, the more imaginative the guide, the greater the chance that students will be enthusiastic about the guide and use it appropriately.

Students Need to Be Prepared for Using Study Guides in the Most Effective Manner

It is critical to prepare students to use study guides. If you simply distribute guides and tell students to complete them, you are setting yourself up for disappointment. Students need grooming and coaching to take full advantage of study guides. We recommend that you begin by "walking through" one of the guides, explaining its features, intent, and benefits. Allow students to meet in small groups and complete the guide in class under your supervision and with your assistance. Engage the class in discussion based on their responses to the guide, and use this feedback to provide additional explanation and to make any necessary modifications to the guide. Above all, keep in mind your purpose for using study guides. They should not be used as tests because promoting a right-or-wrong attitude among students undermines your intent—to encourage elaboration and critical thinking. It is important, however, that students be responsible for rationalizing and defending their responses to the guide. Make this an integral part of the study guide activity. Finally, at every opportunity, reinforce the connection between the mental activity required to complete the guides and your expectations of how and what students should be learning.

Examples of Guides from Various Content Areas

Study guides have been used successfully by teachers and students in nearly every content area with a wide variety of topics. As you look over the following guides, observe the format of each and reflect on how students are encouraged to think critically about the concepts. In addition, consider how you can adapt these formats to fit the textbooks, films, demonstrations, or discussions you use in your classroom.

Literature. The study guide in Figure 3.8 was developed by an English teacher for her sophomores as they completed their analysis of characters in *To Kill a Mockingbird.*

Driver's Education. For a unit in a driver's education class, students were provided with the guide shown in Figure 3.9 to help them compare and contrast the characteristics of motorcycles and automobiles. The information was presented in a film rather than a textbook. After the film, the students were asked to answer the questions that followed each section. These questions then served as a stimulus for classroom discussion.

Foreign Language. In the final example of content-area study guides shown in Figure 3.10, you can see that guides can even be applied to foreign languages to promote more critical thinking. The Spanish teacher who constructed this guide found it to be very useful in helping her students expand their understanding of the central character. The guide is presented in English, but was, of course, given to her students in Spanish.

A Final Word About Study Guides

As this section has demonstrated, study guides can be a very effective and versatile means of promoting higher-level thinking about the concepts in your

Directions: Below you will find a copy of today's want ads from the *Maycomb Daily Times,* a fictitious newspaper straight from the pages of *To Kill a Mockingbird.* Below each ad, write the name of the character from the novel that you feel would best fit the ad's description. All ads apply to at least one character, and some ads may have more than one responder. Be prepared to justify your answers.

Wanted: Individual who is interested in donating baked goods to be sold at the next PTA meeting to raise money for a school function.

____

The Caucasians of America need information on the ghetto life of Negroes in contemporary America. Only those with personal experience need apply.

____

Needed: Local newspaper is in need of an owner. Must have experience in printing, distribution, and sales.

____

Gun Club looking for good shooter to give seminar.

____

Help! The Kane County Rehabilitation Center is looking for a spokesperson for its drug unit.

____

Child abuse is a crime. Report all cases to authorities.

____

Wanted: A disciplinarian. A child who everyone considers a BRAT needs some old-fashioned disciplining.

____

Teacher needed. Patience a plus but not necessary. Will train.

____

The rape crisis hotline is a free public service for the community. If you know of anyone who needs our help, encourage them to call us.

____

Penpals are wonderful. If you know of anyone who is interested in being a summer friend, a winter writer, send us his/her name.

____

Seamstress Opening. Easy mending duties. Pick your own hours. Work at home if it's more convenient.

____

Stop being a neighborhood gossip. Join Tale Enders today. Nobody likes to hear what everyone else has been up to.

____

FIGURE 3.8 Study Guide for Literature: *To Kill a Mockingbird*

content area. In addition to their usefulness in promoting learning from text, they can be used for lectures, films, and demonstrations. But they are just one means. And, as we have pointed out, they are teacher initiated. Here and in other sections of this book, we emphasize the importance of developing independent readers and learners. Therefore, we present a variety of strategies

Check which vehicle is affected most by the following adverse surface conditions. Be prepared to defend your decisions in class discussion.

	Automobile	**Motorcycle**
1. Loose gravel		
2. Gravel surface		
3. Sand on pavement		
4. Snow		
5. Mud		
6. Washboard		
7. Potholes		
8. Wet pavement		

How can a motorcycle operator compensate for the shortcomings of the machine under adverse surface conditions?

FIGURE 3.9 Study Guide for Automobile and Motorcycle Safety

Directions: In your reading about Sor Juana, you discovered that she could be considered one of the first advocates of the feminist movement. In addition, she was a very caring person, and her strong convictions often led her to step into situations on behalf of other people. *Evaluate* the following statements according to whether Sor Juana would agree or disagree with them. Just for fun, also consider your own reactions. Use the numbers 0–5 (5 = *total agreement;* 0 = *total disagreement*). You will be asked to justify your reactions in the class discussion.

Sor Juana	**Me**	
________	________	1. The greatest contribution of women to society is that of producing babies.
________	________	2. Although men and women are physically different, there is very little difference in their intellectual capacities.
________	________	3. If a job that a man holds is essentially the same as the job held by a woman employed by the same company, the man should receive a higher salary because he is most likely the main breadwinner for his family.
________	________	4. There is no excuse for racial or religious discrimination. If you suspect that either of these situations is occurring in your community, you should talk to your neighbors about it.
________	________	5. If you are passing in front of a store and see a robbery taking place, you should discreetly enter the store, assess the situation, and, if possible, somehow try to overpower the thief.
________	________	6. Because of past discrimination, society should now make certain allowances for women. For example, companies should be strongly urged to hire a woman when given the choice between a man and a woman with equal qualifications.
________	________	7. Although both men and women are eligible for the armed services, only men should be assigned combat roles.
________	________	8. If a company is marketing something that you believe may be harmful, you should discuss your feelings with the manager of the store that is selling the product. If he continues to sell the product, you should picket his store.

FIGURE 3.10 Study Guide for a Foreign Language: Spanish Article "Sor Juana Ines de la Cruz: Monja y Feminista"

for teaching students how to generate their own guides and study aids, such as maps, summaries, and other study products that reflect elaborative processing of text and promote long-term retention (see Chapter 9).

Using Discussion Webs to Encourage Critical and Elaborative Thinking

As teachers, we all remember one situation in which we anticipated a lively discussion among our students because we had assigned them an intriguing selection to read. In addition, we entered the classroom armed with a list of thought-provoking questions to help stimulate the discussion. Unfortunately, the discussion fell flat because we did the talking and the students did the listening. Some teachers have given up on discussion because of these memories or of other memories of situations where certain students monopolized the discussion while others daydreamed. Discussion, however, can be a positive and productive experience for students and teachers with appropriate preparation.

Discussion Webs Can Prepare Students for Discussing Content Area Concepts in an Active Manner

One strategy that prepares students for discussion is the **Discussion Web** (Alvermann, 1991). Discussion Webs encourage students to think critically because they are examining alternative points of view and offering evidence to support those views. As illustrated in Figure 3.11, the Discussion Web is literally a visual or graphic representation of the thinking processes the students will go through during their discussion. In the center of the Discussion Web is the central issue or question that the students are to discuss in class. The question should be stated so that there is more than one point of view. The example in Figure 3.11 was created by Raymond, an art teacher who wanted his students to consider the

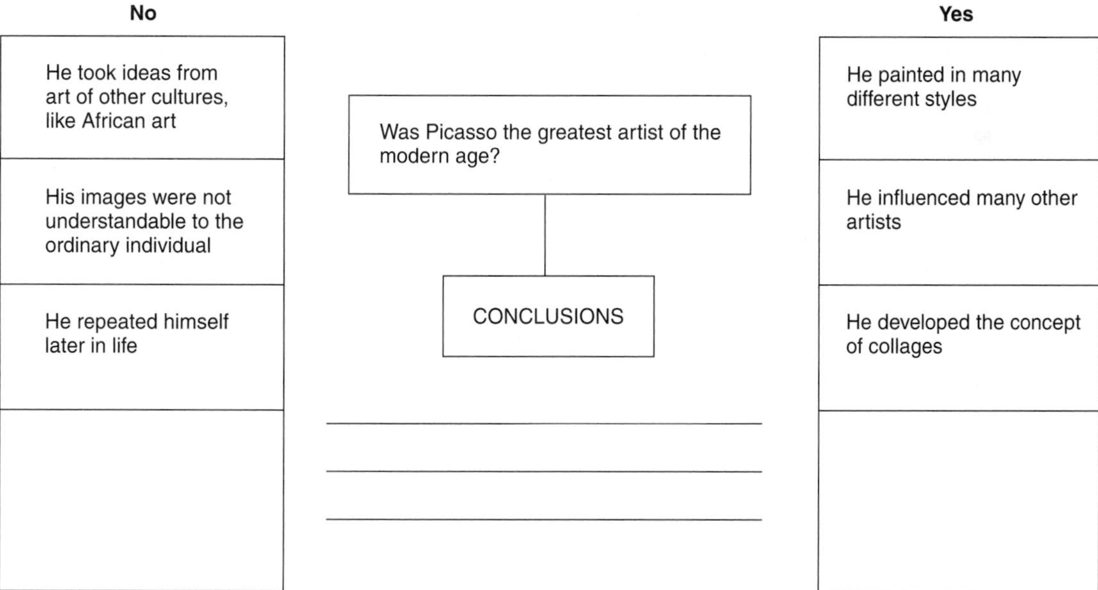

FIGURE 3.11 Discussion Web

central question "Was Picasso the greatest artist of the modern age?" On either side of the Discussion Web are spaces for students to list the reasons why they believe that either "yes" or "no" is the answer to the central question.

When Raymond used the Discussion Web with his art students, he followed these steps recommended by Alvermann (1991):

1. Prepare students for reading or listening by activating their prior knowledge, setting purposes and questions, and asking students to make predictions.
2. Have students read the selection, listen to the lecture, or watch the demonstration or video.
3. Introduce the central question and the Discussion Web. Ask students to work in pairs in discussing both points of view. The partners should take turns jotting down their reasons in the two support columns. Instruct the partners to allow equal time for both sides of the issue.
4. After the partners have jotted down a few of their reasons, combine the partners into groups of four. The four students will compare their Discussion Webs, with the ultimate goal of reaching a consensus. Remind the students to keep an open mind and to listen to the members of their group. If they cannot agree on a point of view, they can offer a minority report as well as a majority report.
5. When the groups have reached a consensus or the students' participation seems to be waning, give them a 3-minute warning. Within those 3 minutes, they are to decide who will report their views to the large group and what the individual will say.
6. Ask each spokesperson to report what his or her group decided and why.
7. After the whole-class discussion has ended, assign students to write their own responses to the central question in the blanks provided under the Conclusion section of the Discussion Web (see Figure 3.11).

Discussion Webs can be used in a variety of ways. Raymond created the Discussion Web in Figure 3.11 as a way of encouraging students to discuss ideas after they had viewed a video on influential artists in the modern art movement. He tells us that he particularly likes the Discussion Web because all the students participate actively in class, even the introverted ones who are afraid to speak up. Raymond believes that most of the students feel more comfortable speaking and sharing their views because they have had time to rehearse what they wanted to say as they worked with their partner and the group of four.

Discussion Webs Can Be Used Before or After Reading or Writing Assignments

Discussion Webs can also be used as a follow-up to a reading assignment. Figure 3.12 shows how a pair of eighth-grade students completed a Discussion Web after reading an assignment on smoking for a health and wellness course. Finally, many teachers report using the Discussion Web to help students brainstorm and prepare for their writing assignments. This use of the Discussion Web has been validated in research studies. For example, Rubin and Dodd (1987) concluded from

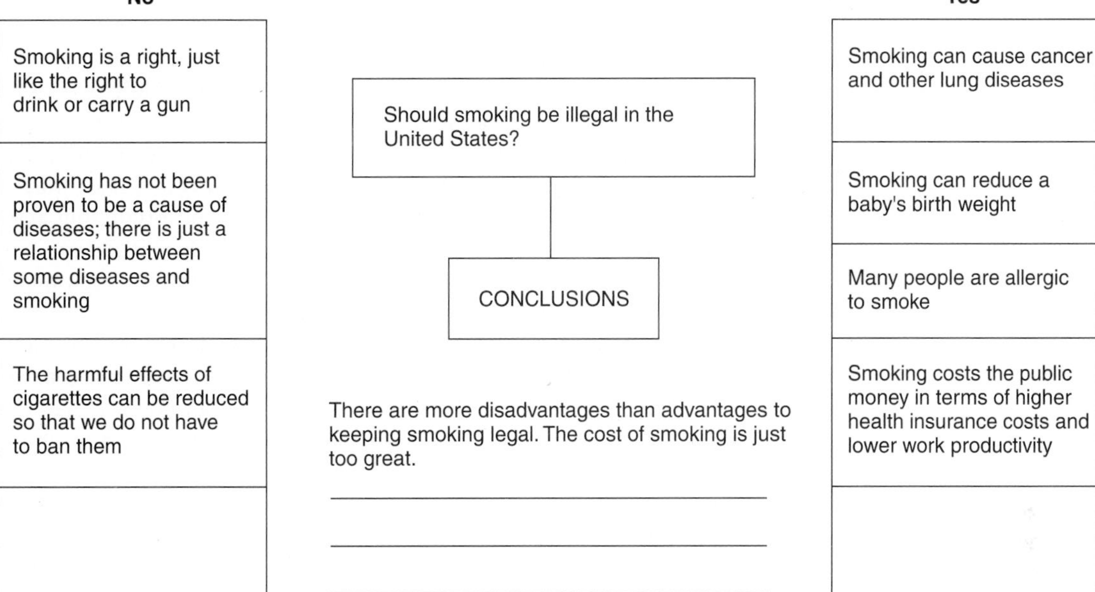

No
Smoking is a right, just like the right to drink or carry a gun
Smoking has not been proven to be a cause of diseases; there is just a relationship between some diseases and smoking
The harmful effects of cigarettes can be reduced so that we do not have to ban them
Should smoking be illegal in the United States?
CONCLUSIONS
There are more disadvantages than advantages to keeping smoking legal. The cost of smoking is just too great.
Yes
Smoking can cause cancer and other lung diseases
Smoking can reduce a baby's birth weight
Many people are allergic to smoke
Smoking costs the public money in terms of higher health insurance costs and lower work productivity

FIGURE 3.12 Discussion Web

their research that oral language activities that require students to debate and switch sides during the debates improve the fluency and coherence of their writing. In sum, Discussion Webs seem to have many advantages for content-area teachers who want less passivity and more critical thinking in their classroom.

ACTIVE LEARNERS ARE METACOGNITIVELY AWARE

We close this chapter by examining strategies that will help students monitor their understanding and gain more knowledge about themselves as learners and the academic tasks they are assigned. Specifically, we examine two strategies to improve students' self-monitoring: reciprocal teaching and fix-up strategies. Then we discuss a planning strategy that both teachers and students can use in setting goals and describing assignments or tasks.

Reciprocal Teaching and Self-Monitoring

To understand a text, you need to split your mental focus. On the one hand, you need to focus on the material itself. At the same time, however, you need to constantly monitor your processing to make sure that you are comprehending and learning (Garner & Alexander, 1989). Unsophisticated readers and learners generally do not monitor their understanding and are unsure about what to do once

Most Adolescents Have Difficulty Monitoring Their Understanding of Content-Area Concepts

they have determined that they are lost or confused (Pressley, 1995; Simpson & Nist, 1997). Fortunately, teachers can help students become more metacognitively aware. One such strategy is reciprocal teaching, an instructional approach that has been found to be extremely successful with at-risk middle school and high school students (Brown & Palincsar, 1982). In classrooms where **reciprocal teaching** takes place, the teacher and student take turns generating questions and summaries and leading a discussion about sections of a text. Initially, the teacher models questioning, summarizing, clarifying, and predicting activities while encouraging students to participate at whatever level they can manage. Gradually, students become more capable of contributing to such discussions and assume more responsibility for their own learning.

Rob teaches a study skills course as one component of exploratory classes for sixth graders. In the class, Rob spends many sessions discussing and modeling what active learners do when they read and think about content area concepts. Here we provide an excerpt of Rob and his students interacting during reciprocal teaching.

Rob began by modeling his active learning processes with a short segment from a science textbook chapter about lightning. He allowed his students to eavesdrop on his thought processes as he attempted to make sense of the chapter.

Students sat at desks arranged in a horseshoe shape, with their copies of the chapter, as Rob commented after reading the first short paragraph:

> What I understand here is that up until very recently we haven't known much about lightning, but now things are changing. I'll probably read something about the technology we're using to figure out how lightning occurs.

During reading he shared comments such as this:

> Right now I'm staring blankly at the page trying to gather my thoughts. I'm not reading anything new. I think I'm just cycling these things around to see if anything seems reasonable.
>
> I'm looking again for key words like *positive* and *negative particles* and *cumulonimbus cloud.* They're going to tip me off as to the big point.

When Rob finished the first major section of the chapter, he attempted to summarize:

> Okay, the first thing is, I went over it and skimmed through the section again, so I can remember where I saw the important things.
>
> It's [the passage] talking about how technology is helping us to better understand lightning so that we can figure out how to protect ourselves from it.

He paused periodically and posed questions to himself ("What's the main idea here?" or "Does that make sense?"). Often after finishing a paragraph, he stated the gist. He made predictions about where the text was going next, and his soliloquy included connecting what he was reading with his store of prior knowledge and personal experiences.

In the next excerpt, Rob and his students were reading and discussing paragraphs from their social studies textbooks. They took turns asking questions about the topic and summarizing. The first paragraph they discussed was about Commander Peary and his quest for the North Pole.

On finishing reading of the short text segment, students immediately responded:

Student 1: I have a question about this. What year did Peary write his diary?

Rob: Not a bad beginning, but I would consider that a question about details. Try to avoid the kind of question you can answer by looking word for word in the paragraph. See if next time you can ask a main idea question, and begin your question with a question word like how, why, when. Go ahead, try that.

Student 2: What if I ask, Why is Peary's diary important?

Rob: A very good question. Notice how your question seems to be getting at the most important idea in the paragraph.

Student 3: And you can't answer it by just looking at the words.

Rob: Right. Very good work! Now, can anyone give me a summary statement for the paragraph?

Student 4: Well, the only way we really know if Peary got to the North Pole is from his diary.

Rob: And why is that?

Student 4: Because there was no one else around who knew for sure where they were.

Student 5: You can't bring back any proof you were there.

Rob: Okay, that explains why some think Peary may not have made it to the Pole first. Isn't that an important part of the summary? (Several students agree.)

Rob: Let me try to make a summary for you. The most important thing we have learned is that we have to take Peary at his word when he said that he reached the North Pole because we don't have any other evidence to support that he did. Does that make sense? Have I left anything important out? Those are important questions to always ask yourself.

Reciprocal Teaching Involves Students in Self-Diagnosing, Summarizing, Predicting, Clarifying, and Questioning

Rob's reciprocal teaching approach seems to be successful because it forces the students to respond, which allows him to evaluate their understanding and provide appropriate feedback. Also, by responding orally, the students are given the opportunity to self-diagnose their understanding and improve their ability to self-question, summarize, clarify, and predict, all processes leading to active learning. Rob does not merely talk to his students about how to read and then tell them to open their texts and read that way. Instead, he demonstrates how he reads and constructs meaning and, through interactions with students, gives them greater responsibility for learning from text.

Middle school and high school students need to learn strategies for monitoring their understanding in all their courses. In addition, they must learn strategies for fixing up the situations in which they are lost or do not understand a concept. In the next section, we outline some fix-up strategies.

Fix-Up Strategies

Metacognitively aware learners know when their understanding breaks down and what techniques to use to reduce their confusion (Wade & Reynolds, 1989). **Fix-up strategies** are the observable or "in the head" techniques that active learners use when they are trying to increase their understanding of a particular content area concept. To illustrate the importance of fix-up strategies, read the following passage and then list all the techniques you used or would use to understand what you had read.

> Recent developments in the self-worth theory of achievement motivation attest to the potential heuristic value of maintaining Atkinson's original quadripolar model. In essence, self-worth theory argues that the need for self-acceptance is the highest human priority and that, in reality, the dynamics of school achievement largely reflect attempts to aggrandize and protect self-perceptions of ability. (Covington & Roberts, 1994, p. 161)

What techniques did you include in your list? Some of the more common fix-up strategies include:

Active Learners Need to Have a Variety of Ways to Fix Up Their Comprehension Breakdowns

1. Rereading the confusing sentence or paragraph
2. Reading more slowly
3. Reading ahead to see if the information becomes clearer
4. Looking back at previous paragraphs, headings, or introductions to see if the author explained the concept in another way
5. Referring to visual aids provided by the author, such as maps, charts, pictures, or graphs
6. Making a picture in your mind of the concept being discussed
7. Drawing or sketching the concept being discussed
8. Looking for text examples that clarify difficult abstractions
9. Checking alternative sources such as other textbooks or references

Most middle school and high school students have limited fix-up strategies, and the ones they do use are usually passive, emphasizing rereading and rote memorization of information (Christen & Searfoss, 1992). Teachers, however, can assist students by modeling and demonstrating effective fix-up strategies appropriate to their content area. If students can see that it is normal to experience comprehension difficulties and that even experts must solve these problems, they are more likely to incorporate the strategies into their behaviors and routines. In addition, teachers can assist students by reiterating in class the diverse ways in which they can improve their comprehension and learning. For example, we know a sixth-grade science teacher who lists fix-up strategies on poster board for all his students to see. And a 10th-grade algebra teacher gives her students a bookmark listing the fix-up strategies she wants them to use when they are attempting to solve word problems.

Building Task Awareness

Task Knowledge Is Essential to Active Learning in a Content Area

Another critical aspect of metacognition involves students in planning their learning by defining the academic tasks they are expected to accomplish. Tasks have two features—a product and a process (Doyle, 1983). The product of a task is what students must do to demonstrate their understanding. In a typical content area class, that product might be an essay exam, a written report, or a project. What students must do to complete the report or project are the processes. For example, to complete a report in a biology class, students may have to identify and locate sources in a library or on a computer database, summarize the information, and then synthesize the ideas into a written paper.

As you would expect, task knowledge is especially important if students are to choose and implement a strategy appropriately (Gibbs, 1990; Simpson & Nist, 1992). Fortunately for students, many content area teachers define academic tasks in a rather explicit fashion. For example, a sophomore English teacher we observed provided her students this task information:

> On Friday you will have an essay exam on the five short stories we have studied thus far. The essay questions will ask you to analyze how the themes of these short stories are alike and different. Your essays will be evaluated on how well you answer the questions and provide specific examples of your points. I will not be grading on spelling and mechanics, but I do expect organization in the form of a thesis statement.

Notice that she shared with students the following task information: (1) what they will be doing—taking an essay test; (2) what thinking processes they would be involved in—analyzing the short stories in order to compare and contrast them; (3) when the test will be given—Friday; and (4) the criteria she will use to evaluate their essay answers—their written answers must be organized, answer the question, and provide specific examples.

The PLAE Strategy Can Help Teachers Clarify Tasks and Organize How They Want to Explain Assignments to Their Students

Some teachers, however, are not so explicit. As a result, students become confused about what they should read and study, and often give up or become extremely frustrated (Simpson & Nist, 1992, 1997). One strategy that can assist students in defining tasks and monitoring their performance is the PLAE strategy (Simpson & Nist, 1984). PLAE is an acronym that stands for *p*replan, *l*ist, *a*ctivate, and *e*valuate. With PLAE, students define the task and establish their goals, select the most appropriate strategies for the task and create a plan of action, activate

Questions to Answer

1. What is the task? A test? Paper? Project? Presentation? ______
2. When is it due? ______
3. What criteria will be used to evaluate the task? ______
4. What kinds of reading, writing, and thinking will I need to do to complete the task? Will the task involve memory-level or higher-level thinking? ______
5. How much does the task count in the total evaluation process? ______
6. What are my other obligations the week that the task is due? ______
7. What is my goal for this task? ______
8. How much time do I need to allot to accomplish this goal? ______
9. How will this goal change my regular schedule? ______
10. When should I begin? ______

FIGURE 3.13 Preplanning to Define Tasks and Establish Goals

their plan, and then evaluate the effectiveness of their plan once they have accomplished the task. We focus on the first step of PLAE, preplanning. In Figure 3.13 you will find the questions that students should pose and then answer during their preplanning. If students do not know the answers to any of the questions, they are encouraged to ask their teacher. Thus, with that information, they can determine which strategies and approaches are most appropriate and create an appropriate plan of action.

Although the preplanning step of PLAE was meant for students to use independently, content area teachers may wish to use these questions as guides in making their own assignments. One teacher we know starts the year using these questions to help her elaborate on the tasks she assigns. In fact, she even hands out the preplanning questions to the students to be answered as she speaks. By the end of the first semester, however, she has transferred the responsibility to the students. On a day she deems appropriate, she announces a test and says, "Any questions?" Admittedly, it took time to cultivate in her students the importance of task knowledge and their responsibility in defining tasks, but the effort was worthwhile because she taught her students a valuable lesson in becoming an active learner.

COMPREHENSION INSTRUCTION ACROSS THE CONTENT AREAS

In Chapters 2 and 3, we deal with an array of information and practical teaching strategies related to comprehension and learning across the content areas. We placed these two chapters near the beginning of the book because we believe they form the foundation for all of the comprehension instruction and learning that is elucidated and demonstrated in the remaining chapters. Ideally, Chapters 2 and 3 will help form the foundation of your lessons and units of instruction.

Many of the same strategies discussed in this chapter appear at other points throughout the book; many new strategies for helping students learn more effectively will also be presented. Nevertheless, all of the strategies are based on the principles of developing active, independent readers and learners.

Comprehension Is at the Core of Content Area Learning

Comprehension should not—and cannot—be taught in isolation from the material from which students are trying to learn. This is especially true in middle school and high school. Consequently, in later chapters, we demonstrate that comprehension is at the heart of reading and learning across the content areas. In Chapter 4, assessment and teaching comprehension are presented as integral instructional activities. You will see in Chapter 5 how schema activation and development guide readiness strategies. In Chapter 6, we show how effective vocabulary instruction develops contextual and conceptual understanding of important textual information and ideas. In Chapter 7, writing is seen as a tool for expanding the comprehension and learning of text material and course content. In Chapter 8, literature is discussed as an alternative and a companion to the textbook for building prior knowledge, generating interest, and expanding comprehension. Chapter 9 demonstrates how students can make comprehension more permanent with student-initiated learning strategies. Adapting comprehension strategies to special students is the focus of Chapter 10. Finally, we demonstrate in Chapter 11 that content area teachers will become more effective if they integrate content with process.

CASE STUDY REVISITED

Charles, the biology teacher introduced at the beginning of this chapter, was searching for ways to engage his students in more meaningful interactions with his course content. Now that you have read this chapter, propose strategies that may help Charles move his students toward more elaborative and meaningful processing of text material related to the topic of genetic engineering.

Charles decided to use a variety of readiness strategies to introduce his students to the new content and gain their interest. He began by exposing them to alternative source material for exploration of the topic. He captured his students' interest by reading aloud daily from a science fiction novel, Hayford Peirce's *Phylum Monsters,* about a genetic engineer called a "life-stylist." The novel helped motivate the class to dig deeper into the content.

Charles also presented examples of exciting experiments done by genetic researchers. For example, he read to students about researchers at the University of California, San Diego, who in 1986 took the gene that makes fireflies glow and inserted it into the DNA of tobacco. The researchers were then able to raise tobacco plants that glowed in the dark.

Charles asked his students to read articles on genetic engineering in news magazines and to generate lists of advantages and disadvantages for this technology. Using the Discussion Web strategy, students met in pairs and groups of four to discuss and prepare what they would say to the whole class on the central question of whether genetic engineering was morally responsible. Finally, Charles helped his students write to the Food and Drug Administration explaining their views on the subject of genetically engineered food.

As a result of these efforts to prepare students for and introduce them to their new learning, Charles saw his students become active learners. They read and participated with enthusiasm, and were motivated to work together in small groups and as a class to explore further the topic of genetic engineering.

■ ■ ■

SUMMARY

Focusing on the principles of active learning, this chapter has described a range of practical strategies to demonstrate all the possible ways in which teachers can enhance student learning in their content areas. The first principle is concerned with students' use of their prior knowledge to interact with text. In relation to this principle, we discussed strategies, such as learning logs and the Content Area DR-TA, for activating and building students' prior knowledge. The second principle focuses on how active learners use text structure to guide their meaning making. We explained the importance of alerting students to the structures of expository and narrative text, and presented a variety of activities and exercises for teaching them how to recognize and manipulate words and structures that connect ideas. The third principle concerns how active learners think critically about text and create their own elaborations. Strategies discussed in relation to this principle included study guides and Discussion Webs. The fourth principle deals with how active learners are metacognitively aware. In connection with this principle, we emphasized the importance of helping students monitor their learning and employ, when necessary, appropriate fix-up strategies to reduce their confusion. We also described how students can be led to think metacognitively through a form of reciprocal or interactive teaching that exploits modeling, active questioning, and discussing. Finally, we pointed out how the principles and strategies discussed in this chapter form the basis for the reading and learning strategies that appear throughout this book.

REFERENCES

Afflerbach, P. (1990). The influence of prior knowledge on expert readers' main idea construction strategies. *Reading Research Quarterly, 26,* 31–46.

Alvermann, D. E. (1991). The discussion web: A graphic aid for learning across the curriculum. *The Reading Teacher, 45,* 92–99.

Alvermann, D., & Hague, S. (1989). Comprehension of counter-intuitive science text: Effects of prior knowledge and text structure. *Journal of Educational Research, 82,* 197–202.

Alvermann, D., & Hynd, C. (1989). Study strategies for correcting misconceptions in physics: An intervention. In S. McCormick & J. Zutell (Eds.), *Cognitive and social perspectives for literacy research and instruction. Thirty-eighth yearbook of the National Reading Conference.* Chicago: National Reading Conference.

Atwell, N. (1987). *In the middle.* Portsmouth, NH: Heinemann.

Brown, A., & Day, J. (1983). Macrorules for summarizing texts: The development of expertise. *Journal of Verbal Learning and Verbal Behavior, 22,* 1-16.

Brown, A., & Palincsar, A. (1982). Inducing strategic learning from texts by means of informed, self-control training. *Topics in Learning and Learning Disabilities, 2,* 1-17.

Brozo, W. G., Stahl, N. A., & Gordon, B. (1985). Training effects of summarizing, item writing, and knowledge of information sources on reading test performance. In J. Niles & R. Lalik (Eds.), *Issues in literacy: A research perspective. Thirty-fourth yearbook of the National Reading Conference.* Rochester, NY: National Reading Conference.

Calkins, L., & Harwayne, S. (1991). *Living between the lines.* Portsmouth, NH: Heinemann.

Christen, W. L., & Searfoss, L. W. (1992). Placing learning and study strategies in the classroom. In E. K. Dishner, T. W. Bean, J. E. Readence, & D. W. Moore (Eds.), *Reading in the content areas: Improving classroom instruction.* Dubuque, IA: Kendall/Hunt.

Covington, M. V., & Roberts, B. W. (1994). Self-worth and college achievement: Motivational and personality correlates. In P. R. Pintrich, D. R. Brown, & C. E. Weinstein (Eds.), *Student motivation, cognition, and learning.* Hillsdale, NJ: Erlbaum.

Dole, J., Duffy, G., Roehler, L., & Pearson, P. D. (1991). Moving from the old to the new: Research on reading comprehension instruction. *Review of Educational Research, 61,* 239-264.

Doyle, W. (1983). Academic work. *Review of Educational Research, 53,* 159-199.

Garner, R. (1988). *Metacognition and reading comprehension.* Norwood, NJ: Ablex.

Garner, R., & Alexander, P. (1989). Metacognition: Answered and unanswered questions. *Educational Psychologist, 24,* 143-158.

Gibbs, G. (1990). *Improving student learning project briefing paper.* Oxford: Oxford Centre for Staff Development, Oxford Polytechnic.

Graff, H. F. (1980). *The free and the brave.* Chicago: Rand McNally.

Greenberg, L. (1992). *AIDS: How it works in the body.* New York: Franklin Watts.

Haggard, M. (1985). An interactive strategies approach to content reading. *Journal of Reading, 29,* 204-210.

Hare, V., Rabinowitz, M., & Schieble, K. (1989). Text effects on main idea comprehension. *Reading Research Quarterly, 24,* 72-88.

Herber, H. (1978). *Teaching reading in the content areas.* Englewood Cliffs, NJ: Prentice-Hall.

Herber, H., & Nelson-Herber, J. (1993). *Teaching in content areas with reading, writing, and reasoning.* Needham Heights, MA: Allyn & Bacon.

Hynd, C., & Alvermann, D. (1989). Overcoming misconceptions in science: An on-line study of prior knowledge activation. *Reading Research and Instruction, 28,* 12-26.

Langer, J. (1981). From theory to practice: A prereading plan. *Journal of Reading, 25,* 152-156.

Marshall, N. (1989). Overcoming problems with incorrect prior knowledge: An instructional study. In S. McCormick & J. Zutell (Eds.), *Cognitive and social perspectives for literacy research and instruction. Thirty-eighth yearbook of the National Reading Conference.* Chicago: National Reading Conference.

Mayer, R. E. (1996). Learning strategies for making sense out of expository text: The SOI model for guiding these cognitive processes in knowledge construction. *Educational Psychology Review, 8,* 357–371.

McNeil, J. (1987). *Reading comprehension: New directions for classroom practices* (2nd ed.). Glenview, IL: Scott, Foresman.

Miller, K. (1988). *Effects of expository passage organizers on sixth graders' reading and writing of text.* Unpublished doctoral dissertation, University of Missouri, Kansas City, MO.

Miller, K., & George, J. (1992). Expository passage organizers: Models for reading and writing. *Journal of Reading, 35,* 372–377.

Palincsar, A. S., & Brown, A. L. (1984). Reciprocal teaching of comprehension-fostering and comprehension-monitoring activities. *Cognition and Instruction, 1,* 117–175.

Pearson, P. D. (1985). Changing the face of reading comprehension instruction. *The Reading Teacher, 38,* 724–738.

Pickle, H., & Abrahamson, R. (1980). *Introduction to business.* Glenview, IL: Scott, Foresman.

Pressley, M. (1995). More about the development of self-regulation: Complex, long-term, and thoroughly social. *Educational Psychologist, 30,* 207–212.

Pressley, M., & Afflerbach, P. (1995). *Verbal protocols of reading: The nature of constructively responsive reading.* Hillsdale, NJ: Erlbaum.

Pressley, M., Yokoi, L., van Meter, P., Van Ellen, S., & Freeburn, G. (1997). Some of the reasons why preparing for exams is so hard: What can be done to make it easier? *Educational Psychology Review, 9,* 1–38.

Raphael, T. E., & Pearson, P. D. (1985). Increasing students' awareness of sources of information for answering questions. *American Educational Research Journal, 22,* 217–235.

Readence, J. E., Bean, T. W., & Baldwin, R. S. (1985). *Content area reading: An integrated approach* (2nd ed.). Dubuque, IA: Kendall/Hunt.

Romano, T. (1987). *Clearing the way.* Portsmouth, NH: Heinemann.

Rubin, D. L., & Dodd, W. M. (1987). *Talking into writing: Exercises for basic writers.* ERIC Clearinghouse on Reading and Communication Skills: National Council of Teachers of English.

Santa, C., & Havens, L. (1991). Learning through writing. In C. Santa & D. Alvermann (Eds.), *Science learning: Processes and applications.* Newark, DE: International Reading Association.

Simpson, M. L., & Nist, S. L. (1984). PLAE: A model for planning successful independent learning. *Journal of Reading, 28,* 218–223.

Simpson, M. L., & Nist, S. L. (1992). A case study of academic literacy tasks and their negotiation in a university history course. In C. Kinzer & D. Leu (Eds.), *Literacy research, theory, and practice: Views from many perspectives. Forty-first yearbook of the National Reading Conference.* Chicago: National Reading Conference.

Simpson, M. L., & Nist, S. L. (1997). Perspectives on learning history: A case study. *Journal of Literacy Research, 29,* 363–395.

Sinatra, R. (1986). *Visual literacy connections to thinking, reading and writing.* Springfield, IL: Charles C. Thomas.

Sinatra, R. (1991). Integrating whole language with the learning of text structure. *Journal of Reading, 34,* 424–433.

Thomas, K. J. (1979). Modified CLOZE: The inTRAlocking guide. *Reading World, 19,* 19–27.

Trends in academic progress. (1991). Princeton, NJ: Educational Testing Service.

Wade, S. E., & Reynolds, R. E. (1989). Developing metacognitive awareness. *Journal of Reading, 33,* 6–14.

Wixson, K. (1983). Questions about a text: What you ask about is what children learn. *Reading Teachers, 37,* 287–293.

CHAPTER 4

Classroom Assessment of Literacy Growth and Content Learning

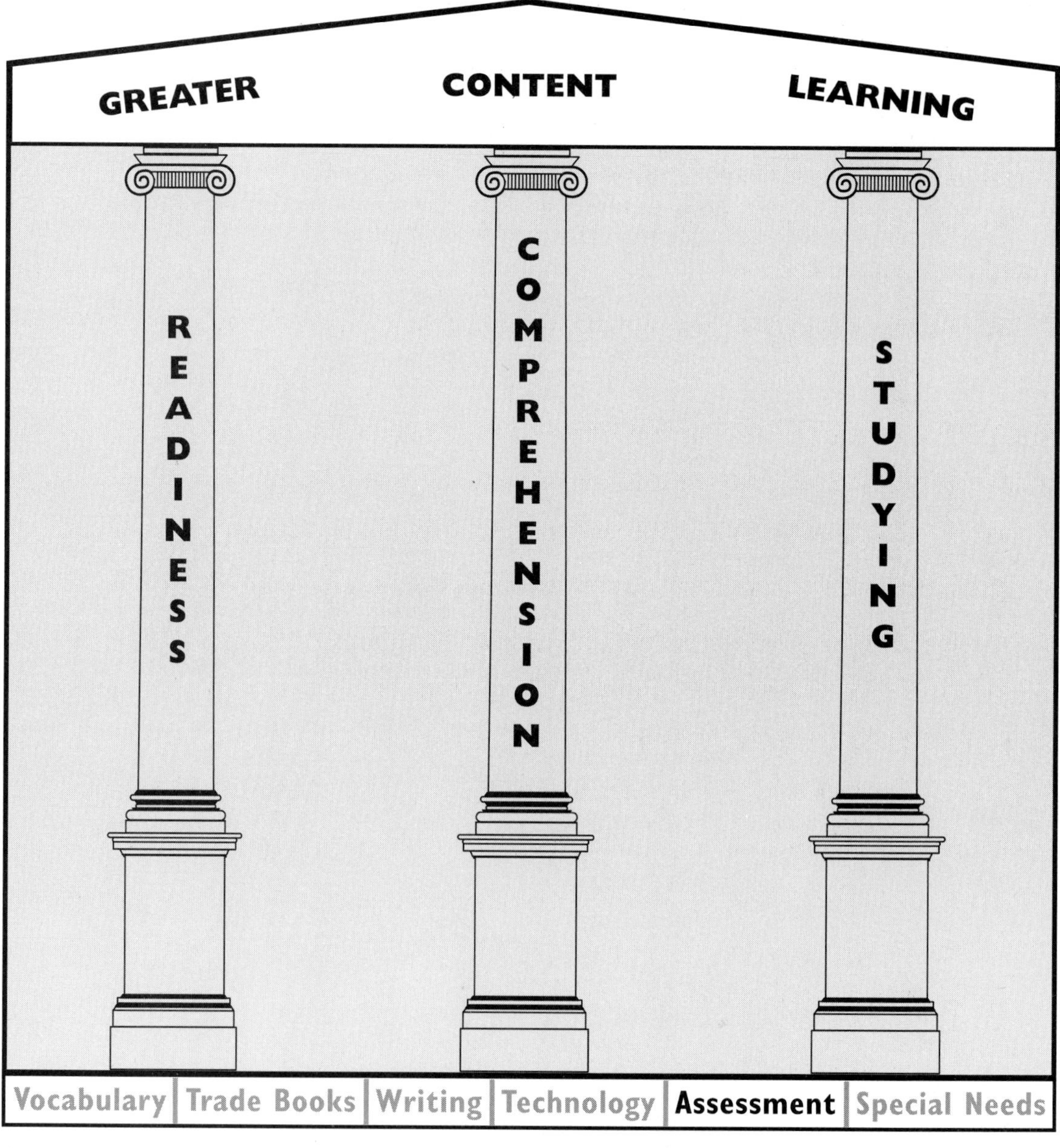

ANTICIPATION GUIDE

Directions: Read each statement carefully and decide whether you agree or disagree with it, placing a check mark in the appropriate *Before Reading* column. When you have finished reading and studying the chapter, return to the guide and decide whether your anticipations need to be changed by placing a check mark in the appropriate *After Reading* column.

	BEFORE READING		**AFTER READING**	
	Agree	*Disagree*	*Agree*	*Disagree*
1. Standardized tests have more disadvantages than advantages.	____	____	____	____
2. Assessment is an activity that occurs primarily at the beginning of the school year.	____	____	____	____
3. Reading specialists should be the ones to assess students' literacy strengths and needs.	____	____	____	____
4. Assessment should focus only on students' reading and writing weaknesses.	____	____	____	____
5. Students should be involved in assessment activities.	____	____	____	____
6. Assessment can inform teaching and learning.	____	____	____	____

There are two primary functions of assessment: optimal learning for all, and a just society. Achieving the former (centrally dependent on teachers as assessors) would accomplish most of the latter. To make serious progress toward this goal, we need a contextualized theory of assessment that is grounded as firmly in moral and social theory as it is in theories of language, literacy, learning, and caring.

—Johnston (1993)

After nearly 20 years of theory development and research that characterizes literacy as an interactive, context bound, purposeful process of meaning construction (Bissex, 1980; Clay, 1975; Pinnell, 1989), we have progressed in our understanding of what literacy behaviors should be assessed, how that assessment should be represented, and what participants or stakeholders should be involved. At the middle and high school levels, these changes have translated into an emphasis on teachers defining what it means to be literate in their classroom and designing a variety of performance-based activities and authentic opportunities to assess their students as they interact with content area concepts. More important, the recent advances in assessment theory and research point out what teachers have always known—that the primary function of assessment is "optimal learning for all" (Johnston, 1993).

In this chapter, issues and strategies of assessment are presented relative to one basic assumption: The goal of literacy assessment is to provide teachers with knowledge about how best to improve and support learning for students and self-knowledge for learners that will allow them to become more reflective, active, and purposeful learners. Because most of you do not administer standardized tests, we have focused on assessment strategies that are most relevant to you in your content classroom. We demonstrate how your assessments can reveal to you and your students important information about students' thinking and language processes, as well as their content knowledge. Because assessment guides and informs instruction and can be integrated into the daily flow of instructional events in the classroom, this chapter provides a foundation for assessment strategies that appear in later chapters. It also builds on the comprehension strategies discussed in Chapters 2 and 3 by demonstrating how assessments can be used to reveal useful information about students' literacy and learning processes.

We are also mindful, however, of two assessment issues that teachers must address on a daily basis. The first issue concerns the proliferation of standardized tests and basic skills competency exams, which more and more states and school districts are mandating (Johnston, 1993; Pearson, 1997). In fact, the Department of Education spends more on the National Assessment of Educational Progress (NAEP, briefly described in Chapter 1) than on any other initiative (Elbow, 1991). The second issue concerns the factors involved in grading and ways in which grades can be better utilized for the improvement of instruction. To help prepare you to deal with these issues, we provide a brief primer on standardized reading tests and examine ways in which the grading process can communicate more to students and parents.

CASE STUDY

Terri is a seventh-grade general science teacher interested in discovering more about her students' ability to comprehend textbook information. After attending in-service workshops on content area assessment procedures, she began to recognize the need for alternative assessments to the chapter check tests in her science textbook. After 5 years of teaching, she discovered that she was relying more and more on these tests for grading purposes and less and less on other "views" of her students as learners and knowledge seekers. Moreover, the results of these tests were not providing Terri with information about why students performed the way they did. She had no way of discovering whether success or failure was tied in any way to students' study processes or to their ability to understand the science text.

The in-service presenter emphasized the need to tie content material to the processes for learning it effectively. Suggestions were made concerning ways teachers could teach and assess at the same time using the class textbook. Terri decided to use this information to develop teaching strategies for improving students' thinking about text structure.

To the Reader:

Think about Terri's concern as you read this chapter, and be prepared by the end of this chapter to suggest possible assessment/teaching solutions for her.

■ ■ ■

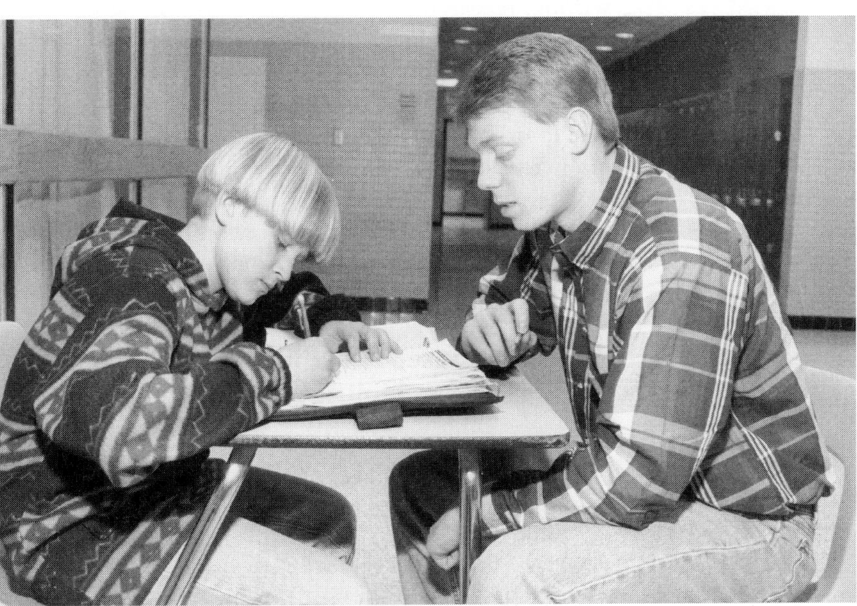

GUIDELINES FOR LITERACY ASSESSMENT

The following five guidelines are based on a synthesis of current research and theory about assessment. These guidelines should determine how you will assess the students in your content area and use that information to plan instructional units.

Assessment Is a Process of Becoming Informed About Authentic Learning

Authentic learning refers to learning that is functional and meaningful. As we stated in Chapter 1, the extent to which students use learning beyond the boundaries of the classroom is directly related to its perceived functionality. For authentic learning to occur, assessments should be rooted in activities that have genuine purposes (Edelsky & Harman, 1988). In this way, acquiring information about student learning does not become an end in itself but is an evolving process of gathering feedback for the teacher and student so that instruction can become more engaging, more tied to real-world issues and concerns, and more personally meaningful.

So, what do we want to know about students that requires us to assess them? We want to know under what conditions they learn best, what instructional strategies we can employ to facilitate their learning, and how to encourage independent, active reading. We also want students to discover more about themselves as learners so that they can expand their abilities as literate knowledge seekers.

Assessment Should Improve Our Instruction and Students' Learning

Middle school and high school teachers want to know whether or not their students are likely to profit from textbook reading, daily instruction, process writing, research projects, and so on. The assessment tools we use for these purposes should therefore be designed to provide insights into students' reading, writing, and thinking strategies with the actual texts they must use daily and in the actual, authentic contexts of their use. In this way, the information gained from assessment can be immediately translated into action, such as promoting elaborative processing (Chapter 3); activating and building relevant prior knowledge (Chapter 5); teaching key concepts and vocabulary (Chapter 6); facilitating thinking and reflection through writing (Chapter 7); developing text study skills (Chapter 9); or improving other important reading, writing, and learning processes.

Assessment of Literacy and Content Learning Should Use Multiple Data Sources Across Multiple Contexts

A basketball coach who wants to find out how well new recruits can play the game does not give a paper-and-pencil test. The players are required to perform on the court, and their ability is assessed while being directly observed. By making multiple assessments of **situated performances** (Valencia, McGinley, & Pearson, 1990), a coach can learn the most about a player's true ability and potential. So it is with the assessment of literacy in content area classrooms.

A sixth-grade health education teacher may feel that she has all the information needed about a student's reading ability when given the test results of the Comprehensive Test of Basic Skills (CTBS). But what do percentiles and grade equivalents have to do with reading and learning from a health education textbook? Perhaps very little, and for obvious reasons. First, the comprehension passages on a test like the CTBS may not cover health issues such as nutrition or exercise. Second, the kind of reading demanded by reading comprehension tests is significantly different from the way a student would read and study a health education textbook. For example, on the test, a student reads one or two paragraphs under strict time limitations. In contrast, the reading assignment in the health education class may require the student to spend an entire week reading and discussing a 20- to 30-page chapter, allowing enough time to learn the material. Finally, the CTBS measures reading performance with multiple-choice questions. The health education teacher may require students to write out answers to short and long essay-type questions.

Rather than relying on one source of information about students, teachers need information from multiple sources in order to plan appropriate instruction. For example, a science teacher could test her students' ability to process and understand the textbook information, and could observe the students' problem-solving abilities and use of experimentation through field notes and logs. The advantage of determining students' progress and understanding with the actual materials used in the science class is that the teacher would then have a much clearer idea about how to modify her instruction to improve students' learning.

This example reinforces an important point we made in Chapter 1: Literacy ability is context bound. No single test (whether the CTBS or any other paper-and-pencil test) can adequately reflect the teaching/learning process. As a former student of ours said, the old "clump theory" of literacy no longer makes sense. Traditional views of literacy held that all of us possess a given, measurable quantity, or "clump," of literacy ability and that reading tests could accurately weigh our clumps. As our conceptions of what it means to be literate have changed to include the dynamic, generative, and idiosyncratic nature of literacy, the most commonly used formal measures of reading and writing have remained largely decontextualized (Collins, Brown, & Newman, 1989; Glazer, Searfoss, & Gentile, 1988). To assess in ways consistent with our best thinking about literacy, our assessment repertoire must be expanded to include multiple demonstrations of ability in situated contexts of authentic teaching and learning.

What It Means to Be Literate Is Very Context Bound

Assessment Is a Continuous Process

A high school teacher of learning-disabled (LD) students recently complained that she is often excluded from the decision-making process concerning student needs and placement. She said that decisions are made about students based on clinical testing in language competencies, intelligence, and behavior, with virtually no input from the teacher who is working closely with and observing the students every day. One of her students, she said, is entirely capable of regular education course work, according to her observations, because he is an excellent reader and possesses some good study skills. When she talked with the clinician, she was shown the student's reading test scores on the Woodcock Reading Mastery Tests (WRMT), which placed him nearly 3 years below his grade placement of 10th grade. It is unlikely, she was told, that he had improved as much as she claimed in the 1 month since he was tested. The question comes down to this: Whose assessment—the clinician's WRMT or the teacher's observations—is more reflective of the student's true ability?

Considering our point about the important influence of context on learning performance, isn't it possible that the context itself—that is, the conditions under which literacy activities and tasks are assessed—has influenced the 10th-grade LD student's reading test performance? The answer is an unequivocal "yes." Carey, Harste, and Smith (1981) discovered that students will often demonstrate much better recall and supply richer information when retelling a story or text to a friend or fellow student than to a teacher, researcher, or test giver. We also have known for some time that when a student is excessively anxious about a task because the perceived consequences of failure are threatening, there is generally a concomitant decrease in performance. The LD teacher's student could have been very threatened by the clinical setting while taking the WRMT, resulting in an artificially low estimate of his reading ability. On the other hand, the student may have perceived the LD teacher in a nonthreatening way and the classroom as a supportive environment. In this context, the student may have demonstrated his true ability. To reiterate, we believe that any test is only a small sample of behavior, and when a single test or observation occurs in isolation (i.e., by a clinician with one test at one point in time), there is insufficient grounds for drawing meaningful diagnostic conclusions.

Besides the influence of context on reading performance, there are other reasons why reading assessment should be a continuous process. Any test result or observed score is partly a reflection of the test taker's true ability, or true score, and a host of other factors we did not plan to measure, referred to as the *error score.* Contextual factors, as in the preceding case with the LD student, contribute to the error score, and there are many others. The reader's health, attitude, tendency to guess, prior knowledge, the test's ability to communicate, and the quality of the test questions, to name a few, are all factors that influence to some degree a test taker's score. Unfortunately, we can never be absolutely certain how much of the observed score is composed of an error score. This critical issue should be considered before we base major decisions on one test or observation—especially if that test or observation is isolated from the conditions under which actual reading tasks are performed—because the observed score may not measure a student's true ability.

All of what we have just said can be applied to classroom teachers who rely exclusively on end-of-chapter, -unit, or -year tests to make decisions about grading and student progress. Learning is a continuous and dynamic process that takes place over time and changes with each new instructional situation. Therefore, to obtain more useful and meaningful information on your students' literacy and learning abilities, we recommend that you base instructional decisions on long-term observations and assessments. Later in this chapter, we provide guidelines and details for assessment formats that use day-to-day information gained from observing students and gathering reflections of their progress over time. Only with such important assessment data can we expect to build a supportive classroom learning environment.

Assessment Should Include Students' Interests and Belief Systems

Carmen begins every new school year with an activity designed to help her eighth graders get to know one another. Using a strategy called "My Bag," Carmen and her students bring in bags filled with objects and items that represent who they are. Students form groups of three or four and share these items. Carmen asks students not to do a "show and tell" but to use an item to elicit questions. For example, Juanita took an onyx ring out of her bag and passed it around for her group members to inspect. Soon students were asking her questions such as "Where'd you get it?", "Was it your mom's?" and "What kind of stone is that?" Juanita revealed that the ring belonged to her *tia,* her aunt, with whom she had a very close and friendly relationship, and said that the ring was given to her just before her aunt died. In another case, Carlos showed his group a model car and a screwdriver. Before long, he was responding to questions that allowed him to go into great detail about his interest in fixing cars with his older brother and his plan to be an auto mechanic.

While students go through the My Bag activity, Carmen circulates throughout the room, taking note of students' interests, desires, needs, and concerns, such as Juanita's relationship with her aunt and Carlos's interest in auto repair. Armed with this knowledge, Carmen tailors certain writing, reading, and group projects to her students' needs and desires. She alludes to particular characteristics of students revealed through the My Bag exercise during class activities, which helps demonstrate her interest in and concern for her students and builds a caring atmosphere in the classroom. In the end, Carmen, too, shares her bag, allowing students to get to know their teacher as a real person who has goals, desires, and interests, just as they do. Carmen has found that in being part of the My Bag activity herself, she can establish an initial foundation on which trust and cooperative problem solving can be built.

There Are Many Creative Ways to Learn about Students' Interests and Beliefs

Through the use of the My Bag strategy, Carmen gathers invaluable assessment information about her students' interests and beliefs in a highly personal, unique, and enjoyable way. While gathering information about how students process text, we should be equally concerned with discovering their habits, interests, and attitudes to reinforce and reward students' use of reading and writing for self-development and learning, and for joy and escape. The benefits that result from putting students in touch with books that match their interests cannot be denied.

An acquaintance described how he had been diagnosed as a remedial reader every year from second to seventh grade. Teachers were beginning to lose hope of ever teaching Tom how to read beyond a rudimentary level. His difficulty affected his achievement in all subjects. Then a particularly enlightened math teacher discovered that Tom's favorite activity was performing magic tricks. The teacher brought Tom some books on magic from the library. He read them. He began reading more and more books on magic. Soon his ability to read and understand other books improved. Eventually Tom graduated from high school with a good grade average and finally took a baccalaureate degree from the University of Illinois—a prominent and respected institution. The lesson here is obvious: By discovering students' interests and introducing them to books that match their interests, we stand a chance of developing enthusiastic and competent readers.

Obtaining information about students' real-world needs and interests—in other words, what they do and what concerns them when they are outside of school—can be as useful in planning ways to teach and reach your students as information about their reading/writing processes and content knowledge. Interest is one of the most potent motivators for young adults, and teachers can take full advantage of this fact in a number of ways (Alexander, Kulikowich, & Schulze, 1994; Hidi, 1990). One obvious strategy is to introduce students to reading materials related to their interests. These materials may be tied to the topic of study in your classroom or may simply be relevant to students on a personal level. In Chapter 8 we explain how teachers can take full advantage of trade literature to help meet students' needs.

In addition to assessing students' interests, teachers need to identify their beliefs systems about learning and how they view themselves as learners (Schommer, 1994). Students with naive conceptions about learning and how knowledge is acquired tend to believe that learning is something that is simple and happens quickly, with very little effort (Schommer, 1994). As a result, they are less likely to use strategies that engage them in elaborative levels of thinking, choosing instead to use rote-level strategies emphasizing the memorization of facts. For example, because many students believe that knowledge about science is simply the memorization of isolated facts, they tend to focus on those facts without thinking about the interrelationships between them and the concepts they represent. This type of learning is obviously something that students can do in a rather superficial fashion rather than invest any mental effort.

Students Who Believe Learning to Be Quick and Easy Will Not Choose to Be Active Learners

These implicit beliefs about learning have a subtle impact on how students comprehend what they read, problem solve, and persist when assigned difficult tasks by their teachers. In addition, Schommer (1994) has found an association between students' grades and their naive conceptions of learning. In her study of 1,000 high school students, a regression analysis that controlled for general intelligence indicated that the more students believed in quick learning, the more likely they were to have a low overall grade point average. Later in this chapter, we will present some assessment activities that will help you identify students' interests and beliefs about reading and learning and discuss how you can use that information to inform your teaching.

Effective Assessment Involves Students in Self-Reflection and Self-Evaluation

Students Must Learn to Set Goals and Evaluate Their Progress

Traditionally, assessment has been interpreted as a professional activity that teachers "do to students" rather than an ongoing activity that involves both students and teachers in the improvement of instruction. Currently, literacy educators recommend that students be involved in assessing their own strengths and needs since that self-reflection and evaluation are important to students' development as independent learners (Zimmerman, Bandura, & Martinez-Pons, 1992). For example, several studies have shown that at-risk students can improve their academic achievement and intrinsic motivation if they are taught how to set goals and evaluate their progress toward those goals (Schunk, 1983; Zimmerman et al., 1992).

There are a variety of ways you can involve students in self-evaluation and self-reflection, one of which is journal writing. These journal entries can be assigned at the beginning of the school year or can be required of students as part of an instructional unit, especially after they have received feedback on how they performed on an exam. For example, Ann, a seventh-grade math teacher, asks all her students to complete a mathematics autobiography as their first entry in their journal. She uses the following directions, which can be modified to fit almost any content area:

> Write your math autobiography. Think and write about the experiences you have had that relate to mathematics. These questions may be used as guides.
>
> 1. How did you feel about math in elementary school?
> 2. What are your experiences with effective and ineffective math teachers?
> 3. Is there one particular experience that stands out?
> 4. What were or are the attitudes of your family members toward math?
> 5. Was there a time when you liked math? Hated it? Why did you feel the way you did?
> 6. Did you have any special strategies for getting through (or around) math classes? Have these strategies worked for you? Why or why not?
> 7. Is there one particular experience you feel is responsible for your present feelings about math?

Learner Autobiographies Can Assess Students' Beliefs and Attitudes

Ann tells us that she quickly learns a great deal of useful information about her students' attitudes, anxieties, and mathematical strategies from this initial journal entry. She then uses classroom observations of her students, as well as their homework and test performance, to validate these self-reports. One of her students, Zena, is the author of the following entry. You will note that this journal entry provided Ann with some useful insights about Zena as she evaluated herself.

> When I was in elementary school I had a little trouble with adding and subtracting. I now have difficulties with my multiplication tables. Story prob-

lems really bother me so my mother tries to help me with these. I still am nervous about math, especially if the test is timed. In stores I always make sure they give me the correct change, but I have trouble figuring out the prices on clothes when they have sales.

If I have good teachers I do great, but when I have poor teachers I do bad. I had a teacher who didn't like me and tried her hardest to make me fail her class. My parents told me to just do the best I can and not to worry about how the teacher feels about me. My father and brothers are all good in math, so I am the only math dummy in our house.

I like math when I understand it, but if I don't understand it, I don't like it. I usually am afraid to ask questions when I am lost—so please be patient with me.

These five guidelines should assist you in determining the assessment procedures appropriate for your content area and your students. Before we describe additional assessment procedures that you can incorporate into your classroom routine, we need to address two controversial issues—standardized tests and grading.

STANDARDIZED READING ACHIEVEMENT TESTS: WHAT YOU SHOULD KNOW

Question

Audrey strained to see the people who were coming through the crowd. Somewhere down there her parents were waiting to welcome her after her voyage.

A. Audrey is standing in a crowd, waiting to meet a plane.
B. Audrey is in a crowd, walking toward her parents.
C. Audrey is on a ship, looking out at a crowd waiting for the ship.
D. Audrey is looking at a ship on which her parents are arriving.
(*Reading Yardsticks,* Form B, 1981, p. 11)

Does the preceding question format look familiar? It should. All of us have taken some form of a reading test that contained short passages and multiple-choice comprehension questions that were very similar to this example. We ascribe almost magical qualities to standardized reading tests. They are "objective measurements," simple to administer and score, with comprehensive tables and charts for deriving a variety of scores. And with more than 100 reading tests on the market, they are accessible and widely discussed in the media. In this section we will discuss the characteristics of standardized tests, outline their uses and potential limitations, and offer some suggestions on how you can communicate with parents and the public about the standardized tests your school administers to students.

Although reading tests have been around since the beginning of this century, only since the 1930s has the question format become the most popular method of assessing comprehension and the basis for current standardized tests of reading achievement (Readence & Moore, 1983). Educators over the past 50 years have regarded the question-answering format as the most convenient, objective, and cost-effective means of comprehension assessment. Why is so much attention given to reading assessment? Most educators and a majority of the public agree that raising students' literacy level is an extremely important goal of public schooling (Goodman, 1992). Since the accountability movement of the 1970s, and given the current glut of national reports, a prominent area of attention for educational improvement initiatives has been literacy (Liston & Zeichner, 1991). To measure the effectiveness of these initiatives, educators have come to rely on students' standardized test scores.

Standardized Tests Have Been Given to a Norm Group That Should Be Similar to the Students in Your Classes

What is a standardized reading achievement test? The term **standardized** means that the test was administered and scored under standard and uniform testing procedures. It is typically constructed by test specialists working with curriculum experts and teachers. Before the test is made available to schools and teachers, it is given to a large number of students, who represent the group for whom the test was intended. This representative group of students is called the **norm group.** The norm group's scores on the test are transformed statistically into **standard scores,** which are usually made available in tabular form in the test's users manual. These standard scores allow teachers and schools to compare their students with a national group of students. The most common standard scores used by schools to interpret student performance on reading achievement tests are grade equivalents and percentiles. A **grade-equivalent** interpretation of a student's reading achievement test score is indicated in terms of years and months—for instance, 10.6, or 10th grade, 6th month. When interpreting reading test performance in terms of a **percentile,** we describe a student's score as a point at or below which a given percentage of other scores falls. For example, a student who scored at the 80th percentile scored as well as or better than 80% of the students in the norm group.

The Uses and Potential Limitations of Standardized Tests

Many of the criticisms of standardized tests focus on how the test scores will be used. Teachers and parents, for example, worry that students will be placed in classes on the basis of one standardized test. What needs to be remembered, however, is that standardized tests, like any other assessment instrument, are only one data source or sample of students' behaviors, skills, and strategies. As the assessment guidelines have suggested, any instructional decision about a student is best made using a variety of sources of information.

Standardized Tests Have Some Uses

If standardized tests should be considered as only one source of information about students, why are these tests given? What are their uses? Why do school districts, school boards, and the public clamor for some form of standardized tests? Standardized tests do have their uses. At the district level, they can be used by principals and superintendents to evaluate a special program or intervention to determine its effectiveness. In addition, the data from a standardized test can often inform administrators and teachers about large-scale trends at the district level. These trends can reflect the skills that are being taught effectively and those that need more emphasis. For example, in Maria's school district, the middle school teachers and administrators examined the results of the Iowa Basic Skills Exam for the sixth graders' strengths and weaknesses. As a result of their analysis, they identified vocabulary as a goal for the next school year because the sixth graders scored much too low on this subtest.

Standardized test results can be used by the classroom teacher, but many middle school and high school teachers do not see their students' test results. If, however, you do have access to the results of a standardized test, you may wish to examine them. Some teachers use these scores as a large-scale screening device to determine possible groupings or skills that need emphasis for the class and for individual students. For example, when Maria examined the test scores for Joseph, an incoming sixth grader, she saw these scores:

Vocabulary	5.1	grade equivalent
Comprehension	2.8	grade equivalent

Joseph's scores suggest that he needs work on reading comprehension but that his vocabulary background is not a contributing factor to his low score on comprehension. Maria hypothesized that Joseph may need help with active reading for main ideas to improve his comprehension. Of course, Maria used that information as a preliminary hunch. She verified that hunch with her own assessment activities to learn more about the strengths and skill needs of Joseph and the other students in her sixth-grade language arts classes.

Standardized Tests Have Some Limitations, as Do All Tests

Maria will use her own assessment activities because she is aware of the limitations of standardized tests:

1. They are only an estimate of a student's reading ability.
2. Each test measures reading in a different way, which means that a student might have five different scores on five different tests.
3. They do not provide information about how students read and learn in their content area classes.
4. They may contain some linguistic or cultural bias that can influence the test scores for students from different cultures or students whose primary language or dialect is not English.

These limitations, of course, can apply to any teacher-designed assessment instrument or activity. Hence, sensitivity to the uses and limitations of standardized tests should help you in planning your own assessment activities.

Communicating with Parents and Students About Standardized Reading Test Results

School districts have an obligation to inform students and parents of reading achievement test results. It is their right to know. While some testing experts have argued that the distribution of assessment results should be limited to those who are prepared to use them, classroom teachers in science, math, history, and language arts may be given printouts of their homeroom students' reading test scores. Furthermore, it is not uncommon for the classroom teacher to be asked by students and parents to explain test scores. These facts point to the need for all teachers to become informed about what these scores mean and how they can be used. Following are several suggestions for reporting and explaining standardized reading test results to students and/or parents. These suggestions come from our own experience as middle school and high school teachers, as well as the experience of others.

Teachers Should Help Parents Understand the Strengths and Potential Limitations of Standardized Tests

1. Put parents at ease. Welcome them and make sure that they are comfortable. If possible, work where there is good lighting and privacy.
2. Before presenting information to parents, find out what information they have already received from other teachers, counselors, or administrators. Failure to do so may put you in the uncomfortable position of contradicting a colleague, having to change your position, or reporting redundant information.
3. Before presenting information, determine exactly what kind of information the parent wants.
4. If assessment information is inadequate or contradictory, be willing to admit the weaknesses of evaluation based on these data.
5. Urge parents not to fixate on standard scores but instead pay close attention to a variety of data sources, such as the student's previous work and the teacher's evaluations.
6. If necessary, explain the limitations of grade equivalents. They are too easily misinterpreted to be given to parents indiscriminately. These norms are often **extrapolated;** that is, they are often estimates based on trends in scores established by the norm group. In other words, if a 10th grader obtains a grade equivalent of 5.5 (5th grade, 5th month) on a reading achievement test appropriate for 10th graders, it is unlikely that students at the 5.5 grade level were actually in the norming group for the 10th-grade test. Therefore, this grade equivalent is merely an estimate based on the hypothetical performance of students at the 5.5 grade level if they had taken the 10th-grade test. As you can tell from this explanation, grade equivalents are very difficult to explain and interpret properly. Another limitation of grade equivalents is that the amount of error may be anywhere from half a year to a full year and a half. So a score of 10.0 could be as low as 8.5 or as high as 11.5—we simply do not know for sure.

Grade Equivalents Are Commonly Misunderstood by the Media and by Parents

7. When explaining percentile scores, make it clear that they are not to be confused with percentages of questions answered correctly. It might be best to say, "In comparison with 10th graders throughout the United States, John is in the upper 10% to 15%, as measured by the Iowa Silent Reading Test when this test was taken last October."

There is no need for classroom teachers to become test and measurement experts simply because occasionally they may be asked to administer and interpret the scores of standardized reading tests. By combining some basic knowledge about these tests with common sense, you can improve your chances of communicating effectively with students and parents.

TEACHERS' GRADES: A FORM OF ASSESSMENT AND EVALUATION

Grading Is a Small Part of Assessment

Grades are another important assessment issue that teachers must address. Although we all would like to avoid those regular and predictable moments when we are expected to assign a grade to a sample of our students' work, the process of grading probably will always be with us. Mindful of this, we offer some thoughts and guidelines based on what we as teachers have done and what teachers have told us they do when they grade. Most important, the uneasiness and ambiguities connected with grading can be lessened if we place grading in the proper context. That is, grading is only a minor part of student assessment (McKeachie, 1994). The major part of assessment and evaluation is the qualitative information we communicate to students and parents on a regular basis. We will, however, examine both aspects of assessment—the quantitative grade we compute and the qualitative information we share.

Admittedly, a music teacher cannot tell a biology teacher how to assign a grade, but there seem to be some basic guidelines that make the quantitative aspects of assessment and evaluation easier. As we talked to teachers, the following guidelines seemed prevalent:

These Seven Guidelines Help Grading to Be Placed in the Proper Perspective

1. *Make explicit how you will determine a course grade.* Teachers need to make explicit what factors are considered in determining students' course grades. That is, will the course grade be based solely on a student's performance or achievement on tests? Will a student's effort count? How much will homework count? What role will a student's participation in class discussion or a cooperative project play in computing a grade? We cannot answer these questions for you, but you should consider them all carefully and then make sure that students and parents understand at the beginning of the school year the factors that you include when you assign a grade.

2. *Make explicit how you will evaluate an assignment.* Although grading is subjective, it can become more objective if you tell students in advance what you expect from them in their work or assignments. The more information you give them on how you will evaluate a lab report on an experiment or a summary of an article, the more comfortable students will be about the grade they receive. Specifically, students need to know in advance the value of the assignment and what a quality product or performance looks like. If, for example, the assignment is to write a summary of a newspaper article, the students could be told the following:

> The summary you will write is worth 20 points. Your summary should be at least six sentences in length, and should include the author's thesis and

an explanation of how the thesis was developed. A summary with these characteristics will receive the full 20 points.

Some teachers like to use a checklist which specifies the evaluation criteria. The checklist in Figure 4.1 is an example used by a vocal music teacher who asked her students to find a current article in a magazine or newspaper that critiqued some type of musical performance. Notice that she informed the students on how the total points for the assignment would be awarded. She tells us that her students also use the checklist as a way of checking and monitoring their own work before they hand it in to her.

3. *Award credit when students try out new strategies or approaches.* Students will not be risk takers if they realize there is an inherent penalty for trying out new strategies or approaches. Hence, it is important to acknowledge these risks and to award proper credit. If, for example, a student tries to develop a map for a chapter rather than outline it, as he usually does, provide the student with substantive feedback on his first attempts at mapping. If the map is not adequate because it overlooks some key points or interrelationships, still award as much credit as possible or allow the student to revise and modify the strategy before a grade is assigned.

4. *Include grading opportunities for both the process and the product.* Although college professors assign grades only for tests, quizzes, and the papers students write, middle school and high school teachers have the opportunity to include in their grading procedures more than just a final product. Sometimes more important than a product is the process of learning because it acknowledges students' attempts to construct meaning in a particular content area.

Directions: Use this checklist to evaluate your assignment before you hand it in to me. The criteria listed below should help you locate strengths and weaknesses in your work. I will also be using the checklist to evaluate your assignment.

______ 1. The references were listed on the index card correctly and completely. (WORTH 6 POINTS)

______ 2. The two articles were appropriate to the assignment. (WORTH 4 POINTS)

______ 3. There was a complete and accurate summary of the key ideas of the two articles you read. (WORTH 10 POINTS)

TOTAL POINTS:

COMMENTS:

FIGURE 4.1 Checklist for Library Project

Those attempts to construct meaning might include strategies to improve recall and understanding, journal entries about difficult concepts, classroom discussions about controversial ideas, or essay revisions. Portfolio assessment is another way in which the process is valued as much as the product.

Teachers also gave us several guidelines on how to communicate qualitative information to students about their performance in a particular content area. The following three guidelines seem particularly pertinent:

Students Need Timely, Qualitative Feedback on Their Performance

5. *Provide students with a variety of qualitative feedback.* The qualitative information connected with assessment and evaluation can occur in many forms. Most common are the comments teachers write on papers, the responses they offer to students' statements or queries, or the checklists they develop to describe the qualities of an activity or strategy that students have completed. The key, however, is to provide students with a variety of feedback in a format that makes sense to them.

6. *Provide students with timely feedback on their work.* We are sure you remember receiving a paper in one of your college writing classes that the professor took 3 weeks to grade. The grade at that point meant little because you had almost forgotten what you had written. Obviously, effective feedback must occur as soon as possible after students have completed a task if they are to improve their performance and learn. Admittedly, this is difficult because middle school and high school teachers receive work from more than 100 students a day. Grading students' summaries or providing them with information on their progress becomes very time intensive. However, substantive and timely feedback can be provided in a variety of ways.

There Are Several Ways to Provide Students with Timely Feedback on Their Work

Checklists are one way to give students quick feedback on how they performed on a particular assignment. Rather than write the same comment 50 times, the checklist allows the teacher to indicate quickly the strengths and weaknesses of an assignment. In addition to the checklist in Figure 4.1, you will find other examples of checklists teachers have devised throughout this textbook.

A second way to make sure that students receive qualitative information about their work in a timely fashion is to create a symbol system and then limit your comments for a particular assignment to that set of symbols. For example, if you have been teaching students how to write a summary that includes the steps and the findings of a lab experiment, the following symbols might be useful in providing students with information about their efforts:

GES: Good explanation of the steps of the experiment

MNS: More information needed on the steps

GEF: Good explanation on the findings

MNF: More information needed on the findings

Some teachers complain that students do not read the qualitative information they are given, but instead focus only on the grades awarded. One middle school language arts teacher told us that she circumvents that difficulty by not writing the letter grade on the assignment until the student writes a response to her comments. Once she reads the student's comments, she places a grade on the paper. Regardless of how it is handled, quick, substantive feedback is important to the learning process.

7. *Involve students in the evaluation process.* Interestingly, all of the qualitative information discussed thus far has emphasized the teacher's responsibility, not the student's responsibility or participation. Assessment, however, should include students in self-reflection and evaluation activities. As we mentioned in the guidelines earlier in this chapter, students should play an active role in setting goals and evaluating whether they have reached those goals. When students are involved in evaluating their work in a content area, they are more likely to link their performance with effort rather than ascribe it to luck or chance or the whims of a teacher.

Taylor, a eighth-grade art teacher, realizes the importance of actively involving students in evaluating their own work. Therefore, she asks her students to evaluate their projects before they hand them in to her for feedback and a grade. She begins the process by asking her students to examine a few projects of her former students. Then she asks them to brainstorm some qualities that make certain projects more memorable than others. Once the class has listed all the possibilities, Taylor returns on the next day with a checklist containing the qualities the students have brainstormed and a few she has added herself. She tells her students to use this checklist to evaluate their own project and then to write a brief paragraph explaining what new techniques they have tried out. Although Taylor does not use a checklist for every project, she and her students find the experience useful.

As we stated earlier, grading is only a minor part of assessment and evaluation. The major part is the qualitative information we share. In the next section, we examine a variety of ways to gather information about students in authentic situations.

AUTHENTIC ASSESSMENT OF LITERACY AND CONTENT LEARNING

Earlier in this chapter, we referred to **authentic learning.** We now use this term to differentiate between standardized tests and those created by teachers and students for their own use with genuine, functional purposes. Over the past several years, we have been collecting what we consider to be some of the best examples of authentic assessment. These examples not only reflect creative methods of discovering how students read and think, but are also consistent with current perspectives on how best to teach and assess literacy and learning processes. Because these assessments are devised and/or adapted by teachers, often in collaboration with students, they invariably yield richer and more meaningful information about student learning than could be gained from traditional testing practices (Johnston, 1989). Furthermore, using authentic assessment helps you rely on your own assessment skills and individual judgment and exercise your own professional prerogative in making important instructional decisions (Valencia et al., 1990).

One of the key principles of reading assessment discussed earlier is to embed assessment in the contexts of actual literacy and learning activities so that the results of assessment will have direct and immediate instructional implications. To this end, middle school and high school teachers need to devise their own approaches to assessment to determine the extent to which their students can read and learn from the various materials used in the classroom and use this new learning in functional and purposeful ways. The approaches teachers have employed to accomplish this goal have taken a number of forms, but all have these four critical characteristics in common:

1. They assess literacy and learning processes with the materials used in the classroom and in the actual contexts of their use.
2. They are so closely related to instruction that assessment and instruction become virtually indistinguishable.
3. They reflect the essential role of the teacher's judgment in student evaluation.
4. They develop students' abilities to think metacognitively and self-reflect.

In the following sections, we will examine two authentic assessment procedures that middle school and high school content area teachers can use with their students: process observations and portfolios.

Assessment by Observation

Suggesting to teachers that they assess through observation is like asking them to breathe or walk; it comes so naturally to most of them that its importance and power as an assessment strategy is often overlooked. Unfortunately, assessments based on teachers' intuition about, interaction with, and systematic observations of students has been devalued (Johnston, 1990).

Teachers' Observations Are a Powerful Assessment Tool

Observational assessment is an excellent source of the critical information the classroom teacher needs to make important instructional decisions. Assessing through observation requires that teachers become more sensitive to the entire instructional situation: the reader, the text, the tasks required of the reader, the processes needed to complete the tasks, and the environment in which the tasks occur. Assessments conducted as students interact with text and complete daily assignments, engage in class discussions, or work cooperatively to solve problems can provide a rich source of information about students' relative strengths and needs, as well as how instruction can be modified to facilitate learning (Readence & Martin, 1988). For instance, teachers can make minute-by-minute decisions and lesson adjustments during classroom learning as they discover which students lack appropriate prior knowledge, fail to understand key vocabulary, or need further concept development (Johnston, 1989).

Observing students over time in a variety of classroom situations can provide teachers with an objective, unbiased view of students. Earlier, we discussed the limitations of making instructional decisions based on a single assessment at one point in time—specifically, that single assessments are not very reliable measures of a student's true reading and learning ability. In contrast, observational assessments are ongoing and occur within the context of normal classroom activities while students are engaged in learning content area concepts.

To determine the extent of students' understanding or lack of understanding and set the scene for observation, many teachers ask students to either write or talk about a concept at the beginning of class. For example, Phil, a seventh-grade science teacher, determines how much his students learned from their reading assignment by asking them to meet in pairs and list all the words they can recall about a topic such as the six different kinds of forces. With this activity, one student talks as the other student writes down the words that his or her partner says. After 2 minutes, the roles are switched and the process begins again. To increase the interest in the activity, Phil sets a kitchen timer, which clicks away as he walks about the room listening to what the students are saying and watching what they are writing.

Strategies Like Word Fluency Can Tell Teachers a Lot about Their Students' Understanding of Concepts

Phil tells us that this **word fluency activity** helps him to determine quickly which students have read the assignment and which ones understand the concepts. With this diagnostic information, Phil can plan more effective lessons and activities for his students. In addition to the word fluency activity, there are many other comprehension and vocabulary strategies that can be used to create rich observation opportunities. These strategies are discussed in Chapters 3 and 6.

In addition to capitalizing on teachable moments, teachers can structure their observations with the use of a checklist. For example, Phil created an observation checklist (Figure 4.2) to collect information on which students may be having difficulty reading his textbook and laboratory activity booklet. With this checklist, he can determine accurately and reliably which individuals need special assistance.

Checklists Can Facilitate Observations

Another teacher put together her observation checklist (Figure 4.3) based on characteristics of good readers (Pearson & Valencia, 1986). With the knowledge she gains about her students' strategies for processing their textbook and other reading material, she determines the relative need for reading and study skills instruction for the group and for individuals.

Because these observations occur as a natural part of the content area lesson, students can demonstrate their true ability. Teachers can obtain highly relevant and useful data by measuring what they choose to measure in the classroom context where students perform actual reading, writing, and learning tasks. The checklists shown in Figures 4.2 and 4.3 are examples of more systematic attempts to assess through observation. They can and should be modified to fit your particular assessment needs.

Student:

1. Avoids eye contact with me, especially when I'm asking questions of the class over the reading assignment.
2. May create the impression that he or she knows the answer to my question by looking intently and flagging his or her hand.
3. During oral reading of the textbook, tries to be the first one to read to get it over with.
4. During oral reading, tries to be the last one to read or tries to avoid being called on to read.
5. Frequently forgets to bring to class books and other materials that may be used for oral reading or needed to do in-class work.
6. Twists and turns restlessly in seat, often talking with neighbor.
7. Attempts to disrupt class.
8. Uses manipulative techniques within and outside of class to try to create a positive perception of his or her ability in spite of poor performance.
9. Uses neighbor for information about assignments and answers to questions.

FIGURE 4.2 Behavioral Clues to Students Needing Special Assistance

Student:

1. Uses prior knowledge to help construct meaning from text.
2. Draws inferences at the word, sentence, paragraph, and text levels.
3. Provides many plausible responses to questions about text.
4. Varies reading strategies to fit the text and the reading situation.
5. Synthesizes information within and across text.
6. Asks good questions about text.
7. Exhibits positive attitudes toward reading.
8. Integrates many skills to produce an understanding of text.
9. Uses knowledge flexibly.

Source: Adapted from P. D. Pearson & S. Valencia, "Assessment, Accountability, and Professional Prerogative," in J. Readence & R. S. Baldwin (Eds.), *Research in Literacy: Merging Perspectives.* © Copyright 1986, National Reading Conference.

FIGURE 4.3 Characteristics of Good Readers

Creating a Portfolio Assessment Culture: Process and Product

As part of a year-long portfolio teaching/assessment research project in collaboration with a high school French and English teacher, we had local professionals speak to students about the importance of portfolios in their work and lives. Frank, a local architect, began his talk to a group of industrial arts, art, and foreign language students by saying, "We are all walking portfolios." Students smiled. "I mean, look around. Each of you projects a certain image by the way you dress, wear your hair, walk, and talk, and this image is open to evaluation and judgment by peers, parents, teachers, and potential employers." Frank continued, "That's why you leave the jeans and sneakers at home when you go to a job interview." Frank's points were extremely helpful because they solidified for students the idea that portfolios are more than a product, a "thing," a container of "stuff"; they are a concept and a process. In our debriefing session after Frank's presentation, students made comments such as "I'm beginning to get the picture that portfolios are anything we want them to be to help someone see what we're capable of." "Like Frank said, I can evaluate my own work and then put together a portfolio that projects the image I want."

We'll return to our experiences and the results of our portfolio research project (Moje, Brozo, & Haas, 1994) a bit later in this section. First, we will briefly explore the definition and history of portfolios and discuss some of the hows and whys of their use.

The **portfolio** for instruction and assessment has become a popular buzz word among teachers in nearly every field. We're sure most of you are already familiar with the term. The idea of using portfolios to document literacy growth has many advocates (Camp & Levine, 1991; DeFina, 1992; Krest, 1990; Lamme & Haysmith, 1991; Murphy & Smith, 1991; Tierney, Carter, & Desai, 1991). One of the best working definitions of a portfolio we have seen was developed at the Northwest Regional Educational Laboratory (Arter, 1990):

> A portfolio is a purposeful collection of student work that exhibits to the students (and/or others) the student's efforts, progress or achievement in (a) given area(s). This collection must include: (1) student participation in selection of portfolio content; (2) the criteria for selection; (3) the criteria for judging merit; and (4) evidence of student self-reflection. (p. 2)

Portfolios are a relatively recent and unique innovation in the areas of literacy and content learning (i.e., math, science, history). Although in fields such as commercial art, modeling, photography, and journalism portfolios have been used for some time to showcase artistic and professional achievement (Tierney et al., 1991), portfolio assessment in writing emerged only in the early 1980s with the work of Judy and Judy (1981) and Elbow and Belanoff (1986) in a freshmen writing course. The growth in portfolio assessment in educational circles since then has been remarkable. It's nearly impossible to pick up a reading, writing, or language arts journal these days without finding an article on portfolios, and this practice is expanding to applied journals in the natural and social sciences and math.

What is the allure of portfolio assessment beyond its bandwagon appeal? Put simply, portfolios offer an assessment framework that reflects our current understanding of the process of literacy and content learning. We know, for instance, that learning takes place over time—portfolios are collections of learning demonstrations over time; that learning occurs in multiple contexts—portfolios sample work from a variety of teaching/learning situations; that effective learning occurs when learners are engaged in meaningful, purposeful learning activities—portfolio teaching/assessment promotes authentic learning; and that effective learning requires personal reflection—portfolios have self-reflection built into the process.

Vavrus (1990) suggests that the following five questions be answered when planning to establish a curriculum that includes portfolio teaching/assessment:

What Will the Portfolio Look Like?

Portfolios Should Have a Physical and Conceptual Structure

All portfolios should have a physical structure as well as a conceptual structure. Physically, a portfolio may be structured chronologically, by subject area, or by style of work. The *conceptual structure* refers to your goals for student learning. After identifying goals, you should decide the best ways to document students' work relative to the goals.

What Goes in the Portfolio?

To determine what goes in the portfolio, several related questions must be answered first: Who will evaluate the portfolios (parents, administrators, teachers)? What will these individuals want to know about student learning? Will portfolio samples document student growth that test scores cannot capture? Or will they further support the results of test scores? What is the best evidence that can be included in the portfolio to document student progress toward goals? Will students include their best work only, or will the portfolio contain a progressive record of student growth, or both? Will the portfolio include drafts, sketches, and ideas in unfinished as well as finished form?

Portfolios Should Contain Samples of Students' Work Across the Year

Because portfolio assessment is authentic in that it represents genuine, meaningful learning activities in the classroom, work samples should come from the variety of daily and weekly assignments and projects students are engaged in. If you are documenting the literacy progress of a seventh grader, for example, then his portfolio would likely contain samples from a writing folder; excerpts from journals and literature logs; early and final drafts of written reports and themes; and copies of assignments from various content areas that required reading and writing.

A 10th-grade biology student's portfolio might include lab reports documenting her ability to conduct an experiment and analyze and interpret the results, actual project hardware, photographs and logs from field work, and questions and hypotheses for further scientific inquiry.

A math student in the eighth grade might include in his portfolio documentation of his improving ability to understand increasingly complex story problems or algebraic equations, samples of computations, descriptions of certain mathematical properties, explanations of why certain mathematical processes work, and evidence of using math to solve everyday problems.

In addition to work samples, portfolios should contain reflective records. Vital to the process of learning through portfolio teaching/assessment, **reflective records** are documentation of students' personal reflections and self-evaluations. Students should study their portfolios at various points throughout the year, focusing on a single work, a set of revisions, evidence of growth in a particular area, or the portfolio materials as a whole. In reflecting on these samples, students should ask themselves questions such as the following:

Students Reflect and Evaluate Their Own Work Samples

Why did I select this piece of work?

Is this a sample of my best work?

What special strengths are reflected in this work?

What was particularly important to me during the process of completing this work?

What have I learned about (math, science, history, writing, etc.) from working on this piece or project?

If I could continue working on this piece or project, what would I do?

What particular skill or area of interest would I like to try out in future works?

Self-evaluative questions concerned solely with writing might include the following:

How has my writing changed since I wrote this?

If I revised this, what would I change?

What have I learned since I wrote this report that I would include in a follow-up report?

How did drafting and revising help me develop this essay?

How have I used this process to create other essays and reports?

Answers to these questions in the form of comments and reflections then become part of the student's portfolio. Students should also date their work and comment briefly on why it was included in the portfolio.

You should also include brief notes about why certain samples of students' work were chosen. At the same time, you should keep personal and anecdotal records of students' work and progress based on classroom observations, inspection of portfolio samples, and conferences on the portfolio with students, parents, and other teachers. These records can complement students' reflective records (Vavrus, 1990). Given most middle school and high school teachers' severe time constraints, record keeping of this kind can often pose the biggest challenge in portfolio assessment.

Jenny, an 11th-grade English teacher, handles record keeping by writing brief comments on adhesive name-tag size labels from rolls she can hold in her hand. She then affixes her comments to the work sample in the portfolio. Comments on each label include identification of the sample, why the activity was completed, why the sample was included, and brief notes about what the sample shows about a student's progress toward achieving instructional and personal goals. Jenny has found her system to be more manageable than others she has tried, especially because she can also hold the roll of labels during classroom activities and make observational and anecdotal records on them quickly and unobtrusively. Later, these notes, too, can be placed in students' portfolios.

Many teachers have found the use of checklists and questionnaires essential for analyzing portfolios and keeping records on them. A math teacher uses the following set of questions to assess students' math work samples:

- What mathematics did the student learn?
- How does this relate to what the student has learned before?
- Of the math the student has done lately, what areas of strength and confidence are exhibited in this work?
- What aspects of this work reflect a lack of or incomplete understanding?

A seventh-grade history teacher uses an overall checklist such as the one shown in Figure 4.4 to keep track of his students' progress relative to portfolio criteria established in collaboration with his class.

Name	Project	Self-Evaluation	Reference Skills	Improvement

FIGURE 4.4 Portfolio Criteria Checklist

How and When Will Samples Be Selected?

Timelines Help Teachers and Students Keep Track of the Portfolio

It's important to establish a clear and efficient system for selecting materials to go into and come out of the portfolio throughout the school year. Most teachers make these decisions at the end of a unit, grading period, semester, or school year. These are all good times to keep and add work samples that provide the clearest and most compelling evidence of student growth and achievement and, where appropriate, to eliminate other samples. Many teachers have found time lines helpful in making the entire class aware of when portfolio checks, revisions, and new entries will occur. In this way, students are brought into the decision-making process about what to include in their portfolios; thus, students further develop the ability to monitor their own progress. As stated, the more students are brought into the teaching/learning process, the more responsibility they take for their own learning.

How Will Portfolios Be Evaluated?

It is essential that evaluative criteria be established relative to the learning goals you and your students set up beforehand. We recommend that the greater part of a student's portfolio be evaluated on the basis of growth, in terms of both academic achievement and self-knowledge, instead of on the basis of comparison with other students' work.

The evaluation process typical in most middle school and secondary classrooms or schools where portfolio assessment occurs looks like this:

1. The teacher discusses and negotiates goals of portfolios with students.
2. Teacher and students develop guidelines and procedures for showcasing portfolios.
3. A showcase portfolio is developed by students with assistance and feedback from peers.
4. Students develop self-evaluation comments and present their portfolio.
5. Students evaluate their portfolio according to criteria they help develop with the teacher (i.e., evidence of improvement, evidence of effort, quality of self-evaluation, range of projects, presentation, future goals).
6. The student submits his or her portfolio to the teacher, who reviews it along with the student's self-evaluations and peer criteria scores. A grade is awarded.
7. The portfolio is returned to the student.

Figure 4.5 shows a **portfolio grade sheet** (Krest, 1990) that can be used to record individual grades for each writing sample and portfolio grades for students' progress.

How Can Portfolios Be Passed On?

As many teachers have noted, one of the special advantages of portfolio assessment is that the records of student progress can be passed on to succeeding

Due Dates: ______
______
______

Name: ____

	Date	Portfolio Grade	Sample	Comments
HP:*				
MP:				
LP:				
HP:				
MP:				
LP:				
HP:				
MP:				
LP:				
HP:				
MP:				
LP:				

*HP = high priority; MP = middle priority; LP = low priority

FIGURE 4.5 Portfolio Grade Sheet

One Advantage of Portfolios Is That They Promote Communication Across Teachers

teachers. In this way, the portfolio process promotes continuity in a student's education and collaboration among teachers at various grade levels. We suggest that as the school year draws to a close, you get together with other teachers at the next grade level to discuss their expectations and to find out what kind of information from portfolios would be most helpful to them in determining student accomplishment. In this process, you can make decisions about what to include or exclude before passing on portfolios. This is also a good time to have a conference with students about their portfolios in terms of the kind of work they believe would best reflect their growth and achievement for next year's teacher.

A Study of Portfolio Assessment: What We Learned

In this section, we discuss the findings of our own research about the benefits of portfolio teaching and assessment. We are vitally concerned about the extent to which the strategies and ideas we offer are implemented in real classroom settings by real teachers. Given this concern, much of our own research over the course of our careers has been devoted to discovering how teachers implement instructional innovations.

We conducted one research project about strategy implementation during the 1990–1991 school year. For 6 months, we worked with and observed an experienced senior high school French teacher, Jayne, as she implemented portfolio instruction and assessment. Our goal was to gain insights into the potential effectiveness of the strategy and the teacher change process itself. Furthermore, we hoped to develop a better understanding of the realities of using portfolios in a secondary school classroom where an individual teacher was attempting to put ideas from the literature into practice.

Our findings suggest that students—their input and voices—are often omitted from reports on the effectiveness of portfolios. Another factor not often accounted for in the rhetoric of educational change is the response and cooperation of students themselves. Yet, we discovered that without student cooperation and involvement, portfolio teaching and assessment is as vulnerable to failure as any other highly touted instructional innovation that has come before it. Perhaps the most important insight we gained from our experience in Jayne's classroom was that *students, like teachers, need scaffolding for change.* In other words, we can't always expect students to take advantage of new strategies simply because we think they should. The change process must include them as well; therefore, we need to prepare students for change, support them as they move through the change process, and provide them with ample opportunities for reflection on and critique of the change process.

With these general findings in mind, and based on our numerous conversations and interviews with several students from Jayne's classroom, we (Moje et al., 1994) offer the following guidelines for implementing portfolios with middle school and secondary school students:

There Are Five Guidelines That Should Help Content Area Teachers Succeed with Their First Attempts to Use Portfolios

1. Start with simple activities.
2. Negotiate firm deadlines.
3. Encourage students to set concrete goals.
4. Provide initial resources.
5. Integrate other classroom activities with the portfolios.

Start with Simple Activities

We suggest that you begin to use portfolios by asking students to complete simple, short writing activities. The activities can take any form. For example, in an advanced algebra class, students could make journal entries that ask them to reflect on their reasons for taking the advanced class, or they could prepare goal statements or biographies that link the class to their needs and interests. Starting with simple activities with foreseeable deadlines will allow students to work up slowly to more comprehensive projects.

Negotiate Firm Deadlines

When students are not used to the cognitive ambiguity and uncertainty of the portfolio process, it is important to help them set deadlines to keep them focused on their work. Despite the fact that the portfolio is designed to be an ongoing activity as opposed to a finite project, students who are accustomed to due dates may require your guidance in setting deadlines to get work completed and to meet project goals.

Encourage Students to Set Concrete Goals

Rather than expecting all students to be able to generate their own projects and samples for the portfolios, we suggest that you conduct conferences with students to create a plan of action. Such a plan would provide students with short-range goals that could be accomplished according to agreed-on deadlines, giving students a clearer view of their progress toward long-range goals. Plans of action can also provide students with a means of self-assessment because students would be able to evaluate both their progress toward meeting steps in the plan and the wisdom of the steps they chose.

Provide Initial Resources

Providing initial resources is critical in classrooms where portfolios will comprise project materials and samples. Students who are not used to conducting extended research that might require finding contacts, following up leads, making phone calls, and the like will need an initial source of specific information to get them started. These sources can help students sustain their research efforts while helping them learn valuable reference skills in the process.

Integrate Other Classroom Activities with the Portfolios

Many content teachers feel the necessity of covering certain concepts that are integral to their content area by means of direct instruction to ensure that the concepts are learned. Jayne, for example, felt it was necessary to continue using the French text and to provide direct instruction in grammar and vocabulary. She understood that students might be unprepared for complete immersion in the portfolio project and consequently moved back and forth between the two types of teaching. The stark contrast, however, between the teacher-led instruction and the student-led portfolios created tension and ambiguity among students.

Although Jayne wanted the portfolio writings to be applications of the book lessons, students didn't readily make the connections on their own. On reflection, Jayne decided that she could have tied activities together in a variety of ways. For example, she could have demonstrated the grammar rules the students read about in the textbook by pointing out the uses of grammatical structures in their portfolio writing samples. Integration helps students see the utility and value of portfolios as an integral part of the learning process in content classrooms.

Perhaps the most outstanding benefit of portfolio assessment is that it invites students and teachers to be allies in the assessment process. When a portfolio culture is established, there is a good chance that students will become more concerned, thoughtful, and energetic learners. At the same time, teachers will find renewed enthusiasm for providing support and guidance of others' learning while growing as learners themselves.

OTHER INFORMAL ASSESSMENT OPPORTUNITIES

In addition to using observations and portfolios in the classroom, content area teachers have other ways of assessing their students' strengths and needs. Some of these assessment opportunities involve students in reading and thinking about content area concepts, some involve students in writing, and some involve students in completing self-report instruments.

The Content Area Inventory

The Content Area Inventory Is a Group Procedure With Many Advantages

The **Content Area Inventory** is extremely valuable because it asks students to demonstrate their thinking and learning processes as they read content area textbooks or any written/oral material teachers may use in their courses (Rakes & Smith, 1992). The results of this type of assessment are far more informative than commercially prepared tests, we believe, because the assessment is based on material that students will be using throughout the year. Hence, when teachers use the Content Area Inventory, they quickly discover which students will have difficulty reading and thinking about the assigned materials used in their course. Moreover, the information gained from a Content Area Inventory can help teachers identify skills that students will need to be taught to succeed in a particular content area.

There Are Usually Two Parts to the Content Area Inventory

Although the Content Area Inventory can be developed in a variety of ways, traditionally it has had two main sections. The first section usually measures students' skills in using book parts, using reference skills, and reading illustrative materials such as diagrams, tables, and charts. As students answer these questions, they are free to use all the parts of the textbook necessary. For the second section, the students read silently a lengthy excerpt from the textbook and then answer a series of questions with the textbook closed. These questions in the second section measure students' skills in understanding technical and general vocabulary words and comprehending what they have read. Music, art, and physical education teachers may wish to have students complete a listening task in this section rather than a reading task since listening skills are more crucial in these content areas.

To develop your own Content Area Inventory, use the following steps:

1. Identify the essential reading, writing, listening, and thinking skills essential to your course.

2. Select a typical excerpt from the textbook or material the class will probably be reading in your course. The selection need not include the entire unit or story, but it should be complete within itself and not dependent on other sections of the chapter. In most cases, two or three pages will provide a sufficient sample of students' behaviors and skills.
3. Read the selection and design at least 25 questions for the first and second sections. These questions should reflect the skills you intend to assess and should be open-ended so that students have to use their recall and writing skills to answer them.
4. To make sure you have created a reliable instrument with no ambiguities, ask a colleague to read the excerpt and answer your questions. Then debrief the experience with the colleague and revise accordingly.
5. Prepare a student answer sheet and a key, noting specific page references for discussion purposes after the testing is completed.

The Content Area Inventory in Figure 4.6 was developed by a driver's education department in a large metropolitan high school. They had determined that it was important for students to be able to use their textbook effectively, to interpret illustrative materials, to understand technical vocabulary, and to identify and paraphrase the key ideas of what they had read. The driver's education teachers administered this assessment during the first week of class at the beginning of the school year. With the results, they were able to determine to what extent students could use their text as a resource and comprehend and process the textual information at a meaningful level. This knowledge led to specific instructional approaches such as cooperative grouping, direct process instruction in comprehension and concept knowledge, and training in designing and using study aids based on text and lecture information.

The teachers in this department have pointed out that it is important to explain the purposes of the Content Area Inventory to the students. That is, the students should do their best work because the information from the Inventory will help in planning appropriate instruction. In addition, students should be told that they will be reading silently and then answering short-answer questions without the assistance of the textbook.

Teachers Should Observe Students As They Take the Content Area Inventory

One middle school team of teachers told us that they observe students as they read in order to note any who are demonstrating behaviors indicating frustration. For example, they make anecdotal notes of their students who appear to use excessive lip movements and who seem restless and generally inattentive. These behaviors may identify students who are experiencing difficulty comprehending what they are reading.

You can choose to grade the Content Area Inventory in class the next day, using that time to discuss the questions and answers with the students, or you can choose to grade the Inventory outside of class. Once the Content Area Inventory has been graded, total the number of items each student answered

Using Book Parts

1. On what page does the unit (section) entitled "When You Are the Driver" begin?
2. On what pages can you find information on smoking and driving?
3. In what part of the book can you find the meaning of *kinetic energy?*

Understanding Graphs and Charts

1. According to the chart on page 61, what is the second most important cause of rural fatal accidents?
2. What does the chart on page 334 imply about the relationship between speed and fuel consumption?
3. Using the chart on page 302 and your own weight, determine what alcohol concentration in your blood would make you legally drunk.

Vocabulary in Context

1. What does the word *converse* mean in the following sentence?
   Do not take your eyes off the road to *converse* with a passenger.
2. What does the word *distracting* mean in the following sentence?
   He should avoid *distracting* the driver.
3. What does the word *enables* mean in the following sentence?
   It *enables* you to carry out your decisions promptly and in just the way you planned.

Summarizing and Sensing Key Ideas

1. Write a one-paragraph summary of the section entitled "A Defensive Driver's Decision Steps" on page 101. Be sure to include the key ideas and any other pertinent information. Use your own words as you write the summary.
2. Using your own words, state the key idea of the following paragraph:

   Not only does a defensive driver have to see all hazards and decide on his defense, he also has to act in time. A defensive driver's thinking shows in his actions as he drives. He anticipates hazards and covers the brake in case a stop is needed. He has both hands on the wheel so that he will be ready to act.

3. Write one or two sentences stating the key idea(s) of Chapter 18, "Controlling Your Emotions and Attitudes."

Creating Study Aids

1. Imagine that you will have a multiple-choice and short-answer test on Chapter 18. Organize the material in that chapter by taking notes on it or by creating some form of study aid.

FIGURE 4.6 Content Area Inventory for a Driver's Education Textbook

correctly in both sections. Enter that total in your gradebook and use the following criteria for interpretation:

80% of the items correct—the student will probably be able to use and comprehend the textbook or materials

79–65%—the student will need some assistance in the form of teacher-directed strategies

Below 65%—the student will require significant assistance because the textbook or material is too difficult

Some teachers like to use a yellow highlighter to note in their gradebook which students are finding the content material too difficult and their frustration level.

The Classroom Summary Form Helps Content Area Teachers See Patterns and Trends

The Content Area Inventory will also help you see patterns in the skills for which students will need additional teaching and reinforcement. Rosa, a sixth-grade math teacher, developed a Classroom Summary Form to help her see these patterns. As illustrated in Figure 4.7, Rosa listed one class of her students on the vertical axis. On the horizontal axis she listed the reading skills she wants her students to master in her math course. Then she placed a check mark in the appropriate column for the students who missed more than half of the questions on a specific skill. For example, any student who missed three Content Area Inventory questions about Understanding Math Symbols received a check on the Classroom Summary Form. Rosa believes that this additional analysis helps her identify the reading and problem-solving skills that most of her students will need to be taught to succeed in mathematics. An added advantage of the Content Area Inventory is that it can be created for any course, regardless of whether you present the objectives and information to your students in written form or in the form of discussions, lectures, labs, and demonstrations.

Assessment Activities Using Students' Writing

Writing is a powerful communication tool because it mirrors what we understand and think about certain ideas. Writing is also permanent, allowing us to reflect upon the meanings that we attempted to construct on paper or on a computer screen. Hence, it is logical to use writing activities as one way to assess students' comprehension of a text (Afflerbach & Johnston, 1986). In the next section, we will consider how you can use summary writing and autobiographical entries as assessment tools. Other assessment and teaching ideas that capitalize on the power of writing are found in Chapter 7.

Summary Writing

When students write a summary of what they have read or listened to, they must think metacognitively, make inferences, select important ideas, and form gists (Brozo & Curtis, 1987). The following letter from P. T. Barnum to General Ulysses S. Grant (*Sequential Tests of Educational Progress,* 1957) was given to 9th-grade American history students at the beginning of a unit on entrepreneurs of the late 19th century. The teacher asked his students to read the letter and then, without looking back, to summarize the key ideas and any other relevant information.

> Honored Sir:
>
> The whole world honors and respects you. All are anxious that you should live happy and free from care. While they admire your manliness in declining the large sum recently tendered you by friends, they still desire to see you achieve financial independence in an honorable manner. Of the unique and valuable trophies with which you have been honored we all

Classroom Summary Form: Content Area Inventory

Names	Using Parts of the Book					Following Directions				Understanding Math Symbols				Understanding Vocabulary				Noting Main Ideas				Drawing Conclusions				
	1	2	3	4	5	6	7	8	9	10	11	12	13	14	15	16	17	18	19	20	21	22	23	24	25	26
Jason	✓					✓	✓	✓		✓	✓	✓		✓		✓	✓	✓	✓	✓	✓	✓	✓	✓	✓	✓
Tamika										✓	✓		✓	✓								✓	✓	✓	✓	✓
Jorge										✓	✓		✓		✓	✓										
Michelle																						✓	✓	✓	✓	✓
Tyrone	✓	✓	✓	✓	✓	✓	✓	✓	✓	✓	✓	✓	✓	✓	✓	✓	✓		✓			✓	✓	✓	✓	✓
Gareth										✓	✓							✓				✓	✓	✓	✓	
Avery	✓					✓				✓	✓	✓		✓	✓	✓		✓	✓	✓				✓		
Judd			✓			✓				✓	✓			✓			✓			✓		✓		✓		
Chanda	✓	✓				✓	✓	✓	✓		✓			✓	✓	✓		✓	✓			✓	✓	✓	✓	
Jennifer		✓				✓	✓	✓	✓					✓				✓	✓	✓		✓	✓	✓	✓	✓

Place a check mark under the number of the question which was missed and alongside the name of the student who missed it.

FIGURE 4.7

have read, and all have a laudable desire to see these evidences of love and respect bestowed upon you by monarchs, princes, and people throughout the globe.

While you would confer a great and enduring favor on your fellow men and women by permitting them to see these trophies, you could also remove existing embarrassments in a most satisfactory and honorable manner. I will give you one hundred thousand dollars cash, besides a proportion of the profits, if I may be permitted to exhibit these relics to a grateful and appreciative public, and I will give satisfactory bonds of half a million dollars for their safe-keeping and return.

These precious trophies of which all your friends are so proud, would be placed before the eyes of your millions of admirers in a manner and style at once pleasing to yourself and satisfactory to the best elements of the entire community. Remembering that the momentoes [*sic*] of Washington, Napoleon, Frederick the Great, and many other distinguished men have given immense pleasure to millions who have been permitted to see them, I trust you will in the honorable manner proposed, gratify the public and thus inculcate the lesson of honesty, perseverance, and true patriotism so admirably illustrated in your career.

I have the honor to be truly your friend and admirer,

P.T. Barnum

("A Letter from the 1870s," 1957)

The three types of summaries produced by the students are representative of the responses obtained by the history teacher. Here is one example:

> Honored sir: The whole world respects you with honor. All are anxious that you should live happily with care. While the whole world worries about the manliness in declining the money tendered you by friends, they respect you to manage with honorable manner.

This response revealed to the teacher a couple of possibilities. First, because the student apparently tried to simply rewrite the letter, the student may have misunderstood the directions. Second, this response could also reflect a reader who, being incapable of understanding the surface logic of the letter (let alone the implied ideas), may have resorted to a strategy intended to disguise this possible serious lack of comprehension by simply writing down the words of the letter. In any case, the history teacher had what he believed to be a student who needed definite follow-up, and he immediately got together with the student for further assessment and discussion.

Another student submitted this summary:

> The passage was a letter sent to Ulysses S. Grant from P. T. Barnum. The letter outlined how Barnum wanted to bring his attractions before millions of admirers with the permission of Ulysses Grant. Barnum was willing to pay $100,000 and a portion of the profits if he was so permitted to be allowed to show his trophies to the American public. Barnum promised $500,000 in

> satisfactory bonds to Ulysses Grant for safekeeping and return to demonstrate how serious Barnum was in bringing his trophies to the people.
>
> Barnum started his letter to Ulysses Grant [by saying] that the people as well as himself respected his position of President and wished him the best of health. Barnum also finished his letter in the same fashion, comparing Grant with other great men such as Frederick the Great, Washington, and Napoleon.

What appeared obvious to the history teacher in this response was that the student had a good grasp of the basic information in the letter. The student recalled the significant details and followed the surface logic of Barnum's proposal to Grant. What is not reflected in this response, however, is any indication that the student appreciated the subtlety and irony in Barnum's letter. Also, this reader apparently had little prior knowledge of the topic because no additional ideas or information, beyond those included in the text, were provided.

A third student turned in this summary:

> The letter from P. T. Barnum to Grant was first a letter honoring and showing Grant how much his public loved him. In other words, a real snow job. Because in the latter part of the letter, Barnum gives Grant a proposal of, first, paying Grant one-hundred thousand dollars to let Barnum exhibit his oddities, or as Barnum puts it, his trophies. Second, Barnum pledged to pay a half a million dollars in bonds for Grant's protection of his trophies. The whole letter came out to be a bribe on Barnum's part. But in real life it worked in favor of Barnum. The reason that one can tell this letter was a real snow job is because Grant wasn't everything Barnum said he was.

The teacher felt this was an impressive response. It reflected not only a basic understanding of the facts of Barnum's proposal, but also an understanding of Barnum's power of persuasion by heaping what history perhaps has proven unfounded, lofty praise on Grant. This student's ability to pick up on the underlying themes and rhetorical devices in the letter indicates a good deal of relevant prior knowledge about the topic and the skill to bring that prior knowledge to bear in constructing a multilevel understanding of the text.

Written Summaries by Students Provide a Lot of Useful Information

Students who show signs of lacking relevant prior knowledge or the literacy skills to interpret the assessment passage meaningfully may be given special assistance. You can provide these students with additional or alternative reading opportunities from books that are content related, including some that are easier and more enjoyable to read than the textbook, to help build prior knowledge. Cooperative learning experiences are helpful for improving students' interpretive powers. Beyond the revelation of your students' reading performance with the texts used in your classrooms, written summaries have another advantage: An entire class can be assessed at one time. This advantage in efficiency, however, can be a disadvantage for students who are poor writers. An alternative to written summaries is to assess students' comprehension of text by having them summarize orally what they remember and learned from the text.

To read and evaluate their students' summaries quickly and efficiently, some teachers have developed scoring rubrics or checklists. Although these scoring devices for writing will be discussed in more detail in Chapter 7, it would be useful to discuss two different approaches. One approach is based on the assumption that within any paragraph, some ideas are more important, more central to the overall meaning than others. Thus, it is possible to rank these ideas on a scale of importance (Winograd, 1984); for instance, an idea of great importance might have a ranking of 3, while an idea of little importance might have a ranking of 1. Suppose you and I are going to read a passage about pollution. The author of the passage makes a few major points about the global consequences of pollution and presents several examples of pollution. After reading, in my summary I mention three specific examples of pollution, while your summary includes two of the author's major points and one specific example. Although we both recalled three ideas, your retelling would receive a higher rating because you recalled two major ideas.

There Are Several Ways Content Area Teachers Can Quickly Evaluate Students' Summaries

A second approach to scoring summaries is more holistic. A holistic scoring rubric was developed by a 10th-grade English teacher (Figure 4.8). His scoring

Directions: Indicate with a check mark the extent to which the student's summary includes evidence of the following:

	No Evidence	**Some Evidence**	**Significant Evidence**
1. Includes verbatim information.			
2. Includes inferred information.			
3. Includes most important ideas.			
4. Connects prior knowledge with text information.			
5. Makes summary statements and generalizations.			
6. Indicates affective involvement with text.			
7. Demonstrates appropriate use of language.			
8. Demonstrates sense of audience or purpose.			
9. Indicates control of the mechanics of speaking.			
10. Indicates creative impressions or reactions to text.			

FIGURE 4.8 Scoring of Students' Summaries

guide for the summaries included many aspects of reading, such as comprehension, metacognitive awareness, strategy use, level of text involvement, and facility with language.

Learner Autobiographies

The Learner Autobiography is an effective method for discovering more about students' interests and belief systems (Gilles et al., 1988). The idea is that students need opportunities to examine their personal histories as readers, writers, and learners both in and out of school. By exploring their past, students might better understand their current approaches and beliefs about learning. To help students reflect on their past experiences as language users and learners, we recommend the following approach:

1. In small groups, ask students to brainstorm their past as readers, writers, and learners. They should try to remember about a time, person, school year, class, event, assignment, textbook or other book, teacher, friend, relative, or the like.
2. After brainstorming, students should write about that event, time, or person that had a positive or negative impact on their thinking and feeling about literacy and learning.
3. Be sure students focus on the questions "What happened that influenced the way you read, write, and learn now?" and "How do you feel about that influence now?"
4. Students should be allowed to write as much as necessary to describe and reflect fully on their past influences and experiences related to how they currently think about themselves as readers, writers, and learners.
5. After thinking and writing, students could be allowed to exchange their drafts with members of their brainstorm group for comment, questions, and feedback.
6. Volunteers could be asked to share their autobiographies.
7. We recommend that you also take part in this activity by writing and sharing your autobiography with the class.

Students and Teachers Profit From Writing Learner Autobiographies

If you feel uncomfortable using these procedures with the Learner Autobiography, you can ask students to write parts of the Autobiography throughout the school year. For example, we know one physics teacher, Hector, who asks his students to write on an index card what they think it means to read, study, and learn in a physics course. He does this activity at the beginning of the class period the first week of classes. After collecting and reading the index cards, Hector discusses with his students his perceptions of what it means to read and learn in physics.

During the school year he follows up this initial assignment by asking students to write on other topics such as these: "This week I really liked ______ because ______"; "What really confused me this week was ______"; and "I would like to know more about ______ because ______". These brief assignments on index cards have two advantages. First, students react positively to them because the required amount of writing seems less intimidating. For Hector, the index cards allow him to assess quickly what his students are thinking, learning, and feeling as they study physics.

The information gained from autobiographies and other writing tasks from your students can help you make instructional decisions, deconstruct maladaptive attitudes and beliefs about literacy, target certain activities and projects to particular students, and improve and support healthy attitudes about literacy and learning.

Self-Report Inventories and Questionnaires

Self-Report Instruments Have Some Limitations

Inventories and questionnaires are the simplest and most direct way of acquiring information about students' skills, interests, attitudes, and belief systems. Although self-report instruments have been criticized because students tend to use the cues embedded in the questions to determine how they should answer in order to be judged competent (Garner, 1987), you can reduce these potential limitations by using a variety of techniques. For example, ask what your students do but not *why,* and ask the question in two different ways to validate the consistency of their responses.

Some inventories and questionnaires, such as the Interest Inventory I (Figure 4.9) and the Survey of Study Strategies (Figure 4.10), require students merely to read and place a check mark in the appropriate place. Other inventories, like the Interest Inventory II (Figure 4.11), ask students to write more elaborate answers to questions regarding their interests. The Writing Strategies Questionnaire in Figure 4.12 has been used by middle school and high school teachers to discover important past experiences their students have had with writing and how they think and feel about writing.

Although your students' attitudes about themselves as learners in your classroom may be difficult to uncover with one simple inventory or questionnaire, they

Directions: Put a check mark on the line to the left of each activity you like to do in your spare time.

Interests Outside of School

______ Television	______ Volunteer work	______ Dancing	______ Cooking
______ Outdoor games	______ Reading	______ Socializing	______ Music
______ Watching sports	______ Hobbies	______ Movies	______ Motorcycles
______ Hiking and camping	______ Playing sports	______ Computer and Internet	______ Cars
______ Video games	______ Fishing or hunting	______ Traveling	______ Other(s):

FIGURE 4.9 Interest Inventory I

Your Name: ______________________________
Date: ______________________________

SURVEY OF STUDY STRATEGIES

	Strongly Agree	Agree	Neutral	Disagree	Strongly Disagree
Time Management					
1. I put off my homework until the last minute.					
2. I plan regular times to study.					
3. I study less than an hour a day outside class.					
4. I cram for tests the night before the exam.					
5. I study with the radio, stereo, or TV on.					
6. I have a specified and quiet place for study.					
Remembering and Understanding					
1. I examine each of my textbooks for its overall organization.					
2. I look over a chapter before reading it in detail.					
3. I have to read a chapter several times before I understand it.					
4. I'm halfway through a chapter before I understand what it is about.					
5. I do not know which information in a chapter is important and which is not.					
6. My mind wanders to other things while I am reading an assignment.					
7. I have trouble remembering what I read.					
8. I try to set purposes and questions to be answered in my reading assignments.					
9. I find reading difficult because of the big words.					

FIGURE 4.10 Survey of Study Strategies

	Strongly Agree	Agree	Neutral	Disagree	Strongly Disagree
Note Taking and Listening					
1. I take notes on my assigned readings.					
2. My notes on my textbooks are unorganized and messy.					
3. My notes don't make any sense to me.					
4. I don't know what to write down in my notes.					
5. I can't find information in my notes when I need it.					
6. I don't get much out of lectures.					
7. I find myself doodling or writing letters during lectures					
8. I can't pick out important ideas from a lecture.					
9. I review my lecture notes as soon as possible after class.					
Test Taking and Test Preparation					
1. I study the wrong things for a test.					
2. I do not perform well on tests.					
3. I have mental blocks when I take a test.					
4. I know how to prepare for an essay exam.					
5. I have an effective strategy for approaching my upcoming exams.					
6. I know techniques for memorization.					
Reading Rate Strategies					
1. I hurry through all my assignments as quickly as I can.					
2. My reading speed is fast enough for my assignments.					
3. It takes me a long time to read any assignment.					
4. I can scan for specific information with little difficulty.					
5. I read most material at the same rate.					
6. I read as quickly as most people in my class.					

FIGURE 4.10 *(Continued)*

Directions: Finish each sentence so that it tells something about you. You may write as much as you wish to finish each sentence.

1. After school I like to ______________________________
2. On weekends I like to ______________________________
3. ________________ is my favorite TV show because ________________
4. The kind of music I like is ______________________________
5. When I graduate from high school, I want to ______________________
6. If I could go anywhere in the world, I'd go to ________ because ________
7. If I could take only one book with me on a trip to Mars, that book would be ________________ because ________________
8. I have seen the movie ________ and wish I could find a book similar to it because ______________________________
9. I have reread the book __________ because ______________________
10. When I read the newspaper or a magazine, I like to read ____________ because ______________________________

FIGURE 4.11 Interest Inventory II

1. If you knew someone was having trouble writing, what would you do to help?
2. What would a teacher do to help that student?
3. If you were told you have to write an essay due in 1 week, what would you do to make sure it is done on time and is well written?
4. Think about someone you know who is a good writer. What makes that person a good writer?
5. What is the best advice you've ever been given about writing?
6. How did you learn to write? When? Who helped you?
7. What would help you improve your writing?
8. Do you think you're a good writer? Why or why not?
9. Why do people write? What are your reasons for writing?
10. Does the writing you do in school interest you? Why or why not?

FIGURE 4.12 Writing Strategies Questionnaire

are a starting point for acquiring more in-depth information about your students. The key is that opportunities are provided on a regular basis for students to explore and share their underlying beliefs and attitudes toward literacy and learning. And remember, the examples of inventories and questionnaires we have presented are merely suggestions of the kinds of issues and questions you may find relevant to your teaching situation. We urge you to use these suggestions to develop your own inventories that suit your particular need to know more about your students.

CASE STUDY REVISITED

Terri, the seventh-grade science teacher introduced in the case study in the beginning of the chapter, wanted to find a classroom-based assessment strategy of her students' ability to understand their science text. Now that you have read about and explored a variety of assessment approaches in this chapter, reflect again on Terri's concerns and generate a few suggestions for meeting her assessment needs. Afterward, read about what she actually did to assess her students.

In our discussion of schema theory in Chapter 2, we pointed out that for students to succeed in school, they need to have a well-developed sense of how authors structure ideas in narrative, especially in expository texts. These schemata for text structure help readers predict, assimilate, and retrieve text information—three critical reading processes. As we discovered, middle school and high school students may have a very good sense of how stories are structured but a relatively poor sense of the structures of complex expository texts they are likely to find in their social science and science books.

Mindful of the problems students have in thinking like writers, Terri decided to combine some of the suggestions she obtained from an in-service workshop with her own ideas. From the workshop she learned how to construct a Content Area Inventory using the materials from her course. The excerpt she selected was about rocks, a typical reading assignment that required students to identify types and characteristics, similarities and differences. Because Terri wanted to assess how well students could read to determine these writing patterns, her Content Area Inventory contained many items like the following:

1. According to the paragraphs you have just read, what are two types of igneous rocks?
2. According to the paragraphs you have just read, what are some characteristics of these types of rocks? Name one characteristic of each rock.
3. According to the paragraphs you have just read, how are these types of rock different?
4. What words or phrases did the author use to cue you that the rocks were different in some ways? One such phrase was "very different." What was the other?

In addition to the information she gained about her students from the Content Area Inventory, Terri carefully observes her students in a variety of settings. For example, she pays special attention to the following signals that her students understand text organization and structure:

- As students are summarizing or discussing an assignment, she determines whether they are using the author's organizational structures as their ideas or comments unfold.

- When students are writing responses to text reading, she looks for indications that they are using text structure knowledge as a framework for developing their writing.

Terri has also found useful a classroom activity that her students really enjoy. She gives her students articles that have been cut up at paragraph boundaries and scrambled and tells them that they will be reading a text that is mixed up. Working in pairs, students are asked to put the article back together in the original fashion. While doing so, they are asked to "think out loud" and explain their decisions during the text reconstruction process to their partners. Terri moves about the room and listens to each pair of students to monitor their progress and provide assistance through modeling or questioning. She looks for evidence that her students grasp the problem–solution pattern employed by the author. Her evidence comes from students' comments and statements such as these:

> Number 5 has to go near the end because it sounds like a summary of the problems with deforestation in developing countries.

By combining text reconstruction activities with the Content Area Inventory and classroom observations, Terri has learned a lot about her students and why they perform the way they do. This information has helped her realize the importance of using a variety of strategies to help her students understand important concepts in science. Furthermore, she has found what researchers before her have found (Mayer, 1996; Richgels, McGee, Lomax, & Sheard, 1987)—that familiarity with expository text structure enhances comprehension and that knowledge of text structure can be directly taught.

■ ■ ■

SUMMARY

Assessment of literacy and content learning is a process of becoming informed about teaching and learning to improve instruction for the teacher and to increase self-knowledge for students. In this chapter we emphasized the importance of authentic assessments that integrate process and content and help make the boundary between assessment and teaching nearly indistinguishable. Because content area teachers need a variety of practical assessment activities and instruments, we described how to use classroom observations during teachable moments, the portfolio approach, students' writing, checklists, and the Content Area Inventory.

Finally, we stressed that when process assessment of literacy is integrated within the content classroom, the result is that assessment and teaching become nearly indistinguishable. Therefore, throughout this book we discuss strategies in relation to how they can be used to assess and teach particular literacy/learning processes. For example, in the next chapter, our discussion of effective strategies for preparing students for content area assignments includes how assessment of prior knowledge and building prior knowledge can be complementary. In Chapter 6, we describe vocabulary strategies that have built-in assessments not only for the teacher but also in the form of self-assessment for the student. This holds true for Chapter 7, in which we demonstrate how students' writing can be used in assessment and development of comprehension. Many of the strategies for teaching with trade literature, developed in Chapter 8, can be used to reveal what students are learning. And in Chapter 9, strategies for developing text study processes are interwoven with teacher assessment and self-assessments of these strategies. Assessment and teaching of important comprehension and literacy processes is at the heart of our chapter dealing with special needs students. Finally, in the last chapter, we discuss the role of assessment as a tool of reflection in improving teaching effectiveness.

REFERENCES

Afflerbach, P., & Johnston, P. (1984). On the use of verbal reports in reading research. *Journal of Reading Behavior, 16,* 307–322.

Afflerbach, P., & Johnston, P. (1986). What do expert readers do when the main idea is not explicit? In J. Bauman (Ed.), *Teaching main idea comprehension.* Newark, DE: International Reading Association.

Alexander, P., Kulikowich, J., & Schulze, S. K. (1994). How subject matter knowledge affects recall and interest on the comprehension of scientific prose. *American Educational Research Journal, 31,* 313–337.

Arter, J. (1990). *Using portfolios in instruction and assessment.* Portland, OR: Northwest Regional Educational Laboratory.

Bean, T. W. (1988). Organizing and retaining information by thinking like an author. In S. Glazer, L. Searfoss, & L. Gentile (Eds.), *Reexamining reading diagnosis: New trends and procedures.* Newark, DE: International Reading Association.

Bissex, G. (1980). *GYNS AT WORK: A child learns to write and read.* Cambridge, MA: Harvard University Press.

Brown, R. (1989). Testing and thoughtfulness. *Educational Leadership, 46,* 31–33.

Brozo, W. G., & Brozo, C. L. (1994). Literacy assessment in standardized and zero-failure contexts. *Reading and Writing Quarterly, 10,* 189–200.

Brozo, W. G., & Curtis, C. L. (1987). Coping strategies of four successful learning disabled college students: A case study approach. In J. Readence & R. S. Baldwin (Eds.), *Research in literacy: Merging perspectives. Thirty-sixth yearbook of the National Reading Conference.* Rochester, NY: National Reading Conference.

Camp, R., & Levine, D. (1991). Portfolios evolving: Background and variations in sixth- through twelfth-grade classrooms. In P. Belanoof & M. Dixon (Eds.), *Portfolios: Process and product.* Portsmouth, NH: Boynton/Cook.

Carey, R. F., Harste, J. C., & Smith, S. L. (1981). Contextual constraints and discourse processes: A replication study. *Reading Research Quarterly, 16,* 201–212.

Clay, M. (1975). *What did I write?* Auckland, New Zealand: Heinemann.

Collins, A., Brown, J., & Newman, S. (1989). Cognitive apprenticeship: Teaching the craft of reading, writing, and mathematics. In L. Resnick (Ed.), *Knowing, learning and instruction: Essays in honor of Robert Glaser.* Hillsdale, NJ: Erlbaum.

DeFina, A. (1992). *Portfolio assessment: Getting started.* New York: Scholastic.

Edelsky, C., & Harman, S. (1988). One more critique of reading tests—with two differences. *English Education, 20,* 157–171.

Elbow, P. (1991). Foreword. In P. Belanoff & M. Dixon (Eds.), *Portfolios: Process and product.* Portsmouth, NH: Heinemann.

Elbow, P., & Belanoff, P. (1986). Portfolios as a substitute for proficiency examinations. *College Composition and Communication, 37,* 336–339.

Garner, R. (1987). *Metacognition and reading comprehension.* Norwood, NJ: Ablex.

Garner, R., Alexander, P., Gillinghan, M., Kulikowich, J., & Brown, R. (1991). Interest and learning from text. *American Educational Research Journal, 28,* 643–659.

Gilles, C., Bixby, M., Crowley, P., Crenshaw, S., Henrich, M., Reynolds, F., & Pyle, D. (1988). *Whole language strategies for secondary students.* New York: Richard C. Owen.

Glazer, S. M., Searfoss, L. W., & Gentile, L. M. (1988). *Reexamining reading diagnosis: New trends and procedures.* Newark, DE: International Reading Association.

Goodman, J. (1992). *Elementary schooling for critical democracy.* Albany, NY: SUNY Press.

Hidi, S. (1990). Interest and its contribution as a mental resource for learning. *Review of Educational Research, 60,* 549–571.

Hidi, S., & Baird, W. (1988). Strategies for increasing text-based interest and students' recall of expository texts. *Reading Research Quarterly, 23,* 465–483.

Johnston, P. (1989). Constructive evaluation and the improvement of teaching and learning. *Teachers College Record, 90,* 509–528.

Johnston, P. (1990). Steps toward a more naturalistic approach to the assessment of the reading process. In S. Legg & J. Algina (Eds.), *Cognitive assessment of language and mathematics outcomes.* Norwood, NJ: Ablex.

Johnston, P. (1992). *Constructive evaluation of literate activity.* New York: Longman.

Johnston, P. (1993). Assessment as a social practice. In D. J. Leu & C. K. Kinzer (Eds.), *Examining central issues in literacy research, theory, and practice. Forty-second yearbook of the National Reading Conference.* Chicago: National Reading Conference.

Judy, S., & Judy, S. (1981). *An introduction to the teaching of writing.* New York: Wiley.

Krest, M. (1990). Adapting the portfolio to meet student needs. *English Journal, 79,* 29–34.

Lamme, L., & Haysmith, C. (1991). One school's adventure into portfolio assessment. *Language Arts, 68,* 629–640.

Liston, D., & Zeichner, K. (1991). *Teacher education and the social conditions of schooling.* New York: Routledge.

Mayer, R. E. (1996). Learning strategies for making sense out of expository text: The SOI model for guiding these cognitive processes in model construction. *Educational Psychology Review, 8,* 357–371.

McKeachie, W. J. (1994). *Teaching tips* (9th ed.). Lexington, MA: D. C. Heath.

Moje, W., Brozo, W. G., & Haas, J. (1994). Portfolios in a high school classroom: Challenges to change. *Reading Research and Instruction, 33,* 275–292.

Murphy, S., & Smith, M. (1991). *Writing portfolios: A bridge from teaching to assessment.* Markham, Ontario: Pippin.

Newman, J. (1985). *Whole language: Theory and use.* Portsmouth, NH: Heinemann.

Pearson, P. D. (1997). Six ideas in search of a champion: What policymakers should know about the teaching and learning of literacy in our schools. *Journal of Literacy Research, 28,* 302–309.

Pearson, P. D., & Valencia, S. (1986). Assessment, accountability, and professional prerogative. In J. Readence & R. S. Baldwin (Eds.), *Research in literacy: Merging perspectives. Thirty-sixth yearbook of the National Reading Conference.* Rochester, NY: National Reading Conference.

Pinnell, G. S. (1989). Reading recovery: Helping at-risk children learn to read. *Elementary School Journal, 90,* 161–183.

Rakes, T. A., & Smith, L. J. (1992). Assessing reading skills in the content areas. In E. K. Dishner, T. W. Bean, J. E. Readence, & D. W. Moore (Eds.), *Reading in the content areas: Improving classroom instruction.* Dubuque, IA: Kendall/Hunt.

Readence, J. E., & Martin, M. A. (1988). Comprehension assessment: Alternatives to standardized tests. In S. Glazer, L. Searfoss, & L. Gentile (Eds.), *Reexamining reading diagnosis: New trends and procedures.* Newark, DE: International Reading Association.

Readence, J. E., & Moore, D. W. (1983). Why questions? A historical perspective on standardized reading comprehension tests. *Journal of Reading, 26,* 306–313.

Reading yardsticks. (1981). Level 14—Grade 8. Chicago: Riverside.

Richgels, D. J., McGee, L. M., Lomax, R. G., & Sheard, C. (1987). Awareness of four text structures: Effects on recall of expository text. *Reading Research Quarterly, 22,* 177–196.

Rief, L. (1992). *Seeking diversity: Language arts with adolescents.* Portsmouth, NH: Heinemann.

Schommer, M. (1994). An emerging conceptualization of epistemological beliefs and their role in learning. In R. Garner & P. A. Alexander (Eds.), *Beliefs about text and instruction with text.* Hillsdale, NJ: Erlbaum.

Schunk, D. H. (1983). Goal difficulty and attainment information: Effects on children's behavior. *Human Learning, 25,* 107–117.

Sequential tests of educational progress. (1957). Princeton, NJ: Educational Testing Service.

Taylor, D. (1988). Ethnographic educational evaluation for children, families, and school. *Theory Into Practice, 27,* 67–76.

Taylor, D. (1989). Toward a unified theory of literacy learning and instructional practices: A critical response to Chall and Carbo. *Phi Delta Kappan, 71,* 184–193.

Thorndike, E. L. (1917). Reading as reasoning: A study of mistakes in paragraph reading. *Journal of Educational Psychology, 8,* 323–332.

Tierney, R., Carter, M., & Desai, L. (1991). *Portfolio assessment in the reading-writing classroom.* Norwood, MA: Christopher Gordon.

Valencia, S. W. (1990). National survey of the use of reading test data for educational decision-making. In P. Afflerbach (Ed.), *Issues in statewide reading assessment.* Washington, DC: American Institutes for Research.

Valencia, S. W., McGinley, W., & Pearson, P. D. (1990). Assessing reading and writing. In G. Duffy (Ed.), *Reading in the middle school.* Newark, DE: International Reading Association.

Valencia, S. W., & Pearson, P. D. (1987). Reading assessment: Time for a change. *The Reading Teacher, 40,* 726–732.

Vavrus, L. (1990, August). Put portfolios to the test. *Instructor,* 48–53.

Wells, G. (1985). *The meaning makers: Children learning language and using language to learn.* Portsmouth, NH: Heinemann.

Winograd, P. (1984). Strategic difficulties in summarizing texts. *Reading Research Quarterly, 19,* 404–425.

Zimmerman, B. J., Bandura, A., & Martinez-Pons, M. (1992). Self-motivation for academic attainment: The role of self-efficacy beliefs and personal goal setting. *American Educational Research Journal, 29,* 663–676.

CHAPTER 5

Initiating Students to New Learning

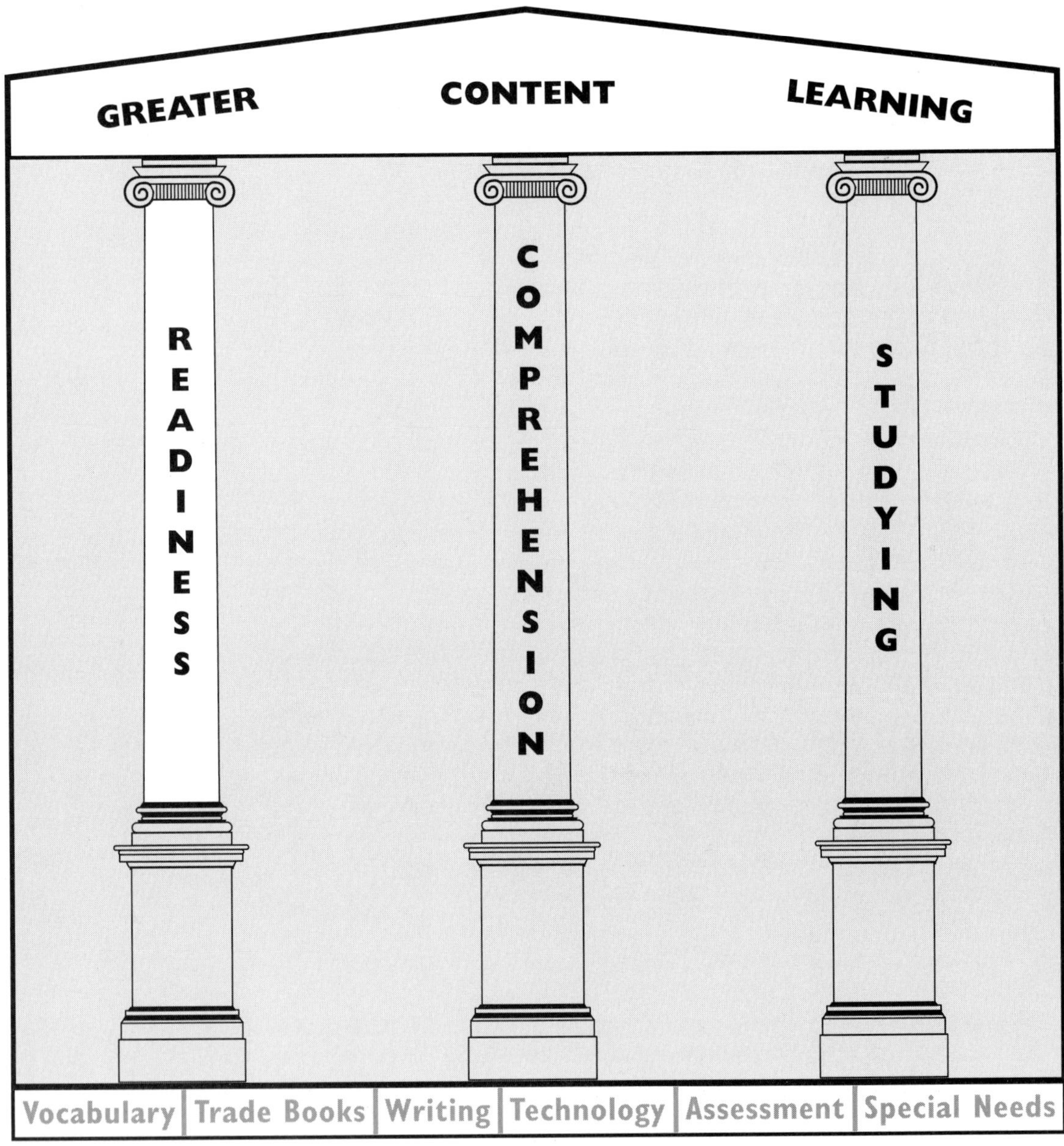

ANTICIPATION GUIDE

Directions: Read each statement carefully and decide whether you agree or disagree with it, placing a check mark in the appropriate *Before Reading* column. When you have finished reading and studying the chapter, return to the guide and decide whether your anticipations need to be changed by placing a check mark in the appropriate *After Reading* column.

	BEFORE READING		**AFTER READING**	
	Agree	*Disagree*	*Agree*	*Disagree*
1. One of the most neglected phases of a content lesson is readiness.	______	______	______	______
2. Most students are automatically motivated to learn new content.	______	______	______	______
3. Students can be helped in setting purposes for reading by being told what to read.	______	______	______	______
4. Writing can be used to prepare for learning.	______	______	______	______
5. Teachers do not have time for readiness activities.	______	______	______	______

It is clear that very little improvement may be expected from formal drill . . . unless at the same time provision is made for the enrichment of experience, the development of language abilities, and the improvement of thinking.

—Ernest Horn (1937)

When Ernest Horn made these comments in 1937, workbooks and skills kits were beginning to flood the reading materials market. These materials were designed to drill students on reading skills and were based on the assumption that drill alone would develop competent readers. Horn's insights into the complex interactions between readers' experiences, language abilities, and cognitive strategies, on the one hand, and the extent to which the context supports meaningful learning during literacy events, on the other, continue to be verified through scholarly research (c.f. Harste, 1989; Hartman, 1995). Today teachers and researchers agree that to create the best conditions for learning, students need to be prepared to learn.

In Chapters 2 and 3, we discussed several important principles of active learning and demonstrated how many useful strategies can be employed by middle and secondary school teachers to promote literacy growth and increase content learning. In this chapter, we explain the important role the preparation phase plays in learning in the content classroom. We argue that when students are adequately prepared for and actively engaged in literacy and content learning activities, their enthusiasm for learning increases and their comprehension of the material improves.

Focus of Chapter 5

Our primary focus in this chapter is on strategies, ideas, and guidelines for preparing students to learn in middle and secondary school classrooms through reading and writing. We also describe class discussion and prediction strategies that teachers have used to help students prepare for listening to lectures. We hope that the principles of effective readiness instruction and the numerous classroom examples described in this chapter will stimulate your own innovative approaches to setting the stage for and engaging students in new learning.

CASE STUDY

Theresa is an eighth-grade social studies teacher. She has noticed that her students appear to have become increasingly uninterested and passive over the past 10 years. Although she has typically taught units from the textbook, her efforts to enlist students in learning social studies content have been moving further and further from the text—with encouraging results. For instance, early in the school year she employed some new strategies to help students develop a broader sense of community responsibility. To her delight, the class took off with the strategy, exhibiting a level of enthusiasm Theresa hadn't seen for some time.

Theresa is in the process of planning a unit on early Native Americans. Last year was the first year she deviated from the textbook approach to teaching about native peoples by having a local Huron tribesman talk to the class about history and

customs. He also shared costumes and artifacts. This year she would like to do more to help students develop a better understanding of what we know about the early Native American cultures and how we learn about these cultures. She wants to devise active, hands-on approaches to engage her class in the study of this important topic.

To the Reader:
As you read and work through this chapter, think about possible strategies and teaching approaches Theresa might use to engage her students in learning about early American cultures. Be prepared to offer your suggestions when we revisit this case study at the conclusion of the chapter.

■ ■ ■

GUIDELINES FOR EFFECTIVE READINESS INSTRUCTION

Engender Interest and Motivation

A self-evident and empirically grounded truth about learning is that students will expend the energy necessary to learn if they are interested in the material (Alexander, Kulikowich, & Hetton, 1994; Renninger, Hidi, & Krapp, 1992; Turner

& Paris, 1995). This is certainly not a recent revelation. Over 80 years ago, John Dewey promoted the idea that when students are interested in a topic or activity they will learn "in a whole-hearted way" (1913, p. 65). Unfortunately, although we all pay lip service to this principle, we often fail to put it into practice. Lack of attention to basic principles of motivation for learning seems to be contributing to a nationwide, and perhaps even a worldwide, decline in students' interest in reading as they move through middle and secondary school (Bintz, 1993).

Current Research Interest in Motivation for Learning

Over the past few years, there has been a resurgence of interest among researchers and practitioners in the influence of motivation on literacy and learning (Gambrell, 1996). The realization that students must have both the *skill* and the *will* to learn has led to a variety of instructional practices designed to support the affective as well as the cognitive aspects of literacy development and school achievement (Cameron & Pierce, 1994). Teachers who motivate for learning do not automatically assume that all students eagerly desire to learn. Instead, they prepare students for learning by helping them become active participants in the learning process, demonstrating how the content can relate to students' lives and concerns, and providing opportunities for students to enjoy learning (Ruddell, 1995).

The Role of Textbooks in Motivation

Another important consideration in sparking motivation and interest in learning for middle and secondary school teachers is the role of the textbook. If you spend any time working with textbooks, you will soon notice that the prose is abstract, formal, and lifeless (Tyson-Bernstein, 1988). To expect students to relish textbook reading is, we believe, unrealistic. Therefore, every effort needs to be made to get students interested in the textbook topic (Hidi & Baird, 1988; Wade, Schraw, Buxton, & Hayes, 1993). This can be accomplished with language experiences, films, games, role playing, guest speakers, field trips, writing, reading-related texts, and fictional works, to name just a few ways. Interest-promoting strategies such as disrupting learners' expectations, challenging them to resolve a paradox, and introducing novel and conflicting information or situations have also been shown to be effective (Mathison, 1989). The unexpected benefit of your efforts to develop imaginative, unique, interest-engendering activities is that you will become more interested in the content as well. And as you know, the more enthusiastic you are about learning, the greater your chance of awakening interest in your students.

Activate and Build Relevant Prior Knowledge

Pearson and Johnson (1978) describe the process of activating and building **relevant prior knowledge** as one of "building bridges between the new and the known." This is a simple yet elegant concept that is neglected far too often in instructional plans.

To demonstrate the importance of being prepared for reading and learning, we have a reading assignment for you. Read the following passage and be prepared to discuss the main points, the supporting details, and the relationships between the themes in the passage and other related passages you have read.

> It is highly unsettling for some to come into close contact with them. Far worse to gain control over them and to deliberately inflict pain on them. The revulsion caused by this punishment is so strong that many will not take part in it at all. Thus there exists a group of people who seem to revel in the contact and the punishment as well as the rewards associated with both. Then there is another group of people who shun the whole enterprise: contact, punishment, and rewards alike.
>
> Members of the first group share modes of talk, dress, and deportment. Members of the second group, however, are as varied as all humanity.
>
> Then there is a group of others, not previously mentioned, for the sake of whose attention all this activity is undertaken. They too harm the victims, though they do it without intention of cruelty. They simply follow their own necessities. And though they may inflict the cruelest punishment of all, sometimes—but not always—they themselves suffer as a result. (Gillet & Temple, 1986, p. 4)

Do you have any idea what this passage is about? Every time we ask our students to read it, they first try desperately to impose a sensible interpretation on the words, offer possibilities that leave them uncomfortable, and finally give up, resorting to protests that sound all too familiar to any classroom teacher: "This is too hard." Most complain that this reading exercise is unfair because the passage has too many unclear referents, which makes it impossible to understand with any certainty. The typical guesses we get include parents and children, concentration camps, corporal punishment, and teachers and students.

Students Need to Warm up to New Learning

With this exercise, we have been able to simulate for you how many students must feel when given reading assignments without any direction, warm-up, or any of the relevant background knowledge necessary for interpreting the statements in the passage. We know that secondary students often finish textbook readings and come away as bewildered as you probably were about the preceding passage.

By the way, the title of the passage is "Fishing Worms." Does that help? Go back and reread it now, and notice as you read how all the ideas seem to fit together, how meaning jumps automatically into consciousness. The title acts as an organizer, a unifying theme, and brings to mind a schema for fishing and worms, which, as discussed in Chapter 2, provides a slot in memory for filing the information presented in this text. Now imagine a ninth grader trying to grapple with the ideas and facts in the following text segment. Without any preparation for this text, the student might find it as unintelligible as our passage above, sans title, was for you.

> A systematic examination of all known rock types shows that two principal kinds predominate. The first are *igneous rocks,* formed by the cooling and crystallization of liquids from deep in the crust or upper part of the

> mantle, called *magmas.* The second are *sedimentary rocks,* formed by compaction and cementation of sediment derived from the continuous erosion of the continents by water, atmosphere, ice, and wind. Most of the sediments are deposited in the sea along the margins of continents. As the marginal piles of sediment grow larger and are buried deeper, increasing pressure and rising temperature produce physical and chemical changes in them. The resulting *metamorphic rocks,* however, generally show whether they were originally sedimentary or igneous rocks. When a sedimentary pile becomes thick enough, material near the bottom may melt to form *magma.* The newly formed magma, being less dense than the rock from which it was derived, will tend to rise up, intruding its parents, and as it cools and crystallizes it will form a new igneous rock.*

Strategies for Building Schemata

What can a teacher do to build a schema and thereby prepare students for reading and learning about rocks in a unit on geology? The possibilities are many and are limited only by the teacher's imagination. The teacher could provide direct experience with rock types by bringing actual examples to class to hold and study. An expert on local geology might give a class demonstration. A field trip to observe natural rock formations could be planned. Students could be asked to find and bring to class examples of rock types. The teacher might prepare a graphic representation of the key vocabulary in the passage depicting the relationships among the ideas. Other high-interest, topically related materials such as Lauber's *Volcano* (1986), a brief but superbly written account of the Mt. St. Helen eruption and its aftermath, could be read before tackling the text. These are only a few suggestions.

For some topics, students will already possess a great deal of background knowledge but simply need to be reminded of what they know. For instance, a class of sophomore history students fails to comprehend the full significance of Julius Caesar's move to publish the activities of the Roman senate. The teacher writes on the board "Jay picks his ears." "Myra sniffs glue." Jay and Myra, students in the class, begin protesting vehemently as the others roar. "The point," she says, "is, how many of you would like to have your foolish acts made public?" Caesar felt that the senators were behaving without decorum, she goes on to explain, and believed that having their behavior posted for all to read would pressure them into changing their ways. She then apologizes to Myra and Jay for libeling them. The teacher, in this example, using information gained from what we might call on-the-spot assessment, modified her instruction to include a concrete example to make her point clearer.

With other topics, students will have great gaps in knowledge that will need to be bridged before they can be expected to profit from their reading and learning (Carr & Thompson, 1996; Gaultney, 1995; McKeown, Beck,

---

*Adapted from Stokes/Judson/Picard, INTRODUCTION TO GEOLOGY: Physical and Historical, 2e, © 1978, pp. 73–75. Adapted by permission of Prentice Hall, Inc., Upper Saddle River, New Jersey.

Sinatra, & Loxterman, 1992). We often take too much for granted when we assign readings or begin lectures or lab activities. We assume students have all the prerequisite knowledge for easy assimilation of the new ideas and facts they will encounter. For instance, in spite of the popularity of a topic such as baseball, many students do not possess a sophisticated baseball schema. Two early studies on the role of prior knowledge in comprehension demonstrated that students who were similar in reading ability performed differently on a comprehension exercise concerning a passage about baseball, depending on their level of prior knowledge about that subject (Spilich, Vesonder, Chiesi, & Voss, 1979). Similarly, Hayes and Tierney (1980) found that high school students who had difficulty reading and recalling newspaper reports of cricket matches improved their performance dramatically when they received instruction on the nature of the game of cricket before reading the newspaper reports. Findings such as these have been replicated in numerous studies over the past decade (Pressley, Johnson, Symons, McGoldrick, & Kurita, 1989; Symons & Pressley, 1993).

Help Set Meaningful Purposes for Learning

Nearly 30 years ago, Illich advocated a curriculum that engendered "self-motivated learning instead of employing teachers to bribe or compel the student to find the time and the will to learn" (1970, p. 104). Two decades later (Gambrell & Morrow, 1995; Schiefele, 1991), Illich's recommendation is as viable as ever. Students become independent knowledge seekers when they perceive what they are learning to be personally meaningful and relevant to their lives and futures. So on one level, we are suggesting that meaningful purposes for learning can be established only when the learning itself is meaningful.

Meaningful Learning Leads to Meaningful Purposes

On a practical level, setting meaningful purposes for learning is essential to remaining focused on an activity. For example, consider this often-repeated scenario. You are assigned a textbook chapter to read as homework. As you read, you realize that your eyes just seem to be moving over words; you're not sure what to concentrate on or what to gloss over. You decide to try to remember facts, but you're not sure why. You realize that you have not been given any direction on *how* to read. In other words, you have not been provided a *purpose* for reading, and figuring out what you are expected to recall as a result of your reading becomes a matter of guesswork. Unfortunately, by studying the facts of the chapter, you guessed incorrectly. Your examination on the chapter is an essay test with conceptual questions. There is a bright spot in this story, however. At least you attempted to set your own purpose for reading, even though you were not provided with one. Many students have not learned to establish a reason for reading before they begin a reading assignment. We have a responsibility for setting clear expectations for students when making reading assignments, and for showing students how to read to meet those expectations. Furthermore, we all need to provide instruction in helping students learn how to set their own purposes for reading.

This guideline applies equally to lectures, labs, and other learning experiences in addition to reading. Students should be made aware of what they are about to learn and, more important, why the content is being discussed and studied. To tell students that "You must learn this because I say so" is not a meaningful purpose for learning. Instead, try to make students aware of real-world purposes for learning. That is, by linking the learning of course content to students' own needs, issues, concerns, and interests inside and outside of school, we can show them the function and meaningfulness of learning: for instance, demonstrating for the athletes in a math class how math can be used to compile sports statistics.

Preteach Critical Concepts and Vocabulary

Emphasize the Most Important Concepts in Preteaching

With some content, particularly content for which students have limited schemata, deciding how much to preteach can seem overwhelming. Obviously, all new concepts and all unfamiliar terms cannot be taught. Some researchers (Nagy, Anderson, & Herman, 1987) have speculated that if teachers concentrated on teaching students unfamiliar words, that is all they would have time to do every day! We recommend here, as we recommend throughout this book, that when deciding what to preteach—or, for that matter, when deciding on any content to teach—emphasize the *most important* ideas and information to be learned. Not all information is vital; not all of it needs to be taught directly, nor should it be. Normally, students are under the impression that every idea and each bit of information in a chapter is of equal importance. The ways in which you prepare students to learn can help dispel this misconception.

CHANNELING KNOWLEDGE AND INTEREST WITH READINESS STRATEGIES

Direct Experiences

While the learning styles debate goes on, one self-evident truth about teaching and learning is that nothing beats direct experience for anchoring new information in memory. As students move through the grades, content becomes increasingly abstract and disconnected from their day-to-day lives. Simple narratives become replaced by complex expository prose; neighborhood and community topics fade away as world-level issues are introduced; manipulatives disappear as students are asked to master complex scientific and mathematical processes using mental operations. Yet, middle and secondary school students continue to need *grounded* approaches to learning that help them make tangible connections to increasingly abstract ideas and processes. Concrete, firsthand learning activities become experiential referents for future learning.

Direct experiences can include any type of field trip. Middle and secondary school teachers in the Detroit area, for instance, often take advantage of the living history museum of Greenfield Village. On more than 100 acres, Henry Ford preserved such American relics as Edison's New Jersey laboratory with the original light bulb and phonographic inventions, the Wright brothers' original bicycle shop, and Henry Ford's garage where his first automobile was built and where the garage wall had to be broken open to allow clearance for the car. Additionally, there are active wheelwrights, coopers, glass blowers, and blacksmiths, along with an original inn serving food in the style of the 1850s. This is a grand site for providing students with a firsthand look at the history of the 19th century. Outside of Seattle, teachers can take students to authentic Indian villages to see dwellings, totems, customs, dress, and more. Along the Texas Gulf, students and teachers journey frequently to the seashore to witness whooping cranes and roseate spoonbills in their winter habitat, endangered species of all kinds in the Arkansas Wildlife Refuge, the state aquarium, and the University of Texas marine biology research center on Padre Island. But even as field trips become less and less common in schools due to costs, logistics, and liability, creative ways can be devised to bring hands-on learning into the classroom.

Experiential Learning Examples

Judy, a sixth-grade science teacher, borrowed her school's old home economics room with its four ovens for a class experiment. She arranged several food items, mixing bowls, and pizza tins on a table at the front of the room. She told her students that they were home alone and were hungry for pizza; however, without money to buy a pizza and no pizzas in the freezer, they would have to create one with the ingredients on the table. Judy divided the class into groups of three, gave each group a sheet for recording the steps involved in their pizza-making adventure, and told them to get started. Under her watchful eye, the groups discussed and gathered, mixed, poured, stirred, baked, and laughed their way through this discovery process. After the fun, Judy asked each group to show off its "pizza," identify its ingredients, and describe the steps taken to create it. Brave volunteers stepped forward to taste test the pizzas. After the class cleaned up and resettled, Judy gave the groups a handout with a detailed description of the five steps of the scientific method. On a poster board with the same five steps listed, she and the students wrote out how the steps they took to create their pizzas corresponded with the steps in the scientific method.

Judy's hands-on class experience satisfied several goals of readiness instruction. First, it immediately generated a great deal of enthusiasm on the part of the class. Second, students were allowed to become purposeful learners as they searched for the best possible ingredients and steps to create pizzas from scratch. Finally, the pizza-making activity provided students with an experiential referent for their ongoing study of the scientific method. In fact, throughout the next several days and weeks, Judy constantly referred back to the pizza-making adventure to remind students of a related aspect of the scientific method they were studying.

Role Playing and Simulations

Martin teaches history to 10th-grade learning-disabled students in a self-contained classroom. One of his principal objectives for a unit about how the American colonies gained their freedom is to develop a thorough understanding of the concept of *taxation without representation.* Martin knew that in the past his students were reasonably excited about the topic, but he found in his assessments that they failed to grasp the significance of the essential concepts leading to a full understanding of the antecedents and consequences of the American Revolution. Martin also knew that the more he transformed lifeless textual information into something tangible and personal, the greater the students' involvement and the more they seemed to learn.

Role Plays Encourage Active Involvement

As a motivator and as a way of personalizing the concept, Martin had his class participate in a simulation activity. He called it a *government experiment* as he handed out written directions and guided the class through them. The students were divided into two groups: one was called the "Oros" and the other, the "Bindus." Martin appointed himself the king of the Oros. Each group was given a set of directions for electing representatives to make laws or rules. The Bindus were told they could only make rules that applied to themselves, while the Oros could impose rules on the Bindus if they chose. Each group also was given a lump sum of 1,000 play dollars for its treasury.

Martin, as king of the Oros, immediately began imposing laws on the Bindus that roughly paralleled the Stamp Act and the Tea Act. The "Paper and Pencil Rule" taxed every Bindu 5 cents for every pencil, pen, and piece of paper used; the "Pop Rule" taxed the Bindus 10 cents for having a soda or any other drink in class (Martin permitted his students to have soft drinks in the classroom). Interestingly, the turn of events in Martin's classroom resembled what had happened between the British and the American colonies. Complaining fell on deaf ears, so at first the Bindus gave in to the Oros's rules. Soon, however, the Bindus began to protest—first by not bringing paper or pencils to class and then by simply ignoring the rule and disdainfully using as many sheets of paper and pencils they wished. The same thing happened with their soda drinking. Soon the Bindus were challenging the Oros's authority by drinking without paying taxes. By week's end, the Oros were debating among themselves as to whether they should drop the taxes or impose penalties and stiffer taxes, while the Bindus were prepared to resist at all costs.

At this point, Martin asked the class to analyze their situation. The Bindus argued that it was extremely unfair for a separate group of people to tell them what to do. They said that they wanted and were able to take care of themselves. One student put it succinctly to the Oros: "What gives you the right to tax us?" The Oros had never really considered this question. They behaved as though there was only one way to behave. Martin took advantage of the students' self-discovery about what can happen when one group imposes rules on another group against their will by having the students draw parallels to the conditions that led to war between the British and the colonies. He asked students to divide a sheet of paper in half. On one side, they were to list the rules imposed by the Oros and the Bindus's reactions to those rules. Then, as they read and studied the chapter, they were to list on the other side of the sheet the events that took place in colonial America just before the Revolutionary War.

Brian introduced the study of carbon bonding to his chemistry class through one of the most unique and clever activities we have ever witnessed. With the desks moved to the walls of the classroom leaving a large open area in the middle, Brian asked his students to stand up and then distributed paper bag vests to each of them that were labeled with a large, colorful H, C, or O (for hydrogen, carbon, and oxygen). After students donned the vests, he gave a fellow teacher a printed square dance call. He then pulled out a fiddle from its case, and with everyone set, he started to play the "Carbon Bonding Hoedown" as the square dance caller called the moves. Meanwhile, students moved around the room searching for partners; by the conclusion of the square dance, all carbon atoms had bonded appropriately, as represented by the students and their vests. Everyone had fun with this activity, and it formed a meaningful introduction to the exploration of the topic. It also provided the class with a memorable experience to which Brian could refer as they progressed through the study of carbon atoms and carbon bonding.

Role Plays Can Be Fun—Even in Chemistry

In yet another excellent simulation experience, Jennifer prepared her sixth graders for the study of westward expansion by setting up a wagonmaster election. After asking four students to join her, she formed groups of three with the rest of the class. The groups were given a scenario describing that they were pioneers in the 1850s about to go on an adventure to the West. Before they took their trip, however, they needed to select the best possible wagonmaster for the job. Groups were given rating sheets with critical criteria for a good wagonmaster, such as being experienced in dealing with Indians, knowledgeable about the best water sources and smoothest trails, and so on. Meanwhile, the four students Jennifer had chosen were to be the individuals vying for the job of wagonmaster. Each was given a name, a brief biography, and a few minutes to prepare for his pitch to the pioneers. When ready, each character, like "Calico Cody," told the groups in impassioned tones why he was the best suited for the job, given the many successful wagon trains he had led back and forth across Indian territories. After all wagonmaster candidates presented themselves, the pioneers checked their ratings and voted on their top choice. This activity and the discussion that followed served as a highly motivating and instructive way to prepare students for the topic.

Role Playing in History Class

Debates and Discussions

As we have said throughout this book, there are obvious differences between classrooms where students are expected to be passive receivers of information and ideas and classrooms where students are active participants in the learning process. Being a good lecturer in the middle and upper grades is not enough; students learn and remember best when they participate (Barton, 1995).

Cheng, a ninth-grade teacher, used writing, cooperative learning, and a class debate in the form of a mock trial to arouse students' interest in the topic of equal rights and opportunities in their American citizenship class. Cheng introduced students to the topic by dividing them into two groups. First, he had the students read about laws and regulations developed in the United States to promote equal opportunity. Then he distributed a written scenario of discrimination to Group 1 and an alternative version of the same scenario to Group 2.

Group 1: You are the lawyers representing the Jackson family in a court case. Mr. and Mrs. Jackson wanted to buy a large house in an upper-middle-class suburb of a major city. They found a house for sale by the owner that was just the right size for themselves and their two children. The Jacksons called in advance to set up an appointment to see the house. The owner, Mr. Simon, was discourteous when the Jacksons arrived and let them into his house only after telling them he was convinced it would soon be sold to another party.

The Jacksons were very impressed with Mr. Simon's house. They were told by their bank that if they chose to buy the house, they would be approved for a loan. When the Jacksons contacted Mr. Simon the next day to make an offer, he told them he was not going to sell it to them. When asked why, he said flatly that he "preferred not to."

Mr. and Mrs. Jackson were very upset. They felt that they were being denied the house because they were African-American.

As the lawyers for the Jacksons, your job is to convince the judge that Mr. Simon was discriminating against the Jacksons on the basis of their race. In your group:

1. List as many reasons as you can why the Jackson family should be allowed to buy Mr. Simon's house. Make sure your arguments make sense and seem fair.
2. Choose a spokesperson who will present your case to the judge.

Group 2: You are the lawyers representing Mr. Simon in a court case. Mr. Simon is a hard-working, law-abiding citizen who has owned his large suburban home for 17 years.

A couple of months ago, he came home from work late in the evening. As he attempted to unlock his front door, he was accosted by two men, who forced him inside at gunpoint. For the next hour, one of the thieves held a gun to his head while the other raced through the house taking valuables and money. Before leaving, the men took Mr. Simon's wallet, watch, and jewelry, then knocked him unconscious. The two robbers were African-American.

Word of the incident swept through the all-white suburb, where fear was mixed with disgust.

Mr. Simon decided to sell his house and move to a more rural part of the state to get away from the crime influence of a nearby large city. An African-American family, the Jacksons, looked through his house and wanted to buy it, but Mr. Simon chose not to sell to them.

Mr. Simon is now being sued by the Jacksons because they feel they were unfairly discriminated against because of their race.

As the lawyers for Mr. Simon, your job is to convince the judge that he, as owner of the property, has the right to decide who may or may not purchase his home. In your group:

1. List as many reasons as you can why Mr. Simon has the right to make the decision he made. Make sure your arguments make sense and seem fair.
2. Choose a spokesperson who will present your case to the judge.

Cheng gave both groups enough time to generate arguments and formulate a defense for their respective clients. He then identified himself as the judge and asked the spokesperson for the Jacksons and Mr. Simon to present their cases. Afterward, Cheng invited further comment from the rest of the class. He thanked the groups for their fine work and said the next step would involve doing more research on how similar cases were resolved in the past. At this point, Cheng directed the students to a section in their textbook that discussed several similar discrimination cases and asked them to read it carefully for homework.

Debates Lead to Higher-Level Thinking

By having his students work together to think about, write, and present their ideas and beliefs, Cheng used conflicting perspectives to generate arguments and discussion about the topic of equal rights. After this activity, students brought a heightened level of enthusiasm and interest to their textbook reading assignment because they were anxious to discover how discrimination cases similar to theirs had been resolved in the past.

Cheng's class readiness activity demonstrates clearly how student talk can lead to meaning making and intertextual tying—critical prerequisites for future learning. With simple and effective class discussions as students begin to explore a new topic, teachers can assess how much students already know about the topic and vary the degree or emphasis of preteaching relative to what they discover. In addition, teachers who use discussion create a learning environment that fosters a free exchange of different viewpoints, which helps students actively shape their own knowledge and enrich and refine their understandings of a topic (Alvermann et al., 1996; Barnitz, 1994; Unrau & Ruddell, 1995).

Teachers who desire to exploit the learning potential of class discussion often tend to undermine it by doing most of the talking and asking most of the questions (Alvermann, O'Brien, & Dillon, 1990; Barton, 1995). These practices inhibit rather than foster the enrichment of understanding through the exchange of viewpoints. The goal is to encourage and orchestrate discussions that result in more student-student interaction patterns rather than student-teacher patterns (Alvermann, Dillon, & O'Brien, 1988; Guzzetti & Williams, 1996). The following alternatives to questioning and teacher-dominated discussions provide strategies for increasing student involvement in class talk and discussion:

- Make a declarative or factual statement.
- Make a reflective statement.
- Describe the student's state of mind.
- Invite the student to elaborate on a statement.

- Encourage the student to ask a question.
- Encourage students to ask questions of one another.
- Maintain a deliberate silence.
- Encourage other students to answer questions posed to you.
- Help students link new information to their prior knowledge.
- Model good listening strategies.
- Allow for small-group brainstorming first before whole-group interaction.

The following example demonstrates how a teacher can employ effective student-centered discussion strategies in preparation for reading and learning.

Discussion Activates Prior Knowledge

An economics class preparing to read and learn about the effects of a recession on the economy watched as the teacher wrote the word *recession* in large letters on the board. Without saying anything, he waited for students to react, question, and elaborate. In no time, students began to make associations with the word. These initial associations with the concept provided students with the opportunity to find associations with their prior knowledge. As students answered, the teacher wrote their responses on the board while purposely avoiding reacting to every response. Responses such as "inflation" and "higher gas prices" were typical, but everyone was surprised to hear the word "grounded" shouted out by a student in the corner. Instead of asking a question himself, the teacher asked if anyone had a question for this student. Students were eager to find out what "grounded" had to do with recession and pressed the student for an explanation. She explained that she had once inflated her parents' already whopping phone bill during a financially tight period that she said was caused by a recession. Her parents punished her by taking away her phone privileges and restricting her after-school activity for a couple of weeks. By using discussion as a readiness-to-learn activity, the teacher helped students develop an awareness of their network of associations and allowed them to listen to one another, weigh, reject, revise, and integrate ideas in their own minds. The grounded student's contribution turned out to be very profitable because the textbook chapter they were assigned to read devoted a major section to the everyday, personal effects of a recession.

After the discussion, the teacher restated students' initial associations with the concept. This allowed students to reflect on their own thinking and offer any new ideas about the concept *recession.* They could verbalize associations that had been elaborated or changed through the discussion and probe their memories to expand on their prior knowledge. Interestingly, several other personal connections with the topic were discovered. One student talked about having to limit his "cruising" because he couldn't afford to waste gas. Another mentioned that his brother had to put off buying a house because interest rates were too high. When the class ended, the students had a better idea of how much they knew about the topic, and the teacher, who encouraged student-centered discussion, had a good picture of his students' existing knowledge. With this information, the preparatory phase of instruction can be adjusted.

Guest Speakers and Performers

We watched the eyes of a group of seventh graders grow to saucer proportions as a local ornithologist walked into the classroom with a great horned owl on one arm and an osprey on the other—both nearly 2 feet tall! The guest speaker explained the life habits of these birds of prey and gave demonstrations. Students asked questions and were nearly able to touch the birds as they gathered around the speaker. It was a memorable day for Diane's science class, especially when the osprey unexpectedly let out a loud whistling call. Thus began Diane's unit on birds of prey.

A group of Alamo battle reenactors tumbled into Hector's eighth-grade history classroom, including a Mexican soldier, a Tennessee volunteer, and a Texas frontiersman. Outfitted in authentic attire, carrying authentic weaponry, and remaining in character for the entire class period, these three performers talked about their lives and the events at the Alamo as though the battle had happened yesterday. Thus, students began the study of the Alamo with the help of these memorable guests.

In both of these cases, Diane, the science teacher, and Hector, the history teacher, were clever enough to recognize the power of bringing into class members of the community with expert knowledge. Students began their study of the topics with increased anticipation and excitement, as well as with a store of useful new knowledge to help them better negotiate the texts and ideas to follow.

Guest Speakers Are an Underexploited Teaching Resource

We believe that guest speakers and performers are perhaps the most underused resources teachers can gather. Even in the remotest communities there is a wealth of knowledge to be tapped—from individuals who lived through critical times in history, to local authors and artists, to members of the political, industrial, and scientific worlds. Often local municipalities have information services about local experts. Colleges and universities have public information offices with names and addresses of professors and notes on their areas of expertise. We recently contacted a city office for information about local Native American groups and were put in touch with a couple of organizations that supplied guest speakers to a ninth-grade teacher's classroom.

We agree with Hoss (1991) and others (*Learning,* 1996) who state that to get the most out of guest speakers and performers, students as well as guests should be prepared. Students should be given time to generate questions, while guests should know in advance your expectations for their visit, how much time they will have, and any special requests. These preparation procedures can avoid potential problems such as embarrassing comments, rambling, or information unrelated to the topic.

Toni, a high school chemistry teacher, invited to her class a woman friend who was an organic chemist in the research and development department of a large local company. She had her students spend a couple of class periods preparing for the guest speaker by first brainstorming their areas of interest about which the guest would likely have information; these included original discoveries and patents, new and future uses of polymers, employment opportunities for women in chemistry, and the day-to-day operation of an R&D department. Toni then asked her students to form small groups based on their interests and generate a set of 10 questions each that they would like answered by the guest chemist. Toni looked over the questions and helped each group refine its list to five good questions. Meanwhile, Toni contacted her friend and told her what the students were most interested in learning. This information made it possible for the chemist to prepare effectively for the classroom visit.

When the day arrived, the school newspaper and science club wanted to cover the presentation, so a video camera was set up to record the event. The chemist gave a brief overview and then asked for questions. Each group was given the opportunity to ask all five of its questions in a set to avoid forcing the guest speaker to jump from topic to topic in a disjointed way. She brought in examples of products developed by her center, as well as diagrams, notes, and computer graphics on future developments. She talked from experience about her interest and schooling in chemistry and the process of gaining employment in the company. She described how patents are obtained and showed the class some of the patented products for which she was responsible. Finally, using a CD-ROM presentation, she took the class through a computer-simulated field trip of her R&D center.

READING YOUNG ADULT LITERATURE TO BUILD PRIOR KNOWLEDGE AND GENERATE INTEREST

Teachers often ask how they can get their students interested in topics about which they themselves are not especially excited. Take a typical topic in art appreciation or history, for example. In such a case, many teachers would be inclined to simply assign the textbook reading, show slides, and then lecture, although they know that students' interest will be minimal. As an alternative, we suggest that they consider reading aloud or asking students to read one of the many outstanding trade books that deal with art and painting, such as Brock Cole's *Celine* (1989), Zibby Oneal's *In Summer Light* (1985) and *The Language of Goldfish* (1990), and Richard Peck's *Unfinished Portrait of Jessica* (1993). In addition to galvanizing the students with their narrative, these stories indirectly provide readers with a living context for art that makes the facts and details more palatable.

Nonfiction Books Can Build Prior Knowledge

Students can also be introduced to topics with nonfiction books. Many teens, especially boys, prefer nonfiction to fiction (Herz & Gallo, 1996). Unfortunately, their experiences with nonfiction in school are usually limited to textbooks (Clary, 1991), which may contribute to their lack of interest in the first place. Many junior and senior high students are never exposed to nonfiction books that have been written specifically for them. The numbers of nonfiction titles for adolescents grows annually, making it easier for classroom teachers to identify appropriate books to incorporate into their content lessons.

Alicia Appleman-Jarman's *Alicia: My Story* (1988) could be offered as a prelude to the study of the Nazis and the Jews during World War II. An autobiography, this gripping account of a young woman who survived the Holocaust is filled with facts and details that help students better understand that tragic period in world history. Relevant prior knowledge of boreal ecosystems could be acquired by reading *Dance of the Wolves* (Peters, 1985), the story of a young researcher's study of wolves in northern Michigan. For students about to begin a creative writing unit, *Chapters: My Growth as a Writer* (Duncan, 1982) is a splendid prelude. This autobiography of a popular young adult writer appeals to adolescents who aspire to a career in writing. With nonfiction books such as these, students develop schemata while reading an interesting and palatable alternative to the textbook. (See Chapter 8 for a comprehensive discussion of strategies for using trade books in the classroom.)

Purpose-Setting Strategies

Many highly effective classroom strategies have been designed to help middle and secondary students set purposes for their reading and develop an anticipatory set for their reading and learning. In this section, we demonstrate how three particularly useful strategies—prediction, KWL, and anticipation guides—can be used to help students set meaningful purposes for and encourage higher-level thinking about class topics. Furthermore, these strategies induce students to attend to text more closely, interact with text in more meaningful ways, and combine their world knowledge with text information, resulting in new understandings.

Prediction

One excellent way of helping students set their own purposes for reading is with prediction activities (Hennings, 1991). Anderson (1984) has proposed that this technique is consistent with a schema-theoretic perspective of optimal reading because it helps students integrate meaningfully what they already know with what is presented on the printed page. Using a **prediction** technique, students either simply generate some form of prediction in advance of reading or read titles, headings, subheadings, or a short segment of text and, based on this limited information, predict what they expect to read in the passage. In this way, they become aware of their prior knowledge and begin to organize what they already know about the subject at hand. By making predictions, they anticipate what they will find in the text, leading them to read for the purpose of finding out if their predictions are corroborated. Countless methods can be used to help students anticipate the content of their reading.

A Prediction Activity in Journalism Class

A wonderful example of the effectiveness of using prediction for purpose setting was provided by a senior high journalism teacher. He was instructing students in editorial writing by sharing examples of editorials and analyzing them.

He handed out a sheet of paper with the title "A No-Lose Proposition," by Stanley J. Lieberman, and the first paragraph, which read:

> America is the most litigious society in the world. We are suing each other at an alarming and increasing rate, and we have more lawyers per capita than any other nation. Since 1950 the number of lawyers in America has increased 250 percent. We have well over half a million lawyers—one for every 450 people. In New York state the ratio is one lawyer per 18. By contrast, the ratio in West Germany is one lawyer per 2,000.

After reading this material, the students worked in small groups and discussed the possible directions the editorial might take, given the title and the first paragraph. Each group was to make two predictions. The teacher moved around the room, listening in on each group, assisting when asked. Next, each group's predictions were presented to the whole class while the teacher wrote them on the board. A lengthy and immensely beneficial discussion then ensued, which included a class-derived definition of *litigious* and an impassioned defense of lawyers by a student whose father and mother were attorneys. An impressive amount of background and related knowledge poured out, as did the exchange and exploration of biases, opinions, and beliefs. The teacher played a facilitative role during the discussion. He prodded when necessary, refocused the conversation when it seemed to stray too far from the task of determining what the author was likely to say in the passage, and clarified points and details. When the debate over which predictions were likely to be verified by the text wound down, the students were eager to finish reading the editorial. Three agreed-on predictions remained on the board, and the students were reminded to read and discover to what extent, if any, the text supported them. After reading, the class discussed the accuracy of their predictions. No one had foreseen that the author would make a pitch for mediation as a way to unblock a clogged court system, although one prediction anticipated some kind of workable solution to this problem based on the editorial's title.

Reflect for a moment on how the preceding scene differs from the way a typical reading assignment is given—with little or no preparation or direction. By the time these students were ready to read the editorial, they had activated and elaborated their schemata for *lawyer* and related legal issues, they had developed an interest in the topic through small-group and whole-class discussions that challenged beliefs and biases and piqued curiosity, and they had developed their own purposes for reading. As a result, attention to the text and comprehension could not help but improve.

Predictions Are Like Hypotheses

Schema theorists say that reading comprehension involves constant hypothesis testing. Predictions are like hypotheses that can be confirmed, refined, extended, or rejected using evidence from the text. In this process, original predictions give way to new predictions as new information from the text is encountered, thus setting further purposes for reading.

Many variations on the prediction theme can help students develop an anticipatory set for the text information. In a 12th-grade sociology class preparing to read about the benefits and limitations of day-care centers, the teacher posed this problem:

> If you were a parent who needed to work to keep the family going, yet you desperately wanted to spend more time with your children, what would you do?

In cooperative learning groups, the students talked among themselves, proposing solutions to the problem. After the entire class discussed possible solutions, their strengths, and their limitations, the teacher invited them to read the essay and find out how a working parent handled this dilemma. The students now had a purpose for reading.

A ninth-grade science class preparing to read a chapter on genetic engineering was given this statement:

> Since scientists have already cloned animals as large as sheep, making exact replicas of dogs, cats, and even human beings through the process of cloning may be possible within the next few years.

The students were then asked to generate five questions based on this statement that were likely to be answered as a result of reading the chapter. After reading, they told which, if any, of their questions were answered. These students also had a purpose for reading.

In a seventh-grade health class, students working in cooperative groups were asked to generate as many words as they could within 3 minutes related to the concept *necessities to sustain life.* At the end of the 3 minutes, students were asked to arrange their words into subcategories and to be prepared to explain the logic behind them. One group clustered their words around *necessities for the body* (oxygen, food, water), *necessities for the heart* (relationships, religion), and *necessities for the mind* (books, music, art). Another group categorized their words with *work* and *fun.* After this exploration of what they already knew about the topic, students were asked to use their words and categories to predict what the reading assignment would be about. Once again, we see how this prediction strategy helped students develop purposes for reading.

Remember, prediction strategies can work equally well before lectures and experiential, hands-on activities such as labs and field trips.

From these examples, you can see that the list of ways of helping students set purposes for reading is limited only by the teacher's imagination. Other variations on the prediction strategy include KWL and anticipation guides.

KWL

KWL focuses on the student as a strategic learner and is based on three principal components: (1) recalling what is **known,** (2) determining what students **want** to learn, and (3) identifying what is **learned** (Carr & Ogle, 1987; Ogle, 1986). We strongly endorse this strategy because it can be carried out before, during, and after reading. Before reading, the student activates background knowledge and sets a purpose for reading; during reading, the student thinks critically about information and monitors learning; and after reading, the student integrates and consolidates the information read. Here we focus on the before-reading benefits of the strategy.

To give you a better idea of the kind of thinking involved in the KWL strategy, let us assume you were asked by the professor using the book to employ the strategy for Chapter 5, the chapter you are reading now. First, you would be directed to read the title, "Initiating Students to New Learning," and in small cooperative groups or as a whole class, you would brainstorm and discuss ideas and information you already hold in prior knowledge about the topic. Through discussion, a good deal of known information will be generated, and unresolved points and unanswered questions also will likely emerge. These will be saved and referred to later as issues about which you desire further information. So, after brainstorming and discussing, you would have a collection of ideas and facts about the chapter topic listed on a chart in the *K* (what is ***known***) column.

KWL as Applied to This Chapter

In the next phase before reading, you would be asked to generate questions based on questions you would like answered by the text. Questions come from the brainstorming and discussion, as well as anticipated information you think will be encountered in the text. These questions comprise the entries in the second column on the chart: *W* (what you *want* to learn). By developing questions in this way, you will tend to define for yourself your purpose for reading. The result is that your reading and self-monitoring during reading will be more focused. As you read, you will pause periodically to monitor your comprehension by checking the questions from the *W* column that can be answered by what you have read. As new information is encountered, additional questions can be added to the list. Thus, purposes are refined and extended throughout reading.

Figure 5.1 depicts what you might have generated for the first two columns of the KWL chart. As you read, you would note in the *L* column new information and information that helps answer the questions you posed in the *W* column. After reading, you would be asked to discuss what you have learned from your reading. You would review the questions asked before and during reading to determine if and how they were answered. For example, in Figure 5.1, the first three questions in the *W* column can be answered fairly thoroughly with the information in this chapter. For the last question, which would remain unresolved because this chapter does not specifically discuss the Directed-Reading-Thinking-Activity strategy, you would be encouraged to conduct some personal research to gather further information about this aspect of the topic. Perhaps the professor would direct you to additional secondary reading methods textbooks or to journal articles that deal with the topic of using Directed-Reading-Thinking-Activity as a prereading strategy.

The KWL strategy can be applied in a variety of content areas with a range of text material. Figure 5.2, for example, is a KWL chart created by an eighth grader reading about the formation of mountains. In this example, note that the student appeared to have little prior knowledge on the topic. As a result of a liberal exchange of ideas in small groups and with the whole class, she asked some excellent questions (in the *W* column) that were answered by the reading. In

K (Known)	W (Want to Know)	L (Learned)
Reading readiness is important for beginning readers. Schema theory says prior knowledge for a topic makes it easer to read about that topic. One strategy is to read the introduction and conclusion before reading the chapter.	What can the classroom teacher do to prepare students for reading assignments? Why is readiness important for secondary school reading? What are all the things that should be done during readiness? Is Directed-Reading-Thinking-Activity a good readiness strategy?	

FIGURE 5.1 KWL Chart for Chapter 5

K	W	L
Volcanoes help form mountains. The Rocky mountains are very tall.	Do mountains grow? How do they erode? Why are the Rockies taller than the Smokies?	Mountains form when heat within the earth pushes bedrock up. Lava forces its way up and hardens into rock, causing mountains to grow bigger. Rain and wind wear them down. Mountains are part of a cycle—ocean sediment to solid rock pushed up to form mountains, then worn down into the sea again. Mountains in the eastern U.S. are very old. Mountains in the West are not as old.

FIGURE 5.2 An Eighth Grader's KWL Chart for the Formation of Mountains

cases in which students' questions cannot be answered by the text, many teachers will ask students to pursue answers to these questions through research and present their findings to the class.

Students will develop the ability to use the KWL strategy on their own through instruction that gradually shifts responsibility for initiating the strategy from you to your students (Carr & Ogle, 1987). After you introduce the strategy with a textbook example and model KWL thinking by describing how you would develop a chart, you should ask students to implement it on their own. Cooperative groups are ideal for helping learn and extend expertise with the strategy. Your role should gradually become one of providing feedback, informally observing, discussing, and reinforcing independence and transfer. As with most content area reading/writing/learning strategies, you can improve the likelihood that students will use this strategy on their own if you demonstrate how using KWL to activate prior knowledge and set purposes for reading facilitates their class performance and helps meet your expectations for learning.

Anticipation Guides

Another highly regarded strategy for activating prior knowledge of text topics and helping students set purposes for reading is the **anticipation guide.** You should be somewhat familiar with this strategy already since you have been asked to complete an anticipation guide for each chapter of this book. This strategy involves giving students a list of statements about the topic to be studied and asking them to respond to them before reading. Guides are particularly useful when they provoke disagreement and challenge students' beliefs about a topic. They should reinforce relevant prior knowledge and modify misconceptions about the topic (Duffelmeyer & Baum, 1992). This function seems especially important given growing research evidence indicating that students' existing prior knowledge and biases will be superimposed on text information when the two are at odds (Marshall, 1989). In other words, if misconceptions about a topic are not cleared up before reading, they may still exist after reading.

Anticipation guides should contain statements that are text and reader based. In addition, Duffelmeyer (1994) recommends the inclusion of certain statements that force students to reconsider existing beliefs. He suggests that four kinds of statements have the potential to do this: (1) those that are related to the major ideas students will encounter; (2) those that activate students' prior knowledge; (3) those that are general rather than specific; and (4) those that challenge students' beliefs. We recommend that guide statements be written to appear correct but incompatible with the information students will encounter or to seem incorrect yet compatible with the information to follow.

Effective Anticipation Guide Statements

The response format for anticipation guides should follow criteria similar to those of study guides. Students should not be asked to write extended answers to questions that resemble discussion or essay questions. Instead, have students respond with simple check marks or brief statements. But make sure the guide includes a feature that tests and confronts students' beliefs. Additionally, we suggest that guides have the extended feature (Duffelmeyer & Baum, 1992). This feature requires students to verify their responses after reading and encountering new content. This form of accountability guards against students making random responses without careful thinking.

Look at Part I of the anticipation guide designed for a health class shown in Figure 5.3. We would like you to respond to this guide so that you will have a better understanding of the points we have just made.

If we had assigned you to use this anticipation guide for an upcoming reading assignment or lecture on diet and nutrition, we would ask you first to meet in small groups and then, with the entire class, to discuss your viewpoints and share information and ideas. As you and other students debate and defend your responses, we would remain neutral by not giving away answers or taking over the discussion. Periodically, we would restate points of view or try to clarify ideas.

The extended feature of this guide is presented in Part II (Figure 5.4). It adds further learning potential to the activity by forcing you to self-interrogate and interact more elaboratively with the text. Part II requires you to find ideas and information from the text or the lecture that either reinforce and verify your existing beliefs, force them to be altered or modified, or require you to completely reject them. During reading and exploration of a topic, as you encounter information related to the statements in Part I of the guide, you are asked to indicate whether the text or lecture material supports or does not support what you had previously asserted. In Part II you would be required to write where you found information that supported your initial anticipations. This can be written in the form of page numbers from a textbook, or class note entries. You would also write information that *corrects* unanticipated information.

Directions: Read each statement. If you believe that a statement is true, place a check in the *Agree* column. If you believe the statement is false, place a check in the *Disagree* column. Be ready to explain your choices.

Agree	Disagree	
______	______	1. About 45% of the total food dollar is spent on food away from home.
______	______	2. More cookbooks are being purchased today than ever before.
______	______	3. Soft drinks are essentially sugar.
______	______	4. The average person's diet consists of between 60% and 70% fat and sugar.
______	______	5. People are eating fewer fruits today than in the 1940s.
______	______	6. Many so-called primitive cultures have more nutritious diets than many affluent Americans.
______	______	7. Vitamin C has been used effectively to treat mental diseases.

FIGURE 5.3 Anticipation Guide for Diet and Nutrition: Part I

Directions: Now you will be reading and listening to information related to each of the statements in Part I of this guide. If the information you read supports your choices in Part I, place a *check* in the *Support* column. If the information does not support your choices, place a check in the *No Support* column. Write in your own words the relevant text and/or lecture information for your answer.

	Support	No Support	Text/Lecture Information
1.	_____	_____	______________________
2.	_____	_____	______________________
3.	_____	_____	______________________
4.	_____	_____	______________________
5.	_____	_____	______________________
6.	_____	_____	______________________
7.	_____	_____	______________________

FIGURE 5.4 Anticipation for Diet and Nutrition: Part II

Anticipation Guides Create a Need in Students to Learn More

As you can see, the anticipation guide takes advantage of prediction as a powerful prereading tool. It forces students to think about what they already know and believe about a topic and then confirm, modify, or disconfirm existing beliefs. Working with anticipation guides helps create the urge in students to know more. They confront the topic ideas and information purposefully and enthusiastically (Nessel, 1988).

Like study guides, discussed in Chapter 3, anticipation guides can be created for virtually any content or topic. The guide in Figure 5.5, for example, was given to students by a science teacher to stimulate prior knowledge about pollution and the environment. In this guide, students first guessed answers to the questions related to real-world problems with pollution. Guesses, in this case, serve as predictions. Then, as students read and studied the topic, they returned to the guide statements and verified the correctness or incorrectness of their initial answers. The situations and questions are designed to encourage various levels of thinking, challenge students' beliefs, and focus on the key issues and points of the topic.

Anticipation guides require time to prepare, but we think you will agree that it is time well spent. By forcing students to make and defend predictions, guides can help sustain interest in topics, promote active involvement with text and in discussion, and facilitate assimilation of new information into existing schemata.

WRITING TO PREPARE STUDENTS FOR READING AND LEARNING

Writing is especially well suited for preparing students to read and learn (Hamann, Schultz, Smith, & White, 1991; Weech, 1994). Writing before learning from text or a lecture allows students to explore what they already know about

Part I

Directions: Below are statements and situations related to the environment. If you agree with the statement, place a check in the *Agree* column. If you disagree with the statement, place a check in the *Disagree* column. Be prepared to explain your responses.

Agree	Disagree	
______	______	1. A poor landowner wants to sell his land to a large chemical refinery. The environmentalists say there is an endangered species on the land. The court says he can't sell the land. Do you agree with the court ruling?
______	______	2. It doesn't matter if I recycle my aluminum cans or not. One person doesn't make a difference.
______	______	3. A small business garage owner goes to a vacant lot to empty motor oil into the ground. The police pick him up for suspicious behavior and find out what he has been doing. He is fined $50,000, which ruins his business and forces him into bankruptcy. Do you agree with the judgment? He says everybody else does it, so what difference does it make?
______	______	4. Your next-door neighbor has a beautiful yard. He sprays the plants almost every day. He never seems to be picking weeds; instead, he sprays his lawn with poison. Do you agree with his technique?
______	______	5. A man and his family saved for years to buy the home of their dreams. After they moved in, the younger child became very ill. He had headaches most of the time. The man eventually found out that he had bought a house on top of an old landfill. He sued the real estate agent and lost the case. Do you agree with the court ruling?
______	______	6. The richest and most diverse terrestrial ecosystems on earth are the tropical forests. Some people want to develop this land for cattle grazing. Do you think that would be a good idea?

Part II

Directions: Now that we have studied facts and issues related to environmental pollution, look back at your responses to the statements in Part I. If you found support for your response, check the *Support* column below; if you didn't find support for your response, check the *No Support* column. Regardless of what column you check, write a sentence in your own words explaining your response.

	Support	No Support	Your Explanation
1.	______	______	______________________________
2.	______	______	______________________________
3.	______	______	______________________________
4.	______	______	______________________________
5.	______	______	______________________________
6.	______	______	______________________________

FIGURE 5.5 Anticipation Guide for the Topic of Environmental Pollution

a topic, thereby building a bridge from their prior knowledge and experiences to the new information. It also is an effective medium for self-reflection. Students can decide where they possess sufficient knowledge and where gaps in knowledge exist. Based on this information, they can seek people and resources to expand their knowledge base. Writing as a readiness-to-learn strategy can also increase student motivation and interest.

Writing as Readiness in Geometry Class

Sena teaches 10th-grade geometry. She had been frustrated with the ways she was teaching vocabulary—using rote memorization techniques, drill sheets, and glossaries. Last year Sena decided to try to make vocabulary learning in geometry class more fun for her students and herself by using a creative writing activity.

Early in the new school year, Sena had her students form groups of three, and then gave each student a list of terms they would encounter often in geometry, along with their definitions. After going over the terms and clarifying the simple definitions, Sena asked her students to write a story with the words. Students were to use at least five of the geometry terms in their story, and use them in an everyday rather than a geometry context. To help clarify the assignment, she wrote on the board, "The sheriff called out, 'Come out with your hands up; we have you circumscribed!' "

The groups worked happily on this assignment, laughing and exclaiming quietly as they completed their stories. All the while, Sena worked on a story of her own. When they had finished, volunteers from each group were asked to share their stories with the class. One group had written the following story:

> A very pretty girl stood nervously as not one but two boys expressed their **paralleled** love for her. Now, her little love **triangle** had been discovered, and she had to choose between the two. She took a stick and **circumscribed** an **area** in the dirt around them. The boys were to fight it out. One of the boys was quick and punched the other bigger boy on his **square** jaw. The big boy fell to the ground, and the girl happily accepted the winning boy's love **axiom**. As the new couple walked away, their arms formed an **angle** that would last forever.

The writing strategy turned out to be fun and helped lay the foundation for future learning of key geometry terminology. Sena noticed that as these terms began to appear and be used in class, her students were much more prepared for them and seemed better able to grasp their meanings in the context of geometry.

WRITING SOLUTIONS TO PROBLEMS POSED BEFORE READING

Many of the purpose-setting activities just discussed can be easily adapted to include a writing component. For instance, a seventh-grade geography class preparing to study the Kalahari bushmen was asked to write a solution to this problem:

> The men have gone to work the big farms for harvest season. The women and children have not eaten meat in several weeks. One morning a herd of giraffe are spotted in the bush nearby. Because you are the most experi-

> enced hunter, you are asked to kill a giraffe. You are sent off alone with only a spear. How will you succeed?

In small groups, the students were given the chance to discuss ideas for solving the problem before writing. After composing their answers, several volunteers shared them with the class. Some of the more inventive solutions are as follows: Dig a big hole and cover it with grass and leaves so that the giraffe will fall into it; wait hidden in a tree that has the giraffe's most irresistible leaves, and when the giraffe comes by to eat, lasso it. Other solutions anticipated what really happens: Put poison on a spear tip, sneak up on a giraffe, and spear it. Many students embedded their solution in stories. The teacher then asked the class to read the text, which explained bushmen hunting strategies and included a description of a giraffe hunt. As they read, students compared their solutions with the text's.

LEARNING LOGS

Another outstanding way of using writing to help students prepare for learning by thinking about new knowledge in terms of preexisting knowledge is with **learning logs** (Newkirk, 1986; Santa & Havens, 1991). First introduced in Chapter 3, this writing strategy involves students in keeping notebooks in content classrooms to record what they already know about a topic; what they desire to know about the topic; and then, after reading, lecture, and class discussion, an amalgamation of these two aspects with what they have learned. The amalgamation is in essence a revision of their first interpretations of the content. Cassie kept a learning log in sophomore history. In preparing to read and study a unit on the American Revolution, which she felt she had gone over 20 times before, she wrote at length about how the war started, some of the battles, Washington's role, the effect of losing on the British and victory on the colonies, and so on. She had little to ask of herself in terms of what she further desired to learn; she thought she had the Revolutionary War down cold. She wrote in her log, "I want to refresh my memory." But then her teacher gave the class a trade book to read as a prelude to reading the text—*My Brother Sam Is Dead* by Collier and Collier (1974). Cassie had never read a fictionalized account of the Revolutionary War and was doubtful about whether she could discover any new fact or detail that had been overlooked by her present or past texts. As she read the book, though, a change began taking place, as reflected in the entries in her log:

> I didn't know families were split about how they felt about the war. I didn't realize there were so many colonists who were against the war and for the British. I wonder how these people were treated during the war?

Further into the book, she found an answer to her question:

> I can't believe how cruel the colonists who supported the war were to those who didn't support the war. They were treated like enemies. Sam's

father was not helping the British. He was just minding his own business, and for that he gets captured and his family isn't even told where he is or whether he's alive. I wonder what's going to happen to Mr. Meeker now, and Tim and his mom, and Sam for that matter.

Learning Logs Force Anticipation and Reflection

The trade book forced Cassie to reconsider her beliefs about the Revolutionary War in light of some new and, to her, startling information. The learning log facilitated this process of reinterpretation. When Cassie completed the book, she wrote another extended entry in her log, where she recorded the same facts she had written before reading the book but this time qualifying each fact with new information and ideas she had gleaned from the trade book.

Preteaching Critical Vocabulary and Concepts

Graphic Organizers and Word Webs

Schema theory informs us that it is best to preteach the overarching concepts and terms that provide the mental framework for building new knowledge structures. One excellent way to teach terms and concepts directly is with **graphic organizers** and **word webs.** These are diagrams of the relationships among the key concepts and terms. The key difference between the two is that the graphic organizer is a teacher-provided structured overview, whereas the word web is developed by students with teacher guidance.

The graphic organizer in Figure 5.6 was given to eighth graders in a history class before they began reading in their texts about the Industrial Revolution. An organizer such as this enables students to see the structure of the text material and anchors in memory the big ideas to which details and facts can be attached.

Word webs are created by branching off from a major concept the related terms and concepts, much like a planet ringed with clustering satellites. The result is a graphic representation of the relationships among concepts and related terminology that approximates a cognitive network of related ideas, or a schema. These semantic networks help students explore and expand their associations with a central concept, thereby building schemata. Figure 5.7 provides a glimpse of a classroom teacher's effective use of a word-web strategy to preteach the critical concept of *prejudice.*

Both graphic organizers and word webs help students focus on the information you deem most important in the text. At the same time, they assist students in assimilating and clustering additional details. (Chapter 6 provides a detailed explanation of how to design and use graphic organizers, as well as many other effective vocabulary strategies.)

CASE STUDY REVISITED

Remember Theresa, the eighth-grade social studies teacher? She was preparing for a unit on the early Americans. Take a moment to write your ideas for Theresa to help her students prepare to study this content and become engaged in learning.

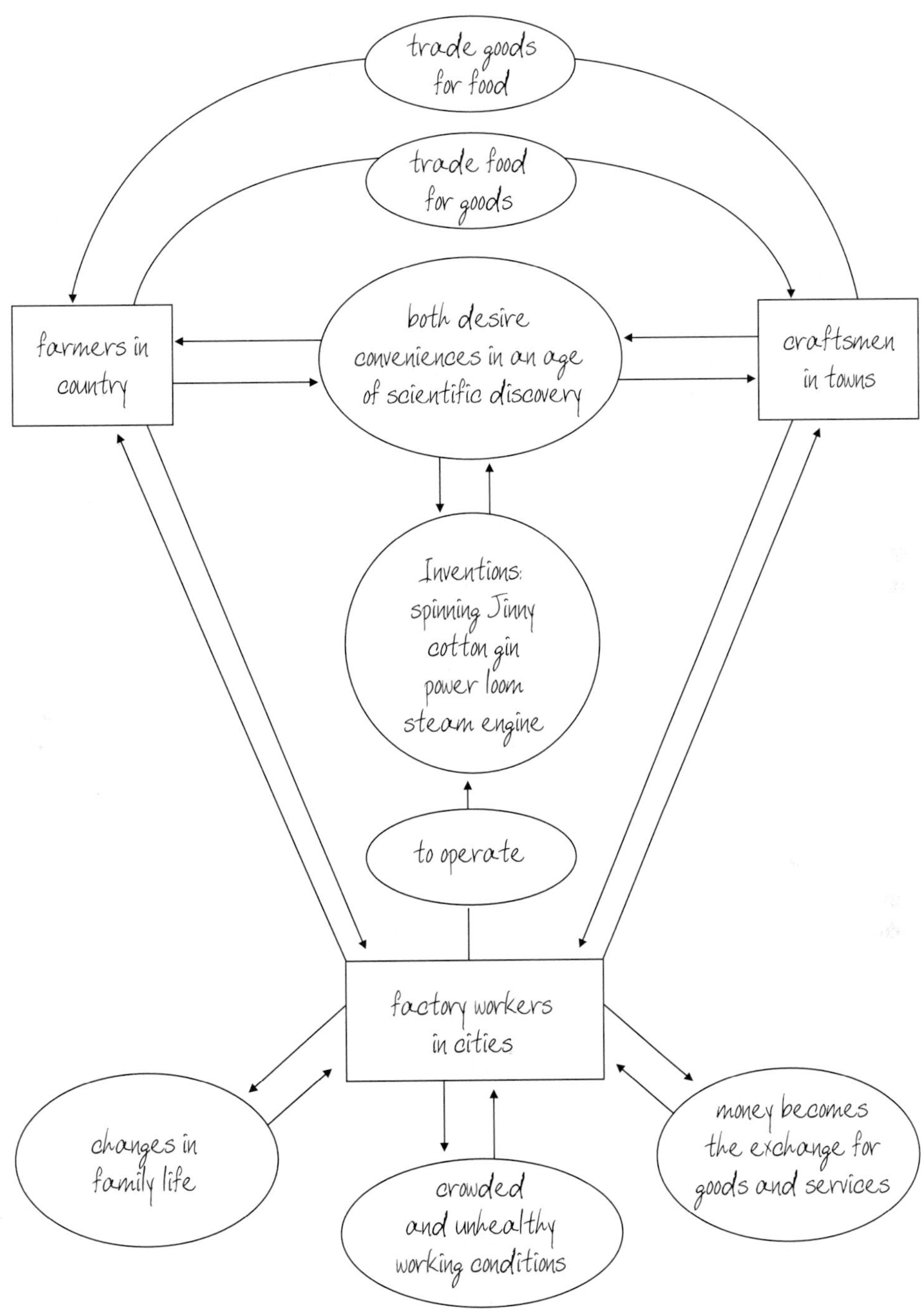

FIGURE 5.6 Graphic Organizer for the Industrial Revolution

Margaret teaches 11th-grade gifted English. In planning a unit around the concept of *prejudice,* she had selected a trade book to use with her students that told a story of racism and prejudice in recent United States history. The book was *Farewell to Manzanar* (Houston & Houston, 1974), a true account of Jeanne Wakatsuki and her family, who spent the World War II years in an internment camp off the West Coast of the United States. Before assigning any reading of the book, Margaret wanted to remind her students of examples of prejudice they were already familiar with to sensitize them to the issues of prejudice and to engage them in a lengthy discussion of the concept.

Margaret first worked with the whole class to create a word web for the broad concept *racial prejudice.* She wrote the words on the board, circled them, and then helped the class come up with an array of related ideas, examples, and terminology. At the conclusion of this activity, the class was divided into groups of four or five, and each group was asked to develop its own word web for one major case of racial prejudice, such as "Nazism," "South African Apartheid," "Southern Blacks in the 1950s," and "Japanese Americans during WWII." Groups were asked to put their webs on transparencies to share them with the class. After working for several minutes, spokespersons from the various groups were asked to share their group's web and explain the rationale for its terms and groupings.

The group working with "Southern Blacks in the 1950s" presented the following word web:

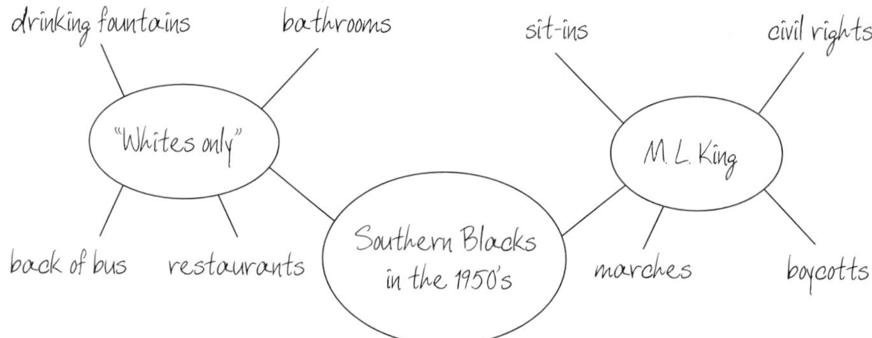

"Well, we knew there were lots of places where blacks couldn't go," said one spokesperson, "and there were signs that said 'Whites only,' or something like that, so we used it as one of our subcategories. Then we listed some of the places where blacks couldn't go . . . like they couldn't use certain bathrooms and drinking fountains . . . and they had to sit in the back of the bus . . . and they couldn't eat in certain restaurants . . . we could have listed more places. We also thought about Martin Luther King, because he was trying to change all that back then, so we listed some of the things he did to try to get rights for blacks. We couldn't remember much about the boycotts and marches, so we just said that."

"Didn't they also go to restaurants that were supposed to be for whites and just take up all the seats and stay there?" a student asked.

"I guess they did, so we could include . . . what would you call that?"

Margaret helped out, "They were called 'sit-ins.' That's an excellent word map."

After each group's spokesperson had an opportunity to present and explain its word web, answer questions, and gather feedback and additional ideas from the class, Margaret then focused the discussion on the commonalities among the major cases of racial prejudice that were depicted in the word maps. The class derived three: (a) one group feels superior to another group, often based on physical characteristics, (b) the superior group denies the rights of the other group, and (c) the superior group often uses violence to gain an advantage over the other group. Students were then asked to pay close attention to the novel they were about to read, *Farewell to Manzanar,* and to be prepared to discuss how the case of prejudice in the story shares common characteristics with the other forms of prejudice discussed in the class that day.

FIGURE 5.7 Classroom Example of Students' Creation of Word Webs to Prepare for a Unit on Prejudice

Theresa introduced students to a prereading activity on the first day that we thought was exceptional. She began by involving the class in a discussion of the role of archaeologists in understanding the relationship of artifacts to past societies. She then explained that one way to understand the past is to relate it to the present, and one way they could do that was by making a time capsule. After defining a time capsule, she asked students to think of objects they felt would be important to include in one that would be buried today and excavated 1,000 years later. Theresa jotted down ideas on the board and asked students to explain why their particular object would help people living 1,000 years later to understand what life was like today. Clearly, the purpose of exploring the idea of a time capsule was to motivate students to learn about the past by making it relevant to their own lives. The students were genuinely enjoying this activity, as reflected in interchanges such as this:

Student 1: Did you see that Coke commercial where this class sometime way in the future is walking through a 20th-century ruin and they find a Coke bottle?

Class: Yeah, I've seen that.

Theresa: What does a bottle of Coke say to these future people about ourselves and our culture?

Student 1: That we like to drink Coke.

Theresa: Would it? How could you be sure? Let's say people aren't drinking Coke a thousand years from now, and let's say these people you're talking about also found a tattered T-shirt with "Madonna" written on it, and a broken television or computer. How would they piece together the way we lived if this is all they found?

Student 2: They might think Madonna was our President or something.

Student 3: They might not even know what a television or computer was. I read a science fiction story about these people who could put this machine on their heads, like a headset, and see images in their heads and feel what you would feel if you were there.

Theresa: That's interesting. So they might not even be able to recognize that it was a television or computer or exactly what it was used for, especially if it was really badly broken up. Do you see now how hard it would be for future people to describe who we were and how we behaved from the few things they might find?

Student 4: Maybe if we put a Coke can in our time capsule, we should tape a piece of paper to it that tells what it is and all about it.

Theresa: If the paper didn't crumble and rot away, that would be very helpful for future people. Good idea. Unfortunately for archaeologists, the original inhabitants of North America didn't leave written directions and explanations with all of their artifacts.

Student 5: Didn't they draw pictures in caves of hunting buffalo and stuff like that?

Theresa: That's right, and those wall paintings help us quite a bit, but they don't tell the whole story. For instance, the wall pictures don't tell whether men and women married like they do today, or whether one man could have several wives. They don't tell us if the Indians were nomadic or whether they lived in one place for long periods of time. Did these people have music or play games, etc.?

Eventually, the class formulated a list of things to put in their time capsule. It was fascinating to listen to the students rationalize why certain items would be appropriate to include. For instance, one young man wanted to contribute his tennis shoes; one was green, the other orange, and both were untied. He argued that they would reflect what young people are like today. The class concluded that his mismatched tennis shoes would give a misleading impression because only a small minority dress that way. Instead, it was decided that pictures from magazines depicting many different fashions would be better. Another student said the time capsule should have a CD of contemporary music. This didn't seem feasible, the class agreed, because in 1,000 years, probably no means of playing the CD would exist.

The final list included a Coke can, accompanied by a picture of someone drinking from a can of Coke, a copy of *Time* magazine, several photographs of cars, fashions, stereos, TVs, computers and other high-tech electronics, houses, lyrics and sheet music to a couple of popular songs, and a class portrait. The activity culminated at week's end with a ceremonial burial on a section of the school grounds of a time capsule (actually a large plastic canister) containing the items the class had decided on.

Theresa conducted a couple of other readiness activities during the week, including a word scavenger hunt, which involves students in a game for learning key words from their readings (see Chapter 6 for details), and viewing a film that traced the journey of the first people to emigrate from Europe to the area we now call Iowa. Students were also provided with a structured overview of the migration patterns, names, and terms associated with the first Americans.

This case study makes clear how varied and yet how effective creative and meaningful activities before reading about and studying class topics can be. It demonstrates how a talented teacher takes her students far beyond the traditional boundaries of a content area lesson in preparing them for learning by generating interest in the topic and activating and building appropriate prior knowledge for the content to be learned.

■ ■ ■

SUMMARY

Because we believe that the degree of success with a topic of study in the content areas depends on how well students are prepared for learning about the topic, we have devoted most of this chapter to presenting a range of classroom practices that teachers in middle and secondary schools have used to hook their students into the topic. The examples included here represent only a few of the potentially endless possibilities for getting students excited about the content to be read and studied. We hope these guidelines and examples help you become more sensitive to the importance of providing preparation activities for all reading and learning experiences and inspire you to expand your notions about what is possible in your classroom before telling students, "Open your books and begin reading Chapter 7."

In the next chapter, you will read more about some of the vocabulary strategies briefly discussed in this chapter. You will also discover a range of additional word-learning strategies designed to expand students' understanding of course concepts.

REFERENCES

Alexander, P., Kulikowich, J., & Hetton, T. (1994). The role of subject matter knowledge and interest in the processing of linear and nonlinear texts. *Review of Educational Research, 64,* 210–253.

Alvermann, D., Dillon, D., & O'Brien, D. (1988). *Using discussion to promote reading comprehension.* Newark, DE: International Reading Association.

Alvermann, D., O'Brien, D., & Dillon, D. (1990). What teachers do when they say they're having discussions of content area reading assignments: A qualitative analysis. *Reading Research Quarterly, 25,* 296–322.

Alvermann, D., Peyton Young, J., Weaver, D., Hinchman, K., Moore, D., Phelps, S., Thrash, E., & Zalewski, P. (1996). Middle and high school students' perceptions of how they experience text-based discussions: A multicase study. *Reading Research Quarterly, 31,* 244–267.

Anderson, R. (1984). Role of the reader's schema in comprehension, learning, and memory. In R. Anderson, J. Osborn, & R. Tierney (Eds.). *Learning to read in American Schools: Basal readers and content texts.* Hillsdale, NJ: Erlbaum.

Barnitz, J. (1994). Discourse diversity: Principles for authentic talk and literacy instruction. *Journal of Reading, 37,* 586–591.

Barton, J. (1995). Conducting effective classroom discussions. *Journal of Reading, 38,* 346–350.

Bintz, W. (1993). Resistant readers in secondary education: Some insights and implications. *Journal of Reading, 36,* 604–615.

Cameron, J., & Pierce, W. (1994). Reinforcement, reward, and intrinsic motivation: A meta-analysis. *Review of Educational Research, 64,* 363–423.

Carr, E., & Ogle, D. (1987). K-W-L Plus: A strategy for comprehension and summarization. *Journal of Reading, 30,* 626–631.

Carr, S., & Thompson, B. (1996). The effects of prior knowledge and schema activation strategies on the inferential reading comprehension of children with and without learning disabilities. *Learning Disabilities Quarterly, 19,* 48–66.

Clary, L. (1991). Getting adolescents to read. *Journal of Reading, 34,* 340–345.

Dewey, J. (1913). *Interest and effort in education.* Boston: Houghton Mifflin.

Duffelmeyer, F. (1994). Effective Anticipation Guide statements for learning from expository prose. *Journal of Reading, 37,* 452–457.

Duffelmeyer, R., & Baum, D. (1992). The extended Anticipation Guide revisited. *Journal of Reading, 35,* 654–656.

Frager, A. (1993). Affective dimension of content area reading. *Journal of Reading, 36,* 616–623.

Gambrell, L. (1996). Creating classroom cultures that foster reading motivation. *The Reading Teacher, 50,* 14–25.

Gambrell, L., & Morrow, L. (1995). Creating motivating contexts for literacy learning. In L. Baker, P. Afflerbach, & D. Reinking (Eds.), *Developing engaged readers in home and school communities.* Mahwah, NJ: Erlbaum.

Gaultney, J. F. (1995). The effect of prior knowledge and metacognition on the acquisition of a reading comprehension strategy. *Journal of Experimental Child Psychology, 59,* 142–165.

Gillet, J., & Temple, C. (1986). *Understanding reading problems: Assessment and instruction: Instructor's manual* (2nd ed.). Boston: Little, Brown.

Guzzetti, B., & Williams, W. (1996). Changing the pattern of gendered discussion: Lessons from science classrooms. *Journal of Adolescent and Adult Literacy, 40,* 38–47.

Hamann, L., Schultz, L., Smith, M., & White, B. (1991). Making connections: The power of autobiographical writing before reading. *Journal of Reading, 35,* 24–28.

Harste, J. (1989). *New policy guidelines for reading: Connecting research and practice.* Urbana, IL: National Council of Teachers of English.

Hartman, D. (1995). Eight readers reading: The intertextual links of proficient readers reading multiple passages. *Reading Research Quarterly, 30,* 520–561.

Hayes, D. A., & Tierney, R. J. (1980). *Increasing background knowledge through analogy: Its effects upon comprehension and learning* (Tech. Rep. No. 186). Urbana: University of Illinois, Center for the Study of Reading.

Hennings, D. (1991). Essential reading: Targeting, tracking, and thinking about main ideas. *Journal of Reading, 34,* 346–353.

Herz, S., & Gallo, D. (1996). *From Hinton to Hamlet: Building bridges between young adult literature and the classics.* Westport, CT: Greenwood Press.

Hidi, S., & Baird, W. (1988). Strategies for increasing text-based interest and students' recall of expository texts. *Reading Research Quarterly, 23,* 465–483.

Horn, E. (1937). *Methods of instruction in social studies.* New York: Scribner's.

Hoss, M. (1991). Guest speakers are our favorite inexpensive reference tool. *Illinois Libraries, 73,* 540–542.

Illich, I. (1970). *Deschooling society.* New York: Harper & Row.

Learning (1996). More than a boring speech. *24,* 64.

Marshall, N. (1989). Overcoming problems with incorrect prior knowledge: An instructional study. In S. McCormick & J. Zutell (Eds.), *Cognitive and social perspectives for literacy research and instruction.* Chicago: National Reading Conference.

Mathison, C. (1989). Activating student interest in content area reading. *Journal of Reading, 33,* 170–177.

McKeown, M., Beck, I., Sinatra, G., & Loxterman, J. (1992). The contribution of prior knowledge and coherent text to comprehension. *Reading Research Quarterly, 27,* 78–93.

Nagy, W., Anderson, R., & Herman, P. (1987). Learning word meanings from context during normal reading. *American Educational Research Journal, 24,* 237–270.

Nessel, D. (1988). Channeling knowledge for reading expository text. *Journal of Reading, 32,* 231–235.

Newkirk, T. (1986). *To compose: Teaching writing in the high school.* Portsmouth, NH: Heinemann.

Ogle, D. (1986). K-W-L: A teaching model that develops active reading of expository text. *The Reading Teacher, 39,* 564–570.

Pearson, P. D., & Johnson, D. D. (1978). *Teaching reading comprehension.* New York: Holt, Rinehart & Winston.

Pressley, M., Johnson, C., Symons, S., McGoldrick, J., & Kurita, J. (1989). Strategies that improve children's memory and comprehension of text. *The Elementary School Journal, 90,* 3–32.

Renninger, K., Hidi, S., & Krapp, A. (1992). *The role of interest in learning and development.* Hillsdale, NJ: Erlbaum.

Ruddell, R. (1995). Those influential literacy teachers: Meaning negotiators and motivation builders. *The Reading Teacher, 48,* 454–463.

Santa, C., & Havens, L. (1991). Learning through writing. In C. Santa & D. Alvermann (Eds.), *Science learning: Processes and applications.* Newark, DE: International Reading Association.

Schiefele, U. (1991). Interest, learning, and motivation. *Educational Psychologist, 26,* 299–323.

Spilich, G. J., Vesonder, G. T., Chiesi, H. L., & Voss, J. F. (1979). Text processing of domain-related information for individuals with high and low domain knowledge. *Journal of Verbal Learning and Verbal Behavior, 18,* 275–290.

Symons, S., & Pressley, M. (1993). Prior knowledge affects text search success and extraction of information. *Reading Research Quarterly, 28,* 250–263.

Turner, J., & Paris, S. (1995). How literacy tasks influence children's motivation for literacy. *The Reading Teacher, 48,* 662–675.

Tyson-Bernstein, H. (1988). *A conspiracy of good intentions.* Washington, DC: Council for Basic Education.

Unrau, N., & Ruddell, R. (1995). Interpreting texts in classroom contexts. *Journal of Reading, 39,* 16–27.

Wade, S., Schraw, G., Buxton, W., & Hayes, M. (1993). Seduction of the strategic reader: Effects of interest on strategy and recall. *Reading Research Quarterly, 28,* 92–115.

Weech, J. (1994). Writing the story before reading it. *Journal of Reading, 37,* 364–367.

YOUNG ADULT BOOKS

Appleman-Jarman, A. (1988). *Alicia: My story.* New York: Bantam Books.

Cole, B. (1989). *Celine.* New York: Farrar, Straus & Giroux.

Collier, J. L., & Collier, C. (1974). *My brother Sam is dead.* New York: Scholastic.

Duncan, L. (1982). *Chapters: My growth as a writer.* Boston: Little, Brown.

Houston, J. W., & Houston, J. (1974). *Farewell to Manzanar.* New York: Bantam Books.

Lauber, P. (1986). *Volcano The eruption and healing of Mount St. Helens.* New York: Bradbury Press.

Oneal, Z. (1985). *In summer light.* New York: Viking Press.

Oneal, Z. (1990). *The language of goldfish.* New York: Puffin.

Peck, R. (1988). *Unfinished portrait of Jessica.* New York: Dell.

Peters, R. (1985). *Dance of the wolves.* New York: McGraw-Hill.

CHAPTER 6

Expanding Vocabulary and Developing Concepts

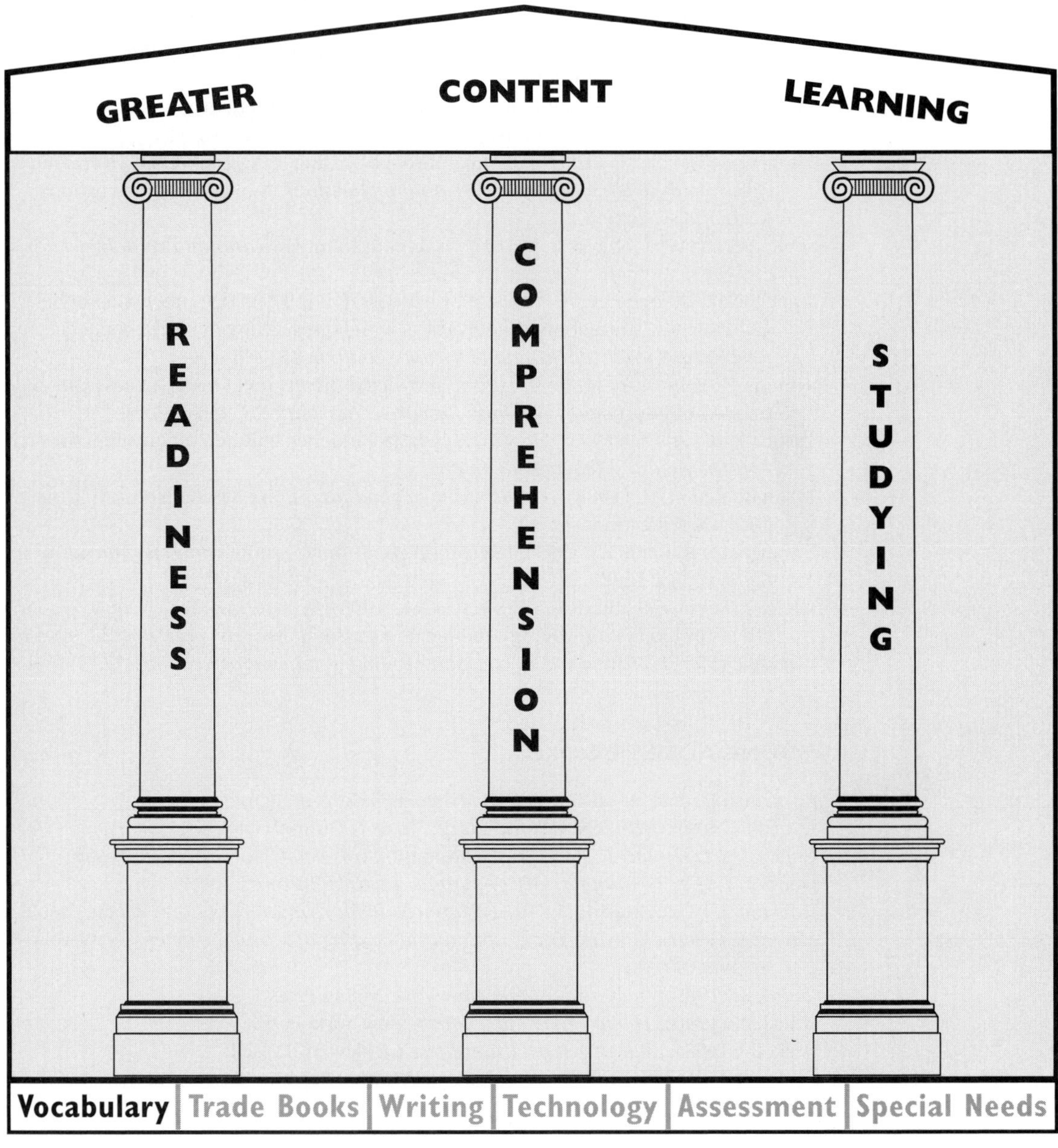

ANTICIPATION GUIDE

Directions: Read each statement carefully and decide whether you agree or disagree with it, placing a check mark in the appropriate *Before Reading* column. When you have finished reading and studying the chapter, return to the guide and decide whether your anticipations need to be changed by placing a check mark in the appropriate *After Reading* column.

	BEFORE READING		**AFTER READING**	
	Agree	*Disagree*	*Agree*	*Disagree*
1. Only high-risk students need to be taught vocabulary words.	_____	_____	_____	_____
2. A student with a deficient vocabulary will probably also have comprehension problems.	_____	_____	_____	_____
3. A student who can define a word for the teacher understands the word.	_____	_____	_____	_____
4. The dictionary can be confusing to many students.	_____	_____	_____	_____
5. Teaching students 20 words a week from a list of high-utility words should improve their vocabulary and comprehension.	_____	_____	_____	_____
6. The best format for evaluating students' word knowledge is a multiple-choice test.	_____	_____	_____	_____
7. Content area teachers should select all the difficult words in a unit and teach them.	_____	_____	_____	_____

The goal for vocabulary development is to insure that students are able to apply their knowledge of words to appropriate situations and are able to increase and enrich their knowledge through independent encounter with words. . . . [T]he best way to reach this goal is to help students add to their repertoires both specific words and skills that promote independent learning of words, and also to provide opportunities from which words can be learned.

—Beck and McKeown (1991)

What does it mean to "know" a word? That question has been debated for about 50 years, starting with Cronbach (1942), who suggested that word knowledge existed in dimensions. In the vernacular, to know a word means to be able to define it. But is this an adequate measure of one's word knowledge? When asked what the word *light* meant, 4-year-old Ryan's reply was "It comes from the sun and helps us see things." However, he had no idea what "light as a feather" meant, nor did he know the meaning of light in the sentence "I saw the birds light on the tree." Does Ryan really know the word *light?*

The Depth and Precision of Word Knowledge Are Critical

One of the primary goals of vocabulary development at the middle and high school levels is not simply to increase the breadth of students' vocabularies (i.e., the number of words for which students have a definition) but also to increase the depth and precision of their word knowledge. In other words, the goal is to help students develop a full and complete understanding of words in order to understand the concepts they encounter across the content areas. This is especially important because most students are expected to read and listen to content packed with concepts and technical vocabulary that they need to understand fully if meaning is to be gained (Jenkins, Matlock, & Slocum, 1989). Without a well-developed conceptual language of a content area, students often become outsiders to the learning process (Moore, Readence, & Rickelman, 1982).

Assuming that a conceptual understanding of key terminology is frequently imperative for content area learning, what are the critical thinking processes involved? What does it mean to understand a word at the conceptual level? Tennyson and Park (1980), in their extensive review of the research relating to concept development, proposed a four-step teaching procedure. Using their work and a review of recent vocabulary studies, Simpson (1987) suggested that conceptual understanding of content area vocabulary words should involve students in the following:

1. Recognizing and generating the critical attributes, characteristics, examples, and nonexamples of a concept.
2. Sensing and inferring relationships between concepts and their own background information or prior knowledge.

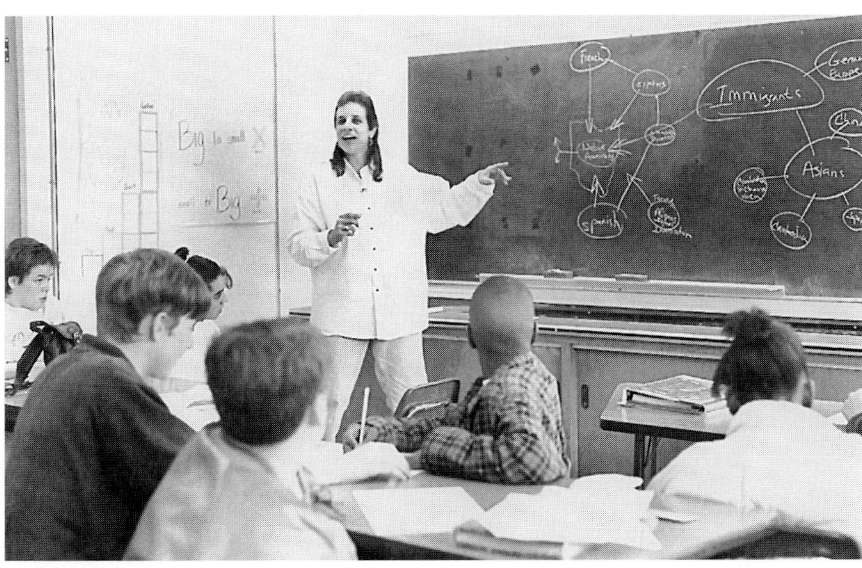

A Conceptual Understanding of a Word Means that Students Should Be Involved in Six Processes

3. Discovering comparisons and contrasts between different concepts to determine meaningful similarities and differences.
4. Determining superordinate and subordinate concepts related to the targeted concept.
5. Applying the concept to a variety of situations.
6. Creating new examples and applications for the targeted concept.

In this chapter, we present a variety of teacher-directed and student-initiated vocabulary strategies that capitalize on these six processes involved in learning words beyond the definitional level. You will notice that the strategies discussed are intended to expand students' comprehension of content area concepts, whether oral or written. We believe the best way to develop word knowledge is by capitalizing on the same effective teaching strategies discussed in previous chapters and throughout this book. Teacher demonstrations and modeling, small-group interactions, class discussions, writing activities, and reciprocal teaching are all powerful teaching tools. As you read this chapter, you will see how these teaching strategies can be effectively applied to word learning.

CASE STUDY

Liz, Curriculum Director of the Parkview School District, analyzed the results of the competency-based reading test that was given to eighth graders in the spring. Much to her dismay, the vocabulary scores were again low. She called the principals to highlight her concerns and to recommend that a district committee be formed to investigate the problem and offer some specific solutions. Consequently, a committee was formed of teachers who taught eighth graders across the district's middle schools. They met regularly during the school year to discuss the problem in more depth, but they could not agree on what should be done. Several committee members thought the language arts teachers should be responsible for improving the vocabulary scores. Other members complained that the additional burden of teaching vocabulary words would rob them of precious instructional time. And three members wanted the school to purchase a computer program promising to teach students 50 words a week. Patience was wearing thin as the school year drew to a close.

To the Reader:

As you read and work through this chapter on expanding vocabulary and concepts across the content areas, consider ways in which this committee could solve their problem. Think about the characteristics of effective vocabulary instruction, what it means to know a word, and possible strategies that this school district might incorporate into the middle school curricula.

■ ■ ■

DEFINITIONAL VERSUS CONCEPTUAL UNDERSTANDING OF WORDS

One of the underlying themes of this chapter is that word-learning strategies should require students to combine new text information with their prior knowledge to yield conceptual understanding of words. The admonitions of our best vocabulary writers and researchers are entirely consistent with this theme (e.g., Baumann & Kameenui, 1991; Beck & McKeown, 1991). Earlier in this chapter, we mentioned 4-year-old Ryan, who had partial definitional understanding of the word *light.* But Ryan did not have a conceptual understanding of light that would have allowed him to interpret its meaning in a variety of contexts.

Steven Stahl (1986) has made the distinction between definitional and contextual word knowledge. **Definitional knowledge** is essentially knowing a dictionary-like definition for a word. It is important word knowledge, but it limits understanding of the word to restricted contexts. **Contextual understanding,** on the other hand, means that the reader has a sophisticated schema for the word that facilitates meaningful interpretations in a variety of contexts.

To help you understand the important distinction between definitional and contextual word knowledge, we have prepared an exercise for you. For the following sentence, two key words have been defined. In the space provided, write what the statement means in your own words.

Surrogate: judge or magistrate
Testator: on making a claim on a will

The learned Surrogate has held that an intent to have an apportionment will be imputed to the testator.

In your own words:

____

____

____

For the next sentence, the topic area is provided. Given the topic, write in your own words the special definition of the two italicized words in the sentence.

Topic: commodities futures
Live hogs *found* November *unchanged.*

Your definition of *found:*

____

____

____

Your definition of *unchanged:*

____

____

____

Now that you have finished the exercise, some explanation is in order. In the first sentence, you undoubtedly discovered that even with a couple of the key terms defined, you were still unable to make sense of it. Why? Because the meaning of the sentence is larger than the sum of the definitions of each of its words. To state it another way, to understand this sentence, you must connect individual definitions to a broad context of meaning. You must possess the schema for these words, for without a schema, the sentence is an unintelligible collection of fragments of definitions. If, however, you were a lawyer of contracts and estate settlements, this sentence would be perfectly understandable.

What about the second sentence? Were you able to supply the appropriate special definitions for the commonly understood words *found* and *unchanged?* If not, it is likely due to the fact that your schema for the language of commodities futures is not especially well developed. Once again, without the necessary schema, or relevant prior knowledge, the sentence is as oblique as a line from a surrealistic poem. Of course, if you are a member of the Chicago Board of Trade familiar with hog futures in the commodities market, the expression would make perfect sense to you.

Word Knowledge Significantly Impacts Students' Comprehension

The difficulty you probably experienced in defining the words in this exercise is not unlike the problems many middle school and high school students often encounter when trying to read their content area textbooks. When students are not given adequate preparation for dealing with the critical terms and concepts in the text, or strategies for discovering word meaning while reading, comprehension can proceed only haltingly or may break down altogether (Schwartz, 1988). For the two sentences you were given, knowledge of the words and, most important, of the concepts they represent is essential if they are to be understood. How students acquire this important prior knowledge, and how they use strategies for elaborative understanding of words and concepts, are the major themes of this chapter.

As you now know from your own experience, definitional word knowledge does not imply conceptual understanding of a word. It is, however, an aspect of word knowledge that allows readers to bring to mind an appropriate schema to aid them in interpreting word meanings in various contexts (Kibby, 1995). Therefore, the principles and strategies of effective vocabulary instruction discussed in this chapter are not meant to make students experts at writing or reciting definitions. If a strategy or program focuses only on correctly matching a word to a definition, then what is obtained is limited in vision and probably has a low chance of being transferred to students' actual reading, writing, listening, or speaking tasks (Beck & McKeown, 1991). Before examining strategies that content area teachers can use to help their students understand content area vocabulary, we present six guidelines that should be considered when planning instruction.

Knowing a Word Involves More than a Knowledge of a Definition

GUIDELINES FOR EFFECTIVE VOCABULARY INSTRUCTION

There Is No One Superior Method of Teaching Vocabulary, but There Are Some Guidelines

After reviewing the literature pertaining to vocabulary instruction, Stahl and Fairbanks (1986) agreed that no single method appears to be consistently superior. Therefore, it seems advantageous for teachers to select a variety of techniques or approaches for increasing their students' vocabulary knowledge. In addition, the following seven guidelines, gleaned from research studies, should be considered when planning vocabulary lessons:

1. Teach vocabulary in context.
2. Emphasize students' active role in the learning process.
3. Give students tools to expand word knowledge independently.
4. Reinforce word learning with repeated exposures over time.
5. Stimulate students' interest in words.
6. Build a language-rich environment to support word learning.
7. Encourage students to read widely.

Teach Vocabulary in Context

Researchers who have reviewed the literature on vocabulary instruction have concluded that vocabulary is best taught in a unifying context (Baumann & Kameenui, 1991; Beck & McKeown, 1991; Stahl, 1986). Words taught in the context of a content area such as biology will be learned more effectively than words taught in isolation because context allows students to integrate words with previously acquired knowledge. The implication, of course, is that students will not improve their long-term vocabulary knowledge and understanding by memorizing the definitions of a list of essential words that high school students should know.

Grouping Words into Categories Is Helpful

Thus, content area teachers need to select or have students select the targeted words for study from textbooks, newspapers, magazines, or novels. For example, if students are reading a short selection from a speech textbook on words and their meaning, words such as *arbitrary, connotation, denotation,* or *syntax* could be studied. Another alternative is to group targeted words into semantic categories (Beck, Perfetti, & McKeown, 1982). One such category could be adjectives that negatively describe a person's actions: *lax, infantile, obsequious, narcissistic.* Whatever approach is used to provide a context and an organizing schema, remember that lists of words that are introduced on Monday and tested on Friday will probably be forgotten on Saturday.

Emphasize Students' Active Role in the Learning Process

Researchers who required their subjects to be actively involved in their own vocabulary development (Beck & McKeown, 1991; Carr, 1985) found that such learners performed significantly better than others on measures designed to evaluate vocabulary knowledge. From their review of the literature, Stahl and Fairbanks (1986) likewise concluded that active processing and involvement are critical for students to improve their vocabulary knowledge.

S. A. Stahl (1985) described active involvement of the learner as "generative processing." Generative or elaborative processing engages students in activities such as (1) sensing and inferring relationships between targeted vocabulary and their own background knowledge, (2) recognizing and applying vocabulary words to a variety of contexts, (3) recognizing examples and nonexamples, and (4) generating novel contexts for the targeted word. In contrast, an example of passive involvement related to vocabulary instruction would be worksheet-type activities asking students to select definitions, whether in multiple-choice or matching formats.

Give Students Tools to Expand Word Knowledge Independently

Generative Approaches to Vocabulary Are Superior Because Students Become Independent Word Learners

Stahl (1986) has differentiated between additive and generative approaches to teaching word knowledge. **Additive approaches** are word specific and emphasize the learning of a predetermined set of words usually taught in lists. **Generative approaches,** on the other hand, emphasize vocabulary-learning strategies that permit students to increase their vocabulary independently, beyond the instruction context. Think about it this way: If you teach students some words, they will be able to recognize and read those particular words; but if you teach students some word-learning strategies, they will be able to expand their vocabulary continually and to read and understand many more texts.

We are not arguing for generative over additive approaches. Instead, we make the point that classroom teachers should strike a balance between these two approaches. Students should be exposed to and actively involved in the learning of key terms and concepts related to text topics. In this case, developing broad understanding of a set of critical vocabulary is relevant and purposeful, as it will contribute to greater comprehension of the text. Indeed, we provide many strategies for this purpose in this chapter. Too often, however, word-specific methods for teaching vocabulary involve handing students a list of arbitrarily selected words without demonstrating a clear connection between remembering definitions and meaningful learning (Stahl, Brozo, & Simpson, 1987). Teachers should also help students become independent word gatherers by helping them develop effective generative strategies (Kibby, 1995).

Reinforce Word Learning with Repeated Exposures Over Time

To really own a word, not only must we possess an elaborative understanding of it, but we must also be able to use it freely in appropriate contexts. Nagy, Anderson, and Herman (1987) discovered that word ownership is reinforced when students receive multiple exposures to targeted words in multiple contexts. A math teacher puts this principle into practice by building vocabulary through (1) extensive discussions of key terms and symbols exploring what students already know about them; (2) previewing how the words and symbols are used in their math textbooks; (3) asking students to record the words and symbols in a vocabulary notebook; and (4) practicing the words and symbols with a variety of activities and exercises that require students to think and write rather than circle answers. These approaches to reinforcing vocabulary ensure students' elaborative understanding and hasten their spontaneous use of the words in spoken and written contexts.

Stimulate Students' Interest in Words

As teachers, we all know the role that interest plays in our content area classrooms. That is, when students are interested in what they hear in class or read about in an assignment, this interest will significantly increase their attention, effort, persistence, thinking processes, and performance (Hidi, 1990). Unfortunately, commercial materials and assignments that ask students to look up 20 words in the dictionary and write sentences using them do not interest or motivate most middle school and high school students. What we need to do as teachers is to create situations where learning new words is fun and intriguing.

Word Learning Can Be Made Fun, and Should Be If We Want Students to Remember Their Content Area Concepts

The best starting point for building word enthusiasm is with you, the teacher. We can hardly expect our students to become sensitive to words and interested in expanding word knowledge if we cannot demonstrate interest in words ourselves. Manzo and Sherk have stated that "the single most significant factor in improving vocabulary is the excitement about words which teachers can generate" (1971, p. 78). As we emphasized in previous chapters, modeling is a powerful teaching tool. If you want students to learn certain words, then talk about words you recently heard on a television show or read in the newspaper. Show students that you use the dictionary to look up words you do not understand or for definitions you need to clarify so that they realize that vocabulary acquisition is a lifelong goal. During class discussion, in conversation with students, or when responding to journal or other student writing, use words you want them to integrate into their written and spoken vocabularies. Above all, be playful with words and exhibit enthusiasm for words.

One way you can be playful with words is to share with students memorable stories and histories of words. We know one sixth-grade middle school team that selects and discusses with their students one word each week that has an unusual origin or history. For example, during the first week of school they taught the word *berserk.* This word originated from Norse mythology. Berserk was a fierce man who used no armor and assumed the form of a wild beast in battle. Supposedly, no enemy would touch him. Today, if you are described as *berserk,* you are wild, dangerous, and crazed. The sixth graders had fun with that word, describing their friends, their brothers and sisters, and their first week in a middle school as berserk. More important, the sixth-grade teachers discovered that their students remembered and then used those words as they were writing and speaking.

Word Histories Can Be Motivating to Students

If you are interested in finding other words such as *berserk* that have fascinating origins, the sources for these stories can be found in reference books such as Funk's (1950) *Word Origins and Their Romantic Stories.* Other such books that are excellent sources are listed in Figure 6.1.

Build a Language-Rich Environment to Support Word Learning

Word learning should occur within a context that supports literacy and language development. Teachers can best promote vocabulary growth by working with students to create an environment where new words and strategies can be learned through genuine communication processes (Cunningham, 1992). Students should be involved in using all of the language systems to learn concepts and expand comprehension. For example, they should be given opportunities to experiment with using words in low-risk situations, to discuss new

Asimov, I. (1961). *Words from the myths.* Boston: Houghton Mifflin.
Asimov, I. (1969). *Words of science and the history behind them.* New York: New American Library.
Asimov, I. (1972). *More words of science.* Boston: Houghton Mifflin.
Funk, C. (1973). *A hog on ice and other curious expressions.* New York: Harper & Row.
Funk, W. (1950). *Word origins and their romantic stories.* New York: Funk & Wagnalls.
Grambs, D. (1986). *Dimboxes, epopts, and other quidams.* New York: Workman.
Jacobson, J. (1990). *Tooposaurus: A humorous treasury of top-o-nyms (familiar words and phrases derived from place names).* New York: Wiley.
Safire, W. (1982). *What's the good word?* New York: Times Books.
Tuleja, T. (1987). *Namesakes: An entertaining guide to the origins of more than 300 words named for people.* New York: McGraw-Hill.
Urdang, L., Hunsinger, W., & LaRoche, N. (1991). *A fine kettle of fish and other figurative expressions.* Detroit: Visible Ink Press.

FIGURE 6.1 Books About Interesting Word Origins

ideas daily, to talk freely and openly about how text concepts relate to their real-world concerns, to read works in a variety of text genres related to concepts, and to write purposeful and meaningful texts that employ key words and demonstrate understanding of important concepts.

Oral Language Interactions Help Build Vocabulary Knowledge

We know teachers who emphasize the oral language use of new words long before students are asked to write a sentence. In these classrooms the students have the opportunity to "try out" a sentence orally using a new word with their partners in order to receive their feedback and suggestions. Then the students share their sentences orally with the entire class. Hence, after 15 minutes, these students hear countless examples of how to use a targeted word correctly and how not to use the word. These oral language activities help students understand the connotative nuances and syntactic rules that govern word knowledge.

Other teachers have told us that they reinforce and extend vocabulary learning by providing regular writing experiences to help their students become more aware of contextual meanings, as well as their lack of specific vocabulary. In addition, the revision and editing stages of the writing process become excellent opportunities to engage students in searches for "that one perfect word" that conveys the precise meaning they have in mind.

Encourage Students to Read Widely

In Chapter 1 we pointed out that many middle school and high school students do not choose to read as a recreational activity. In fact, books and other reading matter are not part of their lives outside the walls of our classrooms. Ironically, students who do read widely and frequently are the ones who have the breadth and depth of word knowledge necessary for success in school and in life (Nagy, 1988; Nagy & Herman, 1987). They are also the students who perform better on standardized achievement tests such as the Scholastic Aptitude Test.

Students Who Read Extensively Will Have a Better Vocabulary

The implication for content area teachers is obvious: If we want our students to understand what they read in our courses, we must encourage them to read beyond what they are assigned to read in our classrooms. Content area teachers should also keep in mind that what students read is not as important as the fact that they are reading. Forcing students to read the "important" works or classics will not instill a love of reading and may, in fact, cause negative reactions. Rather than the classics, many teachers like to stimulate recreational reading by encouraging students to read newspapers, magazines, short stories, and adolescent novels. In Chapter 8 we discuss in detail ways to encourage students' love and interest in reading.

SELECTING KEY TERMS AND CONCEPTS

Word Kowledge Involves Three Differing Tasks That Vary in Difficulty

Learning a new word or key concept for a content area is obviously a complex task dependent upon students' prior knowledge and experiences. Graves (1987) has suggested that there are three tasks involved in word learning. The first task is learning a new word for a concept when the student understands the concept but has not heard of the label for that concept. For example, most students understand the processes involved in defense mechanisms such as rationalization because they have all rationalized their behaviors in some way. The label, however, will probably be new to them. Words such as these are not as difficult to teach students because they have the experiences to draw upon to understand and learn them.

The second and third tasks involved in word learning are more difficult because students are not as familiar with the underlying concept. With the second task, students are learning a new concept for a known word. In psychology and mathematics, for example, the word *set* has a different meaning from what students understand the word to mean when they talk about having to "set the table for dinner." The third task involves students in learning a new concept for which they have no label and minimal, if any, understanding or background. These are the tasks that challenge both students and teachers. For example, in an ecology unit the concept *eutrophication* (a gradual and natural process that turns lakes into marshes because of an excess amount of algae) is probably new to most 10th graders, as is the label. Hence, the science teacher would need to spend more time on this word than on others such as *mercury, detergents,* or *biodegradable.* In addition to understanding the three tasks involved in learning a word, it is important to understand the types of vocabulary in a content area.

Types of Vocabulary

If you were to skim a chapter in this textbook, you would probably discover that the vocabulary words could be classified in two ways. The first type are **general words** that are not particularly associated with any single content area and could be found in any newspaper or weekly magazine. For example, a science teacher who asked his ninth-grade students to read a brief excerpt from Rachel Carson's book *Silent Spring* identified the following general words that he thought should be taught: *maladies, blight, moribund, specter, stark,* and *droned.* A British journalist could have easily used some of these same words to describe a winter day in London because they are common to many communication situations.

The second type are the **technical vocabulary words** that are unique to a particular content area or take on a specialized meaning when used in that content area. As Konopak and Mealey (1992) point out, technical words include general words that are used in a specialized way and technical words that have only one distinct meaning and application—the second and third tasks involved in word learning. Examples of the former are words such as *table, matter, set,* or *drive,* which take on specialized meanings, depending on the content area. Examples of the latter include words such as *alveoli* in science, *sonority* in music, and *matte effect* in art.

A Process for Selecting Words to Teach

Because it is impossible to teach all the general and technical words from a content area chapter, an important first step in teaching vocabulary is to decide which terms and concepts should be taught. Traditionally, teachers have used the

Teachers Must Focus on Certain Key Vocabulary Since It Is Difficult to Teach Them All

textbook as a guide, focusing on the words highlighted in the text. Basing vocabulary instruction on these words alone, however, may not meet your overall goals for teaching the content or unit. Researchers have made it clear that students will learn what is emphasized. If instruction focuses on the important and meaningful details, concepts, and issues, those things will be what students learn and remember. Vocabulary instruction, then, should focus on words related to those important ideas. Sometimes the words the textbook author has chosen to highlight will match the concepts you choose to emphasize; sometimes they will not. It is important, therefore, that you have a system for selecting the appropriate vocabulary terms that help students better understand the key ideas of the unit.

Another issue related to selecting words to teach is that it is impossible to teach students every word that they may not fully understand in their texts. Time constraints alone preclude our doing so (Nagy et al., 1987). Any of you who have tried to identify and teach all the words in a text you think might cause your students difficulty have discovered that your entire lesson can be taken up with vocabulary instruction. It is simply not feasible to attempt to teach every word that might potentially pose trouble for your students. We submit that a far more efficient and effective approach is to select the salient terms and concepts, those that carry and represent the most important ideas, and teach them well. A thorough and elaborative understanding of those vocabulary terms will, in turn, contribute to your students' enhanced understanding of the text itself.

The following process should help you determine what vocabulary words should be taught as a part of a unit of study:

1. Determine what you want your students to learn as a result of reading and studying the content. We might call this the **theme** of the unit. For instance, a music teacher may want students to develop a sense of musical interpretation after covering a unit on opera; an art teacher may wish students to develop a sense of character as a result of reading stories with well-developed characters for a unit on portrait painting; a history teacher covering the Vietnam War may stress the danger of foreign intervention in civil strife.
2. Identify **key terms** that are related to the unit's theme. For example, considering the theme of Sparta and its unique political structure, the teacher would likely select technical terms such as *euphors, assembly, council of elders,* and *helots* because they are important words related to the theme.
3. Decide on appropriate strategies to introduce and reinforce the words. For example, the words related to Sparta could be arranged into a graphic organizer, a strategy introduced in Chapter 5 and discussed in more detail later in this chapter.
4. Identify the general words that are not necessarily central to the theme of the unit but that lend themselves to various word-learning strategies that promote independence, such as modeling words in context.

You should not underestimate the importance of these first steps in teaching key terms and concepts related to a unit of study. The more discretionary you are in selecting vocabulary that potentially has the highest payoff regarding comprehension, the greater the likelihood that students will learn the designated content area material.

TRADITIONAL APPROACHES TO VOCABULARY INSTRUCTION

In this section, we examine two traditional approaches to teaching vocabulary—context clues and the dictionary. This section could have also been titled "Caveats to Vocabulary Instruction" in that we directly discuss the limitations of using context clues and the dictionary, two very traditional and prevalent approaches. Though we offer several caveats to each approach, we also outline ways in which teachers can encourage students to use context clues and the dictionary as methods of vocabulary development.

Using Contextual Analysis

Contextual analysis refers to our attempt to understand the meaning of a word by analyzing the meaning of the words that surround it. Put another way, contextual analysis is figuring out a word by the way in which it is used in a textbook, novel, or magazine. For example, one way in which we figure out the meaning of words is by using extended descriptions or appositives such as the following:

> There was a strange sound *emanating* from the hood of my car. When I opened the hood, I found a stray cat huddling to keep warm and meowing in fear.
>
> The *decadent,* or overindulgent, society in which we live spoils children by buying them whatever they see on television.

Learning Words from Context Is Not as Easy as We Imagine

On the surface, the idea of learning words from context makes a lot of sense. Logical as it may seem, however, the research on students' incidental learning from context seems to indicate that "some learning from context does exist, but that effect is not very powerful" (Beck & McKeown, 1991, p. 800).

One reason the utility of contextual analysis is challenged is that previous research studies have used contrived, unnatural texts as their materials of study and high-frequency words as their target of study (Nist & Olejnik, 1993). The following examples illustrate the oversimplified exercises that have been used in studies and in workbooks designed to teach students how to use context clues. Can you figure out the meaning of the italicized nonsense words?

> The boys bought their tickets for the brand new outer space movie and entered the theater with mystic expectation all over their *whitors.*
>
> Some even looked alive, though no *fome* flowed beneath the skin.
>
> A little later as he sped southward along a Florida *uwurt,* he was stopped by a state police officer.

If you were able to figure out that *whitors* means "faces," *fome* means "blood," and *uwurt* means "highway," congratulations. But is your performance on these sentences indicative of your genuine ability to use contextual analysis? Imagine students who correctly complete 20 sentences similar to those you have just tried. The students may be left with the impression that they have mastered the use of context for determining word meanings. Then imagine their enthusiastic attempt to apply their new skills with a real passage from a history textbook.

To understand the possible frustrations students encounter when told to "use the cues around the word to find its meaning," read the following passage about the Andersonville Prison. As you read, think about the difficulty a ninth grader might have in trying to determine the meanings of the italicized general words using contextual analysis.

> Prisoners from the North during the Civil War who found themselves in Andersonville had to contend with unhealthful, *debilitating* conditions as well as *depredations* by their fellow inmates, who frequently stole food, clothing, and whatever other necessities for survival they could lay their hands on. The Andersonville Raiders were a large, organized group of thieves and murderers. For nearly four months these *notorious predators* controlled what went on inside the prison, committing robbery and murder on a daily basis. Finally, after six leaders were captured and a quick trial by fellow inmates, they were hanged on July 11, 1864.
>
> When the war ended, the *emaciated* survivors of Andersonville returned to their homes amidst *strident* demands in the North for swift *retribution.* It was claimed that prison commanders were responsible for deliberately planned *atrocities.**

As you undoubtedly discovered, trying to figure out the meaning of such words as *emaciated* and *atrocities* using context alone is very difficult. Schatz and Baldwin's (1986) research concurs. In this study, instead of using high-frequency words and researcher-made passages, they chose to use low-frequency words and passages from history and science textbooks. They found the use of context clues ineffective in helping students determine the meanings of those targeted low-frequency words. This is a critical aspect of contextual analysis because students' textbooks are typically lean on clues, and students need to learn how to cope with those contexts.

Teachers Can Help Students to Use Context Clues with Several Different Strategies

If very few clues to meaning are provided for textbook vocabulary, how do we teach our students to use context clues? Despite the fact that real text is not always generous in providing clues to the meaning of unknown words, several approaches can be used to help students become more aware of the importance of contextual analysis. In addition, these teaching approaches can help students develop a habit of using context in conjunction with other strategies to establish or verify word meanings.

---

*Adapted from B. Bowles, Prison site in Georgia marks Civil War horror, *Detroit News,* December 11, 1988, p. 11-H.

Previewing in Context

Previewing in context is a teacher-directed activity that relies on modeling and demonstrating to students how word meanings can sometimes be inferred from the context. Modeling how you go about finding clues to word meanings with actual content reading materials allows students to see the practical application of this skill. As an example of how modeling can be used to help students understand some of the key vocabulary in the passage about the Andersonville Raiders, consider these previewing-in-context strategies employed by a ninth-grade teacher.

First, she read the text carefully, and identified general and specific key vocabulary and all the words and terms likely to pose difficulty for her students. Her list included the following words:

debilitating	predators
strident	inhumane
depredations	emaciated
retributions	notorious
atrocities	expired

Next, she considered the list and pared it down to those words she felt were essential to the overall understanding of the material and consistent with her unit objectives. She included those words that could be used most instructively for teaching contextual analysis. The reason for this step was both to avoid spending too much valuable class time on teaching vocabulary and to leave several unfamiliar words for the students to analyze independently. Through this process, her list was limited to the following:

debilitating	emaciated
predator	expired
inhumane	

When she directed students to each word and its surrounding context, she "thought out loud," modeling using the context to determine word meanings. She questioned students to help them discover a word's probable meaning in the existing context. Some of her specific strategies follow.

1. She spent a considerable amount of time activating students' prior knowledge for the topic. She knew that most of her ninth graders had some information about prison conditions in general. Perhaps they had seen TV documentaries of World War II concentration camps or had read about what it is like to be in prison. Using what her students already knew about the topic, she made it easier for them to figure out many difficult words in this passage, especially the word *emaciated.*
2. She reminded students of what they already knew about syntax and word order in sentences. This clue was helpful in narrowing the contextual

definition of *debilitating* because it appeared between a modifier (*unhealthy*) and a noun (*conditions*).

3. She activated students' prior knowledge acquired in studying other subjects. She thought it likely that the students had encountered the word *predator* in science class as a technical vocabulary word. They were shown how to apply their understanding of the word in science to this context.
4. She impressed on the students the importance of taking advantage of any obvious clues provided. For instance, in the last sentence, the students were given an obvious clue to the meaning of *expired*—died, which was used earlier in the sentence.
5. She alerted students to clues within words—for example, ***in*** in the word *inhumane.*
6. She made students aware of the idea that context is more than just the few words surrounding an unknown word or the sentence in which the unknown word appears. She helped expand their notion of context to include information and ideas within, before, and after the passage.
7. She demonstrated checking the dictionary to validate her hunches about the meaning of a word.

Previewing in context is an honest way of demonstrating how challenging it is for readers to employ contextual analysis for determining word meanings in text. Although students' attempts to use context clues may not always produce precise meanings, the use of contextual analysis in conjunction with other sources and approaches should increase their comprehension and understanding.

Possible Sentences

Possible Sentences Involves Students in Writing, Discussing, and Reading to Confirm Predictions

Possible Sentences is a teacher-directed prereading activity that prepares students for the technical and general vocabulary they will encounter in a reading assignment (Moore & Moore, 1986). During this activity, students make predictions about content, establish connections between words and concepts, write, discuss, and read their assignments carefully to verify their predictions. Stahl and Kapinus's (1990) research with fifth graders indicated that the Possible Sentences Activity could improve students' written recall and long-term understanding of word meanings.

The Possible Sentences Activity requires minimal advance material preparation but a considerable amount of teacher time in thinking and planning. First, the teacher identifies the general or technical vocabulary that is key to the theme of the unit and is adequately defined by the context. For this activity to succeed, at least five to eight words should be taken from a subsection of a chapter rather than three or four words dispersed across an entire chapter. For example, in the Andersonville Prison excerpt, the following words could be used for part of the lesson:

debilitating predators inhumane expired

Teachers need to select the targeted words carefully because students must be able to verify their predictions by reading the text during the third step.

During the second step, the teacher asks students to select at least two words from the list and generate one sentence that they think might possibly be in the text. Students can either write their sentence before sharing or dictate their sentences to the teacher spontaneously. As students share their predicted sentences, the teacher writes them on the overhead transparency or chalkboard. Moore and Moore (1986) stress that it is important for the teacher to write the sentences just as they are dictated, even if students provide inaccurate information or use the word incorrectly. With the Andersonville Prison excerpt, students might pair the following words in this manner:

> In the Andersonville Prison the *predators expired.*
>
> During the Civil War the *inhumane* generals were *debilitating.*

Note that the second example uses the word *debilitating* in a syntactically incorrect manner, but the teacher recorded it. This sharing of predicted sentences should continue until all the words on the list have been included in at least one sentence.

In step three, the teacher asks the students to read their text to verify the accuracy of the sentences the class created. Once students have finished their reading, during step four they evaluate the predicted sentences. Moore and Moore (1986) recommend that students ask these questions to evaluate the sentences: (1) Which sentences are accurate? (2) Which need further elaboration? (3) Which cannot be validated because the passage did not deal specifically with them? For example, with the first possible sentence cited previously, the teacher would want the students to realize that the predators did die, but not a natural death. The Possible Sentence merely needed more elaboration (i.e., "The predators were caught, tried, and expired as a result of hanging"). With the second Possible Sentence, students will need to discuss the meaning and usage of the word *debilitating,* but the context should provide an adequate model for making their evaluations and revisions.

With the fifth and final step of Possible Sentences, students are asked to create new sentences using the targeted words. This activity can be a homework assignment for the next class period, or it can occur during class as students work in pairs or share in the large-group discussion. As students share these sentences, everyone should be involved in checking the text, as well as the agreed-on definitions generated during class discussion.

Possible Sentences Involves Students in Elaborative Thinking Processes

On the plus side, the Possible Sentences Activity involves students in the elaborative thinking processes that characterize active learning. However, as with any teacher-directed activity, it will not work with all units of study. This is especially true for units containing a lot of technical vocabulary for which students may not have any prior knowledge.

Previewing in context and Possible Sentences are two teacher-directed strategies for helping students become more comfortable in using contextual analysis to unlock the meaning of difficult words. If students can learn how to use context clues in conjunction with other word-meaning approaches, they will increase their chances of understanding content area vocabulary.

Using the Dictionary

If you have ever asked someone the meaning of a word, you were probably told to "look it up in the dictionary." You probably can also recall the frustration you felt as you tried to make sense of the entry once you found the word. Often you were given a definition that would help only someone who already knew the meaning of the word. For example, look up the meaning of the word *conservative* in your dictionary. Did you find a definition similar to this one?

> "of or relating to a philosophy of conservatism" (*Webster's Ninth New Collegiate Dictionary*)

Did that definition help you? More important, would that definition help your students understand the word *conservative?* Dictionaries are not a panacea for learning the meanings of unknown words.

Interpreting a dictionary entry and identifying an appropriate and useful definition requires sophisticated thinking skills (Miller & Gildea, 1987). Thus, if students are not taught how to use a dictionary, they will have several predictable problems. One such problem is that many students target only a part of the definition, ignoring the rest of the entry (Miller & Gildea, 1987). In fact, many students do not read beyond the first definition, even though some dictionaries place the oldest and least used definition first. For example, the first meaning of *excoriate* in *Webster's Collegiate Dictionary* (10th ed.) is to "tear or wear off the skin of." Imagine the difficulty students might have in comprehending text if they had only that definition for *excoriate.* A recent magazine article described how Washington officials were about to *excoriate* the FBI for the way in which they conducted their investigation. With only the first definition, students would have a rather grisly interpretation of what the FBI was about to endure. However, had students read the second definition, they would have discovered that the word also means to "denounce or censure strongly."

Students Need Help in Using the Dictionary Since It Is Not Very "Considerate"

A second common problem students have with interpreting entries is that they find a familiar word in the definition and attempt to substitute it for the unknown word. Nist and Olejnik (1995) cite a good example of this with the word *liaison.* They point out that the dictionary definition of the word is "a close relationship, connection, or link." One of their students who read that definition substituted the familiar word *connection* for *liaison* and wrote the following sentence: "The storm caused a *liaison* between the two islands."

A third problem students have in using the dictionary is that they cannot construct an adequate and precise meaning from the vague and disjointed fragments provided in the dictionary entries. As McKeown (1990) points out, dictionaries give "multiple pieces of information but offer no guidance in how they should be integrated" (p. 6). Nist and Olejnik (1995) provide an excellent illustration of this problem with the word *vacuous.* The dictionary entry for *vacuous* is "devoid of matter, empty, stupid, lacking serious purpose." Unable to synthesize the vague

Dictionaries Must Be Used with a Lot of Textual Context and Discussion in Class

parts of this definition, one of Nist's students wrote this sentence: "The glass was *vacuous* because I was thirsty and drank all the Gatorade."

Do these problems that students have with dictionaries mean that we, as teachers, should avoid the dictionary in our classroom? Of course not. What we want to stress is that the dictionary, with all its limitations, can be a tool in building word knowledge. However, it should be used in conjunction with personal experiences and textual context if students are to learn the meanings of unknown words. In short, dictionaries can validate students' hunches about words.

From our experiences as teachers, we believe that students must be taught how to use and interpret the dictionary if we want them to construct useful and precise definitions. How can we help students use the dictionary? Perhaps the most important thing we can do is to avoid giving students lists of words to look up in the dictionary. Without the context of a sentence or paragraph, students will not be able to construct an appropriate definition for the general or technical word and consequently will not be able to apply the word correctly.

We can also help students if we teach and reinforce the following ideas about the dictionary:

We Can Help Students Use Dictionaries If They Learn How to Interpret Entries

1. *The format and organization of a dictionary entry.* For example, each dictionary has its own system or hierarchy for arranging definitions. Many dictionaries, such as *Webster's Ninth New Collegiate Dictionary,* list definitions in order of historical usage, thus making their last definition the most current or most widely used. However, others list the most current or widely used definition first. Students need to know that this information can be found by reading the user's guide or introduction.

2. *The abbreviations and symbols in an entry.* Dictionary entries contain numerous abbreviations and symbols that initially confuse students. These must be mastered so that students can decipher the entries. For example, it is important for students to know that "n, pl" stands for the plural noun form of a word.

3. The *etymological information in a typical entry.* Etymological information usually occurs between square brackets [ ] and may appear before the definitions or after them. Inside the brackets are the origins of a word and some interesting stories connected with words such as *meander* or *snafu.* In addition, students may see how the word has changed meaning over time.

4. *How to select the most appropriate definition for the situation in which they encountered the word.* Because words have meaning only when placed in context, it is important for students to learn how to select the correct definition in a dictionary. This is difficult for students for many reasons. One reason is that dictionary entries contain definitions for words used as different parts of speech and for words used in specialized areas. For example, the word *anchors* can be a noun and a verb and can occur in nautical and sports situations.

Contextual analysis and dictionary use are two ways in which students can begin to understand new words from a content area. However, there are more powerful approaches that content area teachers can use to build students' vocabulary knowledge.

TEACHER-DIRECTED APPROACHES FOR BUILDING VOCABULARY KNOWLEDGE

In this section, we outline several different ways in which teachers can introduce and reinforce the general and technical vocabulary words that are important to students' understanding of content area concepts. Using the principle that students will understand and remember more when they experience concepts in a direct and relevant fashion, we begin by explaining firsthand concept development. The next approach, semantic-feature analysis, emphasizes the importance of students' elaborative understanding of key content area vocabulary. We should point out that in Chapter 5 there are several other strategies similar to semantic-feature analysis that can be used to teach and reinforce vocabulary—strategies such as the graphic organizer.

Activities Encouraging Firsthand Concept Development

Firsthand Concept Development Can Be a Motivating Influence in the Classroom

The terminology in content textbooks is often sterile, abstract, and lifeless, which makes this content especially difficult to understand and retain and leaves students unmotivated to read. Standing before the class and stating glossary-type definitions of textbook vocabulary merely reinforces students' passivity. We need to find ways of making key terms and concepts come alive for students so that they are motivated to read and learn.

Firsthand concept development refers to a variety of approaches that provide students with direct ways of experiencing words (Sartain & Stahl, 1982). Direct or firsthand involvement with words can include dramatized experiences, demonstrations, case studies, field trips, exhibits, television shows or movies, or computer simulations. The premise underlying this vocabulary approach is that information stored in long-term memory is undoubtedly a result of a great deal of mental, emotional, and physical involvement with the content.

Ideally, students should be given opportunities to have direct contact with all the words they encounter. For instance, students about to study a unit about meteorology could be allowed to hold and inspect a barometer or a rain gauge. Unfortunately, many technical vocabulary words are too abstract to be easily represented by a physical object brought into the classroom. Therefore, you must invent ways to make abstract terminology tangible for students. We will examine how three different content area teachers' inventions or approaches helped their students experience concepts in a firsthand manner. Bernard used a demonstration, Margo involved her students in a scavenger hunt, and Tom photographed his students demonstrating adjectives.

You Can Arrange Firsthand Concept Development in a Variety of Ways

Demonstrations

Bernard, a senior high psychology teacher, used an inventive activity to help his students experience and understand a key concept they were preparing to read about in their textbooks. The topic was human memory, and the class was asked to write 10 things they did the first day of second grade. Over the initial moans and groans, Bernard insisted that each student list 10 items within a couple of minutes to "play the game" properly. Eventually, all students were busy working on their lists. When they were finished, Bernard asked them to read the items on their lists and to talk about how they produced the items they could not recall with certainty. Students read off such things as "met the teacher," "talked with my friends from first grade," "took my seat," "received my books," and so on. Most said they could not remember all the details about what they did the first day of second grade, but they listed the things they assumed they had done. Afterward, Bernard explained that the students had been "confabulating" by creating their lists on the basis of related experience rather than definite memory.

Defined in the traditional way, with a textbook definition, *confabulation* is a sterile term. When students were allowed to experience confabulation firsthand, however, they had an experience to which they could affix the meaning of the concept in memory. In turn, the textbook chapter on memory should be easier to understand. Bernard said that his students remembered the meaning of *confabulation* and other concepts long after the unit in which they appeared had been completed if he tied an experience to the process of learning the terms. Firsthand concept development allows for greater student involvement in learning new terminology and concepts, which then encourages deeper understanding of the concepts and improves the likelihood that the textual information you are stressing will be easier to comprehend. Word scavenger hunts also have this potential.

Word Scavenger Hunts

All of us have participated in a real scavenger hunt at some time in our lives. Remember the thrill and excitement of competing with other teams in trying to be the first to gather assorted items in a limited time? Scavenger hunts for helping students build word meanings by collecting real items and pictures are valuable because they are fun, develop cooperative learning skills, and require active involvement. These elements of the strategy ensure that vocabulary learning will be more memorable (Moore, Moore, Cunningham, & Cunningham, 1986).

An eighth-grade science class developed a genuine "learning frenzy" when given the opportunity to work in cooperative groups and compete with other groups in a **word scavenger hunt.** The teacher, Margo, had selected vocabulary words from a textbook chapter on astronomy, words for which she thought students could find actual objects, models, or pictures. She included the key terms that the students needed to learn to gain a full understanding of the important content of the astronomy unit. In compiling her master list, which follows, she included technical words she knew would be easy to collect, as well as difficult words:

comet	meteor	pulsar	nova	cosmic dust
red giant	sextant	black hole	radiation	big bang
telescope	asteroid	gravity	radar	crater

Margo divided her class into teams of four students and explained the scavenger hunt to be sure that all of them understood the rules and purpose. She accomplished this by asking students to share their experiences with scavenger hunting. She then specified the conditions of the competition:

- Students must bring in objects and pictures by a certain date.
- No team should reveal to any other team which items they collected and where they found the items until the hunt is over.

As she handed out the master list of content vocabulary words to each team, Margo explained that teams would earn 3 points for an actual object, 2 points for a model or facsimile, and 1 point for a picture. A few students asked if they were allowed to draw or trace, and Margo said that such art would be admissible; however, the drawing should reflect genuine effort and should not be something put together minutes before the conclusion of the hunt. She went on to explain that an object or a picture cannot count for more than one word. Teams were then given the opportunity to assign specific roles to each of their members and to discuss strategies for finding words. Teams were allowed 1 week to complete the hunt.

During the week, teams met a couple of times to update their progress in finding words and to revise their strategy, if necessary. Periodically, they were reminded to maintain secrecy about the status of the hunt, which heightened the suspense of the competition. By midweek, some students were complaining that they could not find an object or a picture for certain words. Margo told them that it might be impossible to collect objects or pictures for every word. Statements of this kind inevitably push teams to search out difficult words with renewed vigor just to prove the teacher wrong.

At week's end, the teams were allowed to go over their findings and tally the points. Margo double-checked the teams' figures and looked over the drawings to make sure they clearly represented the words and were not thrown together haphazardly. Finally, the team with the most points was declared the winner. They were allowed to gloat over their victory only briefly, however, because Margo rewarded each team for its efforts with an opportunity to display and publish its work.

Giving them the following options, Margo asked the groups to select what they wished to do with their findings and provided the necessary materials to get them started:

- Collages with the words on cards appropriately arranged
- Slide shows developed by photographing the objects and pictures and writing a brief explanation
- Picture books with photographs and illustrations accompanied by a brief explanation
- Newspapers or comic books with pictures and illustrations accompanied by stories
- An exhibit table with objects labeled and briefly described

Not only are word scavenger hunts fun, but they also go a long way toward building relevant prior knowledge for the chapter or unit. Hunts allow students to explore the topic by collecting and reading about key vocabulary words taken from the content. Students gather a great deal of information about the topic and develop an interest in it. The benefits of the hunt last throughout and beyond the unit. For instance, in the classroom just described, students were surrounded during the unit with reminders of the topic's key terms in the form of collages on the wall, a display corner in the back of the room, and books featured on the classroom library shelves.

Word Scavenger Hunts Help Provide Students with More Prior Knowledge for a Unit of Study

The hands-on approach to gathering pictures and objects for words makes scavenger hunting a sound instructional strategy for developing vocabulary and improving comprehension (Cunningham, 1992).

Photographed Vocabulary

Another approach providing firsthand and interesting involvement with a word has been labeled **photographed vocabulary** (Stanley, 1971). This approach involves photographing students as they demonstrate the meaning of one word in a tableau. Tom, a sixth-grade language arts teacher, uses photographed vocabulary because it capitalizes on his students' "unabashed vanity and love of drama." He told us that he begins the process by selecting a list of 25 "actable" words that the class had previously encountered in their literature anthology and discussed. The adjectives the students were to act out or dramatize described people in positive or negative ways and included words such as *garrulous, studious, timid, sinister,* and *eccentric.* Tom then used the following steps to introduce the activity:

Adjectives Work Especially Well for Photographed Vocabulary

1. He told the students that each of them would have responsibility for demonstrating to the class a word from the list. Their demonstration would have to be in a tableau or frozen representation because they would be photographed. While each student was doing his or her tableau, the rest of the class would be writing down the word they felt was being acted out. The entire class would have the list of 25 words, their definitions, and sentences using the words. The students who correctly matched the words to the tableaus would receive 5 extra-credit points.
2. Tom then asked each student to draw from a hat the word he or she would demonstrate. Students were told to be ready with their tableau in 3 days.
3. The next day, the principal visited the class and modeled how she would do a tableau for the word *exasperated.* Tom modeled the word *frenzied.*
4. The day before the assignment was due, Tom checked with all students to make sure they were prepared and offered suggestions for those still groping for ideas.
5. On the day of the photographing, Tom listed the students' names on the board in the order of presentation. As the students posed, he took the pictures and the rest of the class worked to match the word to the tableau.

As a follow-up to the assignment, Tom placed all the pictures on the bulletin board. Even 3 weeks later, students still gathered around the board to check the pictures and discuss the words. Tom told us that this was probably one of the best assignments he had done that year because the students were actually incorporating the words into their writing and speaking, the real touchstone of any vocabulary approach.

Semantic-Feature Analysis

As stated throughout this chapter, to read successfully in the content areas, students must have a deep, elaborative understanding of important concepts. Semantic-feature analysis is a highly effective technique for reinforcing the vocabulary essential to understanding important concepts (Baumann & Kameenui, 1991; Johnson & Pearson, 1984).

Semantic-Feature Analysis Reinforces Many Elaborative Processes Involved in Knowing a Word at the Conceptual Level

Semantic-feature analysis involves building a grid in which essential vocabulary is listed on one axis of the grid and major features, characteristics, or important ideas are listed on the other axis. Students fill in the grid, indicating the extent to which the key words possess the stated features or are related to important ideas. Once the grid is completed, students are led to discover both the shared and unique characteristics of the vocabulary words.

Figure 6.2 is a word grid created for a study of polygons. Notice that the vertical axis contains the names of geometric figures, whereas the horizontal axis contains important features or characteristics of these figures. The extra spaces

	opposite sides parallel	equilateral	equiangular	4-sided	3-sided
square					
rectangle					
triangle					
rhombus					
trapezoid					

FIGURE 6.2 Word Grid for Polygons

allow students to add more vocabulary and features as they work through the reading material.

Another example of the use of word grids (see Figure 6.3) is provided by Aaron, a 10th-grade government teacher, who is particularly effective in teaching key terms and concepts with semantic-feature analysis. He begins by asking his class for the names of fruit, writing them on the blackboard in a vertical list as students call them out. After several fruits are listed, he writes a couple of general features of fruit along the top horizontal axis of the grid, such as "tree grown" and "edible skin"; then he asks for additional features. Finally, he asks the class to consider each type of fruit and whether it possesses any of the listed features. As they go down the list of fruit, they discuss each one relative to the characteristics listed across the top, and Aaron puts a 0, 1, or 2 in the box where the fruit and feature meet on the grid. A 0 indicates that the fruit possesses none of that feature, a 1 indicates that it possesses some of that feature, and a 2 means that it possesses all of the feature. When the grid is entirely filled in, Aaron explains to the students how they can, at a glance, determine the key characteristics of a particular fruit, as well as the similarities and differences between the fruits.

By involving students in the construction of a simple word grid, Aaron introduces them to the semantic-feature analysis process. He goes on to explain how to build word grids for the key vocabulary in their textbook. To help students

	edible skin	tree grown	bunches	citrus	fleshy
banana	0	2	2	0	2
peach	2	2	0	0	2
orange	1	2	0	2	0
apple	2	2	0	0	2
grapes	2	0	2	0	2
grapefruit	0	2	0	2	0

FIGURE 6.3 Word Grid for Fruit

discover how the grid-building process can be applied to the content vocabulary in their texts, he presents a grid based on a section of a recently completed chapter on the Fifth Amendment to the Constitution. Aaron tells them that in building the grid, he first read the selection and identified the major ideas. Next, he listed in a phrase or a single word the vocabulary that represented or was related to each idea. This was followed by an examination of the list to determine which words represent the biggest ideas (indicated by asterisks in Figure 6.4).

Then Aaron identified the words representing the important details related to the major ideas. At this point, he says, he now had enough information to organize the vocabulary and major ideas into a grid, with the major ideas across the top and the related vocabulary listed on the side (Figure 6.5).

Aaron then walks students through the process of deciding on components of the grid, discussing with them the relationship between each major idea and each vocabulary word as they fill in the grid together.

Later, as his students improve their ability to design word grids, Aaron gives them increasing responsibility to complete grids on their own. This is accomplished by providing them with partially filled-in grids containing a few key vocabulary words and major ideas or essential features. As students move through the chapter or unit of study, they expand the grid work to include additional vocabulary and features.

These students are also allowed plenty of time for class discussion and for review of the vocabulary and major ideas. They are given the opportunity to work in cooperative groups where they share their entries on the grids and review each vocabulary word, noting the pattern of numbers (0, 1, 2).

We recommend semantic-feature analysis for three reasons: (1) It is supported by solid theory and research (Baumann & Kameenui, 1991; Bos, Anders, Filip, & Jaffe, 1989; Johnson, Toms-Bronowski, & Pittelman, 1981), (2) it is relatively easy for classroom teachers to implement and for students to use, and (3) it enables students to learn the relationships between and among the key vocabulary and major concepts in the text, thus enhancing both vocabulary development and reading comprehension (Anders & Bos, 1986).

These approaches to vocabulary development—firsthand concept development and semantic-feature analysis—are typically initiated by the content area teacher to improve conceptual understanding. In the next section, we present

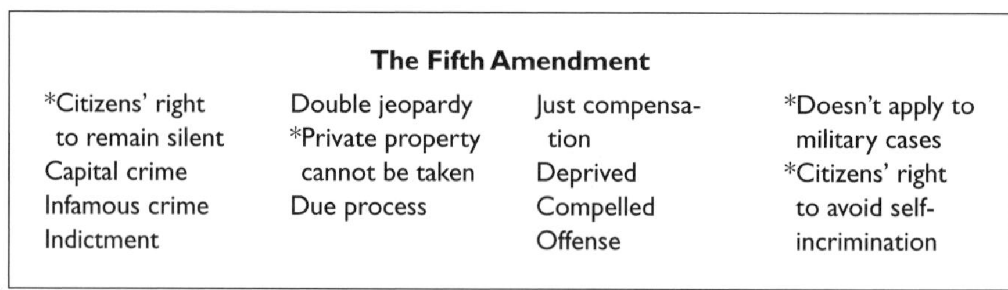

FIGURE 6.4 Key Vocabulary for a Word Grid for the Fifth Amendment

The Fifth Amendment

	citizens' right to remain silent	private property cannot be taken	doesn't apply to military cases	citizens' right to avoid self-incrimination
capital crime				
infamous crime				
indictment				
double jeopardy				
due process				
just compensation				
deprived				
compelled				
offense				

FIGURE 6.5 Word Grid for the Fifth Amendment

some ways in which content area teachers can teach students generative strategies for building their own vocabularies.

PROMOTING INDEPENDENT WORD LEARNING

As we made clear earlier in this chapter, content area teachers should be concerned about two vitally important aspects of vocabulary development. One is to teach key vocabulary and concepts that students need in order to understand the important content, whether in a listening or reading situation. The previous section demonstrated several effective ways in which classroom teachers can help their students develop elaborative understandings of critical terms and concepts. Another equally important aspect of vocabulary development is to teach students a variety of strategies for independently gathering and learning new words. This section describes and exemplifies generative methods of vocabulary development that can be used in a variety of content areas. Below we discuss two generative strategies—word maps and concept cards.

Generative or Independent Means of Knowing a Word Are Also Essential for Active Learners

Word Maps

Students will become more independent in their vocabulary learning if we provide instruction that gradually shifts the responsibility for generating meanings for new words from us to them. One effective way of encouraging this transition is with word maps. Schwartz and Raphael (1985) developed this strategy for helping students establish a concept of definition for content area words. The strategy stresses the importance of teaching students how to use context clues independently, how to determine if they know what a word means, and how to use prior knowledge to enhance their understanding of words.

To build a **word map,** students write the concept being studied, or the word they would like to define, in the center box of a map, such as *quark* in Figure 6.6. Next, in the top box they write a brief answer to the question "What is it?" This question seeks a name for the class or category that includes the concept. In defining *quark,* the category is a "subatomic particle." In responding to the question to the right, "What is it like?" students write critical attributes, characteristics, or properties of the concept or word. In the example, three critical properties of quarks are listed. The question along the bottom, "What are some examples?", can be answered by supplying examples of different kinds of quarks, such as *top* and *charmed.*

Teaching students how to create word maps not only gives them a strategy for generating word meanings independently but also, because of the checking process they go through in asking questions about the context, fosters self-monitoring and metacognitive thinking (Schwartz, 1988). The goal, therefore, is to help students internalize this test-questioning process for all of the important words they must learn. All of us ask similar questions when we encounter unfamiliar words in context, though we rarely, if ever, draw (as in the form of a word map) the information we are seeking about the words. Think of the word map as a visual representation of students' thought processes while trying to figure out word meanings in context. Eventually, after they have demonstrated an understanding of the process by creating appropriate word maps, students should be shown that they do not have to create a map for every word they do not know. Instead, they should go through the questioning process in their heads, as mature readers do.

Word Maps Can Build Students' Metacognition

To help you understand how students can be taught to use word maps in the classroom, we describe the experiences of Tonya, an eighth-grade science

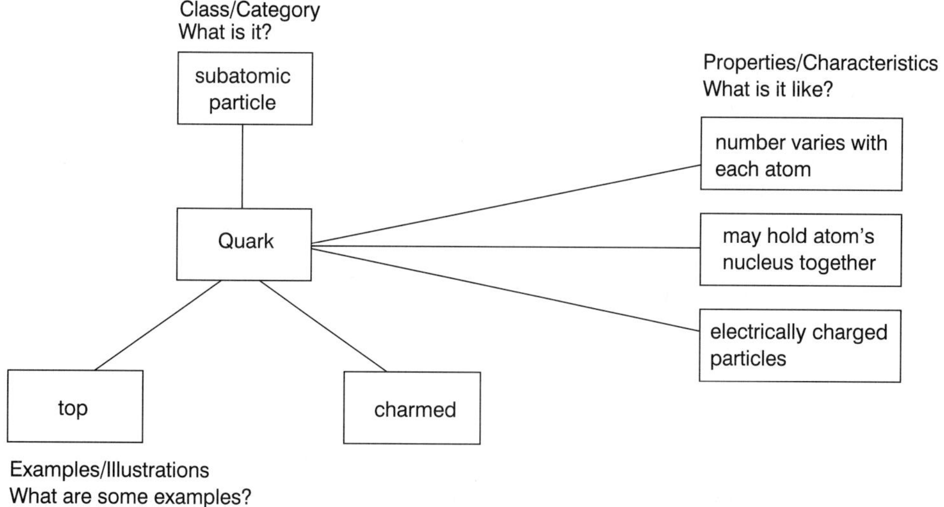

FIGURE 6.6 Word Map for *Quark*

teacher. She began her vocabulary lesson by displaying the structure of the word map and introducing it as a visual guide to remind her students of what they needed to know to understand a new, important word or concept. As the components of the map were discussed, she supplied a concept and filled in answers to the questions on the map with information from a recently studied chapter in their science textbook.

Tonya then directed students to the chapter they were about to read and, with their help, identified a key concept occurring in the first few pages: *conifer.* She asked the students to work in cooperative groups to find information in their texts and in their heads to answer the questions on the word map. As they read about conifers, they discussed the relevant information that helped define the concept and inserted it into the appropriate spaces on the map they were creating. When they completed their maps, Tonya modeled how information about class/category, properties/characteristics, and examples related to the concept could be pulled from the context. She talked about how contexts vary from **complete** (containing rich information) to **partial** (containing scanty information). She encouraged students to include their own information and ideas, especially with stingy contexts, to further their understanding of the word. Drawing on the input from groups, the whole class then worked together to create a word map for *conifer* (see Figure 6.7).

At this point, Tonya asked her students to write a definition for *conifer* based on the word-map activity. Afterward, she asked them to work in their cooperative groups and evaluate each other's definitions to determine if they were complete and, if not, to write down whatever additional information was needed. Definitions were then returned to their owners, who responded to the group's

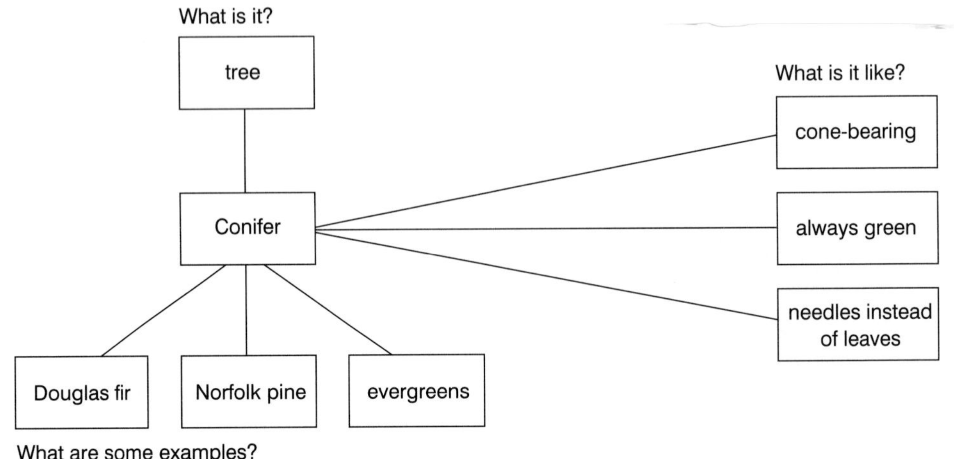

FIGURE 6.7 Word Map for *Conifer*

feedback. With their maps and definitions completed, students were shown that their work can serve as excellent study aids for long-term retention of the concept.

Tonya ended the day's lesson by assigning the students to create word maps for three other key concepts in the chapter. Before leaving, students began their assignment by identifying the possible concepts in the chapter. This procedure of modeling and assigning continued throughout the semester until Tonya was sure that students knew how to apply the word-map strategy independently to their science vocabulary. She also encouraged students to try applying it to their other courses.

Word maps can help students guide their search for new information, monitor their learning of vocabulary, and improve understanding and recall of content area concepts.

Concept Cards

Concept Cards Are More than Flash Cards

Concept cards are another strategy students can use to learn difficult general or technical vocabulary (Nist & Simpson, 1997). You may have used these in your own studying but probably called them *flash cards.* Even though **concept cards** have the same format as flash cards in that they allow students to test themselves, we prefer the term *concept cards* because they involve students in learning more than just definitions for difficult terminology. As illustrated in Figure 6.8, on the front of the concept card, students write the targeted word and the superordinate idea for the word. On the back of the card, they provide the following information, when appropriate: (1) definition(s), (2) characteristics or features, (3) examples from the text and/or personal experiences, and (4) personal sentences. The card in Figure 6.9 illustrates how one 12th grader used concept cards to study the technical terms in her business course. Notice how she adapted the card to fit her purposes.

SUPERORDINATE IDEA

TARGETED WORD

[FRONT OF THE CARD]

1. Definitions
2. Characteristics: features
3. Examples (text or personal)
4. Personal sentences

[BACK OF CARD]

FIGURE 6.8 Content of a Concept Card

Students can use either 4 × 6 or 3 × 5 index cards, but it is important that they use cards rather than pieces of notebook paper because the cards encourage students to test themselves rather than to look at the terminology passively. Cards are also more durable and portable, allowing students to study them while standing in line, riding the bus, or waiting for class to begin.

Concept Cards Can Be Used for Both General and Technical Words

Carol, a teacher for gifted seventh graders, asks students to create concept cards for the general words she wants them to learn during the year. The words she selects for their study come from their integrated history and literature units. Because she wants her students to understand the original context and to apply the word to new situations, Carol asks them to write the original sentence on the front of the card and at least one original sentence on the back. She omits

FIGURE 6.9 A Concept Card by a 12th Grader for Technical Terms in a Business Course

There are 2 types

FORMAL ORGANIZATION

1. Clearly defined relationships, channels of communication, and delegation of authority.
2. Characteristics: clearly defined authority relationships, well-developed communication systems, stable/permanent, capable of expansion.
3. Tools of formal organizations include charts, policy manuals, organization manuals.
4. Example: where my father words (IBM).

the characteristics and personal examples components from the back of the card because they are not typically appropriate. However, she requires students to include antonyms of the targeted word and to state whether the word has a positive or negative connotation. Figure 6.10 illustrates a concept card a student made for the word *turgid* that came from a short story.

To determine the students' accuracy in finding the most appropriate dictionary definition and their precision in writing a sentence that uses the words correctly, Carol usually checks the cards while students are working in groups on another activity. By doing these quick checks of the cards, she knows what words need to be emphasized the next day during discussion. Carol is a strong believer in taking time to discuss words so students can hear the various defini-

adjective

TURGID

The 13-page text includes a poem, an introduction, and a *turgid* opening chapter interpreting the First Seal.

1. Excessively ornate, flashy, wordy, and pompous in style or language
2. Synonym: *bombastic*   Antonym: *plain, simple language*

The minister's turgid sermon put everyone to sleep on the warm Sunday evening.

FIGURE 6.10 Concept Card for the Word *Turgid*

tions and sentences that their classmates have written. She tells us that the nuances and connotations of words are not learned from the dictionary; rather, they are learned from "trying on the words and playing with them" in an environment that invites experimentation.

Carol models for the students how they should study their concept cards because she has discovered that many of them merely look at the front of their cards and then at the back without testing themselves or reciting aloud. While modeling, she makes sure that students realize the importance of saying the definitions and sentences aloud. Moreover, she stresses the importance of practicing from front to back and from back to front on the cards, as well as the usefulness of making piles of cards representing the words that are known and the words that need further study. Carol has been requiring students to make concept cards for about 5 years. She has noticed a substantial improvement in their retention of the words and, more important, their use of the words in their written work.

Word Sorts Using Concept Cards

Word Sorts Are Excellent Reinforcement Activities That Involve Little Teacher Preparation

A **word sort** is an excellent reinforcement activity that students can use with their concept cards. During a word sort, students group their cards into different categories with common features. There are two types of word sorts: closed and open (Gillet & Kita, 1979).

With the **closed sort,** students know in advance the categories in which they must place their cards. For example, the students in Carol's class were asked to sort their concept cards into positive adjectives and negative adjectives. Thus, students sorted words such as *turgid, pretentious, neurotic,* and *condescending* into the negative adjectives category and words such as *charismatic* and *diligent* into the positive adjectives category. Carol tells students to do this activity in small groups and then asks each group to explain and justify their groupings. Being able to manipulate the concept cards makes the word-sort activity more interesting and flexible for students.

Open sorts require students to determine ways in which their general or technical vocabulary can be grouped. Therefore, students search for relationships that might exist among the words rather than depending on the teacher to provide that structure. In a ninth-grade science class, students were studying pollution and were asked to group their concept cards into one or more categories. The following words share some common categories:

biodegradable	photosynthesis
leaching	surface mining
incineration	acid mine drainage
silting	reclamation projects

Can you group the words into some categories? With open sorts, there are no correct categories. Instead, what is important is that students can explain and justify how they grouped the words. Possible sorts or categories with the preceding words include the broad category of land pollution. On a more specific level of sorting, categories might include causes of land pollution (i.e., silting, acid mine drainage, leaching) and solutions (i.e., biodegradable, reclamation projects). Because open sorts demand more elaborative thinking, they probably should be preceded by several closed-sort activities. Students, however, enjoy both types of activities. More important, teacher preparation for this activity is minimal.

In this section, we have discussed two generative strategies for helping students learn the meanings of technical and general vocabulary independently in their content area courses. Other formats emphasizing the processes involved in conceptual understanding are available. For example, Diekhoff, Brown, and Dansereau (1982) have studied the Node Acquisition and Integration Technique, and Carr (1985) has studied the vocabulary overview guide. Both of these vocabulary strategies emphasize processes similar to word maps and concept cards, but each has a different appearance. Teachers can create an appropriate format once they understand the processes involved in knowing a word at a conceptual level and the ways in which students can be taught to employ strategies independently. In the next section, we examine how content area teachers can reinforce and evaluate students' understanding of words with activities similar to word sorts.

ACTIVITIES FOR REINFORCING AND EVALUATING WORD KNOWLEDGE

As mentioned earlier in this chapter, one characteristic of effective vocabulary instruction is that teachers reinforce students' word learning over time. That is, once targeted vocabulary words have been introduced and discussed, students need to use those words in a variety of new situations. Therefore, fewer words will be taught, and more instructional time will be provided for meaningful reinforcement activities and cumulative review if we want to promote students' understanding of content area textbooks.

The first vocabulary review strategies discussed, imagery and key words, can be used across the content areas to help students learn technical and general words.

Imagery and Keywords

Imagery and Keyword Strategies Are Excellent Ways to Reinforce Word Knowledge

Have you ever created a mental picture to remember a difficult word or procedure? Many of us do this routinely because we know that images can be powerful reminders. For example, if the targeted word you need to learn is *acrophobia,* what mental picture could you use to remember that the word means fear of high places? One option would be to focus on the first part of the word, *acro,* and develop the image of an acrobat who is afraid of heights walking on a tightrope high in the sky. You could follow up with a sentence such as this: "The acrobat, who has always been afraid of high places, suffered from acrophobia." When we make pictures in our minds to help us remember what a word means or how it relates to another word or superordinate concept, we are using the strategy of **imagery.** Research suggests that imagery can be a powerful tool for reinforcing vocabulary knowledge (e.g., Levin, 1993; Smith, Stahl, & Neel, 1987).

The **keyword strategy** differs slightly from imagery in that we think of catchy phrases or sentences related to the word we want to remember. For example, if you were having trouble remembering *amorous,* you might think about a phrase such as "more love for us," which sounds like *amorous* but has a synonym for the word in it. Although the research findings on the keyword and imagery strategies are positive and promising, they will not work for every vocabulary word or for every student. In addition, it is important to remember that students' personal images or catchy phrases will always be more powerful than the images or phrases provided by their teacher.

Dale, a 10th-grade biology teacher, uses a combination of imagery and keywords to help his students remember difficult definitions and relationships between concepts. During his unit on the endocrine system, he modeled the procedures he used in creating images and keywords to remember the functions of the glands and hormones in the endocrine system. One of his students, Lara, had difficulty applying the strategies, so Dale met with her during homeroom to help her. The lesson follows.

Dale: Lara, let's start with the pituitary gland and the thyrotropic hormone. To remember the definition, we need to think of something memorable from part of the word *thyrotropic.* I'll start first, and then I'll have you help me. When I hear the word *tropic,* I think of the jungles where rain stimulates extreme growth. Thyrotropic hormones stimulate growth in the thyroid, the other part of the word. Do you see what I did, Lara? I took parts of the word that I could remember because they were already familiar to me. Then I made up a sentence to help me remember the definition. Which word would you like to try next?

Lara: I missed *prolactin* on the pop quiz. Can we try this one?

Dale: Okay, Lara. Let's look at the word carefully—each letter and the parts. Can you divide the word into familiar parts?

Lara: Well, there is the word *pro,* which means a professional, in the word *prolactin.* There is also the word *tin.*

Dale: Okay, Lara. Will either of them help you remember the definition of *prolactin*—a hormone that stimulates milk production?

Lara: No, I don't see how.

Dale: Okay. Let's see if we can play with the middle part of the word, *lac.* This part of the word sounds like what word in our language, Lara?

Lara: Lack?

Dale: That's right! Has your mother ever told you that you lack milk—that you should drink more milk if you hope to be healthy?

Lara: Yes! And I hate the stuff.

Dale: Could we use the letters *l-a-c* to remind us of milk? Many people *lack* the correct amount of milk.

Lara: Yes, but what about the *pro* part of the word?

Dale: Good question. Could we use *pro* to remind us in some way that prolactin is a hormone that stimulates milk? Think about this for a moment, Lara.

Lara: (a few seconds later) Yes! Professional athletes should not suffer from a lack of milk. Will that work?

Dale: Will it work for you, Lara? That is what makes the difference.

Lara: Hmm. Yes, I can use that—it makes sense. Professional athletes should not suffer from a lack of milk. Prolactin stimulates milk production.

Dale: Let's review before we go to the next word, Lara. Give me the definitions of *thyrotropic* and *prolactin.*

Lara: Prolactin stimulates the production of milk, and the thyrotropic hormone stimulates the thyroid. This is easy.

Dale: The next hormone you missed on the quiz is *thyroxine.* Lara, what are the steps in this process of remembering a definition of a difficult word?

Notice how Dale encourages Lara to state the steps of this vocabulary strategy before she applies the strategy independently to another word. Had Lara not been able to use the strategy after this individual lesson, Dale would have shown her another strategy to help her keep straight the definitions and functions of the 47 different technical terms in this unit. He tries to present a variety of choices for his students because he knows that not every student will feel comfortable with concept maps or imagery. With Lara, however, imagery and key words worked once she realized the processes involved in them.

Activities and Test Formats That Reinforce and Evaluate Word Learning

Multiple-Choice and Matching Test Formats Do Not Assess Students' Full, Conceptual Knowledge of a Word

If students are to learn their targeted words at a full and conceptual level of understanding, the activities and test formats we select for reinforcement and evaluation should match that level of thinking. Evidence suggests, however, that a mismatch often exists. For example, in their content analysis of 60 vocabulary textbooks and workbooks, Stahl et al. (1987) found that multiple-choice and matching formats were the predominant ways in which words were reinforced and tested. Beck and McKeown (1991) have argued that multiple-choice vocabulary tests just "do not measure the full continuum of word knowledge (p. 796). Even asking students to write a definition of a word from memory does not stimulate conceptual understanding. Therefore, alternative reinforcement and evaluation activities are needed.

Constructing creative and appropriate reinforcement and evaluative activities can be challenging. However, several activities and formats can be incorporated into any classroom routine, homework assignment, or exam (Simpson, 1987). These activities and formats involve students in a variety of elaborative thinking processes. Some of these activities and test formats follow.

Statement Plus a Request

With the **statement plus a request** activity, students read two related statements, each containing the same targeted word. The second statement, however, asks students to demonstrate their knowledge of the word by exceeding the usual simple definition. In a sophomore history class, a teacher included this question on her unit test:

Directions: Read the first statement carefully. Then read the second statement and answer it. Pay close attention to the italicized word.

1. *Statement:* Robert LaFollette was a *Progressive* with many ideas on what he wanted changed in Wisconsin.
2. *Request:* What are some of the *Progressive* ideas that Robert LaFollette had?

Exclusion

Henry (1974) states that excluding is one of the basic operations involved in concept development. When students practice **exclusion,** they discriminate between, negate, and recognize examples and nonexamples. The following example is a sample from an algebra teacher's homework assignment.

Exclusion Activities Involve Students in Elaborative Levels of Thinking

Directions: Choose the one equation in each group that does not relate to the others and should be excluded. Write the letter of it in the blank after "Exclude." In the blank labeled "General Concept," write the concept that describes the remaining words.

Exclusion Activities

1. a. $x^2 - y^2 = (x + y)(x - y)$
   b. $x^2 + 5x + 6 = (x + 3)(x + 2)$
   c. $ax^2 + a^2x = ax(x - a)$
   d. $3x^2 + 4x^2 + 1 = 7x^2 + 1$

   Exclude: ____________________

   General Concept: ____________________

The following example of an exclusion item is from a French teacher's unit test.

1. la glace   la moutarde   le gâteau   la tarte

   Exclude: ____________________

   General concept: ____________________

Paired Word Questions

The long-term vocabulary study by Beck et al. (1982) employed a question-asking activity that paired two targeted words. To answer these **paired word questions,** students must understand the underlined concepts or words and then determine if any relationships exist between them. The following example is one of several items that an art teacher uses during class when he pairs students for a review. Notice that he tests both technical (*avant-garde*) and general (*incoherent*) vocabulary word knowledge.

Directions: Answer the following questions as completely as possible, making sure you demonstrate your full knowledge of the underlined words.

1. Would an avant-garde painting be incoherent? Why or why not?

The next example is from a review activity that a ninth-grade physical education teacher included in a unit on nutrition and fitness:

1. Would an individual with hyperlipidemia be a candidate for coronary heart disease? Why or why not?
2. Would an individual who had a calorie deficit of 3500 kcal lose 1 pound of adipose tissue? Why or why not?

Seeing the Big Picture

With the format called **seeing the big picture,** students are asked to select the word or phrase that subsumes all the other words or phrases. By completing such an item, students demonstrate that they can discriminate the difference between a major concept and a detail or supporting idea. The following example illustrates how a mathematics teacher used the format in one of her review activities.

Directions: Look at the group of words below and select the one word or phrase that subsumes the other four. Circle it.

1. Distributive properties, axiom, multiplicative inverse, cancellation law, additive identities

Analogies

Analogies are multifaceted in that they can involve students in knowing the synonyms or antonyms of targeted words or can encourage students to sense the relationships between words in a variety of ways. In fact, there are probably 50 different formats to the analogy. The following example is from a French teacher's homework assignment.

There Are Many Kinds of Analogies

Directions: Fill in the blank with the appropriate vocabulary word. You may use each word only once.

1. beau: mauvais :: froid: ____________________

The next analogy is from an 11th-grade art class. The teacher had just finished a unit on film and used items such as this for a review activity.

1. celluloid: film :: matte effect: ____________________

Paired Word Sentence Generation

Traditional sentence-writing activities have never been considered particularly creative or productive. However, **paired word sentence generation** forces students to demonstrate their conceptual understanding of both words and to seek out their implied relationship in order to write a sentence that uses the words correctly. The following example illustrates how a history teacher used this format to reinforce important vocabulary words in a class activity.

> *Directions:* You will find two words below that I have purposely paired because they have some relationship to each other. Your task is to write one sentence that uses both of the words correctly and clearly demonstrates your understanding of them and their relationship to each other. The first item has been done for you as an example.
>
> 1. muckrakers, *McClure's Magazine*
>
> The muckrakers included journalists and novelists who wrote magazines such as *McClure's Magazine* and books such as *The Jungle* to expose the evils and corruption in business and politics.
>
> 2. Wisconsin idea, referendum

The next example comes from a music teacher's lesson.

> *Directions:* Write a sentence using the following word pairs. I have purposely paired the two words because they have some relationship to each other.
>
> 1. cadence, afterphase
> 2. binary form, ternary form

These Alternative Formats Should Be Used to Evaluate Students' Understanding of Content Area Concepts

Because these alternative activities and formats may initially confuse or surprise the students, a few important guidelines about their use should be remembered (Simpson, 1987). First, match the reinforcement or evaluation activity to the unit objectives or goals. Students can only demonstrate the level of conceptual understanding that they have been involved in during the unit. Second, vary the activities and formats across the school year and within the units of study. For example, a history teacher might include five exclusions, five analogies, and five paired word sentence- generation activities into a unit test to represent the different thinking processes underlying conceptual understanding. Finally, inform, practice, and discuss the differing activities and formats with students, especially before they see them on a test. If students are not accustomed to a new activity or test format, their response or score could mask their real understanding. In fact, it is always a good idea to provide a sample item, as did the history teacher for the paired word activity.

CASE STUDY REVISITED

We now return to the Parkview School District, where a districtwide committee of teachers has been meeting throughout the school year to solve the problem of extremely low vocabulary scores in the eighth grade. After reading this chapter, you probably have some ideas on how the committee could solve this problem. Take a moment now to write your suggestions.

By the end of the school year, Liz, the Curriculum Director, and the eighth-grade teachers on the committee had reached only one decision. One eighth-grade science teacher had discussed an article he had read on the characteristics of effective vocabulary instruction, prompting the committee to decide that there were no "quick fixes" and that no single type of commercial material would fully address their school's problems. Perhaps that decision was the most important because it removed as an option the vocabulary computer program that several members were urging the school to adopt. The committee members realized that the computer program expected students to learn the targeted words in lists with no context, and that only rote-level definitional knowledge was emphasized on the activities and quizzes. Hence, they were concerned about whether students would learn the words well enough to be able to apply them to new situations.

Although the committee did reach agreement on the use of commercial materials for Parkview School District, they still disagreed about the language arts teachers' role in improving students' vocabulary. Some teachers saw the teaching of vocabulary as a time-consuming intrusion into an already hectic teaching schedule. Moreover, they viewed vocabulary instruction as a natural and logical part of a language arts curriculum. Consequently, the Curriculum Director suggested that the issue be tabled for a while, at least until they had finished their intensive study of vocabulary acquisition.

During the summer, the committee members were provided with a stipend to read and plan further. The Curriculum Director had the money for their study because expensive commercial materials had not been purchased from the school budget. At their first meeting, she suggested that the committee begin with some general goals rather than adopting commercial materials or another school's approach. With the focus of establishing specific goals for vocabulary instruction at their school, the teachers read intensively about vocabulary development and kept personal learning logs. They chose articles from journals in their own content area, articles from the *Journal of Adolescent and Adult Learning,* and recent books on the topic published by professional organizations such as the International Reading Association. A major breakthrough occurred when one of the more vocal and negative teachers read a review of the literature explaining how vocabulary knowledge was closely related to students' understanding of what they read. She shared that information with the rest of the committee and made a rather compelling case for the importance of vocabulary knowledge to content area learning. From that point on, very few committee members wanted only the language arts teachers to assume responsibility for vocabulary development.

After considerable reading and discussion, the committee developed the following goals for the school district:

1. The students should develop a long-term interest and enjoyment in developing and refining their vocabulary.
2. The students should learn some independent strategies for learning new technical and general vocabulary words.
3. The students should become skilled in the use of the dictionary and, when appropriate, contextual analysis.

Pleased with their goals, the committee members decided that their next step was to outline how each goal could be incorporated into their own curriculum and how the departments could reinforce each other. They also decided that these goals should not be limited to the eighth-grade teachers but should involve all middle school teachers and their students. Their reasoning was that an effective program of vocabulary improvement needed to be comprehensive and cumulative if real growth and change were to occur.

The language arts teachers decided that they would teach students interesting word histories and origins via Greek and Latin mythology. The social studies teachers decided to implement "The Word of the Week," which they would choose together from something they had heard on the news or read in a newspaper. This word would be placed on the bulletin board, discussed on Monday, and reinforced throughout the week. The science and math teachers incorporated that idea with a slightly different twist. Modifying Haggard's (1982) vocabulary self-collection strategy, they had their students select the word or symbol for the week that they wanted to study.

The committee members decided that they also needed to identify the technical vocabulary they would teach their students for each of their units, making sure that they did not try to teach too many words. They had read about the importance of teaching words intensively rather than extensively. The science teachers recommended that they should share these words with each other so they could gain a big-picture perspective of the words students were being asked to learn.

Of course, the committee did not agree on everything. By the end of the summer, they were still debating who should be responsible for teaching the fundamentals of how to use the dictionary. In addition, some teachers wanted everyone to agree that they would assign students to complete concept cards for all the new vocabulary. The others, while conceding the importance of teaching students a vocabulary strategy, wanted more flexibility in selecting the strategies. They all agreed, however, on the importance of selecting and teaching vocabulary strategies that would foster students' conceptual understanding of important new words.

Because the school year was about to begin, the committee decided to implement the first two goals and to evaluate the impact of their unified effort at the end of the school year. They concluded, however, that students' scores on the competency-based reading test would probably not increase suddenly as a result of these small steps toward their unified effort to improve word knowledge and reading comprehension. From their readings and discussions, they realized that their goal of improving students' vocabulary knowledge would involve a long-term commitment by every middle school teacher.

■ ■ ■

SUMMARY

In this chapter we stressed the importance of students having an elaborative understanding of technical and general vocabulary in order to improve their content area learning. Because simple definitional knowledge of a word is not sufficient for textbook comprehension, teachers will need to stress the context links from what students know to what they will learn. This contextual understanding of content area terms and concepts can be facilitated by teacher-directed approaches such as possible sentences, firsthand concept development, and semantic-feature analysis.

Teachers not only should stress the vocabulary of their content area, but should also encourage students to become independent word learners. We therefore discussed generative vocabulary strategies such as word maps and concept cards that students can use as they read and study their assignments. Whether they are teacher directed or student initiated, these vocabulary strategies become even more powerful and useful when anchored in content area lessons that emphasize teachers' demonstrations, modeling, small-group interactions, class discussion, and reciprocal teaching. None of these strategies is mutually exclusive; they can and should be used together. For instance, combining strategies such as firsthand concept development with previewing in context will have a stronger and more long-lasting effect than either of these strategies alone.

Like nearly all of the methods presented in this book, the vocabulary strategies discussed here will not always engender immediate enthusiasm for learning words or produce an immediate impact on reading comprehension. Teachers must take time to warm students up to these methods and must allow their students to develop expertise in using the vocabulary strategies.

Finally, remember that any method, regardless of its novelty, will eventually become ineffective if overused. Therefore, it is wise to vary the vocabulary strategies and reinforcement activities often to sustain students' excitement. In the end, however, any vocabulary development strategies that require students to process terms and concepts in elaborative, meaningful, and unique ways will help them understand words and text more fully and retain important concepts and ideas much longer.

REFERENCES

Anders, P. L., & Bos, C. S. (1986). Semantic feature analysis: An interactive strategy for vocabulary development. *Journal of Reading, 29,* 610–616.

Auten, A. (1985). Building a language-rich environment. *Language Arts, 62,* 95–99.

Baumann, J., & Kameenui, E. J. (1991). Research on vocabulary instruction: Ode to Voltaire. In J. Flood, J. M. Jense, D. Lapp, & J. R. Squire (Eds.), *Handbook on teaching the English language arts.* New York: Macmillan.

Beck, I., & McKeown, M. (1991). Conditions of vocabulary acquisition. In R. Barr, M. Kamill, P. Mosenthal, & P. D. Pearson (Eds.), *Handbook of reading research* (Vol. 2). New York: Longman.

Beck, I., Perfetti, C. A., & McKeown, M. (1982). The effects of long-term vocabulary instruction on lexical access and reading comprehension. *Journal of Educational Psychology, 74,* 506–521.

Bos, C., Anders, P., Filip, O., & Jaffe, L. (1989). The effects on an interactive strategy for enhancing reading comprehension and content area learning for students with learning disabilities. *Journal of Learning Disabilities, 22,* 384–390.

Bowles, B. (1988, December 11). Prison site in Georgia marks Civil War horror. *Detroit News,* p. 11-H.

Carr, E. (1985). The vocabulary overview guide: A metacognitive strategy to improve vocabulary comprehension and retention. *Journal of Reading, 21,* 684–689.

Cronbach, L. J. (1942). An analysis of techniques for systematic vocabulary testing. *Journal of Educational Research, 36,* 206–217.

Cunningham, P. (1992). Content area vocabulary: Building and connecting meaning. In E. K. Dishner, T. W. Bean, J. E. Readence, & D. W. Moore (Eds.), *Reading in the content areas: Improving classroom instruction* (3rd ed.). Dubuque, IA: Kendall/Hunt.

Diekhoff, G. M., Brown, P. J., & Dansereau, D. F. (1982). A prose learning strategy training program based on network and depth-of-processing models. *Journal of Experimental Education, 50,* 180–184.

Gillet, J., & Kita, M. J. (1979). Words, kids, and categories. *The Reading Teacher, 32,* 538–542.

Graves, M. F. (1987). The roles of instruction in fostering vocabulary development. In M. McKeown & M. Curtis (Eds.), *The nature of vocabulary acquisition.* Hillsdale, NJ: Erlbaum.

Haggard, M. R. (1982). The vocabulary self-collection strategy: An active approach to word learning. *Journal of Reading, 26,* 203–207.

Henry, G. H. (1974). *Teach reading as concept development: Emphasis on affective thinking.* Newark, DE: International Reading Association.

Hidi, S. (1990). Interest and its contribution as a mental resource for learning. *Review of Educational Research, 60,* 549–572.

Jenkins, J. R., Matlock, B., & Slocum, T. A. (1989). Two approaches to vocabulary instruction: The teaching of individual word meanings and practice in deriving meaning from context. *Reading Research Quarterly, 24,* 215–235.

Johnson, D. D., & Pearson, P. D. (1984). *Teaching reading vocabulary.* New York: Holt, Rinehart, & Winston.

Johnson, D. D., Toms-Bronowski, S., & Pittelman, S. (1981). *A review of trends in vocabulary research and the effects of prior knowledge on instructional strategies for vocabulary acquisition.* (Theoretical Paper No. 95). Madison: Wisconsin Center for Education Research.

Kameenui, E. J., Dixon, R. C., & Carnine, D. W. (1987). Issues in the design of vocabulary instruction. In M. G. McKeown & M. B. Curtis (Eds.), *The nature of vocabulary acquisition.* Hillsdale, NJ: Erlbaum.

Kibby, M. W. (1995). The organization and teaching of things and the words that signify them. *Journal of Reading, 39,* 208–223.

Konopak, B. C. (1988). Using contextual information for word learning. *Journal of Reading, 31,* 334–338.

Konopak, B. C., & Mealey, D. L. (1992). Vocabulary learning in the content areas. In E. K. Dishner, T. W. Bean, J. E. Readence, & D. W. Moore (Eds.), *Reading in the content areas: Improving classroom instruction* (3rd ed.). Dubuque, IA: Kendall/Hunt.

Konopak, B., & Williams, N. (1988). Using the keyword method to help young readers learn content material. *The Reading Teacher, 41,* 12–18.

Levin, J. R. (1993). Mnemonic strategies and classroom learning: A twenty-year report card. *Elementary School Journal, 94,* 234–244.

Manzo, A., & Sherk, J. (1971). Some generalizations and strategies to guide vocabulary acquisition. *Journal of Reading Behavior, 4,* 78–89.

McKeown, M. G. (1990, April). *Making dictionary definitions more effective.* Paper presented at the annual meeting of the American Educational Research Association, Boston.

McKeown, M. G., Beck, I. L., Omanson, R. C., & Pople, M. T. (1985). Some effects of the nature and frequency of vocabulary instruction on the knowledge and use of words. *Reading Research Quarterly, 20,* 522–535.

Miller, G. A., & Gildea, P. M. (1987). How children learn words. *Scientific America, 257,* 94-99.

Moore, D. W., & Moore, S. A. (1986). Possible sentences. In E. K. Dishner, T. W. Bean, J. E. Readence, & D. W. Moore (Eds.), *Reading in the content areas* (2nd ed.). Dubuque, IA: Kendall/Hunt.

Moore, D. W., Moore, S. A., Cunningham, P. M., & Cunningham, J. W. (1986). *Developing readers and writers in the content areas.* New York: Longman.

Moore, D. W., Readence, J. E., & Rickelman, R. J. (1982). *Prereading activities for content area reading and learning.* Newark, DE: International Reading Association.

Nagy, W. E. (1988). *Teaching vocabulary to improve reading comprehension.* Newark, DE: International Reading Association.

Nagy, W. E., Anderson, R. C., & Herman, P. A. (1987). Learning word meanings from context during normal reading. *American Educational Research Journal, 24,* 237-270.

Nagy, W. E., & Herman, P. A. (1987). Breadth and depth of vocabulary knowledge: Implications for acquisition and instruction. In M. G. McKeown & M. E. Curtis (Eds.), *The nature of vocabulary acquisition.* Hillsdale, NJ: Erlbaum.

Nist, S. L., & Olejnik, S. (1995). The role of context and dictionary definitions on varying levels of word knowledge. *Reading Research Quarterly, 30,* 172-193.

Nist, S. L., & Simpson, M. L. (1997). *Developing vocabulary concepts for college thinking* (2nd ed.). Boston: Houghton Mifflin.

Sartain, H., & Stahl, N. A. (1982). *Techniques for teaching language of the disciplines.* Pittsburgh: University of Pittsburgh Press.

Schatz, E. K., & Baldwin, R. S. (1986). Context clues are unreliable predictors of word meanings. *Reading Research Quarterly, 21,* 439-453.

Schwartz, R. M. (1988). Learning to learn vocabulary in textbooks. *Journal of Reading, 32,* 108-118.

Schwartz, R. M., & Raphael, T. E. (1985). Concept of definition: A key to improving students' vocabulary. *The Reading Teacher, 39,* 198-205.

Simpson, M. L. (1987). Alternative formats for evaluating content area vocabulary understanding. *Journal of Reading, 31,* 20-27.

Smith, B. D., Stahl, N. A., & Neel, J. H. (1987). The effect of imagery instruction on vocabulary development. *Journal of College Reading and Learning, 22,* 131-137.

Stahl, N. A., Brozo, W. G., & Simpson, M. L. (1987). Developing college vocabulary: A content analysis of instructional materials. *Reading Research and Instruction, 26,* 203-221.

Stahl, S. A. (1985). To teach a word well: A framework for vocabulary instruction. *Reading World, 24,* 16-27.

Stahl, S. A. (1986). Three principles of effective vocabulary instruction. *Journal of Reading, 29,* 662-668.

Stahl, S. A., & Fairbanks, M. M. (1986). The effects of vocabulary instruction: A model-based meta-analysis. *Review of Educational Research, 56,* 72-110.

Stahl, S. A., & Kapinus, B. (1990, April). *Possible sentences: Predicting word meanings to teach content area vocabulary.* Paper presented at the meeting of the American Educational Research Association, Boston.

Stanley, J. (1971). Photographed vocabulary. In M. G. McClosky (Ed.), *Teaching strategies and classroom realities.* Englewood Cliffs, NJ: Prentice-Hall.

Tennyson, R. D., & Park, O. (1980). The teaching of concepts: A review of instructional design literature. *Review of Educational Research, 50,* 55-70.

CHAPTER 7

Writing as a Tool for Active Learning

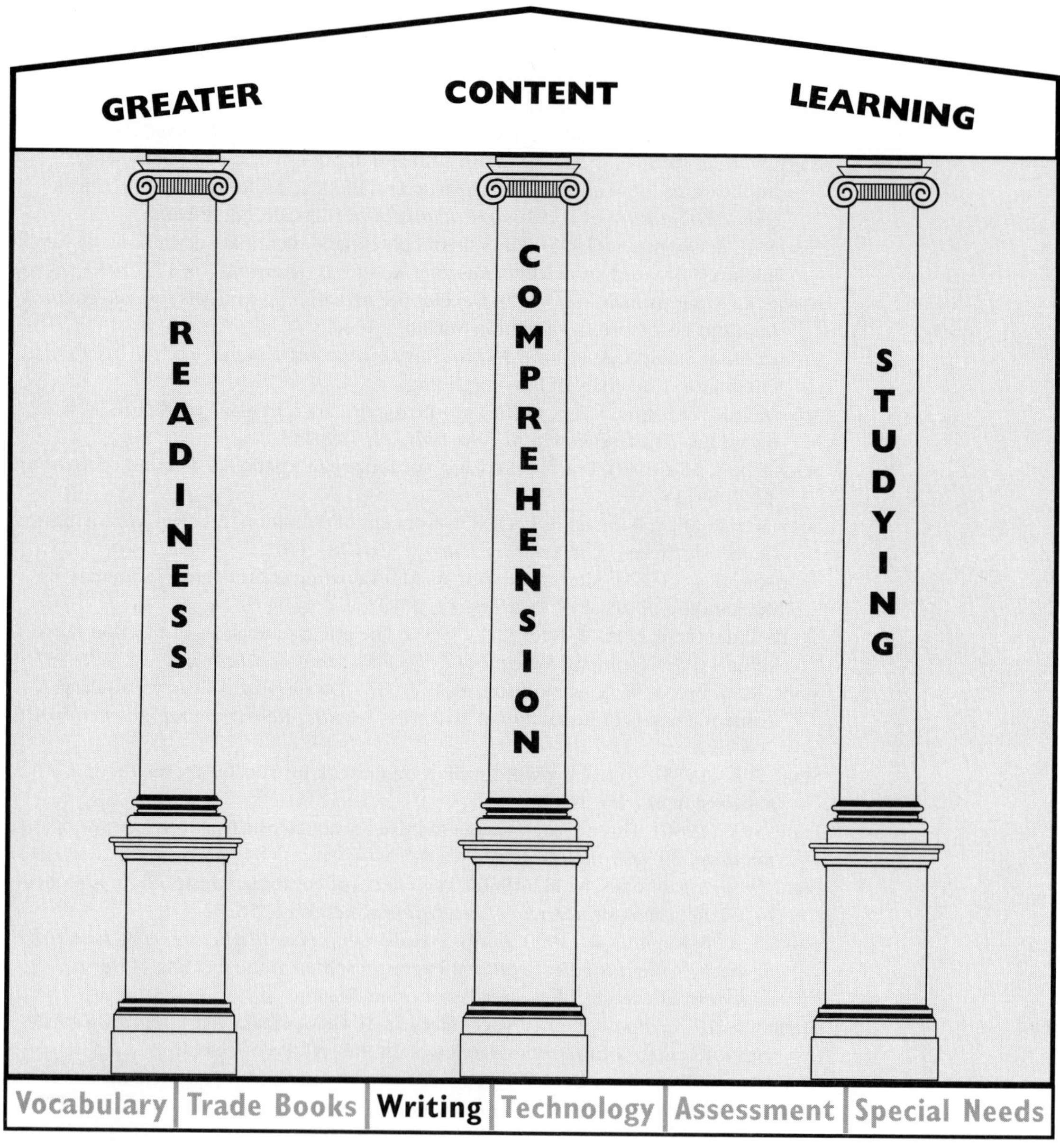

ANTICIPATION GUIDE

Directions: Read each statement carefully and decide whether you agree or disagree with it, placing a check mark in the appropriate *Before Reading* column. When you have finished reading and studying the chapter, return to the guide and decide whether your anticipations need to be changed by placing a check mark in the appropriate *After Reading* column.

	BEFORE READING		**AFTER READING**	
	Agree	*Disagree*	*Agree*	*Disagree*
1. Writing assignments should be reserved for English courses.	______	______	______	______
2. Everything a student writes should be evaluated and graded.	______	______	______	______
3. Writing tasks are best used after students have read their textbook assignments.	______	______	______	______
4. Longer writing assignments are better than shorter ones.	______	______	______	______
5. The best way to respond to students' papers is to write extensive comments on them.	______	______	______	______
6. Most high school students know how to study for essay tests.	______	______	______	______
7. Word processing programs are useful only during the revising and editing stages of writing.	______	______	______	______

Students can write on the first day of class and on the last: they can write during and outside of class. They should recognize that writing is one extremely valuable way of learning, and of finding out what one knows and thinks, as well as showing what one knows. Writing is a way to explore and question, as well as to gain control over and exhibit knowledge of subject matter.

—Draper (1982)

As Draper and others (e.g., Quinn, 1995) have pointed out, when teachers incorporate writing strategies into their content areas, they add a powerful vehicle for enhancing their students' learning. For example, a middle school math teacher used writing to help her students with units on multiplication and geometry. The students wrote explanations that described how to do something, defined new words, and explained their errors on quizzes and homework. At the end of the two units, the teacher found that her students who had used writing as a way of learning mathematics scored significantly better on their posttests than did students who had participated in more traditional activities (Jenkinson, 1988). Other researchers have concluded that writing not only facilitates the learning of content area concepts, but also engages students in higher thinking and reasoning processes (McGinley, 1992; Tierney & Shanahan, 1991).

In this chapter we examine the ways in which teachers can capitalize on the many advantages of writing without sacrificing instructional time or adding another responsibility to their incredibly busy days. We also agree with Gere (1985) that "writing to learn does not mean changing course content." Rather, we view reading and writing as parallel processes that actively involve learners in the construction and monitoring of conceptual understanding. As such, when writing is integrated into the existing curriculum, both teachers and students profit immensely.

CASE STUDY

Dave, a first-year teacher, is a member of the biology department at an urban high school. His students are those who do not plan to attend college, and thus they differ from the students he dealt with during his practice teaching. Dave is a bit frustrated because his first unit did not go well. The students appeared to be very bored with the chapters he assigned, and many did not complete any of the homework. In fact, out of his five classes, only 10 students received an A or B on the first unit exam. Dave's department chairperson has urged him to be stricter with the students. Another new teacher in the English department with whom he shares lunch duty has suggested that he incorporate more relevant reading materials and assignments into his units. Dave considers the English teacher's recommendation more intriguing than the chairperson's but does not know where to begin. He knows he wants to motivate his students to see biology as relevant to their lives, but he needs direction in

planning his next unit. As you read this chapter, think about how Dave might incorporate writing and any other strategies into his next unit on the environment.

■ ■ ■

READING AND WRITING AS CONSTRUCTIVE AND PARALLEL PROCESSES

If your friend observed you reading this book and asked for a synopsis, you probably could provide one with a quick glance at the table of contents. What if, however, you were asked to write a summary? Could you complete this task as quickly and easily? Find out by writing a five-sentence summary of the key ideas of the first six chapters.

Reading and Writing Are Similar Processes

Did you think about the ideas before you began to write your summary? Did you revise your ideas several times? Are your thoughts about the key ideas presented in this book more focused than when you first started to think about the task? Did you learn anything as a result of your writing? If you answered yes to any of these questions, you have experienced the power and permanence of writing. Just as reading is more than moving your eyes across the page, writing is more than "putting ideas" on paper. In fact, reading and writing are very similar activities for the active learner.

Recent research and theory suggest that reading and writing are not mirror images of each other but parallel processes in that they are both constructive (Tierney & Shanahan, 1991). By *constructive,* we mean that students construct meaning; it does not reside in their textbooks or in any written material. Meaning emerges from an interaction among student, text, and context or situation (i.e., the assignment, the classroom, the teacher, the audience). When students read an assignment from a textbook or write a paper, they are involved in the active process of building their own "text world" or internal configuration of meaning (Kucer, 1985). Simply put, when students grapple with questions such as "How can I factor a polynomial?" or "How can I explain in my own words the relationship between time, velocity, and distance?" they are beginning to construct meaning and create their own text.

There Are Recursive Stages to the Writing Process

The writing process, not unlike the reading process, has overlapping and recursive stages (Tierney & Pearson, 1983). Although the labeling of these stages is considerably diverse, the motif common to all appears to be a concern for **prewriting, writing,** and **postwriting.** Just as active learners use what they already know and set purposes before they begin to read, they also spend extended periods of time before the actual writing to plan, to discover ways of approaching the task to self-question and to identify purposes. This stage of the composing process is often ignored because of an inordinate concern for a written product that will be evaluated by the teacher (Florio-Ruane & Dunn, 1987). If students could be provided with more time in class to brainstorm ideas and to discuss writing plans with their peers and their teachers, the quality of their writing would significantly increase.

Teachers Need to Allow More Time for the Writing Process Before They Ask Students to Hand in Their Final Product

The second phase of the writing process focuses on the initial draft. At this point the writer is engaged in the enormous struggle to get words onto paper and into sentences, paragraphs, and sections. As with the reading process, the writer works to make things cohere and fit between the whole and parts and among the parts (Tierney & Pearson, 1983). Most writers, however, do not follow an orderly process in this initial drafting. In fact, research suggests that mature writers engage in extensive revision of their prewriting plans so that thinking and writing shape each other (Florio-Ruane & Dunn, 1987). This stage is often misconstrued by many teachers, causing them to treat the initial draft as if it were the final product and to look for perfection in spelling, punctuation, and other mechanics. Often teachers do not allow enough time in class for this initial drafting or they allow no time at all. Instead, they assign the writing to be done outside of class, where other classmates and the teacher are not available for support and coaching. If students could write their initial drafts during class, teachers would then gain the timely opportunity to meet with their students to discuss their problems in getting ideas down on paper. Moreover, these mini debriefing sessions can often save teachers considerable evaluation time on the subsequent final product.

The third phase of the writing process involves revising, editing, proofreading, and polishing for readability and interest so that the text is ready for sharing with an audience. Just as active readers pause to reflect on their ideas and then reread to verify, elaborate, or evaluate, mature writers take time to read, reflect on, and evaluate their writing as another would. By taking the role of the reader during this third phase of the writing process, students begin to see their "writing" as a piece of "reading" that must make sense to another individual.

The intensity and willingness that students devote to any of these phases depend on the two conditions that we, as teachers, can control. First, most students have a very naive idea of what it takes to be a good writer, just as they do of what it takes to be a good reader. To them, good writing has correct spelling and grammar, whereas good reading is the accurate pronunciation of words. When teachers share with them the processes of their own writing tasks, students are surprised to discover that professionals or mature writers must evaluate and revise extensively before they concern themselves with the surface features of spelling and grammar. Second, students who have never written for anyone but the teacher often feel that their ideas are not worthy of extended writing and revision or that the teacher already understands the ideas, so there is no need to be explicit and clear. They also have difficulty believing in a real audience because the writing task to them is no more than an occasion for a grade (Shaughnessy, 1977). Teachers can change this misconception by providing their students with real and intriguing audiences for their writing so that the urgency of communicating ideas becomes a passion and a drive.

Real Audiences for Writing Is Essential

In short, teachers can help their students understand these recursive and overlapping stages by reserving time in class for brainstorming, planning, drafting, revising, editing, proofreading, and sharing.

HOW CAN THE WRITING PROCESS HELP THE CONTENT AREA TEACHER?

Content area teachers rely heavily on their textbooks, lectures, demonstrations, and question-answer sessions as means of transmitting information to students (Woodward & Elliott, 1990). Unfortunately, many students begin to expect teachers to tell them the important information so that they do not have to think about ideas. Often textbook assignments are not read; at best, the ideas are quickly memorized for examinations and then forgotten. In short, students become passive learners, sponges soaking up details to pass exams.

The following example from a high school government class demonstrates how the sponge theory operates:

Ernesto assigns his 11th graders to read the first part of Chapter 2, which describes the characteristics of public opinion, and to come to class prepared for discussion. In their reading, the students come across one of the characteristics of public opinion, latency, and its corresponding definition—an opinion not yet crystallized or formed.

Marty, an especially diligent student, repeats that definition several times before coming to class, confident that he is prepared for discussion or an unannounced quiz (for which Ernesto is infamous). Ernesto lives up to his reputation. He asks the students to list and define the five characteristics of public opinion and to give an example of each. Marty, confident of the definition of latency, writes the words "not yet crystallized" but gives no example. In fact, none of the students give examples, and they complain loudly about this aspect of the exam. "There were no examples in the textbook! You are not being fair! We really did read the assignment."

Was Ernesto unfair? Did Marty really understand the concept *latency* or the words "not yet crystallized"? Should Ernesto's students be expected to create examples of concepts? Although we believe that Ernesto was justified in not accepting rote memorization by his students, we also believe that he could have prevented this minor student revolt by integrating the processes of reading and writing into his lesson plans. The combined use of reading and writing in this government class would have provided the students with more opportunities to construct their own definitions of the key concepts (e.g., *latency*) and to discover whether or not they understood. Writing is a potent means of learning that can help passive memorizers become active learners and thinkers.

Writing Tasks Help Students Become Less Passive Learners

Writing is a powerful means for learning because the more students manipulate content, the more they are likely to remember and understand that content. In fact, Langer and Applebee's 3-year study of 326 students and their 23 teachers found that "any kind of written response leads to better performance than does reading without writing" (1987, p. 130).

When students are asked to write about content area concepts, they must select and then organize words to represent their understanding of what they have read. To accomplish this, they must relate, connect, and organize ideas from the text. They must establish systematic connections and relationships between words and sentences, the sentences in paragraphs, the paragraphs in texts, and the paragraphs across texts. They must also build interrelationships between the ideas stated in the texts and their own prior knowledge, background, and purposes for reading. These are active processes. In contrast are the passive processes that the students probably employed when they read about the characteristics of public opinion: calling out the words, locating definitions or details, and memorizing word for word those definitions or details. Had they been required to write in some manner about the reading assignment, they would have been better prepared for Ernesto's exam.

Ernesto could have incorporated writing into his classroom routine in three basic ways. Perhaps the most common use of writing is to help students consolidate and review key ideas and experiences once they have finished reading. Ernesto's students could have been assigned to write a brief summary of the chapter's key ideas. In giving the assignment, he could have emphasized the importance of translating ideas into their own words and of creating examples. The students could have compared their summaries at the beginning of the class before the "infamous" and expected quiz.

Writing activities can also be used before students read in order to motivate, to focus their attention, and to help them draw on relevant knowledge and experience. This is the stage at which Ernesto could have capitalized on the power of writing. He could have introduced the chapter and unit by asking the students to take 5 minutes to describe in their journals the typical American's opinion about capital punishment for mass murderers. Then he could have asked them to describe their own opinions. After several students had shared their journal entries with the class, Ernesto could have asked the students to brainstorm reasons why there were so many differences in opinion across the classroom. His students would then have been better prepared to read about the five characteristics that influence political opinion, having brainstormed several of them already.

Writing Can Encourage Students to Think Critically

Finally, writing can be used in the content area classroom to help students think critically and creatively about concepts. This type of writing asks students to explore relationships among concepts, develop classification systems, trace causes and effects, and speculate about future developments—all higher-level and elaborative thinking processes. For the chapter on public opinion, Ernesto could have asked his students to poll a representative sample of 25 individuals about an important issue and then to summarize and explain these findings in light of what they have learned thus far about public opinion.

In short, writing is valuable to you because students cannot remain passive if they are asked to put their ideas on paper. Writing activities demand participation by every student, not just those who volunteer. More important, writing activities can quickly demonstrate which students understand and where the understanding breaks down so that reteaching can be planned. In the next section we discuss several important guidelines for the use of writing in the content area classroom.

GUIDELINES FOR THE USE OF WRITING ACROSS THE CONTENT AREAS

The Writing Process Is More Vital than the Product

You can maximize the potential of writing in your classroom if you remember that writing is a process that may or may not end in a product. Admittedly, there are occasions when you will want your students to write answers to essay questions in a biology class or to summarize their findings in a lab report for a chemistry class. However, a considerable amount of writing should be informal and never shared with others for their editing advice or evaluation. In other words, students need not write a formal paper and have you evaluate that paper for them to profit from their writing. The following six guidelines describe more specifically the implications of the process approach to writing.

Identify Concepts First and Then Determine If Writing Is the Appropriate Strategy for Learning

Before designing a writing activity, ask yourself what you want your students to learn about your content area. Then select the activity that will best accomplish the objective. Applebee, Langer, and Mullis (1986) found that writing may not always be the most efficient and appropriate strategy or approach for learning a content area concept.

Design Writing Assignments That Encourage Active Learning

In Langer and Applebee's (1987) survey of 200 public schools, they found that 40% of the writing activities involved students in merely recording or reciting information in word or sentence increments. These types of assignments ask students to do little more than passively regurgitate information that they have read or heard in class. More important, these assignments do not stimulate active learning. Remember that students learn more when they are required to manipulate concepts actively.

Provide Sufficient Time for Prewriting Activities

Someone once said that frontloading an assignment is the best way to ensure quality thinking and learning from students. By frontloading, this individual meant that the time spent in preparing students to read, listen, or observe was not wasted time but time well spent. Prewriting activities are especially important if you want students to profit from their writing experiences.

There Are Many Written and Oral Activities to Help Students in Their Prewriting

Fortunately, there are a variety of prewriting activities to help students decide on a topic, brainstorm possible ideas, see connections among ideas, and try out the ways in which those ideas could be stated. Some of these activities involve students in brainstorming and predicting questions, such as the KWL strategy discussed in Chapter 5. Other activities involve students in computer programs such as Inspiration, Semantic Mapper, and Semnet. These programs assist students in seeing the interrelationships between ideas and help them develop concept maps, a strategy discussed in Chapter 9.

Finally, there are many prewriting activities that capitalize on the power of oral language or talk. Oral language activities are especially advantageous to at-risk students who may lack experience in the more formal modes of academic thinking and expression (Rubin & Dodd, 1987). For example, in one study researchers found that middle school students wrote more persuasive papers after they had the opportunity to role-play their intended audience before they began writing (Wagner, 1987). In addition to Discussion Webs and word fluency activities (see Chapters 3 and 4), content area teachers can assign students to work in pairs and ask each other questions to help them plan their writing. Rubin and Dodd (1987) recommended the following questions for partners to ask each other during the prewriting phase:

Students Can Ask Each Other Questions to Guide Their Planning

1. What are you going to write about?
2. What are the two most important parts of your topic?
3. What evidence or support will you use?
4. How will you begin? What information could you include in your introduction?
5. Do you have a thesis statement in mind?
6. Who will be the intended audience for your thesis?
7. What might be a good title for your paper?

Design Writing Assignments That Have a Real and Immediate Audience

Whether it be other students in the class, other students in the school, community members, or individuals who support a particular cause in Washington, D.C., students need an audience for their writing. By having a real and immediate audience, students will be able to decide how to state their position, what information to include, and what format best serves their needs. If students write only for their teachers, they will see their audience as someone who "knows it all" already and whose primary reason for reading their work is to give them a grade.

Vary the Assignments and the Discourse Modes

There Are Many Creative Discourse Modes

Allow students to master the narrative or story form before assigning the expository essay. Overreliance on the expository essay can discourage and frustrate many students. The options in Figure 7.1 emphasize many exciting possibilities for your writing assignments. These assignments, such as writing complaints or time capsule lists, not only help students feel more comfortable with writing, but are also inviting, engaging, and motivating tasks that facilitate active learning.

Publish and Celebrate Your Students' Writing

The final phase, postwriting, includes publishing. By publishing we mean that when students finish a piece of writing, it is shared and made public. When students realize that their work will be "published," they know they have an audience and thus a reason for working diligently in revising, editing, and proofreading. You can display their work on the bulletin board, in booklets, or in

Abstracts	Complaints	Instructional manuals	Rebuttals
Advertisements	Correspondence	Jokes and riddles	Recipes
Advice columns	Demonstrations	Journals, diaries	Requests for information
Announcements	Dramatic scripts	Letters (personal, public)	Reviews
Applications	Editorials	Limericks	Scripts, skits, puppet shows
Biographical sketches	Eulogies	Mottoes, slogans	Songs, ballads
Brochures	Feature stories	News stories	Stories
Cartoons	Forms	Oral histories	Tall tales
Case studies	Games and puzzles	Parodies	Technical reports
Character sketches	Guess who/what descriptions	Petitions	Telegrams
Children's books	Historical "you are there" scenes	Posters	Time capsule lists
Coloring books with text	Inquiries	Proposals	Word problems
Commercials		Protests	

FIGURE 7.1 Possible Discourse Modes

school newspapers. Students can also share their work by reading it aloud to their classmates; you too should share your writing with your students.

Adhering to these six guidelines should enhance the quality of writing that students produce when they interact with content area concepts in your classroom. In addition, one critical aspect—assignment making—must be addressed in detail. If you wish, consider it the seventh guideline.

STARTING RIGHT WITH AN EFFECTIVE WRITING ASSIGNMENT

Bad Assignments Will Create Poor Writing

Connelly and Irving (1976) said that the single most important cause of bad writing is bad assignments. Even though bad writing assignments are never intentional, their effect is the same. Bad writing assignments can become good assignments when certain information is communicated to the students orally and in writing. When you communicate your writing assignment to your students, they will first need to know the **purpose of the assignment,** the **topic,** the **audience,** and the **options for discourse modes.** A specific statement of purpose (e.g., "to understand the impact of words on interpersonal communication") will help students understand why this writing is being done. The topic for the writing assignment usually originates from content and course objectives, but you will need to specify how you want the students to narrow that focus without dictating their thesis. The audience will determine the background knowledge, vocabulary, and opinions of the individual who will read the writing, whether that is you, the teacher, another student, or a small child in the community. Ideally, writing assignments should provide students with several suggestions about possible discourse modes rather than just a single option such as the essay. Even the most reluctant student will become intrigued by writing a letter to the editor of a local newspaper or an imaginary diary.

An effective writing assignment should also include information on the recommended process, steps, or strategies that a student might use to complete the assignment. In addition, your writing assignment should include information on your expectations for (1) length; (2) level of polish; (3) format; (4) grammar, mechanics, and spelling; and (5) how the paper will be evaluated. The following writing assignment was used by Jill, an 11th-grade American history teacher, for the unit on the Progressives. Note that she specifies the discourse mode that she wants the students to use, but she gives them choices within that mode.

> We have been studying the Progressive Era for the past week. This assignment will help you summarize the key issues and assess the impact of this intriguing period in our history. I want you to imagine that you are either Dan Rather or Diane Sawyer and you will be interviewing Robert LaFollette or Alice Paul—who have briefly returned from the dead. What would Rather and Sawyer want to ask these individuals? What would the television viewers want to know about these people and this time in history? You are to write out Rather's or Sawyer's questions and LaFollette's or Paul's

replies. Then close the interview with a written commentary by Rather or Sawyer that evaluates the impact of LaFollette or Paul and the Progressive Era. Your audience will be television viewers unfamiliar with this historical period.

Your first step in doing this assignment will be to review the relevant readings that we have done this week. You should also watch several news shows so that you can get an idea of the range of questions that could be asked. In class on Wednesday you will have time to brainstorm and role play with a partner. By Thursday I want you to be prepared for the first draft, which we will write in class.

In grading this assignment I will use these criteria:

A Good Writing Assignment States the Criteria That Will Be Used in Evaluation

1. Your understanding of the Progressive Era and its impact on history.
2. Your creativity and imagination, as demonstrated by your ability to write meaningful and interesting questions, responses, and a commentary.
3. Your quality of writing: It should be clear and free of gross mechanical and spelling errors.

The final draft, which is worth 50 points, will be due at the beginning of class on Tuesday. Please use ink and write on every other line. As for length, the bare minimum is three pages of normal handwriting. These papers will be shared in class.

After assigning this writing activity, Jill also shared some examples of interviews and commentaries from a unit on the Vietnam era so that her students could visualize the finished product. She told us that the time she spends frontloading a writing assignment really pays off in the quality of work she receives from the students.

Because there are a variety of writing strategies that content area teachers can use in their classroom, these strategies will be discussed throughout the remainder of the chapter. It should be pointed out, however, that writing as a way of learning content area concepts permeates this textbook; thus, you will find many other ideas incorporated into other chapters.

WRITING ACTIVITIES THAT PREPARE STUDENTS FOR LEARNING

As discussed in Chapter 5, one way to stimulate students to process and think more elaboratively about content area concepts is to help them make connections between what they already know or want to know and what they are about to read and study. Remember the ease of reading a difficult Russian novel like *War and Peace* after you had viewed the movie? The ease of remembering a fact-filled history chapter on the Civil War after you had visited the Shiloh and Gettysburg battlefields during your summer vacation? The same advantage can be gained by your students if you provide relevant and concrete classroom activities such as discussing, brainstorming, organizing, and writing responses before they read their test assignments. The Guided-Writing Activity and the academic journal are two such activities.

The Guided-Writing Activity

The **Guided-Writing Activity** (Smith & Bean, 1980), an instructional strategy that uses all four of the communication arts, has been researched by Konopak, Martin, and Martin (1987). Using 11th-grade students in a history course, they found that the experimental group who used a modification of the Guided-Writing Activity generated higher-quality ideas and better synthesized information on the written posttest. The steps of this strategy are as follows:

1. On the first day, activate the students' prior knowledge on the topic of study by brainstorming and listing ideas on an overhead or chalkboard.
2. Ask the class to organize and label the ideas collectively.
3. Then ask the students to write individually on the topic using this information.
4. In preparation for the second day, have the class read the text and revise their explanatory writing.
5. In class on the second day, give a follow-up multiple-choice and essay exam on the text's key ideas.

To visualize how the Guided-Writing Activity could be incorporated into a content area classroom, let's examine Lila's eighth-grade health class. Lila began the lesson by asking her students to write any ideas, definitions, or emotions that came to mind when they heard the words *stress* or *stressful.* She then circulated around the room and asked the class to share what they had written while a student wrote these ideas on the chalkboard. The students' reactions were varied. Some mentioned how their parents complained of too much stress in their executive-level jobs, and others commented on the stress their mothers felt in trying to raise a family alone and perform a full-time job at the same time. Some students pointed out that newspapers and television shows constantly focus on how to control stress to prevent serious illnesses. A few students discussed the stress they felt in trying to be accepted by the best college. When Lila was sure that everyone had contributed, she asked the students to help her categorize the list of ideas and emotions on the board. The categories that emerged from this discussion were (1) the causes of stress, (2) the feelings associated with stress, (3) the dangers of stress, and (4) the cures for stress. Next, she asked the students to preview (see Chapter 9) their chapter to discover which of these ideas would be included in their next assignment. The students quickly pointed out that all four ideas were included in the chapter's boldface headings. Lila then asked them to determine the headings in the textbook that were not included in their list. One student suggested that the dangers of stress were subdivided into the physical and mental effects of unrelieved stress, a distinction they had not made in their own list. Another student pointed out that there was a separate section on adolescent stress in the chapter—a comment that generated considerable discussion and excitement.

Lila closed the class period by telling the students to read the chapter, to focus on gathering information on those four areas, and to be prepared for discussing and writing during the next class period. On the second day, Lila began her lesson by asking the students to take out the entry they had written about stress the day before and to reread it for possible revisions. Her directions were: "Imagine that you are explaining the concept of stress to a younger brother or sister. What would you add to your original entry? Jot these ideas down." After a few minutes, she asked the students to share and discuss their ideas. As she recorded their ideas on the board, she was surprised by the number of students who volunteered and eagerly participated in the discussion. In fact, the discussion took longer than she had expected. Then, on the third day of class, Lila returned to the writing task and asked the students to revise their original entry on stress, keeping in mind their audience, a younger brother or sister. Although this activity was not the end of her unit on stress and health, it does illustrate how one teacher used writing as a means of helping students make connections between what is to be learned and what is already known.

Academic Journals

As Fulwiler (1987) has explained, the **academic journal** "stimulates classroom discussion, starts small group activity, clarifies hazy issues, reinforces learning, and stimulates imaginations" (p. 15). Most important, journal writing makes it difficult for passive students to remain passive. Journals, logs, and idea books can be used in class in many different ways. In this section we examine how they can be used to start class discussions and to stimulate passive students to think actively about ideas.

Have you ever begun a class by asking the infamous question "Are there any questions about the assigned reading?" If your students are like most teachers' students, the result is an uncomfortable silence. Rather than asking a question that rarely will be answered, ask your students to take out their journals and spend 5 minutes responding to what they have read. They can summarize key ideas, ask questions, or merely list pages where they became lost. A more focused approach is to write on the board an interesting quotation from the reading assignment or a statement of opinion (e.g., "The pituitary gland is the most important gland in the endocrine system") and ask the students to respond in writing. After 5 minutes you can ask student volunteers to read their entries. To help students feel more comfortable, read your entry first and then ask students to share. This brief writing activity helps the students to focus on the topic of discussion and to identify ideas that they do and do not understand.

Academic Journals Can Stimulate Students to Think About Content Area Concepts

The same procedure can be used before a lecture or lecture-discussion to stimulate students to think about a certain topic. Although we all have used a question at the beginning of class to pique our students' interest, only a few really respond. Writing in a journal for 5 minutes is one way to guarantee that all students are reacting and thinking about the course's objectives. For example, in a seventh-grade math class about to start a unit on averages, the teacher began the lesson by asking the students to answer the following questions in their academic journals:

A Math Teacher Can Use the Academic Journal

1. Where have you heard about averages?
2. Who uses averages and for what?
3. How are averages used?
4. What do you know about forming an average?

As a follow-up to the students' writing, the math teacher could either have the students share their entries or merely use the writing as a way to establish mood and purpose. In the next section we examine writing strategies to help students summarize and monitor what they read.

WRITING ACTIVITIES THAT ENCOURAGE STUDENTS TO CONSTRUCT MEANING AND TO MONITOR THEIR UNDERSTANDING

As mentioned in Chapter 2, active learners can state in their own words the key ideas of what they read, and they can synthesize, evaluate, and apply those ideas to other contexts. Most middle school and high school students are not active learners but rather memorizers who can regurgitate textbook or teacher statements with minimal understanding and involvement. Even though it is admittedly difficult to move a student from memorization to application, this transition can be facilitated through the use of strategically planned writing assignments. The writing activities, however, must require students to do more than merely answer teacher- or text-posed questions. In this section, we will describe three activities to help students construct meaning and monitor their understanding. All of these activities can be easily integrated into the classroom routine and require minimal teacher preparation and response. More important, they are very inviting and approachable for students who have minimal writing skills.

Microthemes

Microthemes Are Small in Size but Large in the Thinking Processes Used by Students

Microthemes are assignments so short that they can be written or typed on a single 4 × 6 index card and read within minutes (Bean, Drenk, & Lee, 1982). They are productive in the content areas because they ask the students to do a small amount of writing preceded by a great deal of thinking. Microthemes can also be designed to emphasize different content area objectives. The most common microtheme asks students to summarize key ideas from a reading assignment, demonstration, experiment, or lecture in their own words. The advantage of a student's summary recorded on an index card rather than in a journal is that the cards are much easier to handle and carry home for your perusal.

The following example illustrates how Ann, a ninth-grade math teacher, uses the microtheme to encourage students to state in their own words their conceptual understanding of exponents.

Integral Exponents

Rule 7 is in addition to previous ones you have worked with in other chapters. In your own words, explain what this rule means and how you might use it to simplify 2^{-4} and $1/4^{-3}$.

Rational Exponents

1. Define *radical, radicand, index,* and *principal root.* Identify each in an example you supply.
2. The *cube root* of a number means ______.

The microtheme can be used in the following ways:

- To emphasize a new and important technique that has just been introduced in science, industrial arts, or home economics class, stop and ask students to write for 5 minutes to describe the technique to another student who was absent from class.
- To focus a class discussion that becomes rambling or dominated by just a few students, stop and ask the class to write for 5 minutes. They could respond to the question "What are we trying to explain?" or to the assignment "Restate the key points that have been made thus far."
- To help students reflect on the key ideas of a specific unit, ask them to review their notes and assigned readings and then to write. This activity works best when announced in advance so that students can think and plan for a while. Such a synthesis is also especially advantageous for the students as a means of preparing for an examination.

Once the students have written their microtheme, the next step is for you to decide what you will do with their written work. Walvoord (1986) suggests several options. First, you could simply go on with the lesson and hope that the writing has served its purpose in helping students summarize and focus on key concepts. Second, you could give the students an immediate chance to ask questions and clear up any confusion they may have discovered while they were writing. They could pose questions for you to answer or issues to clarify, or they could turn to a neighbor to share their answers and resolve their difficulties together. As the students work, you could circulate around the room to eavesdrop and troubleshoot. Finally, you could collect the cards and read them for your own information. The students' writing becomes excellent feedback on whether they learned what you had tried to teach that day. Some teachers grade this type of writing by awarding several points for each microtheme. Others prefer to award pass/fail credit in their gradebooks. Regardless of the evaluating procedure or question posed for the students' writing, the microtheme can facilitate student learning and provide immediate feedback on your teaching effectiveness.

Double-Entry Journals

Double-Entry Journals Help Students Become More Metacognitively Aware

When students write in a journal they can summarize and react to ideas, but they also can reflect on their processes of making sense of what they are reading or learning in a content area. Such journal entries are called **double-entry formats** (Calkins, 1986; Nist & Simpson, 1987). With this format, students use the left-hand column of an evenly divided note page to copy directly from a text quotations, statements, theories, definitions, and other things that are difficult to understand, interesting, of key importance, or require clarification. On the right-hand side, students record whatever thoughts, questions, or comments come to mind as they attempt to make sense of what was copied. Figure 7.2 is an example of a double-entry format that one ninth-grade student, Chris, created for his reading assignment in a government course. The text he copied on the left-hand side of the paper came from a chapter discussing political opinions and attitudes

Text	Responses to Text and Strategy Concerns
Political attitudes may exist merely as potential. They may not have crystallized. But they still can be very important, for they can be evoked by leaders and converted into action. Latent opinions set rough boundaries for leaders. . . . *Source:* J. Burns, J. Peltason, & T. Cronin (1984). *Government by the People* (p. 175), Englewood Cliffs, NJ: Prentice Hall.	I know that this section is supposed to define the key word *latent* because the boldface heading tells me this. However, I am having problems finding a definition. Help! *Okay*—I think the second sentence helps me, but I will need to look up the word *crystallized.* I think, right now, that latent opinions are opinions not formed, but existing as potential for leaders and other people who wish to influence us. *Whew!* I will read on since our teacher has told us that authors often take several pages to define a word. This is hard work and I think the textbook authors made it even harder for us.

FIGURE 7.2 Entry in a Study-Skills Journal

that Chris found confusing. Notice Chris's comments on the right-hand side. By examining his journal entry, his government teacher was able to determine what concepts were troubling him and what strategies he was using to make sense of his reading. More important, Chris gained some information about himself through his writing. The last comment made by Chris was a very honest and perceptive observation about textbooks that typifies the feelings of some students who are very metacognitively aware. Those comments, however, do not occur as a result of one double-entry journal assignment. Teachers must provide modeling and guidance to develop their students' metacognition.

Framed Paragraphs

Framed Paragraphs Provide More Structure for Less Skilled Writers

Some students are so intimidated by writing that they cannot seem to begin the process, even if they view the assignment as intriguing and captivating. In addition to the microtheme, framed paragraphs are another way to provide students with guidance and structure so that they can overcome their paralysis when asked to think and write about content area concepts. As illustrated in Figures 7.3 and 7.4, **framed paragraphs** are skeletal paragraphs with strategically placed transitions or cue words that signal to students a particular way to think and write about a concept (Vacca, Vacca, & Gove, 1995). After students have read an assignment or viewed a demonstration, they complete the framed paragraphs by writing in the missing words and by creating their own sentences in order to produce a total paragraph or mini-essay about a particular topic. Students can then share their framed paragraphs in small groups or with their study partners.

Framed Paragraphs Use Narrative or Expository Text Structure

Framed paragraphs can be constructed for narrative text and emphasize the elements of narrative structure such as plot, setting, characters, and theme. The narrative framed paragraph in Figure 7.3 was written by a sixth-grade language arts teacher to accompany a story in the class's literature anthology. Framed paragraphs can also be created for expository text and emphasize patterns of organization such as problem-solution or comparison-contrast. The framed para-

Manuel was a ______ student. He decided to do a pantomime of Ritchie Valens's "La Bamba" at the school's talent show because ______ . As he watched the various acts done by his classmates, he was ______ . When he went up on stage he felt ______ . Once he began dancing and pantomiming, he ______ . Then suddenly in the middle of his act, ______ . He felt very ______ but decided to keep ______ . Once the talent show was over, the audience ______ . Manuel was surprised because ______ . Ricardo and Manuel's father thought Manuel had ______ . That night when Manuel was alone in his room, he decided ______ . The irony of this story is ______ .

FIGURE 7.3 Framed Paragraph about "La Bamba"

The animal kingdom can be divided into vertebrates and ______ . Vertebrates are animals with a ______ , whereas invertebrates are animals ______ . There are four identifying features of invertebrates. The first distinguishing feature biologists used to group invertebrates is ______ . The name of that subgroup is ______ and an example of such an animal in that subgroup is ______ . The second distinguishing feature is ______ . The name of that subgroup is ______ and an example is ______ . The third ______ ______ . The fourth ______ ______ .

Of all the invertebrates, I have had the most encounters with ______ . As I read about invertebrates, it seemed to me that most of them live ______ . In addition, it seems interesting to me that ______ .

FIGURE 7.4 Framed Paragraph for a Unit on Invertebrates

graph in Figure 7.4 was written by a seventh-grade general science teacher in order to help his students become more aware of the categories, examples, and characteristics of invertebrates and vertebrates.

Many teachers like to use framed paragraphs at the beginning of the school year in order to ease students into the process of writing about content area concepts. After students build their confidence and fluency in writing, the cues in framed paragraphs are reduced so that students then write using alternative formats. Because the framed paragraph and microtheme are not intimidating in their structure and format, your less skilled students will experience success in their writing.

WRITING ACTIVITIES THAT ENCOURAGE STUDENTS TO THINK CRITICALLY

Analytical Writing Assignments Can Encourage Students to Think Critically About Ideas

Langer and Applebee (1987) concluded from their 3-year study of 23 high school teachers that review- or summary-type writing assignments were the predominant choice in most classrooms. Although these forms of writing assignments have their place and are especially useful in courses where students must memorize large quantities of material, they will do little to develop students' higher levels of thinking. One way we can increase our students' ability to think critically is to provide writing assignments that challenge students to extend and reformulate ideas and to think analytically. Analytical writing assignments require students to manipulate a smaller number of concepts in more complex ways, which, in turn, promotes deeper reasoning, thinking, and remembering.

Which type of writing assignment should you emphasize in your content area classroom? Langer and Applebee suggest that a balance is healthy because each type of writing has its "place in school, particularly when writing is used selectively for particular purposes" (1987, p. 136). We have described several writing activities that encourage students to construct meaning and monitor their understanding. In this section we examine the reader-response heuristic, other variations of the microtheme, and the SPAWN mnemonic as writing activities that will encourage critical thinking and active learning in your content area.

Reader Response Applied to Expository Text

As we said earlier, meaning does not reside in any written text. Rather, meaning or comprehension emerges from an interaction among the reader, the text, and the context. This concept puts into perspective your reaction to the reading assignments in your educational methods courses. When you first read those seemingly dry and boring textbook chapters, you almost certainly had no students of your own and no specific problems to solve (e.g., How do I motivate adolescents?). Hence, you probably remember little or nothing from them, even though you were a fluent and highly competent reader. This phenomenon also affects your students as they read unless they are provided with opportunities to explore the connections between what they already know, feel, and want to know and the information contained in their textbooks.

One way to help students make those connections is through the reader-response heuristic. A *heuristic* is a method of inquiry, and the **reader-response heuristic** is a method of self-inquiry in which readers write about their own responses to certain aspects of the text. The reader-response heuristic asks readers first to write what they perceive in the text, then to explain how they feel about what they see, and finally to discuss the thoughts and feelings emanating from their perceptions (Petrosky, 1982). This is a personal type of writing, which is very different from summary-type writing. Summaries are often audience-oriented tasks in that they are written exclusively for other individuals to read. By contrast, reader-response tasks exist for the learner and the reader. Summaries and brief essays require writers to support stances and assertions with public-based information. Conversely, reader-response tasks value the examples, beliefs, and assumptions of the students.

Brozo (1988) has suggested these three generic questions to guide students in making connections to expository text:

These Three Generic Questions Help Students Make Connections

1. What aspect of the text excited or interested you most?
2. What are your feelings and attitudes about this aspect of text?
3. What experiences have you had that help others understand why you feel the way you do?

To visualize how the reader-response journal entry would work in a content area classroom, consider Bob's 11th-grade history and current events class. He introduced the activity by presenting model answers he had created, talking his students through while paying special attention to the way they attempted to answer these three main questions in the self-inquiry process. Bob's essay was a response to an article in *Newsweek* about the former system of apartheid in South Africa. He emphasized how this statement of feeling—that the United States should be doing more to abolish racial segregation in South Africa—was explained and supported by his personal experience of witnessing racial prejudice when he was in the Navy in South Carolina during the early 1960s. He then assigned students to go through the same process of discovering personal connections with several different articles from *Newsweek.* One student, Eric, read an article about Arab-Israeli relations. His ideas blossomed as he moved from brief responses to the three questions to a multiple-page essay. Eric's first response follows:

> Whenever I read that there might be peace among Arabs and Israelis I get real excited. I believe that when they can figure out how to solve the problem for the Palestinians, the entire Middle East will become peaceful. I know Arabs and Jews can live in peace and happiness. I'm part Lebanese and I have friends who are Jewish. If we can get along why can't they? Instead, they fight and every day more people die. My mom told me Lebanon used to be a beautiful country. Now its people and its economy are ruined. (Brozo, 1988, p. 3)

Eric's writing partner thought he had a good start and suggested he find an experience to give his feelings and ideas some authority. Together they brainstormed possible personal connections, which helped Eric explore the roots of his feelings. Bob worked with them too, encouraging and pushing Eric to be more specific about why he felt that way. In the third draft, which follows, Eric created an essay that demonstrated a genuine sensitivity to his readers by linking the text to his strong feelings and attitudes and by explaining his feelings with a vivid experience.

> Whenever I read that there might be peace among Arabs and Israelis I get real excited. I believe that when they can figure out how to solve the problem of the Palestinians, the entire Middle East will become peaceful. It seems like all the problems exist because of the Palestinian issue. I can just think of a time when Israelis and Arabs will work, play, and grow together. I know Arabs and Jews can live in peace and happiness. I hope it happens in my lifetime. [Eric's answer to question one].
>
> I feel so deeply about this issue for two reasons. First, I hate war and how it ruins a country's economy and most importantly, its people. And second, I'm part Lebanese, yet I have real good friends who are Jewish. [Eric's feelings].
>
> Last year I rode twice a week to basketball practice with a Jewish guy named David. I felt close to David right away. We shared ideas and feelings about basketball and our girlfriends and geometry. We talked very personally. We became close even though we didn't get together that often outside of basketball practice.
>
> One day David asked about my ethnic background. He was Jewish and proud of it. But who was I? An American who happens to be part Lebanese (I'm also part Italian and Irish) only by chance. I mean I could have just as easily been born an African bushman or an Alaskan Indian. My

nationality is not a big deal to me. So I didn't know what to say at first to David. I was afraid to tell the whole truth. Then I thought, I like and trust this guy as a friend—he has told me many things about his Jewishness expecting me to accept and respect him, so why should I feel different?

"I'm half Lebanese," I said.

David smiled, "We're cousins. I knew there was something special about us. Salam ah likum," he said.

"Shalom," I replied. [Eric's personal experience]

(Brozo, 1988, pp. 14–15)

With the reader-response heuristic and the assistance of both his writing partner and Bob, Eric was helped to see how his interpretations of the text on Arab-Israeli relations were mediated by his feelings and experiences. His moving responses also created a good, solid essay that supports assertions with an excellent example derived from personal experience.

The next step in the process is the sharing of essays. Bob found it to be a particularly exciting phase of the lesson because multiple viewpoints were exchanged, questioned, and debated. This sharing also gave his students a wider audience and extended feedback for the revision process.

The reader-response heuristic can be easily modified for any content area. Because Brozo's three questions were intended only to be generic stimuli, you can create content-specific questions relevant to your course objectives and your students. Remember, not every student-response entry must be turned into an essay like Eric's. Your students will profit immensely just from the processes of interpreting, questioning, and reacting.

Variations of the Microtheme

There Are Two Other Ways the Microtheme Can Be Used by Content Area Teachers

The **thesis-support microtheme** can help students discover issues and develop arguments and stances that are supported with empirical evidence. When writing a thesis-support microtheme, students must often go beyond the textbook to build a logical, cohesive argument. When students think about and research a particular issue, they actively master the unit's objectives. Most important, they begin to realize that their textbook presents only one point of view and that all content areas are in a constant state of controversy and flux.

An example of a thesis-support microtheme developed by a seventh-grade general science teacher follows:

Directions: The purpose of this assignment is to provide you with an opportunity to examine an issue in depth by taking a stand and developing a logical argument for that stand. You have two choices, so read the choices below carefully and then select one of them. Then determine which side you wish to defend for that issue. For the side you have selected, write a microtheme that defends that position. Use evidence and reasoning from your textbook, from our discussion in class, or from the film we watched in class. Write your final draft on the index card you have been given. Class time will be provided for brainstorming, planning, and prewriting. HAVE FUN WITH THIS!

1. The diversity theory has/has not been proven.
2. People do a lot to the environment that encourages/prevents animal extinction.

The teacher discussed and distributed several examples of thesis-support microthemes after announcing the assignment. Following a discussion of the assignment, he invited the class to help him do an analysis of this seemingly simple assignment so that they could plan appropriately. In addition, he provided one class period for the students who had selected the same issues to meet, debate, and brainstorm. Several days later, he set aside a class period for the students to write their initial draft so that he could be available while they wrote. The teacher reported that the students did have fun with this assignment and, more important, did better than usual on their unit exam.

Another variation of the microtheme, the **data-provided microtheme,** helps students with inductive reasoning and the subsequent arrangement of words, sentences, and paragraphs that signal this type of thinking. Students are provided with data in a list of sentences or in a graph, table, or chart. They then must arrange the data in a logical order, connect the parts with appropriate transitions, and write general statements that demonstrate the meaning they have induced. This type of microtheme is especially useful for students who ignore or who cannot accurately interpret important visual aids, especially in math or science classes.

The secret to the microtheme is in the format of the card. Students must carefully plan what they will say and how they will say it because they receive only one index card to record their ideas. They also learn that more is not always better. Just as a poet carefully chooses words for each poem, so will the students as they write a microtheme. What they write depends on your course objectives and content because these variations are only a beginning.

SPAWN-ing Writing Assignments

Creating unusual and challenging assignments to stimulate students to use higher levels of thinking is not always easy. To help create these assignments, the SPAWN acronym (Martin, Martin, & O'Brien, 1984) is very useful. **SPAWN** stands for **special powers, problem solving, alternative viewpoints, what if,** and **next;** each is a category of writing assignments that can encourage students to move beyond the memorization of facts. To construct such an assignment, you can select one of the categories from SPAWN and combine it with the most appropriate writing form. Refer to Figure 7.1 for some examples of writing forms that are creative and nontraditional.

Beth is a 10th-grade English teacher who decided to use the SPAWN mnemonic to help her construct possible writing topics for the book *Farewell to Manzanar* (Houston & Houston, 1974). The book fit perfectly into the sophomores' unit on prejudice and injustice because it describes the internment of a Japanese girl in an American camp on the West Coast during World War II. Although Beth likes to give her students wide choices for their writing, she also knows that they appreciate some suggestions. Thus, she distributed the following ideas:

Option 1: Special Powers

You have the power to change any event in *Farewell to Manzanar.* You must write and tell what event you changed, how you changed it, why you changed it, and what could happen as a result of the change. For instance, what if Rodine's mother had welcomed Jeanne into the Girl Scouts? Would that affect just that part of the story, or might Jeanne's life have been totally different if she had been accepted right from the first?

After you have completed the written section of this assignment, I will meet in a group with everyone who elected to do this assignment. We will discuss the changes that have been made and the possible consequences.

Option 2: Alternative Viewpoints

We heard Jeanne's viewpoint on her friendship with Rodine. We were told of their experiences as their friendship began to grow through their years at Cabrillo Homes and during junior high school. After entering high school, they began to drift apart. What is Rodine's viewpoint? What happened according to her perspective? How did she feel?

Pretend that you are Rodine. Write several journal entries in which you discuss the beginning of the friendship, a few of the high points, and the time when you finally realized that you were no longer special friends. You will have the chance to share this with others who do this same assignment.

Option 3: What If?

What if this story took place in Japan after World War II? Rodine's father was in the army as an officer in the occupational forces. He wanted her to become familiar with the Japanese culture, so she attended a Japanese school, where she was the only white person. Jeanne was in her class. Starting with Rodine's first day in class, write a story of the experiences Jeanne and Rodine had. How would life be different now that Rodine is the minority and Jeanne is the majority? You may tell your story from either Jeanne's or Rodine's point of view. You will have the opportunity to meet with others in the class to share your story and to discuss the approach that they followed for the same assignment.

Beth reported that the students enjoyed these writing options and that several of them used the SPAWN mnemonic to create their own assignments. More important, this writing assignment measured more completely her students' achievement of unit objectives than any multiple-choice exam she could have created.

Diverse writing tasks are available for content area courses—assignments that effectively smuggle oral and written language into the curriculum, assignments that motivate and intrigue, and assignments that can maximize students' learning and thinking. Several issues must be resolved, however, before teachers and students feel comfortable in using writing as a way of learning. In the next section we discuss four of these issues.

CRITICAL ISSUES CONCERNING THE USE OF WRITING AS A MEANS OF LEARNING

The decision to use writing as a means of encouraging students' active learning changes the way many teachers view their content area, the writing process, and their responsibilities in negotiating the two. As a result, numerous questions and issues are posed that need to be addressed. We deal with four of the more urgent and far-reaching of these:

1. Grading and responding to students' writing
2. Student involvement in evaluation
3. The use of writing in a testing situation to evaluate students' mastery of concepts
4. The ubiquitous research paper

Sane Methods for Grading and Responding

Pearce (1983) found, in his interviews with teachers, that many were hesitant to incorporate writing into their units of study because of the overwhelming amount of work that would be generated by the 100 or more students they see each day. Over the years, we have collected specific techniques from other teachers and from our own experiences that have made it feasible for students to write and teachers to survive. These techniques acknowledge that teachers have personal lives and thus prefer not to spend the weekend glued to the kitchen table writing comments to students about their written work. All of the techniques are based on the premise that responding is more important than grading in the writing process and in students' mastery of content area concepts. The following are some general guidelines to expedite the process of responding and grading:

Students Should Be Told, in Advance, the Role of Mechanisms and Grammar in Any Writing Assignment

1. Remember the purpose of each writing assignment and keep content the center of your focus. If students write a journal entry, the purpose is to help them construct meaning and to learn content area concepts. Hence, the evaluation process should reflect that and not focus on mechanics and spelling. If, however, the students have worked their way through the processes of writing and class time has been provided for feedback at each stage, evaluate the writing as a final draft. Students

should be told, in advance, the importance of their spelling, grammar, and mechanical errors in the total evaluation process. As discussed earlier, the assignment-making process should be thorough to inform students of your expectations and purposes.

2. Avoid zealous error detection as you respond to your students' writing because this type of response can consume huge amounts of your time and energy. Remember that students are more likely to make mechanical errors when they first begin to write on a topic that is unfamiliar or new to them (Shaughnessy, 1977).
3. Write at least one positive comment or reaction: Sometimes a large "yes!" does the trick.
4. Use green, purple, or orange pen, or better yet, use a pencil—any color but red, which connotes a highly punitive message.
5. Use abbreviations for comments you frequently make. For example, instead of writing "Be More Specific" countless times, write BS. Provide students with a list of your abbreviations.
6. Troubleshoot many of the errors that students commonly make by providing them with class time, in advance of the due date, to read and edit their assigned partner's rough draft. This will save you time and provide them with more sensitivity and appreciation for the writing and thinking processes.
7. Consider the possibility of not evaluating every assignment, especially microthemes, academic journal entries, or reader-response entries. Many teachers put a check mark in the upper corner after quickly skimming to make sure the assignment is complete. On other occasions, especially with multiple journal entries or summaries, some teachers determine in advance the one that they will grade thoroughly or ask the students to select their best papers to be graded.

You Need Not Grade Every Paper a Student Writes

8. Severely limit the length of some assignments, as with the microthemes, which are written entirely on an index card. The important criterion should not be length, but rather the students' effectiveness in judiciously selecting the words they will explain or defend. Space limitation not only will save you time, it will also educate your students so that they will not always equate length with quality.
9. Stagger your writing assignments across your classes so that you do not require all your students to hand in their work at the same time. For example, your first- and second-period classes could hand in their writing on Mondays, your third- and fourth-period classes on Tuesdays, and your fifth- and sixth-period classes on Wednesdays.
10. Perhaps the most important thing to remember about grading is to think and plan carefully before assigning. Writing tasks do not facilitate all types of course objectives and help all types of students.

	Below Average	Average	Above Average
1. The essay has an introduction.	______	______	______
2. The essay answers the question and provides key ideas from the text or lecture.	______	______	______
3. The essay provides support for each of the key ideas.	______	______	______
4. The essay personalizes the information by relating it to situations beyond the text and lecture.	______	______	______
5. The writing is clear and organized.	______	______	______
6. The essay summarizes the findings.	______	______	______

FIGURE 7.5 Checklist for Grading a Health Essay

In addition to these general grading suggestions, you can develop some forms (checklists, primary trait evaluation guides, and rubrics) to help decrease the time devoted to providing students with quality comments and responses to their written work (Pearce, 1983). These forms, which can be adapted to any content area and any assignment, are discussed next.

Checklists

Content Area Teachers Can Use Three Forms to Help Them Grade Students' Writing More Quickly

Checklists contain the general criteria that you wish to focus on when you read students' writing, whether their thesis statements or their use of support to defend a position. Rather than writing the same comment over and over again (e.g., "Be more specific," "Support your statements"), you merely circle the item on the checklist. In addition, the checklist allows you to indicate the level of competence the student displayed on the checklist's criteria. Figure 7.5 illustrates a type of checklist that Mary, a health teacher, used when she evaluated her students' papers on heart disease. Notice that it concentrates on content development and organization. You could easily modify such a checklist by adding different criteria.

Primary Trait Evaluations

Much like the checklist, with **primary trait evaluations** teachers focus on the desired traits they want in their students' writing. For example, if Mary had done a primary trait evaluation on her students' essays, it probably would resemble Figure 7.6. You have probably constructed something similar and called it your "grading template." Byers and Brostoff (1979) suggest that teachers write brief comments on students' papers and focus on one or two primary traits, especially

1. The essay lists five of the nine factors impacting heart disease. (age, sex, race, genetic factors; cholesterol and triglycerides; hypertension; diabetes; obesity; smoking; type A behavior; stress; inactivity)	5 points
2. The essay explains these five factors with statistics, examples, support.	15 points
3. The essay relates these factors to personal situations (i.e., the author assesses his/her own risk of developing heart disease).	15 points
4. The essay is clear and well organized.	5 points
	TOTAL 40 points

FIGURE 7.6 Primary Trait Evaluation of Health Essay

with students' first efforts in writing about a concept. In addition, those authors recommend that content area teachers write questions rather than comments such as "Be specific." Questions, they believe, force students to solve problems and interact with the material. For example, instead of writing the comment "Be specific," Mary could write a question such as this: "Can you convince me that fitness relates to general health?"

Rubrics

A **rubric** gives content area teachers more structure for their responses because it summarizes the traits or criteria, as well as the characteristics of high-quality and low-quality papers (Pearce, 1983). Using the rubric as a guide, the teacher can quickly read the students' work and respond specifically and appropriately. For Mary's assignment, the rubric might resemble Figure 7.7.

Regardless of the form you select, it is a good idea to introduce it with the assignment and ask the students to attach it to their writing assignment. In that way, the form becomes a concrete reminder for students of what the criteria will be for your responses and eventual evaluation. In the next section, we will discuss how students can participate and assist in the evaluation of their writing.

Effective Activities for Involving Students in Evaluation

When Students Are Involved in Evaluating Their Writing, They Learn Something About Writing and Lessen Your Burdens as a Teacher

Students should be involved in evaluating their writing and other students' writing if we want them to gain independence as learners and consumers of print. Because many students have been conditioned to respond only on a mechanical level (i.e., "Did I misspell any words?") to their writing, this self-evaluation or peer evaluation takes time to develop. The advantages far outweigh the disadvantages, however, especially in terms of lightening your responsibilities as the sole responder and evaluator. In addition, if students can identify or troubleshoot some common writing problems during class, they can use that information once they begin to revise their final product.

An "A" Essay Would Contain

1. An introduction or thesis statement
2. A list of the factors (five minimum) impacting heart disease
3. Explanations, examples, statistics for each of the five factors
4. A personal application or assessment (i.e., the author would assess himself/herself about the risk of developing heart disease)
5. An implication statement discussing solutions
6. Very good organization, few mechanical errors

A "B" Essay Would Contain

1. An introduction or thesis statement
2. A list of the factors (five minimum) impacting heart disease
3. Explanations, examples, statistics for four of the factors
4. An attempt of a personal application
5. A summary statement
6. Good organization, few mechanical errors

A "C" Essay Would Contain

1. A list of the factors (five minimum) impacting heart disease
2. Explanations, examples, statistics for three of the factors
3. A conclusion or summary
4. Fair organization, some mechanical errors

A "D" Essay Would Contain

1. A list of the factors (three or four) impacting heart disease
2. Explanations, examples, statistics for two of the factors
3. Below-average organization and many mechanical errors

A "F" Essay Would Contain

1. A list of the factors (fewer than three) impacting heart disease
2. Explanations, examples, statistics for one factor
3. A list of points, poor organization, many mechanical errors

FIGURE 7.7 Scoring Rubric for a Health Essay

Over the years, we have discovered several activities that help students learn how to evaluate and respond to writing. We have found it best to begin with a whole-class activity that involves students in judging optimal and nonoptimal written models. Another name for this activity is "The Good, the Bad, and the Ugly" because good writing samples as well as bad ones are shared with the students. It is best not to use actual student work but rather to create samples of student writing that typify what "past students" have written. Usually these samples are combinations of students' work and teachers' concerns about common writing problems. The three essays in Figure 7.8 illustrate what one English teacher developed to help students evaluate short essays objectively. The essays

EXAMPLE 1

We employ categories for the purpose of classifying the stimuli. We note the similarities and the differences. Like the English bulldog and Labrador.

The abstraction process could be termed a stereotyping process. Rather than do that, we employ abstractions and stereotypes. Like doctors.

Abstractions can cause some real problems in interpersonal communication. General semanticists have suggested that the abstraction process causes us to overlook the differences in people and things simply because they are all in the same category.

Always try to check with them to make sure that our responses to words are compatible with theirs.

EXAMPLE 2

The abstraction process is of interest to interpersonal communication. When we use the abstraction process, we employ categories for the purpose of classifying the stimuli we perceive. To conceive of the category *dog*, it is necessary for us to abstract from each of these furry creatures those characteristics they all have in common. To do this, we note the similarities but also overlook the differences.

When we categorize we obviously overlook some significant differences. An English bulldog is short, bowlegged, and waddles. On the other hand, a Lab is incredibly graceful, can jump, and has long silky hair. Yet these two dogs have much in common. Both are interested in chasing birds, barking at strangers, and playing with balls and sticks.

Abstractions can be good in that they help us deal with the incoming stimuli in our day-to-day world and provide us with some predictive ability. However, the abstraction process can also cause some real problems. We often assume that the characteristics of a category will hold true for every member. General semanticists have suggested that the abstraction process causes us to overlook the differences in people and things simply because they are all in the same category.

One way to avoid these kinds of errors with the abstraction process is to use indexing, dating, and quotation marks. What it involves is marking a word by the use of numbers or quotes or dates to indicate that dog 1 is different from dog 2. This should remind us that all dogs are not necessarily friendly and that we must test this assumption with each dog.

EXAMPLE 3

When we use the abstraction process, we employ categories for the purpose of classifying the stimuli we perceive. To conceive of the category *dog*, it is necessary for us to abstract from each of these furry creatures those characteristics they all have in common. An English bulldog is short, bowlegged, and waddles. On the other hand, a Lab is incredibly graceful, can jump, and has long silky hair. Yet these two dogs have much in common. Both are interested in chasing birds, barking at strangers, and playing with balls and sticks.

Abstractions provide us with some predictive ability. The abstraction process could also be termed a stereotyping process. Although the abstraction process is useful, there are some real problems it can create in interpersonal communication. General semanticists have suggested that the abstraction process causes us to overlook the differences in people and things simply because they are all in the same category.

One way to avoid these kinds of errors is to use indexing and dating. Like dog1, dog2, and dog3.

FIGURE 7.8 "The Good, the Bad, and the Ugly" Exercise

were on the abstraction process and fit nicely into her unit on language. See if you can determine the "good," the "bad," and the "ugly" in these essays.

Students are told to read the samples and then assign a grade to each. After grading each sample, they are to rank the writing samples from best to worst. Once they have completed these tasks, the teacher leads a discussion on the grades, ranks, and students' rationales. From our experiences with this activity, students become highly motivated to participate and defend their judgments.

Students Must Remember to Be Positive and Specific as They Evaluate Their Classmates' Writing

When students feel comfortable with the concept of evaluating and responding to their classmates' writing, it is a good idea to pair them for peer evaluation of a writing assignment they have recently drafted. Begin by emphasizing the basic rules for peer evaluation—be positive and be specific. Then explain the process: one student will read his or her paper while the other student listens, using a set of questions to guide the feedback given to the writer. The questions should vary according to the content area and assignment; the following typify some that can be used:

1. What did you like best about your partner's paper?
2. What could be added to make the paper more interesting?
3. What facts, ideas, and evidence could be added to strengthen your partner's paper?
4. What parts are not clear?
5. What two parts should be changed or revised?

To help students remember what their partner has recommended, it is a good idea to provide students with a form, such as the one in Figure 7.9. After the stu-

Author's Name: **Peer Reviewer's Name:**

Authors: Read your paper aloud to your reviewer.
Reviewer: Answer the questions below so that the author has a written copy of the comments you will provide orally.

1. This paper is mainly about
2. The best part of the author's paper was
3. These parts of the author's paper were not clear to me:
   a.
   b.
   c.
4. I think the author's paper could be strengthened by:
   a.
   b.
   c.
5. I think the paper could be even more interesting if the author would

Reviewer and Author: Talk to each other about your ideas.

FIGURE 7.9 Student Evaluation Form for Working in Pairs

dent reads her paper, the partner shares his ideas and responses to the questions as they talk. It is important that they talk to each other about the writing rather than just exchange forms. After the talking and responding, they switch roles. If the activity is difficult for the students or if they feel uncomfortable initially, you can model the procedure for the class by becoming the partner who responds.

A third activity can be done in small groups (Pearce, 1983). A volunteer in each group reads his paper. Then the other members of the group state ideas from their papers that either were or were not present in the paper just read. According to Pearce, each member of the group must respond. Because all students are required to participate, they profit from hearing how others have interacted with the targeted concepts. This information should assist students in revising their papers once they leave class. Moreover, this activity can serve as an excellent review for an examination.

Using Writing to Test Learning

If you have ever used an essay examination in your class as a means of measuring student learning, you probably have shared the reactions of most teachers: "No more essays!" "These students can't write, so why should I waste my time grading these pitiful excuses for essay answers!" or "Did these students even study?" Although the most judicious use of writing is not for testing or evaluating, essay examinations should not be avoided just because students initially are inept with them. As stated in Chapter 4, writing is one of the best means, next to a conference with each student, to assess how well students can think analytically about content. If we expect our students to synthesize, evaluate, and apply course objectives to new contexts, we should design evaluation measures that are sensitive to those objectives. In short, true-false and multiple-choice questions should not be the only examinations that students take.

How then do we prepare students to be adept at taking essay examinations? One way to help students through their first essay test is by teaching them the processes involved in **PORPE (*P*redict, *O*rganize, *R*ehearse, *P*ractice, *E*valuate),** an essay preparation strategy built on research and theory in writing and metacognition (Simpson, 1986). In the initial validation study, the high-risk college freshmen trained in PORPE as a means of preparing for a psychology exam performed significantly better than an equivalent group answering short-answer questions (Simpson, Hayes, Stahl, Conner, & Weaver, 1988). Not only were these students' essays superior in content, organization, and cohesion, but their scores on the multiple-choice exam were also significantly superior to those of the control students. This study demonstrated that any student, with assistance from the teacher, can learn how to apply the steps of PORPE to improve in essay and multiple-choice test performance.

PORPE Helps Students to Study for Essay Exams

PORPE's first step, **predict,** asks students to generate some potential questions that would make good essays. To help students at this point, teachers should introduce the language used for writing essay examinations by providing them with a glossary of commonly used essay-question words such as *explain, discuss, criticize, compare,* and *contrast.* Once students understand the meaning of these

Students Must Understand the Words Used in Essay Questions

essay-word starters, teachers can involve them in brainstorming possible essay questions from a specific chapter. Often the main difficulty students have with essay prediction is that they focus on minute details rather than key ideas. Thus, try telling them to check the boldface headings and summaries for possible essay topics. Essay prediction is not easy, but all students can learn this very important step if given considerable guidance. The following questions illustrate some of the questions students predicted for their essay test on the Modernist Movement in an art appreciation course:

1. Discuss the individuals and types of art that influenced the Modernist Movement in painting.
2. Compare and contrast Kandinsky with Picasso.
3. Trace the development of the Modernist Movement in the United States, noting influential artists as well as critics.

The second step in PORPE, **organize,** involves students in gathering and arranging the information that will answer the self-predicted essay question. This step is very much like brainstorming and prewriting in that students map or outline answers in their own words. Content area teachers can help students with this step by sharing their own maps or outlines that answer a predicted essay question. Students can also work in pairs to brainstorm their own organizational structure for another predicted essay question. Representatives from each pair could then present and discuss their structure and rationale on the chalkboard. As a final step, students could develop their own map or outline for a different essay question and receive brief written or oral feedback from the teacher. This step encourages students to develop connections among ideas so that the course content becomes reorganized into a coherent structure instead of memorized as a list of unrelated bits of information.

The third step of PORPE, **rehearse,** engages students in the active self-recitation and self-testing of the key ideas from their maps or outlines. At this point, teachers should stress the difference between the processes of *recall* and *recognition* so that students will accept and internalize the need for a rehearsal step in their study. Most of the students we have worked with think that studying is the same as looking at the information, and they see no difference in demands between essays and multiple-choice exams. One of the major reasons students have difficulty writing essay answers is that they have not spent the concentrated time rehearsing information to transfer it to long-term memory.

Talk-Throughs Can Be Used to Help Students Prepare for Essay Exams

To help students rehearse, we have found it useful to incorporate the talk-through strategy (see Chapter 9) at this stage. During class, students meet with their partners and practice talk-throughs for a specified amount of time. After discussing and evaluating each other's talk-through, students write, from memory, an answer to one of their self-predicted essay questions.

The fourth step, **practice,** is the validation step of learning because students must write from recall the answers to their self-predicted essay questions in preparation for the real examination. Before students begin their practice, content area teachers should provide them with many examples of essay answers, good and bad, and discuss their relative merits. Teachers can also reduce students' anxiety by outlining the procedures for writing an effective answer in an actual testing situation. For example, students should be taught to read each question carefully before they begin to write, underlining key words. Next, they should be encouraged to sketch their outline or map in the margin of their test paper before they begin writing. Once they begin answering the question, they should make sure that their opening sentence rephrases the essay question and/or takes a position. Finally, students should reread the essay question to ensure that they have answered it directly.

The final step of PORPE, **evaluate,** requires students to evaluate the quality of their practice answers. To facilitate this process, students are given a checklist that requires them to read and evaluate their text as would a teacher. The checklist in Figure 7.10 helps students to evaluate, completely and objectively, both their essay answer and their readiness for the real examination. Content area teachers can introduce this final step of PORPE by arranging brief sessions when students read, discuss, and evaluate the merits of various essay answers.

Directions: Evaluate the quality of your answer by using this checklist. If you score *above average* on the six questions, you are probably ready for the exam. If, however, you find some of your answers to the predicted essay questions to be *below average* or *average,* go back to your notes, annotation, and strategies. Examine your organization (STEP TWO) again—did you leave out some key ideas or details? Repair and then go through the steps again—PREDICT, ORGANIZE, REHEARSE, PRACTICE, AND EVALUATE.

EVALUATING PRACTICE ESSAY ANSWERS

	Below Average	**Average**	**Above Average**
1. I directly answered the question that was asked.	1	2	3
2. I had an introductory sentence which restated the essay question and/or took a position on the question.	1	2	3
3. I organized the essay answer with key ideas or points which were made obvious.	1	2	3
4. I included in the answer *relevant* details or examples to prove and clarify each idea.	1	2	3
5. I used transitions in the answer to cue the reader. (e.g., First, Finally)	1	2	3
6. My answer made sense and demonstrated a knowledge of the content.	1	2	3

Source: Simpson, M. L. (1986), "PORPE: A Writing Strategy for Studying and Learning in the Content Areas," *Journal of Reading, 29,* p. 411. Reprinted by permission of the author.

FIGURE 7.10 Student Checklist for Self-Evaluation

Once students become more accustomed to evaluating writing with a checklist, they can work in pairs to evaluate each other's essays and evaluate their own answers independently.

Even though the steps of PORPE will take some additional class time, it is important to remember that students not only will learn how to prepare for and take an essay exam, but also will learn important course concepts. In addition, the PORPE strategy can help students prepare for multiple-choice exams, especially when the questions ask them to draw conclusions and apply information to new contexts. Thus, the essay test should not be feared by students or teachers but used when appropriate and when students have been taught the *how.*

The Research Paper

Research Papers Involve Students in Many Sophisticated Reading and Thinking Processes

At the college level, the most common writing assignment that students encounter across the curriculum is the **research paper** or **written report** (Simpson, Hynd, Nist, & Burrell, 1997). The research paper or report is also a common assignment in secondary school. These assignments, as Nelson and Hayes (1988) point out, require sophisticated reading and thinking skills because students must be able to identify a focused topic, locate appropriate sources, summarize key ideas, and then synthesize these ideas from the multiple sources into a coherent written product. Because of these sophisticated demands, students and teachers often become frustrated and disillusioned. Students are frustrated because they do not understand the intricate and time-consuming processes involved in writing from multiple sources. Teachers are frustrated because the products students hand in are not what they have anticipated. What is the solution? Should content area teachers avoid research papers or written reports? We think a better solution is to define clearly the goals of such assignments and to provide specific interventions that will help students during the processes of researching, reading, planning, and writing.

The goals of a research paper can vary along a continuum, with one goal emphasizing knowledge telling and the other knowledge transformation (Nelson & Hayes, 1988). Knowledge telling requires students to locate and summarize what other individuals have stated about a certain topic. For example, a student in a history course might decide to do a research paper on blacklisting or the Red Scare. Knowledge transformation involves students in reading and evaluating information in terms of a specific question or goal that they have established for themselves. A student doing a research paper of this type would selectively read, evaluate, and synthesize information from the sources with the goal of answering a question, such as whether or not the activities and behaviors of people during the Red Scare are in any way characteristic of the present era. Knowledge telling differs significantly from knowledge transformation in that students must plan, evaluate, and synthesize more with the latter. If teachers want students to do the type of critical thinking and writing involved in knowledge transformation, then they should inform students of that when giving the assignment. Otherwise, students typically will reinterpret the research report as an assignment in which they gather information and then record it in a paper (Nelson & Hayes, 1988).

In addition to informing students of the goals of a paper, content area teachers can assist students by reviewing the processes or stages involved in writing a research paper:

Students Should Be Told the Steps for Doing a Research Paper to Help Them Avoid Last-Minute Efforts

1. Selecting a topic or issue that is of high interest.
2. Getting started and narrowing the focus of the topic or issue by doing some initial reading and thinking.
3. Searching for more relevant sources and taking notes using your own organizational system rather than the author's.
4. Thinking and planning the structure of the paper.
5. Returning to the library if necessary for additional sources to fill out your structure.
6. Writing the first draft.
7. Evaluating, revising, and editing with the audience in mind.
8. Writing the final version of the paper.

Students can also profit if they are told about the time necessary to move from stage 1 to stage 8. Our experience suggests that students often miscalculate the time necessary to find the appropriate sources in the library. More important, they underestimate the time that must be devoted to the stages that follow the research, thinking that the paper can be written the night before the deadline.

Content area teachers can help students progress through the stages of writing a research paper in several ways. First, they can provide a reading list or key words that students can use in their library or computer searches. Second, they can ask students for progress reports in the form of journal entries where students discuss what they have done and list their concerns or questions. These entries can be shared with the teacher, as well as with other students in group problem-solving sessions during class. Some teachers ask students to hand in writing products as a way of ensuring that students are progressing. For example, students can hand in their initial reference list, outline, or notes to demonstrate that they are on task. Such work, handed in early, also allows teachers to give students specific feedback. Third, teachers can require students to present to the class an oral report of their paper 1 week before the written report is due. In this way, students are forced to think about and organize their ideas for an audience other than the teacher. When students realize that they will be presenting their work to a real audience, they tend to adapt and transform the information they have gathered to meet the needs of their uninformed listeners (Nelson & Hayes, 1988).

Finally, teachers can help students by giving them, in advance, the criteria that will be used to grade or evaluate their work. As mentioned earlier in this chapter, explicitly describing writing assignments can prevent bad writing. Students should understand the role of mechanics, organization, content, and writing style in the grading process. Some teachers use a checklist and ask students to attach it to the first page of their paper. The checklist incorporates the grading criteria and helps students evaluate their work before handing it in. We think this is a good idea that can make the grading process somewhat easier.

The Role of Computers During the Writing Process

The use of computers is addressed more fully in Chapter 10, but it is appropriate to outline briefly how the computer can be used during the writing and learning process. As you undoubtedly have already discovered, computer technology can be initially intoxicating for students. They hope that the computer can think for them and miraculously generate quality text with little or no effort in a short period of time. We must remind students that this technology is not inherently advantageous to the writing process. When used correctly and insightfully, however, a word processing program can develop students' understanding of and sensitivity to how they write and can thus increase their control over their writing process.

Research Suggests That Word Processing Programs Can Help Students Produce Better-Quality Writing

Research tends to support these intuitions about computer technology and writing. For example, in a review of 32 studies, Bangert-Drowns (1993) concluded that word processing programs helped students produce longer documents and better-quality writing. That is, a user-friendly word processing program can facilitate the recursive stages of prewriting, writing, and postwriting so that your students will take more risks in the meaning-making processes of writing and learning. In the next section we examine the role of the computer during each of these three stages.

Prewriting Stages

A word processing program can be advantageous at the prewriting stage by reducing the anxiety that some students feel about writing, especially those who will tell you that they know nothing about the topic or are unsure of where to begin. With a word processing program, students can freely and quickly brainstorm ideas, especially if they know the keyboard. They can then delete, add, and rearrange those ideas into groups, and those ideas can then be labeled and ordered. If students suffer from the "fuzzy-thinking" syndrome during their planning, they can stop and practice what Flower (1985) describes as nutshelling. Nutshelling is helpful to students who have brainstormed many ideas but who lack a focus or precise direction. To **nutshell** on the computer, students must compress into a sentence the key idea they would like to write about and then teach that idea to someone else before they move any further in the composing process. The following example of nutshelling came from a student who was writing an essay about the novel *The Contender.*

> Through boxing and his interactions with several different people, Alfred learned that he could be a contender in life.

By taking the time to nutshell, this student began to understand what he wanted to say about the book he had just read.

There Are Many Inventive Programs to Help Students See Connections Across Their Ideas

In addition to brainstorming and nutshelling, **invention programs** encourage students to "generate, expand, and make connections among their ideas" (Elder, Bowen, Schwartz, & Goswami, 1989, p. 167). These programs provide students with questions or prompts (e.g., "What are the good consequences of your topic?" "Whom do you consider an authority on your topic?"), which help students consider what they already know about a topic and what they still need to research or explore. Other computer programs, such as *Inspiration, Semantic Mapper,* and *Semnet,* help students visualize interrelationships between ideas using concept maps.

Writing Stages

Some of your students will be able to compose at the computer, but the majority will use it only to type their first draft, which they probably have already handwritten. Word processing programs have many advantages at this stage of the writing process. If students know the keyboard, they can be more effective and efficient because their thoughts are almost always ahead of their fingers when they write by hand. With the computer, students are more likely to experiment by trying out ideas, erasing ones they do not like, skipping ahead, and then returning to reword difficult introductions or transition sentences. They even can write two different versions of a sentence or paragraph, marking one with parentheses or capitals, either of which can easily be deleted later. In short, word processing programs encourage flexibility and efficiency during the drafting stages of writing.

Postwriting Stages

The postwriting stages of the writing process include revising, editing, and proofreading. After the draft has been saved and copied on the computer, students will be able to read and revise and/or share copies with their peers or teachers for feedback. This typed, double-spaced draft is far more readable, and gross mistakes, such as misspellings and punctuation omissions, are obvious. Moreover, students are more likely to accept the suggestions for major revisions given by teachers and peers because the computer makes draft writing so easy. Instead of saying "Do I have to do this whole thing over?" students are more likely to say "How else can I make this draft better?" The word processing program allows them to insert new text, combine paragraphs, move entire paragraphs or pages to different places, or delete unnecessary text.

Several word processing commands and software packages can help students with their editing. Some word processing programs have search commands that can identify a character or string of characters, such as a word or a mark or punctuation. The computer will then scan the entire text, stopping each time to highlight the designated character so that the student can change or correct it. The search-and-replace command locates a character and automatically replaces it with another (e.g., *effect* for *affect*). Many word processing programs have a spelling checker, and some have a thesaurus to help students with word choices.

As you can see, word processing programs and software packages have the potential to help your students during the writing process. Because we realize that every teacher does not have access to 30 computers, we offer the following suggestions for capitalizing on the computers to which your students do have access:

Even If You Do Not Have Many Computers, There Are Ways to Circumvent This Problem

1. Make sure that middle school students are taught basic typing and keyboard skills so that they can improve their fluency and speed on the computer.
2. Have students write their first draft in pencil. When they are done, they can sign up for a 20- to 30-minute session on the computer.
3. Ask students to work in pairs on the computer. One student who knows the keyboard can type her paper while the other student reads it to her. Then the students can switch roles.
4. Reserve a certain amount of computer time for printing the students' writing so that they have a written product that can be taken home for reading, revising, and editing.
5. Allow students to decide whether they want to use the computer for brainstorming, drafting, or revising.

Although it is advantageous to use the computer and computer software programs, we should point out the obvious: this technology will not automatically increase students' ability to communicate in writing about content area concepts. What does make a difference in students' learning is how computers are integrated into the process approach to writing and into the classroom environment (Cochran-Smith, 1991).

CASE STUDY REVISITED

At the beginning of this chapter, we described the problems that Dave was experiencing in his first year of teaching biology to non-college-bound students. After reading this chapter, you probably have some suggestions on how he could motivate his students to become more active participants and learners. Write your suggestions now.

After talking to the English teacher and doing some of his own research and planning, Dave decided to spark his students' interest in the environment unit in several ways. Because the unit was to last approximately 9 weeks, he felt he had the time to assign some literature and expository pieces other than just the textbook. In addition, he decided to involve his students actively by asking them to write about their concerns and questions rather than having them merely answer the questions at the end of the textbook chapter.

Dave began the unit with an activity designed to assess his students' present attitudes toward the environment. The students were prepared for a lecture and a textbook assignment when they entered class on the second day of the unit. Instead, they were greeted with Dave's slides of beautiful outdoor scenes and Jethro Tull's "Songs from the Woods" playing in the background. As the song faded, Dave shifted the slides to scenes of human filth and flotsam. Slides of dumps, incinerators, and cities were now shown, and the background music was John Prine's "Paradise." When the slides and song were finished, Dave handed out the following questionnaire:

Directions: Answer as completely as possible. There are no right or wrong answers, so feel free to express yourself.

1. Briefly, tell me how the slide presentation made you feel.
2. What was the message of the second song, "Paradise?"
3. Is there a place outdoors that you especially like to go? Where? Why?
4. Have you ever thought or read or heard about the ideas presented today? If so, tell me about them in more detail. What was the source of those ideas?

Dave read his students' responses before he assigned the next activity, which was designed to provoke them into comparing their personal feelings about the environment with society's attitudes. When his students entered the classroom on the third day, he handed them "a letter from archy," excerpted from *from the lifetimes of archy and mehitabel* by Don Marquis (1950), and asked them to read it. The English teacher had suggested this particular piece to Dave, and he found it especially relevant.

Dave then divided the students into groups of five and gave them a study guide to provide a focus for their discussions. He circulated around the room as they discussed the questions, joining groups and provoking them to think beyond the obvious. One of the statements on the study guide required them to estimate the date of the letter. As Dave interacted with each group, he found that they were shocked to learn that the letter had been written in 1935.

Dave then brought the class together to brainstorm all the actions and decisions people have made that have ignored archy's warnings. Because of recent media coverage, the students were quickly able to list problems like the greenhouse effect, acid rain, deforestation, and the loss of wildlife. At the end of the hour, he told his students that they were going to focus on one issue: the loss of wildlife.

On the next day of class, Dave handed out copies of Farley Mowatt's *Never Cry Wolf* (1963) and said that they would be reading the book for the next few days. To establish an overall purpose for their reading, he asked the students to focus on three questions: (1) Why was the wolf endangered? (2) What was the likely future of the wolf? (3) What must we do to prevent its extinction? He then read aloud the first few pages to elicit their interest and assigned the first 30 pages. Each day the students gathered in their groups to discuss and then write a group response to the "Question for the Day" that Dave had written on the board (e.g., "What were the reasons for Farley's boss giving him this assignment?" "What do you think Farley is going to find out about the wolf?"). When the students finished the book, Dave gave each of them an index card and asked them to respond to the three focus questions he had asked the first day. After reading the students' microthemes, Dave led a class discussion of the book and the three questions. He was pleased with this activity because most of his students had actually read the book and some reported that it was their first.

Because Dave's next unit objective was to have his students localize and personalize the issue of endangered species, he obtained a list of locally endangered animal and plant species from the Department of Natural Resources and asked each student to select a species from the list. The librarian and the English teacher suggested that he give his students a lot of structure for the assignment, so Dave distributed a handout outlining his expectations:

> You are to select one of the species from the list and gather information about its problem of survival. Specifically, I want you to include the following information in your paper: (1) past and present range and population, (2) length of time it has been endangered, (3) reasons for its being endangered, (4) why it is important that this species survive, and (5) actions currently being taken to improve its chances for survival.
>
> You will have 2 weeks to complete this assignment. Your first step in doing the assignment will be to use the classroom library and any resources I have listed for you on the accompanying page. Read extensively and take notes for about 4 days. On the fifth day, begin organizing your ideas into an outline or map, making sure you have answered all five questions. On the sixth day, you will deliver a 3-minute presentation to the class on what you have learned thus far about your endangered species. Rough drafts of your written paper will be due on October 15. I will read them and provide you with feedback. The final paper will be due October 30.
>
> In grading this assignment, I will use these criteria:
>
> 1. How well you answered the five questions concerning your species. Were you complete? Accurate? Did you explain yourself clearly so that your best friend could understand? This part is worth 35 points.
> 2. Your spelling, mechanics, and grammar. This part is worth 15 points. As to length—there are five questions, so I expect 3 pages as a minimum.

Most of Dave's students attempted to do the assignment, so he was pleased. He realized, however, that he probably should have started on a smaller scale with a less intimidating discourse mode. After chatting with the English teacher during lunch, he decided to try letter writing because it was a less formal type of writing and was closer to talking, something his students were good at.

The next week, Dave began his final activity for the unit. The class brainstormed what could be done to stop or slow down the process of environmental degradation. When Dave asked his students what they could do, he received many blank stares. He then suggested to them that education was one answer and that they could be a part of that educational process by becoming informed and involved. Dave explained that involvement can occur in many forms, and that letter writing was one powerful and permanent means of disseminating ideas. With that introduction, he told each student to write a letter to his or her senator or representative asking for support of legislation they considered important for the protection of wildlife. After discussing the proper form for a letter to a government official, the students were given time to begin their rough drafts. Dave provided feedback on all rough drafts, and by the end of the week he had 24 letters to mail to Washington, D.C. Many students doubted whether they would receive a response, but within a month, all of Dave's students had received replies from the senators and representatives. Copies of the 24 letters were placed on Dave's bulletin board and shared with group members. Even after 4 months and several other units of study, the students still gathered at the bulletin board to read those letters and to discuss the status of their environment.

Dave is still struggling with ways to involve his students with the biology curriculum. He has some good days and some bad ones, but he feels that his students are certainly more involved than they were before, when he taught only from the textbook.

■ ■ ■

SUMMARY

In this chapter we have tried to demonstrate that the writing process can be a powerful tool in helping students learn content area concepts. Writing, like reading, is a constructive process that can stimulate passive learners to become active learners as they grapple with the task of putting their own words on paper. Although writing can be extremely useful in teaching content, teachers must also remember that writing is not a product, but a process with overlapping and recursive stages. Sufficient instructional attention and time must be allotted to these stages so that students plan, draft, revise, edit, proofread, and polish their writing before the possibility of grading is even considered. For those teachers wondering how to evaluate students' writing, we offered some practical grading guidelines and suggestions to make the task easier and more reasonable.

This chapter was organized on the assumptions that writing can be used to help students (1) prepare for their reading assignments, lectures, demonstrations, and class discussions; (2) summarize and react to concepts; and (3) think critically and creatively. Using those three assumptions, we presented a variety of activities—the Guided-Writing Activity, the academic journal, the double journal entry, framed paragraphs, the reader-response heuristic, and the microtheme—as well as the SPAWNing method for creating assignments to stimulate students to attain higher levels of thinking. For those teachers who are interested in computers or who have access to computers in their classroom, we also recommended some materials and activities for word processing programs. Any of these writing activities could easily be incorporated into content area lesson plans to challenge and motivate even the most reluctant learner.

REFERENCES

Applebee, A. N., Langer, J. A., & Mullis, I. V. S. (1986). *The writing report card: Writing achievement in American school National Assessment of Educational Progress.* Princeton, NJ: Educational Testing Service.

Bangert-Drowns, R. L. (1993). The word processor as an instructional tool: A meta-analysis of word processing in writing instruction. *Review of Educational Research, 63,* 69–93.

Bean, J. C., Drenk, D., & Lee, F. D. (1982). Microtheme strategies for developing cognitive skills. In C. W. Griffin (Ed.), *New directions for teaching and learning.* San Francisco: Jossey-Bass.

Bridgeman, B., & Carlson, S. B. (1985). Survey of academic writing tasks. *Written Communication, 2,* 247–280.

Brozo, W. (1988). Applying the reader-response heuristic to expository texts. *Journal of Reading, 32,* 140–145.

Burns, J., Peltason, J., & Cronin, T. (1984). *Government by the people.* Englewood Cliffs, NJ: Prentice-Hall.

Byers, B. K., & Brostoff, A. (1979). The time it takes managing/evaluating writing and social studies. *Social Education, 43,* 194–197.

Calkins, L. M. (1986). *The art of teaching writing.* Portsmouth, NH: Heinemann.

Cochran-Smith, M. (1991). Word processing and writing in elementary classrooms: A critical review of related literature. *Review of Educational Research, 53,* 445–459.

Connelly, P. J., & Irving, D. C. (1976). Composition in the liberal arts: A shared responsibility. *College English, 37,* 670–674.

Draper, V. (1982). Writing to assist learning in all subject areas. In G. Camp (Ed.), *Teaching writing: Essays from the Bay Area Project.* Upper Montclair, NJ: Boynton/Cook.

Elder, J., Bowen, B., Schwartz, J., & Goswami, D. (1989). *Word processing in a community of writers.* New York: Garland.

Florio-Ruane, S., & Dunn, S. (1987). Teaching writing: Some perennial questions and some possible answers. In V. Richardson-Koehler (Ed.), *Educator's handbook: A research perspective.* New York: Longman.

Flower, L. (1985). *Problem solving strategies for writing.* New York: Harcourt Brace Jovanovich.

Fulwiler, T. (1987). *Teaching with writing.* Upper Montclair, NJ: Boynton/Cook.

Gere, A. R. (1985). *Roots in the sawdust: Writing to learn across the disciplines.* Urbana, IL: National Council of Teachers of English.

Houston, J. W., & Houston, J. (1974). *Farewell to Manzanar.* New York: Bantam.

Jenkinson, E. B. (1988). Learning to write/Writing to learn. *Phi Delta Kappan, 69,* 712–717.

Konopak, B. C., Martin, M. A., & Martin, S. H. (1992). Reading and writing: Aids to learning in the content areas. In E. K. Dishner, T. W. Bean, J. E. Readence, & D. W. Moore (Eds.), *Reading in the content areas: Improving classroom instruction* (3rd ed.). Dubuque, IA: Kendall/Hunt.

Konopak, B. C., Martin, S. H., & Martin, M. A. (1987). An integrated communication arts approach for enhancing students' learning in the content areas. *Reading Research and Instruction, 26,* 275–289.

Kucer, S. L. (1985). The making of meaning: Reading and writing as parallel processes. *Written Communication, 2,* 319–336.

Langer, J. A. (1986). Learning through writing: Study skills in the content areas. *Journal of Reading, 29,* 400–406.

Langer, J. A., & Applebee, A. N. (1987). *How writing shapes thinking: A study of teaching and learning.* Urbana, IL: National Council of Teachers of English.

Marquis, D. (1950). *from the lifetimes of archy and mehitabel.* Garden City, NY: Doubleday.

Martin, C. E., Martin, M. A., & O'Brien, D. G. (1984). Spawning ideas for writing in the content areas. *Reading World, 11,* 11-15.

McGinley, W. (1992). The role of reading and writing while composing from sources. *Reading Research Quarterly, 27,* 227-248.

Mowatt, F. (1963). *Never cry wolf.* Boston: Little, Brown.

Nelson, J., & Hayes, J. R. (1988). *How the writing context shapes college students' strategies for writing from sources* (Tech. Rep. No. 16). Berkeley: Center for the Study of Writing, University of California at Berkeley.

Nist, S. L., & Simpson, M. L. (1987). Facilitating transfer in college reading classrooms. *Journal of Reading, 30,* 62-65.

Pearce, D. L. (1983). Guidelines for the use and evaluation of writing in content classrooms. *Journal of Reading, 27,* 212-218.

Petrosky, A. R. (1982). From story to essay: Reading and writing. *College Composition and Communication, 33,* 19-36.

Quinn, K. B. (1995). Teaching reading and writing as roles of learning in college: A glance at the past and a view to the future. *Reading Research and Instruction, 34,* 295-314.

Rubin, D. L., & Dodd, W. M. (1987). *Talking into writing: Exercises for basic writers.* ERIC Clearinghouse on Reading and Communication Skills. Urbana, IL: National Council of Teachers of English.

Shaughnessy, M. P. (1977). *Errors and expectations.* New York: Oxford University Press.

Simpson, M. L. (1986). PORPE: A writing strategy for studying and learning in the content areas. *Journal of Reading, 29,* 407-414.

Simpson, M. L., Hayes, C., Stahl, N., Conner, R., & Weaver, D. (1988). An initial validation of a study strategy system. *Journal of Reading Behavior, 20,* 149-180.

Simpson, M. L., Hynd, C. R., Nist, S. L., & Burrell, K. I. (1997). College academic assistance programs and practices. *Educational Psychology Review, 9,* 39-87.

Smith, C. C., & Bean, T. W. (1980). The guided writing procedure: Integrating content reading and writing improvement. *Reading World, 19,* 290-294.

Tierney, R. J., & Pearson, P. D. (1983). Toward a composing model of reading. *Language Arts, 60,* 568-580.

Tierney, R. J., & Shanahan, T. (1991). Research on the reading/writing relationships: Interactions, transactions, and outcomes. In M. Kamill, P. Mosenthal, P. D. Pearson (Eds.), *Handbook of reading research* (Vol. 2). White Plains, NY: Longman.

Vacca, J. L., Vacca, R. T., & Gove, M. K. (1995). *Reading and learning to read.* New York: HarperCollins.

Wagner, B. J. (1987). The effects of role playing on written persuasion: An age and channel comparison of fourth and eighth graders. *Dissertation Abstracts International, 47,* 4008A.

Walvoord, B. E. F. (1986). *Helping students write well: A guide for teachers in all disciplines.* New York: Modern Language Association.

Woodward, A., & Elliott, D. L. (1990). Textbook use and teacher professionalism. In D. L. Elliott & A. Woodward (Eds.), *Textbooks and schooling in the United States. Eighty-ninth yearbook of the National Society for the Study of Education, Part I.* Chicago: University of Chicago Press.

CHAPTER 8

Literature Across the Curriculum and Throughout Life

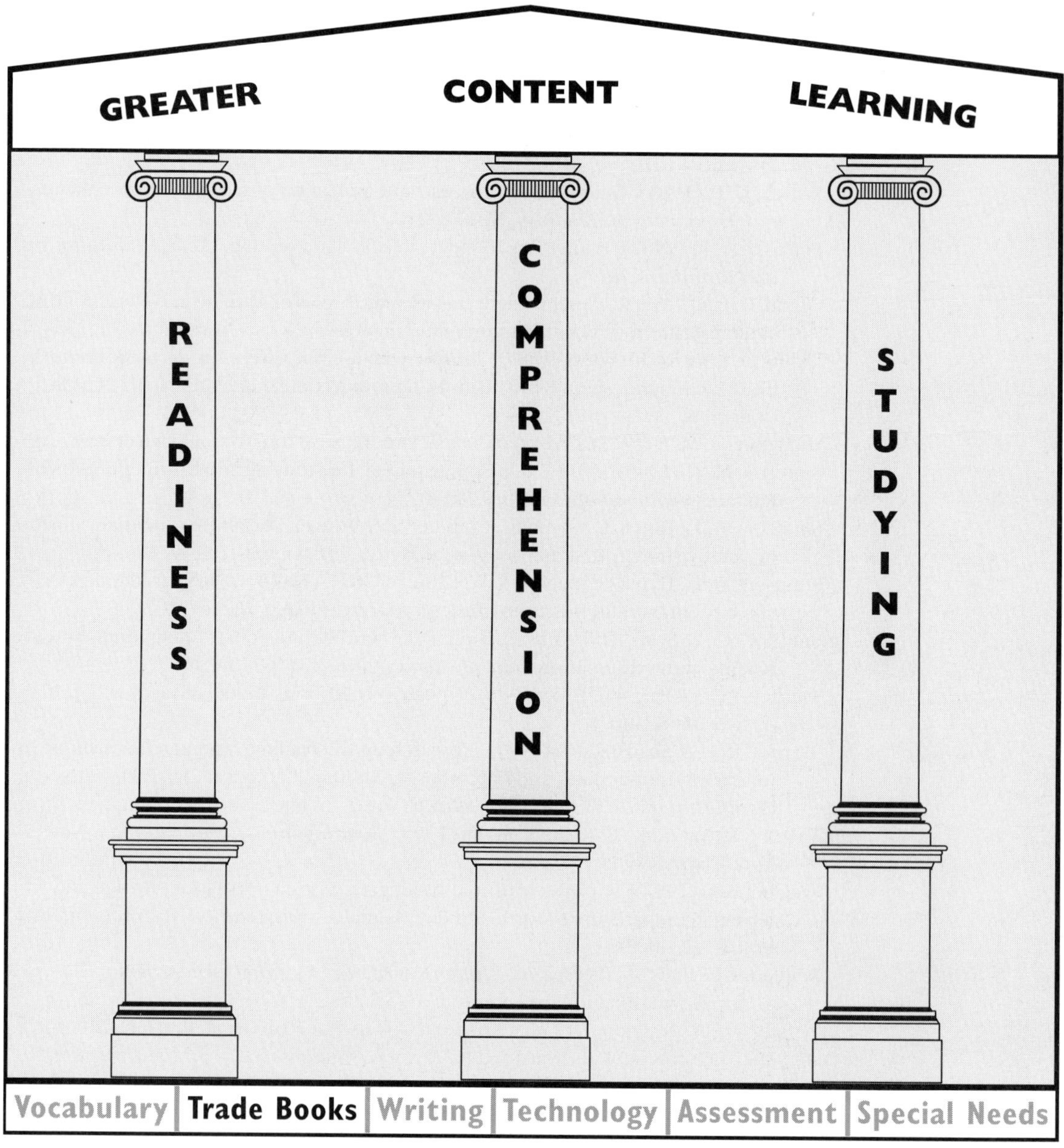

ANTICIPATION GUIDE

Directions: Read each statement carefully and decide whether you agree or disagree with it, placing a check mark in the appropriate *Before Reading* column. When you have finished reading and studying the chapter, return to the guide and decide whether your anticipations need to be changed by placing a check mark in the appropriate *After Reading* column.

	BEFORE READING		**AFTER READING**	
	Agree	*Disagree*	*Agree*	*Disagree*
1. Using novels and picture books in the content areas is a recent innovation.	√	______	______	______
2. Trade books can educate the heart and the mind.	√	______	______	______
3. Certain trade books supply many useful facts about a variety of topics.	√	______	______	______
4. Literature has limited utility in science and math classrooms.	______	√	______	______
5. Middle and secondary students enjoy being read to just as much as younger learners do.	______	√	______	______

> *Real books are wonderful. These are the books you find in public places like libraries, bookmobiles, bookstores, and sometimes even in supermarkets. Real books rest beside your bed, clutter the coffee table, and stand on shelves at the ready—waiting to be lifted, opened and brought to life by your reading. Real books—each one with its own individual binding, each one sized just right for the story it houses—are written by authors who know how to unlock the world with words and to open our eyes and our hearts. Each real book has its own voice—a singular, clear voice—and each speaks words that move us toward increased consciousness.*
>
> —Peterson and Eeds (1990)

Many junior and senior high school students receive their first serious look at different cultures, historical eras and events, politics, and scientific advances of the human race through content area textbooks. As we stated earlier, because of the demands of limited space, adoption committees, and readability constraints, textbook publishers often present a distilled version of content area information. Emphasis is placed on important facts, broad views, pivotal characters, and general effects on whole populations, resulting, inevitably, in a detached tone and dry material. But we must not forget that within each of these cultures, social movements, historical eras, and scientific advances lie richly detailed stories about the people who made them or who watched them being made and were affected by them. The narrative element—the stories that lie within all human interactions—is often left out of many content area lessons. Yet, it is narrative that can bring the content to life.

Stories Lie Behind All Topics in the Content Areas

One of the most instructive precedents for bringing content material to life is Selma Lagerlof's book *The Wonderful Adventures of Nils* (1912), an earlier edition of which had been written for and adopted by the public schools of Sweden in 1907 and a rare example of textbook and trade book successfully written as one. In this adventure-filled story, Nils, a boy-turned-to-elf, sails back and forth across Sweden astride a barnyard goose as the author subtly acquaints the reader with an encyclopedia of knowledge about that country. Lagerlof recognized the value of story and exploited it fully by stringing dry, educational subjects on the thread of exciting adventures and the engaging character of Nils Holgersson.

Children learn to read with stories. In fact, their early reading experiences involve stories exclusively. So it is not surprising that for many children the transition to content textbooks employing expository structures leads to their first difficulties with reading (Frew, 1990; Richgels, Tomlinson, & Tunnell, 1993). We believe that one very effective response to the difficulties students may experience with reading textbooks, not only in the transitional middle grades but in secondary school as well, is for the content area teacher to continue to exploit students' past successes with literature by using children's and young adult books in conjunction with textbooks.

In Chapter 2, we described some important instructional requisites for developing the higher levels of literacy many middle and secondary students seem to lack. Trade books, when used appropriately with textbooks, can become a powerful teaching tool for expanding literacy. This approach builds relevant prior knowledge, capitalizes on the student's skill in reading narrative, engenders interest and motivation, and, consequently, promotes a deeper understanding and appreciation of the content in both trade books and textbooks (Tomlinson, Tunnell, & Richgels, 1993).

Main Purposes of Chapter 8

This chapter has two main thrusts. It is devoted primarily to ways in which young adult literature can be skillfully integrated into the content curriculum to make it more palatable, comprehensible, and memorable. Additionally, we discuss ways in which teachers can encourage students to make reading an integral part of their lives outside the classroom.

CASE STUDY

Linda is a high school teacher who has two junior-level American history classes. In planning the unit "Immigration to the United States," she established three primary goals. First, she wanted her students to recognize and appreciate that the United States is made up of immigrants from virtually every country of the world, who have played a role in the creation of our country and our culture. Second, she wanted her students to recognize, explain, and describe the concept of *cultural diversity* and determine the advantages and challenges that cultural diversity has brought to this country. Finally, she wanted her students to recognize and appreciate both the specific contributions and the specific problems associated with Jews and African-Americans in the United States.

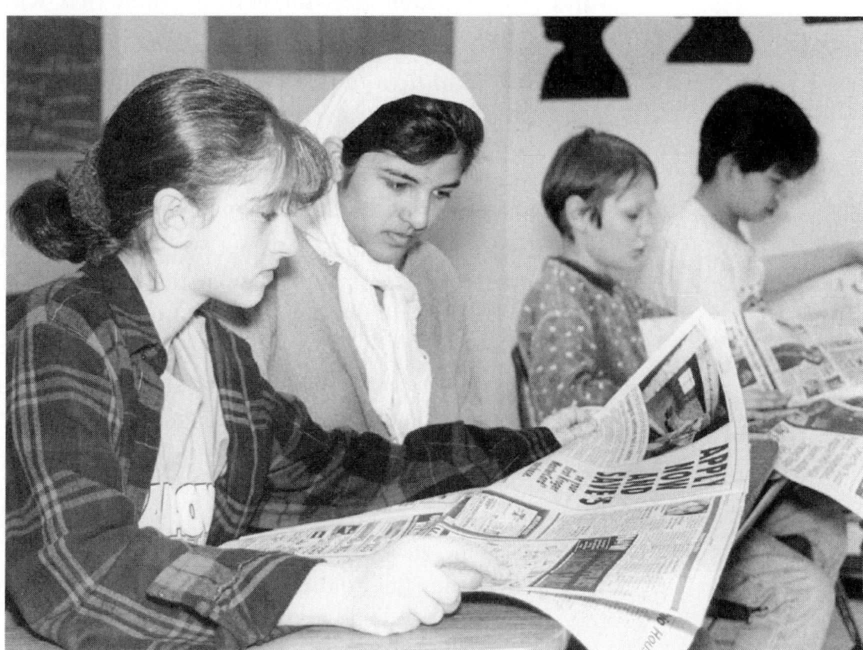

During the year, the class discussed immigration several times as it related to various eras of our country's history. For example, they studied Spanish, French, English, German, and Swedish immigration during colonial times; Irish immigration in the 1820s and 1840s; and the forced immigration of blacks into slavery.

To the Reader:
As you read and work through this chapter on the use of literature to improve content learning and develop the reading habit, consider ways in which Linda could incorporate young adult books and other literature sources into her unit in order to meet her goals. Think about how the strategies described and those from your own experience and imagination could be applied to the teaching of a unit on immigration.

■ ■ ■

WHAT IS YOUNG ADULT LITERATURE?

According to Carlsen and Sherrill (1988), any literature read by young adults is considered young adult literature. Although we know that adolescents read a large variety of texts, there is a type of literature that is especially relevant to their interests and needs. For our purposes, young adult literature, adolescent literature, and trade books for young adults all refer to books written or marketed primarily for teens and preteens.

There are several major genres or types of young adult books. Indeed, the world of young adult literature is wonderfully rich, with countless high-quality books of fiction and nonfiction that cover a wide range of topics.

Genres of Young Adult Literature

- *Historical fiction:* Historical fiction allows adolescents to appreciate important historical events in human terms through the eyes of adolescents who lived through them (Spencer, 1994). Because these books deal with events of the near and distant past, they often have a timeless quality which permits their use for many years.
- *Coming-of-age books:* Most young adults enjoy reading books about characters who are grappling with the transition from childhood to adulthood. These books are capable of moving young adults toward maturity (Estes, 1994).
- *Science fiction:* Young adults who are interested in science are often great fans of science fiction. By the same token, quality science fiction books can play an important role in developing students' interest in science (Hartwell & Cramer, 1994).
- *Fantasy:* Reed (1988) points out that fantasy may be the most appropriate genre to meet the needs of adolescents who are trying to discover where they fit into the world. The dominant theme of fantasy books is the quest for good and for truth.

- *Mystery and suspense:* This genre has been a timeless favorite among young adults, going back to the Nancy Drew and Hardy Boys books. Today, many excellent tales of mystery and suspense are available to adolescents (Spencer, 1994).
- *Nonfiction:* A very important genre of adolescent literature, nonfiction books written for young adults draw them into the reading and learning process the way no textbook ever could. Nonfiction books, often referred to as *informational* books, are typically written by authorities who cover topics from dinosaurs to dating using engaging and informative writing styles and writing from the perspectives of young adults. According to some (Sebesta & Donelson, 1994), nonfiction is the most frequently read literature among adolescents.

In this chapter and in this book we make essentially one broad recommendation: regardless of the genre, use as many types of trade books and alternative text sources as your resources will allow to complement and enrich the teaching and learning of content area subjects.

GUIDELINES FOR INTEGRATING LITERATURE INTO CONTENT CLASSROOMS

Research and Theoretical Support for Combining Trade Books and Textbooks

The contributions that young adult literature can make to the teaching of subject matter are limited only by your own sensibilities because the union of trade book and textbook seems to rest on firm theoretical underpinnings (Richgels et al., 1993). Researchers (Alexander, Kulikowich, & Hetton, 1994; Dillon, 1989) have shown that attitudinal and motivational factors have a direct influence on students' literacy development and content learning. Pennac (1994) has observed that teenagers will quickly turn off to reading if they find texts difficult or boring. On the other hand, Gambrell (1996), in reviewing research on the influence of affect in the reading process, observed that when students find reading pleasurable and interesting, their positive attitudes toward reading rapidly become generalized to most other subjects, which leads to a deeper love of reading as a primary source of information and enjoyment. Furthermore, students' reading comprehension has been shown to be greater with high-interest materials because interesting material maintains their attention more effectively and provides motivation (Baker, Afflerbach, & Reinking, 1995; Frager, 1993).

Although literature can be a powerful motivator for reading and writing, combining its use with content area textbooks is also compelling from a schema-building perspective. In earlier chapters you learned that schema theorists posit that the more developed the knowledge structures readers possess about a particular topic, the greater the likelihood that they will be successful in dealing with new information related to that topic. The most important instructional implication of schema theory is that teachers should build bridges between new information to be learned and students' prior knowledge (Hartman, 1995). Stories written in familiar narrative style can provide the background information and call to mind related ideas, building the foundation for easier assimilation of new textual information.

Vye, Rowe, Kinzer, and Risko (1990) point to another major advantage of combining textbooks with trade books. When literacy instruction is kept separate from mathematics, science, and social studies, students believe that math knowledge is relevant only in math class, science knowledge only in science class, and social studies only in social studies class. Labeling this compartmentalized approach to teaching and learning "inert" knowledge (Brandsford & Vye, 1989), Vye and her associates demonstrated that using literature in social studies helps to circumvent the problem of inert knowledge. By integrating literature into the social studies classroom, the teacher in their research project was able to help students use the cross-curricular content to better understand the social studies information and the functionality of their learning.

The union of trade book and textbook can be supported theoretically, as we have shown, and continues to be widely recommended in the literature for virtually every content area (Jacobi-Karna, 1995; Lightsy, 1996; Lombard, 1996; Miller-Hewes, 1994; Royce & Wiley, 1996).

The duration and scope of any lesson or series of lessons that integrates trade book and textbook will depend on the topic and on your judgments and preferences. Throughout this book we have noted the benefits of planning and teaching in units, whereby students experience a series of lessons often lasting up to several weeks that revolve around a unifying theme with related subtopics. The primary benefit of this approach to both you and your students is time—sufficient time to investigate a topic thoroughly through reading, discussion, writing, and research and, therefore, time to get interested in and excited about learning while producing considered responses. The following guidelines and methods are most applicable to unit-based teaching.

Identify Salient Themes and Concepts

The process of identifying important themes and concepts for a unit of study is essential for integrating appropriate trade literature. Trade books and textbooks should be bridged by overarching themes and concepts related to the most important information and ideas of the unit. The process involves, first, deciding what you want your students to know as a result of the unit and then using this theme as a guide, identifying the related concepts and subtopics.

We Recommend Unit Plans with Trade Books

Textbooks are usually organized by units, which makes them helpful in identifying broad themes for unit plans. As we have recommended before, however, you should develop unit themes that are meaningful to you and your students, regardless of the extent to which the topics are dealt with in the textbook. In this way, you can take advantage of your own and your students' special skills or interests. We have stressed the importance of this step many times throughout this book. It involves deciding what students should take away from their study of the content so that instruction can focus on the ideas and information that are most important to you and your students.

Unfortunately, while textbooks are excellent dispensers of facts, they often lack explicit development of important themes. Therefore, you must infer essential ideas and information from texts. Try asking yourself the following questions as you look over a textbook unit:

Critical Questions for Identifying Textbook Themes

- What are the driving human forces behind the events?
- What phenomena described in the textbook have affected ordinary people (including me and my students) or may do so in the future?
- What universal patterns of behavior related to this reading should be explained?

Answers to these questions will go a long way toward helping you decide what students should know as a result of the unit and thereby will provide direction for selecting appropriate trade books to tie in with the theme. For example, when Debbie, a seventh-grade social studies teacher, applied these questions to the textbook's unit on Australia, she inferred that the geography of a place affects the lives of its inhabitants. Because this theme seemed particularly apparent in the case of Australia, with its curiously evolved wildlife and bush country lifestyles, Debbie believed that this would be an advantageous context in which to teach it.

To further illustrate the process of establishing important themes related to textbook topics, consider the following excerpt about the Nazis, the Jews, and the Holocaust taken from an eighth-grade history/social studies book. Indeed, the quoted paragraphs are the extent of text related to the Holocaust in this history book. As you read the excerpt, ask yourself the three questions just posed. Then write down a theme you believe would be important to teach in relation to this content.

> As Allied forces were advancing, they found prison camps called *concentration camps* in various parts of Germany. The Nazis had herded millions of people into these camps. The largest group of prisoners was made up of Jews, both from Germany itself and from the conquered countries. Other prisoners included thousands of non-Jews who had opposed the Nazis.
>
> Many people had died of disease and starvation in the camps. Thousands of others had been put to death, most commonly in gas chambers. This was part of Hitler's plan to kill off all the people he considered "unacceptable." No one was spared—not even the young and the very old. Six million Jews and perhaps as many non-Jews were murdered in what is now known as the Holocaust (that is, the terrible destruction). (Graff, 1980, p. 660)

You probably found that this preceding text is like most textbook prose. It covers the details but offers few ways of identifying the underlying critical

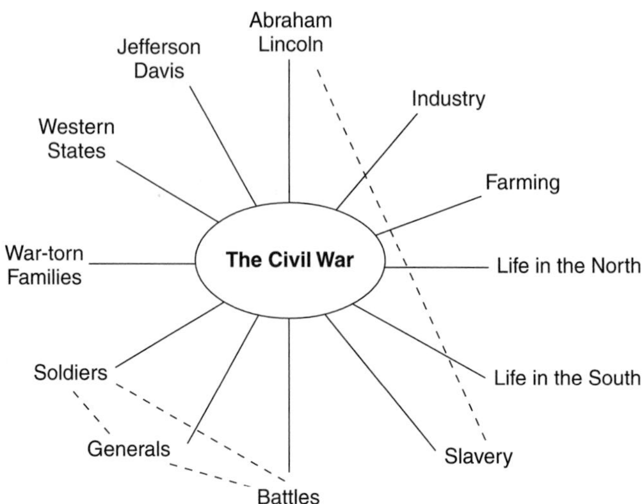

FIGURE 8.1 Web for a Unit on the Civil War

themes and concepts. By asking our three recommended questions, however, we believe you can identify one of the most important themes of this content—*the dangers of prejudice*—only hinted at in the sweeping, factual account of Nazism and the Holocaust.

After establishing a theme for a unit of study, we recommend that you explore the content further to identify important concepts and subtopics related to the unit's theme. To accomplish this, we recommend that you create a visual display or a web (Pappas, Kiefer, & Levstik, 1995). Beginning with the unit topic or theme written in the center of a large piece of paper, you, with help from your students, generate related subtopics and write them around the main topic. These ideas may come directly from the text or from prior knowledge. Figure 8.1 is an example of a web constructed by Debbie and her seventh-grade social studies class for their unit on the American Civil War.

The connections between subtopics (indicated by the broken lines in Figure 8.1) are indicative of another important benefit of unit teaching: The scope of a unit is broad enough to reveal relationships between different aspects of a topic, thereby helping students knit information together, expand schemata, and improve their overall understanding of the topic. With the completed web, Debbie then decided which subtopics were most relevant to the theme of the unit. Rarely is there time to cover every aspect of a topic generated in the webbing process, and some subtopics must be deemphasized or omitted entirely—even though the information may be covered in the textbook. Finally, under the subtopic headings to be included in the unit, Debbie listed related literature and activities (Figure 8.2). We will talk more about how Debbie organized instruction with multiple trade books later in this chapter.

Make Topic Sub-Topic Webs

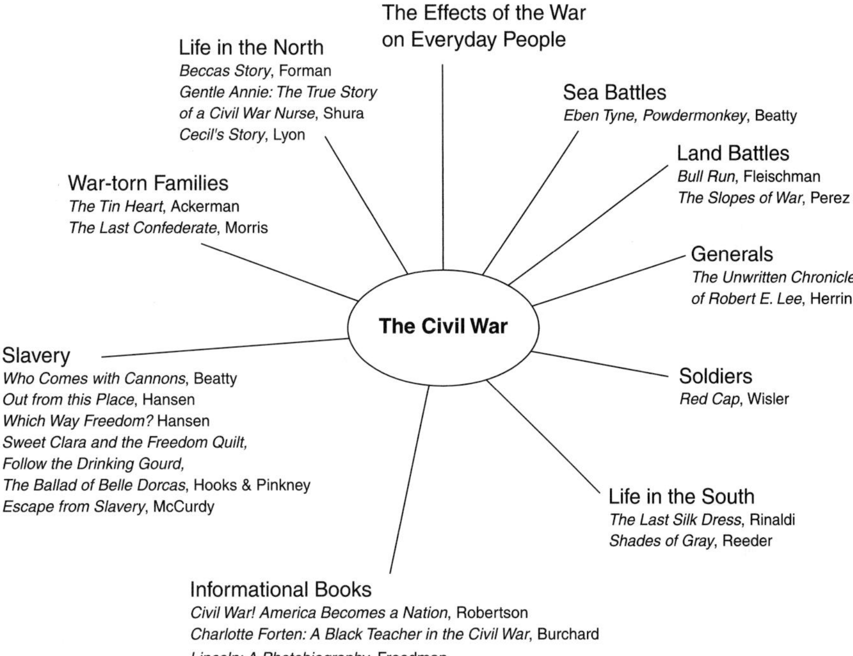

FIGURE 8.2 Web for a Unit on the Civil War, Including Appropriate Young Adult Books

Identify Appropriate Literature to Help Teach Concepts

Once an important theme for the unit is established and related subtopics and concepts have been identified, the next step is to find trade books that are thematically and conceptually related.

Obviously, this approach to content area instruction requires you to be familiar with a great variety of young adult books. To make selection easier, many bibliographies, reference guides, lists, and reviews of current young adult literature are available. In most cases, the selections in these guides are based on quality, and reading levels are often included. Some of the most helpful references are found in Figure 8.3.

Regarding our topic of Jews in Europe during World War II, we find a wealth of related young adult books listed in these references, including one of our favorites, *Friedrich* (Richter, 1970), and many other fine selections, such as *Briar Rose* (Yolen, 1992); *The Children of Bach* (Dillon, 1992); *Waiting for Anya* (Morpurgo, 1991), *Touch Wood: A Girlhood in Occupied France* (Roth-Hano, 1988), *Shadow of the Wall* (Laird, 1990), *The Devil's Arithmetic* (Yolen, 1988), *Behind the Secret Window* (Toll, 1993), and *Number the Stars* (Lowry, 1990).

Obviously, teachers need to read these books before using them in class. We have found that as teachers begin a reading program of their own, they rediscover

Adamson, L. G. (1994). *Recreating the past: A guide to American and world historical fiction for children and young adults.* Westport, CT: Greenwood Press. An immensely useful resource, filled with complete annotated bibliographies for a wide selection of books related to each historical time frame in American and world history.

American Library Association. (1995). *Selecting materials for children and young adults: A bibliography of bibliographies and review sources.* Chicago: Author. This extremely useful guide contains annotations of over 300 books and review sources of children's and young adult literature.

Benedict, S., & Carlisle, L. (1992). *Beyond words: Picture books for older readers and writers.* Portsmouth, NH: Heinemann. This edited book is filled with classroom examples of teachers using picture books with middle and secondary school students. Contributors include Linda Reif and Tom Newkirk. An excellent bibliography of picture books is in one of the appendices.

Bogart, G. L., & Carlson, K. R. (1993). *Senior high school library catalog.* New York: Wilson. An annotated bibliography of fiction and nonfiction, updated every 5 years and supplemented annually.

Bushman, K. P. (1993). *A thematic guide to young adult literature—annotations, critiques and sources.* Ottawa, KS: The Writing Conference, Inc. Teachers can take full advantage of this resource for planning units with quality trade books.

Carlsen, G. R. (1988). *Books for young adults.* Iowa City: Books for Young Adults, University of Iowa. This list is based on a poll conducted by Robert Carlsen of the University of Iowa of readers between ages 16 and 19 reacting to some 300 new books. The list contains 30 fiction and nonfiction titles and a special list of titles that are especially useful for classroom study. The list usually appears in the January issue of the *English Journal.*

Carter, B. (1994). *Best books for young adults.* Chicago: American Library Association. This guide includes genre and age/grade appropriateness of the highest-quality literature for teens and preteens.

Carter, B., & Abrahamson, R. (1990). *Nonfiction for young adults: From delight to wisdom.* Phoenix, AZ: Oryx Press. This guide covers several nonfiction topics in separate chapters. Each chapter concludes with an interview of a reknowned author of nonfiction for young adults, such as Milton Meltzer and Brent Ashabranner.

Children's Science Book Review Committee. (1994). *Appraisal: Science books for young people.* Arlington, VA: National Science Teachers Association. This work (published triannually) rates books and provides grade levels of primarily nonfiction science books. A very useful guide for selecting literature to use in science classrooms.

Donelson, K., & Nilsen, A. P. (1989). *Literature for today's young adults.* Glenview, IL: Scott, Foresman. A textbook with many ideas and strategies for teaching with adolescent literature.

Dreyer, S. S. (1993). *The book finder: A guide to children's literature about the needs and problems of youth aged 2–15.* Washington, DC: American Guidance Service. This very useful guide includes an index cross-referenced by subject, author, and book title and a book of summaries that are organized thematically with indications of age-level appropriateness.

Estes, S. (1993). *Genre favorite for young adults.* Chicago: American Library Association. Over 100 topics are provided with annotations of fiction and nonfiction books for middle- and secondary-level students.

Gillespie, J. T. (1990). *Paperback books for young people: An annotated guide to publishers and distributors.* Chicago: American Library Association. An especially useful guide to discount distributors of hard-to-find paperback books.

Gillespie, J. T. (1991). *Best books for junior high readers.* New York: R. R. Bowker. This resource is particularly helpful to teachers working with students in Grades 5 through 8.

Herz, S., & Gallo, D. (1996). *From Hinton to Hamlet: Building bridges between young adult literature and the classics.* This book will support any language teacher's effort to find and use contemporary young adult books as preludes to an exploration of classic literature.

FIGURE 8.3 A List of Useful Guides to Young Adult Books

International Reading Association. Books for adolescents. *Journal of Adolescent and Adult Literacy.* 800 Barksdale Road, P.O. Box 8139, Newark, DE 19711. Reviews of current young adult literature appear in all nine issues of the volume year.

International Reading Association. Children's choices. *The Reading Teacher.* This list is similar to Carlsen's for younger readers but contains many titles that can be used profitably with middle grade students. The list appears in the October issue of each volume year.

Jane Addams Peace Association and the Women's International League for Peace and Freedom. (annually). *Jane Addams children's book award.* This award is given to honor books that promote peace and social justice. Works of adolescent literature are frequent award winners.

Kobrin, B. (1988). *Eye openers. How to choose and use children's books about real people, places and things.* New York: Viking Penguin. A helpful guide to selecting and teaching with books for students in the middle grades.

McBride, W. G. (1990). *High interest easy reading for junior and senior high school students.* Urbana, IL: National Council of Teachers of English. An annotated bibliography of the best adolescent literature for reluctant readers.

New York Times Book Review, 299 W. 43rd St., New York, NY 10036. The weekly edition of book reviews includes reviews of new books for teens and preteens.

Scales, P. (n.d.). *Communicating through young adult books.* New York: Bantam. This book has plenty of useful strategies for teaching with adolescent literature.

Schecter, I. R., & Bogart, G. L. (1995). *Junior high school library catalog.* New York: Wilson. An annotated bibliography of fiction and nonfiction, updated every 5 years and supplemented annually.

The School Library Journal. P.O. Box 1978, Marion, OH. In the nine issues published annually are reviews of current young adult literature.

Spencer, P. (1994). *What do young adults read next? A reader's guide to fiction for young adults.* Detroit: Gale Research, Inc. This is perhaps the most comprehensive guide to young adult literature available today. Books are listed in alphabetical order by author but are grouped in two useful appendices according to genre and topic. Annotations are provided for each selection.

Webb, C. A. (1993). *Your reading: A booklist for junior high and middle school students.* Urbana, IL: National Council of Teachers of English. This list comprises annotations of 3,100 books of fiction and nonfiction.

Wurth, S. (1992). *Books for you: A booklist for senior high students.* Urbana, IL: National Council of Teachers of English. This is a comprehensive annotated guide to literature appropriate for teenagers. Books are grouped by topic.

Young Adult Services Division of the American Library Association. (annually). *Best books for young adults.* Chicago: Author. This list contains approximately 50 books published the previous year that are recommended reading for young adults.

On the Internet

Amazon.com Books (Earth's Biggest Bookstore)

Aunt Ella's Bookshop (www.localaccess.com/books/)

From Page to Screen: Children's and Young Adult Books on Film and Video (www.thomson.com)

Morris, E. (1996). *The book lover's guide to the Internet: Where and how to find on-line.* New York: Fawcett.

Publishing Houses (http://dns.uncor.edu/links/siteprnt.htm)

their love of good literature, they develop fresh perspectives on the topic, and their enthusiasm for teaching grows. In *Friedrich* the reader meets a German boy and his Jewish playmate and learns how both are gradually victimized by Nazi propaganda and pogrom during the years 1925 to 1942. In *Briar Rose,* Grandmother Gemma weaves the fairy tale of briar rose with life in Poland during the Holocaust as she tells her story to Becca. After Gemma's death, Becca travels to Poland to locate her grandmother's "castle in the sleeping woods," her safe and beautiful house before the Nazis arrived. Peter and his musician friends are left to fend for themselves in *The Children of Bach* after their parents are taken by the Nazis from their Budapest home. They survive alone for several days until miraculously Peter's Aunt Eva returns, and they plot their escape to Italy. Twelve-year-old Hannah Abramovicz goes on a harrowing time travel when she opens a symbolic Passover door in her grandparents' home in New York and suddenly finds herself among hundreds of Jewish families in Poland being loaded into cattle cars headed for the concentration camps. In the unforgettable *Shadow of the Wall,* Misha and his younger sisters are sent to an orphan's home in Warsaw by their dying mother. While there, Misha witnesses the deportation of one of his sisters to Treblinka. As a result of this tragic loss of his beloved sibling, Misha decides to join the resistance movement in Poland. In *Touch Wood: A Girl in Occupied France,* Renee Roth and her family are Jewish refugees fleeing the French countryside just ahead of the German advance. After arriving in Paris, Renee and her two sisters are sent to live in a convent in Normandy, where they struggle to survive. A beautiful story of love and heroism is told in *Waiting for Anya.* As Jo Lelande's French village of Lescun is overrun by Germans, the townsfolk band together to distract the soldiers so that tens of Jewish children can escape. Nelly Toll shares her personal story of fear and triumph in *Behind the Secret Window* as she recounts how she and her family survived the Holocaust by hiding in a small secret bedroom of a Gentile couple's house in Lwow, Poland. Her book includes her own childhood watercolors made while in hiding that reflect her fantasies of bright skies, school friends, and happy families. Finally, Lois Lowry's *Number the Stars* recounts the story of how a Danish family was able to hide Jews and eventually help them escape the tightening grip of Nazi persecution.

Excellent Trade Books for Use with the Topic of the Holocaust

On reading these stories, you will note that they and others like them are, first of all, human. You will understand that the effects of distant, large-scale events such as war will become real to students only when translated into terms of what they mean to characters such as Friedrich, Nellie, and their parents, friends, and neighbors. After hearing her teacher read *Waiting for Anya* (Morpurgo, 1991), for example, a ninth-grade student commented, "This book describes the life of these people so well you'd think the Lelandes and the other people were a part of your own family." Were it not for works of literature like these, most historical events of national and international scope and most notable human achievements and tragedies would remain for many young adults distant or even mythical notions with no emotional connection to their own lives and experiences.

A second notable characteristic of quality young adult literature is that the authors take time to describe the effects of large-scale events on ordinary people. Within the narration of realistic human interaction, concepts can be made understandable and real to young readers. Earlier, we referred to *prejudice* as an important concept to be explored in the study of Nazism and World War II. Excellent passages exploring the nature of this concept can be found in all of the previously mentioned books. Consider, for example, the following passage from Richter's *Friedrich*. In it, the 13-year-old Jewish boy is trying to retrieve his clothes from a swimming pool attendant in Germany in 1938.

> "Just take a look at this!" the attendant said. "You won't get to see many more of them." Everyone could hear his explanation: "This is one of the Jewish identification cards. The scoundrel lied to me. He claims his name's Friedrich Schneider—it's Friedrich *Israel* Schneider, that's what it is—a Jew that's what he is! A Jew in our swimming pool!" He looked disgusted.
>
> All those still waiting for their clothes stared at Friedrich.
>
> As if he could no longer bear to touch it, the attendant threw Friedrich's identification card and its case across the counter. "Think of it! Jewish things among the clothes of respectable human beings!" he screamed, flinging the coat hanger holding Friedrich's clothes on the ground so they scattered in all directions. (Richter, 1970, pp. 76–77)

When reading passages such as this, students cannot help but be affected by the injustice and humiliation suffered by this character they come to know as decent, likable, and intelligent. Furthermore, the theme of the dangers of prejudice—its meaning, its effect on people, and its often terrible results—is made startlingly clear. After reading *Friedrich*, a seventh-grade student wrote:

Trade Books Bring Out Deep Feelings and Reactions

> The book made you feel how you would have felt if you were Jewish or German at the time. I learned how brave the Jewish family was in the book. I also learned how cruel and unthinking people can be and not caring and thinking that these people are the same as we are—human. Another thing I learned is that war is horrible. I hope, even though I doubt it, that there will be no more wars and discrimination in this world. The book really touched me.

Organize the Content and the Classroom for Literature

Clearly, good literature affects young adults deeply; even so, teachers who have never used trade books often ask us questions such as "How can I find the time to work literature into my daily plans when I barely have enough time to cover the chapters?" or "I have 20 to 25 students per class. How can I manage my classroom if I use literature, the textbook, and other sources?"

The first concern is easy enough to understand when you consider the fragmented, fact-laden curricula that so many content area teachers try to operate within. Not only is each content area taught as a separate entity, but each subject is broken down into bits of information that students are required to memorize (Brown, Collins, & Duguid, 1989; O'Brien, Stewart, & Moje, 1995). Almost invariably, so much time is spent learning the small details that no time is left to experience holistic treatments of the topic and to understand the big picture. As a result, many students rarely enjoy or see the point in studying history or science facts, forget them, and often have to relearn them the next year. In contrast, time spent reading good literature can be both efficient and effective because it gets students interested in learning the content and, when the books are chosen appropriately, can serve as a source for content instruction (Brandsford & Vye, 1989). For example, one of the trade books used in Debbie's unit on the Civil War was Beatty's *Eben Tyne, Powdermonkey* (1990). From this book, students learned accurate information about the ironclad ships of the North and South, as well as historically sound facts about Civil War prison camps, and at the same time benefited from the experience of reading a whole, well-written book with an exciting message.

Place Instructional Emphasis on Important Themes

We believe the best way to approach the problem of finding time for trade literature is to choose the most important themes and overarching concepts to be taught and then place instructional emphasis on this information. Naturally, some of the textbook content is not as pertinent to the important themes as other content and, consequently, should be given less attention; deciding on a focus thus frees up time that can be spent on relevant, important information. For example, in his unit on the American Revolution, Frank decided to emphasize three important themes: (1) freedom, both for countries and for people, has a price (the heavy toll of war, even on the victor; the responsibilities that accompany self-government and personal independence); (2) war affects all citizens of a country; and (3) alternatives to war exist. Frank then selected several possible trade books that would help to reinforce these themes, finally deciding to use one primary book, *Johnny Tremain* (Forbes, 1945), and to suggest others for students' independent reading. *Johnny Tremain* is a classic of accurate and compelling historical fiction. Next, Frank went through the 12 chapters in the text unit and, keeping his salient themes in mind, made decisions about how to teach each chapter (Figure 8.4) and listed potential writing activities for many of the chapters (Figure 8.5).

We can address the second concern—how to manage the content classroom with literature—by describing the experiences of three different teachers whose approaches represent three management systems.

Read Aloud Trade Books for Science Topics

Don uses the simplest of systems. He reads to his ninth graders literature that is thematically linked to the science topics under consideration. When studying the topic of genetics and genetic engineering, for instance, Don read *Mutation* (Cook, 1989), the plot of which concerns the genetic development of a "perfect" child who grows up to become a monster. Don made other books available to students that were related to the topic of genetic alteration including *Cry Havoc* (Forman, 1988), about a hysterical town under siege from genetically engineered dogs; *Tina's Chance* (Leonard, 1988), the story of a teenager who is determined to find her mother whose genetic disease led to her death; and *Alien Child* (Sargent, 1988), a futuristic tale of genetically designed humans

Chapter	Suggested Activity
1.	Life in New England—Students read; compare w/trade book; write (see writing suggestions).
2.	Work, Church, & School same as Chapter 1.
3.	Life in Southern Colonies Teacher lecture—brief.
4.	Life in Middle Colonies Teacher lecture—brief.
5.	Life in the Wilderness Teacher lecture; book talk: *Distant Thunder* (Moore).
6.	Government in the English Colonies Teacher lecture; debates (see writing suggestions).
7.	Furs and Farming in New France Teacher lecture—brief.
8.	French & English Fight Students read; map study; develop time line, write (see suggestions); book talk and sharing: *The Matchlock Gun* (Edmonds).
9.	England Tightens Its Grip Students read.
10.	Colonists Become Angry Students read; prioritize value of ways to cause change; compare text & trade book; write (see suggestions); book talk and sharing: *My Brother Sam Is Dead* (Collier & Collier).
11.	Liberty or Death Students read; list causes of war, rank order, & defend rankings.
12.	New Nation Is Born Students read; discuss Johnny Tremain's change of mind.

FIGURE 8.4 American Revolution: Teaching Ideas

and the moral and personal struggles to restart a race of humans who had decimated themselves through violence.

Farley Mowat's *Never Cry Wolf* (1979), about a scientist's struggle to survive and study wolves in the Arctic Circle, was read during the study of scientific explorations of the Arctic. Along with Mowat's narrative, Don used *Buried in Ice: The Mystery of a Lost Arctic Expedition* (Beattie & Geiger, 1992), with its vivid, gripping photographs of mummified explorers found in the Arctic permafrost, to grab his students' interest in the topic. Isaac Asimov's *Fantastic Voyage* (1966) was used in conjunction with a unit on the systems of the body. His students also used Schultz's light and informative *Looking Inside the Brain* (1992) during this unit.

As Don reads, he asks his students to be active listeners, paying attention not only to plot developments but also to how the ideas in the story relate to those in the text. With this approach, only a single trade book is needed. Don reads 15 to 20 minutes daily and is able to complete a book of average length in 2 1/2 weeks. Over 9 months, he often reads as many as 15 books to his classes. Over the same period, he exposes his students to countless other novels, picture books, and informational books.

Chapters 1 & 2

Let Johnny Tremain have a dialogue with a person of today about the living conditions in the 1700s. Make comparisons.

Write a position paper for living in the 18th century or today.

Compare & contrast women's roles in the 18th century and today, based on reading in *Johnny Tremain.*

Chapter 6

Debate: Develop arguments explaining the points of view of British and colonists. Placards and posters can support either side.

Chapter 8

Thumbnail sketches of important Revolutionary War personalities.

Newspaper articles for *Colonial Times.*

Editorial about British taxation.

Dialogue between a colonist and King George III.

List personal freedoms you have and value today. Which of these can be traced to the events of the 1770s? Which were actually fought for in the Revolutionary War?

Chapter 10

Prioritize relative value of various means of gaining one's ends and producing change.

1. Voting
2. Physical force
3. Vigilante (scare) tactics
4. Terrorism
5. Diplomacy

Chapter 12

You have just read *Johnny Tremain.* What part of this story did you react to most strongly? Do you see any connection between this part of the story and your own life?

FIGURE 8.5 American Revolution: Suggested Composition Assignments

As an alternative to the teacher's reading aloud, the whole class can read a single book. Patty's eighth-grade social studies classes read Lois Lowry's *The Giver* (1994) during a unit on political systems. This trade book dovetailed nicely with her textbook instruction, which focused on the theme of ways in which governments can control citizens. Lowry's book follows the life of Jonah, a 12-year-old boy living in what seems to be a utopian community. When Jonah discovers that the government is secretly murdering babies who aren't "perfect," he plots his escape. Students read the trade book and the textbook as homework, and then engaged in classroom activities designed to help tie the two texts together. For example, they developed a chart that depicted the similarities and differences between Jonah's society and that of the Soviet Union.

A more complex but exciting and powerful management system involves student-directed, cooperative learning groups for reading and sharing multiple novels. Earlier, we described how Debbie, a seventh-grade social studies teacher,

Reading Assignment ________________ **Date** ________________ **Name** ________________

LITERARY LUMINARY—guides oral reading for a purpose

Page	Reason (1–5)	Plan for Sharing Reading

Choices Could Include

1. Good dialogue between characters
2. Vivid description
3. Setting a mood
4. Examples of:
   a. Simile/metaphor
   b. Flashback or foreshadowing
   c. Other literary device
5. Other instance of the author's craft

Source: Abraham, B. *Using Novels in the Classroom: A Management System.* Unpublished manuscript.

FIGURE 8.6 Literary Luminary for a Cooperative Learning Assignment

builds webs for her units to identify salient concepts and subtopics and appropriate literature. For her Civil War unit she decided to focus on the subtopics of the generals, slavery, the major battles, and war-torn families. She secured sets of four of the following trade books: *The Unwritten Chronicles of Robert E. Lee* (Herrin, 1989), *Which Way Freedom?* (Hansen, 1992), *The Long Road to Gettysburg* (Murphy, 1992), and *The Last Confederate* (Morris, 1990). Debbie then introduced the books through book talks and allowed students to form their own cooperative groups based on self-selection of these four books. Independent reading schedules were set for each book, and each group member was given a daily assignment that related to the reading.

Specific Cooperative Roles Ensure Full Participation in Studying Trade Books

Figures 8.6 to 8.9 provide a more detailed description of cooperative literature group members' assignments. The student assigned to be the "literary luminary" identified three to five passages in that day's assignment for discussion or oral reading (Figure 8.6). The "vocabulary enricher" prepared a list of four to six unfamiliar words or word usages for discussion (Figure 8.7). The "discussion director" prepared five to eight questions about the assignment (Figure 8.8). The "checker" questioned each group member about completion of the assignment,

Reading Assignment ______________ **Date** ______________ **Name** ______________

VOCABULARY ENRICHER—clarifies word meanings and pronunciations

Page	Word	Definition	Plan

Presentation Plan Possibilities

1. Have the group find the word and figure out the meaning from context clues.
2. Use the dictionary. Choose the correct definition.
3. Use a thesaurus. Find a synonym to substitute in the sentence.

Source: Abraham, B. *Using Novels in the Classroom: A Management System.* Unpublished manuscript.

FIGURE 8.7 Vocabulary Enricher for a Cooperative Learning Assignment

evaluated participation, and urged everyone to enter into the discussion (Figure 8.9). Discussions focused on daily independent reading assignments that were usually completed the day before at home.

In the beginning, Debbie carefully modeled each cooperative group assignment and helped students tie together trade and text learning through questions and discussions. Debbie devised these cooperative learning group roles because they contribute to students' learning in the manner she desires. It is important to note that you can create your own cooperative learning group roles, depending on what kinds of learning you want to take place within the groups.

Such a system is admirably suited to teaching units because a variety of trade books, each emphasizing a different aspect of the unit theme, will contribute much to the scope and depth of students' understanding. In Debbie's unit on the

Reading Assignment ____________ **Date** ____________ **Name** ____________

DISCUSSION DIRECTOR—asks questions to increase comprehension

Why do you think the author put ____________________ in this place in the story?

How is ____________________ like/different from ____________________?

If you had been ________________ how would you have ________________?

How did you feel about ____?

What happened after ____?

What do you think caused ____?

Compare ____.

If the author had left out ____

how would the story have been changed?

Summarize ____.

Predict ____.

What happened that you think will be important later on?

Who? Where? When? ____

____

Source: Abraham, B. *Using Novels in the Classroom: A Management System.* Unpublished manuscript.

FIGURE 8.8 Discussion Director for a Cooperative Learning Assignment

Reading Assignment ________________ **Day #** ________________ **Name** ________________

CHECKER—checks for completion of assignments, evaluates participation, helps monitor discussion for equal participation

Names	Job	Done?	Participation or Cooperation	Read Assignment

Participation Key:

✓ for each answer

+ for other contributions and cooperative behaviors

− for interrupting, distracting, "goofing-off" incidents

Reading Key:

+ appears to have read

− little, if any, proof

Process Evaluation:

Our group ____

____

____

Source: Abraham, B. *Using Novels in the Classroom: A Management System.* Unpublished manuscript.

FIGURE 8.9 Checker for a Cooperative Learning Assignment

Civil War, one group of students reading *The Unwritten Chronicles of Robert E. Lee* learned of the great deeds and masterful battle strategies of Lee, Stonewall Jackson, and other prominent Confederate generals. Another group looked at the life on the Mason-Dixon line during the war, and how families and friends were torn apart by their strong feelings over slavery and secession in *The Last Confederate.* Another group of students read compelling history of the battle of Gettysburg from the authentic journals of two young soldiers who were there in *The Long Road to Gettysburg,* while in *Which Way Freedom?* students learned of the brutality and hardship of slavery from the story of Obi, a young boy who is sold and separated from his family.

TEACHING WITH TRADE BOOKS AND TEXTBOOKS: SYMBIOSIS

Precisely how you develop plans for relating literature to themes and concepts in the text will depend on your individual style. Generally, you should be prepared to use texts and trade books interchangeably throughout any teaching sequence. Toward that end, we recommend the following instructional combinations that are likely to deepen students' understanding of content material.

Use the Trade Book as a Schema and Interest Builder

Science

A sixth-grade science teacher had her students read Robert Lipsyte's *The Chemo Kid* (1993) as a prelude to a unit on ecology. The story is about two boys who try to stop the pollution of their town's reservoir. The adventures the boys have and the lessons they learn set the stage for the theme of the ecology unit and class discussion by establishing an overall picture of how a human can live and thrive in harmony with nature. In addition, the story gave students a store of unusual, dramatic examples of the interdependence of species, food chains, and habitats, which they then read about in expository form in their science textbooks.

Mathematics

Tenth-grade students were introduced to the study of geometry by reading and exploring Doris Schattschneider's *Visions of Symmetry: Notebooks, Periodic Drawings, and Related Works of M. C. Escher* (1990). The repetitive patterns in Escher's drawings provided students with excellent models for creating their own repetitive designs. Students read about Escher's descriptions of his drawings—"regular division of the plane." Then they were given the opportunity to find examples of a variety of regular geometric shapes in Escher's works. Students enjoyed finding parallelograms, rhombi, hexagons, rectangles, triangles, and squares in the artist's other-worldly illustrations. These patterns were found on floors, walls, pillars, and even some of Escher's creatures, which seem to grow out of geometric patterns. With these experiences, the 10th graders were much more enthusiastic about continuing their study of geometry.

Students in a senior math class were introduced to probabilities and inferential statistics with the book *Death Qualified: A Mystery of Chaos* (Wilhelm, 1991). Barbara Holloway quits her own law practice to help her father in a murder case. In so doing, she enters a new world of fractuals, chaos theory, and computers—necessary for developing the case for the modern attorney.

Physical Education

Before starting the softball season, a physical education teacher read aloud to his students the interesting sports novel *Striking Out* (Weaver, 1993). Billy Baggs, the central character in the story, possesses almost unbelievable pitching and hitting ability, yet his struggle to find himself and realize his potential while dealing with the hardships of family and farm life nearly cause him to lose everything. The teacher used this particular book because he wanted his students to develop realistic expectations for themselves as ball players and as teenagers. The novel allowed students to become aware of their own strengths inside and outside of sports.

A group of senior high students who had volunteered to be counselors for summer camp were asked to read *Downriver* (Hobbs, 1991) in their training class. In the book, four 15-year-old Outward Bound trainees steal a guide's equipment and raft and attempt to take on the mighty Colorado River on their own. They learn about responsibility the hard way, with disastrous consequences. The seniors read and discussed the book each evening. While they enjoyed the gripping adventure and the adolescent mischief, the book forced them to look seriously at their role as counselors and served as a focal point for discussions about behavioral problems and health emergencies.

English

In preparation for reading, studying, and doing dramatic interpretations of William Shakespeare's *Hamlet,* an English teacher had her 12th-grade students read Grant and Mandrake's (1990) picture book version of the play. Lavishly illustrated, this work remains faithful to the story and retains much of the original dialogue and narration. Although the teacher knew there is no substitute for the actual work, she nonetheless recognized the value of this illustrated book for introducing her students to the exciting world and remarkable ideas of *Hamlet.* In this way the book served as a bridge to the original, offering students a story with rich artwork and skillful expressions of Hamlet's anguish and torment.

Because you know which concepts and information will be encountered later in the textbook when choosing to read literature orally, you can easily highlight key passages by reading them with particular emphasis or by reading them again after cueing the students. When trade books are read independently or in small groups, you can alert students to these passages before reading. You can also use discussion and demonstrate context strategies for learning terminology that appears in the trade book and later in the textbook.

The Interest Factor Is Built in with Quality Literature

One benefit of using good literature in content classes is that the interest factor is built in. Good narrative, by its very nature, drives readers and listeners on to discover what happens next. But you should not depend on reading alone to build schemata. Because students learn best through active participation, you should encourage discussion and written responses after daily reading sessions. Worthwhile topics could include favorite passages, alternative courses of action for characters, characters' personalities, and possible future developments in the story.

Use the Trade Book to Extend Textbook Ideas

During reading, students can work in small groups to discuss particular issues focused on in the text and elaborated on in related trade books. Students can share what they have found to be particularly informative sections of the trade book or passages that support and extend the text. For instance, the teacher and class could read a section of text and then search trade books for additional and supporting information, as occurred in the following classroom examples.

Social Studies

Eighth-grade students studying the Age of Exploration in the New World in their social studies texts also read in small groups Scott O'Dell's trilogy *The Captive* (1979), *The Feathered Serpent* (1981), and *The Amethyst Ring* (1983), which chronicle the 16th-century world of the Maya, Aztec, and Inca empires, respectively. Students were asked to find passages in the trade books describing events from the indigenous people's point of view, a perspective often omitted in textbook treatments. Likewise, students found passages that helped to explain how and why a mere handful of Spaniards were able to overtake three enormous empires. As we have noted before, too often the driving human forces behind important historical events are not made clear in textbook accounts. In O'Dell's trilogy, however, the reader is brought face-to-face with the greed and religious zeal that drove many explorers and their followers to fanatical behavior.

Music

A 12th-grade music teacher asked her orchestral class to read *Lohengrin* as they prepared for a performance of the overtures that accompany Wagner's enchanting opera. Much more than a libretto, *Lohengrin,* written by the composer, resembles a novella. Because of its length, the story of Lohengrin is well developed and character descriptions are rich. These features make the book ideally suited to instruction in musical interpretation. As the class read the book, they also worked on the operetta. Cooperative groups were formed on the basis of orchestral sections (strings, woodwinds, percussion instruments, etc.). During each class session, groups were responsible for reflecting on the story, discussing plot and character, and then, based on story interpretations, presenting possible musical interpretations. After whole-class discussions and teacher input, the student musicians attempted to operationalize their interpretations in rehearsals.

Terrence used reading and writing in his music composition class. Every week his inner-city students gathered newspapers and used the headlines for inspiration in their composing. In another example, his class read a book about musical instrument makers of medieval times. The book was filled with illustrations of instruments, some rather exotic, that have long since vanished. The author explained how some contemporary craftspersons were attempting to recreate these extinct instruments. This book inspired the class to create their own instruments. So, with junk from garages, closets, attics, and alleys piled in the classroom, students fashioned horns, drums, and stringed instruments. With this motley assemblage, they wrote and performed an original composition. The female students were complaining that they were reading about and hearing compositions only by male composers. Terrence acquired information on and addresses of several contemporary female classical music composers, and his students wrote letters to them. A couple of them wrote back, sending samples of their work on tape and on CDs, as well as sample scores. The class performed a composition given them by one of the women and allowed her to listen and watch via a telecommunications hookup.

History

For the study of the American Revolution, a 10th-grade history teacher selected the following themes: Broaden the students' awareness of all the colonists' attitudes toward the war, and sensitize them to the tragic consequences war brings its participants. She selected the trade book *My Brother Sam Is Dead* (Collier & Collier, 1974) to use in conjunction with text study. In this story, students learned about the hardships and realities of the war as told by Tim Meeker, a young boy who watches his loyalist father killed by bandits and his brother Sam unjustly accused of stealing by his comrade in the colonial army and hung.

Study Guides Are Useful with Trade Books

As students read chapters in their textbook and trade book, they responded to study guides (discussed in Chapter 3) that were designed to help students see connections between material in both sources, apply their new learning beyond the parameters of the unit, and involve them in dynamic class discussions. In the first guide (Figure 8.10), students were asked to make inferences about the attitudes of story characters. In this way, students were helped to understand the various points of view on the war. With another study guide (Figure 8.11), students were asked to consider the human elements of war—so poignantly brought out in the trade book—by reminding them that the problems and conflicts the revolutionists faced are still real today where other wars are being waged.

Directions: Listed across the page are 9 events or statements from *My Brother Sam Is Dead.* Listed down the left side are the names of characters involved in the story plot. In each box indicate whether that character would agree or disagree with the words stated above. Use the symbols in the key below. You must make some inferences to answer the questions. Be prepared to support your answers with examples from the book.

Key: **A** = Agree with **D** = Disagree **X** = Doesn't apply **?** = Not enough info	Children should respect and obey their parents.	Battles of Lexington and Concord.	Men should be free to govern themselves.	Render unto Caesar the things that are Caesar's.	I'm an Englishman but have more say in government as a colonist.	The end justifies the means.	I'm interested in making a living but not in fighting a war.	I'm just against wars.	Declaration of Independence.
Sam Meeker, rebel soldier									
Mr. Meeker, Sam's father									
Mrs. Meeker, Sam's mother									
Tim Meeker, Sam's brother									
Mr. Beacher, minister									
Betsy Read, Sam's girlfriend									
Col. Read, Betsy's father									
Mr. Heron, Meekers' neighbor									
General Putnam									
Captain Betts									

FIGURE 8.10 Study Guide for *My Brother Sam Is Dead*

In a study of immigrants to the United States in the early 20th century, Tom read aloud to his juniors from the award-winning book *Letters from Rifka* (Hesse, 1992). Rifka and her Jewish family flee Russia in 1919 to avoid Russian soldiers and a pogrom. Her dream of finding a new, safe world is finally realized when the family arrives in America. Rifka records her journey in her treasured volume of Pushkin poetry, bringing the reader intimately close to her ordeal: humiliating examinations by doctors and soldiers; deadly typhus; separation from family, friends, and homeland; deadly ocean storms; detainment on Ellis Island; and the loss of her beautiful golden hair.

"Principle, Sam? You may know principle, Sam, but I know war. Have you ever seen a dear friend lying in the grass with the top of his skull off and his brains sliding out like wet oats? Have you ever looked into the eyes of a man with his throat cut and the blood pouring out between his fingers, knowing that there was nothing you could do, in five minutes he would be dead, yet still trying to beg for grace and not being able because his windpipe was cut in two? Have you ever heard a man shriek when he felt a bayonet go through the middle of his back? I have, Sam, I have. I was at Louisbourg the year before you were born. Oh, it was a great victory. They celebrated it with bonfires all over the colonies. And I carried my best friend's body back to his mother—sewed up in a sack."

Both men had their own principles. Think about what your principles might be about war and the exercise of our freedoms. Immense human sacrifice was made by both sides during the American Revolution. Thomas Paine, a patriot, wrote, "The cause of America is in a great measure the cause of ali mankind." What do you think he means by this? Was there another way besides war to achieve the same end? "Could the United States have made its way without all that agony and killing?" ask James and Christopher Collier.

Part I. Pretend you are a United States senator. Indicate whether you would vote yes or no on the suggested imaginary bills on the floor of the United States Senate. Give your reason.

	U.S. Senate bill, proposed	*Reason*
______	The U.S. government should lift the oil embargo on Iraq.	
______	The U.S. government should cut spending on nuclear arms.	
______	The U.S. government should create a fund to give aid to other countries' rebels or patriots.	

Write a bill of your own to be voted on.

FIGURE 8.11 Study Guide for *My Brother Sam Is Dead*

While studying the details and facts of immigration in their textbooks, students in Tom's class were discovering the human drama of immigration through the words in Rifka's diary. Tom had his students trace Rifka's journey on a map of Europe and the United States. Students compared immigration procedures on Ellis Island, as discussed in the textbook, with Rifka's experiences. He also had them adopt the persona of an immigrant and create a record of that person's experiences in the form of a diary or personal travelogue modeled after Rifka's. Students were given regular opportunities to read entries from their diaries to the class.

Mathematics

Lori had been struggling to help her geometry students expand their perceptions of geometry and to look for real-life parallels to geometric terms, postulates, and theorems. Her efforts accomplished little until she boldly decided to have her class read and discuss novels. She began her search for appropriate literature with some incredulity, but with the help of a local reference librarian she soon discovered several books that appeared ideally suited to teaching geometry, including Abbot's *Flatland* (1927), Hinton's *An Episode in Flatland* (1907), and Dewdney's *The Planiverse* (1984). She finally chose *Flatland,* a 19th-century British novel of science fiction, as an important tool in trying to humanize students' understanding of geometry.

In *Flatland,* all of the characters are two-dimensional geometric figures that represent different social classes. The first part is essentially a social satire. In the second part, the main character travels to other dimensions to describe the relative merits of different points of view. *Flatland* can be read for its straight geometric descriptions, as well as for its social commentary and satire.

Lori found that *Flatland* could be incorporated into her geometry course without ignoring any of the basic material. She tied the book to a unit in the textbook dealing with geometric models of the universe. Class discussion centered on the basic plot: why it was written, its social context, details of Flatland, other lands and their inhabitants, and the symbolism. In small groups, students were asked to brainstorm solutions to problems in Flatland (not explained by the author) such as rain and snow patterns, locomotion, food, writing, and so on. Then the whole class compared their solutions. As a writing activity, students were asked to select a known person and tell which Flatland class (geometric figure) he or she would be in and why.

Lori's geometry unit was very well received. Many students asked that more novels be used in the class. Lori found her efforts worthwhile because she was able to get to know her students better, how they thought and felt, as a result of the many opportunities to interact during the unit. She also accomplished her goal of humanizing the learning of geometry.

In Latife's physics class, she read aloud during the first grading period *The Uncertainty Principle* (Sommers, 1990). The central character in the story, Kathy, quits the cheerleading squad and takes physics instead. To the dismay of all the boys in class, she excels. For the first time in her life she feels a genuine challenge, and begins to dream and plan for a future as a physicist. There are obstacles, of course, among them Kathy's father, who can't accept the idea of sending his daughter to Cal. Tech. Latife used this book as a prod, especially for the girls in class, to keep up the work and effort, and to accept problems in physics as challenges to be met and overcome.

French

To help a group of freshmen develop an appreciation for the similarities and differences in French and American cultures, Faith had her students read *Mystery of the Metro* (Howard, 1987). In this story, a 16-year-old American girl finds herself alone in France and is forced to deal with all of the challenges of getting by in a foreign country. The story also has a tinge of mystery that makes it even more engaging. As students read the book, Faith had them compare the French styles of eating, transportation, and other customs with the American way of life. Students were also required to research a particular aspect of French culture that presented the main character in the book with problems and report back to the class.

Current Events

Glen's senior class was focusing on the former system of apartheid in South Africa. Resources for the unit included government and United Nations reports, essays by Nelson Mandela, music lyrics by black South African folk song writers, and two masterful novels written by Norman Silver. *No Tigers in Africa* (Silver, 1990) tells the story of Selwyn Lewis and his white racist upbringing in Cape Town, South Africa. When his family moves to England, however, Selwyn's new experiences force him to confront his racism and look within himself to find moral solutions to prejudice. In *An Eye for Color* (Silver, 1991), Basil Kushenovitz narrates interconnecting stories about growing up white and Jewish in Cape Town. About his ambivalent position in a racist culture, Basil says that like a lizard, "My one eye sees one thing, and my other eye sees something quite different." Basil must try to reconcile his split vision—between his comforts and others' deprivation; between what is expected of a white man and what he himself is willing to become. Glen's goal in having his students read both of Silver's honest and painful novels was to rivet them to the compelling human stories of apartheid, making it possible for them to understand that racist systems leave victims on both sides of the color/culture fence.

Science

An eighth-grade teacher captured her students' attention and enthusiasm for learning by using the illustrated informational book *Looking Inside Sports Aerodynamics* (Schultz, 1992). Filled with young teens' favorite sports figures, from Michael Jordan in basketball to Monica Seles in tennis, this colorful, enjoyable book deals with unseen forces that affect objects in motion. By combining sports and science, the teacher found that students learned the facts of aerodynamics and understood the principles more thoroughly than when the textbook was the sole resource.

In another classroom, Gail taught a unit on the consequences of science and technology through the use of science fiction. Her goal was to promote problem-solving skills and help students clarify values regarding scientific technology. Knowing that science fiction can motivate students to take a greater interest in science (Schmidt, 1996), Gail used *Star Trek: The Next Generation* (Bornholt, 1989) to instigate discussion on controversial issues associated with cloning. In the story, members of the *Enterprise* spaceship, while on a planet populated by original clone settlers, are asked to allow their own tissues to be used to spawn a new generation of clones to replace a line that is malfunctioning. The crew members refuse but find that their tissues have been stolen while they were rendered unconscious. They return to the planet and destroy their clone look-alikes. The colony claimed that without the new clones they would die out in a few generations.

Given these story events, Gail poses the following question to her students and asks them to take a stand on a values continuum: Did the *Enterprise* crew members have the right to destroy the clones?

Pro-choice	Right-to-life
Do not provide tissue for cloning	Provide tissue for cloning

First, students were asked to write their positions on their own. Then they went to the board and plotted their positions on the values continuum by writing their names along it. This was followed by small-group interaction to crystallize their positions and respond to those of others. The activity concluded with class discussion. Gail has found science fiction to be a rich resource for teaching science because it motivates students to become more active learners and thinkers.

Art

Many students who are not blessed with artist's hands can learn something of how the artist sees the world through related trade books (Hurst, 1995; Stover, 1988; Tallman, 1990; Whitin, 1996). Cal, a high school art teacher, began to recognize the connection between good books and art appreciation after reading sleuth books by Gash and Malcolm relating to crimes in the art world. This led him to investigate books for adolescents that would help students who struggle with drawing and painting assignments gain some insights into the way artists see the world and approach compositions. In his search he found several good books and began using them in his art classes. Among students' favorites are *The Broken Bridge* (Pullman, 1992) and *Unfinished Portrait of Jessica* (Peck, 1991), where contemporary adolescents learn about art while grappling with typical adolescent concerns; *Visions: Stories about Women Artists* (Sills, 1993), the lives and visions of women who share a commitment to art and creative imagination; and *I, Juan de Pareja* (de Trevino, 1965), which deals with the slave and friend of the Spanish painter Velasquez who becomes a painter himself under the tutelage of his master. Cal has read these books aloud to his students, drawing their attention to their central theme: the artist's struggle to capture a vision on canvas. In addition, he has found that his students come to care deeply for the engaging characters, both fictional and real, who populate these books, thus learning things from them about artistic expression that Cal himself cannot teach.

Use Follow-up Activities That Allow Students to Personalize New Trade/Text Knowledge

Because follow-up activities often help students to assimilate concepts and information and allow you to evaluate students' learning and to check for misconceptions, they are essential to a complete teaching and learning experience with trade books and textbooks.

Writing, Drama, and Art Are All Excellent Ways to Follow Up Trade and Textbook Reading

With writing, drama, and art, all viable discourse forms, and with the array of electronic and graphic media available in today's schools, follow-up activities that help students synthesize textbook and trade book learning can be as diverse as the people who create them. The following strategies, which are drawn from the same classroom experiences referred to throughout this chapter, are representative of the unlimited possibilities for rewarding follow-up activities. Moreover, they facilitate deep, meaningful comprehension of the critical unit themes and concepts.

Writing

Writing activities can be as simple as on-the-scene descriptions of places or events mentioned briefly in the text and detailed in a trade book or letters to historical figures from students who assume the persona of fictional characters. Both activities allow students to use factual knowledge in a personal way. A more involved writing activity is composing a dialogue between historical figures and fictional characters. One teacher had students write dialogue between Misha, from *Shadow of the Wall* (Laird, 1990), and Hitler. A science teacher asked students to present a conversation between a fictional and a real-life character based on a study of the environment and the novel *Deadeye* (Llewellyn, 1991). The main character, Harry, a teenager on a sailing vacation off the coast of Scotland, becomes embroiled in a dangerous plot to foil criminals dumping toxic waste into the North Sea. Students wrote and presented imaginative scenes involving Harry and an industrial polluter. These composing activities elicited responses in which concepts, issues, and information were reviewed and reconsidered. As an overall review of the Civil War unit, groups of students wrote and illustrated an informational picture book containing facts from both the textbook and their trade books. Fact sheets were written about the Aztec chieftain Montezuma as one culminating activity for students studying exploration of the New World. Students finishing their unit of the American Revolution assumed the persona of a character from *My Brother Sam Is Dead* (Collier & Collier, 1974) and composed a short diary from April 1775 through April 1776. They also wrote personal letters from Tim Meeker to George Washington explaining his feelings about the war and its effects on the Meeker family.

Drama

Drama, unrehearsed and without an audience, serves students well in providing nonthreatening, active contexts for trying out new roles and language forms and experiencing different perspectives. Students can extemporaneously reenact scenes or events mentioned in their reading, or use text material and stories to provide models for original scenes pertaining to the same concepts. Informal, on-the-spot interviews of characters or figures encountered in texts or trade books allow students to play with newly acquired content area ideas, concepts, and facts as they formulate questions and answers. Interviewers armed with facts reported in their texts and the knowledge of the characters from trade book reading interviewed peers posing as Friedrich (Richter, 1970) and his German friend as they lived through different stages of the Nazification of Germany; Tina (Leonard, 1988) in her search for her mother; Jesse and her friends (Hobbs, 1991) as they embark on their perilous journey down the Colorado River; Julian Escobar (the main character, a young seminarian, in *The Captive,* by O'Dell, 1979) in the Mexican jungle; and the Redding townspeople gathered to watch the execution of Sam Meeker. For the World War II unit, some students interviewed local people who actually lived in Europe during the war as a means of personalizing and extending their knowledge of that era.

Radio plays are a natural adjunct to reading and writing. In this dramatic form, students select a scene or invent a probable scene from a historical event, write a script with dialogue and action, and tape-record it with sound effects for later "broadcast." Free of the demands of staging and acting, students can concentrate on accurate representation of facts, characters' motives, and appropriate language production. Imagine the language and composing skills, thinking, and relevant concepts and information called into play by students who reconstructed the scene surrounding Pizarro's decision to burn his ships off the Mexican coast to prevent his fearful, disgruntled soldiers from deserting. Drama—an enjoyable, valuable form of composition—is too seldom used in our secondary school classrooms.

Follow-Up Activities Should Encourage Higher-Level Thinking and Application

We recommend activities that require students to plan, think, and, in many cases, write and revise. Although these can be time-consuming processes, we believe much is gained from higher-order follow-up activities, including abundant oral and written language production; opportunities for independent thinking and decision making; and application of newly acquired concepts, ideas, and information. As you begin and continue to integrate trade books into your curriculum, we think you will agree that its benefits more than justify the time it requires.

PROMOTING LIFELONG READING HABITS

We now shift our attention away from specific instructional strategies that combine textbook and trade book learning to ways in which classroom teachers can help students develop the reading habit, encouraging them to read outside of school as well as inside the classroom for information, self-growth, and the sheer pleasure of reading.

In Chapter 1, we described the growing phenomenon of aliteracy—capable readers choosing not to read. We argued that the seeds of aliteracy are planted when reading lessons become drudgery; when the books students must read are uninspiring or have little connection to their real-world needs, concerns, and interests; and when reading is perceived as a separate subject instead of a functional tool for intellectual and personal growth. Unfortunately, many students who enter junior and senior high school rarely read, not because they can't but because they won't. Some have given up reading altogether and will likely become nonreading adults (Davidson & Koppenhaver, 1993).

Reaching Students in the Content Areas Through Meaningful Reading

Because many adolescents are reluctant readers (Bintz, 1993), all teachers have a responsibility to do more than teach the content in their subject areas. Teachers must try to reach students by developing curricula that encourage them to read interesting and personally meaningful books, and that help them realize that reading for its own sake can be a pleasurable and rewarding experience.

What Classroom Teachers Can Do to Keep Students Reading

Classroom teachers who employ strategies similar to those described in this chapter will go a long way toward encouraging students already in the reading habit to read even more and toward rekindling a desire to read among students whose interest has faded. Along with these strategies, there are many additional ways to promote independent reading.

Discover and Use Students' Interests

In Chapter 4 we offered some suggestions for assessing students' interests to introduce them to informative and exciting books that match their interests. We reiterate that it is important for you to discover the particular interests of the students in your classroom, not only to turn them on to your subject but to turn them on to reading.

A simple sentence-completion inventory, such as those suggested in Chapter 4 and in the example that follows, can reveal a great deal about what students find pleasurable. Remember that students who may be nonreaders or reluctant readers will have little to say in response to questions or incomplete statements about reading. Therefore, interest inventories should reveal more than reading interests; they should uncover students' real-world interests, concerns, needs, dreams, hobbies, and so on.

Use Journals to Discover Students' Interests

Teachers who use journals often get to know their students in ways that would be impossible with simple inventories and questionnaires. In journals, students often disclose important aspects of their lives related to their community, family, relationships, as well as what makes them laugh and cry. With this information, a teacher is better able to respond with appropriate suggestions for reading material that speaks to their real-world concerns. For instance, a teacher who learned that one of her students was pregnant responded in the young woman's journal with suggested books about pregnancy, such as *Teen Pregnancy: The Challenges We Faced, The Choices We Made* (Ewy & Ewy, 1985), an honest guide through the practical, moral, and legal issues associated with childbirth and parenting.

Other teachers have used letters from reluctant readers to gain insights into their reading and outside interests (Isakson, 1991). Receiving letters from students and writing letters back to them makes it possible for the teacher to offer book suggestions in a nonthreatening and confidential way. One student confided in a letter to his teacher that he loved "stuff" about the Civil War but was having a very difficult time finding books on the topic that were easy for him to read. The teacher loaned him a copy of *Civil War!: America Becomes One Nation* (Robertson, 1992), a photographic picture book written in a lively and accessible style—just right for the student. He eventually wrote back that it was one of the best books about the Civil War he had ever read and wondered if the teacher had more suggestions.

Demonstrate That Reading Is Valued

Teachers who are bored with their own texts can hardly be expected to entice students into the "literacy club" (Sanacore, 1996). Likewise, if students believe that only the teacher and the text possess the important and correct ideas and information, they will likely remain uninvolved and uninterested readers.

Creating an atmosphere in the classroom in which you and your students are free to share enthusiasm for books is the best way we know to demonstrate that reading is valued. To do this, time must be allocated for building and browsing through the classroom library and visiting the school library to select books, magazines, and newspapers for recreational reading, sharing books, and gathering students' responses and reactions to books.

Create a Print-Rich Environment in the Content Classroom

Sanacore (1992) recommends cluttering up the classroom with as much print material as possible. In an environment where students are surrounded by reading material of all varieties, they are more likely to browse and read some of these materials. Instead of becoming anxious over what students choose to read, we should be reminded of Nell's (1988) discovery that as readers become more experienced in reading for pleasure, they tend to select appropriate materials. Making the environment conducive to reading by arranging a few comfortable reading spots with good seating and lighting and adding colorful posters, book jackets, and mobiles for decoration will make it clear to students that you value pleasurable personal reading (Clary, 1991).

Within a print-rich classroom, there must also be time for pleasure reading. We strongly recommend a **sustained silent reading (SSR)** program as a useful strategy to encourage the leisure reading habit. SSR provides you and your students with time to do nothing but read in an atmosphere free of assignments, grades, and reports. Students are allowed to read anything that interests them. For many, SSR may be the only free reading time all day. Ideally, the entire school should be involved in SSR, even though you and your classroom alone can have a successful program. SSR programs have been shown to promote more positive attitudes toward reading (Sanacore, 1988) and greater independence (Sanacore, 1994). The following sections present a few guidelines for your classroom SSR program.

Give students assistance in finding something to read. In time, most students will come prepared for SSR with material selected in advance. Others, particularly reluctant readers, may need help in finding something to read. Talk with these students about their interests, and allow them to visit the classroom or school library to select a book, magazine, newspaper, or other reading material that matches their interest.

Accept any reading material that students bring for SSR. Avoid the tendency to push your tastes on students, even if they have selected material you consider to be of poor literary quality. The key is that you are providing a supportive environment for students to read material that is meaningful to them. One qualifier: Many teachers experienced with SSR programs find that they must eventually make it clear that certain material is absolutely inadmissible, such as pornography. You may want to head off any problems before they occur by restricting certain materials that are clearly inappropriate for the SSR program.

Never link reports or grading to SSR. SSR is free reading. The best way to undermine this intent is by turning SSR into schoolwork. Occasionally, school-related activities will flow naturally from SSR reading. For instance, a student may use a book being read in SSR for a research project or story writing, but these activities should never become requirements. SSR should allow students to explore the pleasures of reading. Your support of the program will clearly demonstrate that you value daily reading of personally meaningful and interesting materials.

Use as much time as you can allow for SSR. For adolescents, SSR periods of 15 minutes or more should be the goal. Keep in mind that those 15 minutes may be the only time all day that many students read self-selected materials simply for pleasure or personal use.

Read Aloud to Students

Earlier in this chapter, we mentioned that reading aloud is one way to integrate trade books into content area classrooms. Reading aloud to students on a regular basis is also an excellent way to motivate them to read and is a highly pleasurable experience for listeners of any age (Daisey, 1993; Erickson, 1996). Jim Trelease, the noted storyteller, says that teachers should read aloud "to reassure, to entertain, to inform or explain, to arouse curiosity, and to inspire—and to do it all personally" (1989, p. 2). We recommend that you try to re-create the same intimate atmosphere of a parent reading a favorite story to a child (Mathews, 1987). In a warm, trusting environment, you and your students can "get lost" in books. Read-aloud resources can range from short, appealing magazine articles to full-length novels. Sharing with students a variety of materials through read-alouds models expressive reading, transmits the pleasure of reading, and invites listeners to be readers while expanding their tastes (Richardson, 1994).

Reading Aloud Promotes Positive Perceptions about Books and Learning

The following read-aloud guidelines offered by Erickson (1996) have proven to be highly useful for identifying and working with quality selections:

- The books hold the interest of both teacher and students.
- The books stimulate discussion.
- The books lead to additional readings.
- The books involve dilemmas whose solutions are open-ended.
- The books include main characters who are both male and female.
- The books have authors from many cultures.
- The books match listeners' social and emotional levels.

Other aspects of read-alouds that we have found critical to their success include (1) practicing reading aloud a selection beforehand, (2) stopping the selection if it clearly doesn't work for your students, (3) keeping each read-aloud to about 15 or 20 minutes, and (4) encouraging but not insisting on discussion of the selection.

We have witnessed teachers take risks with hundreds of selections, abandoning many but keeping many that students enjoy. Over the course of a few years, you will develop a growing collection of "winners" that will appeal to most all middle and high school students.

Make Reading Fun

Many teachers and parents are quick to point out that reading cannot possibly compete with television viewing as a leisure-time activity. It is well documented that most adolescents spend from a few to several hours per day watching TV (Neuman, 1988). It is also apparent that reading performance is negatively correlated to TV viewing, especially for those who watch for 4 or more hours daily (Campbell, Donahue, Reese, & Phillips, 1996). A surprising finding by Neuman, however, is that students choose to watch TV during their leisure time because it is more interesting than other activities, such as reading. In other words, take TV out of the lives of students who are not interested in reading, and those students will fill the void with other nonreading activities. Get those students more excited about books, however, and they will consciously make time for reading, even if it means eliminating some TV viewing. One way to help students choose reading as a leisure-time activity is to make it fun.

We must remember that junior and senior high school students enjoy playing with language and should be encouraged to read books that are fun. Reed (1988) recommends that teachers, as well as parents, suggest humorous young adult books such as joke books and even comic books, especially for reluctant readers, to keep them active members of the literacy club. These books can act as a bridge to more sophisticated reading materials.

Humorous Books Help Students Enjoy Reading

A seventh-grade teacher we know demonstrates how enjoyable reading can be through read-alouds. Regionalized versions of well-known fables and fairy tales from such books as Chase's *Grandfather Tales* (1948) and *Jack Tales* (1943) have become perennial favorites. The Christmas season is made all the more festive with humorous holiday favorites such as Garner's *Politically Correct Holiday Stories: For an Enlightened Yuletide Season* (1995) and Jacobs's *Cajun Night Before Christmas* (1973). The teacher involves students in role plays to her compelling narration. The texts and her interpretations often leave the class full of laughter. She has noted the influence of the read-alouds on her students' own enthusiasm for reading these and other humorous books.

Make Reading a Real-Life Experience

As we have emphasized throughout this chapter, your goal as a teacher is to do more than teach the content of your subject area. You must also be involved in reaching students through reading to help them take responsibility for their own literacy development beyond the schoolroom. This can be accomplished by taking every opportunity to bring real-world reading materials into the classroom so that, through interesting and meaningful classroom activities, adolescents come to understand how reading needs to be a part of their adult lives. Newspapers, magazines, and various other print sources found in the adult world should be used in daily classroom instruction and made available in the classroom library or reading corner.

A prime example of integrating everyday reading materials into classroom instruction comes from a literature teacher who was helping his students understand *metaphor.* He knew that metaphors are often found in newspapers. And because they are inexpensive, easy to obtain, and contain articles that are generally short and concise, newspapers are a very good source for figurative language instruction.

The teacher began by distributing to small groups of students headlines that used metaphorical language, such as "Still Limping, Oil Patch Exits Intensive Care" and "Experts Zero In on Magic Bullet to Kill Cancer Cells." Using a reciprocal teaching strategy (explained in Chapters 2 and 3), the teacher modeled a question-asking and -answering process out loud to demonstrate for students how he interpreted the metaphors in the headlines. For instance, with the first headline, he began by asking "What is an oil patch?" Then he dug into the article until he found information that helped him answer the question. The oil patch is a group of four states whose net worth and economic stability depend heavily on the production and sale of oil—namely, Louisiana, Oklahoma, Colorado, and Texas.

The next question he asked was, "In what way could four oil-producing states exit intensive care?" He pointed out that the statement clearly made no sense if interpreted literally, which, by default, made it a metaphor. This question led immediately to his next question, "Who would normally exit, 'limping,' from the intensive care ward?" Students were quick to respond by identifying a sick or injured person who is getting better but is basically still ill or injured. In this way students began to see the similarities between the oil patch and a patient just released from intensive care.

At this point, the teacher asked students working in their groups to come up with an explanation of the metaphor. Most were able to explain that the oil-producing states were in trouble but were in far better financial shape than they were a few years ago, just as the hospitalized person who limps out of intensive care is still in trouble but in better physical condition than not long before.

The teacher went on to engage students in a discussion of why the author chose to use a metaphorical headline in the first place. To make the article more attractive and "catchy" was one explanation. Another was that the author was "teasing" readers to entice them to read the article. The teacher pointed out that by linking the troubled economies of distant states with something familiar—hospitals, illness—the author was trying to make his subject accessible to more readers.

There are many more examples of teachers who routinely integrate real-life reading materials into their content instruction to help students see connections between literacy development inside and outside the classroom boundaries.

- A health teacher has students bring in menus from restaurants and cookbooks from home when working on food preparation and nutrition.
- A business education teacher, for his unit on career explorations, brings in several examples of employment applications. He also urges students who may be applying for part-time jobs to bring in their applications.
- A chemistry teacher asks students to bring in labels from household cleaning products and foods indicating that certain chemicals are being used.
- A government teacher uses popular news magazines to relate text topics to current events.
- An accounting teacher asks students to bring in actual bills and account statements to teach accounting terms and budgeting.
- A math teacher asks students to write/create math problems using tables, maps, and graphs from the local newspaper.

Real-Life Reading Material in the Content Classroom

The list could go on and on because the possibilities for integrating everyday reading materials into the content classroom are virtually limitless.

According to Davidson and Koppenhaver (1993), adolescents today live in a world of instant food, appliances, entertainment, and information. Unfortunately, the technology that makes life easier for young adults is also decreasing their motivation to develop literacy skills beyond the classroom. To help students see the importance and utility of real-world literacy, we recommend that teachers bring into the classroom familiar, everyday texts that students encounter outside school. These strategies, along with others that emphasize the personal-growth benefits and pleasure of leisure reading, are the best ways we know to encourage young adults to make reading an integral part of their lives.

Help Students See the Importance of Real-World Literacy

CASE STUDY REVISITED

Remember Linda, the history teacher? She was preparing a unit on "Immigration to the United States," and we asked you to think of trade book strategies that might be helpful to her as she developed activities for her students. Write your suggestions now.

Linda taught the unit using the history textbook and a variety of trade books. She chose books for their quality representation of the immigrant experience of four primary ethnic groups: (1) European-Americans (*Immigrants:* Sandler, 1995); (2) African-Americans (*The Slave Dancer:* Fox, 1973); (3) Asian-American (*I Am An American:* Stanley, 1994); and (4) Hispanic-Americans (*Spanish Pioneers of the Southwest:* Anderson, 1989; *Voices from the Fields:* Atkin, 1993). Additional sources included Mitsumasa Anno's *Anno's U.S.A.* (1983) and a featured article in *The Atlantic Monthly* called "The Price of Immigration" (Kennedy & Borjas, 1996).

The class began the study of immigration by reading, analyzing, and discussing *Anno's U.S.A.* in small groups and then as a class. Each student was asked to look for historical and literary events, figures, and ideas found in the book. This wordless picture book was a favorite among many of Linda's students. Some of them borrowed the book over and over again, impressed that the Japanese author knew so much about the United States but that they knew so little about the country and history of Japan. *Anno's U.S.A.* provided Linda's American history classes with an excellent introduction to the topic of immigration through detailed and accurate illustrations.

Linda then introduced the other trade books with brief booktalks. She divided the class into small groups and assigned each group one of the books. As she circulated among the groups, they talked about what they read and what they saw in the illustrations. As each group finished, she asked them to write down their reactions to what they read: what they liked and did not like, what the illustrations brought to the text, what the illustrations told them that the text did not, and their overall impressions.

Each group was responsible for making a daily oral report summarizing what had been read and learned from the trade books. In this way, all students could gain essential content about the immigration experience for different major ethnic groups.

Students who read *Immigrants* thoroughly enjoyed sharing with their classmates information about transatlantic travel by young European children without parental supervision and guidance, procedures on Ellis Island, and life on Hester Street in New York City at the turn of the century. The group representing Asian-American immigrants discovered fascinating information about early Japanese and Chinese settlers and workers in the Western United States. This group was especially taken by the treatment of Japanese-American citizens during World War II. Separate groups read and shared their trade books about Hispanic immigrants. In *Spanish Pioneers of the Southwest,* students learned how Spanish, Mexican, and Native-American cultures combined to form a unique blend of original American customs among the early immigrants to the territory once called New Spain. In *Voices from the Fields,* students were brought face-to-face with Mexican-American children and youth living a hazardous yet proud itinerant life as farmworkers. All of these engaging informational picture books provided a refreshing contrast to their regular textbook reading and class discussion.

During this time, Linda also read *The Slave Dancer* to both classes so that her students would have a clearer understanding of black immigration. In it, students learn about Jesse, a New Orleans boy who is kidnapped and taken aboard a slave ship where he's forced to play his fife so that the slaves will dance and maintain their good physical condition. Students also learned a wealth of information about how slaves were obtained in Africa and the routes taken to bring them to the United States. They enjoyed the novel immensely. In discussion groups, they explained the role of African tribal chiefs who sold blacks to white captains like Cawthorne (the captain of the ship in the story); they described the living conditions aboard the slave ship; and they debated the reasons for slavery in America.

The next activity also involved small-group and then class discussion as Linda asked students to brainstorm possible ways of sharing the material they found in their trade books. After they compiled a list of activities and projects, she asked each student to pick an activity or project to do individually and share it with the class. (Figure 8.12 shows the list of activities the students brainstormed.) As a class, they focused on the contributions of each of the major ethnic groups to the culture of the United States.

Anno's U.S.A.

1. Draw a map of the United States to show Anno's route.
2. Draw a time line to accompany the pages of the book.
3. Write a text for several pages of the book. Choose an age group and an audience to write it for.
4. Analyze a page with historical and literary explanations.
5. Write a list of questions to ask the author and then incorporate them in a letter.
6. Choose an activity or write a paper explaining an incident or a character found on a page of the book.
7. Add a double-page spread to update the book to 1998.
8. Add a double-page spread to include the history of Pearl City.
9. Construct a model of a page or part of a page.
10. Share the book with a younger student and provide the student with explanations.
11. Design a cover or book jacket for *Anno's U.S.A.*

Immigrants

1. Write a list of questions and possible answers for a European immigrant from the book.
2. Dramatize the above interview and tape-record it.
3. Contact a recent immigrant, develop a list of questions, interview the immigrant, and then write a report of the interview.
4. Write a description of an immigrant from the book's first week in the United States.
5. Write a diary as the narrator of life aboard ship.
6. Read and discuss the book with younger students.
7. Research some aspect of immigration (transportation, routes, conditions aboard ship, Ellis Island, etc.) and prepare a written report.
8. Design a cover or a book jacket for *Immigration.*
9. Research and write a short paper on why people from a particular European country immigrated to the United States.
10. Research conditions in one European country that led to the immigration of some of its citizens to the United States.
11. Research the contributions made by a European immigrant to the United States.

Spanish Pioneers of the Southwest

1. Keep a journal for 1 week as if you were one of the pioneer children.
2. Make a model of the *placita* where the Baca family lived.
3. Create articles for a pioneer newspaper (front page, cartoon, living, entertainment, etc.).
4. Create a colorful map that charts the path taken by the Baca family.

Voices from the Fields

1. Write a letter to a congressperson explaining the living conditions of migrant farmworkers and asking for policies to help improve them.
2. Create a map that charts the travel of a farmworker family for 1 year.
3. Write dialogue and reenact a scene between farmworkers and farm owners.
4. Interview a current or former migrant farmworker and present the results of your interview.
5. Write and perform a rap or Tejano song about your life as a farmworker.

The Slave Dancer

1. Design a cover or a book jacket.
2. Design a picture book based on one aspect of the book.
3. Write a letter to the main character expressing your thoughts and opinions about slave trading.
4. Write a book review.

FIGURE 8.12 Project Choices for Immigration Unit

After students completed the trade books and Linda finished reading *The Slave Dancer* to the class, they turned their attention to the issue of cultural diversity, its advantages and disadvantages, and the specific contributions and problems that have resulted from America's brand of cultural diversity. Using the article on immigration in *The Atlantic Monthly,* the class explored a variety of social, economic, and political issues surrounding current immigration practices and policies in the United States. These ideas were handled in a number of lively discussions. Topics included anti-semitism and racism in the last decade, the recent arrests of white supremacy group members, U.S. Supreme Court decisions, the Ku Klux Klan and the American Nazi Party, superiority, inferiority, economic disparity, and even the firing and censorship of athletic officials after their racist remarks about black athletes.

The classes charted the problems each major group of immigrants has faced in American society and the ways in which society has sought to address and solve those problems. Linda's students did not affix blame to any one racial or ethnic group; rather, they recognized that we are all responsible for the problems and for finding the solutions.

■ ■ ■

SUMMARY

This chapter has been devoted to two themes: (1) strategies for combining trade book and textbook instruction in the content classroom and (2) strategies for helping students develop lifelong reading habits.

First, we presented a theoretical rationale, specific recommendations, and practical considerations for integrating young adult books and textbooks into content area teaching. We have shown that the practical use of trade books can be supported by theories of learning. Trade books can help students build on past literacy successes, create interest and motivation, and develop schemata.

In this chapter we provided an in-depth explanation of how trade books and textbooks can be used together. Specific instructional recommendations were made for (1) developing a unit overview and identifying key themes and concepts within the unit topic, (2) choosing trade books to help teach concepts, (3) teaching with textbooks and trade books, and (4) following up a unit of study with exciting learning activities.

The union of textbook and trade book is feasible and has produced elaborate processing of textual information, greater enthusiasm for learning, and long-term recall in field tests that we have conducted in junior and senior high schools (Brozo & Tomlinson, 1986, 1987). The probability of success with this approach is enhanced when teachers responsible for content area subjects look for opportunities to integrate trade books with their texts and when the literacy support staff work with these teachers to help bring about such an integration. Moreover, using trade books in content classrooms should not be perceived as a device or gimmick to create interest in a topic on Monday that is forgotten by

Friday. To use trade books and textbooks effectively, you need to make long-range plans, carefully considering how each unit's themes and salient concepts will be developed, and how trade books and text will interplay from the introduction to the conclusion of the unit.

Good literature, once discovered, sells itself. Students return again and again to favorite books, and teachers who know good young adult literature find ways to use it in their classes. The key is knowing the literature. Unfortunately, many teacher training and certification programs still offer literature courses as electives only. We endorse the trend toward making these courses mandatory and further suggest that all content area methods courses include a literature component to increase the likelihood that students will graduate with skills and knowledge related to using trade books across the curriculum. Most important, we recommend that you establish and maintain an independent reading program of literature geared to the students and subject you teach.

The content areas deal with interesting, vital information, but if you rely on textbooks as your sole teaching resource, you may render this information dry and lifeless. Use trade books in conjunction with texts to help ensure that students are more actively involved in learning and that the vitality and spirit inherent in the content area material are kept alive. In later chapters, you will discover once again how young adult literature can play an integral role in content area learning.

Finally, this chapter discussed ways in which the classroom teacher can demonstrate the importance and pleasure of developing independent reading habits. Students who are led to see the connection between their real-world needs, concerns, and interests and books, newspapers, magazines, and the myriad print sources in the adult world will likely remain active, lifelong members of the literacy club.

REFERENCES

Alexander, P., Kulikowich, J., & Hetton, T. (1994). The role of subject matter knowledge and interest in the processing of linear and nonlinear texts. *Review of Educational Research, 64,* 210–253.

Baker, L., Afflerbach, P., & Reinking, D. (1995). *Developing engaged readers in school and home communities.* Mahwah, NJ: Erlbaum.

Bintz, W. (1993). Resistant readers in secondary education: Some insights and implications. *Journal of Reading, 36,* 604–615.

Brandsford, J., & Vye, N. (1989). A perspective on cognitive research and its implications for instruction. In L. Resnick & L. Klopfer (Eds.), *Toward the thinking curriculum: Current cognitive research.* Alexandria, VA: Association of Supervision and Curriculum Development.

Brown, J., Collins, A., & Duguid, P. (1989). Situated cognition and the culture of learning. *Educational Researcher, 18,* 32–42.

Brozo, W. G., & Tomlinson, C. (1986). Literature: The key to lively content courses. *The Reading Teacher, 40,* 288–293.

Brozo, W. G., & Tomlinson, C. (1987, October). *A trade book/textbook approach versus a textbook-only approach on student learning and attitudes during a social studies/history unit.* Paper presented at the meeting of the College Reading Association, Baltimore, Maryland.

Campbell, J., Donahue, P., Reese, C., & Phillips, G. (1996). *NAEP 1994 reading report card for the nation and the states.* Washington, DC: U.S. Department of Education.

Carlsen, G., & Sherrill, A. (1988). *Voices of readers: How we come to love books.* Urbana, IL: National Council of Teachers of English.

Clary, L. (1991). Getting adolescents to read. *Journal of Reading, 34,* 340–345.

Daisey, P. (1993). Three ways to promote the values and uses of literacy at any age. *Journal of Reading, 36,* 436–440.

Davidson, J., & Koppenhaver, D. (1993). *Adolescent literacy: What works and why* (2nd ed.). New York: Garland.

Dillon, D. (1989). Showing them that I want them to learn and that I care about who they are: A microethnography of the social organization of a secondary low track English Reading classroom. *American Educational Research Journal, 26,* 227–259.

Erickson, B. (1996). Read-alouds reluctant readers relish. *Journal of Adolescent and Adult Literacy, 40,* 212–214.

Estes, S. (1994). *Growing up is hard to do: A collection of booklist columns.* Chicago: American Library Association.

Frager, A. (1993). Affective dimensions of content area reading. *Journal of Reading, 36,* 616–622.

Frew, A. (1990). Four steps toward literature-based reading. *Journal of Reading, 34,* 98–102.

Fuhler, C. (1991). Add spark and sizzle to middle school social studies: Use trade books to enhance instruction. *The Social Studies, 82,* 234–237.

Gambrell, L. (1996). Creating classroom cultures that foster reading motivation. *The Reading Teacher, 50,* 14–25.

Graff, H. F. (1980). *The free and the brave.* Chicago: Rand McNally.

Hartman, D. (1995). Eight readers reading: Intertextual links of proficient readers reading multiple texts. *Reading Research Quarterly, 30,* 520–561.

Hartwell, D., & Cramer, K. (1994). *The ascent of wonder: The evolution of hard science fiction.* New York: TOR Books.

Hurst, C. (1995). Bringing art into the library. *Teaching Prek-8, 26,* 84–86.

Isakson, M. (1991). Learning about reluctant readers through their letters. *Journal of Reading, 34,* 632–637.

Jacobi-Karna, K. (1995). Music and children's books. *The Reading Teacher, 49,* 264–270.

Kennedy, D., & Borjas, G. (1996, November). The price of immigration. *The Atlantic Monthly, 278,* 51–77.

Lightsey, G. (1996). Using literature to build fifth grade math concepts. *Reading Horizons, 36,* 412–419.

Lombard, R. (1996). Using trade books to teach middle level social studies. *Social Education, 60,* 223–230.

Mathews, C. (1987). Lap reading for teenagers. *Journal of Reading, 30,* 410–413.

Miller-Hewes, K. (1994). Making the connection: Children's books and the visual arts. *School Arts, 94,* 32–38.

Nell, V. (1988). *Lost in a book: The psychology of reading for pleasure.* New Haven, CT: Yale University Press.

Neuman, S. B. (1988). The displacement effect: Assessing the relation between television viewing and reading performance. *Reading Research Quarterly, 23,* 414–440.

O'Brien, D., Stewart, R., & Moje, E. (1995). Why content literacy is difficult to infuse into the secondary school: Complexities of curriculum, pedagogy, and school culture. *Reading Research Quarterly, 30,* 442–463.

Pappas, C., Kiefer, B., & Levstik, L. (1995). *An integrated language perspective in the elementary school* (2nd ed). White Plains, NY: Longman.

Pennac, D. (1994). *Better than life.* Toronto: Coach House.

Peterson, R., & Eeds, M. (1990). *Grand conversations.* Richmond Hill, Ontario: Scholastic-TAB.

Reed, A. J. S. (1988). *Comics to classics: A parent's guide to books for teens and preteens.* Newark, NJ: International Reading Association.

Richardson, J. (1994). Great read-alouds for prospective teachers and secondary students. *Journal of Reading, 38,* 98–103.

Richgels, D., Tomlinson, C., & Tunnell, M. (1993). Comparison of elementary students' history textbooks and trade books. *Journal of Educational Research, 86,* 161–171.

Royce, C., & Wiley, D. (1996). Children's literature and the teaching of science: Possibilities and cautions. *The Clearinghouse, 70,* 18–23.

Sanacore, J. (1988). Schoolwide independent reading: The principal can help. *Journal of Reading, 31,* 346–353.

Sanacore, J. (1992). Encouraging the lifetime reading habit. *Journal of Reading, 35,* 474–477.

Sanacore, J. (1994). Lifetime literacy through independent reading: The principal is a key player. *Journal of Reading, 37,* 602–606.

Sanacore, J. (1996). An important literacy event through the grades. *Journal of Adolescent and Adult Literacy, 39,* 588–591.

Schmidt, G. (1996). Of pulp, substance, and science fiction. *Children's Literature Association Quarterly, 21,* 45–60.

Sebesta, S., & Donelson, K. (1994). *Inspiring literacy: Literature for children and young adults.* New Brunswick, NJ: Transaction.

Spencer, P. (1994). *What do young adults read next? A reader's guide to fiction for young adults.* Detroit: Gale Research.

Stover, L. (1988, September). What do you mean, we have to read a book for art class? *Art Education,* 8–13.

Tallman, S. (1990). Cultural literacy. *Arts, 64,* 17–18.

Tomlinson, C., Tunnell, M., & Richgels, D. (1993). The content and writing of history in textbooks and trade books. In M. Tunnell & R. Ammon (Eds.), *The story of ourselves: Teaching history through children's literature.* Portsmouth, NH: Heinemann.

Trelease, J. (1989). *The new read-aloud handbook.* New York: Penguin.

Vye, N., Rowe, D., Kinzer, C., & Risko, V. (1990, April). *The effects of anchored instruction for teaching social studies: Enhancing comprehension of setting information.* Paper presented at the meeting of the American Educational Research Association, Boston.

Whitin, P. (1996). Exploring visual responses to literature. *Research in the Teaching of English, 30,* 114–140.

Young Adult Books

Abbot, E. (1927). *Flatland.* Boston: Little, Brown.

Ackerman, K. (1990). *The tin heart.* New York: Atheneum.

Anderson, J. (1989). *Spanish pioneers of the Southwest.* New York: E. P. Dutton.

Anno, M. (1983). *Anno's U.S.A.* New York: Philomel.

Asimov, I. (1966). *Fantastic voyage.* Boston: Houghton Mifflin.

Atkin, S. B. (1993). *Voices from the fields: Children of migrant farmworkers tell their stories.* Boston: Little, Brown.

Beattie, O., & Geiger, J. (1992). *Buried in ice: The mystery of the lost Arctic expedition.* Toronto: Madison Press Books.

Beatty, P. (1990). *Eben Tyne, powdermonkey.* New York: Morrow.

Beatty, P. (1992). *Who comes with cannons?* New York: Morrow.

Bornholt, J. (1989). *Star trek: The next generation.* New York: Dell.

Burchard, P. (1995). *Charlotte Forten: A black teacher in the Civil War.* New York: Crown.

Chase, R. (1943). *Jack tales.* Boston: Houghton Mifflin.

Chase, R. (1948). *Grandfather tales.* Boston: Houghton Mifflin.

Cook, R. (1989). *Mutation.* New York: Putnam.

Collier, J. L., & Collier, C. (1974). *My brother Sam is dead.* New York: Scholastic.

de Trevino, E. (1965). *I, Juan de Pareja.* New York: Farrar, Straus & Giroux.

Dewdney, A. K. (1984). *The planiverse.* New York: Poseidon Press.

Dillon, E. (1992). *The children of Bach.* New York: Scribners.

Edmonds, W. (1991). *The matchlock gun.* New York: Troll.

Ewy, D., & Ewy, R. (1985). *Teen pregnancy: The challenges we faced, the choices we made.* New York: New American Library.

Fleischman, P. (1993). *Bull Run.* New York: HarperCollins.

Forbes, E. (1945). *Johnny Tremain.* Boston: Houghton Mifflin.

Forman, J. (1988). *Cry havoc.* New York: Scribners.

Forman, J. (1992). *Becca's story.* New York: Scribners.

Fox, P. (1973). *The slave dancer* (E. Keith, Illus.). New York: Bradbury.

Freedman, R. (1989). *Lincoln: A photobiography.* New York: Clarion.

Garner, J. (1995). *Politically correct holiday stories: For an enlightened Yuletide season.* Thorndike, ME: G. K. Hall.

Grant, S., & Mandrake, T. (1990). *William Shakespeare's Hamlet.* New York: Berkley.

Hansen, J. (1988). *Out from this place.* New York: Walker.

Hansen, J. (1992). *Which way freedom?* New York: Avon.

Herrin, L. (1989). *The unwritten chronicles of Robert E. Lee.* New York: St. Martin's Press.

Hesse, K. (1992). *Letters from Rifka.* New York: Henry Holt.

Hinton, C. H. (1907). *An episode in flatland.* London: Swan Sonnenschein.

Hobbs, W. (1991). *Downriver.* New York: Macmillan.

Hopkinson, D., & Ransome, J. (1993). *Sweet Clara and the freedom quilt.* New York: Random House.

Howard, E. (1987). *Mystery of the metro.* New York: Random House.

Hooks, W., & Pinkney, B. (1990). *The ballad of Belle Dorcas.* New York: Alfred A. Knopf.

Hunt, I. (1965). *Across five Aprils.* New York: Grosset & Dunlap.

Jacobs, H. (1973). *Cajun night before Christmas.* New York: Pelican.

Lagerlof, S. (1912). *The wonderful adventures of Nils* (V. S. Howard, Trans.). New York: Doubleday, Page.
Laird, C. (1990). *Shadow of the wall.* New York: Greenwillow.
Leonard, A. (1988). *Tina's chance.* New York: Viking.
Lipsyte, R. (1993). *The chemo kid.* New York: HarperCollins.
Llewellyn, J. (1991). *Deadeye.* New York: Summit Books.
Lowry, L. (1990). *Number the stars.* New York: Dell.
Lowry, L. (1994). *The giver.* New York: Dell.
Lyon, G. (1991). *Cecil's story.* New York: Orchard/Watts.
McCurdy, M. (1994). *Escape from slavery: The boyhood of Frederick Douglass in his own words.* New York: Alfred A. Knopf.
Moore, R. (1991). *Distant thunder: A sequel to the Christmas surprise.* Scottdale, PA: Herald.
Morpurgo, M. (1991). *Waiting for Anya.* New York: Viking.
Morris, G. (1990). *The last confederate.* Minneapolis: Bethany House.
Mowat, F. (1979). *Never cry wolf.* New York: Bantam Books.
Murphy, J. (1992). *The long road to Gettysburg.* New York: Clarion.
O'Dell, S. (1979). *The captive.* Boston: Houghton Mifflin.
O'Dell, S. (1981). *The feathered serpent.* Boston: Houghton Mifflin.
O'Dell, S. (1983). *The amethyst ring.* Boston: Houghton Mifflin.
Peck, R. (1991). *Unfinished portrait of Jessica.* New York: Delacorte Press.
Perez, N. (1990). *The slopes of war.* Boston: Houghton Mifflin.
Pullman, P. (1992). *The broken bridge.* New York: Alfred A. Knopf.
Reeder, C. (1989). *Shades of gray.* New York: Macmillan.
Richter, H. P. (1970). *Friedrich* (E. Kroll, Trans.). New York: Holt, Rinehart & Winston.
Rinaldi, A. (1988). *The last silk dress.* New York: Holiday.
Robertson, J. (1992). *Civil War!: America becomes one nation.* New York: Alfred A. Knopf.
Roth-Hano, R. (1988). *Touch wood: A girlhood in occupied France.* New York: Macmillan.
Sandler, M. (1995). *Immigrants.* New York: HarperCollins.
Sargent, P. (1988). *Alien child.* New York: Harper & Row.
Schattschneider, D. (1990). *Visions of symmetry: Notebooks, periodic drawings, and related work of M. C. Escher.* New York: W. H. Freeman.
Schultz, R. (1992a). *Looking inside sports aerodynamics.* Santa Fe, NM: John Muir.
Schultz, R. (1992b). *Looking inside the brain.* Santa Fe, NM: John Muir.
Shura, M. F. (1991). *Gentle Annie: The true story of a Civil War nurse.* New York: Scholastic Books.
Sills, L. (1993). *Visions: Stories about women artists.* Morton Grove, IL: Albert Whitman.
Silver, N. (1990). *No tigers in Africa.* New York: E. P. Dutton.
Silver, N. (1991). *An eye for color.* New York: E. P. Dutton.
Sommers, B. (1990). *The uncertainty principle.* New York: Fawcett.
Stanley, J. (1994). *I am an American.* New York: Crown.
Toll, N. (1993). *Behind the secret window.* New York: Dial.
Weaver, W. (1993). *Striking out.* New York: HarperCollins.
Wilhelm, K. (1991). *Death qualified: A mystery of chaos.* New York: St. Martin's Press.
Wisler, G. C. (1991). *Red cap.* New York: Lodestar/Dutton.
Yolen, J. (1988). *The devil's arithmetic.* New York: Viking.
Yolen, J. (1992). *Briar rose.* New York: Tor.

CHAPTER 9

Strategic Learning Across the Content Areas

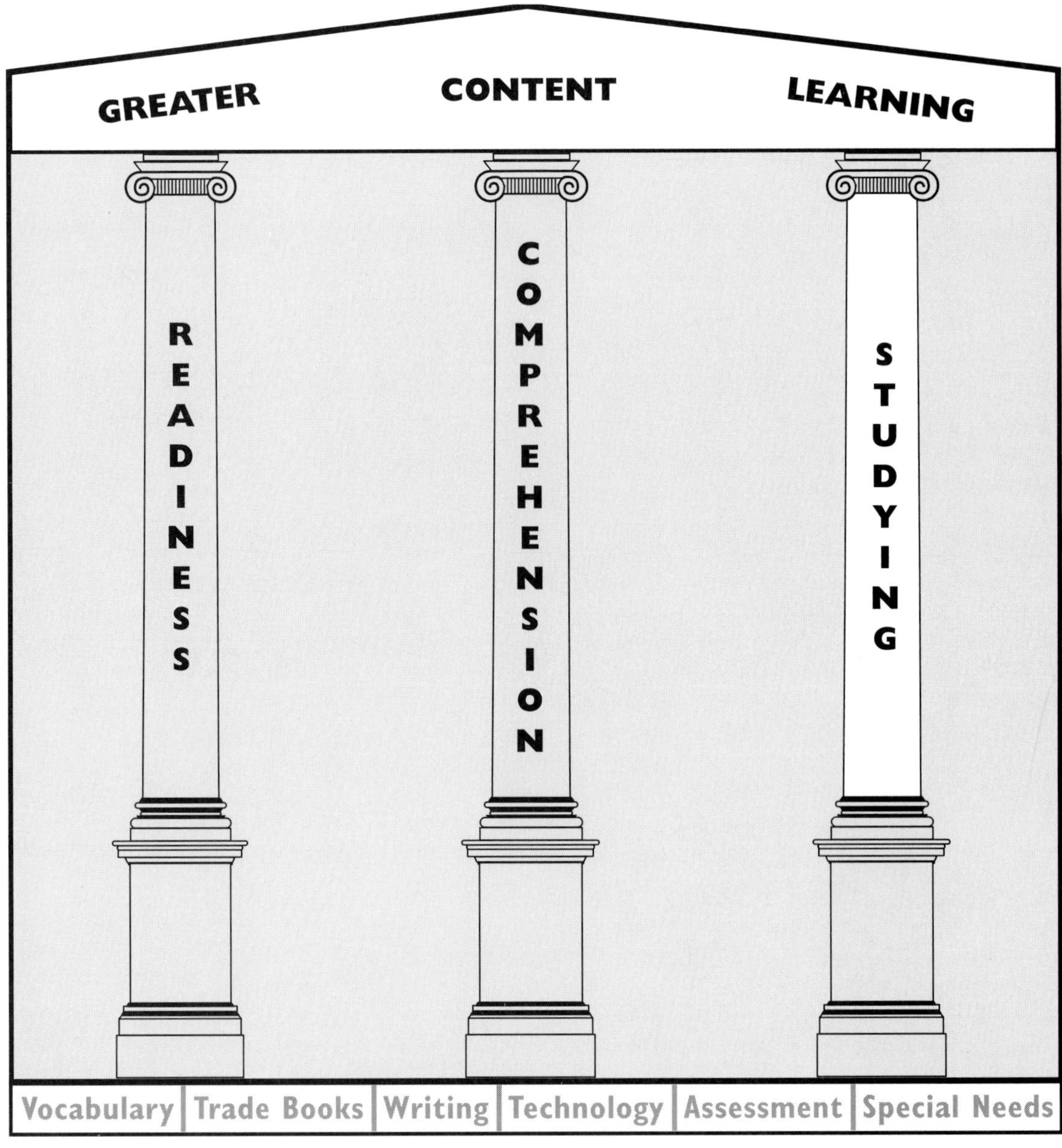

ANTICIPATION GUIDE

Directions: Read each statement carefully and decide whether you agree or disagree with it, placing a check mark in the appropriate *Before Reading* column. When you have finished reading and studying the chapter, return to the guide and decide whether your anticipations need to be changed by placing a check mark in the appropriate *After Reading* column.

	BEFORE READING		**AFTER READING**	
	Agree	*Disagree*	*Agree*	*Disagree*
1. Research has shown that there is a best strategy for studying.	______	______	______	______
2. By the end of elementary school, most students have learned how to summarize what they have read.	______	______	______	______
3. If teachers tell students about a strategy, they will begin using it.	______	______	______	______
4. By high school, most students know how to take class notes.	______	______	______	______
5. Students' beliefs about themselves and learning have an impact on the strategies they choose to use.	______	______	______	______
6. Homework can be used as a way of reinforcing study strategies.	______	______	______	______

Shifting the responsibility for learning from the teacher to the student and improving the capabilities of students for engaging in self-directed learning might be expected to have benefits for both students and teachers. First, with respect to teachers and schools, these changes might provide an economical way to increase total learning without the need to allocate additional teaching or instructional time.... Giving students more responsibility for their learning might also be expected to reduce somewhat the burden that teachers bear for effecting student achievement. Having students share in this responsibility might be expected to reduce teachers' anxiety that they alone are the cause of students' successes and failures.

—Thomas, Strage, and Curley (1988)

Study Strategies Make a Difference

As the preceding quotation suggests, students who are strategic learners will profit, as will their teachers. Students will profit because the use of study strategies is positively related to their academic performance. In general, students who use strategies that demand their critical thinking and elaboration are more likely to do better on their assignments, exams, and papers (Nist, Simpson, Olejnik, & Mealey, 1991; Pintrich & Garcia, 1994; Zimmerman, Bandura, & Martinez-Pons, 1992).

Study strategies are deliberate, planned, and conscious activities that students select to achieve a particular goal. Students typically employ study strategies when they need to retain material for the purpose of taking a test, writing a paper, participating in class discussion, or any other demonstration of their learning. When does the need for strategy training begin? As soon as students are required to retain material for a later purpose, typically, when they encounter their first expository textbook—around fourth grade.

As we mentioned in Chapter 2 in our fifth principle of active learning, middle school and high school students must have a variety of strategies to be effective in their studying and learning. Researchers (e.g., Thomas, Rohwer, & Wilson, 1989) have suggested that the strategies we teach students should include important cognitive and metacognitive processes such as being able to:

Essential Processes in the Content Areas

1. Select important ideas and restate them in your own words.
2. Reorganize and elaborate on these ideas.
3. Ask questions concerning the significance of targeted information and ideas.
4. Monitor when you know and when you do not understand.
5. Establish goals and define your tasks.
6. Evaluate plans and the usefulness of the strategies you selected.

Because of their importance, these cognitive and metacognitive processes are reflected by the strategies we present in this chapter.

We should also note that this chapter is an extension of Chapter 3; both describe and discuss how to build active learners. Whereas Chapter 3 emphasizes

This Chapter Will Emphasize Student-Initiated Learning Strategies

teacher-generated strategies that encourage elaborative processing of text and reflection (e.g., discussion webs and study guides), this chapter emphasizes student-initiated strategies that promote strategic reading and independent learning. In particular, this chapter is devoted to ways of incorporating strategy training into your classroom instruction.

CASE STUDY

Khaled is a ninth-grade English teacher who has been required by his department chairperson and the district-level Language Arts Coordinator to teach study strategies to his students. They have provided him with a workbook that contains the SQ3R method and other techniques for improving vocabulary, time management, and reading rate. Khaled has organized his curricula so that Mondays are reserved for study skill instruction. During class, students complete the workbook pages by reading the brief passages and answering questions. As the students work, he walks

around the room to answer questions and provide help. Unfortunately, his students have complained bitterly about these activities. Even more disheartening is the fact that they have not seen the connection between the workbook activities and their other courses. Students seem to be reading, listening, and studying the same way in his English class, and other teachers report the same result. That is, students still seem to be passive memorizers and learners. Khaled believes study skills are important for his students, but he is growing increasingly frustrated.

To the Reader:
As you read and work through this chapter on study strategies, decide what Khaled might do to improve his approach. Consider the strategies we examine and the conditions necessary for students to become strategic learners.

■ ■ ■

GUIDELINES FOR TEACHING STUDY STRATEGIES

There Are Eight Guidelines

In order to develop active learners who have a variety of strategies for learning in your content area, there are some basic guidelines drawn from current research and theory. The eight guidelines presented below describe the conditions that are necessary for students to become active learners. A discussion of these guidelines follows.

Emphasize the Importance of Task Knowledge

Imagine that you are training to run a machine in a factory, and you prepare for your job by reading a manual about how to operate it. You read the manual a couple of times, skimming over it before you begin working. Then you are put on the machine and told to get started. Every few minutes you need to consult the manual; eventually, the machine breaks down, and your boss is at your throat. The reason for your failure? A clear mismatch between the way you trained and the task's demands.

Now imagine that a student is studying for a biology test by using flash cards with the names of the hormones secreted by the endocrine system on one side and their definitions on the other. On the test, students are asked to interpret several diagrams, explaining the relationship between the hormones and their impact on other glands and human behavior. What grade would you predict for this student? Would she pass the test? Was there a match between the way she studied and what she needed to know for the test?

Like the factory worker, this student experienced a mismatch between the strategy and the demands of the task. That is, the biology test required the students to integrate the information about the hormones in the endocrine system. The student, however, focused on rote memorization of definitions rather than the relationships between concepts.

These two examples point out the importance of the principle of **transfer appropriateness.** This principle states that the more appropriate the match between a study process and an academic task, the more easily information can be transferred to long-term memory. When students select strategies that match the tasks they have been assigned, their academic performance will be enhanced (Butler & Winne, 1995; Pintrich & Garcia, 1994). Conversely, many failures or mediocre performances by students can be explained by a mismatch between their perceptions of the task and their teacher's perceptions (Simpson & Nist, 1997).

Tasks Must Match Strategies

The implication of this principle is that students must be taught how to analyze the tasks they will encounter in their content area courses. Tasks, according to Doyle (1983), can be characterized in terms of their products and thinking processes. The products are the papers, projects, lab reports, or tests that students must complete for a course. More important than the product are the thinking processes that a student must employ in order to complete the product. For example, if students are assigned a paper for a government class, that paper is the product. If the teacher asks the students to read an editorial by George Will and critique it, the thinking processes for that paper are far more involved than those required for a paper summarizing Will's key ideas. Students must be able to determine and understand the levels of thinking demanded in their academic tasks. More important, they need to be shown that it is acceptable for them to seek information about the nature of their tasks and about other ways they will be held accountable for their learning. With that information, they can make informed decisions about which study strategy to employ.

Not only should we teach students how to analyze an academic such as the one required by the government teacher, but we, as teachers, should provide clear and explicit information about what we want students to do and how we want them to do it. By sharing product and process information with our students, we ensure that they will have the task knowledge to make informed strategy decisions.

Teachers Need to Be Explicit About Tasks

Remember the When, Why, and How of Strategy Use

In Chapter 2, we described active learners as those who have knowledge (i.e., declarative, procedural, and conditional) and control of strategies. Here we reiterate that active learners need to develop a repertoire of adaptive, flexible strategies and an ability to use the most appropriate ones to match the task demands of the content areas they are reading and studying. To do this, we need to teach students the *when,*or best specific applications of the strategy; the *whys,* or advantages; the limitations; and the *hows,* or steps of the strategy. If students lack procedural and conditional knowledge about a strategy, they will not be likely to abandon their typical approaches of memorizing, which they find more comfortable and accessible, in favor of more elaborative and appropriate strategies (Butler & Winne, 1995).

Take the Time to Develop Students' Strategic Expertise

Workbooks May Not Be Effective in Teaching Students How to Be Strategic

Pressley (1995) and others have pointed out that students do not quickly transfer or use a new strategy they just have been taught. Most study strategies involve complex processes that cannot be mastered in brief teaching lessons or artificial exercises packaged in workbooks. Admittedly, students may learn the steps of a strategy from such instructional approaches, but they will not gain the conditional and procedural knowledge necessary for them to transfer the strategy to their own tasks.

We believe it is critical for any teacher interested in training students to use study strategies to accept this principle; otherwise, the teacher and the class may give up on a strategy, in spite of its potential, too early, before students have had a chance to develop control and expertise.

There are Five Characteristics of Effective Strategy Instruction

Validated training approaches and models (e.g., Simpson, Hynd, Nist, & Burrell, 1997) are numerous, but they all agree that instruction should be direct, informed, and explanatory. In other words, students can be taught to employ a strategy if they receive intensive instruction over a reasonable period of time that is characterized by (1) a description of the strategy and its characteristics, (2) an explanation of why the strategy is important, (3) think-alouds about how the strategy is used, including the processes involved, (4) explanations as to when and where it is appropriate to apply the strategy, and (5) guidelines for evaluating whether the strategy is working and what to do if it is not. In addition, teachers should provide students with strategy examples from their content area textbooks or materials, guided practice during class, and qualitative feedback on their strategy attempts.

We have found that it takes at least a few weeks before students begin to feel comfortable with a particular strategy. One way we have found to facilitate this process is by allowing students to practice the strategy with material that is easy to understand. In this way, students avoid overcrowding the cognitive workbench and can focus most of their attention on learning the strategy. Gradually, we increase the difficulty of the material until students demonstrate that they can apply the strategy to their own textbooks. This may take several weeks, but the time is well spent because our primary goals of study strategy training are to develop students' strategic expertise and ultimate independence in learning.

Know the Study Strategies You Teach

We could restate the principle "Know the study strategies you teach" by saying "Practice what you preach." In our experience, students respond most favorably to strategy instruction when the teacher is credible and enthusiastic. This means that you must be very familiar with the strategies you offer. If you plan to teach your students a text-study system, for instance, you need to know the system inside and out, including its strengths, limitations, and applications. One way to gain this knowledge is to learn and practice the system with your school reading. If you are taking university course work, use the strategy you are teaching your students in your own studying. Then, when students have questions about the strategy, you will be able to answer them from firsthand experience. Examples of your own strategies can also be very illuminating for students because they often hold the misconception that "sophisticated readers" can read and remember everything on the first try. One of our graduate students shared with her students the chart she had created to learn the different theories of reading as one way of explaining the strategy of comparison and contrast charts. Students are sensitive to your attitudes about what you teach; if you can demonstrate your belief in the value and utility of study strategies, they will respond to your enthusiasm.

Create Situations in Which Students Can Transfer Strategies to Realistic Content Area Tasks

Students need real, meaningful purposes for reading and studying. To teach them how to take notes in a particular way that has little to do with how they are actually supposed to organize and process the material in your class and other classes may mean that they will know how to take notes your way, but they will find no reason to do so. What good is it that students can list the steps of a strategy or complete a workbook activity using that strategy? As we have said many times, strategies should never be taught in isolation from authentic reading and study tasks.

One way to increase the likelihood that students will actually use the strategies they are taught is by linking strategy training to learning across the content areas. A nearby high school provides an example of this approach. The high school requires all incoming freshmen to take a reading and study skills course during their first quarter. The course is designed to teach them how to read and study their textbooks, manage their time, and prepare for and take tests. In addition, they are taught to take notes from their class discussions or lectures in a specific form, called the *split-page method* (Palmatier, 1973). Split-page notes are taken on note paper that is divided into two columns, the left side for key idea statements or questions and the right side for the information presented during class (this method is explained in greater detail later in this chapter). Here is what is so special about the way students in this high school learn this strategy: Although they are taught and practice the strategy in reading class, they are given the opportunity to apply it in their biology class. Biology teachers reinforce this method of note taking by talking to their students about how split-page notes can be taken for text content and for their lectures. To facilitate this process, they show students examples of their lecture material organized in the split-page format, and they constantly remind and encourage students to use the method. In sum, all teachers must carefully orchestrate strategy transfer.

An All-School Approach Helps to Build Active Learners

Acknowledge the Importance of Students' Motivation and Belief Systems

As mentioned in Chapter 2, students' "will," or motivation, is as important as their strategy "skill" (Paris, Lipson, & Wixson, 1983). In fact, motivation is what makes active learning in your content area possible. When students are motivated, they value academic tasks and view themselves as learners who know whether or not they understand the concepts in a particular content area (Pintrich & Garcia, 1994). Rather than attributing academic success to chance or the whims of a teacher, active learners with high **self-efficacy** ratings attribute what they learn to their own effort and strategy use. In contrast, students with low self-efficacy are more likely to attribute their failures to external factors (e.g., the test was not fair) or to a fixed ability that they cannot change (Dweck, 1986). As a result, these students decide to give up before they even enter the classroom, or at the first setback or challenge. Interestingly, you will find that students' self-efficacy varies across the content areas. For example, a student may have a strong sense of self-efficacy in a math course but feel totally overwhelmed or frustrated in an English course that requires her to write critical or creative responses to what she reads (Pintrich & Garcia, 1994).

Self-Efficacy Is Important to Students' Learning

In addition to considering your students' motivation, it is important to remember the importance of their belief systems about learning. As stressed in Chapter 2, because some students believe learning involves only the memorization of facts, they perceive most academic tasks as situations involving minimal effort or mental energy. As a result, it will be very difficult for you to convince them that they need to use strategies that encourage them to think critically and elaboratively about content area concepts. The best way to counteract students' naive conceptions about learning is to persuade them that learning is often hard and rarely quick or absolute (Pressley, 1995).

Encourage Students to Modify Strategies to Meet Personal Needs and Styles

It never fails. After a semester of teaching study strategies, say a note-taking system, none of the students' notes look exactly like ours or like anyone else's in the class. But this should be expected because there are no prototypes, no answer keys. We all make choices and decisions based on what we think is the most important information to include in our notes, and we modify the format to fit those perceptions. Students need to be able to make these choices and changes. After all, each of our study needs is personal, and what better time to learn how to stress personal adaptations than when students are being trained to use study strategies? Help students develop ownership of the strategies by allowing them to decide how study strategies should be modified to meet their needs.

Students Should Learn How to Modify Strategies

The fundamental point is this: Do not be too prescriptive, mechanical, or formulaic when teaching students study strategies. Otherwise, you shift emphasis away from your intention of having students modify study processes to making judgments about their products.

Use Homework and Other Assignments to Reinforce Study Strategies

The topic of homework is often overlooked in teacher education programs. Yet, anyone who is or has been a middle school or high school teacher knows that students who study study at home. In fact, students equate studying with time outside the classroom spent poring over books and notes in preparation for tests.

With regard to high school students, increasing time spent on homework is systematically related to high academic achievement (e.g., Keith, Reimers, Fehrmann, Pottebau, & Aubey, 1986). While this correlation seems to indicate that more homework is better, we contend that homework itself does not necessarily promote and extend classroom learning, in spite of the chidings from national educational figures and major national reports. We briefly take up this topic here because we believe that homework, when appropriately assigned, can play an important role in reinforcing students' developing study strategies. Our data for this discussion do not come from empirical research but rather from anecdotal evidence, interviews with content area teachers, and our teaching experience.

Homework Is Linked to Students' Academic Achievement

Classroom teachers interested in helping students see the connection between how they read and study their textbooks and the course expectations and requirements should assign homework that asks students to integrate particular strategies with the learning of the course content. For example, a biology teacher who wants her students to learn the different glands and hormones in the endocrine system could assign homework requiring them to create a chart to summarize those concepts. In class, the students could brainstorm what information might be contained in the charts (e.g., locations, functions) and examine possible formats. The following day, students could meet in groups to compare and discuss their charts and identify any ambiguous information. The teacher could also give the students a quiz about the endocrine system, allowing them to use their newly created charts. In this way, the teacher receives feedback on how students are progressing in their mastery of the study strategy simultaneously with how well they are learning the course content.

There Are Six Guidelines for Assigning Strategy Homework

In addition to these ideas for using homework to apply newly learned study strategies, we offer the following guidelines for assigning strategy homework:

- Study strategy homework assignments should be made as a result of careful initial planning of a unit's themes and concepts.
- Homework should be related to the amount of instruction given and the time spent teaching a study strategy.
- If study strategy homework is given, it should be given to all students, and adjustments should be made for various ability levels.
- Homework should be used as feedback on students' progress toward strategy mastery.
- Study strategy homework should be meaningful and functional.
- Specific feedback should be provided on students' homework assignments in a timely fashion.

Students frequently perceive homework as an infringement on their time for extracurricular activities, part-time jobs, or recreation. When homework is given judiciously and when it is meaningfully related to the course expectations, there is a greater chance that it will be completed. In turn, students who practice applying strategies to their course content will become competent readers and successful independent learners.

Based on these eight guidelines of effective study strategy instruction, we next describe some basic processes that are important to almost any content area.

BASIC PROCESSES IMPORTANT TO ACTIVE LEARNING

Students who are active learners understand how their textbooks are organized, how to interpret and record an assignment, how to begin reading their assignments, and how to interact with the material. As content area teachers, we cannot assume that students have mastered these basic processes in the elementary grades.

Knowing the Format and Organization of a Textbook

Students Must Understand How Their Textbook Is Organized

One basic strategy that students often overlook is the effective use of the textbook. We have known college students who have carried their psychology textbook around for 6 weeks without knowing that there was a glossary at the back or that a list of key terms was included at the end of each chapter. If students can learn how their textbook is organized and capitalize on those features as they read and study, they can increase their concentration, understanding, and remembering.

Carolina, an eighth-grade social studies teacher, had attended a district workshop where the speaker stressed the importance of introducing the format and organization of textbooks to students. Before the workshop she had assumed, as had many other teachers, that most students take the time to explore their textbooks once they receive them. Like most, she had merely handed out her textbook and assigned the first chapter of reading. Taking part of a class period to explain the "obvious characteristics" of a textbook seemed a bit unnecessary, but she decided to give it a try. She began her discussion by explaining that textbooks contain only the theories, perspectives, and conclusions of certain scholars under contract from a publisher. She then asked the students to read the title page and preface of their textbook to gain information about their authors. The students discovered that three individuals had written their text. After a discussion of the authors, Carolina stressed that the content of all their readings would be filtered through the biases and personal opinions of the authors.

After that brief orientation, which many students found intriguing, Carolina distributed a textbook introduction activity designed to orient her students further to their textbook (Figure 9.1). In the workshop, she had learned that many students know neither where important textbook parts are located nor how they function. She therefore paired her students and gave them 15 minutes to familiarize themselves with the parts of the textbook through the questions on the activity sheet. Each chapter, as the students soon discovered, had a general introduction; a summary that listed key ideas; and boldface headings, subheadings, and italicized words. Carolina closed the period with a discussion of how these aids could help them as they read and studied their first assignment.

Title of textbook ______
Author(s) ______
Copyright date ______ Has the book been revised? ______

1. Read the ***preface*** carefully and completely. Summarize briefly what it says.
2. Find the ***table of contents.*** Answer these questions after studying it:
   a. Are the chapters broken down into many or few subheadings?
   b. Can you list five or six major topics included in the table of contents?
3. Find the ***index.*** On what page does it begin? Name two or three types of information you find there.
4. Find the ***glossary.*** How can it help you?
5. Find the ***appendix.*** What type of information can you find in it?
6. Find one ***bibliography.*** List two authors or titles that interest you.
7. Examine Chapter 1. Check the organizational features available in this textbook:
   a. Introduction ______
   b. Marginal notes ______
   c. Italicized or underlined words ______
   d. Boldface headings ______
   e. Pictures ______ Graphs ______ Maps ______ Charts ______
   f. Internal summaries ______ Summary ______
   g. Questions at the end ______

FIGURE 9.1 Getting Acquainted with Your Textbook

Carolina received positive feedback from her students on this lesson and decided to incorporate it into her beginning-of-the-year routine. We know some school districts that insist that all teachers take the time during the first week of school to introduce their textbook with an activity like the one in Figure 9.1. The form can obviously be modified to fit any content area textbook. What Carolina and many other teachers hope is that students will become critical and savvy consumers of text who will conduct their own "get-acquainted" activities before they begin reading.

Recording and Interpreting Assignments Correctly and Completely

As previously mentioned, if students are to select the appropriate strategies, they must understand all the nuances of their academic tasks. They must also record these tasks or assignments correctly and completely so that they can refer to them while they read and study at home. We, as content area teachers, can help students with this basic process by providing predictable questions that they should ask themselves about an assignment:

1. What is the assignment? What am I to produce? What is the purpose of the assignment?
2. What resources should I use? Textbook? Class discussion notes? Computer databases? Outside reading? Videos? Class demonstrations or laboratory experiments?

Questions Students Should Ask Themselves about an Assignment

3. What are the requirements for format, length, or size? Must the assignment be typed? In ink? Stapled?
4. When is the assignment due? Are there any penalties for late work?
5. How will this assignment be evaluated? How much does it count in the total evaluation process?
6. Do I understand all the words that the teacher used to explain the assignment?

The last question is particularly critical because we often use words such as *critique* or *respond creatively* when we give students assignments, assuming that they know what we mean. More often than we would like, students do not understand these words and the processes they embody (Simpson & Nist, 1997).

Parents Like this Strategy!

We know a team of seventh-grade teachers that have these six questions listed on a poster in their classroom in order to encourage students to "get all the information" when they write their assignments in their notebooks. In addition, they encourage and reinforce students for asking questions about assignments. A serendipitous result of training students to record their assignments in this fashion has been vocal endorsement from the students' parents, who are frequently bewildered by what homework their children should be doing each night. These six questions have reduced students' and parents' bewilderment and frustration.

Previewing

Dominique and Turkessa were preparing to go to a performance of the local symphony. As they were dressing, Turkessa suggested that they read about the composer, Bach, to learn about his life and musical philosophy. Dominique rummaged through their stacks of books in the basement and eventually found the trusty music appreciation text he had used years ago in undergraduate school. He read aloud about Bach as they finished dressing and continued reading to Turkessa as she drove downtown. They arrived at Symphony Hall early and read further from the program about the compositions to be performed that evening. By the time the first note sounded, they had established a context for the music that greatly aided their interpretation and appreciation of what they heard.

This kind of context setting is at the heart of the **previewing strategy.** Students often seem to begin a reading assignment much like those people who entered Symphony Hall and scurried to find their seats just before the conductor's entrance on the stage. The music rushed over them, but because they did not plan for listening, they may not have known what the composer intended to communicate with his music. Likewise, when students are expected to gain a complete understanding of their text but approach their reading by opening their books to the beginning of the assignment and simply plowing forward, they fail to prepare for the flood of words they encounter and may find themselves in the middle of the chapter unsure about what the author is trying to convey.

To prepare for the reading assignments, students should be taught how to preview. The previewing strategy is a logical follow-up to learning the format and organization of a textbook because it requires students to know and use those features. As indicated in Figure 9.2, as students preview, they note the introductory paragraphs, summaries, topic markers or boldface headings, visual aids, summaries, and questions or problems provided by the author. Once students have previewed these text features, they need to take a moment to reflect on this information, allowing the ideas to sink in. They might ask themselves such questions as these: What is the chapter about? What are some key vocabulary words I will learn? How should I read this chapter and divide up this task? With a mental picture of the key ideas and information in the text, students can employ appropriate strategies, and their reading can proceed more purposefully and appropriately.

Previewing Has Many Advantages

Why should students preview? Because students may initially resist such a strategy, it is important to discuss the advantages of previewing with them. In these discussions, stress the fact that previewing provides a meaningful organization of the material to be learned. As students read introductory paragraphs and look over headings and subheadings, they will form a mental outline of the major topics and subtopics. This information will provide students with the data they need to make judgments about their readiness to learn the material, the difficulty of the material, and the actions they may need to take to learn the material. In addition, when students take the time to preview their textbooks before they read, they should observe an improvement in their reading fluency, concentration, and comprehension (Neuman, 1988).

As a strategy, previewing is neither relevant nor appropriate for all texts and tasks. Some texts are not considerately organized, and many literature anthologies do not contain textbook markers or summaries. Hence, students will need to modify the preview strategy (i.e., read the first sentence of each paragraph when there are no textbook markers) or select a more appropriate strategy. Occasionally, some teachers may not want their students to read and study an entire chapter but instead may tell them to memorize specific processes, steps, or formulas. For example, if a chemistry teacher told her class that all they would be required to know from Chapter 3 in their textbook was the symbols and atomic weights for five specific elements, extensive previewing would not be appropriate. This example points again to the importance of students' knowing what they will be responsible for as a result of reading and studying so that they can employ the most relevant study strategy.

Previewing, although not a panacea, certainly will engage students in more active reading and learning. Moreover, previewing is one of the strategies that can be initially introduced by teachers, modeled and reinforced, and then gradually shifted to the students for their own responsibility and control.

Once students have previewed their text and started their reading, they must be able to identify and transform key ideas using their own words. We address that essential process next.

- ***Table of contents.*** A look through the table of contents for a chapter provides students with a broad level of organization.
- ***Topic markers within the chapter.*** These markers provide the reader with a more specific view of the organization of the chapter. Students should look over titles, headings, and subheadings and concurrently ask themselves these questions: How much do I already know about this topic? What does the author expect me to learn from this chapter? How are the topic markers related? The following topic markers, from a chapter in a history textbook over the Civil War, are listed in the order in which they appeared in the text to demonstrate how much students can learn about the material from merely surveying these markers.

1. Bloodshed
    - Fort Sumter Leads to War
        - Other Southern States Secede
        - The Border States
    - The North Against the South
        - The Northern Position
        - The Southern Position
    - Surprise at Bull Run
2. The Read War Begins
    - Machinery of Modern War
        - New Guns
        - Better Warships
    - Early Battles
        - The Battle of Shiloh
        - A Naval Blockade
        - The Peninsula Campaign
        - Antietam
3. The Goals of War Change
    - England Remains Neutral
    - Slavery Becomes the Main Issue
    - The Emancipation Proclamation
    - Drafting Begins

- ***Introductory paragraphs and summaries.*** Students can gain a great deal of information about the purpose of the chapter, the author's goals, and the major concepts by reading these sections of text. With this information in mind, students can focus their attention while reading about these important ideas.
- ***Graphs, diagrams, and pictures.*** Students should be shown that authors include visuals to highlight important information and ideas.
- ***Questions or problems.*** Textbook authors often include questions for consideration at the beginning of a chapter and/or questions at the end of a chapter that help students reflect on what they have read. Keeping these questions in mind will help students focus their reading on important information.

Source: Adapted from Jordan, W. D., Greenblat, M., & Bowes, J. S. (1985). *The Americans, the History of a People and a Nation,* Evanston, IL: McDougal, Littell. Copyright 1985. Adapted by permission of the publisher.

FIGURE 9.2 Important Textbook Features to Be Previewed

Summarizing

When you ask your colleague in the hall, "How are you?" and she says, "Fine," she is summarizing—categorizing her collective experiences and feelings and labeling them with a single word. When you ask a fellow student about the weather and he says, "Gloomy," this also is a summary, the selection of a single word that embraces a variety of weather characteristics.

All of us summarize many times during the course of a day. **Summarizing** is condensing information and ideas; it is getting to the heart of a matter; without it, communication might be tediously protracted. Imagine those two simple questions being answered by a litany of feelings, emotions, and experiences and by a detailed description of every weather feature. Despite our experience with summarizing, many students find it difficult to summarize what someone else has written or has said (King, 1992; Wittrock, 1990).

Summarizing Is a Difficult Skill

The ability to summarize text is perhaps one of the most essential and sophisticated reading skills (Wittrock, 1990; Wong, Wong, & Perry, 1986). In fact, if you return to Chapter 2 and review the five principles that characterize active learners, you will note that summary generation involves students in all of them. Because summarizing involves students in so many cognitive and metacognitive processes, a great deal of time can be required to develop expertise in summarizing. If, however, students can learn how to construct a summary using their own words, their understanding and metacognition will be enhanced (Wittrock, 1990). In addition, students can use their self-generated summaries to study and prepare for examinations. For example, Simpson and Nist (1990) found that students who had been trained to summarize and annotate key ideas performed significantly better on three different content area exams than students who used traditional study methods (e.g., rereading, outlining). Even more interesting was the finding that the students who had summarized and annotated spent half as much time studying as their counterparts.

The process of constructing summaries has been found to be rule governed (Brown & Day, 1983); that is, the mental steps involved seem to be the same from person to person. These rules have been turned into steps and have been used effectively to train students in summary writing:

There are Steps We Can Teach Students for Summarizing What They Read

1. Delete unimportant and redundant information.
2. Categorize information.
3. Select or create key idea statements.
4. Synthesize ideas across paragraphs.

These steps are a logical place to begin teaching students how to summarize. Loris, a ninth-grade English teacher, uses these steps and extensive modeling to teach summarization to her students. Mindful of process writing, Loris begins summary-writing instruction by emphasizing the *process* of constructing written summaries, thereby freeing students from worries about correct structure and perfect grammar and allowing them to focus on learning the process.

After the class discusses what a summary is and looks over examples, Loris passes out a short article and, without having previously rehearsed it, begins reading and thinking aloud as she works through the summary-writing process. She believes that demonstrating the summarizing process with brand-new text gives students a glimpse of how she struggles to make meaning and to reveal the genesis of her summary thinking. Loris has discovered that by giving only polished summaries, she misses the opportunity to teach them the strategies she used to construct them, that is, the process of working from confusion to understanding (Pradl, 1987).

A ninth grader in the class offered Loris his history textbook and asked her to summarize a subsection from his reading assignment for the upcoming week. Selecting a short section entitled "The Yellow Press," Loris made copies and distributed them the next day. Without rehearsing, she then modeled the entire summary-writing process, talking about how she made sense of the text and the decisions behind what to include in her summary. Compare the textbook segment with Loris's think-aloud while modeling the summarizing process.

> The Yellow Press
>
> While supporters of the rebel cause were active in the United States, newspaper tycoons William Randolph Hearst and Joseph Pulitzer were carrying on a circulation war. Each was determined that his paper would outsell the other. So both began to play up Spanish "atrocities." Legitimate accounts of suffering in the concentration camps were mixed with fake stories of wells being poisoned and little children being thrown to the sharks. American correspondents, who were not allowed to enter areas where fighting was going on, would sit around the bars of Havana and make up reports about battles that never took place. One, artist Frederic Remington, who had been illustrating reporters' dispatches, cabled Hearst saying that war between the United States and Spain seemed very unlikely. Back came Hearst's reply, "You furnish the pictures and I'll furnish the war."*
>
> Loris's Think-Aloud
>
> *Loris:* Remember that I'm looking at this section without having read what comes before, so I'm reading it in isolation. You would have read the entire chapter. But I can clearly see by looking at the other subheadings on these couple of pages that the topic is about Cuba and its struggle for independence from Spain around the turn of the century.
>
> Okay, right from the start, the term *yellow press* means something like bad journalism or false reporting. This is something I just already know, so I'm thinking that the section will describe false reports about the

---

*Jordan, W. D., Greenblat, M., & Bowes, J. S. (1985). *The Americans, the history of a people and a nation.* Evanston, IL: McDougal, Littell. Copyright 1985. Used by permission of the publisher.

Cuban-Spanish war. I don't remember much about that time in history except for Teddy Roosevelt and his Rough Riders, so I'll have to read on to find out which side the press is writing bad news about. (*Loris reads the first three lines aloud.*)

I know of Hearst and Pulitzer and the fact that they made their fortunes in the newspaper business. Remember Patti Hearst? She's part of that family . . . and you've heard of the Pulitzer Prize for journalism and fiction writing, haven't you?

I've learned here that they were reporting falsely about the Spanish to make them look bad and capitalize on all the Cuban supporters in the United States who might buy their papers. I figured this out because it said they wanted "to outsell the other" so they played up Spanish "atrocities." *Atrocities* are terrible acts of inhumanity, like the Nazis' concentration camps, and the word is in quotes, which tells me that it's being used in a sarcastic or exaggerated way. (*Loris reads the next sentence.*)

These are examples of the exaggerated stories about how the Spaniards were supposedly torturing helpless Cubans, throwing babies to sharks, and poisoning water. Because these are specific examples, I probably won't include them in my summary. (*Loris reads the last three sentences.*)

Okay, so the reporters made up the false stories, and the last example points up how far Hearst was willing to go. He would actually lie about a war between the U.S. and Spain just to sell more papers.

I noticed Remington was an illustrator. He's famous for his paintings of Western scenes, cowboys and Indians.

Now I'm going back to write a summary for this. First, I'm thinking about what the overall point is . . . something like how newspapers reported lies during the Cuban war of independence just to sell more papers. With this idea in mind, I'm going to *delete* some specific details here, like the fake stories of atrocities and the fact that the reporters sat in bars and thought up their stories, and even the last example about Hearst and a make-believe war. (*As she reported aloud on her thinking, she went to the board and crossed out the lines she wished to delete.*) Instead I want to group or *categorize* these things with an expression like, well, I could use this one: "The press printed false stories about Spanish atrocities."

So I might say in my summary (*Loris writes using a grease pencil and an overhead transparency while saying the words aloud*): "During the Cuban war of independence, major U.S. newspapers were competing with one another to sell the most papers. To do this, some papers printed false stories about Spanish atrocities."

Now, if it's important to remember that Hearst's and Pulitzer's papers were the primary ones engaged in false reporting, then I suppose they should be mentioned in the summary.

Student: You said that when we summarize, we should also look for topic sentences if the author gives them to us, so couldn't you just take the first three lines of that section, since they say just about what you've said?

Loris: They do sound similar, don't they? If those three sentences said it all for you, then I guess there would be no reason why you couldn't use them. But one thing I'm trying to encourage you all to do is to put the information into your own words as much as possible because, by paraphrasing, you can usually save on words and condense even more. I suppose if I were summarizing this entire chapter, then mention of the Cuban war of independence in my first sentence would not be necessary either, and I could cut it out.

Modeling Is Helpful in Teaching How to Summarize

As this session demonstrates, allowing students to eavesdrop on her thinking and decision making provided students with a model for interacting with Loris in constructing summaries for other pieces of text. Working and struggling together, they added and deleted information, created topic sentences, and tied together remaining ideas into condensed paragraphs.

It is important to begin strategy training with text that is relatively easy for students to understand so that they can concentrate on learning the strategy instead of being bogged down in trying to understand what they are reading. Loris likes to begin training by providing students with articles from popular magazines that are interesting and well organized. Eventually, students bring in their own articles to summarize, and gradually their practice includes passages and chapters from their textbooks.

Like other teachers who have taught students how to summarize, Loris uses a variety of activities to teach and reinforce the steps of summarization. Once students feel somewhat comfortable summarizing, Loris asks them to share their own summaries with their classmates to help each other. Figure 9.3 shows a record of Cheng, Juan, and Andrea, members of Loris's class, discussing Juan's summary of an article about a radical high school principal from New Hampshire.

Loris has also given students models of summaries to evaluate. We have used this activity and have found it productive to provide two or three versions of a summary, ask students to rank them from best to worst, and give a rationale for their decisions. This activity can be done in pairs or in small groups. In Chapter 7 there are additional examples of activities like the ones that Loris has used with her students.

STRATEGIES FOR TAKING CLASS NOTES

If you have ever wondered why it is so difficult for your students to take notes during class discussions or during one of your demonstrations of a concept, consider all the prerequisite skills involved in note taking. Students must be able to:

1. Paraphrase and summarize
2. Select key ideas and discard irrelevant details

Juan's Summary

> Dennis Little took over as principal of Thorne High School 6 years ago. Before he came and got involved the dropout rate was high, and reading and math scores were below average. Now that everything is up, the townspeople and the school board are trying to get rid of him because he is very intimate with students.

Cheng asked why the townspeople would want to get rid of Little when their students were doing better.

Juan: He's too close with the students.
Cheng: But it says here that he knows all the students and helps them out, like the girl who got pregnant when she was a junior and he helped her graduate and now she's in college.
Andrea: Sounds like a great principal to me. Ours just tells us to go to class and stuff like that.
Cheng: That's what I mean. If he's doing such a great job, why do they want to get rid of him?
Juan: I think this town is weird. They don't know how good Little is.
Andrea: I think what Cheng is asking is, is it only because Little's close to the students that they want him out, or is there something else?

Juan looked back over the article, studying certain sections intently.

Juan: It's a small town. They're set in their ways.
Cheng: Yeah, that's what I think. So how can you say that in your summary?
Juan: Something like, because he's so different and the town is so . . .
Andrea: Conservative.
Juan: Yeah, conservative, they want him out even though students like him and more are going to college.
Cheng: And fewer drop out, and they have higher reading and math scores, like you said already.
Juan: Okay, anything else you think I should change?
Andrea: I think you should say how Little made the change—you know, like where it says he raised discipline and academic standards.
Cheng: And he puts students first.

After assisting Juan with other minor concerns, his partners helped him rewrite his summary to read:

> Dennis Little took over as principal of Throne High School 6 years ago. Before he came the dropout rate was high, and reading and math scores were below average. Because he required high academic standards and discipline and got involved in students' lives, Little's students have made big improvements. But even though they have improved, the conservative townspeople and school board think Little doesn't set a good example, and they are trying to get rid of him.

FIGURE 9.3 Cooperative Group Interaction During Summary Writing

Taking Class Notes Is Difficult for Many Reasons

3. Establish purposes for listening or observing
4. Identify organizational patterns such as problem-solution or cause-effect
5. Record information quickly using abbreviations and symbols.

In addition to these skill prerequisites, students need some prior experiences or background information in order to make sense of the concepts being discussed or presented during class. In sum, taking class notes is a difficult skill for most middle school and high school students. In fact, note taking is a difficult skill for most college students (Simpson & Nist, 1997). Fortunately, this skill can be taught and reinforced across the content areas.

We have collected a variety of suggestions from content area instructors about how they teach notetaking. The following are some of the activities they use:

1. Begin the year with a discussion of your classroom note-taking expectations. Include the *why* of taking notes, whether notes will be checked by you, how notes will be utilized, and in what you would like the notes to be kept (i.e., in a spiral or three-ring notebook).
2. Discuss the qualities of good notes in your course. Include general physical formats, organization, and content. Show examples of your own class notes or previous students' notes via handouts, the overhead projector, a web page on the computer, or the bulletin board.

Content Area Teachers Can Use Framed Outlines to Help Students Take Class Notes

3. Model note-taking behaviors by using a **framed outline** during class. At the beginning of class, distribute a handout with the major points to be covered that day but with ample room for the development of your ideas. Specific cue words could be added for learning-disabled students (e.g., "The second step of the tennis serve"). Then deliver your presentation and fill in the major points and details on the framed outline using the overhead projector. Require students to add your notes to their framed outline. Repeat this procedure at least once a week and gradually reduce the cues until you no longer present the notes on the overhead or on the framed outline.
4. Teach the patterns of organizations that are common to your content area (e.g., comparison–contrast, sequence). For example, after discussing the problem–solution organizational format, the science teacher could deliver a brief lecture and assign students to note the nature of a problem, the courses of action proposed, and the advantages and disadvantages of the solutions.
5. Teach and model physical and verbal cues that teachers commonly use during class presentations. Include physical cues such as tone, facial expressions, pace, and gestures. Include verbal cues such as "Now we will consider the second point" or "In summary." Reserve time in class to discuss the students' notes to check if they recorded the important points that were cued.
6. Teach the common symbols and abbreviations and those unique to your specific content area. For example, students should be taught to use abbreviations such as *ex* to represent *examples* and = to represent the words *equals* or *equivalent.* And government teachers should teach students to use abbreviations such as *jud.* and *leg.* to represent the words *judiciary* and *legislation.*

In addition to these activities, it is important for content area teachers to continually reinforce the usefulness and advantages of taking class notes. Stu-

Students Must See Note Taking as Useful

dents will not continue to use a strategy unless they see it as effective and worthy of their effort (Paris et al., 1983). There are a variety of ways in which you can reinforce and reward your students' efforts in taking class notes. We particularly like these four ideas and have found them to be successful with middle school and high school students:

1. Give unannounced quizzes in which students can use their class notes. Make sure that the questions asked pertain to the information and concepts you presented during the class. Students will quickly learn that it is important to listen and take detailed, organized notes.
2. After some instruction on how to take class notes, collect students' notes without warning, either at the end of the class period or the next day. Evaluate the notes and then discuss them the next day with the students.
3. Have a weekly review of class notes. Ask questions that could be answered by using the notes. Points could be awarded for correct answers. This procedure could also be used at the beginning of each class period.
4. Provide students with class time to review their notes with a partner, especially after an important lesson or before a test or quiz.

The Split-Page Note-Taking Format

The Split-Page Strategy Can Be Used in Several Ways

Some content area teachers like their students to take class notes in a predictable format such as the **split-page format** (Palmatier, 1973). With this format, during class students record their notes on the right-hand side of a piece of paper. Later, perhaps as a class assignment, they write on the left-hand side of the paper key idea statements in order to reduce the information and to see the big picture. The notes in Figure 9.4 illustrate how one student used the split-page format in his math class. In addition to writing key idea statements in the left-hand margin, students could be assigned to incorporate key ideas from their textbooks or other sources. In that way, they can collect and synthesize all the information about a particular concept.

Bob, a 10th-grade biology teacher, teaches his students the split-page format. He begins by asking them to take notes during class in their usual fashion. This assignment provides him and his students with some self-assessment data. Samples of actual notes produced by students are put on the overhead projector and analyzed. Bob asks the students to consider the note samples relative to the goals of studying, which stimulates discussion of the relevance and transfer appropriateness of note-taking strategies. When he introduces split-page notes, he first describes the format; then, unrehearsed, he creates a set of notes. This gives students a view of Bob's thoughts and decisions during the note-taking process, similar to Loris's way of introducing her students to the summary-writing process. In addition, Bob demonstrates how he would study the notes by covering the right column and using the left-column entries as recall prompts, and vice versa.

"To Be Good Is Not Enough When You Dream of Being Great" 1/16/97 ①

What is the slope of a line tangent to $y=x^2$ at (x, x^2)?	* Problem Find the slope of a line tangent to the parabola $y=x^2$ at (x, x^2) Q $(x+h, (x+h)^2)$ P (x, x^2)
How do you find the slope of a tangent line?	* The slope of the line thru P + Q is given by $M_{PQ} = \frac{(x+h)^2 - x^2}{(x+h)-x}$ * To find the slope of a tangent line, let $h \to 0$. Equivalently, let Q tend to P.
Simplify the equation $x^2+2xh+h^2-x^2$	* Simplify $\frac{x^2+2xh+h^2-x^2}{h} = \frac{2xh+h^2}{h}$ $= \frac{h(2x+h)}{h} = 2x+h$ So: $M_{PQ} = 2x+h$

FIGURE 9.4 Sample of Split-Page Notes from a Math Course

When students take class notes, they are involved in several elaborative reading and critical thinking processes. These processes cannot be mastered in a week or two. We emphasize that if you believe a study strategy is worth teaching, students should be given the opportunity to learn it well. More important, students need to develop facility with the strategy so that they can personalize it to the task and the course in a controlled, comfortable manner. In the next section we discuss some strategies that will assist students in synthesizing information from multiple sources.

STRATEGIES FOR SYNTHESIZING CONTENT AREA CONCEPTS

Students Find It Very Difficult to Synthesize

Students have great difficulty organizing and synthesizing ideas from multiple sources (Nist, 1993). Thus, when you assign students to write a paper or present a speech using several outside sources, or when you ask them to combine their class notes with the information presented in their textbooks, what they produce will often be mediocre at best. Moreover, students may inadvertently resort to copying what they have read and listing these "borrowed ideas" without thinking about overall patterns or generalizations. What students need are organizational strategies that stimulate them to synthesize and think about content area generalizations. We will discuss three such strategies in this section: mapping, time lines, and synthesis journals. Other strategies explained elsewhere in this text, such as charting in Chapter 3, could certainly be used by students as an organizational strategy for reading and studying. The difference, however, is that students, not the content area teacher, create the chart.

Mapping

Carol, a learning disability resource-room teacher, was working recently with her students on study strategies. Instead of talking to them about strategies, she spent the day meeting with students individually to discover what their study needs were and how they were presently trying to meet those needs. While sitting with Mark, a congenial, conscientious 12th grader, she listened as he tried to explain the characteristics and relationships among the three major aspects of Freud's theory of personality. He was studying for a test in his psychology course. As Mark moved back and forth from *id* to *ego* to *superego,* Carol soon became lost and said, "I need to see what you're talking about. Can you draw me a picture?" As Mark drew and Carol questioned, they created a diagram to represent Freud's theory (Figure 9.5). When finished, they both looked at the diagram they had created and realized they had taken their understanding of the material to a new level. The diagram was an attempt to infer and make clear the organization and relationships in the content. Mark and Carol then talked about how students can create diagrams of complex material to use as study aids. Mark agreed that drawing out how ideas are related forces students to get their thoughts together.

Mark's discovery that creating a diagram of the material helped organize his thinking and provided a useful study aid is perhaps the best way to learn the value of the **mapping strategy.** Moreover, research has clearly demonstrated that it is a valuable strategy (Baumann & Kameenui, 1991). Like other elaborative study processes, however, mapping should not be taught as a series of steps that, when followed, will automatically lead to greater comprehension and retention. Instead, students should discover through experimentation an approach to mapping that is personally meaningful and appropriate to the study task. The reason is that there is actually no set way to map content. The material itself, the individual style and preference of the

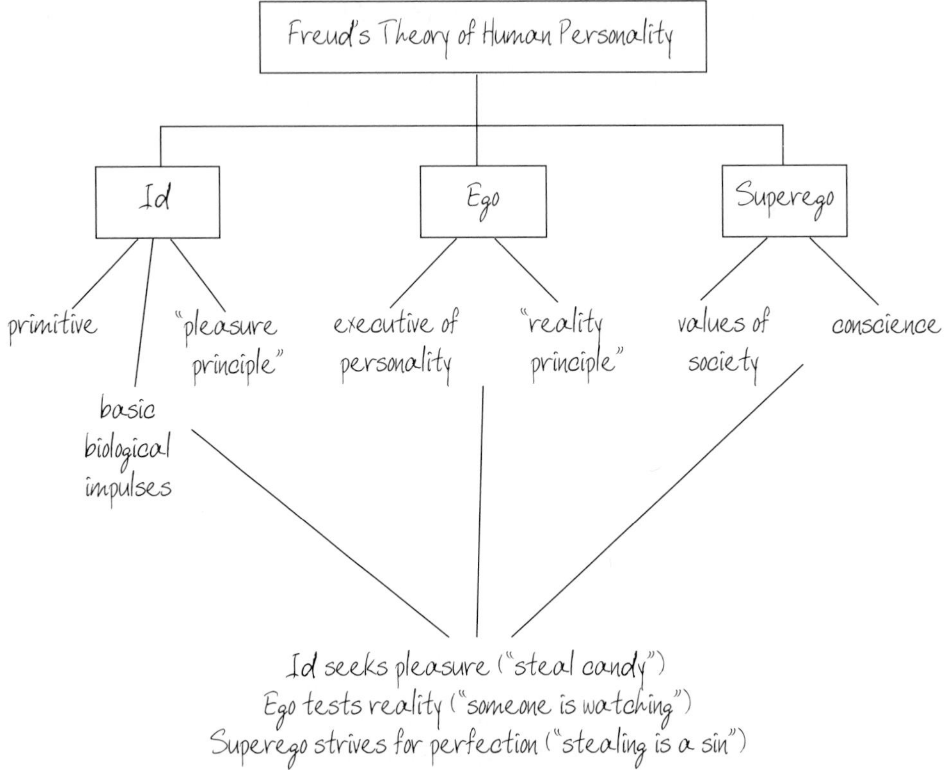

FIGURE 9.5 Map for Freud's Theory of Human Personality

reader, and the study demands will all influence any map design. Notice how the specific designs of the examples of maps in Figures 9.6 and 9.7 differ yet retain these common features:

- The major theme, topic, or concept is emphasized.
- Other important ideas, concepts, and terms are boxed, circled, or otherwise set off in some way.
- Lines are used to connect related ideas.
- Information becomes more specific as map lines radiate from the major theme or topic.

There Are Many Kinds of Maps

We encourage students who prefer to create maps and other diagrammatic representations of text to develop a sensitivity to the clues the author provides to the organization of the content so that they can create the most accurate and useful map. For example, some content may best be represented by a cycle or flow chart, whereas other content may best be summarized in a

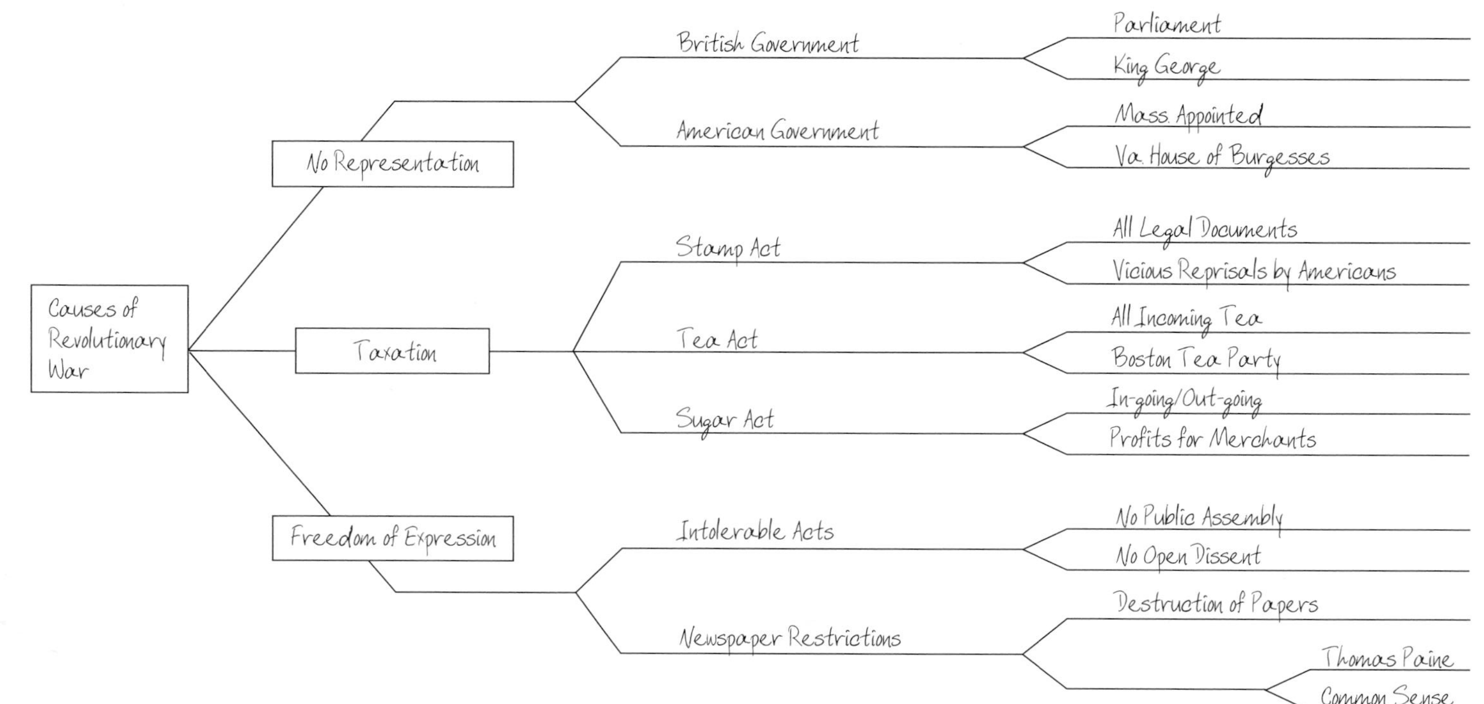

FIGURE 9.6 Map for the Causes of the Revolutionary War

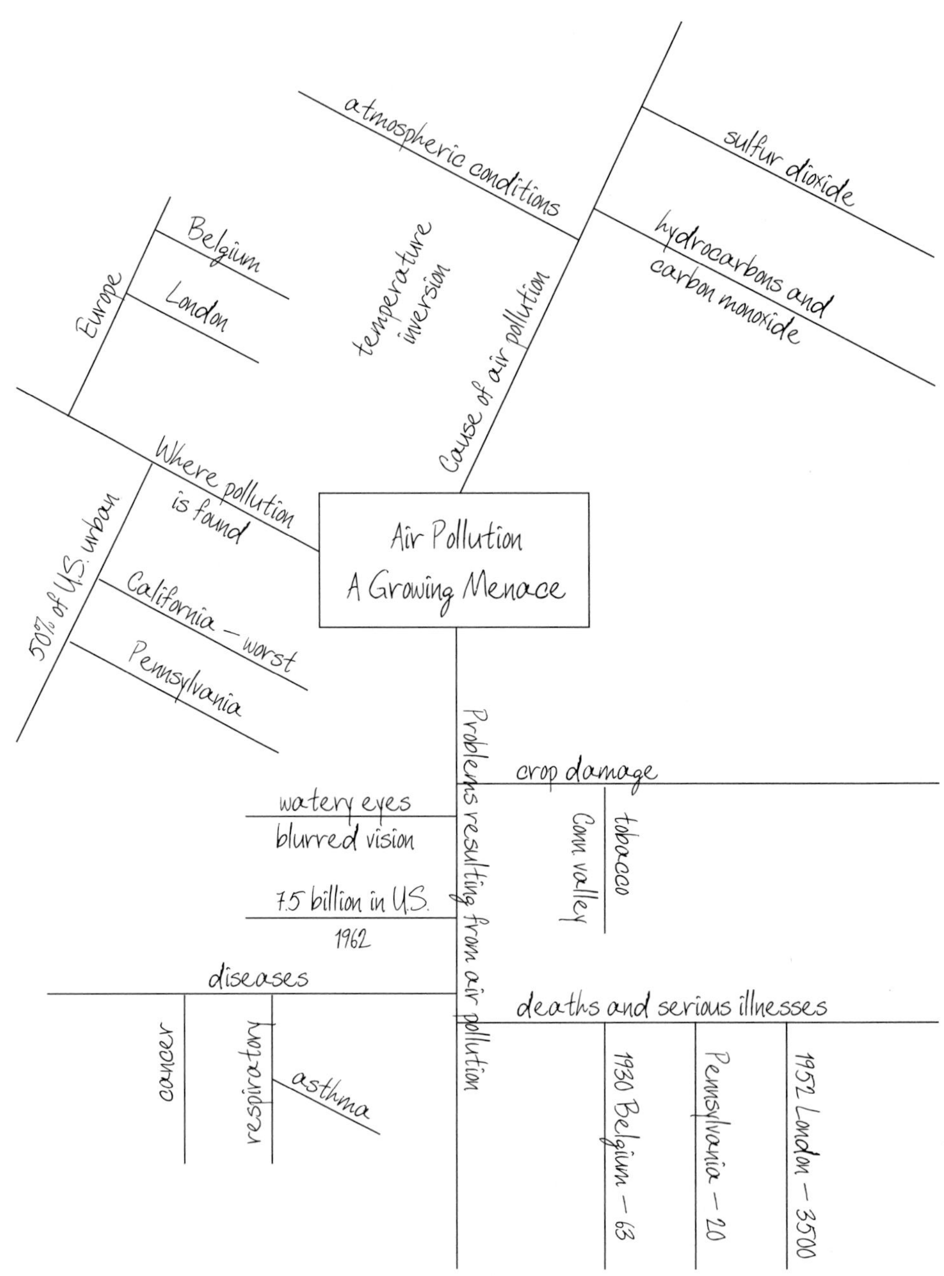

FIGURE 9.7 Map of a Chapter on Air Pollution

tree diagram. The following suggestions have also helped students as they map sections from their textbooks:

1. Read and think about the information before beginning to map.
2. Make sure you do not crowd your map with information because you want a memorable and precise image to study from. Consider using legal-size or computer paper and colored pencils and pens to differentiate ideas and make them stand out visually.
3. The act of constructing a map is a way of studying, but you will learn even more if you review your map by talking through the ideas.

Our experiences with teaching the mapping strategy have led us to believe that students either initially love the strategy or find it confusing and cumbersome. Hence, we have found it useful to encourage students to try out the strategy before rejecting it as a possible way to study. The best way to encourage students to try out any strategy is to begin with some very structured practice on easy, interesting material. With the mapping strategy, you can provide initial structure by asking students to complete a skeletal or unfinished map in small groups or pairs. Students can then discuss the experience and brainstorm ways to study from their finished product.

You may remember that a graphic organizer, useful as a readiness strategy (see Chapter 5), is a visual representation of the key vocabulary and concepts in a text that the teacher creates and gives to students. Although maps often strongly resemble graphic organizers, the major difference between the two is that maps are student generated. This is a critical difference. Providing students with organizational aids will promote learning; however, teaching students how to generate their own strategies will ensure that they become successful independent learners. As teachers, we need to determine how to walk that fine line between providing and promoting content area learning.

Time Lines

Timelines Can Be Formatted in a Variety of Ways

Time lines can be used in any course where it is important for students to understand a sequence or chronology of events. As with mapping, the act of constructing a time line helps students organize and synthesize ideas, especially if they come from multiple sources such as a textbook, a lecture, and a newspaper article. In Kent's 11th-grade English class, he teaches a unit on the struggle for civil and economic rights in the United States. In this way he can ask his students to read a variety of essays, short stories, poems, and novels that illustrate differing perspectives and ideas. One of the unit activities that students can select is the time line. Charisse and Erik, two of Kent's students, created the time line in Figure 9.8 after viewing a television documentary and reading the book *The Autobiography of Malcolm X* (Haley, 1964). Their time line arranged important events during the 1960s and 1970s vertically, but time lines can also be arranged in a horizontal fashion. As with the chart or any other organizational strategy, Charisse and Erik learned a considerable

1960	Sit-in at a lunch counter, Greensboro, NC.
1962	Meredith tries to enter U. of MS; Kennedy sends forces and two die, many are injured in disagreement.
1963	MLK campaigns against discrimination in Birmingham, AL; violence against peaceful demonstrators.
	Governor Wallace of AL tries to stop blacks from entering the U. of AL.
	Kennedy on television pleads for civil rights legislation.
	MLK leads (August) 200,000 peaceful demonstrators in the "March on Washington."
	Medgar Evers, a civil rights worker, is shot in MS.
	Explosion in a Baptist Church kills four black girls in Birmingham.
	Malcolm X becomes national spokesperson for Black Muslims.
1964	Civil Rights Act of 1964.
	24th Amendment.
	MLK wins Nobel Peace Prize.
	Voter registration effort begins in Mississippi; blacks and Northern whites work together; three are killed.
	Mississippi Freedom Democratic Party sends delegation to national Democratic Convention; refused seating.
	Malcolm X goes to England.
1965	Student Nonviolent Coordinating Committee (SNCC) launches new tactic, voter registration drives in AL; Black Panther Party is started.
	Violence in Selma, AL, as MLK, Malcolm X, and S. Carmichael register voters.
	Johnson sends through Congress Voting Rights Act of 1965.
	Riots in Watts, Los Angeles.
	Malcolm X is shot.
1966	Voter registration in Lowndes County, MS.
	SNCC and S. Carmichael criticize MLK's methods.
	Meredith begins march from Memphis to Jackson, MS (March Against Fear) and is shot. MLK and Carmichael continue march for him, and 4,000 blacks are registered to vote. This is the last great march in the South. The movement now moves North.
1967	Riots in Newark, NJ, and Detroit; 43 people die.
1968	MLK is killed.

FIGURE 9.8 Civil Rights Time Line During the 1960s and Early 1970s

amount of information merely from the decisions they had to make about formatting, identifying, and arranging the events.

Synthesis Journals

Synthesis journals (McAlexander & Burrell, 1996) are not really journals per se but a format that encourages students to identify, organize, and then synthesize various perspectives on an issue. As illustrated in Figure 9.9, when completing a synthesis journal, students determine and then write in the appropriate place

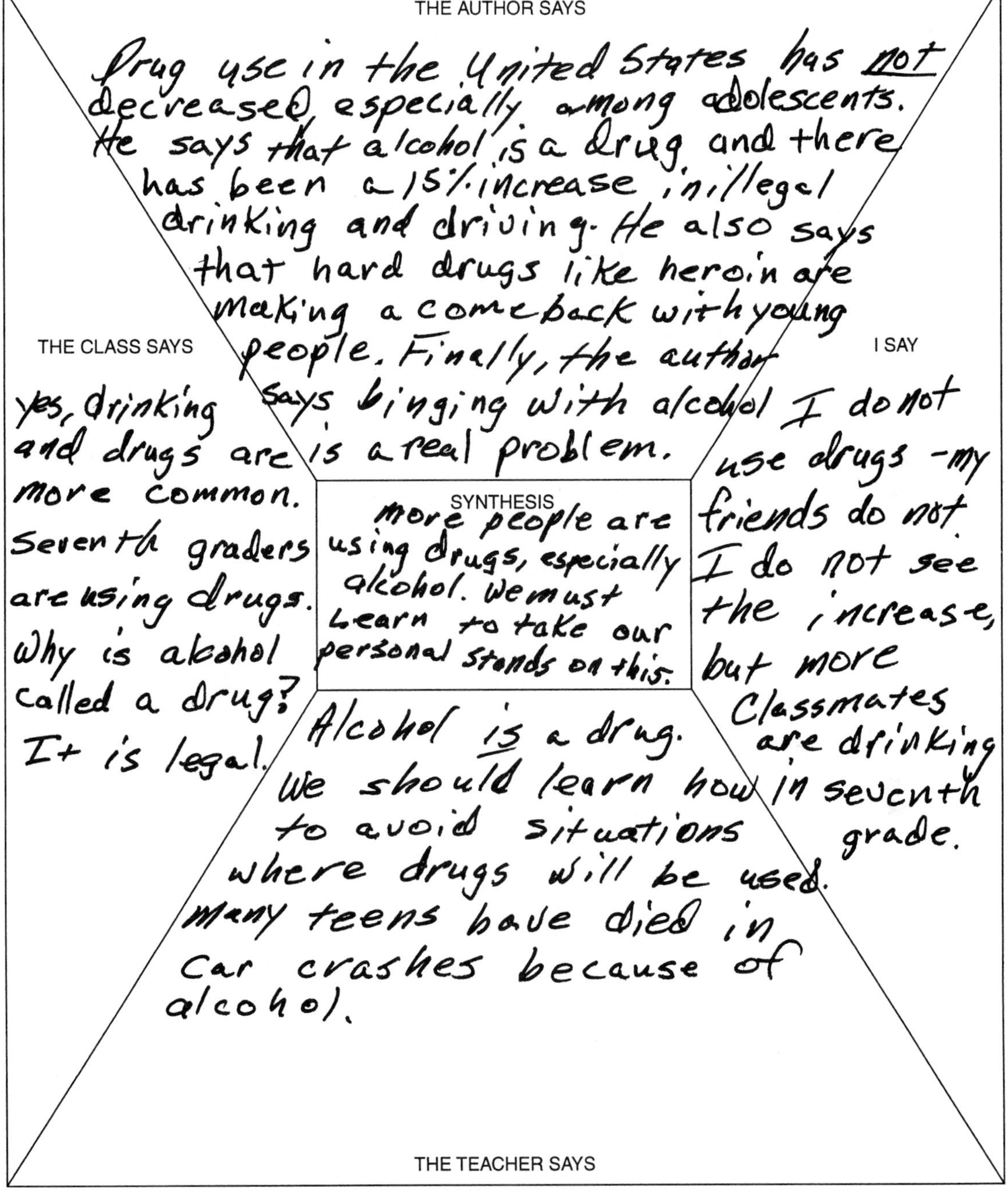

THE AUTHOR SAYS

Drug use in the United States has not decreased especially among adolescents. He says that alcohol is a drug and there has been a 15% increase in illegal drinking and driving. He also says that hard drugs like heroin are making a comeback with young people. Finally, the author says binging with alcohol is a real problem.

THE CLASS SAYS

yes, drinking and drugs are more common. Seventh graders are using drugs. Why is alcohol called a drug? It is legal.

I SAY

I do not use drugs -my friends do not. I do not see the increase, but more Classmates are drinking in seventh grade.

SYNTHESIS

more people are using drugs, especially alcohol. We must Learn to take our personal stands on this.

THE TEACHER SAYS

Alcohol is a drug. We should learn how to avoid situations where drugs will be used. Many teens have died in car crashes because of alcohol.

FIGURE 9.9 A Synthesis Journal

the viewpoints and statements of authors they have read, of their teacher, of their classmates, and finally, their personal viewpoints. The center is reserved for the students to synthesize the viewpoints and then write a generalization. The synthesis journal entry in Figure 9.9 was created by a seventh grader during a unit in his health course about drug use and adolescents.

Synthesis journals obviously have many advantages. Not only do they encourage students to think critically about an issue and synthesize multiple sources, but they also stimulate students to identify and explain various perspectives, a problem many middle school and high school students have with their writing (McAlexander & Burrell, 1996). Moreover, synthesis journals give students a strategy that assists them in taking notes during discussions. Far too often, what the teacher says in class during a discussion becomes more important than what other classmates say about the issue being discussed. In fact, we have observed students' note-taking behaviors during discussions and discovered that they rarely took notes. If they did, they included only what the teacher said. The synthesis journal validates students' viewpoints as well as the teacher's. Finally, the synthesis journal provides content area teachers who may use only a few written sources in their classrooms with a strategy for students to use in summarizing and thinking about ideas that have been presented orally during a unit. For example, under the "Author Says" column in Figure 9.9, students could write the ideas and viewpoints presented in a video, film, or class presentation by a guest speaker.

Synthesis Journals Help Students Think Critically

Although there are many ways in which to use the synthesis journal with your students, Adrian, a seventh-grade health teacher, likes to begin by explaining to the students the purpose of the format. She tells them that every perspective on a controversial issue deserves consideration; the synthesis journal recognizes and supports these viewpoints. For a unit on drug abuse and teenagers, Adrian began by asking the students to read an article from a local newspaper about two well-known high school students, a football player and a cheerleader, who died in a car accident while under the influence of alcohol. She tells them to briefly summarize the article and write it in the "Author Says" section. For students who tend to write too much or have difficulty summarizing key ideas, she suggests that they think about these questions before they start writing: (1) What is the topic of this assignment? (2) What does the author say about the topic? and (3) How does the author explain, support, and defend his or her position on this topic?

The next day in class, Adrian begins the discussion by asking students to share what they have written in their synthesis journals about the author's viewpoint. Before she invites students to share their own perspectives in a class discussion, she asks them to complete the "I Say" corner. Because Adrian reserves the synthesis journal for the more controversial issues in her health course, it does not take much prompting for students to voice their opinions after writing them. Perhaps the most difficult part of the lesson is to stop the discussion so that students will take the time to record what other students believe in the "Class Members Say" section. Adrian leads the discussion but also offers her viewpoints, giving her seventh graders opportunities to fill in the last section—"The Teacher Says."

During the last 15 minutes of class, Adrian asks the students to fill in the middle section, "Synthesis." Because this synthesis was initially difficult for her students, Adrian explained what was meant by a synthesis and then modeled the process for them on an easier topic. In addition, she described how other students had completed their "Synthesis" section on issues they had discussed in her health course. The next day in class, Adrian likes to have students share what they have written. For this unit on drugs, she had students meet with their study partners to read each other's entries. Adrian's unit did not end with the synthesis journal, but it certainly started it in the right direction. She believes that the synthesis journal, like the Discussion Web, encourages her students to think critically about highly charged issues like the ones she addresses in her health course.

The three study strategies discussed in this section will definitely help students master content area concepts and encourage their active learning. Because metacognitive awareness is also an essential characteristic of active learners, in the next section we examine strategies for developing this characteristic.

STRATEGIES FOR CREATING METACOGNITIVE AWARENESS

As we stated in Chapter 2, active learners are metacognitively aware, that is, they monitor and evaluate their own reading, studying, and learning. The strategies we discuss in this section—self-generated questions, talk-throughs, and strategy evaluation—should definitely help middle school and high school students to become more metacognitively aware.

Self-Questioning Strategies for Expository Text

Students Must Be Taught How to Ask Effective Questions

Tom Newkirk says that our schools develop "polite readers" who are "deferentially literate. . . . Like good guests, they do not ask impertinent questions" (1982, p. 455). Instead of encouraging students to ask their own questions, teachers typically ask the questions or the text provides questions at the end of the selection. These questioning practices convey a number of messages to students: (1) what appears in print is unassailable, (2) the teacher's and the text's questions are the important ones, and (3) comprehension cannot be monitored. Yet the ability to generate and then answer appropriate questions is essential to becoming metacognitively aware (King, 1992; Pressley, 1995).

One strategy for increasing students' active processing of text is to teach them how to pose and then answer task-relevant questions about what they study. Because nearly every form of testing comprises questions, asking and answering questions while studying makes good sense. The key, of course, is knowing the kinds of questions to ask.

Students can learn how to ask thought-provoking questions by using high-utility stems as question starters (King, 1992). The following question stems are useful in most content areas:

1. In my own words . . . what does this term mean?
2. What are the author's key ideas?
3. What is an example of . . . ?
4. How would you use . . . to . . . ?
5. What is a new or different example of . . . ?
6. In my own words, explain why. . . .
7. How does . . . affect . . . ?
8. What are the results or consequences of . . . ?
9. What are the likenesses between . . . and . . . ?
10. How is . . . different from . . . ?
11. What are the advantages of . . . ?
12. What are the disadvantages/limitations of . . . ?
13. What are the functions of . . . ?
14. What are the characteristics of . . . ?
15. Do I agree or disagree with this statement: . . . ?
16. What were the contributions/influences of . . . ?
17. How would you evaluate . . . ?

Question Stems Can Help Students Ask Good Questions

Asking Good Questions Can Impact Students' Learning

King found that students working in pairs who generated elaborative answers to question stems like those in the preceding list perform better on a content area objective test than those who did not.

Students have options in organizing and answering their questions about expository text. They could, as did the subjects in King's studies, meet in pairs and quiz each other. They could also write their questions and answers in a format that encourages self-testing. One such format is the questions–answers strategy.

Questions–Answers Strategy

Figure 9.10 illustrates how one student used the **questions–answers strategy** to prepare for a test in an ecology course. When the questions and answers are written and organized this way, students can test themselves by folding the paper in half and reading the questions aloud. They can also test each other because a permanent written artifact is available for them to share. Because the questions–answers strategy is written, it also can be handed in to teachers for their feedback. For example, by looking at the students' self-generated questions, teachers can determine what misconceptions or difficulties students are encountering with a particular concept.

Questions	Answers
1. What is the major source of solid waste? 2. What is the effect of silting on our environment? 3. What causes acid mine drainage? 4. What is the danger of acid mine waste? 5. Why was DDT banned? 6. What chemical compound affects the central nervous system of humans and animals? 7. What is the specific problem associated with thermal pollution? 8. Give an example of a material that is *not* biodegradable.	Agriculture Silting reduces oxygen production and the food supply for fish; also fouls spawning beds of fish.

FIGURE 9.10 Questions–Answers Strategy in Preparing for a Test

Questions like the ones in Figure 9.10 do not spout from students' mouths at the first try. In fact, we have found that modeling, coaching, and specific feedback are necessary in teaching students how to ask and answer meaningful questions. One math teacher we know distributes index cards to his students and requires them to write a question every day of the year. He collects the cards, groups the questions, and then responds to them at the beginning of class. Although it may take time to teach this strategy, the results are worth the effort because students learn how to control and monitor their own learning. In the next section, we discuss how this strategy can be modified to narrative text.

Narrative Text and Self-Generated Questions

In Chapters 2 and 3, we presented the idea that texts have predictable structures and that we can teach students to take advantage of inherent properties of text to improve their reading and studying. One way to capitalize on the predictable rhetorical structure of narratives is to ask and answer questions related to story elements. The following are typical of the kinds of questions that could be asked:

1. Who is the main character?
2. What did you learn about the main character from his actions? From what he said? From what others said about him?
3. How is the setting important to this story? Could this story have taken place somewhere else?
4. What are the goals of the main character? Of the supporting characters?
5. How does the main character attempt to achieve these goals?

6. Is the main character successful in reaching his goals?
7. What is the author saying about human nature?

Singer and Donlan (1982) devised such a set of story-structure questions and taught them to 11th-grade students. They found that compared with a group of students who simply read and reread, the students who asked questions of the story elements have a more complete understanding of the stories.

An 11th-grade literature teacher taught his students to use the story-structure questions as a basis for creating their own questions. The teacher emphasized that this questioning process could be useful for understanding the stories they would read in their literature text, which in turn would aid them in class discussion and on examinations. To reinforce the relevance of this study strategy, the connection between these criterion tasks and studying stories through questioning was made explicit by giving the students typical discussion and exam questions and relating them to specific questions based on the story-structure questions. Modeling the process of question construction, the teacher described how he created specific questions to prompt his understanding of essential elements in simple, familiar stories. He then asked students to work in small groups to generate questions for other simple, familiar stories. Gradually, students began working with the stories from their literature anthology. Figure 9.11 illustrates one group's set of questions developed for Hemingway's "The Short Happy Life of Francis Macomber," a short story in their literature anthology.

The Leading Character

Who is Francis Macomber?
What do we learn about him from what Wilson and Margot say about and to him?
What do we learn from what the author says about him?

The Goal

Why does Macomber want to kill the lion?
What does this reveal about Macomber's personality?

The Obstacles

What prevents Macomber from killing the lion?
Why does Macomber go after the buffalo with such a vengeance?

The Outcome

Why did Macomber run from the grass when the lion charged?
What does this reveal about his character?
Was Margot trying to shoot Macomber or the buffalo?

The Theme

Macomber's struggle is with himself and his self-confidence. He also struggles with the forces of nature in the lion and buffalo. And he struggles with his wife because of what she thinks about him.

FIGURE 9.11 Story-Specific Questions Based on Story-Structure Questions for Hemingway's "The Short Happy Life of Francis Macomber"

What is most impressive about story-structure questions is that they reflect the student's attempt to personalize and control the questioning process. Students learned that questioning can be modified to match the structure of a story and to focus their attention on its most important aspects.

The Talk-Through

If you have ever verbally rehearsed what you wanted to tell the life insurance agent who kept pestering you with phone calls, you have conducted a talk-through. A **talk-through** is a study strategy that involves verbal rehearsal of content area concepts (Simpson, 1994). Many of the study strategies previously discussed (e.g., timelines, mapping) rely on written products. The talk-through, by contrast, involves students in expressing and explaining themselves orally. In fact, the talk-through is very much like teaching, except that the audience is imaginary. We tell students that when they conduct talk-throughs, they should imagine themselves giving a lecture on a topic to a very uninformed audience.

Since most of us have used informal talk-throughs to practice delivering important information, it is not surprising to learn that talk-throughs, as a study strategy, can improve understanding and remembering of content area concepts. Simpson's (1994) research demonstrated that students who had been trained to generate talk-throughs performed significantly better on an objective exam (i.e., multiple-choice and true-false) and an essay exam than their counterparts who were not so trained. Even more interesting was the finding that these students predicted more accurately their overall performance on the test and on each item. In other words, the subjects who did talk-throughs were more metacognitively aware of their performance on the exam than their counterparts.

Talk-Throughs Can Be Used in Many Content Areas

Talk-throughs can be used in any content area, but they must be tailored to the demands of the course. Depending on the course, a talk-through could contain any of the following information:

1. Key ideas, using the student's own words
2. Examples, characteristics, processes, steps, causes, effects
3. Personal or creative reactions
4. Summary statement or generalizations
5. Personal applications or examples

Consequently, an effective talk-through in an American history class would probably differ from an effective talk-through in a geometry or physical education course.

Ann, an algebra teacher, has found that students profit from using the talk-through strategy in her classes, especially when it comes to internalizing the steps for solving word problems. She begins the school year by teaching the following steps to her students:

1. Read the problem carefully, underlining key words or phrases.
2. Reword the problem using the necessary facts.
3. Ask yourself, What problem do I have to solve? What is unknown?

4. Translate the reworded problem into an equation.
5. Solve the equation.
6. Check the answer by substituting the answer in the equation. Ask yourself, Does this answer make sense?
7. State the answer to the problem clearly.

Talk-Throughs Can Include Visual Aids

Ann posts these seven steps on her bulletin board and distributes them to every student on a bookmark. Throughout the first 9 weeks, she provides her own talk-throughs on how to implement the seven steps with sample problems taken from the textbook. However, Ann has added an extra dimension to the talk-through: She uses the chalkboard as a support to her talk-through, sketching situations and setting up equations from the word problems. She has found that the verbal and visual involvement of the talk-through has greatly increased her students' attention and subsequent learning.

The following is an example of a talk-through that one of Ann's students, Damien, did in class with his study partner:

> This is the problem. "As a chef's assistant in a fancy restaurant, Kendra earns in 1 year a salary of $19,000. This is two fifths of the head chef's salary. What is the head chef's salary?" First, I will reword the problem. Two fifths of the head chef's salary is Kendra's salary. I was able to reword the problem because I knew that the word *this* in the second sentence referred to Kendra's salary. I also took out the extra words and reduced the problem to just the necessary facts and words.
>
> Second, I will translate these 10 words into symbols and numbers to create an equation. My goal for this problem is to find the chef's salary, which I do not know. Thus, I will represent this *unknown* with an X (he uses the chalkboard to do this and to reinforce the rest of his talk-through). I do know Kendra's salary: It is $19,000. I also know that two fifths of the chef's salary, or 2/5 of X or 2/5 *times* X, is $19,000. Or, stated in another way, 2/5 times X = $19,000 *or* 2/5 ($X$) = $19,000. I used the parentheses to stand for "multiplied by." Now I am ready to solve the problem, which is step five of the process.

Although many of the math problems in Ann's class could probably be answered without using the seven steps or the talk-through, Ann believes that verbal rehearsal on the simple problems will help students later on in the school year with the more demanding problems.

We have found, from our experiences with the talk-through strategy, that it helps to explain to students the steps in developing an effective talk-through. A talk-through, like Damien's, involved considerable cognitive and metacognitive effort and planning. The following steps, while generic, can be modified according to the content area:

1. Think about the key ideas, trends, issues, and problems. Make sure you are using your own words when you explain them.

2. Organize the key ideas in some way. This can be done on an index card, but be brief because these notes are meant only to prompt your memory.
3. Find a quiet place, close your textbook or class notes, and use your card to deliver your talk-through out loud.
4. After practicing your first talk-through, check your card to make sure you were precise and complete. Ask yourself if you made sense.
5. Find someone to listen to your talk-through. Ask them if you made sense.

Because Ann knows that her students will not use the talk-through strategy unless they find it has more benefits than costs, she asks them to generate a list of advantages to the strategy after they have used it several times. The following comments typify what Ann's students and other students have seen as the advantages of the talk-through strategy: (1) Talk-throughs help me determine what information I know and what information is still unclear. (2) Talk-throughs improve my understanding of key terms because I am using my own words. (3) Talk-throughs help store information in my long-term memory. (4) Talk-throughs make me more actively involved in my learning.

Encouraging Students to Evaluate

Active Learners Know How to Evaluate

Active learners reflect upon the strategies they have employed and evaluate whether these strategies were appropriate for the task and content area (Butler & Winne, 1995). In addition, active learners determine whether their self-selected strategies were appropriate for themselves as learners and make adjustments, when necessary, to remedy the situation and improve their academic performance. Reflecting and evaluating in this manner are highly sophisticated processes that make students even more metacognitively aware and successful in their independent learning across the content areas (Butler & Winne, 1995; Nist & Simpson, 1989).

There are a variety of techniques that content area teachers can use to encourage their students to reflect and evaluate. One effective technique is to ask students to write a brief evaluation paragraph once they have finished taking a test in your class. In this paragraph, students would address some or all of the following questions:

Questions Students Can Ask Themselves as They Evaluate Their Performances

1. Was the exam what you expected? Explain.
2. What grade do you think you will receive on this exam?
3. Did you follow a study plan? Explain why or why not.
4. How long did you study? When did you begin your serious studying? Did you cram at the last minute?
5. Describe how you read and studied. For example, did you reread? Solve problems? Memorize?
6. What strategies worked best for you? Explain.
7. What strategies did not seem to help you? Explain.

8. If you could take this exam over, how would you change your reading and studying behaviors and strategies?
9. If you could take this exam over, what strategies would you continue to use?
10. Did you learn anything about yourself as a learner from this test? If so, what?

If you tell students that it is important to be honest in giving their answers, and if you take the time to evaluate their performance and the strategies they used, you will gain some very useful assessment information about them. More important, by thinking about these questions, your students will realize that they are the ones in control of their academic performance, not you.

Kim, a 10th-grade biology teacher, asked her students to answer the first five evaluation questions before she handed back their scores on the first exam. Then, after discussing the exam during class and going over the answers, Kim asked them to answer the second five questions. One student, Jason, wrote the following evaluation paragraphs, labeled *before* and *after.* As you read them, think about his strengths and weaknesses as an active learner.

Jason's Evaluation Paragraphs

> *BEFORE:* Well, I predict that I will get an A on this test. I have always been smart in science. The test was about what I expected—not too hard, not too easy. I didn't think we would have to diagram the female reproductive cycle—that was a surprise. I studied by skimming the chapters and looking at my notes during homeroom. I probably studied about 10 minutes—science is my thing, so I really did not need to study much. By the way, did we talk in class about the regulation of glucose?
>
> *AFTER:* Well, I guess I did not do as well as I predicted—I got a D on the test. I missed all the questions on the diagrams. My other science teachers never asked me to label and explain diagrams. I probably should have read the chapters rather than skimming them. I also should have looked at my class notes longer. If I could take the test again, I would certainly study longer, and I would memorize those diagrams you discussed with us in class. Otherwise, if I could take this test over, I probably would not change my strategies that much. I learned from this first test that biology may be different from general science.

What did you learn about Jason? What did you decide his strengths were? His weaknesses? After receiving Jason's evaluation paragraph, Kim hypothesized that Jason was not using active strategies for studying. He was merely skimming or looking at material—very passive strategies. Because Kim requires her students to integrate concepts, Jason's strategies were definitely not appropriate for the thinking processes she emphasizes in her course. Moreover, Jason probably was not listening very intently in class because Kim had stressed the importance of studying the diagrams and being able to explain how hormones interact with each other. Kim decided to watch Jason carefully and to work on his definitions of what it means to read and study in a biology course. We know from our teaching experiences that you will learn similar information about your students if you ask them to evaluate their strategies and approaches in your content area.

CASE STUDY REVISITED

Return to the beginning of the chapter, where we described Khaled, the English teacher assigned to teach study strategies. After reading this chapter, you probably have some ideas about how he could be more creative and effective in his teaching. Take time now to write your suggestions.

Khaled decided that his present approach of using a workbook to teach study strategies needed modification. His most important realization was that he had no idea of what strategies his ninth graders needed to know to be successful learners in their other courses. Khaled therefore decided to talk with his colleagues and visit some of their classes during his planning period to determine the tasks they assigned or the academic demands they made on their students. He also borrowed textbooks from the teachers and read a chapter in each. By doing this, he determined what the students were being asked to read.

Armed with this information and with comments from the students, he decided to downplay the importance of the workbook. As he explained to his department chairperson, "The students do not like the workbook, and neither do I. Commercial materials are not relevant to what students are being asked to do in their other courses. They do not typically read short passages and answer questions about the main idea and tone. If I am to teach students how to study, then I should teach them using the materials they are expected to master."

During the school year, Khaled also read a few articles about the teaching of study strategies in professional publications such as the *Journal of Adolescent and Adult Learning.* From his reading, he realized that he needed to teach strategies more directly rather than merely assigning students to complete activities. One teaching technique he found particularly intriguing was modeling, or the think-aloud. After looking through the units he used to teach, he decided that he would probably have to teach less material but in more depth if he wanted his students to modify and transfer the strategies to their own courses.

During the summer, Khaled planned his curriculum, making sure that he would emphasize basic processes or techniques, such as knowing the parts of a textbook, that students could use in all classes. He also included content-specific strategies such as how to read and solve a word problem in mathematics. He knew his goal was to show his students how to become active learners rather than passive memorizers.

We caught up with Khaled at the end of the first quarter, and he filled us in on what he perceived, thus far, to be his successful units as well as his failures. On the positive side, Khaled thought his unit on teaching the students how to use their textbook and how to preview was well received by the students and the other ninth-grade teachers. In fact, the civics teacher was so thrilled that her students this year knew how to use the index, appendix, and glossary of her textbook that she agreed to reinforce the preview strategy in her class. Khaled and his students also thought the unit on solving mathematical problems was successful.

Khaled also spent considerable time teaching his students to summarize sections in their textbooks. He learned, however, not to have them practice a difficult new process with material they find demanding. The first time he taught summarization, he told the students to summarize a section from their biology textbook. The lesson was a complete disaster. Some students did not do it, and others became frustrated and resorted to almost verbatim copying from their textbook rather than paraphrasing. After analyzing the problem, Khaled realized that his students were struggling with the process of summarization and certainly did not need the added stress of a difficult text to confound the situation. He replaced the textbook with an interesting, well-organized article about gene splicing from the newspaper. This easier, more accessible material made all the difference.

As Khaled looks to the next quarter, he is excited. His students participate more in class and do not complain as much about their assignments, even though they are probably doing more work than they did when they completed workbook pages. Many of his students are reading and listening more actively, but some are not monitoring their understanding. With those students he hopes to introduce self-questioning. He also plans to introduce the mapping strategy to the students who have resisted the idea of summarizing. The first quarter has taught Khaled many things. Most important, he has realized that students will not be able to transfer study strategies to their own tasks if they do nothing but complete workbook activities.

■ ■ ■

SUMMARY

Study strategies should be taught as processes instead of as a series of steps that, when followed, will automatically produce greater learning and retention. We have emphasized the learner as an important part of strategy instruction. Without giving students opportunities to help shape the study strategies they are being taught, we run the risk of offering them a series of meaningless formulas that have little relevance to their genuine study needs. This has important implications for content area teachers who want their students to be active rather than passive learners. Your role should be to inform students of each study process and its best possible applications, and then to guide them in developing personally meaningful adaptations that transfer to actual study tasks.

We purposely limited our presentation to a few effective study-reading processes because we wish to reiterate the idea that it takes a great deal of time to develop expertise in using them. We also made it clear that no single text-study strategy will be appropriate for every study need. Consequently, students should be encouraged to learn a few flexible, meaningful study processes so that they can select the most appropriate one for their purposes and tasks. Finally, we stressed that the development of strategic, active learning should be the goal of every content area teacher.

REFERENCES

Berkowitz, S. (1986). Effects of instruction in text organization on sixth-grade students' memory for expository reading. *Reading Research Quarterly, 21,* 161-178.

Brown, A. L., & Day, J. (1983). Macrorules for summarizing texts: The development of expertise. *Journal of Verbal Learning and Verbal Behavior, 22,* 1-14.

Butler, D. L., & Winne, P. H. (1995). Feedback and self-regulated learning: A theoretical synthesis. *Review of Educational Research, 65,* 245-281.

Calkins, L. M. (1986). *The art of teaching writing.* Portsmouth, NH: Heinemann.

Doyle, W. (1983). Academic work. *Review of Educational Research, 53,* 159-199.

Dweck, C. S. (1986). Motivational processing affecting learning. *American Psychologist, 41,* 1040-1048.

Garner, R. (1988). *Metacognition and reading.* Norwood, NJ: Ablex.

Haley, A. (1964). *The autobiography of Malcolm X.* New York: Ballantine Books.

Hare, V. C. (1992). Summarizing text. In J. Irwin & M. Doyle (Eds.), *Reading/writing connections: Learning from research.* Newark, DE: International Reading Association.

Keith, T. Z., Reimers, T. M., Fehrmann, P. G., Pottebau, S. M., & Aubey, L. W. (1986). Parental involvement, homework, and TV time: Direct and indirect effects on high school achievement. *Journal of Educational Psychology, 78,* 373-380.

King, A. (1992). Enhancing peer interaction and learning in the classroom through reciprocal questioning. *American Educational Research Journal, 27,* 664-687.

McAlexander , P., & Burrell, K. (1996). *Helping students "get it together" with the synthesis journal.* Paper presented at the annual conference of the National Association of Developmental Education, Little Rock, AR.

Neuman, S. B. (1988). Enhancing children's comprehension through previewing. In J. E. Readence & R. S. Baldwin (Eds.), *Dialogues in literacy research. Thirty-seventh yearbook of the National Reading Conference.* Chicago: National Reading Conference.

Newkirk, T. (1982). Young writers as critical readers. *Language Arts, 59,* 451-457.

Nist, S. L. (1993, Fall-Winter). What literature says about academic literacy. *Georgia Journal of Reading,* 11-18.

Nist, S. L., & Simpson, M. L. (1989). PLAE: A validated study strategy. *Journal of Reading, 33,* 182-186.

Nist, S. L., Simpson, M. L., Olejnik, S., & Mealey, D. L. (1991). The relation between self-selected study processes and test performance. *American Educational Research Journal, 28,* 849-874.

Palmatier, R. A. (1973). A notetaking system for learning. *Journal of Reading, 17,* 36-39.

Paris, S. G., Lipson, M. Y., & Wixson, K. K. (1983). Becoming a strategic reader. *Contemporary Educational Psychology, 8,* 293-316.

Pintrich, P. R., & Garcia, T. (1994). Self-regulated learning in college students: Knowledge, strategies, and motivation. In P. R. Pintrich, D. R. Brown, & C. E. Weinstein (Eds.), *Students motivation, cognition, and learning.* Hillsdale, NJ: Erlbaum.

Pradl, G. (1987). Close encounters of the first kind: Teaching the poem at the point of utterance. *English Journal, 76,* 66–69.

Pressley, M. (1995). More about the development of self-regulation: Complex, long-term, and thoroughly social. *Educational Psychologist, 30,* 207–212.

Simpson, M. L. (1994). Talk throughs: A strategy for encouraging active learning across the content areas. *Journal of Reading, 38,* 296–304.

Simpson, M. L., Hynd, C. R., Nist, S. L., & Burrell, K. I. (1997). College academic assistance programs and practices. *Educational Psychology Review, 9,* 39–87.

Simpson, M. L., & Nist, S. L. (1990). Textbook annotation: An effective and efficient study strategy for college students. *Journal of Reading, 34,* 122–131.

Simpson, M. L., & Nist, S. L. (1992). A case study of academic literacy tasks and their negotiation in a university history course. In C. Kinzer & D. Leu (Eds.), *Literacy research, theory, and practice: Views from many perspectives. Forty-first yearbook of the National Reading Conference.* Chicago: National Reading Conference.

Simpson, M. L., & Nist, S. L. (1997). Perspectives on learning history: A case study. *Journal of Literacy Research, 39,* 363–395.

Singer, H., & Donlan, D. (1982). Active comprehension: Problem-solving schema with question generation for comprehension of complex short stories. *Reading Research Quarterly, 17,* 166–186.

Thomas, J. W., Rohwer, W. D., & Wilson, M. (1989, March). *Hierarchical models of studying.* Paper presented at the meeting of the American Educational Research Association, San Francisco.

Thomas, J. W., Strage, A., & Curley, R. (1988). Improving students' self-directed learning: Issues and guidelines. *Elementary School Journal, 88,* 313–326.

Wittrock, M. C. (1990). Generative processes of comprehension. *Educational Psychologist, 24,* 345–376.

Wong, B. Y., Wong, R., & Perry, N. (1986). The efficacy of a self-questioning summarization strategy for use by underachievers and learning-disabled adolescents in social studies. *Learning Disabilities Focus, 2,* 20–35.

Zimmerman, B. J., Bandura, A., & Martinez-Pons, M. M. (1992). Self-motivation for academic attainment: The role of self-efficacy beliefs and personal goal setting. *American Educational Research Journal, 29,* 663–676.

CHAPTER 10

Expanding Literacy and Content Learning Through Computer Technology

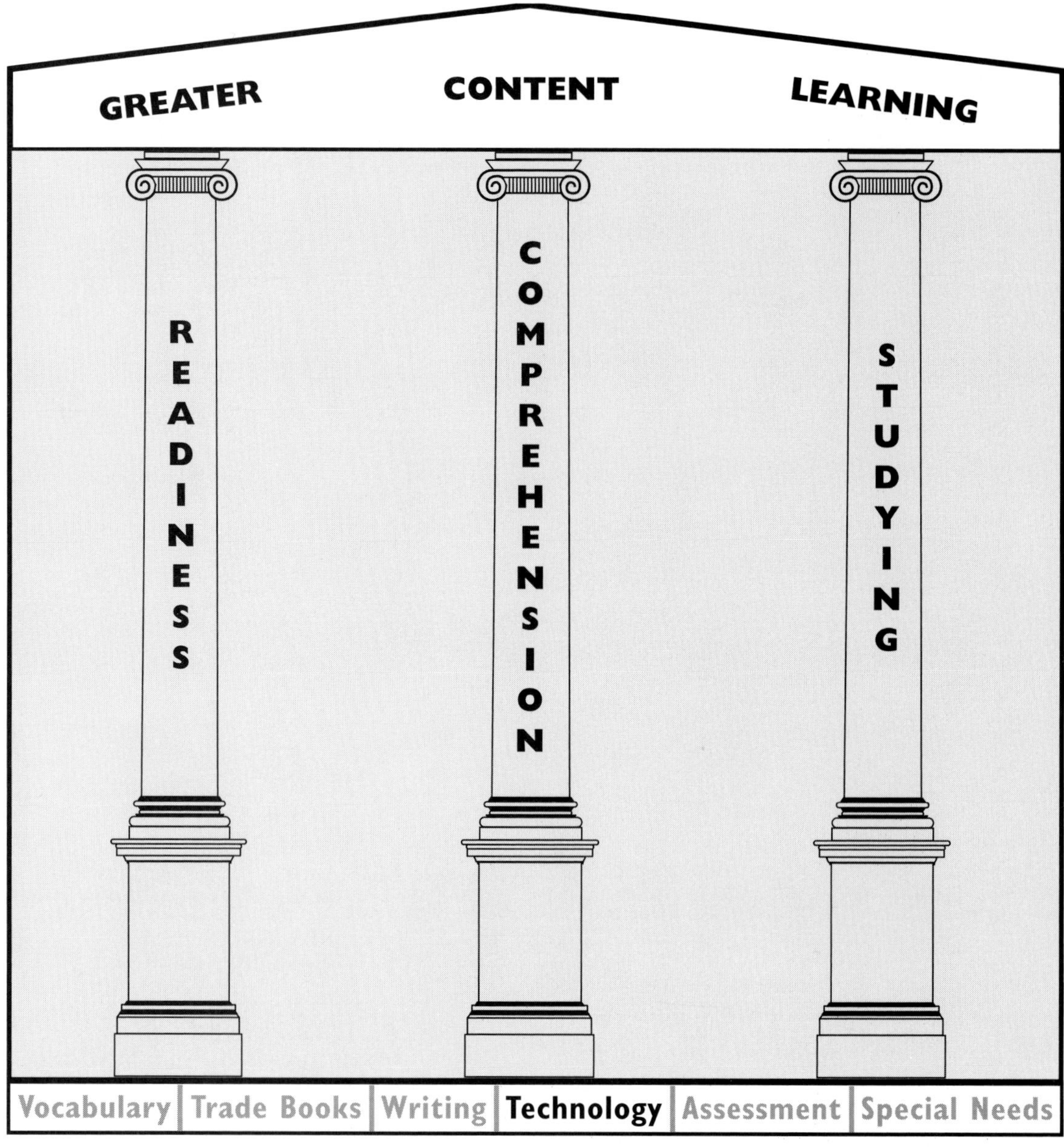

ANTICIPATION GUIDE

Directions: Read each statement carefully and decide whether you agree or disagree with it, placing a check mark in the appropriate *Before Reading* column. When you have finished reading and studying the chapter, return to the guide and decide whether your anticipations need to be changed by placing a check mark in the appropriate *After Reading* column.

	BEFORE READING		**AFTER READING**	
	Agree	*Disagree*	*Agree*	*Disagree*
1. Computer technology is incompatible with a language-based approach to content area teaching.	_____	_____	_____	_____
2. Computers are limited learning tools in the content classroom.	_____	_____	_____	_____
3. Reading and writing are necessary skills for operating computers effectively.	_____	_____	_____	_____
4. The Internet can be used to promote higher-level thinking in virtually every content area.	_____	_____	_____	_____
5. Word processing is the only computer application supportive of students' literacy growth.	_____	_____	_____	_____
6. Electronic field trips will be possible in the next century.	_____	_____	_____	_____
7. Databases and spreadsheets are difficult to use in content areas other than math and science.	_____	_____	_____	_____

[W]hen students work with computer technology, instead of being controlled by it, they enhance the capabilities of the computer, and the computer enhances their thinking and learning.

—Jonassen (1996)

The overriding principle that guides our selection of strategies for this book is that they engage students in ways that lead to meaningful and active learning. It is clear that computer technology holds great promise for engaging students and helping them think in meaningful ways. Over the past 10 years remarkable developments in hardware, software, and access to information have made computers more important than ever as tools for expansive thinking (Negroponte, 1995). For example, consider the explosion of interest in the Internet. Five years ago, very few teachers even knew of its existence. Just a couple of years ago, many more teachers knew of its existence but few used it. Today, however, teachers all over the country, from remote villages to major cities, have knowledge of and experience with the Internet (Ryder & Graves, 1997). Other computer technologies, such as telecommunications, multimedia, and word processing, have seen similar growth.

In this chapter we will explore these and other types of computer technology and their use in middle and secondary school classrooms. We will also provide useful information for helping teachers become more informed about these technologies while developing strategies to use them with their students.

CASE STUDY

In 1997 José and his colleagues in the science and math department of a large urban high school received a state-funded technology grant. The grant was designed to be used by teachers of math and science to train their students in the ways in which computer technology could improve learning in those subjects. José received funds to purchase computers, computer software, networked Internet connections, and teacher training in the new uses of computer technology.

In staff development workshops, José discovered a number of exciting applications of computer technology to his biology subject matter. In one workshop session, he and other faculty were asked to think of ways of using the computer to facilitate their students' learning of especially challenging content. José's students seemed most challenged by the sheer volume of detail they were required to learn. For example, for the study of cell types in advanced biology, students had to learn and remember hundreds of facts related to 10 to 20 different cell types. They were having a great deal of difficulty organizing and remembering this information. José had tried to devise study schemes for his students, but they were either too complex or did not provide motivation.

To the Reader:

as you read and study the remainder of this chapter, think about José and his goal to help his students organize their biology content more effectively. What computer-based strategies could José use to achieve this goal?

WHY USE COMPUTER TECHNOLOGY?

Over the past few decades our ideas about literacy have undergone major transformations. Literacy is no longer viewed as the ability to decode and encode printed words. Theorists now assert that there are multiple literacies (Gallego & Hollingsworth, 1992) that we need to learn if we are to participate fully in our increasingly complex global society (Anderson & Lee, 1995). We agree with John Willinsky (1993), who believes that computer technology will continue to expand our conceptions about how literacy is learned, taught, and used.

Schools Are Making Technology an Integral Part of the Curriculum

National and state educational initiatives over the past few years have included major efforts to increase and improve the use of computer technology in public elementary and secondary schools. President Bill Clinton set a goal of providing Internet access to every school child in America (Leyden, 1995). The president, like many educators, parents, and students, believes that technology should be an integral part of K–12 education. The belief that computer technology can enhance learning in schools appears to be based on the following assumptions (Roblyer, Edwards, & Havriluk, 1997):

Most school-related computer technologies require students to use reading and writing skills. Even for skeptics of computers as learning tools, it is indisputable that reading and writing are essential for electronic navigation and information retrieval (Ryder & Graves, 1997). Current findings about how best to teach comprehension make it clear that students need ample time for reading and writing for authentic purposes (Fielding & Pearson, 1994). The reading and writing involved in typical computer tasks in schools can provide some of that much needed time for authentic literacy activities. Consider the literacy requirements of a ninth grader's computer research of the rocky planets in our solar system. First, he must read a variety of directions for accessing specific databases on planets. Then he must select the most relevant "hits" to review. Next, he must follow additional directions to find texts and other information about the planets of interest. All the while, the student is reading, making critical judgments, and typing key words and phrases to hone his search. There may come a time when students will be able to complete similar tasks with mere voice activation; but for the foreseeable future, reading and writing skills will continue to be a necessity for school-related computer tasks.

Assumptions Behind the Benefits of Computer Technology in Schools

Computer technology is widespread. Computers are certainly a part of the landscape of society. From the checkout point at a local food store to a stock broker's office in a Wall Street high-rise, computers are necessary for commerce, business, and everyday life. Given the widespread use of computers, many conclude that students need training in the use of technology in order to be prepared for challenges in the workplace. This connection between technology and business has resulted in the perception that high-quality education is synonymous with technology-based methods of teaching and learning (Landow, 1992).

Computer technology is an effective tool of instruction. Because legislators have been stressing the need for advanced computer training in schools and because computer technology has become so widespread, many assume that there is abundant research evidence to demonstrate the teaching advantages of technology-based methods over traditional approaches. Unfortunately, although there is a growing number of investigations of computer-based teaching methods, the literature remains largely inconclusive with respect to the superiority of such methods over other approaches (Clark, 1994; Kozma, 1994; Thompson, Simonson, & Hargraves, 1992).

Although there is a lack of consensus in the research literature on computer-based teaching, some studies clearly support the use of computers in teaching reading and writing. Reinking (1996), for instance, found that students reading computer-based texts investigated more word definitions, recalled the definitions of more words, and comprehended more of the text than students reading traditional printed texts. He believed that electronic texts should not be taught in place of printed texts but should be used as one of several tools for enhancing literacy teaching and learning.

In spite of findings like Reinking's, there remains a lack of research consensus on the benefits of educational applications of computer technology. For this reason, caution seems warranted when rationalizing financial and training investment in computer technology in schools on the basis of research evidence alone. Nevertheless, promising lines of research are underway, and several as-

Observed Outcomes of School-Based Computer Technology

pects of computer technology have improved educational practice and are likely to continue to facilitate teaching and learning in the future (Roblyer, 1993). Roblyer et al. (1997) have suggested that computer technology in education can be justified on the basis of the following outcomes already observed by teachers and students:

- *Increased student motivation.* Pask-McCartney (1989) and Summers (1990–1991) have found that many technology resources with visual and interactive features can help focus students' attention and encourage them to spend more time on learning.
- *Unique instructional capabilities.* Computers and other electronic media can help students visualize content to be learned in novel ways. For example, virtual reality programs and programs that allow students to work with geometric figures in hyperspace are made possible only through computer-based instructional technology (Marcus, 1995).
- *Support for new instructional approaches.* Polin (1992) has asserted that technology-based activities can support new instructional initiatives such as critical thinking, cooperative learning, and collaborative problem solving by linking learners from different regions of the country and the world.
- *Increased teacher productivity.* A growing number of teachers have been discovering how to delegate time-consuming paperwork and record-keeping chores to the computer. Because teachers spend less time on these tasks, they are able to have more direct contact with students (Roblyer et al., 1997).

Computers foster constructive learning. One of our expressed goals in this text is to help teachers develop students who are independent learners. Learning independently means that students are able to construct their own knowledge rather than simply recall information supplied by teachers (Simons, 1993). Salomon (1993) argues that unlike most other tools for learning, computers can serve as intellectual partners that take on unproductive memorizing tasks while allowing learners to think more deeply and meaningfully. One way to think about this is to consider how scientists and mathematicians who have come into their own in the past 20 years have done so in the age of computers. And yet, no one claims that these thinkers and scholars are less capable than their predecessors because of computer technology. On the contrary, computers have become a necessary tool allowing scientists and mathematicians to find practical expression for their most imaginative ideas. For instance, it is safe to say that without computers to handle the staggering number of calculations necessary for manned exploration of the moon and the planets, our space program would be far less advanced than it is today. The point is that when computers are used as partners in learning, students and teachers alike can free their imaginations to explore content on a more meaningful and critical level than they might without this technology.

COMPUTER TECHNOLOGY IN SCHOOLS TODAY

Ten years ago, when we were finishing the final draft of the first edition of this book, we made some predictions about trends in schools' use of computer technology most likely to expand in the future. We're proud to say that our predictions have been highly accurate. For example, we said that telecommunications, multimedia, and databases would become increasingly prominent in educational computing. A safe prediction, you might say. However, at that time, it was impossible for us to know with certainty how rapidly instructional computing would change the way we think about teaching and learning. Some (Newby, Stepich, Lehman, & Russell, 1996) have said that if the automobile industry had progressed as quickly as the computer industry, we would be able to own a vehicle capable of traveling at jet engine speeds while getting a million miles to the gallon, for only a few dollars! Over the past 10 years, personal computers have become remarkably more powerful, more compact, and less expensive, making it possible for a single machine to handle a number of complex tasks. Four areas of computer technology are changing the face of education in junior and senior high schools in virtually all subject areas: (1) *telecommunications,* including *networking;* (2) *word processing,* including *desktop publishing* and creating *home pages;* (3) *database management systems;* and (4) *multimedia.*

Telecommunications

Telecommunications technology involves electronic communication of information using computers. Although telecommunications has been in use for some time in business and industry, a growing number of telecommunications applications are being explored in schools. Massive webs of phone lines, bulletin board systems, and international networks are now available to bring a world of people and information within reach for teachers and students (Harris, 1994; Kelly & Wiebe, 1994).

Electronic Networking with Computers Has Become Accessible and Affordable

Communicating with computers has provided teachers in reading and language arts, as well as all other subject areas, with powerful support for literacy and content learning (Roblyer et al., 1997). Today, with advances in telecommunications technology along with steadily declining costs for the use of this technology, electronic links between students and teachers have become an affordable and effective option for delivery of instruction. Teachers who value students' active exploration of information and collaborative exchange of ideas will find numerous applications of telecommunications technology (Armstrong, 1995).

The Internet, including e-mail, is one of the most common ways in which telecommunications technology can be used by teachers.

What Is the Internet?

The **Internet** is not one system, but a collection of thousands of computers from areas such as education, business, government, and the military (Mike, 1997). It can be thought of as the network of networks, at least 30,000 of them (Lewis,

1994), that connects computers throughout the world into one global communication system (Cooke & Lehrer, 1993). Given the dimensions of the Internet, it is possible to access information on virtually every conceivable topic (Ryder & Hughes, 1997). This is what makes it so appealing to teachers, students, and parents.

Unlike previous technologies such as television and radio, once thought to have the potential to transform education, the Internet offers teachers and students a blend of communication and retrieval functions within a worldwide framework. More significantly, while the Internet is an electronic machine, it nonetheless runs on literacy (Mike, 1997). People interact with the Internet almost exclusively through reading and writing. Reinking (1994) has described this electronic communication as a new literacy that will have an increasingly significant impact on the design and outcomes of education.

Benefits of the Internet

Mike (1997) has described several potential benefits for students and teachers who use the Internet as a communication and knowledge tool:

- *Promoting higher-level thinking.* Imagine a science teacher posing a question to the class such as "Could the *Star Trek* 'wormhole' for intergalactic travel actually exist?" To solve this problem, student groups might be assigned different tasks. For example, one group could be responsible for locating and consulting with physicists, science fiction authors, and futurists. Another group could be given the task of searching for and retrieving information about limitations on human space travel, as well as hypothesized and exotic solutions to the problems of long-distance space exploration. Groups would be asked to report their findings to the entire class, including what they learned and which electronic path was taken to uncover the information.

  To answer the question posed above, students would have to make extensive use of higher-level thinking. Search strategies would need to be constructed and refined. After the search, the results would have to be reviewed and evaluated. Finally, the pieces of information would have to be synthesized into a coherent report. Furthermore, throughout the search, sort, and report assignment, students would have had ample opportunities to use and develop higher-level literacy skills, such as (1) setting purposes for reading, (2) adjusting the reading rate, (3) evaluating text content for relevant and significant information and ideas, and (4) synthesizing textual information. Mike (1997) argues that cognitive abilities exercised in this kind of Internet assignment will transfer to other similar electronic and nonelectronic activities involving gathering, evaluating, and communicating information.

- *Promoting a sense of the audience for literacy activity.* Research has demonstrated that sensitivity to one's audience is a critical factor in developing sophisticated reading and writing skills (Fielding & Pearson, 1994). Students who communicate on the Internet are writing for an actual audience of one or perhaps hundreds or thousands. Likewise, students who read Internet communications become part of an audience. Teachers can take advantage of this experience by helping students develop audience sensitivity with writing assignments on the Internet for various purposes. For example, students can use the Net to write simple missives to chat groups, letters to pen pals, and formal inquiries to companies and organizations.

- *Promoting authentic literacy purposes.* While the Internet is not expected to replace textbooks and other classroom print sources anytime in the near future, it is likely to become an increasingly popular supplement to help students expand their access to current real-world information.
- *Promoting cooperative learning.* Internet use can promote literate interaction among students within the same classroom and with students around the world (Leu, 1996). In collaborating electronically, students communicate through reading and writing e-mail.

Internet services and educationally oriented sites. Some of the most commonly accessed Internet services include the following:

- *World Wide Web (WWW).* This is the most popular Internet service. The WWW allows users to point and click to access information. Using the WWW browser, Netscape, you can navigate the Web, create e-mail,participate in on-line discussion groups, or download text and graphics to your computer.
- *Electronic mail (e-mail).* E-mail makes it possible for you to send messages to and receive them from anyone in the world who has an e-mail address. This is the most widely used service of the Internet.

There are many different Internet sites that continue to be of great interest to middle and secondary school teachers and students. Some examples of the more interesting sites include:

- *Integrating the Internet.* Developed by a teacher in Arizona, this site contains many useful ideas for integrating the WWW into your classroom.
- *Web66.* This site provides a comprehensive list of K–12 schools that are currently accessing the Internet. This list is especially useful to teachers and classes involved in collaborative efforts to explore topics from the perspective of students throughout the country. The site also provides the Web pages of more than 6,000 elementary and secondary schools throughout the world.
- *Teachers@work.* One thousand rated sites for students grouped by age and subject are available at this site.
- *Hubble Space Telescope.* This Internet site contains pictures and movies of astronomical phenomena gleaned from the Hubble telescope. It is a highly useful source of information for science teachers.

- *National Science Foundation.* There are many useful resources and interactive experiences for science students and teachers at this web site. Among the more often used educational resources are science fair "starters"; Science in the Home, a site for learning about scientists, scientific investigations, and interactive science activities; *Dragonfly* magazine; and student-scientist partnerships that allow whole classes to take part in real scientific investigations with researchers throughout North America.
- *FedWorld.* This site provides access to information from many U.S. government agencies and departments. Social studies, history, and government teachers will find it very useful.
- *The Library of Congress.* History and social studies teachers will find this site extremely useful for helping students explore topics such as the San Francisco earthquake, the Civil War, and countless other historical phenomena over the past 200 years.
- *CIA World Factbook.* This encyclopedia provides detailed descriptions of every country in the world.
- *Weather Information Superhighway.* Current and forecasted weather from the National Weather Service is available at this site, including color satellite imagery of storms and fronts.
- *KidPub.* This site serves as a clearinghouse for students' writing. Students can place their writing here, and they can read and respond to written works by students from different countries.
- *History/Social Studies Web Site for K-12 Teachers.* This is a very rich site for teachers interested in developing thematic lessons and units for social studies.
- *Ask ERIC Virtual Library.* Locations at this site contain lesson plans and easy search paths for topic bibliographies for teachers at all grade levels.

Telecommunications Strategies in Content Classrooms

Thousands of junior and senior high school teachers around the country are exploring new ways of teaching and helping their students learn via telecommunications. In the following section we will describe several examples of teachers using e-mail and the Internet to engage students in meaningful learning projects. Common to all of these activities is the use of computers for authentic and purposeful communication. In this way, we hope you will see how students' language and literacy skills, necessary for electronic communication, can be used and reinforced (Anderson & Lee, 1995) while learning content from virtually any content area.

Electronic pen pals.

Foreign language. Janette, a Spanish teacher, and her class had been studying the cultures of Spain for several weeks (as described in Newby et al.,

1996). Her students enjoyed reading about the people from different regions of Spain, and she wanted them to have the opportunity to interact directly with Spaniards. As a student herself, Janette had carried on a pen pal relationship with a young girl from Barcelona. She remembered how enjoyable it was to write and receive letters with interesting information and items, such as stamps, coins, and photographs. Eventually the exchange of letters dwindled and then stopped as the girls grew older; but Janette always regretted never being able to meet and speak with her pen pal in person. Janette's knowledge of telecommunications technology helped her decide to arrange for an audio teleconference between her Spanish language students and students from Spain.

Electronic Pen Pals Promote Language Development and Cultural Appreciation

After making arrangements with a high school English language teacher in Seville, Janette and her students prepared questions for their Spanish counterparts. Using a speakerphone from the school's technology center, Janette called the classroom in Seville and the two classes held a 20-minute conversation. The students in Spain got to practice their English, while Janette's students got to practice their conversational Spanish. In the end, everyone seemed to understand each other, and both classes of students were enthusiastic about continuing to interact.

After the teleconference, Janette had her students initiate e-mail conversations with their new pen pal class in Spain. Students were able to practice their writing skills while gaining valuable cultural and language information from their electronic pen pals. Janette felt that the experience had been a success, since several of her students continued to correspond with Spanish students months after they were introduced to the long-distance education technologies.

Social studies. Last year, as middle school students in a small community in Alaska began to prepare for their class trip to Disney World in Orlando, Florida, they tried something a little different (as described by Roblyer et al., 1997). In April they established a computer link with eighth-grade students in Orlando. Using e-mail, students exchanged information, eventually met each other in Orlando, and continued to contact one another after the trip via e-mail. The Alaskan students were mostly native Alaskans, so they were able to share a great deal about their culture and daily lives with the Orlando junior high students while gaining greater knowledge of telecommunications technology.

Biology. Students in Wisconsin established e-mail links with classrooms all along the migratory route of the whooping crane. Students initiated reports on the movement of the cranes during their migration and created an informational guide to their migration habits.

Computer-mediated communication.

Science. Though land-locked, middle graders in Iowa kept track of a U.S. Coast Guard "tall ship" during a training journey using telecommunications technology. Students gathered updates on its movements and activities through the SAILING forum, which can be accessed through the Internet. The topic was of great interest to the students and included a variety of related learning experiences. Students researched more about the ship. They adopted a sailor or cadet aboard the ship and exchanged e-mail letters and pictures. They read books such as *Mutiny on the Bounty* because the Coast Guard ship was following a route similar to Captain Bligh's. Log sheets were kept, and weekly updates via computer were received. Students learned about time zones and the international date line, as well as about meteorology and weather's effects on the seas. They developed their map-reading skills. Telecommunications technology stimulated and supported the students' exploration of a 20th-century sailing voyage.

Biology. A group of 10th-grade biology students in Massachusetts used the National Geographic Society's Kids' Net to tap into a national science project. Kids' Net was designed for science classrooms around the country to share in-class science experiments. The students tried various experiments with seeds that had been sent into space aboard the space shuttle to see how space travel had affected them. After collecting data on their experiments, the students sent their results across the country through Kids' Net on the Internet.

Mathematics. High school students in several cities throughout the country polled the local population on their views of national issues, such as gun control, smoking bans in public places, female presidential candidates, and abortion. Using e-mail, the classes exchanged the data they collected, and all the participating schools shared in an overall analysis of the findings.

Across the curriculum. Reil (1993) studied students involved in the Global Learning Circles Project. The project facilitates collaboration through telecommunications among a small group of classrooms for exploring and seeking solutions to social, environmental, and geopolitical problems. The outcome of the project is the publication of jointly authored booklets and papers based on the students' collaborative problem solving. Several learning circles projects have taken place over the past few years, including the following (Reil, 1990):

Solving Global Problems through Telecommunications

- Students in Saudi Arabia, along with their partner students in other countries, explored solutions to problems in the Persian Gulf. The students discussed issues such as world dependence on Arabian oil, political freedom, and religious and cultural conflicts.
- West Virginia students are conferencing with prison inmates to discuss a range of social issues. Inmates provide information from their personal life experiences so that students can better understand the origins of crime.
- Students from several urban areas around the country collaborated on studies of homelessness, illiteracy, and substance abuse. Data were compiled and written in a booklet.
- Students from Belgium worked with collaborating schools in the United States and other industrialized nations on a research project concerned with excessive packaging of goods. They gathered local products and evaluated them from the standpoint of their pricing and their effects on the environment.

Reil (1993) found that students' written communication for a larger networked audience of their peers was more fluent, better organized, and more clearly written than work produced merely for a grade. Electronically supported collaborative authoring involving partner students around the world resulted in better use of grammar and syntax as well.

Electronic field trips. Experiential learning is one of the most highly valued forms of learning promoted in this book. We believe strongly that when students are given the opportunity to explore content firsthand, they are much more likely to learn information and ideas and to commit new learning to memory than they are without direct experience. A common source of frustration among teachers, however, is the lack of resources to make experiential learning possible. Undoubtedly, there are countless "Ms. Frizzles" out there who would like nothing more than to be able to arrange field trips for virtually every topic in the curriculum. Fortunately, this goal is rapidly becoming more achievable through the use of telecommunications technology.

An electronic field trip turns students into "virtual travelers" capable of going to places they could only imagine. Unlike prerecorded video programs of distant places, electronic field trips make it possible for students to interact with other learners and teachers at remote locations (Armstrong, 1995). Using telephone, e-mail, and fax, students interact with peers and local experts as they explore interesting locations around the world.

Science. One of the most exciting electronic field trip projects available to teachers today is the Jason Project (U.S. Congress, Office of Technology Assessment, 1989). Through a complex network of advanced satellite technology, underwater robotics, two-way audio, and television screens, viewers at participating schools in many locations in the United States and other countries can observe actual exploration sites and participate in the exploration itself. Jason, a remotely operated vehicle for underwater navigation and research from which the project gets its name, has made it possible for students to go on interactive scientific explorations of sites such as the Mediterranean Sea, the Galapagos Islands, and the bottom of Lake Ontario. The project allows students live participation via satellite-delivered images and two-way audio interaction. Teachers and students can pose questions, receive answers, and conduct remote experiments. A special curriculum guide developed by the National Science Teachers Association can be obtained to help teachers and students study and prepare for each expedition. During Jason's expedition, students and teachers record its progress, communicate through e-mail, and participate by completing assignments and experiments.

Electronic Field Trips Are Less Expensive and More Safe than Traditional Ones

Electronic field trips are becoming increasingly popular because of their ease and relatively modest expense. With insurance, travel, safety, and time issues forcing many middle and secondary schools to limit or even eliminate conventional field trips, we're likely to see tremendous growth in electronic explorations over the next several years.

Opportunities for electronic communication in the classroom are endless, limited only by the imagination of teachers and students. As Roblyer and his colleagues (1997) point out, the biggest challenge is for teachers to take the first step. We believe that as teachers become more familiar with the benefits of communicating via computers across distances, an increasing number from all content areas will take advantage of this technology for motivating students to read, write, and exchange meaningful information.

Word Processing for Meaningful Communication

Word processing is, at its simplest, typing on a computer. Word processing programs facilitate nearly any assignment or activity that was previously done by longhand or a typewriter. Word processing is more versatile and powerful than older writing methods. Since a word processed document is typed and formatted on a screen before being printed, editing, revising, and correcting can all take place before a finished written product is produced.

Those of us who have been around long enough to remember know what writing and publishing were like before access to computers became easy and commonplace. It would be difficult to return to the days of lumbering and spotty computer technology. The advantages of word processing seem obvious, but there is some dispute over whether this new technology has actually helped produce better writing (Halio, 1990). Nevertheless, we believe that writing as a conceptual and creative process is facilitated by productivity tools such as word processors. That is why we have included examples of teachers and students using computers for word processing in other sections of this book, such as in Chapter 7.

Applications of word processing programs are becoming increasingly varied. Today students and teachers alike are using word processing for creating imaginative documents, brochures, books, newsletters, and more with desktop publishing programs. Other programs have been developed to facilitate student note taking. Word processors are now being used to create home pages and other printed information on the WWW.

Desktop Publishing

Desktop publishing software gives teachers and students more powerful formatting capabilities for printed material than regular word processing programs. Recently, older distinctions between word processing and desktop publishing software have disappeared since word processors are now including more and more desktop publishing features (Roblyer et al., 1997). With desktop publishing, users have a great deal of control and flexibility in the composition and layout of the printed page, including text and graphics. Today many schools are using high-quality desktop publishing software to produce colorful and visually appealing school newspapers and yearbooks, as well illustrated material for the classroom.

Mathematics. Sixth-grade students at a middle school in the Southwest planned all of the second semester for a math fair in early May. Not only did individuals and groups work tirelessly on projects to be displayed at the fair, but students also worked diligently to make the fair one of the best the school had ever had. Early in the planning stages for the fair, the classes decided to emphasize publicity of the event as a way of increasing participation by the school and the community. Hector, one of the math teachers, aided students in their publicity efforts by introducing them to desktop publishing. Using Microsoft's *Publish It!* software, Hector taught students how to create a variety of eye-catching and professional communications combining page setup, text format, and graphics elements.

Students first learned how to design their own stationery, blending the school's mascot, an owl, with their own creative arrangement of print and figures. The desktop publishing program made it possible to generate colorful flyers and brochures describing the upcoming math fair. These were mailed in the desktop-generated envelopes to local business, churches, and school and community organizations. Additionally, large posters were created and displayed throughout the school and community. With the desktop publishing software, students even discovered the ease of creating a math school newsletter containing updates on the math fair events. The newsletter featured students who had records of high achievement in math, real-world math problems, and a math "puzzler."

The students' advertising campaign paid off. The math fair brought more people to the school to observe, judge, and participate in related activities than any previous math fair. Desktop publishing provided students with an important tool for promoting their event and helped them learn valuable information about using the computer.

Computer-Assisted Outlining

Another way to use word processing as a learning tool involves computer-based outlining programs. Outlining is one of the most commonly recommended strategies for organizing textbook and classroom information. That's why we offer suggestions for teaching text organization strategies to students in Chapter 9. As we discuss in that chapter, organizational strategies have been found to be an excellent way to promote active learning (Anderson & Armbruster, 1984) and provide students with a record of study for future use, such as in tests, projects, and class discussion (Nist, Simpson, Olejnik, & Mealey, 1991). Many students will tell you, however, that creating paper-and-pencil outlines can be very inefficient. What makes this form of note taking so difficult is not knowing how much space to allot to each heading and subheading because it's impossible to know with certainty in advance the number of significant points within each subsection of a textbook chapter. Furthermore, even though students are often urged to incorporate lecture and class information into a unified outline of notes, it becomes very difficult and messy to reorganize, make room for new information, and elaborate on prior information using paper and pencil. Scratch-outs and erasures, changes and additions written in between lines and in margins, drawings,

Note Taking Is Made Easier with the Computer

and arrows inevitably force students to recopy everything they've written or to try to learn and study from disorganized notes.

Anderson-Inman (1995–1996), at the Center for Electronic Studying at the University of Oregon, has been investigating ways in which teachers can help students improve their independent study skills by using the computer to record and organize information. Her work has led to the development of computer-based outlining programs designed to make outlining easier and more efficient for students. Outlining programs operate similarly to word processing programs, but the typed text consists only of formats into an outline. Electronic outlining is an effective form of recording and organizing information from the text and the class (Horney & Anderson-Inman, 1992) for the following reasons: (1) **expandability**—students can modify electronic outlines in an infinite number of ways; (2) **focusability**—program functions such as "hide" and "show" allow students to display particular sections of their outline for concentrated attention; and (3) **juxtaposability**—electronic outlines allow students to bring together two or more sections from different places in the outline for instant and easy comparisons and for information elaboration. Afterward, the sections can be returned to their original places in the outline.

Music. Music students in a ninth-grade class created electronic outlines for the topic of historical periods of music (Figure 10.1). The students were taught a five-step process for creating the outline using *Inspiration* 4.1 (1995) software. First, they went through the primary music textbook and crafted a skeletal outline of the chapter's major headings and subheadings. Second, they summarized textual information using important words and phraseology under each heading in the skeletal outline. Third, they read information on the topic in alternative text sources supplied by the teacher and inserted relevant information in the outline. Fourth, class notes from teacher- and peer-led discussions and demonstrations were integrated into the outline. Finally, students restructured the headings and subheadings by adding and consolidating and rearranged information in the outline to fit the new structure. When their outlines were completed, the music teacher showed students how they could use the outlines to prompt themselves during study and test themselves in anticipation of a test on the content.

Creating Home Pages and Other WWW Writing

An ever-increasing number of teachers and students are creating information on the Internet by designing their own **home pages,** screens on the WWW that identify a particular site. For example, the home page for Texas A & M University in Corpus Christi (www.tamucc.com) contains colorful graphics including the school's logo and mascot, printed information, and point-and-click hot spots for particular information about the university. One such spot provides information about the College of Education and lists all degree programs, admission requirements, and faculty—including Dr. Bill Brozo (coauthor of this book). This site will eventually have course syllabi for browsers to peruse. More and more

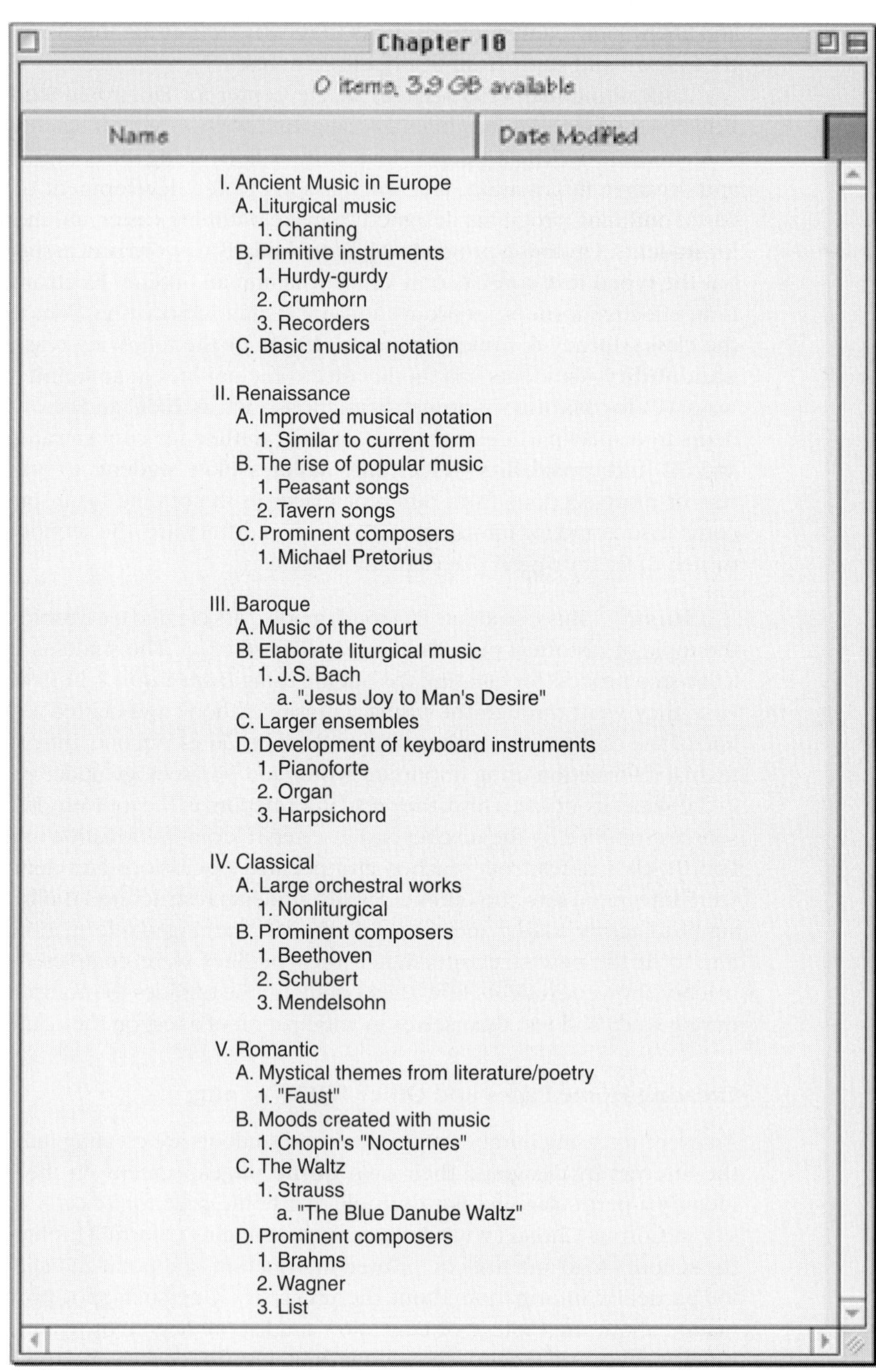

Chapter 10
0 items, 3.9 GB available
Name
Date Modified
I. Ancient Music in Europe
A. Liturgical music
1. Chanting
B. Primitive instruments
1. Hurdy-gurdy
2. Crumhorn
3. Recorders
C. Basic musical notation
II. Renaissance
A. Improved musical notation
1. Similar to current form
B. The rise of popular music
1. Peasant songs
2. Tavern songs
C. Prominent composers
1. Michael Pretorius
III. Baroque
A. Music of the court
B. Elaborate liturgical music
1. J.S. Bach
a. "Jesus Joy to Man's Desire"
C. Larger ensembles
D. Development of keyboard instruments
1. Pianoforte
2. Organ
3. Harpsichord
IV. Classical
A. Large orchestral works
1. Nonliturgical
B. Prominent composers
1. Beethoven
2. Schubert
3. Mendelsohn
V. Romantic
A. Mystical themes from literature/poetry
1. "Faust"
B. Moods created with music
1. Chopin's "Nocturnes"
C. The Waltz
1. Strauss
a. "The Blue Danube Waltz"
D. Prominent composers
1. Brahms
2. Wagner
3. List

FIGURE 10.1 Electronic Outline for Periods of Music

Web sites have colorful and informative home pages designed to draw browsers deeper into the site.

Home Pages Turn Students into WWW Contributors

It seems to be a natural progression for students as they become skillful at accessing information on the Web; eventually, they are not satisfied with this activity and want to create their own information. Home page construction seems to support active learning, group problem solving and planning, and interactive teaching (Ryder & Hughes, 1997). Various types of home pages have been created by students, including personal home pages, multimedia newspapers, online portfolios, class supplements, and community resources.

Art. A group of students in a high school art class were prompted to develop a home page for other art students after they found it difficult to locate resources on contemporary artists and art movements. The advantage of the Internet over the limited resources available in their school's library became immediately apparent to the students when they initiated their search on the WWW for information about current active artists. Hundreds of relevant sites were identified that included artists' names, biographies, illustrations of their works, and more. The art students decided to design their home page with a collage of photographs of original works they had done. They entitled their home page "The Demon of Curiosity: A 12th Graders Guide to Modern Art" after a painting by Penck done in the 1980s. The site was designed as a resource for any student wishing to gather information about the current art scene. Students included a brief history of their effort to create the site, as well as art autobiographies, links to relevant Internet sites, additional readings about artists and their work, and suggestions of assignments and activities to develop modern painting and sculpting techniques.

Word processing technology generally has been viewed as the most versatile tool for teaching and learning in most subject areas. In communication, it offers significant advantages over traditional writing tools such as typewriters and paper and pencil. Word processors eliminate many of the difficulties associated with editing and producing texts. With sophisticated desktop publishing capabilities, students can integrate word processing with graphics to create professional-looking materials. Finally, when word processing is combined with the WWW to create home pages and Web sites, students can make their texts available to a global audience.

Expanding Learning in Content Classrooms with Databases and Spreadsheets

Databases are extremely versatile computer programs that allow students to collect, organize, and retrieve information. Databases are very popular computer applications second only to word processing programs (Jonassen, 1996). Similar to phone books, recipe files, and catalogs, databases enable students to find, cross-reference, classify, and sort data and search for specific topics and information quickly and easily. Most libraries store reference materials, including encyclopedias, in databases. The exceptionally large storage requirements for works such as encyclopedias, the complete works of Shakespeare, and world almanacs require the optical storage technologies of **CD-ROMs.** Similar to audio CDs, CD-ROMs can store hundreds of millions of bits of information. One small CD can hold up to 250,000 pages of information, making it possible to store entire reference works on a single CD, along with an extensive index that allows searchers to access the information within seconds. Using CD-ROMs, students have been able to expand their research skills, improve their ability to organize information, and learn a great deal about a particular topic by authoring their own databases (Turner & Dipinto, 1992). Teachers have found databases excellent ways of developing higher-level thinking skills through questioning (Hancock, Kaput, & Goldsmith, 1992).

Database Authoring Expands Content Learning

Spreadsheets are computerized, numerical recordkeeping systems. A spreadsheet is composed of a grid, table, or matrix with columns and rows. Each cell may contain values, formulas, or functions, using either numbers or words. Spreadsheets are used to store, calculate, and present information. Most spreadsheet programs allow the learner to display information in a variety of ways, including graphs and charts. Spreadsheets help users manage numbers in much the same way that word processors help them manage words. In fact, Bozeman (1992) described spreadsheets as a way to "word process numbers" (p. 908). Teachers from a variety of content areas have used spreadsheets to engage and support problem solving and other forms of higher-level thinking.

Following are brief descriptions of how databases and spreadsheets have already been used by middle and secondary school teachers to improve student motivation and learning in content classroom.

Social Studies. An eighth-grade social studies teacher had her class compile a database on current events using information from local newspapers about happenings in countries around the world. Each student was assigned 10 newspaper articles per quarter, which were summarized in a database field that included the country, subject, date, title, publication, and student's name. At the end of the year, the class organized their articles into their own encyclopedia containing more than 2,000 newspaper articles. The students developed a convenient retrieval system for accessing articles with key words.

Current Events. Tenth graders engaged in a letter-writing campaign to political prisoners, which grew out of a unit on Amnesty International, and built databases to keep track of their prisoners. They entered such information as the reason for the arrest, the length of the prison term, the current length of imprisonment, the reason for incarceration, health status, and addresses of persons or groups to contact. With the database, they could monitor changes concerning the prisoners, update the record on any prisoner as new information became available, and analyze the information for patterns such as similarities among charges brought against prisoners.

Databases and the Internet

Combining use of the Internet with database systems is an excellent way for teachers to exploit both technologies. Students researching information on the WWW can use a database for organizing and storing information, making study and recall of the information convenient and easy.

Art. An art teacher had his students research information about artists ranging from Leonardo DaVinci to Frida Kahlo. Using a database program, students first created a framework for recording critical information about each artist, including dates of birth and death and the movement he or she represented or defined (Figure 10.2). Students searched Web sites with information about the artists, downloaded and printed what they wanted to retain, and then placed the relevant information in the database. When the databases were completed, students printed them and used them to recall information for class discussion and study for a test.

Kinesiology. Each student in a middle school physical education class was required to maintain a database for the entire school year for recording personal information related to each exercise and athletic activity (Figure 10.3). The purpose of the assignment was to help students learn important information about fitness and muscle development while tying this information to class sports and activities. Students recorded the type of activity (basketball, sit-ups, flag football, etc.), necessary equipment, the type of motion required to perform the activity, the primary muscle groups involved, and the cardiovascular and other fitness benefits. Students also made notes on their databases of particularly useful Web sites for acquiring additional information relevant to the activity. Using their direct experience as well as information from the Internet, the students filled in their databases. Throughout the year, they used their databases to retrieve specific information as needed for class participation and examinations. The teacher often asked students to show the rest of the class an especially helpful Web site and explain how it was used.

FIGURE 10.2 Database of Artists

Artist	Birth	Movement	Death
Leonardo DaVinci	1452	High renaissance	1519
Édouard Manet	1832	Impressionism	1883
Vincent Van Gogh	1853	Impressionism	1890
Salvador Dali	1904	Surrealism	1983
Frida Kahlo	1910	Surrealism	1954
Henri Matisse	1869	Fauvism	1954
George Bellows	1882	Realism	1925
Käthe Kollwitz	1867	Expressionism	1945
Jackson Pollock	1912	Abstractionism	1956
Andy Warhol	1928	Pop art	1987
Mildred Howard	1945	Postmodernism	

Activity	Equipment	Type of Motion	Muscle Group	Benefits
sit-ups	none	sitting, bending	abdominis	toning stomach
walking	shoes		longus, lateralis	toning, cardiovascular
cycling	bicycle	pedaling	femoris, soleus	toning, cardiovascular
running				
curls				
chin-ups				
push-ups				

FIGURE 10.3 Database for Personal Exercise and Health

Databases and Hypertext/Hypermedia

Hypertext and **hypermedia** refer to nonsequential linking of information in a computer database. The information can include print, sound, video, animation, graphics, and pictures (Landow, 1992; Tolhurst, 1995). With the development of software such as HyperCard (Apple), CD-ROM Bookshelf (Microsoft), Hyperstudio, and SuperLink (Roger Wagner) it is possible to create and use databases containing an immense amount of multidimensional information (Kozma, 1991).

Physics. A high school physics teacher had her students create a hypertext database on Nobel Prize winners in physics over the past 10 years. First, using the Internet to establish an initial roster of prize winners, students developed links to news stories, books, scholarly articles, their university and research centers' home pages, three-dimensional models of their award-winning work, photos of the physicists, biographical information, and more. When the projects were completed, they were "tested" by other students working through the stacks and links of information in each database on the physicists to determine ease of access and creativity in making connections. In the course of this project, students demonstrated imagination and a great deal of valuable research experience.

History. Dillner (1994) describes the work of an American history teacher who created a hypermedia database for the Bill of Rights. She designed the computer-based lesson to be friendly to even her most inexperienced computer users. When students turned on the classroom computer, a title page with the words *The Bill of Rights* and a graphic of an American flag appeared on screen, while the music of "Yankee Doodle" flowed from the computer speakers. When the song ended, directions appeared on the screen. Using the mouse, students highlighted an arrow at the bottom of the screen and a new page appeared. The new page was a menu with a list of all 10 amendments. Students were asked to highlight an amendment to acquire more information about it. For example, highlighting "Right to Bear Arms" brought on a screen with the amendment title surrounded by five choices (*Interpretation, Definition, On your own, Examples, Assignments*). When students highlighted *Examples,* a videotaped clip ran of a student broadcaster and student actors replaying the scene of the day former President Ronald Reagan and his press secretary, James Brady, were shot by John Hinckley. The video was accompanied by audio information about how, since the assassination attempt, James and Sarah Brady have been lobbying against Americans' easy access to handguns. The other choices on each of the amendment screens provided additional media support for learning about the amendments and directing learning of the textbook chapter on the Bill of Rights.

Spreadsheets in the Content Classroom

Science. As Earth Day approached, a junior high science teacher had his students develop a spreadsheet assignment for analyzing lunchroom trash (Ramondetta, 1992). Students spent a week organizing trash items into recyclable and nonrecyclable categories, weighing trash samples, and projecting annual waste and costs. Using color pie charts, bar graphs, and grids, students organized and exhibited their findings at the school's Earth Day fair and assembly. Thought-provoking questions were included with the exhibit to help students understand the seriousness of the problem.

In another science class, Sixth graders created a spreadsheet to display information concerning relative gravity on Earth and the other planets. The students designed a grid with statistics on all the planets and individual bar graphs comparing Earth with each planet. Feeding the spreadsheet program with the appropriate formulas for calculating relative gravity, students filled in columns with each planet's relative gravity and their body weight on Earth. The program then automatically calculated the students' weights on the other planets. The information was blown up and put on a large chart board to be displayed in class during the study of gravity.

Math. High school math students were given the assignment of calculating the dimensions of the Milky Way. Using a scale model, they plugged their formulas into a spreadsheet that provided a calculation function. This function proved to be critical as students modified their formulas up to the last minute and used the spreadsheet to recalculate all of the new values based on the formula changes. As a result of this project, students developed a much better appreciation for the enormity of space.

Algebra. To better organize and understand nonlinear equations, an algebra teacher had her students develop a spreadsheet (Figure 10.4). The spreadsheet was created as students moved through the text and class material on hyperbolas. As students learned new examples, these were added to the spreadsheet along with additional characteristics and definitional information. When the spreadsheet was completed, the teacher showed her students how to use it to study and prepare for tests she designed based on how the information in the spreadsheet was organized. For example, she asked students to compare and contrast different types of hyperbolas and to describe a particular hyperbola based on its critical features.

	Intersects itself	Function?	Has a defined range	Has a defined domain	Has an x^2 term	x^2 term + or –	Has a y^2 term	y^2 term + or –	Coefficient of x^2 and y^2 terms are equal
Parabola									
Parabola									
Parabola									
Parabola									
Circle									
Ellipse									
Hyperbola									
Hyperbola									

FIGURE 10.4 Spreadsheet for Nonlinear Equations In Algebra

Database management systems offer teachers and students organized formats for storing and retrieving information. Higher-level thinking skills can be fostered through the use of this computer technology as students comprehend and analyze information to be included in the databases. Furthermore, students can gain an encoding and recall benefit when they are given responsibility for putting information into the database and creating a record of their study for a later purpose, such as a quiz, test, or class discussion.

Active Learning Through Multimedia and Hypermedia Presentations

Multimedia and Hypermedia Can Improve Communication Skills and Increase Motivation for Learning

Multimedia technology involves blending two or more media to enhance the presentation of information. Computer-based interactive multimedia include hypermedia and hypertext. Since publication of the previous edition of this book, an increasing number of students and teachers around the country are using hypermedia and hypertext programs to develop computer-based multimedia productions using text, sound, graphics, animation, video, and spatial modeling (Tolhurst, 1995; von Wodtke, 1993). Given students' familiarity with electronic images, multimedia and hypermedia presentations in schools are growing in popularity because they are excellent for gaining and holding attention and because they are multisensory (Jonassen, 1996). Student-developed multimedia and hypermedia projects have been shown to strengthen written and oral communication skills, increase motivation, and further creative processes (Troxclair, Stephens, Bennet, & Karnes, 1996).

Science. Some highly motivated junior high students worked together to create a touch-sensitive multimedia kiosk that was installed at a local zoo (Beichner, 1994). Using HyperCard and other hypermedia technology, they designed an information program, working with an on-screen audio recorder, a video tool to operate the videodisc player, color painting and text tools, and a data-linking tool for connecting pieces of information. Hot spots were created on the screen that, when touched by zoo visitors, made it possible to see and hear animals, gather additional information, and even obtain printouts, such as a map and student-generated questions and comments about zoo animals. Students demonstrated great enthusiasm for this project because they saw a real-world connection between their developing technology and science skills and the product of their efforts—the information kiosk for zoo visitors.

Social Studies. Middle school students, using the tools available in HyperStudio, created a hypermedia presentation on the civil rights movement of the 1960s for a class project during African-American Month. Their research resulted in several hypermedia topics of interest including music, images (photographs and video), major players, historical background, and more. The program was on display in the school library during February for all students to access. By clicking on a topic of interest, students could read about Rosa Parks, see a video clip of George Wallace, or listen to President John Kennedy make a brief speech.

Multimedia technology seems to be an ideal way to motivate today's youth to explore information in realistic and multimodal ways. Integrating sights, sounds, texts, graphics, and computers into an overall presentation can be an enriching and memorable learning experience for students in virtually all subject areas. Multimedia projects are becoming excellent alternatives to traditional papers and tests as measures of students' overall understanding of a unit or topic. The projects students create can also become part of the classroom collection of resources to be accessed by future students to enrich their learning. Interactive video disk technology allows teachers and students to control video information through the computer. Any segment of the disk can be accessed quickly and easily without having to scan the entire disk. In a physics class, for example, while reading, writing, or answering questions about subatomic particles on a computer screen, students can call up moving video images that further demonstrate and explain how these particles are detected by cyclotrons.

Electronic Media Productions Can Become Part of the Learning Environment

ACCESSING INFORMATION ABOUT COMPUTER TECHNOLOGY

Because of the rapid developments in computer technology, keeping up with innovations in hardware, software, and related technologies is a daunting task, especially for busy teachers. Perhaps the most challenging task for the classroom teacher is the selection of appropriate software. While microcomputers have the potential to improve teacher effectiveness, this can occur only when quality computer programs are put in the hands of quality teachers. Concerns about quality software are especially critical for those of us promoting the integration of literacy processes into content area classrooms.

Select Software on the Basis of Meaningful Learning

It is generally accepted that most software can, at best, cover only a small portion of the curriculum (Jonassen, 1996). Although vigorous efforts are being made to change the nature of learning software, much of what is currently available is not designed to instruct students but rather to drill them on material presented previously (Kulik & Kulik, 1991). More significantly, more programs are needed that provide instruction based on an interactive model of the reading, writing, and learning processes (Bangert-Drowns, 1993; Reinking, 1994). Given the current status of instructional software, we recommend that it be selected on the basis of whether it contains meaningful content and can be used for purposeful learning. In addition, software programs should require active participation by the learner and emphasize elaborative thinking instead of repetitive drill.

One fairly easy way to find appropriate software is by reading reviews of software in educational computing and general microcomputer magazines as well as in professional journals. A list of the more popular and relevant publications can be found in Figure 10.5.

CASE STUDY REVISITED

After exploring this chapter, you should now have many new ideas about how to utilize computer technology in the content classroom for increasing student motivation and active involvement and for promoting higher-level thinking. José, the biology teacher who is the focus of this case study, was fortunate enough to discover some of the outstanding instructional applications of computer programs for helping his students better organize, analyze, and study biology information.

José brainstormed with another biology teacher and decided that a database management system held the most promise for helping their students organize a large number of related bits of information. José used the Microsoft Works integrated software package provided with the DOS-based computers purchased through his school's grant.

José introduced his students to the database management system approach to organizing and studying by presenting a database he had completed as an example. José knew that with the students' first exposure, it was critical that the database not be too complex, leading to possible frustration and failure. Wisely, he began with a familiar database of lunch menu items from the previous month, his likes and dislikes, meat and vegetable content, and choice of beverage. First, he projected his database

Byte
One Phoenix Mill Lane
Peterborough, NH 03458

Computer Assisted English Language Learning Journal
International Society for
Technology in Education (ISTE)
1787 Agate St.
Eugene, OR 97403-1923

Computer Science Education
Ablex Publishing Corp.
355 Chestnut St.
Norwood, NJ 07648

Computers and Education
Michigan Technological University
Department of Humanities
Houghton, MI 49931

Computers and Education
Pergamon Press
600 White Plains Rd.
Tarrytown, NY 10591-5153

Computers, Reading and Language Arts
Modern Learning Publishers, Inc.
1308 E. 38th St.
Oakland, CA 94602

Curriculum Product News
Educational Media, Inc.
992 High Ridge Rd.
Stamford, CT 06905

ED-TECH Review
Association for the Advancement of
Computing in Education (AACE)
Box 2966
Charlottesville, VA 22902

Educational Technology
720 Palisade Ave.
Englewood Cliffs, NJ 07632

Instruction Delivery Systems
Communicative Technology Corp.
50 Culpepper St.
Warrenton, VA 22186

Interactive Learning Environments
Ablex Publishing Corp.
355 Chestnut St.
Norwood, NJ 07648

Internet World
20 Ketchum St.
Westport, CT 06880

Journal of Adolescent and Adult Literacy
International Reading Association
800 Barksdale Rd.
Box 8139
Newark, DE 19714-8139

Journal of Computers in Mathematics and Science Teaching
AACE
Box 2966
Charlottesville, VA 22902

Journal of Computing in Teacher Education
ISTE
1787 Agate St.
Eugene, OR 97403-1923

Journal of Educational Computing Research
Baywood Publishing Co., Inc.
26 Austin Ave.
Box 337
Amityville, NY 11701

Journal of Educational Multimedia and Hypermedia
AACE
Box 2966
Charlottesville, VA 22902

Journal of Research on Computing in Education
ISTE
1787 Agate St.
Eugene, OR 97403-1923

Learning and Leading with Technology
(formerly *The Computing Teacher*)
ISTE
1787 Agate St.
Eugene, OR 97403-1923

FIGURE 10.5 Technology Journals and Magazines for Middle and Secondary School Teachers

MacWorld
MacWorld Communications, Inc.
501 2nd St.
San Francisco, CA 94107

PC Magazine
Ziff-Davis Publishing Co.
One Park Ave.
New York, NY 10016

Personal Publishing
Hitchock Publishing Co.
191 S. Gary Ave.
Carol Stream, IL 60188

The Reading Teacher
International Reading Association
800 Barksdale Rd.
Box 8139
Newark, DE 19714-8139

School Library Journal
Box 1878
Marion, OH 43305

Science Teacher
1742 Connecticut Ave., NW
Washington, DC, 20009

Teaching and Computers
Scholastic, Inc.
Box 2040
Mahopac, NY 10541-9963

Tech Trends
Association for Educational Technology and Communications
1025 Vermont Ave. NW, Suite 820
Washington, DC 20005

Telecommunications in Education (T.I.E.) News
ISTE
1787 Agate St.
Eugene, OR 97403-1923

T.H.E. Journal–Technological Horizons in Education
150 El Camino Real
Tustin, CA 92680

Via Satellite
Phillips Business Information, Inc.
7811 Montrose Rd.
Potomac, MD 20854

Windows Magazine
CMP Publications
600 Community Dr.
Manhasset, NY 11030

Windows Users
Wandsworth Publishing, Inc.
831 Federal Rd.
Brookfield, CT 06804

The Writing Notebook, Creative Word Processing in the Classroom
Box 1268
Eugene, OR 97440-1268

FIGURE 10.5 ***continued***

on a large screen using a liquid crystal display (LCD) acquired with grant monies. LCD panels are compact, flat units that fit on top of overhead projectors and allow large groups equal viewing access to computer screen information. After explaining how he constructed his database, he posed several questions to the class, and then had them work in pairs using the database to answer the questions.

José's next step was to have students complete a partially completed database by using their biology textbooks to fill in the gaps. This approach is highly consistent with the ways teachers can help students enjoy the encoding benefits of learning we describe in this book. Again, working in pairs, his students keyed in information re-

Type of Cell	Shape	Function	Location
astocyte	radiating	supply nutrients	central nervous system (CNS)
basal	cube-like	make new cells	stratum basale
cardiac muscle	branched	pump blood	around heart
erythrocytes	disc	move O^2, remove CO^2	blood plasma
fibroblast	flat	fiber production	connective tissue
keratinocytes	round	strengthen cells	stratum basal
osteoclast	ruffled	bone restoration	bone
sensory neurons	long, thin	impulses to CNS	cell body
simple columnar	columnar	secretion, absorption	digestive tract, glands
simple squamous	flat	diffusion of materials	lungs, blood vessels, kidneys
skeletal muscle	long	movement, posture	bone, skin
smooth muscle	disc	movement	organ walls

FIGURE 10.6 José's Class Database

lated to several different animals, their diets, and their habitats. Several sessions were spent monitoring and coaching the students, as well as demonstrating the desired thinking and computer skills needed to complete the database. Students were encouraged to ask frequent questions of José and their peers as they gained greater facility and confidence in using the process of database construction.

At this stage, José was ready to begin applying the database technology to the study of cell types. As before, he placed a database (this time, blank) on the overhead projector using an LCD panel. Students sat in pairs around a common terminal, with their own blank database on screen and their textbooks open to the chapter on human cells. José read through the chapter with his students and engaged them in discussion about key terms and descriptions of cell types. As they progressed through the first few pages of the chapter and talked about information they were learning about cells, José demonstrated on the overhead how and where to place critical information into their databases. Finally, essential categories were agreed upon and written into their database grids; these included cell type, shape, function, and location (Figure 10.6). With each subsequent class session, as students read, studied, and engaged in meaningful learning activities related to cells, they were given the opportunity to input relevant information into their databases. At the end of each class session, José engaged students in an exchange of questions about their expanding databases. Students asked questions of each other and of José, as he asked questions of them in a model/elicit format. In this way, José was stimulating critical decision making and higher-level thinking as he prepared his class for a test on the material at the end of their study of the chapter. Through this process, students were able to see how test-like questions were related to their databases and could be answered using information in their grids.

José was proud to report that after his class created, queried, and studied their databases on cells, they scored higher on his chapter test than any previous group. His colleague, who used the same approach, had similar results. Students demonstrated much more enthusiasm for learning the content of the chapter using the computer and reported that they could concentrate and understand the material more easily using a database.

■ ■ ■

SUMMARY

We have included this new chapter in the third edition of *Readers, Teachers, Learners* because of the incredibly rapid growth in instructional applications of computer technology. We believe the ultimate outcome of this growth is the inevitable use of computers as teaching and learning tools in an increasing number of middle and secondary schools. We also believe that with this growth comes responsible use of computer technology for meeting the learning needs of adolescents. Consequently, we advocate in this chapter that teachers use computers in meaningful ways to encourage active learning, to provide students with opportunities for unique learning experiences, and to help them organize and synthesize information across the content areas. Teachers of today and the future will need to increase their knowledge of classroom applications of computer technology in order to be wise and purposeful consumers. It is our hope that with this knowledge, teachers will discover ways to make computers a tool compatible with the other interactive, prosocial, language-based strategies recommended throughout this book.

REFERENCES

Anderson, J., & Lee, A. (1995). Literacy teachers learning a new literacy: A study of the use of electronic mail in a reading education class. *Reading Research and Instruction, 34,* 222–238.

Anderson, T. H., & Armbruster, B. B. (1984). Content area textbooks. In R. Anderson, J. Osborn, & R. Tierney (Eds.), *Learning to read in American schools: Basal readers and content texts.* Hillsdale, NJ: Erlbaum.

Anderson-Inman, L. (1995–1996). Computer-assisted outlining: Information organization made easy. *Journal of Adolescent and Adult Literacy, 39,* 316–320.

Armstrong, S. (1995). *Telecommunications in the classroom.* Palo Alto, CA: Computer Learning Foundation.

Bangert-Drowns, R. L. (1993). The word processor as an instructional tool: A meta-analysis of word processing in writing instruction. *Review of Educational Research, 63,* 69–93.

Beichner, R. J. (1994). Multimedia editing to promote science learning. *Journal of Educational Multimedia and Hypermedia, 3,* 55–70.

Bozeman, W. (1992). Spreadsheets. In G. Bitter (Ed.), *Macmillan encyclopedia of computers.* New York: Macmillan.

Clark, R. E. (1994). Media will never influence learning. *Educational Technology Research and Development, 42,* 21-29.

Cooke, K., & Lehrer, D. (1993). The Internet: The whole world is talking. *The Nation, 257,* 60-64.

Dillner, M. (1994). Using hypermedia to enhance content area instruction. *Journal of Reading, 37,* 260-270.

Fielding, L. P., & Pearson, P. D. (1994). Reading comprehension: What works. *Educational Leadership, 51,* 62-68.

Gallego, M., & Hollingsworth, S. (1992). Multiple literacies: Teachers' evolving perceptions. *Language Arts, 69,* 206-213.

Halio, M. P. (1990). Student writing: Can the machine maim the message? *Academic Computing, 6,* 18-19.

Hancock, C., Kaput, J. J., & Goldsmith, L. T. (1992). Authentic inquiry with data: Critical barriers to classroom implementation. *Educational Psychologist, 27,* 337-364.

Harris, J. (1994). Teaching teachers to use telecomputing tools. *The Computing Teacher, 22,* 60-63.

Horney, M. A., & Anderson-Inman, L. (1992, April). *Computer-based outlining programs as tools for gathering, organizing and studying information across the curriculum.* Paper presented at the annual conference of the American Educational Research Association, San Francisco.

Inspiration Software, Inc. (1995). *Inspiration 4.1.* Portland, OR: Author.

Jonassen, D. H. (1996). *Computers in the classroom: Mindtools for critical thinking.* Englewood Cliffs, NJ: Prentice-Hall.

Kelley, M. G., & Wiebe, J. H. (1994). Telecommunications, data gathering, and problem solving. *The Computing Teacher, 21,* 23-26.

Kozma, R. (1991). Learning with media. *Review of Educational Research, 61,* 179-211.

Kozma, R. (1994). Will media influence learning? Reframing the debate. *Educational Technology Research and Development, 42,* 5-17.

Kulik, C., & Kulik, J. (1991). Effectiveness of computer-based instruction: An updated analysis. *Computers in Human Behavior, 7,* 75-94.

Landow, G. P. (1992). *Hypertext: The convergence of contemporary critical theory and technology.* Baltimore: Johns Hopkins University Press.

Leu, D. J. (1996). Sarah's secret: Social aspects of literacy and learning in a digital information age. *The Reading Teacher, 50,* 162-165.

Lewis, P. H. (1994, August 9). Who's the coolest Internet provider? *The New York Times,* p. 120.

Leydon, P. (1995, June 4, 11, 18, 25). On the edge of the digital age. *The Minneapolis Star Tribune,* Section T.

Marcus, S. (1995). E-meliorating student writing. *Electronic Learning, 14,* 18-19.

Mike, D. (1997). Internet in the schools: A literacy perspective. *Journal of Adolescent and Adult Literacy, 40,* 4-13.

Negroponte, N. (1995). *Being digital.* New York: Alfred A. Knopf.

Newby, T., Stepich, D., Lehman, J., & Russell, J. (1996). *Instructional technology for teaching and learning.* Englewood Cliffs, NJ: Prentice-Hall.

Nist, S. L., Simpson, M. L., Olejnik, S., & Mealey, D. L. (1991). The relation between self-selected study processes and test performance. *American Educational Research Journal, 28,* 849-874.

Pask-McCartney, C. (1989). *A discussion about motivation.* Proceedings of selected research presentations at the annual convention of the Association for Educational Communications and Technology (ERIC Document Reproduction No. ED 308 816).

Polin, L. (1992). Looking for love in all the wrong places? *The Computing Teacher, 20,* 6–7.

Ramondetta, J. (1992). Learning from lunchroom trash. *Learning Using Computers, 20,* 59.

Reil, M. (1990). Cooperative learning across classrooms in electronic learning circles. *Instructional Science, 19,* 445–466.

Reil, M. (1993, April). *The writing connection: Global learning circles.* Paper presented at the annual meeting of the American Educational Research Association, Atlanta.

Reinking, D. (1994, December). *Reading and writing with computers: Literacy research in a post-typographic world.* Paper presented at the meeting of the National Reading Conference, San Diego, CA.

Reinking, D. (1996). *Electronic literacy.* (Tech. Rep. No. 4). Athens, GA: National Reading Research Center.

Roblyer, M. D. (1993). From the editor's clipboard. *The Florida Teachnology in Education Quarterly, 5,* 2.

Roblyer, M. D., Edwards, J., & Havriluk, M. A. (1997). *Integrating educational technology into teaching.* Upper Saddle River, NJ: Prentice-Hall.

Ryder, R. J., & Graves, M. F. (1997). Using the Internet to enhance students' reading, writing, and information-gathering skills. *Journal of Adolescent and Adult Literacy, 40,* 244–254.

Ryder, R. J., & Hughes, T. (1997). *Internet for educators.* Upper Saddle River, NJ: Prentice-Hall.

Salomon, G. (1993). On the nature of pedagogic computer tools: The case of the writing partner. In S. P. LaJoie & J. Derry (Eds.), *Computers as cognitive tools.* Hillsdale, NJ: Erlbaum.

Simons, P. R. (1993). Constructive learning: The role of the learner. In T. Duffy, J. Lowyck, & D. Jonassen (Eds.), *Designing environments for constructive learning.* Heidelberg, Germany: Springer-Verlag.

Summers, J. (1990–1991). Effects of interactivity upon student achievement, completion intervals, and affective perceptions. *Journal of Educational Technology Systems, 19,* 53–57.

Thompson, A., Simonson, M., & Hargraves, C. (1992). *Educational technology: A review of the research.* Washington, DC: Association for Educational Communications and Technology.

Tolhurst, D. (1995). Hypertext, hypermedia, multimedia defined? *Educational Technology, 35,* 21–26.

Troxclair, D., Stephens, K., Bennett, T., & Karnes, F. (1996). Teaching technology: Multimedia presentations in the classroom. *Gifted Child, 19,* 34–47.

Turner, S. V., & Dipinto, V. M. (1992). Students as hypermedia authors: Themes emerging from a qualitative study. *Journal of Research on Computing in Education, 25,* 187–199.

U.S. Congress, Office of Technology Assessment (1989). *Linking for learning: A new course for education.* OTA-SET-430. Washington, DC: U.S. Government Printing Office.

von Wodtke, M. (1993). *Mind over media: Creative thinking skills for electronic media.* New York: McGraw-Hill.

Willinsky, J. (1993, April). *Qualities of learning and connection in computer-mediated communication.* Paper presented at the annual meeting of the American Educational Research Association, Atlanta.

Zeitz, L., Hornety, M., & Anderson-Inman, L. (1992). Empowering students with flexible text. *The Computing Teacher, 19,* 16–20.

CHAPTER 11

Meeting the Literacy Needs of Special Students

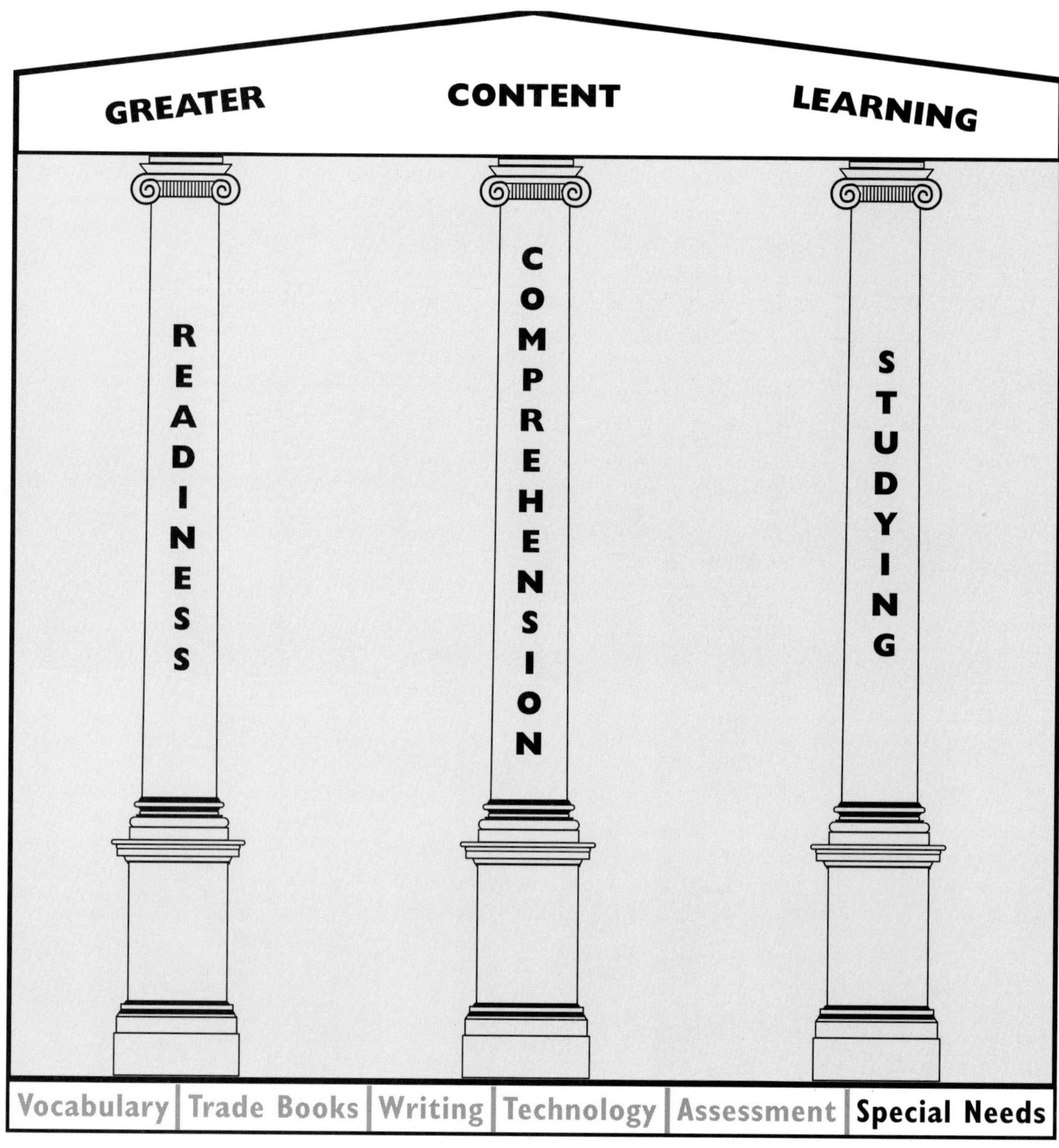

ANTICIPATION GUIDE

Directions: Read each statement carefully and decide whether you agree or disagree with it, placing a check mark in the appropriate *Before Reading* column. When you have finished reading and studying the chapter, return to the guide and decide whether your anticipations need to be changed by placing a check mark in the appropriate *After Reading* column.

	BEFORE READING		**AFTER READING**	
	Agree	*Disagree*	*Agree*	*Disagree*
1. All students with special needs are poor readers.	______	______	______	______
2. Strategies that emphasize basic skills are best for special needs students.	______	______	______	______
3. Students of color are not necessarily at risk for reading and learning failure.	______	______	______	______
4. Definitions and characteristics of gifted students are consistent and unambiguous.	______	______	______	______
5. Trade books should be used sparingly with special needs students.	______	______	______	______

Only as we meet our students, observe them intelligently, and use them as informants are we able to draw from the potential curriculum appropriate and suitable objectives, assignments and strategies. Teachers with their students create, change, and are in charge of curriculum.

All the fuss about knowing students, both in general and specifically, comes from the belief that learning occurs when it is personalized and positive, and when it focuses on the strengths and unique abilities of individuals.

—Watson (1988)

In previous chapters of this book, we have laid down the foundations for effective content area instruction and literacy development for middle and secondary students. In many ways, these instructional foundations find their most powerful expression in applications for students with special needs. Students with reading difficulty should receive our best strategies and not simply more structure, more routines, and more basic remedial lessons (Banks, 1994). Similarly, excellent readers should not be asked to complete, in an accelerated fashion, a larger number of low-level, basic-skills tasks (Cain & Brewer, 1992). Students with unique needs, such as those who are culturally different, those who speak another language or a dialect, those who are poor readers, those with specific learning disabilities, or those who are academically gifted, make up a varied and diverse group. Consequently, blanket generalizations about these students are inappropriate (Carlson, 1992). Yet, these students can be taught to improve their reading, thinking, and language use if we apply our knowledge of literacy, language development, and learning strategies to them as we do to other so-called normal or regular students (Dole, Brown, & Trathen, 1996; Rios, 1996; Wood & Algozzine, 1994). For students with individual needs, as for all students, literacy development should be seen as a process of meaning making in which reading and writing are vehicles for helping students make sense of their world and course content and the classroom is the supportive environment where growth in literacy occurs (Miller, 1993). Throughout this chapter, therefore, we will be emphasizing approaches that capitalize on what students with unique needs bring to the classroom in terms of their prior knowledge, skills, experiences, beliefs, and culture.

Special Needs Students Are a Diverse Group

CASE STUDY

Rene is a biracial daughter of an Asian mother and a Hispanic father. She is in the 11th grade and attends a high school in a major urban center in the Midwest in a community of ethnic and socioeconomic diversity. The school is a large, decaying, fortress-looking building with no windows. Its grounds are littered and unattended. Rene has been in special education classes since the third grade. She recalls with bitterness the experience that led her to initiation into these classes:

> It was the first or second day of school. My mom was real sick, she was having a miscarriage I think. I was really afraid. I thought she was going

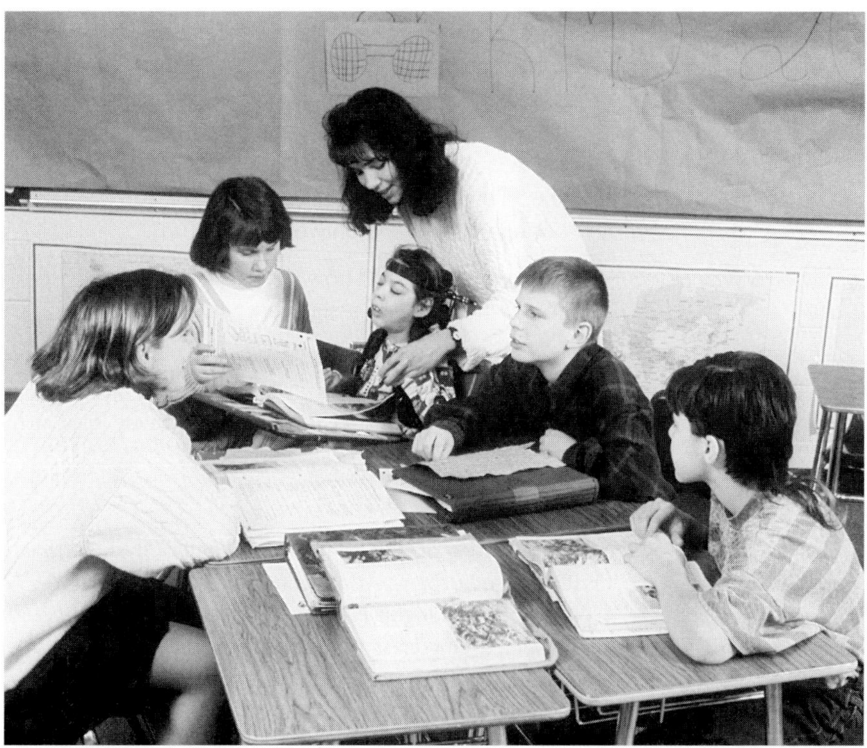

to die. Anyway, the teacher would write a word on the board, erase it, then go around the room and call on someone to say the word and spell it. Well, she finally called on me, but I wasn't paying attention because I was so upset about my mom. I had to stand up . . . I just couldn't remember the word. The class started laughing, and the teacher told me to sit down and for not paying attention I would have to write the word 50 times. It seems like from that time on I started having a lot of trouble reading, and they put me in special ed.

As an 11th grader, Rene was still in a special reading class. The class included 23 students; all but two were members of ethnic minorities. The classroom was small, cramped, and cluttered. During the winter, the radiators generated stifling heat and clanged uncontrollably. According to the teacher of this special reading class—a former shop teacher with 4 graduate hours of reading instruction from a nearby university—students were supposed to be working on their own in self-paced workbooks and programmed materials. Reading kits with 25-year-old copyright dates and some programmed spelling and phonics books were stacked irregularly on the one small bookcase next to the teacher's desk. Very few of these materials were being used, however. Most of the students were either sleeping, listening to music on headphones, or talking quietly. On one of our visits, the teacher spent the period balancing his checkbook.

Rene used the time to visit with the only other female in the class. She commented on her experiences in remedial reading:

> It's a joke. I'm wasting my time in there. Nobody works. We just catch up on what's going on, you know, who's pregnant, who's going with who and stuff. Mr. Willis hates it too, so he just says, "Don't bother me and I won't bother you." That's cool, but my reading is still bad and I have to take general courses because they're the only ones I can pass.

Rene commented on how she gets by in her other classes, such as history, science, and math, where reading assignments are required for successful class performance.

> Math's no problem for me. I've always been good in math. History is harder. I sit next to my girlfriend, Stella. She's real smart; she tells me what to do. I don't like that teacher. . . . I never look at him, and he never calls on me.

To the reader:
When reflecting on this challenging scene of dysfunctional teaching and learning in a disadvantaged urban setting, consider ways in which Mr. Willis's class could become a place for meaningful literacy opportunities. How could Rene be reached? How could her reading class be restructured so that it is no longer a waste of time for students like her? Be prepared to write down your ideas and recommendations after reading this chapter.

■ ■ ■

WHO ARE STUDENTS WITH SPECIAL NEEDS?

As stated earlier, there are many different, unique needs that students in middle and secondary schools bring to the classroom. These needs may be based on factors of culture, instruction, ability, motivation, attitude, learning, and even gender (Brozo & Schmelzer, 1997). Consider, for example, the growing literacy needs boys bring to the middle and upper grades. Did you know that boys of all ages fail in reading more often than girls (Flynn & Rahbar, 1993)? National test results in reading consistently show superior achievement for girls. Also, boys populate remedial reading classrooms, lower-track classrooms, and learning disabilities programs far more often than do girls (Page, 1991).

Teachers Need To Become Sensitive to the Growing Needs of Special Students

To confound matters, factors often and necessarily interact, resulting in myriad variations of unique needs. We believe that to expect teachers to be knowledgeable about and expert in dealing with all of students' needs is unrealistic. Nonetheless, we all need to become more sensitive to the increasingly diverse concerns of students as we move into the new century. In this section we briefly describe three principal populations of students: culturally diverse, learning disabled, and gifted. We enter into this discussion with a clear understanding of the pitfalls of categorizing students into neat, tidy groups for the sake of academic simplicity. We ourselves are generally uncomfortable with the proclivity for creating "otherness" or self-fulfilling prophecies (Eaker-Rich & Van Galen, 1996) through our professional discourse; we address this concern later in this chapter as it applies to the term *at risk*. Ever mindful of these concerns, we believe nevertheless that it can be productive for us to try to better understand these three groups of students who are entering middle and secondary school classrooms in increasing numbers. These groups have been studied and described extensively by researchers and scholars, many of whom have offered considered and sensitive insights into the unique learning needs of each.

Culturally Diverse Students

On a recent professional trip to California, we encountered a school administrator who documented nearly 120 distinct language groups of students in his district. If that fact alone doesn't alert you to the ineluctability of American cultural pluralism, we don't know what will! A clear indication of growing cultural diversity in our society and schools is that students of color comprise nearly one-third of the public school population in the United States and are projected to make up almost 50% of all students by the year 2020 (Cushner, McClelland, & Stafford, 1992). Significantly, this multicultural trend is not regional but is evident in neighborhoods and schools that were once monocultural (Diamond & Moore, 1995). The dramatic shift toward cultural diversity in our schools means that teachers who have traditionally taught students of one culture may expect to teach students with wide-ranging language and linguistic backgrounds, levels of acculturation, countries of birth, and socioeconomic statuses (Rios, 1996).

Students of Color Will Comprise Nearly Half of the School Population by 2020

Accommodating and celebrating diversity are ideals that are not always easily achieved. Nonetheless, you can acknowledge and affirm diversity by modeling behaviors of tolerance and acceptance and by linking the curriculum to the unique experiences of your students. Banks (1994) proposed that multicultural education be considered a basic part of a student's general education. This means that all students become bilingual and all students study different cultural perspectives. According to Banks, multiculturalism should pervade the curriculum and all aspects of school life, including bulletin boards, lunch rooms, and assemblies. All teachers and subjects should reflect a multicultural perspective.

Learning-Disabled Students

Learning disabilities can refer to a variety of problems, including difficulties in reading and language, math, memory, and nonverbal communication. However, in most instances, learning disabilities are generally diagnosed with reading assessments and, more often than not, refer to some type of reading disability (Spafford & Grosser, 1996). While the incidence of learning disabilities seems to be increasing, the U.S Department of Education reported in 1995 that 5.25% of the entire school-age population was learning disabled. Furthermore, 2.625% of all students were identified as dyslexic, that is, having a learning disability in the area of reading.

Dyslexia has never been easy to define, largely because a unanimously acceptable definition has not yet been formulated (Hynd, 1992). Some have challenged its very existence (Coles, 1987), while others, who have devoted their professional careers to the study of dyslexia, continue to refer to it as an "elusive disorder" (Spafford & Grosser, 1996). Dyslexia is elusive because it is difficult to capture and understand the true nature of this disorder. Despite a host of correlating behaviors, including delayed language development, memory deficits, and social behavior problems, the most common form of dyslexia is characterized by extreme difficulty in learning to read and spell words. Students may be diagnosed with dyslexia if they have average intelligence and have been given conventional reading instruction, yet continue to fail to learn to read. Experts have long thought that brain dysfunction is the true origin of dyslexia. With rapid developments in brain scanning technology, dyslexia researchers are trying to zero in on the precise location of neural dysfunctioning in processing written language (Grosser & Spafford, 1995).

Dyslexia Is Difficult to Define Even by the Experts

Students with serious reading and learning disabilities are showing up in growing numbers in regular middle and secondary school classrooms. This means that teachers of all subjects should be aware of the unique needs of these students in order to improve their chances for successful learning. Does this mean that you will be required to understand the complexities of the brain in order to deal with students diagnosed as dyslexic? Not at all. Many of the strategies offered in this textbook have been shown to be effective with students who have reading disabilities or dyslexia (Spafford & Grosser, 1996).

How Does It Feel to Be a Remedial Reader?

To empathize fully with students with reading disabilities, we would have to be able to trade places with them, "crawl into their skin," see the world through their eyes. Anyone who has journeyed to another country and has tried to communicate and get by in a brand-new culture where English is not spoken can begin to appreciate the frustrations some special needs students experience as they grapple to understand new, complex language forms in middle and secondary school classrooms and textbooks. For obvious reasons, we cannot know fully the feelings and experiences these students have when trying to learn, although we can help you come closer to understanding these students through a simulation. Read the following passage; then write your interpretation of it in your own words.

A Simulation of Reading Failure

The Correct Interpretation of the Thirty-Fourth Section

The thirty-fourth section refers to the construction thereof adopted by the local tribunals, and to rights of things having a permanent locality, and other matters immovable and intraterritorial in their nature and character. It never has been supposed that the section did apply, or was intended to apply to questions of a more general nature, not at all dependent upon a fixed

> and permanent operation, as, for example, to the construction of written instruments, where the state tribunals are called upon to perform, that is, to ascertain upon general reasoning and legal analogies what is the true exposition of the instrument.
>
> Based upon this interpretation, it seems to us that it would be at least as reasonable to assume an intent that the power should be imperative as to property known to be productive but which later becomes unproductive. We think under the facts of this case the existence of an intent that the power of sale was to become imperative upon failure of productivity with likelihood of continuance of that status, is the correct interpretation of the thirty-fourth section.

Now that you have read the passage and written your own interpretation of the thirty-fourth section, how does it feel to be a remedial reader? We are only half serious when we ask this question because we know you are not a remedial reader—most of the time. Occasionally, however, we all encounter texts that leave us totally bewildered, confused, and frustrated. This is how many poor readers must feel when they try to read textbooks filled with abstract concepts and unfamiliar vocabulary, and about which they have little interest or prior knowledge. As you work through the remainder of this chapter, keep in mind your experiences with the thirty-fourth section. Remember how it felt to have little or no meaning to grab on to in the passage. Then, perhaps, you will see more clearly the relevance and importance of the ideas and strategies we recommend for helping these students expand their literacy.

Gifted Students

The concept of giftedness may be as controversial as the concept of dyslexia in the sense that it is almost as difficult to define (Walker, 1991). Furthermore, gifted programs in junior and senior high school have been criticized for their exclusionary policies and for the fact that students of color are often seriously underrepresented in advanced academic classes (Van Galen, 1996).

Typical Classrooms Have a Wide Range of Academic Abilities

Giftedness refers to a syndrome of special learning talents exhibited by certain students, including high intelligence, unique problem- solving abilities, high standards, an inquiring mind, alertness, creative imagination, and an enjoyment of school (Albert & Spangler, 1992). Human nature suggests that few teachers would be displeased with an entire classful of students with these attitudes and abilities. Typical middle and secondary school classrooms, however, are populated by students of all abilities and multiple cultures, requiring teachers to accommodate to learners who may range from dyslexic to academically gifted (Shields, 1996). Many teachers have found ways to incorporate especially challenging learning experiences into their content lessons to keep students who are academically accelerated actively involved (Cain & Brewer, 1992). We believe that most of the strategies described in this book can be used successfully with gifted students.

INSTRUCTIONAL GUIDELINES FOR TEACHING STUDENTS WITH SPECIAL NEEDS

As we have indicated, there are many types of students who require extra teacher attention. Some, like those with reading disabilities, need better instruction in order to become competent language users and good readers and thinkers in dealing with subject area information and ideas. Others, like academically gifted students, need special instruction that helps them to maintain their high level of motivation and to grow as active, independent learners. We hope you will gain a sense of how the guidelines and methods of effective reading and writing instruction set forth in previous chapters and those that follow in this chapter may be applied to meet the literacy needs of these special students.

Reading-Disabled and Gifted Students Should Not Be Permanently Separated from Regular Students or Each Other

In her learning disabilities resource room, Carol provides sound reading and study skills assistance, but she cannot take care of all the literacy needs of her students. Much of her time outside of class, therefore, is spent in consultation with subject area teachers to discover ways to work cooperatively. She often finds this aspect of her work the most challenging because many teachers feel that the 45 minutes these students spend in resource instruction daily is all the time they need. The result of this attitude is that classroom teachers give up responsibility for assisting the language and literacy development of learning- and reading-disabled students. Resource should play a supplementary and supportive role; it should not replace the work of the classroom teacher, who should be highly involved. The key concern here is that without coordination between reading and writing instruction in resource and the kind that occurs in other classrooms, these students will likely continue to experience difficulty learning content area subject matter and adequate reading strategies.

Resource Should Not Replace the Classroom

Lack of coordination can lead to another problem—the failure to demonstrate adequately how special needs students can transfer their reading and writing skills learned in resource classes to reading tasks in other classrooms and outside of school. Classroom teachers can facilitate this transfer by helping students apply text study processes to their own textbook reading and other assignments. Working with the resource teacher, the classroom teacher can discover the particular needs of all special students and plan valuable reading and writing opportunities for them. By taking time to integrate reading and study skills instruction into their content lessons, teachers will assist special needs students without singling them out or making them feel inferior.

Gifted learners and readers also need regular opportunities to interact socially and academically with students of all abilities. In diverse classrooms, gifted students can learn how to respect others, value everyone's gifts, expand leadership skills, and provide role models for classmates (Shields, 1996).

A Word about Inclusion

Regardless of your position on the most appropriate environment for learning-disabled students, the growing popularity of inclusion makes it increasingly likely that you will be responsible for teaching content area curricula to these students in your classroom (Rogers, 1993). *Inclusion* involves keeping students with disabilities in the regular classroom during the entire school day while providing support services from resource teachers, reading specialists, and others (Roberts & Mather, 1995). Though not without controversy (Pearman, Huang, & Mellblom, 1997), inclusion has been successfully implemented in middle schools (Fishman & Goss, 1996) and high schools (Touchette, 1996).

Effective Guidelines for Inclusion

To improve the likelihood of successful inclusion in the middle and upper grades, Sanacore (1996) presents the following guidelines:

- Develop curricula that integrate reading, writing, speaking, listening, studying, and thinking as interactive processes.
- Immerse students in meaningful, interesting, and content-based activities.
- Use multiple forms of assessment to ensure that students' responses to instruction are fully and appropriately observed and documented.
- Involve parents in their children's learning.

Earlier, we cited Banks, who argues that all students benefit from being part of a multicultural setting and educational experience. Similarly, students with and without disabilities can benefit from being part of the same community of learners. Students can learn tolerance and cooperation, and can gain a better understanding of the full range of human diversity when interacting daily in inclusive environments.

Instruction Should Emphasize Meaningful Reading and Writing Experiences

Poor readers are often penalized. They are usually recycled through a regimen of basic skills instruction that failed to produce reading competence in the first place (Marr & Allington, 1994). Basic skills instruction that focuses on spelling accuracy and word attack, and requires memorizing rules and performing mechanical behaviors, fails to capitalize on how language is learned best (Brozo & Brozo, 1994; Goodman, Bird, & Goodman, 1992). As for minority students, Reyhner and Garcia (1989) point out that many teachers falsely assume that these students can be successfully diagnosed with standardized reading tests and then treated prescriptively through "basic" skills instruction. This approach "focuses a teacher's efforts on testing and remediation rather than on finding meaningful reading materials and culturally appropriate ways to teach and motivate students" (Reyhner & Garcia, 1989, p. 86). Poor readers and students from divergent cultures can expand their literacy skills when they are given opportunities to explore their own interests through meaningful reading and writing experiences (Abt-Perkins, 1996; Field & Aebersold, 1990). Based on an extensive review of the literacy research, Knapp and Needels

(1991) posit the following instructional guidelines for working with students experiencing failure in reading:

Research-Based Teaching Guidelines for Students Having Reading Difficulty

- Instruction should be active and focused on comprehension of meaning.
- Instruction should use a wide variety of authentic texts.
- Instruction should use students as resources for one another's learning.
- Instruction should place reading in real-world contexts.

You probably recall the story we told earlier in this book about the young man who was diagnosed as learning disabled in the second grade because of his inability to read. To refresh your memory, just when special education and reading teachers were ready to give up on him, his seventh-grade math teacher discovered that the young man had a great interest in magic. The teacher gave him books on magic, which he struggled through initially but eventually began reading with growing confidence. Soon he was able to apply his increasing reading skills to his school textbooks. The young man went on to graduate from high school and, finally, from the University of Illinois. We remind you of this story to demonstrate the power of meaningful learning.

It should not be assumed that students with learning disabilities require inordinate structure and routines to expand their language and literacy skills. Using reading and writing to help them explore personal interests and satisfy cultural needs can increase their language competence and motivate them to become better language learners.

Gifted readers and learners also need meaningful learning experiences, not simply an accelerated diet of "more of the same." We know of school settings where students classified as gifted are asked to complete the same basic skills tasks as their peers, who are not categorized as gifted, but more rapidly and in greater number. This approach may keep gifted readers busy, but it is likely to do little to motivate them to learn. Instead, gifted students, like all learners, should be constantly challenged by stimulating, thought-provoking, and useful academic tasks and projects.

Each Student's Unique Contribution Should Be Valued

In *Seeking Diversity,* Linda Rief (1992) says about her junior high students, "I don't believe any one system of learning works for every child. Everyone learns differently. As a teacher I believe my job is to find out what works best for each child" (p. 3). In valuing student diversity, we discover ways to reach and teach young adults that are personally meaningful and culturally responsive. Banks puts it this way:

> When teachers have gained knowledge about cultural and ethnic diversity, looked at that knowledge from different ethnic and cultural perspectives, and taken action to make their own lives and communities more culturally sensitive and diverse, they will have the knowledge and skills needed to help transform the curricular canon as well as the hearts and minds of their students. (1991, p. 140)

Curricular Control Should Be Shared with Diverse Learners

In contrast to this open, diversity-seeking stance is the very definite message that is communicated to students when the teacher and the text completely dominate and control instruction. The message is that only the teacher and the text can ask the questions, only their questions are worth asking, students cannot learn from one another, and the students' job is to answer questions correctly. A vise-like grip on the curricular controls denies the important contributions each student can make to the development of literacy in the classroom. More significantly, it reinforces the feeling of inferiority in students with a history of learning failure because they learn that their ideas, attitudes, and experiences have little value.

As stated many times in this book, the process of meaning making, whether in reading or writing, depends on an individual's perceptions and is enhanced through students' interaction and cooperation within the social context of the classroom. Literacy theory refers to classrooms as **interpretive communities** (Fish, 1980; Harste, 1986) made up of individuals who share many approaches to life and models of reality, but who also hold separate and unique models of reality based on interactions in other interpretive communities outside the classroom (home, community, church, social groups, etc.). Through cooperative grouping and other forms of student interaction, academically gifted, learning-disabled, and regular students can share thoughts, feelings, and experiences; question and expand their own models of reality; and learn to value each other's cultures, perceptions, and input. This student-centered approach to language learning assigns a great deal of value to the social interactions within the classroom. When special needs students see that their input is valued because it has helped reshape someone else's perceptions about a text, this gives them the chance to be recognized as successful thinkers and learners.

The unique academic talents of gifted learners can and should be viewed as assets by middle and secondary school teachers. These students can be a vital part of the classroom community as academic resources and models. There appears to be evidence that when gifted learners interact frequently with other members of the class during meaningful learning tasks, academic achievement increases for all students (Shields, 1996).

All Dialects of a Language Should Be Valued

What do you call a person who knows two languages?
Bilingual.
What do you call a person who knows one language?
An American.

We found this graffiti on a university corridor, and it occurred to us that ethnocentricity rooted in monolingualism is so prevalent in our society that it cannot help but creep into our schools and classrooms. It also occurred to us that it is not necessarily bilingualism that marks a speaker as being less of an American, but rather which ethnic group is speaking. For instance, why do the speech patterns of many African-Americans, rural Southerners, Eastern European immigrants, or Hispanic immigrants receive a negative response, whereas descendants from Western Europe find that their speech patterns are quite acceptable—for example, those with French, Swedish, or German accents? Pietras claims that understanding and accepting language variation is "more a matter of which racial, ethnic, or social group is doing the speaking than it is of language variation per se" (1984, p. 240). The serious danger in an illogical response to language variation is that some teachers may judge students negatively just by the sound of their speech. In fact, research in teacher expectancy suggests that low expectations about a student's ability to learn are formed unconsciously based on dialects and use of language (Banks, 1994).

Not All Dialect Variations of English Are Perceived Equally

According to linguists (Barnitz, 1994; Labov, 1982), all of us who speak English use a dialect or version of the English language. Teachers who understand this, who are knowledgeable about language, fail to be swayed by dialects; instead, they incorporate this information into their curriculum to help students understand the functions of language and literacy in all aspects of everyday communication and social interaction.

To be sure, issues of dialect are often highly charged, controversial, and rarely clear-cut. Lisa Delpit (1988, 1995), an African-American educator, suggests that schools fail students of color when schools ignore the importance of the ability to use standard forms of English. She asserts that standard English, the form of English used by the dominant culture, becomes a power lever for students of color and nonstandard dialect users as they attempt to advance economically and politically. Without this ability to shift their speaking and writing into the dialect of the dominant culture, students will find few avenues of advancement. Delpit quotes an angry African-American mother, who discovered that the school her son was attending placed little or no emphasis on teaching students standard forms of English, as saying "My son already knows how to be Black!" (1988, p. 285).

From another perspective, those of us who are privileged, who may be white, and who are members of the dominant culture are asked to change our perceptions of what constitutes appropriate language use (Arnold & Swadener, 1993). Swadener (1990) poses these stirring questions:

> What if teachers and teacher educators were required to show evidence of bi- or multi-cultural competence,rather than merely mastery of dominant culture approaches to pedagogy and mastery of "general knowledge," drawing entirely from Eurocentric traditions? (p. 34)
>
> What if those of us who are monolingual were considered at risk? (p. 35)

Situation and Purpose Should Guide Language Instruction

Although all dialects of a language should be valued, situation and purpose may require a certain form of the language. Perhaps the responsible position is to respect variant forms of language while helping students use the dialect expected of them when they participate in the institutional life of our society, especially as it applies to writing standard English.

Engage Students in Literacy Experiences That Reverse Cycles of Passive Failure and Learned Helplessness

The constructs of *passive failure* and *learned helplessness* come from a line of psychological inquiry known as **attribution theory** (Fenwick, 1995; Singhal & Kanungo, 1996). This theory posits that students' performance on a task is influenced by their perceptions of the causes of past behavior. Over the past two decades, researchers (Butkowsky & Willow, 1980; Diener & Dweck, 1978; Graham, 1997; Hersh, Stone, Brian, & Ford, 1996; Mikulincer & Averill, 1995) have repeatedly found that students who attribute their performance to stable, controllable factors, such as effort, maintain their effort in the face of failure. Students who attribute performance to uncontrollable factors, such as luck, the task, the teacher, and ability, are likely to give up in the face of failure.

Whether they are aware of it or not, teachers generally treat less successful students differently than their more successful peers (Hamilton, 1996; Robinson & Good, 1987), which makes it easier for less successful students to attribute their failure to low ability. Johnston and Winograd (1985) have described teacher behaviors that apparently contribute to students' feelings of helplessness and passivity. The list of teacher behaviors, derived from classroom observation research by Good and Brophy (1984), suggests that teachers reinforce passive failure when they do the following:

Ways That Passive Failure Is Reinforced in the Classroom

1. Give less successful students the answers or shift to another student instead of refocusing or readjusting the question.
2. Reward inappropriate behavior or answers.
3. Criticize less successful students more often for failure.
4. Praise less successful students less frequently for success.
5. Pay less attention to and interact less with less successful students.
6. Give less successful students less time to answer questions.
7. Demand less from less successful students.
8. Come to the aid of less successful students more quickly.
9. Give terminal feedback more often.
10. Interrupt more often before the end of a sentence during oral reading.*

The teacher–student interactions in this list tell students that they cannot control their own learning, reinforcing the feeling of incompetence. We are not sure that any of us can totally eliminate differential behaviors from our interactions with students. Nonetheless, it is important to become more sensitive to these behaviors so that we can try to modify them. Indeed, it has been shown that when teachers are made aware of behaviors and attitudes that potentially may have negative effects on students, they can change (Brophy & Good, 1985).

---

*Adapted from Johnston and Winograd (1985, p. 285).

Students' feeling of incompetence is often rooted in reading experiences in very early grades and becomes so entrenched that it persists into adulthood. In a study of college upper-class students who had been diagnosed as learning disabled as early as grammar school, Brozo and Curtis (1987) found that these students continued to view themselves as failures. This was evidenced by statements they made about themselves:

> I see it as stuff I wasn't born with.
> I'm not smart.
> There's not a lot I can do to change myself.

The key to helping students break the cycle of passive failure in reading is to force them to attend to the connection between effort and outcomes. Less successful learners who have become helpless or passive need to accept more responsibility for their failure and success. Metacognitive strategies, such as those discussed in Chapters 3 and 9, that make students aware of what they are doing while learning will help them know when effort pays and when it does not. Getting students actively involved in the learning and teaching processes through cooperative learning, for instance, is essential for developing independence and a sense of control over their literacy (Rhodes & Dudley-Marling, 1996). When placed in the role of teacher, students see that they are valued and respected for their strengths rather than ignored or hounded because of their disabilities and disruptions (Watson, 1988). We should also provide these students with engaging texts and opportunities to explore personal connections and real-world applications through the use of all the communications systems: reading, writing, speaking, and listening.

Reinforce Effort–Outcome Connections for Students

E. Garcia (1990) presents the following list of curriculum principles for moving linguistically and culturally diverse secondary students beyond passivity and engaging them in meaningful learning:

- The more diverse the students we teach, the more content must be related to their own environment and experience.
- The more diverse the students, the more the curriculum should involve them in active rather than passive learning experiences.
- The more diverse the students, the more the curriculum should offer opportunities for them to apply new learning in meaningful contexts.
- The more diverse the students, the more the curriculum should deemphasize excessive practice and drill while providing more time for informal activities such as group work on projects.
- The more diverse the students, the more the curriculum should be integrated to provide opportunities for in-depth study of topics and for skill application.

Promote New, Positive Ways of Communicating About Students' Special Needs

Our professional educational discourse is replete with labels. We mentioned earlier that as authors we are not always comfortable using glib labels of the popular educational vernacular to describe students with unique characteristics. Unfortunately, although labels are used by professionals to better understand and communicate about behavioral, psychological, and sociological phenomena, they can also stigmatize and engender self-fulfilling prophecies of student failure. The field of reading has been especially responsible for promoting a lexicon of pejorative labels. Consider the terms used over the past century about students who demonstrate reading difficulty, such as *congenital word blindness, reading retarded,* and even the term we use in this chapter, *disabled reader.* Is it possible that the very words and terms we use to describe students influence our expectations about them and, in turn, influence the brand and type of instruction they receive? In attempting to answer this question, let's consider the growing use of the term *at risk.*

Our Professional Language Can Influence Our Perceptions and Actions

The pervasiveness of the term *at risk* hardly needs an introduction. The language of risk has gained such currency in educational circles that it can be found as the focus of specialized books on teaching, journal issues, conferences, and national centers for research. What does it mean to be at risk? Does it signal a useful way of identifying students for assistance who would otherwise fail, or is it just another labeling device that perpetuates a deficit view of literacy education?

Ironically, one of the first applications of the at-risk label was to African-Americans at a time when they were not legally educated. African-American children were referred to as children "at risk" of literacy (Swadener, 1990). Over the last century, educators and public officials have most often framed the problem of poor school achievement by at-risk students in the following ways (Banks, 1994; Cuban, 1989; Rios, 1996):

- Students who perform poorly in school are responsible for their performance. They lack ability, character, and motivation.
- Families from certain cultural backgrounds fail to prepare their children for school and provide little support for them in school. They are poor, lack education, and do not teach their children what is proper and improper in the dominant culture.

Notice how these two explanations locate the problems of being at risk in the students and families themselves. From this deficit perspective, students are presumed to have an affliction or a disease that must be treated. Using the medical metaphor, students at risk need "immunization" and "treatment" in the form of special classes and tracks or compensatory pull-out programs.

But what if we reframed the at-risk issue as one whereby schools and political institutions acknowledge their responsibility in helping to create living and learning conditions that result in failure for certain students and their families? Remember Rene, the student we focused on in this chapter's case study? We believe the very learning conditions she was subject to in her special reading class helped to perpetuate her risky status. Twenty years ago, McDermott and Gospodinoff said:

> Without learning how to read, there are few other paths for upward mobility for minority children in modern nations. . . . If we wanted a mechanism

> for sorting each new generation of citizens into the advantaged and the disadvantaged, into the achieving and underachieving, we could have done no better than to have invented the school system we have. (1979, p. 192)

Sometimes the Ways We Teach Put Students at Risk of Failure

Pellicano says that the at-risk label "reflects the dysfunctions of both the larger society and the school" (1987, p. 49). From this perspective, schools that are inflexible in dealing with the linguistic and cultural needs of their students may be creating conditions that breed academic failure and unsatisfactory student performance (Gillette, 1996). From this perspective, certain teaching practices and curricula can actually increase the likelihood of students' reading and learning failure in school (Polakow & Brozo, 1993).

So we see that labels themselves can be deceiving. Some labels, such as *at risk,* may do little more than blame the victims and perpetuate conditions of failure both at home and in school. In recognition of this problem, all of us can make efforts to reverse the detrimental effects of labeling and deficit-driven instruction. We can begin this reversal process by changing the educational vernacular used to describe students with special needs. For instance, it has been demonstrated that by transposing our deficit-laden language to a language of hope for and expectation of success, teachers can make profound differences in the ways students perceive, use, and grow into literacy (Brozo, 1991). Although we have used the terms *disabled reader* and *learning disabled* in this chapter, we believe we should be working to replace language of deficits with language that refers to ways literacy progress can be improved for students or, better yet, completely turned around to become *at promise* of literacy growth (Brozo, 1995; Lee & Neal, 1992–1993). We believe that an at-promise view of special needs students will lead to more interesting and meaningful teaching and learning.

Establish Home–School Connections and Use the Community as a Cultural Resource

Teachers are well aware of the importance of parental support for achieving their instructional goals. And although we know this is especially true at the middle and high school levels, we generally fail to be proactive about establishing or eliciting parental support for the academic growth of adolescents. Henry (1996) found that parents were reluctant to get involved with their children's junior and senior high schools because they felt that:

- Homework was often too difficult for them to be of much use.
- Teachers view themselves as being content experts, not experts in relating to youth.
- High schools are very big and less intimate than elementary schools.
- Parental demands are seen as a threat to educators' professionalism.

In spite of the perceived and actual barriers to home-school cooperation, we believe, like others (Rioux & Berla, 1993; Swap, 1993), that there is an urgent need to find ways to support the academic success of all our youth. The research

Higher Achievement Is Strongly Related to Parental Involvement

appears to offer a unanimous finding—one element that contributes to more successful students and more successful schools across populations is parents' involvement in their children's education (Rich, 1993).

The broader community should be exploited as a cultural resource to promote the academic success of middle and high school students (Jackson, 1993–1994). Hilliard (1989) urges teachers to use community members as "touchable role models," who bring to life the words and ideas being explored in the classroom. Saravia-Shore and Arvizu's (1992) extensive investigation of literacy programs for Hispanic students led to their contention that instructional approaches without parent participation are not adequate. They argue that it is only through home-school linkages that the cultural resources of the surrounding community are utilized. They assert that for programs for Hispanic children to succeed, "students and parents need to participate actively with school personnel in creating and testing innovative approaches" (p. 50).

In our personal experience with eighth-grade Mexican-American students, we have discovered the crucial role parents and community can play in content learning (Brozo, Valerio, & Salazar, 1996). Throughout a unit on Hispanic-American culture, we had students explore their cultural roots within their families. One way we were able to bring about a community-school dialogue and exchange of cultural resources was through the use of Integrated Parent Involvement Packets (IPIPs) (Prouty & Irby, 1995). The IPIPs we used were housed in a three-ring binder with the following components: Introducing the IPIP was a letter to the parents thanking them for taking the time to participate in the unit. On the flip side of the letter was a sign-out chart with a place for the parents' and students' signatures when they completed the IPIP. Next, there was an explanation of what was required to complete the IPIP successfully. This was followed by a story by a Hispanic author along with a short biography of the author. The stories reflected authentic Hispanic cultural experiences and were meant to be read aloud by the parents and the students to one another (Hayden, 1995).

A Strategy for Parental Involvement

The final component of the IPIP was a hands-on activity for student and parents to share. The activities were typically suggested by the IPIP readings. For example, in one of the stories we included in the IPIPs, Sandra Cisneros's (1990) "Three Wise Guys: Un Cuento de Navidad," a Mexican-American family celebrates Christmas with the smell of cinnamon in the holiday air. We then asked parents and students to make cinnamon sticks from the ingredients we provided in a zippered plastic pouch in the IPIP binder. After reading Rudolpho Anaya's (1990) "Salomon's Story," which contains information about brewing traditional teas from local herbs, parents and students were given directions and ingredients for making their own native tea, manzanilla.

We also made sure that students connected with the broader Hispanic community as often as possible. For example, we took a field trip to the garden of a school neighborhood resident who gave students a tour and an explanation of the healing powers of plants and herbs. Students also went to the local university to participate in Cinco de Mayo (a Mexican-American holiday) festivities.

The eighth graders also enjoyed a talk and demonstration from a local Mexican-American scholar on "green medicines."

Overall, our efforts to create community-school collaboration during the Hispanic culture unit resulted in the eighth graders exhibiting greater enthusiasm for learning, improved literacy behavior, and heightened awareness of their positive cultural identity.

READING AND WRITING STRATEGIES FOR STUDENTS WITH SPECIAL NEEDS

As we stated earlier, the strategies advocated in this chapter for increasing the literacy of readers and learners with special needs follow naturally from those described and demonstrated in previous chapters. For all students, be sure to include the readiness activities in Chapter 5, the vocabulary strategies in Chapter 6, and the comprehension activities in Chapter 3. Writing experiences (Chapter 7), opportunities to read, listen, and respond to young adult trade books (Chapter 8), and study skills training (Chapter 9) are essential for helping special needs students become enthusiastic and independent readers and writers. Finally, take advantage of computer technology (Chapter 10) to increase the motivation for learning. In addition to activities in the preceding chapters, the strategies that follow are particularly useful for meeting the literacy needs of special students.

Sustained Silent Reading and Writing

In Chapter 8 we introduced the **sustained silent reading (SSR)** strategy for promoting the reading habit. We once again extol its virtues by demonstrating how SSR, as well as **sustained silent writing,** can be particularly helpful for special needs students.

SSR Provides Meaningful Reading Practice for Special Needs Students

We agree with Frank Smith (1985), who says that students improve their reading and writing by reading and writing. Sustained silent reading and writing provide daily uninterrupted silent time for personal and pleasurable reading and writing. This time not only helps poorer readers improve but promotes positive attitudes toward reading and toward themselves as literate young adults.

A local high school has an exemplary SSR program that has had a very positive influence on special needs readers. Immediately after lunch, every day, all other activities cease and everyone reads for 20 minutes, including teachers, the principal, secretaries, the custodial and food service staff, and any visitors to the school. Even a work crew that was repairing the roof of the school for 2 weeks got into the act, taking out their books, newspapers, and magazines to read with the rest of the school.

Judith teaches 10th-grade journalism. She finds that the most challenging aspect of the SSR program is helping reluctant readers, who claim they do not like reading, choose just the right book. She knows that the right book can often get a student hooked on reading. She recalls how one of her formerly poor readers literally discovered his calling after reading a book on paleontology. He went on to major in anthropology in college and is currently studying artifacts of cave-dwelling Native Americans in Colorado. Judith attributes this student's self-discovery to the fact that he was able to find the book in her well-stocked classroom library, which contains paperbacks from a variety of genres that appeal to students of varying abilities and interests and, most important, provide opportunities for personal choice. She has acquired books and magazines in a number of ways, including garage sales, library benefit book sales, thrift shops, student donations, and bake sales, using the proceeds to take advantage of several paperback suppliers' good discounts. She regularly gives personal introductions to new books with book talks, suggests three or four books that might appeal to particular students, and lets students know what she is reading for enjoyment by discussing her current book and why she likes it. After the SSR period, she allows students to talk about their books if they wish. Students are also allowed to talk to their friends about their interests and to recommend books. Time is also provided for browsing through books that were discussed or introduced. The key, says Judith, is that book sharing and recommendations are pressure free; students therefore realize that they can freely choose the books they would like to read, instead of being told what to read, and that reading can be enjoyable instead of punitive.

Sustained Silent Writing Described

A nearby suburban junior high school has a sustained silent writing program that operates much like the SSR program just described. Everyone in school writes for 15 minutes during a set time—in this case, after lunch. The program has been most successful in stimulating reluctant writers to write. By engaging in personally meaningful writing experiences, students establish the habit of writing, which improves their writing skills and helps them develop healthy attitudes about writing. Many students keep journals or make diary entries during this time. Some write letters or "to do" lists. No one, however, does homework or work-related writing because the intent of the program is to help students see the pleasurable and personally meaningful side of writing.

In her eighth-grade language arts classroom, Madelyn, like the other teachers in the building, does not restrict what her students write during sustained silent writing. However, she helps reluctant writers find personally meaningful reasons for writing by suggesting and demonstrating a variety of purposeful written exchanges. Two of her writing strategies we find particularly stimulating for special needs readers and writers are the **message board** and **dialogue journals.**

Message Board: Encouraging Purposeful Writing

Kurt,

Yesterday I was talking with Sean and he told me that extinct animals have been found frozen in ice. I don't believe him, do you?

Neal

> Neal,
>
> It's true. I saw a show about it. They found one of them long haired elephants. There's a book in the resource center that has pictures of them. Want to see?
>
> Kurt
>
> Kurt,
>
> Okay. What are you doing 6th period? I got study hall, but Mr. Williams will let me go to the library.
>
> Neal

And so go the typical kinds of exchanges students pin to the message board. Madelyn explains that many of her poor writers have never enjoyed writing so much since she introduced the message board and allowed them to write notes (which are forbidden in most classrooms) to one another and to her.

As we demonstrated in Chapter 7, reading and writing—indeed, all of the language systems—complement and support each other. When Madelyn's students write, they read what they are writing: They read to regain their train of thought or their momentum, to check the "sound" of their text, to check for errors, or for any of a variety of reasons. When given real-world reasons to communicate, students will take the time to edit, revise, and correct spelling and punctuation errors (Rhodes & Dudley-Marling, 1996).

Dialogue Journals

In addition to face-to-face conferencing with her poor writers, Madelyn corresponds with them about their writing, reading, and personal concerns in dialogue journals (Wells, 1992–1993). Using an approach developed by Nancie Atwell (1984, 1987), she gives reluctant writers a folder with the following letter inside:

> This folder is a place for you and me to talk about books, reading, authors, writing, and us. You write letters to me, and I'll write letters back to you. In your letters, talk with me about what you've read. Tell me what you thought and felt and why. Tell me what you liked and didn't like and why. Tell me what these books meant to you and said to you. Tell me about your interests and dreams, what you do when you're outside of school. Ask me questions or for help. And write back to me about my ideas, feelings, and questions.

The writing folder provides Madelyn with a forum for getting to know her special needs students as readers and writers and as people with real-life concerns, interests, experiences, strengths, weaknesses, self-concepts, hang-ups, and gripes. She can exploit what she learns about these students by introducing them to books and engaging them in writing experiences that match their interests and experiences. Through the dialogue journal, she can offer specific advice and suggestions, as well as carry on a dialogue between one interested reader/writer/person and another. The journals are ungraded and free of red pen marks and circles highlighting spelling, syntax, and punctuation errors. Instead,

Madelyn subtly influences student writing and attention to these errors by using their misspelled words in her own responses, spelling them correctly.

As her class grew increasingly excited about an upcoming field trip to a museum downtown, Madelyn read and responded to many journal entries about the trip. In one of the journals, a very shy young lady talked about how depressed she was because she was unable to go on the trip since her mother didn't have the money. Madelyn was so moved by the student's concern that she wrote back: "Ask your mother if she'll allow you to go if I pay your way." A broad smile on the girl's face the next day gave away the answer. Without the opportunity to communicate through the journal, it's likely that Madelyn would never have learned of her student's problem. The dialogue journal makes it easier for special needs students to follow through on their natural impulse to use language to communicate genuine feelings, ideas, needs, desires, and interests.

By Talking through Journaling, Teachers Can Discover a Student's Uniqueness

Exploring Personal Connections to Text

Several summers ago, Carol, a special education teacher, was teaching special needs students in a small junior high school in rural Illinois. Just a few days into the term, she became frustrated with their antipathy toward reading and their inability to generate more than a few lines when given writing assignments. We talked about how she could find out who her students were outside of school—their experiences and interests, their concerns and attitudes. With this knowledge, she could begin to identify texts that would help them make connections between their personal lives and why they read.

She began by revealing herself to the group through the "My Bag" strategy (discussed in Chapter 5). To refresh your memory, the strategy involves filling a bag with personal items and symbols that represent aspects of your personality, interests, experiences, and beliefs. Students empty the bag, then make guesses and ask questions as they pass around the items. This strategy has often been used as a catalyst for writing based on questions and interests others have about a particular aspect of one's personality or experiences.

Carol first emptied her bag, which contained a picture of a female runner, a copy of an Agatha Christie mystery, a photograph of her husband, some sheet music, and an old brooch. After talking about the items and answering questions, the students wanted to know more about the brooch. The next day, Carol read aloud an account of how the brooch came from her grandmother and brought back many wonderful memories of summer visits to her grandparents' house on the Missouri River. Students then revealed themselves with their bags. They had great fun with this strategy, and Carol discovered some very useful information about each student.

Another strategy she used to help students get closer to text, to interact with text, and to find personal connections with text was a **reader-response heuristic.** This strategy, which was discussed in detail in Chapter 7, involves creating an essay based on three questions about text:

1. What aspect of what you read excited or interested you the most?
2. What are your feelings and attitudes about this aspect of the text?

3. What experiences have you had that help others understand why you feel the way you do?

This response heuristic gives readers an opportunity to present their own visions of literacy by writing expressive and explanatory prose in response to what they read. When the heuristic is used as a catalyst for writing, it can, with revisionary assistance from other writers and the teacher, yield a sophisticated essay (Brozo, 1988). The response heuristic should guide the writer in the development of an essay with specific personal support for feelings and assertions. Examples and illustrations should come from the reader's experiences, beliefs, knowledge, and perceptions of the text. In contrast, traditional, formal essays require writers to support positions and claims with information accessible to all writers, with little concern for personal validation. Yet, it is through a personal connection that a text is made meaningful and memorable.

Carol modeled the essay-writing process by reading her own essay, which was a response to an article about sons and daughters dealing with their aging, infirm parents and by describing the decisions that went into creating the essay. She explained her attitude that children should accept responsibility for their parents when they grow old and helpless, and she related this attitude to an anecdote that captured the special relationship she has with her mother. She shared the article with the class, read her personal response, and talked through her reasoning processes in reading, writing, and revising. She also answered students' questions about her response.

Reader Response Can Impel Special Needs Students to Communicate through Writing

Colt, a hulking, slow-moving 14-year-old, could barely finish two sentences in a 45-minute period. When Carol discovered from the "My Bag" strategy that he had a motorcycle, she found a human interest article in the newspaper related to bikes and invited him to read it and respond to it, if he liked, in a manner similar to the one she used in responding to her article. The newspaper clipping was about motorcycle gang members who were out for a Sunday ride when they came upon the scene of an accident. A car had veered off the road and plunged into a small lake. A dozen or so people were standing on shore watching as the car's hood dipped below the surface. One of the bikers ran down to the scene. Quickly grasping the problem, he screamed at the crowd in bewilderment: Why hadn't anyone tried to save the people in the car? The crowd had been unable to act. He kicked off his boots and dove into the water. Before long, he bobbed up with two children in his arms; then a woman came to the surface. Only when they were near shore did some of the people help them out of the lake. The biker gathered his boots, voiced a few parting criticisms for the crowd, got on his bike, and left.

Carol could not help noticing at the end of the period that Colt was still working. He had written two full pages! He said he wanted to take it home and finish it. The next day Colt raised his hand when Carol invited members of the class to share what they had written. Slowly and methodically, he described the contents of the article; then he moved to his personal response. "Bikers get a raw deal," it began. Colt went on to read his moving essay about how important it is to be brave, like the biker in the article. He related the experience of finding someone, on one of his rides, who had flipped a dirt bike and broken his arm. His essay went on to describe how he positioned the boy on his own bike seat, sat behind him so that he could reach around to hold the handle bars and keep the boy from falling, and rode to the emergency room. Colt concluded his essay by saying, "Bikers should be treated with respect because you never know when you might need a brave one to come along."

We have known for some time that individual perceptions (Anderson, 1984) and cultural schemata (Pritchard, 1990) shape one's comprehension. Providing special needs students with vehicles for responding to the texts they read that begin with references to the text and then move into personal narratives helps these readers explore the roots of their perceptions. In supportive classrooms, teachers can exploit the reader-response heuristic as a catalyst for reading and writing.

By the end of the summer, Colt and the other students had written several essays that tied their experiences to an aspect of the texts they read. Their written products grew longer and more sophisticated as a result. More important, these students began to view themselves differently as readers. Colt's comments on one of the last days of school are revealing:

> I've changed the way I feel about reading things. I never cared about reading before. Now I look for something that interests me, something I can connect to.

Trade Books

Trade Books Can Be Matched to the Unique Needs of Learners

We emphasized in Chapter 8 that abundant reading of quality young adult literature provides a powerful means of helping students acquire information, gain insights into themselves and others, and enrich their leisure hours. It is also clear that bringing young adults into contact with trade books is a very effective means of helping them learn language, extend vocabulary, and come to grips with new and complex syntax. From improving young women's self-concept (Miller, 1993) and offering detained juveniles a chance to enjoy reading (Hill & Van Horn, 1995) to giving teenage mothers a second chance at literacy (Doneson, 1991) and gifted readers emotional strength (Halsted, 1988), providing regular opportunities to hear, read, and respond to quality young adult trade books can make it possible for all special needs students to become better language learners and users (Erickson, 1996).

Picture Books and Wordless Books

We often associate picture books and wordless books with very young readers. Yet, these books can be used profitably with poor readers and culturally different readers at the middle and high school levels to help them develop a sense of story, make predictions, produce language, generate their own texts, build schemata, and expand their repertoire of study skills (Benedict & Carlisle, 1992; Jimenez,

1997). Picture books can also be used to sensitize all students to issues of diversity (Godina, 1996; Jimenez & Gamez, 1996). Furthermore, Bishop and Hickman point out that "Picture books are a source of personal pleasure and aesthetic satisfaction for all ages" (1992, p. 4). "We also value picture books, fiction and nonfiction alike, for what they can teach us through their content" (p. 5).

The list in Figure 11.1 represents an excellent assortment of picture books and wordless books that are especially useful with middle and secondary students.

Chris uses picture books with high school English as a Second Language (ESL) students as a catalyst for oral language production and writing. First, he gives personal introductions to several books by describing the pictures and eliciting responses and predictions about the stories and characters. Then groups of two or three students select a picture book for which to write a story, script, or text to be shared with the class. Some students sit in an "author's chair," with class members gathered around them, and read their texts while holding up the pictures for all to see. Others give dramatic interpretations of the pictured events and characters in the books using their scripts as guides. Chris eventually types what the students have written and places these accounts with the picture books in the class library.

Saravia-Shore and Arvizu (1992) have demonstrated that we can speed up the learning of English in bilingual contexts if we exploit the use of good stories. We recommend building up a stock of materials geared to the students' natural curiosity, their love of narrative, of excitement, of humor, and their easy identification with characters like themselves. Picture books allow students to interpret the events of stories and the personalities and motives of characters from their own cultural perspectives and experiences while experimenting with the English language.

According to Stotsky, "Teachers are responsible, in a highly multireligious and multiethnic society, for creating and cultivating common ground through the literature they teach in all its many forms" (1992, p. 56). As we stated in Chapter 8, many important stories of cultural victimization and ethnic prejudice often go unmentioned or are only hinted at in content area textbooks. Trade books may be the only sources that examine these issues closely and in personal terms. For example, in the picture book *Encounter* (Yolen, 1992), the author describes how the Taino Indian culture and civilization were all but lost after Columbus landed on their beaches.

Multicultural Trade Books Help Students Value Themselves and Others

The number of multicultural trade books written by ethnically diverse authors is on the rise (Diamond & Moore, 1995), so that it's possible for most junior and senior high school teachers to find quality picture books covering a range of important topics. Picture books are an excellent way to introduce cultures to students. For example, Amelda had her eighth graders read two recent picture books, ***The Fortune-Tellers*** (Alexander, 1992) and ***Red Thread*** (Young, 1993) so that they could compare Cameroon and Chinese cultures regarding young men, their need to understand what the future holds for them, and marriage. Her students also explored their own beliefs about the future and marriage.

Karen Ackerman
Song and Dance Man
Jon Agee
The Incredible Painting of Felix Clousseau
Aliki
The King's Day
A Medieval Feast
Linda Altman
Amelia's Road
Laurie Anderson
The Package
Maya Angelou
Now Sheba Sings the Song
Mitsumasa Anno
Anno's Animals
Anno's U.S.A.
Anno's Britain
Anno's Italy
Anno's Journey
Dr. Anno's Magical Midnight Circus
Gloria Anzaldua
Friends from the Other Side
Frank Asch
Topsy Turvies: Pictures to Stretch the Imagination
George's Store
Linda
The Blue Balloon
Beth Atkins
Voices from the Fields
Elisa Bartone
Peppe the Lamplighter
Graeme Base
My Grandma Lived in Gooligulch
Byrd Baylor
I'm in Charge of Celebrations
Tony Blundell
Beware of Boys
Julie Brinckloe
The Spider Web
Eve Bunting
Fly Away Home
Eric Carle
The Very Long Train
Ruth Carroll
The Dolphin and the Mermaid
Omar Castanada
Abuela's Weave
Gary Chalk
Yankee Doodle
Lynne Cherry
A River Ran Wild
The Great Kapok Tree
Armadillo from Amarillo
Joanna Cole
The Magic School Bus (series)
George Crespo
How the Sea Began
Lois Czarnecki
The Six Wrinkled Woos
Rick Dupre
The Wishing Chair
Michael Emberly
Ruby
Leonard Fisher
The Tower of London
Russell Freedman
Kids at Work: Lewis Hine and the Crusade Against Child Labor
Sherry Garland
The Lotus Seed
Christian Garrison
The Dream Eater
Giovannetti
Max
Paul Goble
Beyond the Ridge
John S. Goodall
The Story of a Castle
An Edwardian Christmas
An Edwardian Holiday
An Edwardian Summer
Shrewbettina's Birthday
Story of an English Village
The Ballooning Adventure of Paddy Park
Joy Hakim
The First Americans
John Hamburger
The Lazy Dog
Bud Howlett
I'm New Here
Roberto Innocenti
Rose Blanche
Tony Johnston
The Tale of Rabbit and Coyote
Janet Klausner
Sequoyah's Gift
Fernando Krahn
The Flying Saucer Full of Spaghetti
The Great Ape
Gregory Kreikemeier
Come With Me to Africa
Judi Kurjian
In My Own Backyard
Riki Levison
Watch the Stars Come Out
Richard Lewis
All of You Was Singing
Bill Littlefied
Champions
Susan Lowell
The Three Little Javelinas
David Macaulay
Black and White
The Way Things Work
Castle
Pyramid
Cathedral
Betsy Maestro
The Story of the Statue of Liberty
Mercer Mayer
Frog Goes to Dinner
Oops
Two Moral Tales
Patricia McKissack
Mirandy and Brother Wind
Judith Mellecker
Randolph's Dream
Margaree Mitchell
Uncle Jed's Barbershop
Ken Mochizuki
Baseball Saved Us
Guillermo Mordillo
The Damp and Daffy Doings of a Daring Pirate Ship

FIGURE 11.1 Wordless Books and Picture Books for Young Adults

Margaret Musgrove
Ashanti to Zulu: African Traditions
Peter Parnall
Woodpile
Denise Patrick
Red Dancing Shoes
Diane Patrick
Family Celebrations
Felix Pitre
Juan Bobo and the Pig
Richard Platt
Stephen Biesty's Incredible Cross-Sections (series)
Kjell Ringi
The Winner
Cynthia Rylant
All I See
Uri Shulevitz
Dawn
Treasure
Diane Siebert
Heartland
Virginia Driving Hawk Sneve
Dancing Teepees
Peter Spier
Noah's Ark
Diane Stanley
Peter the Great
Shaka, King of the Zulus
Fay Stanley
The Last Princess: The Story of Princess Ka'iulani of Hawai'i
Bryna Stevens
Handel and the Famous Sword Swallower of Halle
Brinton Turkle
Deep in the Forest
Ann Turner
Katie's Trunk
Heron Street
Nettie's Trip South
Dakota Dugout
Wayne Ude
Maybe I Will Do Something
Mircea Vasiliu
What's Happening
David Vozar
Yo, Hungry Wolf!
Alice Walker
To Hell with Dying
Lynd Ward
The Biggest Bear
The Silver Pony
The Wild Pilgrimage
David Weisner
Free Fall
Holden Wetherbee
The Wonder Ring: A Fantasy in Silhouette
Peter Wetzel
The Good Bird
Nadia Wheatley
My Place
Margaret Wild
The Very Best of Friends
Brian Wildsmith
Brian Wildsmith's Circus
Sherley Anne Williams
Working Cotton
Val Willis
The Secret in the Matchbox
Jeanette Winter
Follow the Drinking Gourd
Laura Wittstock
Ininatig's Gift of Sugar

FIGURE 11.1 ***continued***

Dean's freshmen explore trickster tales from a variety of Native American cultures as a way of demonstrating what is considered antisocial behavior in these particular cultures. In their exploration, they have read about tricksters called *Raven* by Native American tribes of the Pacific Northwest and *Coyote* by tribes in the Southwest in *Song for the Ancient Forest* (Luenn, 1993) and called *Iktomi* by Plains Indians, as illustrated in *Iktomi and the Boulder: A Plains Indian Story* (Goble, 1988).

Numerous books have African-American characters and themes due largely to the growing pool of talented African-American authors and illustrators. During African-American History Month, Sylvia worked with two excellent picture books. In *Follow the Drinking Gourd* (Winter, 1989), students learned about slavery and how slaves escaped from their masters. In Hopkinson's *Sweet Clara and the Freedom Quilt* (1993), Sylvia's students discovered how slaves hand sewed quilts in designs that provided a map of the Underground Railroad.

Picture books have been used to present the wonderful diversity among cultures both within and outside our borders. Middle and secondary school teachers who involve their students in reading, writing, discussing, and listening to these books have found that all students develop greater empathy and understanding of other cultures. This is critical in light of our criticisms of many typical textbooks that fail to deal adequately with issues of diversity and multiculturalism.

Other Books That Promote Cultural Pluralism

> A people's dream died at Wounded Knee
> The nation's hoop is broken and scattered.
> There is no center any longer, and the
> sacred tree is dead.

These words—spoken by Black Elk, an Oglala medicine man—open the first chapter of *A Boy Becomes a Man at Wounded Knee* (Wood & Afraid of Hawk, 1992). In this haunting and exciting photographic picture book, we follow the story of Wanbli Numpa Afraid of Hawk, an 8-year-old Sioux, as he journeys with his Lakota tribe 150 miles from his reservation to Wounded Knee Creek. The trip is the fifth and final one taken on the anniversary of the Wounded Knee massacre foretold by a medicine man as the only way to mend the "sacred hoop" and restore the dreams and hopes of the Lakota (Sioux) nation. Wanbli Numpa tells of braving -50°F temperatures and treacherous mountainous terrain along the way as a ritual of sharing the suffering borne by his ancestors.

Nonfiction trade books such as *A Boy Becomes a Man at Wounded Knee* are ideally suited to the cultural and personal interests of certain special needs students. The goal is to find just the right book to reach them in ways the textbook and the packaged curriculum never could (J. Garcia, Hadaway, & Beal, 1988; Glasgow, 1996).

An interesting and easy-to-read biography of Colin Powell, *Colin Powell: A Man of War and Peace* (Senna, 1992), could bring joy and inspiration to many special needs young adults. Two recent books that deal with the horror and reality of drug addiction (*The House That Crack Built* by Taylor, 1992) and homelessness (*No Place to Be: Voices of Homeless Children* by Berck, 1992) are excellent sources for helping special needs students better understand these growing social problems and help them explore ways of improving their own lives and the lives of others.

Within the past 10–15 years, a great volume of outstanding young adult fiction has been produced with main characters from ethnically diverse backgrounds. Consequently, it has become easier for teachers to find good books with Hispanic-American, African-American, Asian-American, and Native-American themes to share with students and/or integrate into the curriculum. Encountering characters, settings, and themes that resonate with students' own cultural backgrounds improves their self-esteem and pride in their cultural heritage (Brozo et al., 1996) and enhances their comprehension skills (Peregoy & Boyle, 1993). A list of suggested young adult works of fiction with multicultural themes for middle and secondary students is provided in Figure 11.2.

African-American

Kenyette Adrine-Robinson
Black Image Makers
Burton Albert
Where Does the Trail Lead?
Jennifer Armstrong
Steal Away
James Berry
Ajeemah and His Son
Gillian Bradshaw
Imperial Purple
Kay Brown
Willy's Summer Dream
Barbara Hood Burgess
Oren Bell
Neil Cohen
Jackie Joyner-Kersee
J. California Cooper
Family
Michael Cooper
Playing America's Game: The Story of Negro League Baseball
Jean Darby
Martin Luther King, Jr.
Ossie Davis
Escape to Freedom: A Play about Young Frederick Douglass
Just Like Martin
Barry Denenberg
Nelson Mandela: No Easy Walk to Freedom
Jeri Ferris
What Are You Figuring Now?
M. K. Fullen
Pathblazers
Peter Golenbock
Teammates
Keith Elliot Greenberg
Magic Johnson: Champion with a Cause
Patricia Baird Greene
The Sabbath Garden
Rosa Guy
The Friends
Louis Haber
Black Pioneers of Science and Invention
Virginia Hamilton
Anthony Burns: The Defeat and Triumph of a Fugitive Slave
Cousins
Many Thousand Gone: African Americans from Slavery to Freedom
Joyce Hansen
Out from This Place
Philip Hart
Flying Free: America's First Black Aviators
James Haskins
Against All Opposition: Black Explorers in America
Black Dance in America: A History Through Its People
Get On Board: The Story of the Underground Railroad
One More River to Cross: The Stories of Twelve Black Americans
Outward Dreams: Black Inventors and Their Inventions
Merle Hodge
For the Life of Laetita
Toyomi Igus
Book of Black Heroes, Volume II: Great Women in the Struggle
Angela Johnson
Toning the Sweep
William Katz
The Black West
Breaking the Chains: African-American Slave Resistance
Bud Kliment
Ella Fitzgerald
Jacob Lawrence
The Great Migration
Mary Lyons
Letters from a Slave Girl: The Story of Harriet Jacobs
Sorrows Kitchen
Robert Lypsyte
The Brave
Jan Marino
The Day Elvis Came to Town
Tina McElroy
Baby of the Family
Patricia McKissack
The Dark Thirty: Southern Tales of the Supernatural
Kate McMullan
The Story of Harriet Tubman, Conductor of the Underground Railroad
Caroline Meyer
White Lilacs
Walter Dean Myers
Brown Angels: An Album of Pictures and Verse
Malcolm X: By Any Means Necessary
Now Is Your Time: The African American Struggle for Freedom
Somewhere in the Darkness
N. Y. Nathiri
Zora!: Zora Neale Hurston, A Woman and Her Community
Jim O'Connor
Jackie Robinson and the Story of All-Black Baseball
Rosa Parks and James Haskins
Rosa Parks, My Story
A. P. Porter
Jump at de Sun: The Story of Zora Neale Hurston
Brenda Seabrooke
The Bridges of Summer
Beatrice Siegel
The Year They Walked: Rosa Parks and the Montgomery Bus Boycott
Susan Straight
I Been in Sorrow's Kitchen and Licked Out All the Pots
Eleanora Tate
Thank You, Dr. Martin Luther King

FIGURE 11.2 Multicultural Literature for Young Adults

Mildred Taylor
Let the Circle Be Unbroken
The Road to Memphis
Theodore Taylor
Timothy and the Cay
Mildren Pitts Walter
Mississippi Challenge
Rita Williams-Garcia
Blue Tights
Fast Talk on a Slow Track
Jacqueline Woodson
The Dear One

Arab-American

Brent Ashabranner
An Ancient Heritage: The Arab-American Minority
Wayne Grover
Ali and the Golden Eagle
Florence Heide and Judith Gilliland
Sami and the Time of the Troubles
Francesc Sales
Ibrahim
Suzanne Staples
Shabanu
Francis Temple
The Beduin's Gazelle

Asian American

Frank Chin
Donald Duk
Sook Nyul Choi
Echoes of the White Giraffe
Year of Impossible Goodbyes
Shirley Climo
The Korean Cinderella
Linda Crew
Children of the River
Demi
The Magic Boat
Sherry Garland
Song of the Buffalo Boy
Sara Gogol
Vatsana's Lucky New Year
Minfong Ho
The Clay Marble
Diane Hoyt-Goldsmith
Hoang Anh: A Vietnamese-American Boy
Joanna Kraus
Tall Boy's Journey
Holly Kwon
The Moles and the Mireuk
Gus Lee
China Boy
Marie Lee
Finding My Voice
Steven Lo
The Incorporation of Eric Chung
Margaret Mahy
The Seven Chinese Brothers
Milton Meltzer
The Chinese Americans
Janet Nomura Morey
Famous Asian Americans
Karen O'Connor
Dan Thuy's New Life in America
Katherine Paterson
The Tale of the Mandarin Ducks
Jayne Pettit
My Name Is San Ho
Nami Rhee
Magic Spring: A Korean Folktale
Marcia Savin
The Moon Bridge
Allen Say
El Chino
Grandfather's Journey
Amy Tan
The Kitchen God's Wife
A. Tompert
Bamboo Hats and Rice Cake
Betty Torre
The Luminous Pearl: A Chinese Folktale
Yoshiko Uchida
The Invisible Thread: An Autobiography
Lynette Vyong
Sky Legends of Vietnam
Rosalind Wang
The Fourth Question
Yoko Watkins
Tales from the Bamboo Grove
Gloria Whelan
Goodbye Vietnam
Paul Yee
Tales from Gold Mountain: Stories of the Chinese in the New World
Laurence Yep
American Dragons: Twenty-Five Asian American Voices
The Lost Garden
The Star Fisher
Tongues of Jade

Hispanic-American

Julia Alvarez
How the Garcia Girls Lost Their Accents
Rudolfo Anaya
Bless Me, Ultima
The Legend of La Llorana
George Ancona
Pablo Remembers: The Fiesta of the Day of the Dead
Robert Baden
And Sunday Makes Seven
T. Ernesto Bethencourt
The Me Inside of Me
David Nelson Blair
Fear of the Condor
Maria Brusca
The Blacksmith and the Devils
Lori Carlson and Cynthia Ventura
Where Angels Glide at Dawn: New Stories from Latin America
Sandra Cisneros
The House on Mango Street
Woman Hollering Creek and Other Stories
Carol Dines
Best Friends Tell the Best Lies
Roberta Fernandez
Intaglio: A Novel in Six Stories

Joan Mazzio
The One Who Came Back
Kevin McColley
The Walls of Pedro Garcia
Milton Meltzer
The Hispanic Americans
Carolina Meyer
Rio Grande Stories
Ben Mikaelsen
Sparrow Hawk Red
Victor Montejo
The Bird Who Cleans the World and Other Mayan Fables
Anne Neimark
Diego Rivera: Artist of the People
Gary Paulsen
The Crossing
Consuelo Rodriguez
Cesar Chavez
Gary Soto
A Summer Life
Baseball in Aril
Fire in My Hands
Local News: A Collection of Stories
Neighborhood Odes
Taking Sides
Faythe Turner
Puerto Rican Writers at Home in the USA
Paul Walker
Pride of Puerto Rico: The Life of Roberto Clemente

Native-American

Sara Banks
Remember My Name
Natalia Belting
Moon Was Tired of Walking on Air
Noel Bennett
Halo of the Sun
John Bierhorst
Lightning Inside You and Other Native American Riddles
Joseph Bruchac
Return of the Sun: Native American Tales from the Northeast Woodlands
The Faithful Hunter: Abenaki Stories
A. E. Cannon
The Shadow Brothers
Louise Erdrich
Tracks
Russell Freedman
Buffalo Hunt
Paul Goble
Death of the Iron Horse
Her Seven Brothers
Kirkpatrick Hill
Toughboy and Sister
Tony Hillerman
Coyote Waits
Arlene Hirschfelder and Beverly Singer
Rising Voices: Writings of Young Native Americans
Will Hobbs
Bearstone
Stan Hoig
People of the Breaking Day: The Southern Cheyenne Today
James Houston
Akavak
Diane Hoyt-Goldsmith
Cherokee Summer
Totem Pole
William Katz
Black Indians: A Hidden Heritage
Michael Lacapa
The Flute Player
Rafe Martin
The Rough-Face Girl
Susanne Page
A Celebration of Being: Photographs of the Hopi and Navajo
Russell Peters
Clambake: A Wampanoag Tradition
Marsha Qualey
Revolutions of the Heart
Gordon Regguiniti
The Sacred Harvest: Ojibway Wild Rice Gathering
Sue Stauffacher
S'gana the Black Whale
Stephen Trimble
The Village of Blue Stone
Helen Hughes Vick
Walker of Time

FIGURE 11.2, *continued*

Reading Aloud

Hearing Well-Written Trade Books Is Critical for Students Learning the English Language

Special needs students, particularly bilingual students, need to become familiar with written English, which differs, of course, from spoken English. Poor readers need to know that reading is more than drill sheets and workbooks. Therefore, daily experience with listening and responding to literature is extremely important for these students for developing knowledge about and interest in language (Richardson, 1994). Jim Trelease, in talking about the importance of reading aloud to students, says:

> Reading aloud . . . stimulates their interest, their emotional development, and their imagination. There is also a fourth area which is stimulated by

> reading aloud and it is a particularly vital area in today's world . . . language. They will speak the language primarily as they have heard it spoken. (1985, p. 11)

Students who are exposed to excellent young adult literature through regular read-alouds will also develop reading and writing schemata. These schemata will help them understand more complex language structures in their reading and will help them create richer written discourse.

Our concerns about language development in special needs students are rooted in the fact that many of them, especially poor readers, have role models who do not stimulate language growth or come from homes where language experiences are not encouraged. In such cases, your classroom may be one of the few environments these students have for language development opportunity. We urge you to take advantage of this opportunity by exposing students to quality literature.

We have found the books in Figure 11.3 to be excellent read-alouds for young adult readers with special needs. These books should be used to stimulate discussion, writing, and further reading. The ideas and suggestions in Chapter 8 will provide you with options for helping special needs students respond to and extend their experiences with literature.

The most commonly asked question we receive from teachers who work with special needs students is, How can my ESL and remedial students who are reading well below grade level understand these stories? Daniel Fader (Fader, Duggins, Finn, & McNeil, 1976) supplies the most convincing answer to this question. Based on his work with delinquent boys at the W. J. Maxey Boys' Training School in Michigan, where he helped transform them from uninterested nonreaders into willing and excited readers, he says:

> *Semi-literate readers do not need semi-literate books. The simplistic language of the life-leached literature inflicted upon the average schoolchild is not justifiable from any standpoint. Bright, average, dull—however one classifies the child—he is immeasurably better off with books that are too difficult for him than books that are too simple.... Reading is a peculiarly personal interaction between a reader and a book ... but in no case does this interaction demand an understanding of every word by the reader. The threshold ... even in many complex books, can be pleasurably crossed by many simple readers.* (p. 106; emphasis in the original)

Young Adult Books with Characters Who Have Special Needs

Students with special needs are like all of us. They have complex personalities, and are as talented in many areas and as untalented in just as many areas as any other people. They exhibit all of the emotions and in the same proportions as other people; therefore, literature should portray them realistically. Characters with disabilities, for instance, should be respected and not pitied. "They should be shown coping with their disability," says Marsha Rudman (1995), "rather than

Avi
Nothing but the Truth
Wolf Rider
Patricia Beatty
Lupita Manana
T. Ernesto Bethancourt
The Dog Days of Arthur Cane
William Brooke
Untold Tales
Mel Cebulash
Ruth Marini, Dodger Ace
Ruth Marini of the Dodgers
Alice Childress
A Hero Ain't Nothin' but a Sandwich
Rainbow Jordan
Eth Clifford
The Rocking Chair Rebellion
Barbara Cohen
Thank You, Jackie Robinson
James L. Collier and Christopher Collier
Jump Ship to Freedom
My Brother Sam Is Dead
When the Stars Begin to Fall
Caroline Cooney
Flash
Robert Cormier
Tunes for Bears to Dance to
We All Fall Down
Joe Cottonwood
Quake!
Chris Crutcher
Goin' Fishin'
Ironman
Staying Fat for Sarah Byrnes
Karen Cushman
Catherine, Called Birdy
The Midwife's Apprentice
Robert Davies
The Ghost Who Vanished By Degrees
Lois Duncan
Killing Mr. Griffin
Thomas Dygard
Rebound Caper
Winning Kicker
Allan W. Eckert
Incident at Hawk's Hill
Clyde Edgerton
Raney
Paul Fleischman
Path of the Pale Horse
Robert Fulghum
It Was on Fire When I Lay Down on It
Donald Gallo
Center Stage: One-Act Plays for Teenage Readers and Actors
Jean George
Julie of the Wolves
My Side of the Mountain
Judith Gorog
A Taste for Quiet and Other Disquieting Tales
Bob Greene
American Beat
Virginia Hamilton
M. C. Higgins, the Great
Sid Hite
Dither Farm
It's Nothing to a Mountain
Anne Holm
North to Freedom
Felicia Holman
Slake's Limbo
Lee Kisling
The Fool's War
Annette Klause
Alien Secrets
R. R. Knudson
Zanbanger
Zanboomer
Sibley Lampman
The Potlach Family
Madeleine L'Engle
A Ring of Endless Light
Jack London
The Call of the Wild
Lois Lowry
A Summer to Die
The Giver
Harry Mazer
Snow-Bound
Willie Morris
Good Old Boy
Robert Murphy
The Pond
Walter Dean Myers
Hoop
Somewhere in the Darkness
Won't Know Till I Get There
Phillip Naylor
Send No Blessings
Robert Newman
The Case of the Baker Street Irregular
Joan Lowrey Nixon
The Other Side of Dark
Scott O'Dell
Sarah Bishop
Sing Down the Moon
Gary Paulsen
Canyons
Hatchet
The Monument
The River
Robert Newton Peck
A Part of the Sky
The Day No Pigs Would Die
Annie Proulx
Postcards
Otto Salassi
And Nobody Knew They Were There
Gary Soto
Mother and Daughter
New and Selected Poems
Two Dreamers
Ivan Southall
Josh
Elizabeth George Speare
The Witch of Blackbird Pond
Jerry Spinelli
Maniac Magee
Robert Stine
The Girlfriend
Susan Straight
I Been in Sorrow's Kitchen and Licked Out All the Pots
Todd Strasser
On the Bridge
Joyce Sweeney
Free Fall
Mildred Taylor
Mississippi Bridge
The Friendship and the Gold Cadillac
Rosemary Wells
When No One Was Looking
Tim Winton
Lockie Leonard, Human Torpedo
Lawrence Yep
Child of the Owl
Dragon's Gate

FIGURE 11.3 Read-Aloud Books for Young Adults

being rewarded with a miraculous cure because of their positive thoughts and/or good behavior." Gifted students, too, should be exposed to books with themes and characters to help them develop a realistic sense of themselves and useful emotional and social skills for interacting with others (Hauser & Nelson, 1988).

Find and Use Books About Special Needs Young Adults

An excellent way to draw special needs students with reading difficulties into the literacy club and keep gifted readers motivated is by finding young adult books that interest them by dealing with themes relevant to their personal situations. Again, these books can be used most profitably when tied to the kinds of learning experiences suggested in Chapter 8. Students should receive personal introductions to books; the books should be used as catalysts for small-group and whole-class interactions and discussions; and students should be given plenty of opportunities for extending their understanding through personal research, writing, and additional reading.

Figure 11.4 is a list of books that we and other teachers have found to be of great interest to adolescents with special needs. These fiction and nonfiction books deal with typical problems special needs students must face. A separate list of books found to be especially useful with gifted readers is included.

Charles, a physical education teacher, has his students who are preparing to work in summer camps and recreation programs read *The Acorn People* (Jones, 1976). This true story about a group of handicapped children at summer camp explores how counselors first react to them. Slowly, the counselors realize how human the new campers are and how much they share. Charles has found that the book is useful in sensitizing his students to the emotional and physical dimensions of working with children with mobility impairments. Dean's senior sociology students read Miklowitz's *Secrets Not Meant to Be Kept* (1987), a trade book that deals creatively with the very sensitive but current social problem of child sexual abuse. Dean contends that this personalized view of child abuse helps make real the facts and statistics reported in the textbook and brings his students to a new level of awareness of and empathy for victims of abuse.

"Other Englishes"

Literature for ethnic and racial minority students should represent the emotional and intellectual reality of a world that is important to them (Pugh, 1989). Reyhner and Garcia (1989) argue that these students can benefit from reading materials that are linguistically and culturally related to their backgrounds. Literature that is both thematically relevant and linguistically accessible to ethnic and racial minorities can motivate them to read and provide an ideal vehicle for illustrating language use (Lukens & Cline, 1995).

A rich source of literature for helping ethnic and racial minorities learn more about themselves, expand their knowledge of English, and extend reading for its own sake is the literature written in "other Englishes"—that is, written in English by nonnative English speakers. The result is an English shaped by native styles, tempos, and themes, yet still quality English (Pugh, 1989). Much of this

Geoffrey Austrian
The Truth About Drugs
Avi
Something Upstairs
Sometimes I Think I Hear My Name
Graeme Base
The Sign of the Seahorse
James Bennett
I Can Hear the Mourning Dove
Joanne Bernstein and Bryna Fireside
Special Parents, Special Children
Janet Bode
Rape: Preventing It; Coping with the Legal, Medical, and Emotional Aftermath
Bruce Brooks
The Moves Make the Man
Betsy Byars
The Summer of the Swans
Vera and Bill Cleaver
Me Too
Robert Cormier
I Am the Cheese
Chris Crutcher
Chinese Handcuffs
N. B. Dorman
Laughter in the Background
Linna Due
High and Outside
Lois Duncan
A Gift of Magic
Don't Look Behind You
Jeanne Gehret
The Don't Give Up Kid and Learning Differences
Arthur Geisert
Pigs from A to Z
Jamie Gilson
Do Bananas Chew Gum?
Mel Glenn
Class Dismissed: High School Poems
Virginia Hamilton
Sweep Whispers, Brother Rush
The Planet of Junior Brown
Joyce Hansen
Yellow Bird and Me
Deborah Hautzig
Second Star to the Right
Florence Parry Heide
Growing Anyway Up
Irene Hunt
The Lottery Rose
Margaret Hyde
Cry Softly! The Story of Child Abuse
Knowing About Alcohol
Mind Drugs
Ann Irwin
One Bit at a Time
Paul Janeczko
Preposterous: Poems of Youth
Norma Johnston
Of Time and Seasons
M. E. Kerr
Dinky Hocker Shoots Smack
Ursula K. LeGuin
Very Far Away from Anywhere Else
Jane Claypool Miner
Why Did You Leave Me?
Joyce Slayton Mitchell
See Me More Clearly: Career and Life Planning for Teens with Physical Disabilities
Jocelyn Riley
Only My Mouth Is Smiling
Colby Rodowsky
What About Me?
Harriet Savitz
Run, Don't Walk
Marlene Shyer
Welcome Home, Jellybean
Ivan Southall
Let the Balloon Go
Sam Teague
The King of Hearts' Heart

Books Especially for Gifted Students

Tom Birdseye
Just Call Me Stupid
Eth Clifford
I Hate Your Guts, Ben Brooster
Emily Crofford
Frontier Surgeons: A Story About the Mayo Brothers
Madeleine L'Engle
A Ring of Endless Light
Norma Fox Mazer
I, Trissy
Patricia McKillop
The Riddle-Master of Hed
Robin McKinley
The Blue Sword
Claudia Mills
Fifth Grade, The World!
Robert O'Brien
Mrs. Frisby and the Rats of NIMH
Katherine Paterson
The Great Gilly Hopkins
Marilyn Sachs
Dorrie's Book
Harriet Sobol
Encyclopedia Brown Carries On
Zilpha Synder
Libby on Wednesday
Jane Yolen
Dragon's Blood
Zheng Zhensun
A Young Painter: The Life and Paintings of Wang Yani—China's Extraordinary Young Artist

FIGURE 11.4 Young Adult Books with Special Needs Topics

literature deals with a dilemma that ethnic and racial minorities face daily—the tension in non-Western immigrant families in which the parents' past is in one culture and the children's future is in another. (The Appendix is an extensive list of works in English by nonnative speakers.)

Once he or she begins the search, the responsive teacher will soon tap into a rich vein of trade literature that can help special needs students learn more about themselves and their disabilities, link them with their immediate culture, dissipate the effects of cultural discontinuity, spark interest in further reading, and demonstrate the power and promise of literacy.

Verbal Reports

In Chapters 3 and 9, we demonstrated the value of modeling for and eliciting from students verbal reports of thought processes while they occur during reading and writing. The goal of this strategy is to make readers more aware of how they make sense of what they read. According to our best knowledge about poor readers, from research and teacher observations, they lack knowledge about themselves as learners and lack metacognitive awareness of their reading strategies (Wong, 1988). Helping these students verbalize thoughts while reading can lead to a level of self-awareness necessary for recognizing the demands of the reading task—to use the most appropriate strategies—and for recognizing when comprehension is breaking down—to use fix-up strategies (Dana, 1989; Gentile & McMillan, 1992; Reyes & Molner, 1991; Young & Bastianelli, 1990).

Teachers Must Model Effective Thinking About Text

To demonstrate comprehension processes for special needs students effectively, you need to become aware of your own cognitive activity during reading. To describe your mental activity in terms your students will understand and eventually be able to model, you need to learn the language of process. To illustrate what we mean, Figure 11.5 contains examples of *content statements,* essentially, paraphrases of the text, and *metacomments,* statements that describe how the reader thinks about and makes meaning of the text. Notice how the metacomments describe, as accurately as possible, the type of processing the reader is engaged in so that students can clearly see the relationship between these processes and the comprehension strategies they are being taught to use.

As we indicated in Chapters 2 and 3, you will undoubtedly discover that attempting to talk about how you make sense of a text is not very easy at first. Sophisticated readers, such as you and I, process text so automatically that we are hardly aware of our own mental operations during comprehension. Helping poor readers develop conscious control of their text-processing strategies will require that they "see" what goes into effective comprehension. Verbal reporting can help them see how a sophisticated reader negotiates a text and derives meaning.

In the next section, "Case Study Revisited," we reconsider the problems of dysfunctional teaching in Rene's remedial reading class. You will also read about a teacher who employs a number of the strategies discussed in this chapter to expand the literacy levels of her remedial readers.

- **Making and Checking Predictions**
  Content Statement: Okay, based on the title and this first subheading, I think the author is going to explain why the number of nurses is declining.
  Metacomment: What I'm doing now is *predicting* what the text is going to be about, and as I read further I can check to see if my predictions need to be changed.
- **Using Contextual Strategies for Word Learning**
  Content Statement: It says here that the Romans had agrarian laws giving all citizens equal shares of land, so agrarian probably refers to land or agriculture.
  Metacomment: See how I'm using *context clues* right within this sentence to figure out what the word *agrarian* means.
- **Imaging**
  Content Statement: I can picture this guy, Ian, trapped in a mine shaft, with no light, and not knowing which way to turn.
  Metacomment: By *creating an image* in my mind of the events of the story, I can almost see them happening, and they become more understandable.
- **Linking Prior Knowledge to Text**
  Content Statement: The truck broke down on their way to California. That reminds me of the time I was driving to Boston and . . .
  Metacomment: I'm thinking about something in my *prior knowledge and experience* that I can relate to what I'm reading so I can better understand it.
- **Verbalizing Points of Confusion**
  Content Statement: The text says that the sun is actually slightly closer to the earth during the winter than it is during the summer.
  Metacomment: This is very *confusing* to me. It makes more sense to me to think about it in just the opposite way.
- **Demonstrating Fix-Up Strategies**
  Content Statement: (Same as previous content statement)
  Metacomment: Maybe I wasn't paying close enough attention to the explanation on this page. I'm going to *reread* this section about the earth's orbit around the sun and its relationship to the seasons.

FIGURE 11.5 The Language of Process

CASE STUDY REVISITED

We hope that by now you have had a chance to give some thought to Rene's situation. We're sure it became obvious as you read this chapter that a variety of potentially very effective literacy strategies can be used with special needs students. The fact that Mr. Willis is providing very few meaningful literacy experiences for Rene and the class is, we believe, largely inexcusable. Here is your chance to suggest ways of transforming Rene's special reading class to make it a more culturally and intellectually responsive environment for language learners. Take a moment to write your suggestions now.

We next offer our suggestions for transforming Mr. Willis's classroom. To do so, we describe the outstanding work of a remedial reading teacher who we believe embodies what it means to teach meaningful literacy to special students.

Carolyn teaches remedial reading in a suburban high school. Many of her students are nonnative English speakers, and all of them have a history of poor academic achievement. In her classroom, she has created a literacy environment that supports authentic uses of print. She also regularly demonstrates for students her own comprehension processes, thereby allowing them to observe effective reading and writing strategies. Carolyn believes that development in reading and writing can take place only in environments where students regularly engage in reading and writing, and where there are frequent opportunities for them to read and write whole, meaningful texts.

Students who enter her classroom are immersed in a language-rich environment characterized by the following:

- A reading center: a comfortable corner of the classroom crammed with fiction and nonfiction books, magazines, newspapers, pamphlets, taped stories, high-interest/easy-reading books, and other sources of printed material
- Displays of students' work, including stories, themes, essays, and artwork
- Functional reading opportunities, including a message board for exchanging notes and information among students and between Carolyn and her students, lunch menus, part-time job notices, classified ads, and more

Carolyn demonstrates how reading and writing can be functional and enjoyable. Fifteen minutes of every class are devoted to reading aloud from young adult books. Students have enjoyed the experiences of hearing and discussing books such as *Scorpions* (Myers, 1988), *Just Like Martin* (Davis, 1992), and *Bless Me, Ultima* (Anaya, 1972). Another 15 minutes of each class period are set aside for SSR, time for Carolyn and her students to read anything they like.

Carolyn not only writes to her students on the message board and through response journals, she also writes with them by collaborating on such projects as letter and report writing, a class diary, and language experience stories.

Carolyn helps her students see themselves as growing and maturing into literacy by providing frequent opportunities to read and write what they choose, which helps consolidate their less-than-sophisticated strategies. In this way, they can self-correct and teach themselves more readily.

Carolyn exploits students' own concerns, interests, and individual needs to know more about certain topics through reading and writing. Students are asked to respond to books being read in class by finding links between the text and their personal experiences. For instance, two of her students, Raymond and Renque, teamed up to write a compelling piece about their experiences as "graffiti artists" in response to an editorial Carolyn read to the class about the influence of the media on public opinion. Raymond and Renque argued that newspapers gave graffiti artists a bad reputation by erroneously linking their activity to gangs.

Modeling and demonstrating the editing process begins early in the year in Carolyn's classroom. Daily, she makes overheads of her own and students' writing, and for 10 minutes or so she edits them for the whole class to see, commenting aloud as she works through a piece. Students are encouraged to take notes on what they observe and keep them in a special section of their notebooks labeled "Editor's File," which also contains procedures and editor's marks. Gradually, as students develop a feel for the editing process, she receives more and more comments about the writing displayed on the overhead. As students' writing is displayed and edited by the class, they become sensitized to their own strengths and weaknesses with conventions and focus attention on weak areas during the writing process.

As students develop skill in the editing process, Carolyn establishes an editor's table (Burke, 1985) where students rotate responsibility for editing their own and others' writing before it is prepared for publication. Carolyn reports that as students take turns at the editor's table, she begins to see substantial growth in their own work. We strongly endorse this process of helping special needs students learn by assuming the role of teacher.

To establish a close relationship between the regular and remedial programs, Carolyn meets frequently with her students' subject area teachers. From them, she discovers as much as possible about her students' strengths and weaknesses in each subject area and learns about the content and type of instruction they receive. Her efforts have led to collaboration with teachers on various units of study. For example, she worked with a history teacher during his unit on Reconstruction because several of her students were in the history class. She gathered the history teacher's notes and other materials on the topic. In her classroom, she introduced the students to Armstrong's book *Sounder* (1972) and Smothers' book *Down in the Piney Woods* (1992), which were used to help students connect with and assimilate many of the concepts and details related to race relations during that period in American history.

Carolyn says her classroom is a place where students can take risks and learn to take advantage of the power and joy of literacy. All of her students come to her with histories of negative and maladaptive attributions for their failure as readers and learners. In her class, however, they are given abundant opportunities to view themselves as successful and competent communicators. This feeling of competence has a way of leavening their global self-concepts and generalizing across school subjects.

■ ■ ■

SUMMARY

We have stressed that regardless of whether students are learning disabled or academically gifted, they should receive our best strategies if we are to help them become effective language users and motivated learners.

We agree with Allington, Boxer, and Broikou (1987), who recommend that instruction in remedial and special language programs move away from workbooks and skills exercises that fractionalize literacy learning and leave few or no opportunities for teacher–student interaction. Instead, we have described methods that emphasize meaningful, whole, and enjoyable reading and writing experiences appropriate for students of all abilities. Meaningful literacy experiences should include those that are personally and culturally relevant to the students, as well as those that assist students in applying effective reading and writing strategies to subject area learning. Special needs students and those who teach them should be involved in demonstrations of and interactions throughout the process of comprehending and constructing whole texts. Finally, special needs students should be led to discover the enjoyment and power of mastering language forms.

REFERENCES

Abt-Perkins, D. (1996). Teaching writing in a multicultural classroom: Students and teacher as storytellers. In F. Rios (Ed.), *Teacher thinking in cultural contexts.* Albany, NY: SUNY Press.

Albert, R., & Spangler, D. (1992). Giftedness, creative efforts, and identity: Their relationships to one another. In J. Carlson (Ed.), *Advances in cognition and educational practice.* Greenwich, CT: Jai Press.

Allington, R. L., Boxer, N. J., & Broikou, K. A. (1987). Jeremy, remedial reading, and subject area classes. *Journal of Reading, 30,* 643–645.

Anderson, R. C. (1984). Role of reader's schema in comprehension, learning, and memory. In R. C. Anderson, J. Osborn, & R. Tierney (Eds.), *Learning to read in American schools: Basal readers and content texts.* Hillsdale, NJ: Erlbaum.

Arnold, M., & Swadener, E. B. (1993). Savage inequalities and the discourse of risk: What of the white children who have so much green grass? *The Review of Education, 15,* 261–272.

Atwell, N. (1984). Writing and reading literature from the inside out. *Language Arts, 61,* 240–252.

Atwell, N. (1987). *In the middle.* Portsmouth, NH: Heinemann.

Banks, J. (1991, Spring). Multicultural literacy and curriculum reform. *Educational Horizons, 69,* 135–140.

Banks, J. (1994). *Multiethnic education: Theory and practice* (3rd ed.). Boston: Allyn & Bacon.

Barnitz, J. G. (1994). Discourse diversity: Principles for authentic talk and literacy instruction. *Journal of Reading, 37,* 586–591.

Benedict, S., & Carlisle, L. (1992). *Beyond words: Picture books for older readers and writers.* Portsmouth, NH: Heinemann.

Bishop, R. S., & Hickman, J. (1992). Four or fourteen or forty: Picture books for everyone. In S. Benedict & L. Carlisle (Eds.), *Beyond words: Picture books for older readers and writers.* Portsmouth, NH: Heinemann.

Brophy, J., & Good, T. (1985). Teacher behavior and student achievement. In M. Wittrock (Ed.), *Third handbook of research on teaching.* New York: Macmillan.

Brozo, W. G. (1988). Applying a reader-response heuristic to expository text. *Journal of Reading, 32,* 140–145.

Brozo, W. G. (1991, October). *Who is at risk?: A critical literacy perspective.* Paper presented at the annual meeting of the College Reading Association, Washington, DC.

Brozo, W. G. (1995). Literacy without "risk": Reconsidering cultural and curricular differentiation in literacy. *The State of Reading, 2,* 5–12.

Brozo, W. G., & Brozo, C. L. (1994). Literacy assessment in standardized and zero-failure contexts. *Reading and Writing Quarterly, 10,* 189–208.

Brozo, W. G., & Curtis, C. L. (1987). Coping strategies of four successful learning disabled college students: A case study approach. In J. Readence & R. S. Baldwin (Eds.), *Research in literacy: Merging perspectives. Thirty-sixth yearbook of the National Reading Conference.* Rochester, NY: National Reading Conference.

Brozo, W. G., & Schmelzer, R. V. (1997). Wildmen, warriors, and lovers: Reaching boys through archetypal literature. *Journal of Adolescent and Adult Literacy, 41,* 4–11.

Brozo, W. G., Valerio, P., & Salazar, M. (1996). A walk through Gracie's garden: Literacy and cultural explorations in a Mexican-American junior high school. *Journal of Adolescent and Adult Literacy, 40,* 164–170.

Burke, C. L. (1985). Editor's table. In J. Harste, K. M. Pierce, & T. Cairney (Eds.), *The authoring cycle: A viewing guide.* Portsmouth, NH: Heinemann.

Butkowsky, I., & Willow, D. (1980). Cognitive-motivational characteristics of children varying in reading ability: Evidence for learned helplessness in poor readers. *Journal of Educational Psychology, 72,* 408–422.

Cain, L., & Brewer, F. (1992). Toward accommodating the gifted and talented in high school American history. *Illinois Schools Journal, 72,* 35–52.

Carlson, J. (1992). *Advances in cognition and educational practice.* Greenwich, CT: Jai Press.

Coles, G. (1987). *The learning mystique: A critical look at learning disabilities.* New York: Pantheon.

Cuban, L. (1989). The "at-risk" label and the problem of urban school reform. *Phi Delta Kappan, 70,* 780–801.

Cushner, K., McClelland, A., & Safford, P. (1992). *Human diversity in education: An integrative approach.* New York: McGraw-Hill.

Dana, C. (1989). Strategy families for disabled readers. *Journal of Reading, 33,* 30–35.

Delpit, L. (1988). The silenced dialogue: Power and pedagogy in educating other people's children. *Harvard Educational Review, 58,* 280–298.

Delpit, L. (1995). *Other people's children.* New York: New Press.

Diamond, B., & Moore, M. (1995). *Multicultural literacy: Mirroring the reality of the classroom.* White Plains, NY: Longman.

Diener, C., & Dweck, C. (1978). An analysis of learned helplessness: Continuous changes in performance, strategy, and achievement cognitions following failure. *Journal of Personality and Social Psychology, 34,* 451–462.

Dole, J., Brown, K., & Trathen, W. (1996). The effects of strategy instruction on the comprehension performance of at-risk students. *Reading Research Quarterly, 31,* 62–88.

Doneson, S. (1991). Reading as a second chance: Teen mothers and children's books. *Journal of Reading, 35,* 220–223.

Eaker-Rich, D., & Van Galen, J. (1996). *Caring in an unjust world: Negotiating borders and barriers in schools.* Albany, NY: SUNY Press.

Erickson, B. (1996). Read-alouds reluctant readers relish. *Journal of Adolescent and Adult Literacy, 40,* 212–214.

Fader, D., Duggins, J., Finn, T., & McNeil, E. (1976). *The new hooked on books.* New York: Berkley.

Fenwick, A. (1995). On attribution theory: Challenging behaviour and staff beliefs. *Clinical Psychology Forum, 79,* 29–43.

Field, M. L., & Aebersold, J. A. (1990). Cultural attitudes toward reading: Implications for teachers of ESL/bilingual readers. *Journal of Reading, 33,* 406–410.

Fish, S. (1980). *Is there a text in this class? The authority of interpretive communities.* Cambridge, MA: Harvard University Press.

Fishman, J., & Goss, B. (1996). Inclusion in an urban middle school. *Middle School Journal, 27,* 24-36.

Flynn, J., & Rahbar, M. (1993). The effects of age and gender on reading achievement: Implications for pediatric counseling. *Developmental and Behavioral Pediatrics, 14,* 304-307.

Garcia, E. (1990, November-December). *An analysis of literacy enhancement for middle school Hispanic students through curriculum integration.* Paper presented at the annual meeting of the National Reading Conference, Miami.

Garcia, J., Hadaway, N., & Beal, G. (1988, November-December). Cultural pluralism in recent nonfiction tradebooks for children. *The Social Studies,* 252-255.

Gentile, L., & McMillan, M. (1992). Literacy for students at risk: Developing critical dialogues. *Journal of Reading, 35,* 636-641.

Gillette, M. (1996). Resistance and rethinking: White student teachers in predominantly African-American schools. In F. Rios (Ed.), *Teacher thinking in cultural contexts.* Albany, NY: SUNY Press.

Glasgow, J. (1996). Motivating the tech prep reader through learning styles and adolescent literature. *Journal of Adolescent and Adult Literacy, 39,* 358-367.

Godina, H. (1996). The canonical debate—implementing multicultural literature and perspectives. *Journal of Adolescent and Adult Literacy, 39,* 544-549.

Good, T., & Brophy, J. (1984). *Looking into classrooms* (3rd ed.). New York: Harper & Row.

Goodman, K., Bird, L., & Goodman, Y. (1992). *The whole language catalog: Supplement on authentic assessment.* New York: SRA Macmillan.

Graham, S. (1997). Using attribution theory to understand social and academic motivation in African American youth. *Educational Psychologist, 32,* 21-40.

Grosser, G., & Spafford, C. (1995). *Physiological psychology dictionary.* Boston: McGraw-Hill.

Halsted, J. W. (1988). *Guiding gifted readers: From preschool to high school.* Columbus: Ohio Psychology Publishing.

Hamilton, M. L. (1996). Tacit messages: Teachers' cultural models of the classroom. In F. Rios (Ed.), *Teacher thinking in cultural contexts.* Albany, NY: SUNY Press.

Harste, J. C. (1986, December). *Good readers as informants: What it means to be strategic.* Paper presented at the annual meeting of the National Reading Conference, San Antonio, TX.

Hauser, P., & Nelson, G. (1988). *Books for the gifted child* (Vol. 2). New York: R. R. Bowker.

Hayden, R. (1995). Training parents as reading facilitators. *The Reading Teacher, 49,* 334-336.

Henry, M. (1996). *Parent-school collaboration.* Albany, NY: SUNY Press.

Hersh, C., Stone, B., Brian, J., & Ford, L. (1996). Learning disabilities and learned helplessness: A heuristic approach. *International Journal of Neuroscience, 84,* 103-116.

Hill, M., & Van Horn, L. (1995). Book club goes to jail: Can book clubs replace gangs? *Journal of Adolescent and Adult Literacy, 39,* 180-188.

Hilliard, A. (1989). Teaching and cultural styles in a pluralistic society. *National Education Association, 7,* 65-69.

Hynd, G. (1992). Neurological aspects of dyslexia: Comment on the balance model. *Journal of Learning Disabilities, 25,* 110–123.

Jackson, F. (1993–1994). Seven strategies to support a culturally responsive pedagogy. *Journal of Reading, 37,* 298–303.

Jimenez, R. (1997). The strategic reading abilities and potential of five low-literacy Latina/o readers in middle school. *Reading Research Quarterly, 32,* 224–243.

Jimenez, R., & Gamez, A. (1996). Literature-based cognitive strategy instruction for middle school Latina/o students. *Journal of Adolescent and Adult Literacy, 40,* 84–91.

Johnston, P., & Winograd, P. (1985). Passive failure in reading. *Journal of Reading Behavior, 17,* 279–301.

Knapp, M., & Needels, M. (1991). Review of research and instruction in literacy. In M. S. Knapp & P. M. Shields (Eds.), *Better schooling for the children of poverty: Alternatives to conventional wisdom.* Berkeley, CA: McCutchan.

Labov, W. (1982). Objectivity and commitment in linguistic science: The case of the black English trial in Ann Arbor. *Language and Society, 11,* 165–202.

Lee, N., & Neal, J. (1992–1993). Reading rescue: Intervention for a student "at promise." *Journal of Reading, 36,* 276–283.

Lukens, R., & Cline, R. (1995). *Critical handbook of literature for young adults.* New York: HarperCollins.

Marr, M. B., & Allington, R. (1994). Changes in the identification and instruction of high-risk readers. In K. Wood & B. Algozzine (Eds.), *Teaching reading to high-risk learners: A unified perspective.* Boston: Allyn & Bacon.

McDermott, R., & Gospodinoff, K. (1979). Social contexts for ethnic borders and school failure. In A. Wolfgang (Ed.), *Nonverbal behavior.* New York: Academic Press.

Mikulincer, M., & Averill, P. (1995). Human learned helplessness: A coping perspective. *Contemporary Psychology, 40,* 1049–1066.

Miller, D. (1993). The literature project: Using literature to improve the self-concept of at-risk adolescent females. *Journal of Reading, 36,* 442–448.

Page, R. (1991). *Lower-track classrooms: A curricular and cultural perspective.* New York: Teachers College Press.

Pearman, E., Huang, A., & Mellblom, C. (1997). The inclusion of all students: Concerns and incentives of educators. *Education and Training in Mental Retardation and Development, 32,* 11–19.

Pellicano, R. (1987). At risk: A view of "social advantage." *Educational Leadership, 44,* 47–49.

Peregoy, S., & Boyle, O. (1993). *Reading, writing, and learning in ESL.* New York: London Press.

Pietras, T. (1984). Cultural variation and textbook publication vis-à-vis jelly beans and designer genes. In R. C. Anderson, J. Osborn, & R. Tierney (Eds.), *Learning to read in American schools: Basal readers and content texts.* Hillsdale, NJ: Erlbaum.

Polakow, V., & Brozo, W. G. (1993). Special section editors' introduction. *The Review of Education, 15,* 217–221.

Pritchard, R. (1990). The effects of cultural schemata on reading processing strategies. *Reading Research Quarterly, 25,* 273–295.

Prouty, J., & Irby, B. (1995, February). *Parent involvement: Integrated packets.* Paper presented at the Student/Beginning Teacher Conference, Nacogdoches, TX.

Pugh, S. (1989). Literature, culture,and ESL: A natural convergence. *Journal of Reading, 32,* 320–329.

Reyes, M., & Molner, L. (1991). Instructional strategies for second-language learners in the content areas. *Journal of Reading, 35,* 96–103.

Reyhner, J., & Garcia, R. (1989). Helping minorities read better: Problems and promises. *Reading Research and Instruction, 28,* 84–91.

Rhodes, L., & Dudley-Marling, C. (1996). *Readers and writers with a difference: A holistic approach to teaching struggling readers and writers.* Portsmouth, NH: Heinemann.

Rich, D. (1993). *Megaskills: How families help children succeed in schools and beyond.* New York: Houghton Mifflin.

Richardson, J. (1994). Great read-alouds for prospective teachers and secondary students. *Journal of Reading, 38,* 98–103.

Rief, L. (1992). *Seeking diversity.* Portsmouth, NH: Heinemann.

Rios, F. (1996). *Teacher thinking in cultural contexts.* Albany, NY: SUNY Press.

Rioux, J. W., & Berla, N. (1993). *Innovations in parent and family involvement.* Princeton Junction, NJ: Eye on Education.

Roberts, R., & Mather, N. (1995). The return of students with learning disabilities to regular classrooms: A sellout? *Learning Disabilities Practice, 10,* 46–58.

Robinson, R., & Good, T. (1987). *Becoming an effective reading teacher.* New York: Harper & Row.

Rogers, J. (1993). The inclusion revolution. *Research Bulletin—Phi Delta Kappa, 11,* 1–5.

Rudman, M. (1995). *Children's literature: An issues approach* (3rd ed.). New York: Longman.

Sanacore, J. (1996). Ingredients for successful inclusion. *Journal of Adolescent and Adult Literacy, 39,* 588–591.

Saravia-Shore, M., & Arvizu, S. (1992). *Cross-cultural literacy: Ethnographies of communication in multiethnic classrooms.* New York: Garland.

Shields, C. (1996). To group or not to group academically talented or gifted students? *Educational Administration Quarterly, 32,* 295–303.

Singhal, S., & Kanungo, R. (1996). Learned helplessness among university students: A bi-national test of the attributional model. *Psychologia, 39,* 42–66.

Smith, F. (1985). *Reading without nonsense.* New York: Teachers College Press.

Spafford, C. S., & Grosser, G. (1996). *Dyslexia research and resource guide.* Boston: Allyn & Bacon.

Stotsky, S. (1992). Whose literature? America's! *Educational Leadership, 49,* 53–56.

Swadener, E. B. (1990, Fall). Children and families "at risk": Etiology, critique, and alternative paradigms. *Educational Foundations,* 17–40.

Swap, S. M. (1993). *Developing home-school partnerships: From concepts to practice.* New York: Teachers College Press.

Touchette, R. (1996). Implementing inclusion in the high school: The first year teacher's perspective. *American Secondary Education, 25,* 33–45.

Trelease, J. (1985). *The read aloud handbook.* New York: Penguin.

U.S. Department of Education. (1995). *Sixteenth annual report to Congress on the implementation of the Individuals with Disabilities Education Act.* Washington, DC: U.S. Government Printing Office.

Van Galen, J. (1996). The limitations of compassion in facilitating diversity. In D. Eaker-Rich & J. Van Galen (Eds.), *Caring in an unjust world: Negotiating borders and barriers in schools.* Albany, NY: SUNY Press.

Walker, S. Y. (1991). *The survival guide for parents of gifted kids.* Minneapolis: Free Spirit.

Watson, D. (1988). Knowing where we're coming from: The theoretical bases. In C. Gilles, M. Bixby, P. Crowley, S. Crenshaw, M. Henrich, R. Reynolds, & D. Pyle (Eds.), *Whole language strategies for secondary students.* New York: Richard C. Owen.

Wells, M. C. (1992–1993). At the junction of reading and writing: How dialogue journals contribute to students' reading development. *Journal of Reading, 36,* 294–303.

Wong, B. (1988). Metacognition and learning disabilities. In T. Waller, D. Forest, & E. MacKinnon (Eds.), *Metacognition, cognition, and human performance.* New York: Academic Press.

Wood, K., & Algozzine, B. (1994). *Teaching reading to high-risk learners:A unified perspective.* Boston: Allyn & Bacon.

Young, P., & Bastianelli, C. (1990). Retelling comes to Chiloquin High. *Journal of Reading, 34,* 194–196.

Young Adult Books

Alexander, L. (1992). *The fortune-tellers.* New York: E. P. Dutton.

Anaya, R. (1972). *Bless me, Ultima.* New York: Warner.

Anaya, R. (1990). Salomon's story. In C. Tatum (Ed.), *Mexican-American literature.* Orlando, FL: Harcourt Brace Jovanovich.

Armstrong, W. (1972). *Sounder.* New York: Harper & Row.

Berck, J. (1992). *No place to be:Voices of homeless children.* Boston: Houghton Mifflin.

Cisneros, S. (1990). Three wise guys: Un cuento de navidad. In C. Tatum (Ed.), *Mexican-American literature.* Orlando, FL: Harcourt Brace Jovanovich.

Davis, O. (1992). *Just like Martin.* New York: Simon & Schuster.

Goble, P. (1988). *Iktomi and the boulder:A Plains Indian story.* New York: Orchard.

Hopkinson, D. (1993). *Sweet Clara and the freedom quilt.* New York: Alfred A. Knopf.

Jones, R. (1976). *The acorn people.* New York: Bantam Books.

Luenn, N. (1993). *Song for the ancient forest.* New York: Atheneum.

Miklowitz, G. (1987). *Secrets not meant to be kept.* New York: Dell.

Myers, W. D. (1988). *Scorpions.* New York: Harper & Row.

Senna, C. (1992). *Colin Powell:A man of war and peace.* New York: Walker.

Smothers, E. F. (1992). *Down in the piney woods.* New York: Alfred A. Knopf.

Taylor, C. (1992). *The house that crack built.* San Francisco: Chronicle Books.

Winter, J. (1989). *Follow the drinking gourd.* New York: Alfred A. Knopf.

Wood, T., & Afraid of Hawk, W. N. (1992). *A boy becomes a man at Wounded Knee.* New York: Walker.

Yolen, J. (1992). *Encounter.* San Diego, CA: Harcourt Brace Jovanovich.

Young, E. (1993). *Red thread.* New York: Philomel.

CHAPTER 12

Becoming an Effective Literacy Professional

ANTICIPATION GUIDE

Directions: Read each statement carefully and decide whether you agree or disagree with it, placing a check mark in the appropriate *Before Reading* column. When you have finished reading and studying the chapter, return to the guide and decide whether your anticipations need to be changed by placing a check mark in the appropriate *After Reading* column.

	BEFORE READING		**AFTER READING**	
	Agree	*Disagree*	*Agree*	*Disagree*
1. To answer questions about the best instruction to provide students, teachers should rely solely on expert opinion and research.	_____	_____	_____	_____
2. Introducing new ideas is usually a smooth and enjoyable process for all involved.	_____	_____	_____	_____
3. Change, no matter how minor it may seem to others, can be difficult for most teachers.	_____	_____	_____	_____
4. Meaningful change in teaching methods can happen only if teachers work alone.	_____	_____	_____	_____
5. Reflective teachers are constantly striving to understand how to provide more effective instruction.	_____	_____	_____	_____

I have to learn beyond my classroom. I have to put myself in situations that challenge my thinking, my comfort. I take courses that push my knowledge. I find myself hiding behind other students, hoping the professor won't call on me because I'm having trouble understanding the vocabulary and the concepts. But I push myself to figure it out. I listen hard. I reread. I rewrite what I think. And I try to relate it all to my experiences. I have to be a learner in and out of my classroom so I won't lose sight of what it's like for my students—so I will continue to hear their voices.

—Rief (1992)

Just as effective reading does not result from prescriptive teaching, effective teaching cannot be achieved by following a set of prescriptions. What makes literacy professionals effective is often what makes them unique. They create classroom learning environments and engage students in experiences that break from tradition, that make learning exciting and memorable. The strategies in this book, then, should be viewed as examples of possibilities that, when modified to fit your needs, your students' needs, and the instructional context, will lead to greater learning and enthusiasm for learning.

Purpose of Chapter 12

This chapter deals with several important issues related to literacy professionalism as it concerns middle and secondary classroom teachers and student literacy. First, we explore personal, contextual, and political factors that influence teachers' use of innovative reading and learning strategies. Within this discussion, we propose a model of teacher change. We then discuss how teacher reflections and classroom action research can provide teachers with insights into themselves, their evolving philosophies of teaching, and their students. We also present collaborative strategies for solidifying support among teachers and students, parents, other teachers, and administrators. We argue that through these collaborative relationships, teachers become more effective in arousing students' enthusiasm for learning, increasing content area learning, and expanding literacy. As part of this discussion, we present what we believe to be the most effective role a literacy professional can play in an overall middle and secondary school reading and writing program.

CASE STUDY

Melinda hadn't used centers for 10 years, since the last time she taught first grade. But last summer just before the new school year, she decided to see if her sixth graders would get just as excited about centers as her little ones did. Melinda, a language arts teacher, knew a change was needed in her classroom, though she had been uncertain about exactly what and how to change. Student performance was not necessarily slipping; it was Melinda's own sense of professionalism that impelled her to explore other instructional possibilities for her sixth graders. Remembering vividly how centers helped her children problem solve, work cooperatively, use their imaginations more creatively, and enrich their skills, Melinda reasoned that centers

could bring about the same results with older readers and learners, provided that they were designed appropriately. Part of her goal in implementing centers was to determine their effectiveness throughout the year so that modifications could be made whenever needed.

To the Reader:
As you explore Chapter 12, consider all of the possible steps Melinda can take to study the effectiveness of her centers. Keep in mind that the context for this research is an actual sixth-grade language arts classroom, with all of its dynamics and complexities. Also keep in mind Melinda's goals for the centers.

■ ■ ■

LITERACY INNOVATIONS IN THE CONTENT CLASSROOM: CHALLENGES TO CHANGE

Those of us who teach content area reading courses for undergraduate and graduate preservice and in-service teachers from a variety of subject area disciplines are engaged in a constant struggle to convince our students that the methods we advocate have validity. A ubiquitous concern is that we are being hypocritical as teachers of teachers if we tell our students to teach content in a way that makes it personally meaningful and functional to their students while we discuss and demonstrate strategies that are not functional or personally meaningful to our own students (Short & Burke, 1989).

Several researchers (Bintz, 1997; Holt-Reynolds, 1992; O'Brien, Stewart, & Moje, 1995; Palmer & Stewart, 1997; Ratekin, Simpson, Alvermann, & Dishner, 1985; Ruddell & Sperling, 1988; Sturtevant, 1993; Wilson, Konopak, & Readence, 1992) have offered explanations for why classroom teachers do not practice the strategies learned in content reading courses. Collectively, these reasons include the following:

Reasons Teachers Do Not Use Content Area Reading Strategies

- Teachers construct simplified approaches to content instruction based on the perceived constraints of their particular school setting.
- Teachers view content reading and writing strategies as instructionally worthless because they were learned from lecture and textbooks, essentially in isolation from real classroom settings with groups of students. They have not been able to try out the strategies, observe them in practice, or make judgments and decisions about them.
- The organization and power structure of schools inhibit teachers' attempts to try new ideas such as content reading and writing strategies. Preservice teachers are also acutely sensitive to the potential ramifications of nonconformity and innovation.
- Teachers perceive that content reading and writing strategies encroach on valuable time spent covering content.
- Teachers perceive that content reading and writing instruction does not produce measurable gains on standardized tests, where such tests are seen as the most important gauge of successful teaching.

To determine your own attitudes and beliefs about teaching reading and writing strategies in your classroom, follow the directions in Figure 12.1 to complete the inventory of attitudes and beliefs about implementing reading and writing strategies in your content classroom.

STRATEGY, TEACHER, AND ORGANIZATIONAL CHARACTERISTICS INFLUENCING THE KNOWLEDGE AND USE OF READING AND WRITING STRATEGIES

Ruddell and Sperling (1988) have identified teacher, strategy, and structural characteristics that influence the extent to which reading and writing strategies are implemented in the classroom. These are discussed in the following paragraphs.

Strategy

For any new strategy to be effectively incorporated into practice, teachers must perceive it in one or more of the following ways:

1. The new strategy must have an advantage over alternatives. We believe it has been made abundantly clear in this book that when strategies for reading,

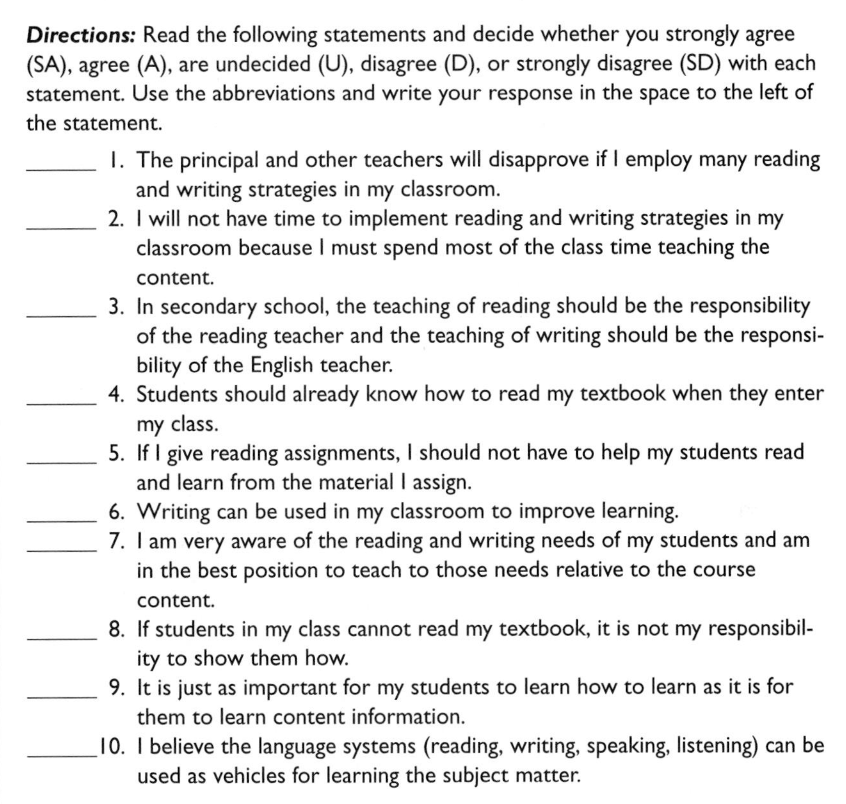

Directions: Read the following statements and decide whether you strongly agree (SA), agree (A), are undecided (U), disagree (D), or strongly disagree (SD) with each statement. Use the abbreviations and write your response in the space to the left of the statement.

______ 1. The principal and other teachers will disapprove if I employ many reading and writing strategies in my classroom.

______ 2. I will not have time to implement reading and writing strategies in my classroom because I must spend most of the class time teaching the content.

______ 3. In secondary school, the teaching of reading should be the responsibility of the reading teacher and the teaching of writing should be the responsibility of the English teacher.

______ 4. Students should already know how to read my textbook when they enter my class.

______ 5. If I give reading assignments, I should not have to help my students read and learn from the material I assign.

______ 6. Writing can be used in my classroom to improve learning.

______ 7. I am very aware of the reading and writing needs of my students and am in the best position to teach to those needs relative to the course content.

______ 8. If students in my class cannot read my textbook, it is not my responsibility to show them how.

______ 9. It is just as important for my students to learn how to learn as it is for them to learn content information.

______ 10. I believe the language systems (reading, writing, speaking, listening) can be used as vehicles for learning the subject matter.

FIGURE 12.1 Inventory of Attitudes and Beliefs About Implementing Reading and Writing Strategies in Your Content Classroom

Content Area Literacy Strategies Have Many Advantages Over Traditional Ones

writing, and literacy development are integrated within the content classroom, there are a number of advantages over traditional instructional delivery systems. Students can learn more quickly and easily by improving the process of acquiring the content. They can become more motivated to learn, remember, and apply the content when innovative language-learning strategies are used as vehicles for expanding knowledge. The teacher can become more enthusiastic and involved in the teaching/learning process when there are abundant opportunities for demonstrations, multidirectional interactions, reflections, and personal and group explorations.

2. The new strategy must be compatible with what the teacher already knows or believes. What do you know and believe about teaching reading in middle and secondary school? In this book we have attempted to expand your understanding of the reading process, as well as your knowledge about how best to teach reading and writing in the middle and secondary school class-

room. Figure 12.2 is a table adapted from Ruddell and Sperling (1988) that summarizes what we know about skilled readers and writers and implications for teaching based on this knowledge. We believe their summary may also serve as a summary for the reading and writing processes and strategies discussed in this book.

Reading	Writing	Implications for Practice
We learn to comprehend written text using prior knowledge—life experience as well as academic knowledge.	We construct written text using prior knowledge and experience.	*Reading.* Connecting students' prior knowledge and experience to reading content. *Writing.* Using students' own life and school experiences as topics for writing or as the basis for developing content for more general topics.
We develop basic perceptual and decoding processing to a level of automaticity, freeing attention for text analysis and construction of meaning.	We master conventions of style and mechanics to a level of automaticity, freeing attention for construction of meaningful content.	*Reading.* Attending to the meaning of text, allowing decoding skills to develop in the service of meaning. *Writing.* Attending to development of ideas in writing, allowing skills in style and mechanics to develop in the service of communicating ideas.
Our reading purpose and the nature of the text material influence our self-monitoring and comprehension of text.	We learn to write guided by our own writing purposes, the nature of our material, and awareness of the audience.	*Reading.* Introducing students to notions of genre and reading for different purposes based on the reading genre. *Writing.* Having students write in different genres to achieve a variety of real-world communicative purposes, addressing real readers other than the teacher.
Our attitudes and interests focus and sustain attention, leading to improved understanding and lifelong development of values.	Our attitudes toward writing as a valuable communicative process serve to focus and sustain attention while composing and lead to lifelong writing development.	*Reading.* Giving students books and articles to read that address their individual interests and curiosities. *Writing.* Valuing students' own ideas, including their experience and knowledge, to be communicated through their writing.
We modify our knowledge in assimilating and comprehending new text-based information and related aesthetic experiences.	We modify our knowledge in the process of writing it down.	*Reading.* Encouraging students' predictions about story outcomes and using these predictions to emphasize reading as a discovery process. *Writing.* Having students write for the sole purpose of discovering their ideas and working out solutions to problems.

Adapted from R. B. Ruddell & M. Sperling (1988), "Factors Influencing the Use of Literacy Research by the Classroom Teacher: Research Review and New Directions," in J. Readence & R. S. Baldwin (Eds.), *Dialogues in Literacy Research* (pp. 322–323), Chicago: National Reading Conference. Used by permission of the author.

FIGURE 12.2 Skilled Readers and Writers and Instructional Implications

3. The new strategy must not be too complex. Although it is true that the reading process comprises many complex interactions, we have tried to point out that it is also true that teachers can be effective if they recognize self-evident truths about learning. For instance, it does not take volumes of research to tell us that students will be more motivated to read and learn if we give them something interesting to read. By the same token, students will become better language users if we give them plenty of opportunities to use language in meaningful and functional ways. We have purposely tried to eliminate unnecessary complexity from our discussions and have not laden our explanations of reading and writing processes and strategies with dense, abstract theoretical terminology because we believe that theory and practice are transactional (Burnaford, 1996; Lee & Patterson, 1987; Zeichner & Liston, 1996). In other words, reading theory ought to be grounded in experience (Harste, 1988; Wells, 1992). In this connection, we have tried to demonstrate what competent language teachers and users do to facilitate text comprehension.

4. The new strategy must be tried out and/or observed in practice. For some of you who have yet to enter a classroom, nearly every teaching strategy discussed by a professor or presented in a textbook must seem a bit hollow and leave you a bit incredulous. We are especially sensitive to these reactions among students. Although the laws of physics prevent us from projecting you into an actual classroom/instructional setting, we have tried our best to offer realistic applications for the strategies discussed. The constant references to actual classroom practices and anecdotal evidence for the successful implementation of strategies are intended to help you see how the strategies worked in one setting and reflect on the possibilities for you and your classroom.

Teacher

Reasons Teachers Are Likely to Put Content Area Strategies into Practice

Ruddell and Sperling, as well as others who have investigated the complexities of teacher change (Hargreaves, 1995; Lieberman & McLaughlin, 1992), claim that teachers are highly likely to accept and put into practice innovative literacy strategies if they (1) view themselves as supportive and productive; (2) have open lines of communication in the classroom and with colleagues and others in the profession; (3) are self-initiating, cooperative, and highly motivated; and (4) are intellectually curious. Aronowitz and Giroux (1991) recommend that teachers explore the ramifications of the cultural/political role of schooling—how schools define teachers' roles as technicians and students' roles as passive receptors of information. Through this exploration, these authors claim, teachers can actively transform their perceptions of themselves and of students.

Organization

Several factors related to the organizational system of the school, including communication networks through which teachers obtain new information about reading and writing, can strongly influence how much a teacher knows about innovative reading and writing strategies and whether knowledge is translated into practice.

The Ease or Difficulty of Access to Professional Development Opportunities

The ease or difficulty of access to professional development opportunities is directly related to how much support is provided to a teacher for professional development, as reflected by a school's formal policies that structure a teacher's time and activities. For instance, ease of access to professional workshops and conferences and access to professional journals can dramatically influence a teacher's knowledge and use of reading and writing strategies. Some school systems have formal policies that provide many opportunities for professional development, whereas the opportunities in other systems are less formalized and less abundant (Hargreaves, 1995).

The Extent to Which Change Agencies Are Highly Formalized

In the complex organizational system of many schools, responsibility for change is often centralized and highly formalized. In some school systems, boards, superintendents, and principals are the exclusive change agencies responsible for implementing formal policies related to such issues as standardized testing and textbook adoptions, which in turn influence curriculum choices and changes. It has been found that in organizations where the change agencies are not so formalized, innovative teaching strategies are more easily and quickly implemented in classrooms.

According to O'Brien et al. (1995), before teachers will take full advantage of content literacy strategies, they should be informed of the realities of school organizations in which they must function on a day-to-day basis. They should be given the opportunity to explore reasons behind an organization's resistance to change, as well as the social and political constraints that define school policy and acceptable and unacceptable teaching practices.

SUPPORTING MEANINGFUL CHANGE IN TEACHER PRACTICE

As you might infer, promoting change in the ways middle and secondary school teachers integrate and apply content area literacy strategies is not always a simple or clear-cut process. Educational innovations do not happen in schools merely because teachers or administrators say they should. The expanding literature on teacher change suggests that ignoring teachers' beliefs (Griffiths & Tann, 1992; Richardson, Anders, Tidwell, & Lloyd, 1991), classroom cultures (Moje, Brozo, & Haas, 1994), the structure and organization of schools (Hargreaves, 1995), teachers' personal attributes (Brozo, Brobst, & Moje 1994–1995), and teachers' knowledge of the realities of their own teaching situations—referred to as *practical knowledge* (Liston & Zeichner, 1996)—in the change process could lead to disappointing results.

Researchers involved in exploring how educational innovations are adopted and used by teachers have begun to paint a more detailed picture of the variables involved in the change process. For instance, teachers are no longer viewed as intractable, ignorant, and blindly resistant to innovation. Instead, teacher change involves a complex blend of variables ranging from personal attributes of teachers to the structure of the organizations in which they work. To understand the interrelationships among these variables more fully, Richardson (1990) proposes that the following questions should be explored:

Important Questions to Ask About the Teacher Change Process

- *Who is in control of change?*

  Teachers should feel a genuine sense of investment in the change process.

  Teachers should see a relationship between their efforts and change outcomes.

  Teachers should be provided with opportunities to reflect on their practical knowledge, theoretical frameworks, and activities associated with the educational innovation.

- *What is significant and worthwhile practice?*

  Teachers must be actively involved in making judgments about which changes are worthwhile and significant.

- *What is the context of change?*

  Individual teacher change should be viewed within the context of the culture and norms of teachers, administrators, other school personnel, and students in a particular school.

Given these questions, we present a model for promoting meaningful change in teacher practice in Figure 12.3. The model suggests that changes in teaching practices are most likely to come about when teachers' own beliefs, attitudes, theories about learning and teaching, and their everyday knowledge about the realities of teaching are taken into account when an educational innovation is introduced to them. *Structural support* refers to all of the ways school administrators and staff can support each other in the change process, including providing necessary and desired resources, as well as time to problem-solve and commiserate collectively. A critical component of this model is the need for teachers to reflect on the change process in order to assess regularly the efficacy of the educational innovation and the ways in which it is being implemented.

CHARACTERISTICS OF EFFECTIVE TEACHERS

Although we know that effective teaching cannot be distilled, bottled, and taken as an elixir, we do know that effective middle and secondary classroom teachers exhibit certain general characteristics that can serve as guidelines for helping you become a better teacher.

FIGURE 12.3 A Model for Promoting Meaningful Change in Teaching Practice

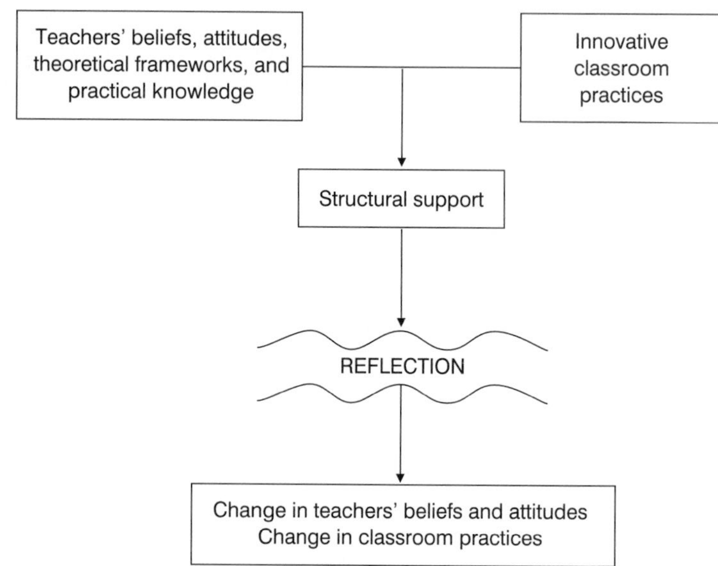

Effective Teachers Are Reflective Teachers

Reflective teaching is a powerful way to consider your teaching carefully and to become a more thoughtful and alert student of teaching (Henderson, 1992; Tremmel, 1993). First, we know from Zeichner and Liston (1996) what doesn't constitute reflective teaching:

> If a teacher never questions the goals and the values that guide his or her work, the context in which he or she teaches, or never examines his or her assumptions, then it is our belief that this individual is not engaged in reflective teaching. (p. 1)

Valverde (1982), on the other hand, provides a very useful operational definition of *reflection:*

Definition of Reflective Teaching

> The teacher must examine his/her situation, behavior, practices, effectiveness, and accomplishments. Reflection means asking basic questions of oneself. The basic and comprehensive question during reflection is, What am I doing and why? . . . Reflection then, is an individual's needs assessment and continued self-monitoring or satisfaction with effectiveness. As with any type of evaluation, reflection should be formative, that is, periodic, constructive, and deliberate. (p. 86)

Reflective teachers do not rely on routine, tradition, and authority to simplify their professional lives, nor do they uncritically accept the everyday reality of schools. Instead, they constantly and carefully reconsider beliefs and practices (Valli, 1993).

Reflection allows the teacher to examine critically the assumptions that schools make about what are and are not acceptable goals and practices. According to McLaughlin (1992), although teachers must work within some constraints, they often accept as predetermined by authority or tradition far more than is necessary. Although we have seen that school structures do place constraints on teachers' policies and decision making, a fair degree of latitude exists nonetheless. For instance, teachers within the same school will vary widely on such matters as evaluation and classroom management practices, goals, political beliefs, treatment of special needs students, and adherence to textbooks. We believe there is ample room for teachers to exercise their professional prerogative and individuality in teaching.

Urging you to be a reflective teacher, then, means urging you to depend on yourself as a decision maker and to trust your judgments of what you know and believe.

Reflection and Developing a Personal Philosophy of Teaching

Reflective thinking can be a tool for helping you develop and refine your personal philosophy of teaching, your professional identity. Reflection forces you to engage in inquiry about teaching that ultimately requires self-analysis and appraisal. If you reflect on your professional experience throughout your career, your personal philosophy of teaching will evolve over the years. This evolution is a sign of professional growth.

A Teaching Journal Can Promote Professional Growth

One way to become a reflective teacher, to determine where you stand and what you believe relative to your specific school environment, is to record events and your analysis of them in a **Reflective Thinking Journal (RTJ).** Keeping a daily or weekly journal allows you to keep track of events and reflect privately on what they mean to you and what they mean within a broader context. What happened? Why did it happen? What was my role? What beliefs did my actions reflect? Did my actions reflect beliefs and assumptions of which I was not aware? Did the consequences of my actions raise doubts or reinforce beliefs? How should I act in the future based on what happened?

An RTJ not only can lead you to discoveries about how you teach, it can help you teach. It can offer you a way to think about strategies, to plan their implementation, to question the social and dynamic conditions that will influence their success, to appraise their effectiveness, and to reconsider and modify them (Santa, Short, & Smith, 1993).

We suggest the format depicted in the sample RTJ in Figure 12.4. Any format is adequate, however, if it helps you focus on particularly significant events and facilitates the recording of necessary information about events and analysis of events. A discussion of the components of the RTJ follows.

Events. Select one or two events that you felt were significant. They may be significant because what you tried to teach or what you observed bothered you (such as the earth science teacher's concern about trying a prereading writing assignment); excited you; caused you to rethink your initial ideas, plans, or goals;

Event	Analysis Reflections
I began Chapter 7 a little differently today. Instead of jumping into the text like I normally do, I asked the class to write before they read the chapter. The chapter was concerned with important environmental issues related to nuclear power, and I asked students to get together in small groups and talk about possible solutions to the nuclear energy problems and then write a short paper discussing their solutions. Collective groans went up when I explained the assignment. It took a few students several minutes to find a group. As I moved around the room, I discovered that many students were not participating in the group discussions; some were staring out the window or had their heads on the desk; some were talking about anything but the topic. I asked them to hand in their papers at the end of the period—I got 7 out of 27 back!	I'm not sure what happened, but this strategy of writing before reading sure fell on its face. I felt embarrassed and confused. I wanted to demand that students get involved and take advantage of this "fun," different approach to the chapter, but it didn't make any sense to try that. They seemed just as confused and unenthusiastic as I must have appeared. As I think some more on it, I'm beginning to realize that I came out of nowhere with this exercise. The class has done very little group work and not much writing other than term papers and reports. Maybe if we try this again—but move into it more gradually and I prepare the class for writing—I might get a better response. I think I also have to get clearer in my head why I'm asking students to do this in the first place. I read that it was a good idea; perhaps I need more information.

FIGURE 12.4 An RTJ: Sample Format and Entry for an 11th-Grade Earth Science Classroom

or convinced you that your initial ideas were valid. Whether your events reflect successful or unsuccessful experiences or something in between, they are significant if they provide fodder for reflection and learning.

Describe the significant event(s) in detail. Think about what you felt during the event(s), your perceptions of your students' responses to your actions and words, and who or what significantly influenced and shaped the outcome of the event(s). Rich description here will provide you with the material you need for further analysis and reflection in the other section of the journal.

Analysis/Reflection. In this section of the journal, you should include a discussion of *why* the event was significant to you and how you interpret it. Posner (1985) points out the critical importance of this section:

> Try to figure out what you accomplished, identify problems that emerged and how you plan to follow up, and distill from the episodes what you learned. This last point is the most important. You may have learned what

works in this situation and what does not. If so, describe what you conclude. But you may also have learned something about your philosophy of teaching (your perspective). Does the episode confirm your ideas or force you to reconsider them? Maybe initial ideas you held rather dogmatically depend, to a large extent, on the situation that affected the applicability of the ideas. (p. 25)

A Teaching Journal Will Help You Answer Important Teaching Questions

After analysis and reflection, you may be left with more questions than answers. We view questions as an essential part of the inquiry process of reflective thinking. The RTJ can be used to search for answers to your questions, explore your evolving feelings and philosophy about teaching, and help you modify approaches over time.

To help you "experience" reflective thinking, take a moment to do a reflective thinking exercise. Set up a piece of notebook paper in the format shown in Figure 12.4, using the headings "Event" and "Analysis/Reflection." Fill in this "page" of an RTJ based on one of the following: (1) a strategy you implemented in your classroom, (2) a strategy you observed a teacher implement, or (3) a recent classroom experience in which you were a student. Try to provide a full description of the event and a complete analysis of and reflection on the event.

In summary, reflective teaching is a process that causes teachers to think deeply about their experiences and calls on them to self-assess and produce insights and new perspectives that will guide their practice.

Effective Teachers Use the Research Process as a Learning Process

Effective teachers expand their knowledge about their practice and themselves in many ways. They learn by reading the professional literature, by observing students in their own classrooms, by observing teachers and students in other classrooms, by reflecting on their observations alone and with others, and by sharing their knowledge and experience. They also learn through systematic investigations of their teaching effectiveness (Goff, 1996). According to Harste (1988), "As a learning process, nothing beats research" (p. 9).

Teacher researchers, interested in improving practices within their own settings, undertake research to better understand their students, themselves, and their particular educational environment. In simple terms, teacher researchers use research to do a better job of teaching (Branscombe, Goswami, & Schwartz, 1992).

Classroom action research is research undertaken by teachers to improve practice. It can also be used to provide verification and produce evidence that certain strategies are making a difference (Cochran-Smith & Lytle, 1993). You and most teachers work hard and are constantly searching for new methods and strategies to improve instruction, but rarely do you gather the kind of proof about the effectiveness of your strategies that makes superintendents, principals, and other teachers take notice. As a result of action research, your teaching practices improve, and support for your efforts increases. This type of research also encourages ownership of strategies, as well as improvement in student achievement. Effective teachers view teaching as research.

A Seven-Phase Plan for Teacher Research

We recommend a seven-phase plan for helping you conduct research in your classroom (Green, 1987): (1) identify an issue, interest, or concern; (2) seek knowledge; (3) plan an action; (4) implement the action; (5) observe the action; (6) reflect on the observations; and (7) revise the plan. For you to better understand classroom action research and how it works, we discuss the seven phases in some detail.

Phase 1: Identify an Issue, Interest, or Concern

There are several reasons why teachers conduct classroom research: (1) they want to learn more about an aspect of their students' reading and writing development; (2) they want to observe the reading and writing development of certain students (e.g., special needs students); (3) they want to observe over time students' responses to and development of particular strategies; (4) they want to observe the effect of the learning environment on student development; (5) they want to determine differences in students' responses to and development of various strategies.

For example, Michael, an 11th-grade history teacher, was dissatisfied with the departmental unit tests that had been developed before he joined the faculty. He felt they placed too much emphasis on memorization of detailed information and not enough emphasis on understanding concepts. After presenting his concerns to the history faculty and gaining their general support, he decided to test some alternative teaching strategies to determine how well students learned important history concepts.

Phase 2: Seek Knowledge

There Are Many Sources of Information About Teaching

A variety of sources are available for acquiring information about teaching strategies, including (1) college undergraduate and graduate courses and notes; (2) professional books, journals, and magazines; (3) university faculty; (4) district curriculum specialists; (5) professional conferences, workshops, and inservice training; and (6) colleagues.

For example, Michael began to seek information related to teaching concepts in history. He got the idea of teaching history using a thematic unit approach centering on critical concepts from an undergraduate history methods class. He found reinforcement for the idea from presentations at a state social studies conference and from a class project in a graduate content area reading class. Returning to the handouts and texts from the presentations and courses, he began putting together a unit plan on the Civil War. In addition, he consulted with his former university professors and the district curriculum specialist, and he brainstormed with a colleague in the history department to round out the particulars of the unit and ways in which students' knowledge of concepts could be assessed. Michael decided to focus his instruction on helping students apply their understanding of the concept of civil war to examples of civil strife that have occurred before and since and are occurring today around the globe (e.g., in the former Soviet Union and in Lebanon).

Phase 3: Plan an Action

In this phase the teacher researcher should refine the research goals. One way to do this is to pose questions that the classroom research might help answer. Brainstorm as many questions as possible related to the issue, interest, or concern of the research. During this phase, plan how the action will be observed or assessed.

For example, Michael formulated three main questions:

1. Will students acquire the basic factual information about the Civil War (e.g., battles, generals, dates, places)?
2. Will students demonstrate an understanding of the concept of *civil war?*
3. Will students exhibit greater enthusiasm for this unit over previous ones?

To answer the first question, the existing questions on the departmental unit test would be used. In this way, his students' performance could be directly compared with the performance of students in other classes.

To answer the second question, Michael wrote some additional questions for the unit test that required knowledge and application of the critical concept. In addition, he designed an assessment requiring students to generate a personal essay that would provide insights into their ability to apply their knowledge of the concept.

To answer the third question, Michael designed an attitude and interest inventory that would be given to students at the conclusion of the unit. The inventory asked students to reflect on their learning experiences during the unit, and decide how they felt about them and how they compared with other learning experiences in other history units.

Phase 4: Implement the Action

The plan that has been devised to investigate an issue, interest, or concern should be put into action. A plan of action in classroom action research generally involves a teacher's trying out a strategy or series of strategies related to the five reasons for classroom research outlined in Phase 1. The strategies may be new or they may be existing. In both cases, the teacher desires information about students' responses to the strategies and their effectiveness.

For example, during the unit, Michael engaged his students in a variety of learning experiences intended to help them explore the concept of *civil war.* As students read and learned about our Civil War, they also learned about civil strife in other countries and at other times in history using fiction and nonfiction trade books, current events magazines, films and videos, discussions and debates, and many other strategies.

Phase 5: Observe the Action

Teachers Can Use a Variety of Methods for Gathering Observations of an Action Plan

Teacher researchers employ a variety of data-gathering methods as part of their investigations. The most common methods include observations, field notes, teacher and student journals and learning logs, interviews, and questionnaires. Normally, teachers gather feedback and interpret students' responses throughout an investigation period as a part of everyday classroom assessment.

For example, Michael kept a daily log of classroom events in which he recorded observations, perceptions, and reflections. The log provided a means of formative evaluation concerning how well he was teaching the critical concept and the extent to which students were learning it. The log was also used to monitor students' enthusiasm and interest in the unit. With this information, he was able to make ongoing adjustments to the unit plan.

Phase 6: Reflect on the Observations

In this phase, data collected through various methods to provide information for the teacher researcher concerning the issue, interest, or concern should be collated. Teacher researchers typically analyze data informally; however, formal analyses are made in more tightly structured investigations.

For example, Michael analyzed data from four primary sources: (1) his daily log, (2) the end-of-unit department test, (3) his end-of-unit essay test, and (4) the attitude inventory. At the conclusion of the unit, all students from all the history classes took the departmental test, the essay test, and the attitude inventory. Results clearly demonstrated that Michael's students came away from the Civil War unit with not only a collection of newly learned details but also the ability to recognize other examples of civil strife and explain their significance. Students in the other history classes seemed only to be able to demonstrate memory of detailed information.

Phase 7: Revise the Plan

A scrutiny of the results of the investigation should lead to some important decision making. The teacher researcher should ask: Were the investigation's questions answered? Is more information needed? Was useful unanticipated information obtained? Answers to these questions will help the teacher determine whether or not students benefited, further investigations should be planned, new strategies should be implemented, or changes in the way data are collected and analyzed should be made.

For example, Michael's demonstration of the effectiveness of a concept approach to teaching history led to several important changes. It helped solidify the history faculty's resolve to place a more balanced emphasis on critical concepts and important details; departmental goals were revised; cooperation increased among the history faculty; and changes were made to the unit tests. In addition, the principal made more money available to the history department for trade books and other alternative resources.

Benefits of Classroom Action Research

Why do we encourage classroom action research? To reiterate, we believe there are many benefits to individual teachers and teacher teams conducting classroom-specific research, including the following:

- Provide verification that instructional practices work.
- Promote more open-mindedness among the faculty and the administration to try new ideas.
- Expand instructional possibilities and enhance a teacher's own teaching.
- Develop ownership of specific strategies based on theory and research.
- Help teachers learn more about themselves and their students.
- Build a teacher's self-confidence and feeling of empowerment.

In short, we concur with the words of Dorothy Strickland (1988):

> In an age when our nation is calling for excellence in teaching, there is no more promising trend than the teacher-as-researcher movement. The demystifying of research, professionalization of teaching, and empowering of teachers are part of the plan. (p. 763)

Effective Teachers Employ Innovative Strategies That Link Content and Literacy Learning

All of the ideas in this book for expanding reading, writing, and other language processes are suggestions, ways of demonstrating possibilities. These suggestions come from our own work, from research, and most prominently from the exceptional teachers who have developed them and used them successfully. They are to be considered guidelines because, obviously, not all will work in your particular setting and not all of the suggested strategies will work in precisely the ways we describe. Effective teachers are constantly on the lookout for new ideas, suggestions, and strategies that they can modify and adapt to their particular needs. This process of modification and adaptation is innovation. In fact, we expect that the strategies we suggest will take on new shapes and forms in the hands of generative teachers.

For example, a 10th-grade music teacher who wished to incorporate trade books into her music classes was having difficulty finding appropriate young adult fiction books that dealt with music themes. She solved this problem by locating and bringing in the original stories for the suites her students were performing. Together, they read the stories, analyzed them, and based much of their musical interpretation on what they learned about the characters and the action. In another example, a sixth-grade science teacher created a language-rich environment in his classroom by establishing a class library, including a variety of science textbooks and information books dealing with many different topics, science magazines, young adult fiction books with science themes, picture books, biographies of scientists, and other young adult books unrelated to science but available to students who simply wished to read. Next to the shelved books was an old overstuffed couch, a couple of beanbag chairs, and a table with chairs for relaxation reading and personal research. Students were given opportunities during nearly every class period to use the class library to work on personal and class projects and to simply read as their interests dictated.

Effective Teaching Involves Creating Strategies to Meet Students' Needs

To restate our key point, you do not become an effective teacher by simply following the suggestions of others. Teaching effectiveness will result if you create new strategies based on reframing and expanding existing strategies that are more ideally suited to the needs and interests of you and your students.

Effective Teachers Understand Literacy Processes

A common concern among the teachers we meet is expressed in the question "How can I stay abreast of all the new trends and developments in the fields of reading and writing?" In response, we strongly advocate that teachers take graduate courses in reading or as part of a graduate or certification program and attend workshops and conferences on reading and writing. Another inevitable answer we must give to this question is that to become aware of current teaching developments in reading and writing, you must read the professional literature. We admit, however, that trying to decide what professional literature to read can be a daunting task. Some guidelines follow.

Become a member of the International Reading Association (IRA) and the National Council of Teachers of English (NCTE). As a member of either of these organizations, you will receive a journal that deals with reading and writing issues, concerns, and practical teaching suggestions for adolescent students. IRA members find the *Journal of Adolescent and Adult Literacy* most helpful for presenting many fresh ideas each month on such topics as teaching vocabulary, writing in the content areas, and using young adult literature. NCTE's *English Journal* is most appropriate for teachers looking for ideas and strategies to facilitate students' written expression. Select two or three articles from these journals every month and read them closely. Integrate the ideas and suggestions into your instructional plans, and modify them to meet your particular needs. In this way, you will gain regular exposure to the current perspectives on reading/writing processes and on developing skill at translating ideas and others' suggestions into your own personally meaningful and useful strategies.

Benefits of Professional Organization Membership

Another benefit of membership in IRA and NCTE is the availability of discounted books on a wide range of reading/writing topics, most of which can be purchased only through these professional organizations. New books are added annually. As you peruse the IRA or NCTE catalog, you will undoubtedly find three or four publications on topics of interest. Regularly reading these publications will help to expand your knowledge about reading and writing processes. It will also provide you with many more strategies for developing these language processes and helping students use them in learning your classroom content.

International Reading Association
800 Barksdale Road
P.O. Box 8139
Newark, DE 19714-8139

National Council of Teachers of English
1111 Kenyon Road
Urbana, IL 61801

Given the staggering number of journals that publish reading and writing articles, and the professional texts that appear annually, we suggest that you ease into the current literature in a modest way. Set aside a couple of hours per week to devote to reading journals and books. After reading a journal article or book, jot down notes about the topics on an index card and file the card so that you can consult it when you need some ideas for teaching course content using reading and writing strategies. Your file categories might include "Developing Prior Knowledge," "Developing Vocabulary," "Teaching Text Study Strategies," and "Writing in the Content Areas."

A second common concern, related to the one just discussed, is expressed in the question "How do I determine whether reading strategies are appropriate for my students and are based on sound theory and research?" This question, dealing with how to choose appropriate, sound, research-based strategies for teaching reading and writing, is not easily answered. Perhaps the biggest challenge for the concerned professional is to determine the most important criteria related to a research study or methods paper: Is the research based on actual practice in actual school settings with students like mine, or is it based on populations of students and conducted in contexts dissimilar to my own?

It is safe to say that because of the mind-boggling number of research studies and reports that continually appear in the professional literature, many literacy professionals, including those in higher education, do not always know what is research based. To confound matters, articles appearing in the same journal often contain conflicting findings. So it is not surprising to find many concerned teachers confused about how best to teach reading and writing.

One way of breaking through the confusing maze of reading research is to follow our advice given in previous sections of this chapter in our discussion of reflective teaching and classroom research. Begin defining your personal philosophy about teaching language processes. Your philosophy will be influenced by what you have learned and are learning about reading and writing from course work, journals, textbooks, other teachers, your students, and, most important, your own classroom research experiences and reflections. Then look for and generate strategies that are consistent with your evolving knowledge about yourself and your students and about the best conditions for teaching and learning.

We certainly hope that your developing philosophy encompasses beliefs similar to our own:

Our Beliefs About Student Learning

1. Students grow in language when it is whole, meaningful, and functional.
2. All classrooms should immerse students in a language-rich environment.
3. The learning environment should be arranged in such a way as to promote and encourage regular and frequent student–student interactions.
4. Teachers should demonstrate the reading, writing, and learning processes they expect their students to acquire.

These beliefs have guided the selection of strategies for this book. If your beliefs about language development are similar, then it should be easy for you to modify and adapt many of the strategies contained in this book to help improve your ability to develop your students' content knowledge and literacy. Also, as you read about other strategies that may derive from a different philosophical base, you will be better able to decide what, if any, aspects of the strategies can be adapted for your use and what can be left out of your instructional practices.

Effective Teachers Establish Personal Reading Programs

Middle and secondary school teachers often protest when we suggest that they should read several young adult books every year so that they can use good books to enlist their students in the *literacy club,* as Frank Smith (1985) terms it. "We haven't the time," they respond. "We're too busy with our required work to read all those books."

We are not naive; we understand the time constraints placed on secondary school teachers. Teaching often entwines itself around teachers' entire lives, so that outside the classroom they are thinking about their students, their existing methods of instruction, and new ways to improve their instruction, as well as grading papers and preparing lessons. Yet many teachers also have a family, children, house chores, and cooking, and may even be taking additional university courses. Teachers lead incredibly busy lives! However, reading young adult books may be as integral to your role as a teacher as any other teaching-related activity.

It Is Vitally Important That We Be Active Readers Ourselves

We can reach adolescents in many ways. Experienced and insightful teachers often discover how to capitalize on subtle teaching moments that are not part of a preconceived lesson or curriculum. We know, for instance, that young adults can be dramatically influenced by teachers who simply show genuine concern for them as individuals with real-world needs and problems. Often, books recommended to teenagers by a concerned teacher can make a significant difference in the young adults' lives, their way of viewing a problem or relationship, their strategies for coping with a personal difficulty, or their interest in knowing more about a topic. It is not uncommon for us to learn from our undergraduate and secondary reading students that certain books that really moved them as teenagers were recommended by teachers. One student recalled how in seventh grade he was talking with his English teacher, whom he regarded as a friend, about the difficulty he was having in geometry. The teacher suggested that he read the book *The Planiverse* (Dewdney, 1984), which describes life in a two-dimensional world. The student became very excited about the ideas in the book and began approaching his geometry lesson with renewed enthusiasm, which helped him pass the course. Another student recounted how her music teacher, who knew her mother had recently died, passed her the book *When the Phone Rang* (Mazer, 1985), which tells the story of three teenagers who have to deal with the tragic death of their parents. It wasn't the book itself that made a difference in her ability to cope, she said, but the fact that her teacher cared enough for her to suggest the book.

Young adult books can obviously play a more direct role in lesson planning and content area instruction, as demonstrated in Chapters 8 and 10. Because of the tremendous influence these books can have on students' lives, we recommend that all teachers become knowledgeable about how to use adolescent literature to stimulate students' interest in the topic of study, to help them learn the content information in a more palatable way, and to reach them by introducing them to books related to their needs outside of the classroom. To get started on a personal reading program, we suggest that you take as little as 15 minutes a day to read a young adult book. Try reading the book before bed. We think you will discover that this kind of teaching preparation is much easier and much more exciting than traditional school-preparation tasks. You will have the pleasure of enjoying quality literature while learning about the power of books for reaching the students in your classroom.

The following list indicates where you can find young adult books for your own reading and for stocking your classroom library:

Everyday Locations for Finding Young Adult Books

- Locally owned bookstores and bookstore chains
- Supermarkets, drugstores, and discount department stores
- Used-book stores
- Libraries (will often sell duplicate or unused books at a fraction of the original cost)
- Book fairs
- Book clubs (paper and illustrations are often inferior, but the prices are low)
- Garage sales

Effective Teachers Collaborate with Students, Teachers, Parents, and Administrators

Many people share an interest in your students' reading, writing, and learning development, including the students themselves, other teachers, parents, and school administrators. The prospects of students becoming active learners and developing lifelong reading habits greatly increase when all persons concerned work collaboratively to help students use literacy for information and pleasure. And with these collaborative efforts, your teaching effectiveness increases as well.

Following are suggestions for developing collaborative relationships with teachers, parents, administrators, and students.

Let All Interested Groups Know Your Expectations for Reading, Writing, and Learning

To work collaboratively, it isn't necessary to convert others to your approach to teaching, but it is important that they be made aware of the nature of your curriculum and the rationale behind it. Otherwise, suspicion, distrust, and confusion may develop. Before others make judgments about you based on piecemeal or incorrect information, share with them as honestly and as accurately as possible your teaching philosophy and classroom strategies.

Make Sure Students Understand Your Expectations for Them as Readers, Writers, and Learners

Students must "revalue" reading and writing as meaningful, functional processes that can be used as vehicles for learning and expanding on subject matter. All the strategies discussed in this book are intended to help you incorporate into your content curriculum learning experiences that demonstrate this revaluing of literacy.

Develop Collaborative Relationships with Students

Rhodes and Dudley-Marling (1988) put it well when they said, "We can teach but we can't force learning; learning is a student's prerogative" (p. 273). Students in the middle and upper grades should be used as curricular informants and should be allowed a hand in determining course topics, materials, learning experiences, projects, and evaluation. Involving students in course decisions will encourage cooperation and commitment; they will be vested in the learning process. Without students' active involvement, the chances of expanding their content knowledge, as well as their literacy skills, are greatly diminished.

Develop Collaborative Relationships with Parents

Parents play a vital role in the literacy development and motivation of students (Bean & Valerio, 1997; Brozo, Valerio, & Salazar, 1996). Teachers and parents can work together to facilitate students' literacy at home. Most of the suggestions that teachers make to parents should be reminders of how parents have been supporting literacy at home for generations. When support for literacy at school is provided at home, students discover the importance of reading and writing (Saravia-Shore & Arvizu, 1992). Parents, in turn, can be useful informants about their students' attitudes, interests, hobbies, and other behavioral and personality insights that the teacher can use when selecting trade books and planning research projects.

One of the best ways parents can be involved in their adolescent son's or daughter's literacy development is by encouraging and modeling personally meaningful reading. Adolescents who daily "catch their parents in the act" of reading—whether it's an executive in Los Angeles with *The Wall Street Journal,* a hog farmer in Illinois with the farm report, or a teacher in Florida curled up on the couch with a mystery novel—are likely to develop positive attitudes about reading (DeBruin-Parecki, Paris, & Siedenburg, 1997). Encourage parents to make sure they let their adolescents observe them reading. Instead of ordering and demanding them to read, parents should set an example for their adolescents of the importance and joy of literacy.

Parents Can Be Helpful Models of Meaningful Reading

Another way to involve parents in the literacy development of their sons or daughters is to encourage them to make a variety of reading materials available at home. A student in one of my graduate reading courses told me recently how she had been struggling to get her 12-year-old son to read. She had subscriptions to youth and teen magazines, but he wouldn't read them. She handed him one book after another, only to have each rejected. One day she left Gary Paulsen's *The Haymeadow* (1992) on his bedstand. Later that night she noticed light spilling out from under his bedroom door. To her delight, she found her son engrossed in the book. She almost had to wrestle it from him to get him to go to sleep. The next day a blizzard kept students at home, and he picked up the book on waking and stayed in bed until he was finished. "Man, that was a great book," he said. "Are there any more like that?"

Indeed, there are many more outstanding young adult books that can make the difference between whether or not adolescents become lifelong readers. Figure 12.5 presents guidelines adapted from Reed (1988) for helping parents select books for adolescents.

The best way to assist adolescents in developing the reading habit is to be a model. As adolescents observe influential adults reading functional and meaningful materials and observe adults' selection processes, they are likely to imitate this behavior. Teachers and parents can work together to discover what adolescents will enjoy reading, and use thoughtful and sensitive guidance to help them become mature readers.

Develop Collaborative Relationships with Other Teachers

In Chapter 9 we described how Bob, a reading and study skills teacher, teamed up with a biology teacher to help reinforce instruction in the split-page method of note taking. The beneficiaries of their collaboration were new freshmen grappling with the demands of high school textbook reading. This example of cooperative planning between teachers demonstrates the power of collaboration as an effective way to influence teachers' beliefs about reading, writing, and learning.

A great many demands are placed on classroom teachers, and more seem to be added yearly. Although most teachers are interested in incorporating effective reading, writing, and learning strategies into their plans, real or perceived

1. Use the book lists in Chapters 8 and 11 as guides.
2. Check local bookstores, and public and university libraries, for the best source of books.
3. Consult librarians, bookstore clerks, university faculty, and teachers who are knowledgeable about young adult books.
4. Become a keen observer of your adolescent's interests, including favorite television shows, hobbies, leisure-time activities, and the kinds of books he or she had read and enjoyed in the past.
5. Consider how well your daughter or son reads when deciding the appropriateness of young adult books.
6. Take a close look at the books to determine whether they match your adolescent's interests.
7. Enroll your son or daughter in a young adult book club.
8. Be sure the main character in the book approximates the age of your adolescent. Characters who are too young are likely to be poorly received; characters who are a bit older are often preferred.
9. Try to make a variety of books available to your adolescent; then allow her or him to select a favorite one.
10. Don't impose your tastes on your adolescent; use your child's selection to guide you in selecting or purchasing future books.
11. Don't jam the books down your adolescent's throat or lay on a thick, hard sales pitch.
12. Try to increase gradually the literary quality of books.
13. Avoid the tendency to make reading a requirement at home; be patient.
14. Try to gradually induce your adolescent to select young adult books. Help by (a) encouraging regular visits to the public library and bookstore, (b) introducing librarians and clerks who are knowledgeable about young adult books and sensitive to the needs of adolescents, (c) purchasing and sharing annotated bibliographies of young adult books (see the reference guides in Chapter 8), (d) discussing the book your young adult is reading, and (e) suggesting books your young adult might enjoy.

Adapted from A. J. S. Reed (1988), *Comics to Classics: A Parent's Guide to Books for Teens and Preteens,* Newark, DE: International Reading Association.

FIGURE 12.5 A Parents' Guide to Selecting Books for Adolescents

constraints limit how much they can do in this area. One way teachers can support each other is by collaborating on thematic units. For example, an eighth-grade history teacher teamed up with the language arts teacher on a World War I unit. In the language arts classroom, students read *No Hero for the Kaiser* (Frank, 1986), wrote responses and themes related to the book and what they were learning in the history class, researched their own family histories to determine who fought in the war, built charts relating battles described in their history books to the effects of the battles on the characters in the trade book, and

Teacher Collaborations Can Lead to More Effective Instruction

engaged in many other literacy experiences designed to integrate trade and text reading. This support of the history teacher's unit led to greater student learning of details and concepts related to World War I, as well as increased enthusiasm for the unit on the part of the students and teachers alike. In this way, the history teacher had time to cover the content he felt was important, while the language arts teacher engaged students in functional and meaningful literacy experiences. And in the process, everyone benefited.

A few middle and secondary schools have a reading specialist to serve students and teachers. If your school has such an individual, introduce yourself immediately to discover what specific services the specialist can offer you to help your students. The reading specialist can take referred students from your class who are having difficulty learning your content area concepts. The specialist will often team teach with you to develop effective study strategies for learning material from course texts and class notes. The specialist might conduct demonstration lessons for your students on certain strategies, such as mapping or the survey procedure using your content materials. The reading specialist can also provide you with teaching ideas for students who have been mainstreamed into your classroom.

Finally, you should develop an effective relationship with your school librarian. Librarians can be invaluable friends and colleagues when you plan units and projects with your students. Librarians are excited about identifying relevant resources for your upcoming topics. They can provide your class with helpful presentations and demonstrations in using reference material, accessing computer databases, and conducting research. Finally, as mentioned in Chapter 8, librarians are your best link to quality young adult books.

Develop Collaborative Relationships with Administrators

In most buildings, school administrators (principals, supervisors, etc.) possess a great deal of decision-making power. Therefore, they can be important allies. The extent to which they share their power may depend on how actively you cultivate cooperative relationships with them.

We recommended earlier that to begin, you should make clear your expectations for the learning environment in your classroom. Most administrators are happy to hear of your innovative efforts and are more likely to provide support if they are kept abreast of the reading, writing, and learning strategies you are attempting to incorporate into your classroom. Principals can play an instrumental role in developing and implementing a sustained silent reading or writing program. They can find funds for alternative resources, such as trade books, and can provide the necessary support for book drives, sales, and other plans you devise for finding books and raising money for books. Administrators can help create a supportive environment for teacher collaboration and classroom research. With your cooperation, they can help arrange important and enlightening in-service training and facilitate parent–teacher programs. They can also make critical links to community resources for donations of reading, writing, and other curricular materials.

Teachers Need Administrative Support to Make Effective Curricular Change

The more you communicate with administrators about your students' growth, the greater the chance that they will appreciate your efforts, understand your needs, and support your curricular changes.

One last word about collaboration. We do not want to give the impression that students, parents, teachers, and administrators are the only individuals who can contribute to the overall learning and literacy development of your students. We recommend that you also develop links with other members of the community who can assist you, including local poets, writers, musicians, senior citizens, retired teachers, university student volunteers, and others. Sometimes persistent inquiry can lead to the discovery of some wonderful local resources. Recently, for example, one of our students, an English teacher, while preparing a unit on the Arthurian Legend, found out about a local group of actors known as the Guild of Creative Anachronisms. Several members came into his classroom dressed in Arthurian garb and gave an exciting and informative demonstration on the life, culture, and music during that period and place in history. This strategy enlivened the unit and provided his students with a truly unforgettable experience.

CASE STUDY REVISITED

We hope that as a result of reading and studying this chapter you now have a much better idea about how a teacher like Melinda can go about systematically and contextually discovering the best ways to implement centers for junior high students in her language arts classroom. In this chapter we described processes of reflection and steps in teacher research that allow teachers to ask and answer their own "local" questions about student learning. Take some time now to write your suggestions for Melinda.

Melinda began the process of introducing centers to her seventh graders by talking with colleagues about the feasibility of using centers with older students. The feedback she received was frank and useful, with overall support for her ideas. In fact, one other sixth-grade language arts teacher wanted to keep in close touch during the implementation process to discover whether centers might also work for him. One extremely helpful recommendation from other teachers was for Melinda to give her centers a name more appropriate for sixth graders. The idea was to eliminate any possible childish associations students might have with centers. With the brainstorming help of her colleagues, Melinda decided to call her centers *language think tanks.* Melinda also had a discussion with the curriculum director in her school district, who loaned her an IRA publication entitled *Teachers as Researchers: Reflection and Action* (Santa, Short, & Smith, 1993). With this book as a guide, Melinda organized a plan of action for implementing centers.

Though time-consuming and not always a high priority, Melinda followed one of the book's suggestions and kept a log or, as she called it, a *research journal* throughout her teaching with centers. In the journal she recorded just about anything that came to mind regarding this aspect of her teaching. Some of her entries consisted of questions, others of inner talk about her doubts or concerns; still others described actual scenes and observations of students using centers. Melinda tried to make entries while observing students; though more often than not, she found herself later in the evening with a cup of coffee in one hand and her pen in the other trying to reflect on the experiences of the day, groping through her memory for anything that might inform her about the effectiveness of the centers.

After using the centers for a couple of weeks, Melinda began to modify her observations and analysis. It soon became apparent that trying to account for the responses of all of her students to the centers would be an overwhelming task, so she decided to track three particular students. She identified the students she believed would provide highly useful information about the effectiveness of the centers. One student, Tony, was a high performer; another student, Amy, was average; and Kaley was below average. These students became informants both through direct observation of their work in the centers and via formal and informal interviews Melinda had with them throughout the year.

Melinda focused her exploration of the centers' effectiveness by asking three broad questions: (1) Will students find centers enjoyable and motivating, resulting in more task-focused activity? (2) Will students' reading, writing, and language abilities improve through the use of centers? and (3) Will students work more cooperatively to problem-solve and share language? Melinda employed a variety of methods for gaining information to answer each of these questions, including observation notes, informal and formal interviews, assignments and other materials completed at the centers, and quiz/test results.

One of the first discoveries resulting from her scrutiny of the three students was that the term *language think tank* appeared to be acceptable. Students were using the term themselves; Tony even began calling them *LTTs*—a term that caught on. This certainly was an indication that students were finding centers interesting, if not entirely engaging.

Kaley seemed to be taking the fullest advantage of the centers. In her observation notes, Melinda noted that Kaley was spending most of her time on the center's activities and completing her assignments on time. For example, in one note Melinda observed Kaley sitting at an LTT devoted to the study of cover material for young adult books. The goal was to look over at least three books, read all the cover text, inside and out, and then rate the cover information using a sheet with scaled questions and open-ended questions. Kaley was seen completing this activity with enthusiasm and focus. She was proud to describe for the class her finding: that of the four books she reviewed, the most enticing cover material concerned *Maniac Magee* (Spinelli, 1990), followed by *Monkey Island* (Fox, 1991), *The Crossing* (Paulsen, 1987), and *Off and Running* (Soto, 1996). Her detailed explanation of the features of each book made it abundantly clear to Melinda that this center activity was valuable as a language builder and motivator for Kaley.

To see how effective centers were in promoting group problem solving and cooperation, Melinda formed groups of three, including one group consisting of her three students of concern: Amy, Tony, and Kaley. Their center activity involved creating poems from a bag filled with words and expressions cut out of magazines. Then the students were asked to identify all of the possible figures of speech evident in the poems and to share their results with the class. Melinda observed how Amy, who was normally uncomfortable working in groups, took on a leadership role, directing Tony and Kaley through this activity with confidence and enthusiasm.

Every couple of weeks, Melinda found time to gather feedback from her three students on the centers. From these conversations, she learned which centers were most motivating and which activities needed to be modified. For example, one of the LTTs for grammar was designed to drill students on parts of speech using traditional approaches. Melinda felt that this practice was necessary and that coaching in a center might create more of an incentive to complete. All three of her students told her, however, that this was one of their least favorite LTTs. Amy suggested that music lyrics be used to study parts of speech. Picking up on that suggestion, Melinda set up a listening center with rap, folk, country, and rock music. With printed lyrics available, students listened to the music and did a variety of grammatical analyses, such as (1) identifying parts of speech, (2) looking for and correcting subject–verb agreement errors, and (3) identifying figures of speech. This LTT quickly became one of the most popular with the three students and the rest of the class.

At midyear, Melinda took stock of her centers, noting some significant results that helped answer her guiding questions. First, overall, centers appeared to be motivating for most students. As the year progressed, there was less and less grousing and grumbling about center work. Students seemed to enjoy being able to get out of their seats and move around the classroom from center to center. Their behavior appeared to be focused and task related when they worked at centers. Second, Melinda noted improvement in writing and grammar, which she attributed at least in part to the centers. Her three student informants, especially Kaley and Amy, showed good progress from August to December, as evidenced on quiz grades and themes. Finally, Melinda found ample evidence that the centers instigated freer language exchanges among students. Center group work was often the most enjoyable for the class, and students often generated high-quality answers and solutions to language-related problems.

Answering classroom questions through a systematic approach is one of the best ways for a teacher to discover the effectiveness of her or his teaching. Melinda's discoveries about the centers impelled her to continue their use and modification throughout the year. She now collaborates with her language arts team, all of whom have adopted centers, improving and refining them through regular and frequent discussion and feedback from her colleagues. These developments would not have been possible without Melinda's initiative and willingness to introduce an instructional innovation into her classroom and her commitment to scrutinize and reflect on her teaching in order to maximize student success.

■ ■ ■

SUMMARY

This chapter was devoted to issues related to teacher professionalism. We organized the chapter around factors that influence the degree of literacy instruction that classroom teachers provide and around characteristics of effective teachers.

We know that junior and senior high school teachers must deal with real and perceived constraints on what they can do in the classroom. We suggested that innovative literacy strategies are likely to find their way into the classrooms of teachers who (1) are able to explore their own beliefs, theories, and practical knowledge when preparing to implement an innovative literacy practice; (2) are provided with the necessary support from administrators and staff to follow through with implementation; and (3) are given plenty of opportunities to reflect on the change process.

We describe characteristics of effective teachers that contribute significantly to students' achievement and attitudes. In particular, we have much to learn about teaching effectiveness from teachers who are reflective; who test their strategies in classroom action research; who understand the importance of providing literacy instruction within the content classroom; and who develop collaborative relationships with students, parents, teachers, and administrators.

REFERENCES

Aronowitz, S., & Giroux, H. (1991). *Postmodern education.* Minneapolis: University of Minnesota Press.

Bean, T., & Valerio, P. C. (1997). Constructing school success in literacy: The pathway to college entrance for minority students. *Reading Research Quarterly, 32,* 320–327.

Bintz, W. (1997). Exploring reading nightmares of middle and secondary school teachers. *Journal of Adolescent and Adult Literacy, 41,* 12–25.

Branscombe, N., Goswami, D., & Schwartz, J. (1992). *Students teaching, teachers learning.* Portsmouth, NH: Heinemann.

Brozo, W. G., Brobst, A., & Moje, E. B. (1994–1995). A personal story of teacher change. *Childhood Education, 71,* 70–73.

Brozo, W. G., Valerio, P. C., & Salazar, M. (1996). A walk through Gracie's garden: Literacy and cultural explorations in a Mexican American junior high school. *Journal of Adolescent and Adult Literacy, 40,* 164–170.

Burnaford, G. (1996). A life of its own: Teacher research and transforming the curriculum. In G. Burnaford, J. Fischer, & D. Hobson (Eds.), *Teachers doing research: Practical possibilities.* Mahwah, NJ: Erlbaum.

Cochran-Smith, M., & Lytle, S. (1993). *Inside outside: Teacher research and knowledge.* New York: Teachers College Press.

DeBruin-Parecki, A., Paris, S. G., & Siedenburg, J. (1997). Family literacy: Examining practice and issues of effectiveness. *Journal of Adolescent and Adult Literacy, 40,* 596–605.

Goff, S. (1996). Experienced teachers and action research: A model for professional development. In G. Burnaford, J. Fischer, & D. Hobson (Eds.), *Teachers doing research: Practical possibilities.* Mahwah, NJ: Erlbaum.

Green, J. L. (1987). *Colloquial materials.* Unpublished manuscript. Columbus: The Ohio State University.

Griffiths, M., & Tann, S. (1992). Using reflective practice to link personal and public theories. *Journal of Education for Teaching, 18,* 69–84.

Hargreaves, A. (1995). *Changing teacher, changing times: Teachers' work and culture in the postmodern age.* New York: Teachers College Press.

Harste, J. C. (1988). Tomorrow's readers today: Becoming a profession of collaborative learners. In J. Readence & R. S. Baldwin (Eds.), *Dialogues in literacy research. Thirty-seventh yearbook of the National Reading Conference.* Chicago: National Reading Conference.

Henderson, J. (1992). *Reflective teaching: Becoming an inquiring educator.* New York: Macmillan.

Holt-Reynolds, D. (1992). Personal history-based beliefs as relevant prior knowledge in course work. *American Educational Research Journal, 29,* 325–349.

Lee, S., & Patterson, L. A. (1987, December). *The nature of transactional theory: Not static, but dynamic.* Paper presented at the annual meeting of the National Reading Conference, St. Petersburg, FL.

Lieberman, A., & McLaughlin, M. (1992). Networks for educational change: Powerful and problematic. *Phi Delta Kappan, 73,* 673–677.

Liston, D., & Zeichner, K. (1996). *Culture and teaching.* Mahwah, NJ: Erlbaum.

McLaughlin, M. (1992). What matters most in teachers' workplace context? In M. McLaughlin & J. Little (Eds.), *Cultures and contexts of teaching.* New York: Teachers College Press.

Moje, E. B., Brozo, W. G., & Haas, J. (1994). Challenges to change: Portfolios in a high school classroom. *Reading Research and Instruction, 33,* 275–292.

O'Brien, D., Stewart, R., & Moje, E. B. (1995). Why content literacy is difficult to infuse into the secondary school: Complexities of curriculum, pedagogy, and school culture. *Reading Research Quarterly, 30,* 442–463.

Palmer, R., & Stewart, R. (1997). Nonfiction trade books in content area instruction: Realities and potential. *Journal of Adolescent and Adult Literacy, 40,* 630–641.

Posner, G. J. (1985). *Field experience: A guide to reflective teaching.* New York: Longman.

Ratekin, N., Simpson, M., Alvermann, D., & Dishner, E. (1985). Why teachers resist content reading instruction. *Journal of Reading, 28,* 432–437.

Reed, A. J. S. (1988). *Comics to classics: A parent's guide to books for teens and preteens.* Newark, DE: International Reading Association.

Rhodes, L., & Dudley-Marling, C. (1988). *Readers and writers with a difference: A holistic approach to teaching learning disabled and remedial students.* Portsmouth, NH: Heinemann.

Richardson, V. (1990). Significant and worthwhile change in teaching practice. *Educational Researcher, 19,* 10–18.

Richardson, V., Anders, P., Tidwell, D., & Lloyd, C. (1991). The relationship between teachers' beliefs and practices in reading comprehension instruction. *American Educational Research Journal, 28,* 559–586.

Rief, L. (1992). *Seeking diversity: Language arts with adolescents.* Portsmouth, NH: Heinemann.

Ruddell, R. B., & Sperling, M. (1988). Factors influencing the use of literacy research by the classroom teacher: Research review and new directions. In J. Readence & R. S. Baldwin (Eds.), *Dialogues in literacy research. Thirty-seventh yearbook of the National Reading Conference.* Chicago: National Reading Conference.

Santa, C., Short, K., & Smith, K. (1993). *Teachers as researchers: Reflection and action.* Newark, DE: International Reading Association.

Saravia-Schore, M., & Arvizu, S. (1992). *Cross-cultural literacy: Ethnographies of communication in multiethnic classrooms.* New York: Garland.

Short, K., & Burke, C. (1989). New potentials for teacher education: Teaching and learning as inquiry. *The Elementary School Journal, 90,* 193–206.

Smith, F. (1985). *Reading without nonsense.* New York: Holt, Rinehart & Winston.
Strickland, D. S. (1988). The teacher as researcher: Toward the extended professional. *Language Arts, 65,* 754–764.
Sturtevant, E. G. (1993). Content literacy in high school social studies: A focus on one teacher's beliefs and decisions. In T. Rasinski & N. Padak (Eds.), *Inquiries in literacy learning and instruction. Fifteenth yearbook of the College Reading Association.* Pittsburgh, KS: College Reading Association.
Tremmel, R. (1993). Zen and the art of reflective practice. *Harvard Educational Review, 63,* 434–458.
Valli, L. (1993). Reflective teacher education programs: An analysis of case studies. In J. Calderhead (Ed.), *Conceptualizing reflection in teacher development.* Albany, NY: SUNY Press.
Valverde, L. (1982). The self-evolving supervisor. In T. Sergiovanni (Ed.), *Supervision of teaching.* Alexandria, VA: Association for Supervision and Curriculum Development.
Wells, G. (1992). *Constructing knowledge together.* Portsmouth, NH: Heinemann.
Wilson, E., Konopak, B., & Readence, J. (1992). Examining content area reading beliefs, decisions, and instruction: A case study of an English teacher. In C. Kinzer & D. Leu (Eds.), *Literacy research, theory, and practice: Views from many perspectives. Forty-first yearbook of the National Reading Conference.* Chicago: National Reading Conference.
Zeichner, K., & Liston, D. (1996). *Reflective teaching: An introduction.* Mahwah, NJ: Erlbaum.

Young Adult Books

Dewdney, A. K. (1984). *The planiverse.* New York: Poseidon Press.
Fox, P. (1991). *Monkey island.* New York: Bantam Doubleday.
Frank, R. (1986). *No hero for the Kaiser.* New York: Lothrop, Lee & Shepard.
Mazer, H. (1985). *When the phone rang.* New York: Scholastic.
Paulsen, G. (1987). *The crossing.* New York: Bantam Doubleday.
Paulsen, G. (1992). *The haymeadow.* New York: Dell.
Soto, G. (1996). *Off and running.* New York: Delacorte Press.
Spinelli, J. (1990). *Maniac Magee.* New York: HarperTrophy.

APPENDIX

Literature in and for Students Who Speak "Other Englishes"

	TYPE	REGION
Abiakam, J. (n.d.). *The game of love: A classical drama from West Africa.* Onitsha, Nigeria: J. C. Brothers Bookshop.	Play	Nigeria
Achebe, C. (1959). *Things fall apart.* New York, Astor-Honor.	Novel	Nigeria
Achebe, C. (1969). *No longer at ease.* Greenwich, CT: Fawcett.	Novel	Nigeria
Achebe, C. (1985). *African short stories.* Portsmouth, NH: Heinemann.	Stories	Nigeria
Achebe, C. (1988). *Anthills of the Savannah.* New York: Anchor Press.	Novel	Nigeria
Achebe, C. (1989). *A man of the people.* New York: Anchor Press. (Original work published 1966)	Novel	Nigeria
Achebe, C. (1989). *Arrow of God.* New York: Anchor Books. (Original work published 1974)	Novel	Nigeria
Allen, P. G. (1983). *The woman who owned the shadows.* Boston: Beacon Press.	Novel	Native American (Laguna-Sioux)
Allen, P. G. (1986). *Recovering the feminine in American Indian traditions.* Boston: Beacon Press.	Nonfiction	Native American (Laguna-Sioux)
Allen, P. G. (1989). *Spider woman's granddaughters.* Boston: Beacon Press.	Stories	Native American (Laguna-Sioux)
Amadi, E. (1971). *The great ponds.* London: Heinemann.	Novel	Africa
Amadi, E. (1972). *The concubine.* London: Heinemann. (Original work published 1965)	Novel	Africa
Amand, M. R. (1970). *Untouchable.* Delhi: Orient. (Original work published 1935)	Novel	India
Anorue, J. C. (n.d.). *The complete story and trial of Adolph Hitler.* Onitsha, Nigeria: J. C. Brothers Workshop.	Play	Nigeria
Chan, A. B. (Ed.). (1983). *Gold mountain: The Chinese in the new world.* Vancouver: New Star Books.	Poetry	China
Coffer, J. O. (1989). *The line of the sun.* New York: Harper & Row.	Autobiography	Puerto Rico
Colon, J. (1961). *A Puerto Rican in New York and other sketches.* New York: Mainstream.	Stories	Puerto Rico
Day, L. B. (1874). *Govinda samanta or history of a bengal raivat* (2 vols.). London: Macmillan. (Reprinted 1878 under the title *Bengal peasant life*)	Novel	India
Desai, A. (1980). *Clear light of day.* New York: Harper & Row.	Novel	India
Desai, A. (1982). *Games at twilight and other stories.* New York: Harper & Row.	Stories	India

	TYPE	REGION
Dinh, T. V. (1983). *Blue dragon, white tiger: A Tet story.* New York: TriAm Press.	Nonfiction	Vietnam
Erdrich, L. (1984). *Jacklight.* New York: Holt, Rinehart & Winston.	Poetry	Native American (Chippewa)
Erdrich, L. (1984). *Love medicine.* New York: Holt, Rinehart & Winston.	Novel	Native American (Chippewa)
Erdrich, L. (1986). *The beet queen.* New York: Holt, Rinehart & Winston.	Novel	Native American (Chippewa)
Erdrich, L. (1988). *Tracks.* New York: Holt, Rinehart & Winston.	Novel	Native American (Chippewa)
Ekwensi, C. (1961). *Jagua Nana.* Greenwich, CT: Fawcett.	Novel	Nigeria
Ekwensi, C. (1962). *Burning grass.* London: Heinemann.	Novel	Nigeria
Ekwensi, C. (1966). *The drummer boy.* Cambridge, England: Cambridge University Press.	Novel	Nigeria
Ekwensi, C. (1966). *Lokotown and other stories.* London: Heinemann.	Stories	Nigeria
Ekwensi, C. (1969). *The people of the city.* Greenwich, CT: Fawcett. (Original work published 1963)	Novel	Nigeria
Ekwensi, C. (1971). *The passport of Mallam Ilia.* Cambridge, England: Cambridge University Press. (Original work published 1960)	Novel	Nigeria
Ekwensi, C. (1975). *Restless city and Christmas gold: With other stories.* London: Heinemann.	Stories	Nigeria
Ekwensi, C. (1986). *Jagua Nana's daughter.* Nigeria: Spectrum.	Novel	Nigeria
Fernando, L. (1968). *Twenty-two Malaysian stories.* Kuala Lumpur: Heinemann.	Stories	Malaysia
Gonzalez, N. V. M. (1961). *The bamboo dancers.* Denver: A. Swallow.	Novel	Philippines
Gonzalez, N. V. M. (1964). *Selected stories.* Denver: A. Swallow.	Stories	Philippines
Gonzalez, N. V. M. (1977). *Children of the ash-covered loam and other stories.* Manila: Bookmark.	Stories	Philippines
Hagedorn, J. (1990). *Dogeaters.* New York: Pantheon.	Novel	Philippines
Harth, D., & Baldwin, L. (Eds.). (1974). *Voices of Aztlan: Chicano literature of today.* New York: New American Library.	Poetry, stories	Mexico/U.S.
Javellana, S. (1976). *Without seeing the dawn.* Quezon City, Philippines: Alemar-Phoenix.	Novel	Philippines
Latin American Literature Review Press (Ed.). (1991). *Scents of wood and silence.* Pittsburgh: Latin American Literature Review Press.	Stories	Latin America
Lim, C. (1978). *Little ironies: Stories of Singapore.* Singapore: Heinemann.	Stories	Singapore
Lim, C. (1980). *Or else the lightning god and other stories.* Singapore: Heinemann.	Stories	Singapore
Ludwig, E. (Ed.). (1972). *The Chicanos: Mexican-American voices.* Baltimore: Penguin Books. (Original work published 1971)	Poetry, stories	Mexico/U.S.

	TYPE	REGION
Momaday, N. S. (1968). *Journey of Tai-Me.* New York: Harper & Row.	Novel	Native American (Kiowa and Cherokee)
Momaday, N. S. (1969). *The house made of dawn.* New York: Harper & Row.	Novel	Native American (Kiowa and Cherokee)
Momaday, N. S. (1969). *The way to rainy mountain.* New York: Ballantine.	Novel	Native American (Kiowa and Cherokee)
Momaday, N. S. (1974). *Angle of geese and other poems.* Boston: D. R. Godine.	Poetry	Native American (Kiowa and Cherokee)
Momaday, N. S. (1987). *The names: A memoir.* Tucson: University of Arizona Press. (Original work published 1976)	Autobiography	Native American (Kiowa and Cherokee)
Momaday, N. S. (1989). *The ancient child: A novel.* New York: Doubleday.	Novel	Native American (Kiowa and Cherokee)
Naipaul, V. S. (1964). *The mystic masseur.* New York: Penguin. (Original work published 1957)	Novel	Trinidad
Naipaul, V. S. (1967). *A flag on the island.* New York: Macmillan.	Stories	Trinidad
Naipaul, V. S. (1969). *A house for Mr. Biswas.* New York: Penguin. (Original work published 1961)	Novel	Trinidad
Naipaul, V. S. (1972). *The overcrowded barracoon.* London: Andre Deutsch.	Stories	Trinidad
Naipaul, V. S. (1975). *Guerrillas.* London: Andre Deutsch.	Novel	Trinidad
Naipaul, V. S. (1979). *A bend in the river.* New York: Alfred A. Knopf.	Stories	Trinidad
Naipaul, V. S. (1984). *Finding the center: Two narratives.* New York: Alfred A. Knopf.	Novel	Trinidad
Narayan, R. K. (1966). *The guide.* New York: New American Library.	Novel	India
Narayan, R. K. (1967). *The vendor of sweets.* New York: Viking.	Novel	India
Narayan, R. K. (1970). *A horse and two goats.* New York: Viking.	Stories	India
Narayan, R. K. (1972). *The dark room.* Delhi: Hind Pocket Books.	Novel	India
Narayan, R. K. (1972). *Lawley Road and other stories.* Delhi: Hind Pocket Books.	Stories	India
Narayan, R. K. (1972). *Next Sunday.* Delhi: Hind Pocket Books.	Novel	India
Narayan, R. K. (1974). *My days.* New York: Viking.	Novel	India
Narayan, R. K. (1974). *The reluctant guru.* Delhi: Hind Pocket Books.	Novel	India
Narayan, R. K. (1976). *The painter of signs.* New York: Viking.	Novel	India
Narayan, R. K. (1985). *Under the banyan tree and other stories.* New York: Viking.	Stories	India
Nau, C. (Ed.). (1977). *Singapore writing.* Singapore: Woodrose Publications.	Poetry, stories	Singapore
Neihardt, J. G. (1961). *Black Elk speaks.* Lincoln: University of Nebraska Press.	Novel	Native American (Oglala-Sioux)

	TYPE	REGION
Okara, G. (1970). *The voice.* London: Heinemann.	Novel	Nigeria
Ong, J. (1975). *Run tiger run.* Kuala Lumpur: Eastern Universities Press.	Novel	Malaysia
Orfalea, G. (1988). *Before the flames: A quest for the history of Arab Americans.* Austin: University of Texas Press.	Nonfiction	Syria
Panunzio, C. (1921). *The soul of an immigrant.* New York: Macmillan.	Novel	Italy
Qoyawayma, P. (E. White). (1964). *No turning back: A Hopi Indian woman's struggle to live in two worlds,* as told to V. F. Carlson. Albuquerque: University of New Mexico Press.	Novel	Native American (Hopi)
Rao, R. (1963). *Kanthapura.* London: Oxford University Press. (Original work published 1943)	Novel	India
Rao, R. (1965). *The cat and Shakespeare: A tale of India.* New York: Macmillan.	Novel	India
Rao, R. (1968). *The serpent and the rope.* Delhi: Hind Pocket Books.	Novel	India
Riis, J. (1909). *The old town.* New York: Macmillan.	Novel	Denmark
Riis, J. (1957). *How the other half lives.* New York: Hill & Wang.	Nonfiction	Denmark
Rolvaag, O. E. (1929). *Giants in the earth: A saga of the prairie.* New York: Harper.	Novel	Norway
Rolvaag, O. E. (1929). *Peder victorious.* New York: Harper & Brothers.	Novel	Norway
Rivera, E. (1983). *Family installments.* New York: Macmillan.	Novel	Puerto Rico
Santos, B. (1979). *Scent of apples.* Seattle: University of Washington Press.	Novel	Philippines
Seng, G. P. (1972). *If we dream too long.* Singapore: Island Press.	Novel	Singapore
Singh, K. (1983). *The interview and other stories.* Singapore: Chopmen Publishers.	Stories	Singapore
Tan, K. S. (1972). *Son of Singapore.* London: Heinemann.	Novel	Singapore
Thumboo, E. (Ed.). (1970). *The flowering tree: Selected writings from Singapore/Malaysia.* Singapore: Educational Publications Bureau.	Poetry, stories	Malaysia, Singapore
Thumboo, E. (Ed.). (1976). *The second tongue. An anthology of poetry from Malaysia and Singapore.* Singapore: Heinemann.	Poetry	Malaysia, Singapore
Tutuola, A. (1953). *The palm-wine drinkard.* London: Greenwood Press. (Original work published 1952)	Novel	Nigeria
Tutuola, A. (1954). *My life in the bush of ghosts.* New York: Grove Press.	Novel	Nigeria
Tutuola, A. (1987). *Pauper, brawler, and slanderer.* London: Faber and Faber.	Novel	Nigeria
Ulasi, A. L. (1973). *Many things you no understand.* London: Collins (Fontana).	Novel	Nigeria
Yeap, J. K. (1975). *The patriarch.* Singapore: Times Printers.	Novel	Malaysia

	TYPE	REGION
Yeo, R. (Ed.). (1978). *Singapore short stories.* Singapore: Heinemann.	Stories	Singapore
Yezierska, A. (1920). *Hungry hearts.* New York: Grosset & Dunlap.	Stories	Poland
Yezierska, A. (1923). *Children of loneliness.* New York: Grosset & Dunlap.	Novel	Poland
Yezierska, A. (1925). *The bread givers.* Garden City, NY: Doubleday, Page.	Novel	Poland
Yezierska, A. (1927). *The arrogant beggar.* Garden City, NY: Doubleday, Page.	Novel	Poland
Yezierska, A. (1932). *All I could never be.* New York: Harper.	Novel	Poland
Yezierska, A. (1950). *The red ribbon on a white horse.* New York: Harper.	Novel	Poland

NAME INDEX

SUBJECT INDEX